PARKIN ◆ BADE

MACROECONOMICS

CANADA IN THE GLOBAL ENVIRONMENT   TENTH EDITION

MICHAEL PARKIN   ROBIN BADE

ACQUISITIONS EDITOR: Anne Williams
MARKETING DIRECTOR: Leigh-Anne Graham
CONTENT MANAGER: Emily Dill
PROJECT MANAGER: Avinash Chandra
MANAGER OF CONTENT DEVELOPMENT: Suzanne Schaan
DEVELOPMENTAL EDITOR: Leanne Rancourt
DIGITAL CONTENT MANAGER: Nicole Mellow
SENIOR MEDIA DEVELOPER: Olga Avdyeyeva
PRODUCTION SERVICES: Cenveo® Publisher Services

TECHNICAL ILLUSTRATOR: Richard Parkin
PERMISSIONS PROJECT MANAGER: Joanne Tang
PHOTO PERMISSIONS RESEARCH: iEnergizerAptara®, Ltd.
TEXT PERMISSIONS RESEARCH: iEnergizerAptara®, Ltd.
INTERIOR DESIGNER: Emily Friel, Integra Software Services/
Anthony Leung
COVER DESIGNER: Anthony Leung
COVER IMAGE: © Orangeline / Dreamstime
VICE-PRESIDENT, DIGITAL STUDIO: Gary Bennett

Pearson Canada Inc., 26 Prince Andrew Place, North York, Ontario M3C 2H4.

978-0-13-468683-7

2 18

Library and Archives Canada Cataloguing in Publication

Parkin, Michael, 1939-, author
    Macroeconomics : Canada in the global environment / Michael Parkin, Robin
Bade. — Tenth edition.

Includes index.
Issued in print and electronic formats.
ISBN 978-0-13-468683-7 (softcover).—ISBN 978-0-13-482984-5 (loose-leaf).—
ISBN 978-0-13-482989-0 (HTML).—ISBN 978-0-13-483530-3 (PDF)

    1. Macroeconomics—Textbooks. 2. Canada—Economic conditions—1991- —
Textbooks. 3. Textbooks. I. Bade, Robin, author II. Title.

HB172.5.P363 2018   339   C2017-906394-4
                                      C2017-906395-2

TO OUR STUDENTS

Michael Parkin is Professor Emeritus in the Department of Economics at the University of Western Ontario, Canada. Professor Parkin has held faculty appointments at Brown University, the University of Manchester, the University of Essex, and Bond University. He is a past president of the Canadian Economics Association and has served on the editorial boards of the *American Economic Review* and the *Journal of Monetary Economics* and as managing editor of the *Canadian Journal of Economics*. Professor Parkin's research on macroeconomics, monetary economics, and international economics has resulted in over 160 publications in journals and edited volumes, including the *American Economic Review*, the *Journal of Political Economy*, the *Review of Economic Studies*, the *Journal of Monetary Economics*, and the *Journal of Money, Credit and Banking*. He became most visible to the public with his work on inflation that discredited the use of wage and price controls. Michael Parkin also spearheaded the movement toward European monetary union. Professor Parkin is an experienced and dedicated teacher of introductory economics.

Robin Bade earned degrees in mathematics and economics at the University of Queensland and her Ph.D. at the Australian National University. She has held faculty appointments at the University of Edinburgh in Scotland, at Bond University in Australia, and at the Universities of Manitoba, Toronto, and Western Ontario in Canada. Her research on international capital flows appears in the *International Economic Review* and the *Economic Record*.

Professor Parkin and Dr. Bade are the joint authors of *Foundations of Economics* (Addison Wesley), *Modern Macroeconomics* (Pearson Education Canada), an intermediate text, and have collaborated on many research and textbook writing projects. They are both experienced and dedicated teachers of introductory economics.

BRIEF CONTENTS

Flexibility

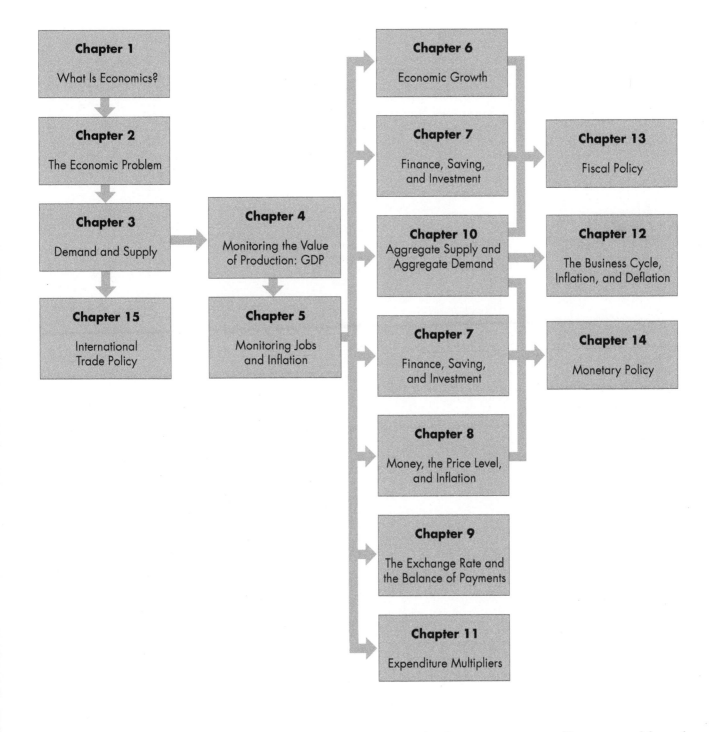

Chapter 1
What Is Economics?

Chapter 2
The Economic Problem

Chapter 3
Demand and Supply

Chapter 15
International
Trade Policy

Chapter 4
Monitoring the Value
of Production: GDP

Chapter 5
Monitoring Jobs
and Inflation

Chapter 6
Economic Growth

Chapter 7
Finance, Saving,
and Investment

Chapter 10
Aggregate Supply and
Aggregate Demand

Chapter 7
Finance, Saving,
and Investment

Chapter 8
Money, the Price Level,
and Inflation

Chapter 9
The Exchange Rate and
the Balance of Payments

Chapter 11
Expenditure Multipliers

Chapter 13
Fiscal Policy

Chapter 12
The Business Cycle,
Inflation, and Deflation

Chapter 14
Monetary Policy

Start here ...

... then jump to
any of these ...

... and jump to any of these after
doing the prerequisites indicated

◆ New To This Edition

All data figures, tables, and explanations thoroughly updated to the latest available; five main content changes; 21 new Economics in the News items based on recent events and issues; almost 80 new news-based problems and applications; and all seamlessly integrated with MyLab Economics and Pearson eText: These are the hallmarks of this tenth edition of *Macroeconomics*.

Main Content Changes

Chapter 1 now contains an entirely new section, "Economists in the Economy," which describes the types of jobs available to economics majors, their earnings compared with majors in other related areas, and the critical thinking, analytical, math, writing, and oral communication skills needed for a successful career in economics.

FIGURE 1.3 Earnings of Economics Majors

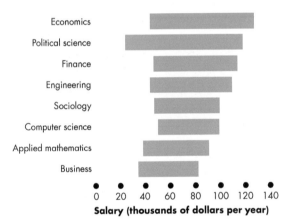

The bars show the range of earnings for eight majors in a sample of jobs monitored by the jobs survey firm PayScale. Economics graduates are the highest earners among the eight majors shown here.

Source of data: payscale.com

MyLab Economics Animation

Chapter 2 has a new section prompted by the ongoing concern about the rust-belt economy, its causes and cures, which describes and illustrates the changing patterns of production as an economy expands, and explains how technical change and economic growth first shrinks the share of agriculture as manufacturing expands and later shrinks the share of manufacturing as services expand.

Chapter 2 also has an expanded explanation and graphical derivation of the outward-bowed *PPF*.

Chapter 5 now includes the three new measures of core inflation: CPI-trim, CPI-median, and CPI-common.

FIGURE 5.8 Core Inflation

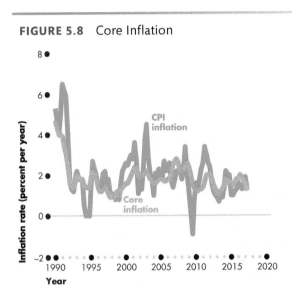

Chapter 7, Finance, Saving, and Investment, has been reorganized and streamlined with less emphasis on the 2007–2008 financial crisis and more on the current extremely low real interest rate.

Chapter 14, Monetary Policy, has a new final section on macroprudential regulation and the roles of the Bank of Canada and other federal institutions in ensuring broader financial security.

Economics in the News

The new *Economics in the News* features are listed at the back of the book. They are all chosen to address current issues likely to interest and motivate the student. An example is the one in Chapter 2 on expanding production possibilities of a B.C. First Nation.

ECONOMICS IN THE NEWS

Expanding Production Possibilities

B.C. First Nation Gives Nod to Proposed LNG Export Facility
The Canadian Press
March 27, 2017

A First Nation on Vancouver Island has approved a proposed liquefied natural gas export facility on its traditional territories.

Leaders of the Huu-ay-aht First Nation and the CEO of Vancouver-based Steelhead LNG held a joint news conference in Vancouver on Monday to announce what Chief Robert Dennis said was the First Nation's "official entry into the international business world."

Members of the small First Nation voted Saturday to approve development of the LNG facility at Sarita Bay, on the west coast of Vancouver Island ...

The company's plans could even include building a new pipeline linking Vancouver Island and the B.C. mainland ...

The company planned to make a final investment decision on Sarita Bay by 2019 or 2020, with first production targeted for 2024, he said ...

John Jack, executive councillor with the Huu-ay-aht, said it's time the First Nation took its place within Canada and British Columbia.

"This is an example of a First Nation working with business and working with the people of B.C. and Canada in order to create value that fits both of our interests."

© The Canadian Press

ESSENCE OF THE STORY

- The Huu-ay-aht First Nation on Vancouver Island has approved a liquefied natural gas export facility on its traditional territories.
- Steelhead LNG will build and operate the facility.
- A new pipeline linking Vancouver Island and the B.C. mainland is a possible part of the plan.
- Production is targeted to start in 2024.

MyLab Economics Economics in the News

News-Based Problems and Applications

Just a sample of the topics covered in the 80 new news-based problems and applications include: Shrinking brick-and-mortar retail and expanding online shopping; Canada's economic growth triples U.S.'s; jobs data highlights divergence between Canada, U.S.; thousands of robots improve human efficiency; after a summer bond binge, signs of angst are growing in the market; Poloz's best option: increase the money supply; Bank of Canada raises benchmark rate to 1%; and U.S. tariffs on Canadian softwood lumber.

◆ Solving Teaching and Learning Challenges

To change the way students see the world: this is our goal in teaching economics, in writing this book, and in playing a major role in creating content for MyLab Economics.

Three facts about students are our guiding principles. First, they want to learn, but they are overwhelmed by the volume of claims on their time and energy. So, they must see the relevance to their lives and future careers of what they are being asked to learn. Second, students want to get it, and get it quickly. So, they must be presented with clear and succinct explanations. And third, students want to make sense of today's world and be better prepared for life after school. So, they must be shown how to apply the timeless principles of economics and its models to illuminate and provide a guide to under-standing today's events and issues, and the future challenges they are likely to encounter.

The organization of this text and MyLab arise directly from these guiding principles. Each chapter begins with a clear statement of learning objectives that correspond to each chapter section.

The learning resources also arise directly from the three guiding principles, and we will describe them by placing them in five groups:

- Making economics real
- Learning the vocabulary
- Seeing the action and telling the story
- Learning interactively—learning by doing
- MyLab Economics

Making Economics Real

The student needs to see economics as a lens that sharpens the focus on real-world issues and events,

and not as a series of logical exercises with no real purpose. *Economics in the News* and *At Issue* are designed to achieve this goal.

Each chapter opens with a student-friendly vignette that raises a question to motivate and focus the chapter. The chapter explains the principles, or model, that address the question and ends with an *Economics in the News* application that helps students to think like economists by connecting chapter tools and concepts to the world around them. All these news exercises are in MyLab with instant targeted feedback and auto-grading and constant uploading of new, current exercises.

In many chapters, an additional briefer *Economics in the News* (shown here) presents a short news clip, supplemented by data where needed, poses some questions, and walks through the answers.

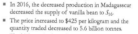

◆ ECONOMICS IN THE NEWS

The Market for Vanilla Bean

Price of Ice Cream Set to Spike
A poor harvest in Madagascar has exploded the price of vanilla bean, the flavouring in Canada's top ice cream.
Source: *The Toronto Star*, April 7, 2016

THE DATA

Year	Quantity of Vanilla Bean (billions of tonnes per year)	Price of Vanilla Bean (dollars per kilogram)
2015	7.6	70
2016	5.6	425

THE QUESTIONS

- What does the data table tell us?
- Why did the price of vanilla bean rise? Is it because demand changed or supply changed, and in which direction?

THE ANSWERS

- The data table tells us that during 2016, the quantity of vanilla bean produced increased and the price of vanilla bean increased sharply.
- An increase in demand brings an increase in the quantity and a rise in the price.
- A decrease in supply brings a decrease in the quantity and a rise in the price.
- Because the quantity of vanilla bean decreased and the price increased, there must have been a decrease in the supply of vanilla bean
- The supply of vanilla bean decreases if a poor harvest decreases production.
- The news clip says there was a poor harvest in Madagascar. This decrease in production brought a decrease in the supply of vanilla bean.
- The figure illustrates the market for vanilla bean in 2015 and 2016. The demand curve D shows the demand for vanilla bean.
- In 2015, the supply curve was S_{15}, the price was $70 per kilogram, and the quantity of vanilla bean traded was 7.6 billion tonnes.

- In 2016, the decreased production in Madagascar decreased the supply of vanilla bean to S_{16}.
- The price increased to $425 per kilogram and the quantity traded decreased to 5.6 billion tonnes.
- The higher price brought a decrease in the quantity of vanilla bean demanded, which is shown by the movement along the demand curve.

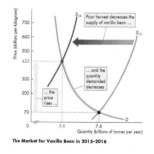

The Market for Vanilla Bean in 2015-2016

MyLab Economics Economics in the News

Four *At Issue* boxes engage the student in debate and controversy. An *At Issue* box introduces an issue and then presents two opposing views. It leaves the matter unsettled so that students and the instructor can continue the argument in class and reach their own conclusions.

Economics in Action boxes make economics real by providing data and information that links models to real-world economic activity. Some of the issues covered in these boxes include five Asian economies like fast trains on the same track; intellectual property rights propel growth; Canadian and U.S. banks compared; the tale of two central banks; Canada's 2016 budget deficit; and the size of the fiscal stimulus multipliers.

Interviews with leading economists, whose work correlates to what the student is learning, are the final component of making economics real. These interviews explore the education and research of prominent economists and their advice for those who want to continue studying the subject.

ESTHER DUFLO is the Abdul Latif Jameel Professor of Poverty Alleviation and Development Economics at the Massachusetts Institute of Technology. Among her many honours are the 2010 John Bates Clark Medal for the best economist under 40 and the Financial Times and Goldman Sachs Business Book of the Year Award in 2011 for her book (with Abhijit Banerjee) *Poor Economics: A Radical Rethinking of the Way to Fight Global Poverty*. Professor Duflo's research seeks to advance our understanding of the economic choices of the extremely poor by conducting massive real-world experiments.

Professor Duflo was an undergraduate student of history and economics at École Normale Supérieure and completed a master's degree at DELTA in Paris before moving to the United States. She earned her Ph.D. in economics at MIT in 1999.

Michael Parkin and Robin Bade talked with her about her work, which advances our understanding of the economic choices and condition of the very poor.

Professor Duflo, what's the story about how you became an economist and in particular the architect of experiments designed to understand the economic choices of the very poor?

When I was a kid, I was exposed to many stories and images of poor children: through my mother's engagement as a doctor in a small NGO dealing with child victims of war and through books and stories about children living all around the world.

I remember asking myself how I could justify my luck of being born where I was. I had a very exaggerated idea of what it was to be poor, but this idea caused sufficient discomfort that I knew I had to do something about it, if I could.

Quite by accident, I discovered that economics was the way in which I could actually be useful. While spending a year in Russia teaching French and studying history, I realized that academic economists have the ability to intervene in the world while keeping enough sanity to analyze it. I thought this would be ideal for me and I have never regretted it. I have the best job in the world.

… imagine living on under a dollar a day after your rent is paid in Seattle or Denver. Not easy!

The very poor who you study are people who live on $1 a day or $2 a day. … Is $1 a day a true measure that includes everything these poor people consume?

For defining the poverty line, we don't include the cost of housing. The poor also get free goods, sometimes of bad quality (education, healthcare) and the value of those is also not included. Other than that, yes, it is everything.

Moreover, you have to realize this is everything, taking into account the fact that life is much cheaper in many poor countries because salaries are lower, so anything that is made and consumed locally (e.g., a haircut) is cheaper.

For example, in India, the purchasing power of a dollar (in terms of the real goods you can buy) is about 3 times what it is in the United States. So the poverty line we use for India is 33 cents per day, not a dollar.

All told, you really have to imagine living on under a dollar a day after your rent is paid in Seattle or Denver. Not easy!

Learning the Vocabulary

Learning the vocabulary isn't exciting, but it is the vital first step to every discipline and it needs to be effective and quick. Highlighted key terms simplify this task. Each key term is defined in the sentence in which it is highlighted and appears in an end-of-chapter list and the end-of-book glossary (both with its page number); boldfaced in the index; and in MyLab Economics in a Flash Card tool and an auto-graded Key Terms Quiz with targeted student feedback.

Key Terms   MyLab Economics Key Terms Quiz

Change in demand, 60   Demand curve, 60   Quantity demanded, 59
Change in supply, 65   Equilibrium price, 68   Quantity supplied, 64
Change in the quantity   Equilibrium quantity, 68   Relative price, 58
  demanded, 63   Inferior good, 62   Substitute, 61
Change in the quantity supplied, 66   Law of demand, 59   Supply, 64
Competitive market, 58   Law of supply, 64   Supply curve, 64
Complement, 61   Money price, 58
Demand, 59   Normal good, 62

Showing the Action and Telling the Story

Through the past nine editions, this book has set the standard of clarity in its diagrams; the tenth edition continues to uphold this tradition. Our goal is to show "where the economic action is." The diagrams in this book continue to generate an enormously positive response, which confirms our view that graphical analysis is the most powerful tool available for teaching and learning economics at the principles level.

Recognizing that some students find graphs hard to work with, we have developed the entire art program with the study and review needs of the student in mind.

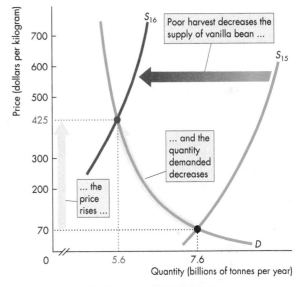

Poor harvest decreases the supply of vanilla bean …

… and the quantity demanded decreases

… the price rises …

The Market for Vanilla Bean in 2015–2016

The diagrams feature

- Axes that measure and display concrete real-world data, and where possible and relevant, the most recent data
- Graphs paired with data tables from which curves are plotted
- Original curves consistently shown in blue
- Shifted curves, equilibrium points, and other important features highlighted in red
- Colour-blended arrows to indicate movement
- Diagrams labelled with boxed notes that tell the story
- Extended captions that make each diagram and its caption a self-contained object for study and review

Learning Interactively—Learning by Doing

At the end of every chapter section, a *Review Quiz* invites the student to rework the section with questions that cover the key ideas. A parallel set of questions in MyLab Study Plan enable the student to work the questions and get instant targeted feedback.

As part of the chapter review, the student has an opportunity to work a multi-part problem called *Worked Problem* that covers the core content of the chapter and consists of questions, solutions, key points, and a key figure. This feature increases the incentive for the student to learn-by-doing and review the chapter actively, rather than passively. The Worked Problems are available in MyLab Study Plan.

MyLab™ Economics

Reach Every Student with MyLab Economics

Pearson MyLab provides a rich menu of teaching and learning resources that support your course needs and serve the learning style of each individual student.

At the core of MyLab is the Study Plan, an online learning experience that continuously adapts to the student's individual performance. MyLab learning resources also include animations of textbook figures, student PowerPoint lecture notes, and Dynamic Study Modules.

Among MyLab's instructor tools are the Assignment Manager, which enables you to create homework, quiz, test, media, and experiment assignments; the Study Plan Manager, which lets you control chapter coverage; and the Gradebook, with which you can review and manage student results.

MyLab's weekly update of *Economics in the News* brings current issues to your classroom to motivate students, and exercises arising from these stories are available to be assigned and auto-graded.

Teach Your Course Your Way
Your course is unique. So whether you'd like to build your own assignments, teach multiple sections, or set prerequisites, MyLab Economics gives you the flexibility to easily create *your* course to fit *your* needs. For instructors who want to make the most recent data a central part of their course, **Real-Time Data Analysis** exercises communicate directly with the Federal Reserve Bank of St. Louis's FRED site, so every time FRED posts new data, students can see the most recent data update automatically.

Improve Student Results
When you teach with MyLab, student performance improves. That's why

instructors have chosen MyLab for over 15 years, touching the lives of over 50 million students.

◆ Developing Employability Skills

The economic way of thinking is a foundational skill for citizenship and career. Every feature of the text helps the student develop this skill, repeatedly using its central ideas of tradeoff; opportunity cost; the margin; incentives; the gains from voluntary exchange; the forces of demand, supply, and equilibrium; the pursuit of economic rent; and the tension between self-interest and the social interest.

The new section of Chapter 1, "Economists in the Economy," identifies a further five general skills that are crucial for getting a job and developing a successful career. The table lists these skills and the features of this text that promote them.

CAREER SKILLS AND THE FEATURES THAT PROMOTE THEM

Skill	Feature
Critical thinking	Economics in the News
	At Issue
Analytical skills	The economic way of thinking
	Manipulation of models
	Application of models
	Graphical analysis
Math skills	Math appendices
Writing skills	Review Quiz and end-of-chapter problems and applications as short-answer written assignments
Oral communication skills	Economics in the News and At Issue as topics for classroom discussion and debate

◆ Table of Contents Overview and Flexibility

You have preferences for how you want to teach your course, and we've organized this book to enable you to choose your teaching path. The chart on p. xiii illustrates the book's flexibility. By following the arrows through the chart you can select the path that best fits your preference for course structure. Whether you want to teach a traditional course that blends theory and policy, or one that takes a fasttrack through either theory or policy issues, this text gives you the choice.

◆ Instructor Teaching Resources

The program comes with the following teaching resources.

Supplements available to instructors at www.pearsonhighered.com/irc	Features of the Supplement
Instructor's Manual *Macroeconomics* Instructor's Manual	• Chapter-by-chapter overviews • List of what's new in the tenth edition • Ready-to-use lecture notes
Solutions Manual *Macroeconomics* Solutions Manual by Jeannie Shearer, University of Western Ontario	• Solutions to Review Quizzes • Solutions to the end-of-chapter Study Plan Problems and Applications • Solutions to the end-of-chapter Additional Problems and Applications

Test Bank
 New questions for the *Macroeconomics* Test Bank by Jeannie Shearer of University of Western Ontario Jeannie reviewed all questions to ensure their clarity and consistency
	• Nearly 5,000 multiple-choice, true/false, short-answer, and graphing questions with these annotations:
	   ■ Difficulty level (1 for straight recall, 2 for some analysis, 3 for complex analysis)
	   ■ Type (Multiple-choice, true/false, short-answer, essay)
	   ■ Topic (the chapter section the question supports)

Computerized TestGen	• TestGen enables instructors to:
	   ■ Customize, save, and generate classroom tests
	   ■ Edit, add, or delete questions from the Test Item Files
	   ■ Analyze test results
	   ■ Organize a database of tests and student results

PowerPoints	• Slides include:
	   ■ Lectures with the textbook figures and tables animated and speaking notes from the Instructor's Manual
	   ■ Large-scale versions of all textbook figures and tables animated for instructors to incorporate into their own slide shows
	 • A student version of the lectures with animated textbook figures and tables
	 • Accessibility PowerPoints meet standards for students with disabilities. Features include, but are not limited to:
	   ■ Keyboard and screen reader access
	   ■ Alternative text for images
	   ■ High colour contrast between the background and foreground

◆ Acknowledgments

We thank our current and former colleagues and friends at the University of Western Ontario who have taught us so much. They are Jim Davies, Jeremy Greenwood, Ig Horstmann, Peter Howitt, Greg Huffman, David Laidler, Phil Reny, Chris Robinson, John Whalley, and Ron Wonnacott.

We also thank Doug McTaggart and Christopher Findlay, coauthors of the Australian edition, and Melanie Powell and Kent Matthews, coauthors of the European edition. Suggestions arising from their adaptations of earlier editions have been helpful to us in preparing this edition.

We thank the several thousand students whom we have been privileged to teach. The instant response that comes from the look of puzzlement or enlightenment has taught us how to teach economics.

We thank the management team at Pearson Canada who have built a culture that brings out the best in its editors and authors. They are Marlene Olsavsky, General Manager Higher Education, and Anne Williams, Vice President, Editorial, Higher Education. It is a special joy to thank the outstanding editors, media specialists, and others at Pearson Canada who contributed to the concerted publishing effort that brought this edition to completion. They are Emily Dill, Content Manager; Avinash Chandra, Lead Project Manager; Leanne Rancourt, Developmental Editor; Nicole Mellow, Digital Content Manager; Joanne Tang, Permissions Project Manager; Susan Bindernagel, Copy Editor; and Leigh-Anne Graham, Marketing Manager.

Leanne Rancourt was our lifeline. She kept the production process on track, provided outstanding management, and gave our manuscript a most thorough proofread and accuracy check.

Anthony Leung designed the cover and package and yet again surpassed the challenge of ensuring that we meet the highest design standards.

We thank the many exceptional reviewers who have shared their insights through the various editions of this book. Their contribution has been invaluable.

We thank the people who work directly with us. Jeannie Shearer and Sharmistha Nag provided research assistance and created exercises for MyLab Economics. Richard Parkin created the electronic art files and offered many ideas that improved the figures in this book.

Classroom experience will test the value of this book. We would appreciate hearing from instructors and students about how we can continue to improve it in future editions.

Michael Parkin
mparkin@uwo.ca

Robin Bade
robin@econ100.com

◆ Reviewers

Syed Ahmed, Red Deer Community College

Ather H. Akbari, Saint Mary's University

Doug Allen, Simon Fraser University

Benjamin Amoah, University of Guelph

Torben Andersen, Red Deer College

Terri Anderson, Fanshawe College

Syed Ashan, Concordia University

Fred Aswani, McMaster University

Iris Au, University of Toronto, Scarborough

Keith Baxter, Bishop's University

Andy Baziliauskas, University of Winnipeg

Dick Beason, University of Alberta

Karl Bennett, University of Waterloo

Ronald Bodkin, University of Ottawa

Caroline Boivin, Concordia University

Paul Booth, University of Alberta

John Boyd, University of British Columbia

John Brander, University of New Brunswick

Larry Brown, Selkirk College

Sam Bucovetsky, York University

Bogdan Buduru, Concordia University

Lutz-Alexander Busch, University of Waterloo

Beverly J. Cameron, University of Manitoba

Norman Cameron, University of Manitoba

Emanuel Carvalho, University of Waterloo

Francois Casas, University of Toronto

Alan Tak Yan Chan, Atlantic Baptist University

Robert Cherneff, University of Victoria

Jason Childs, University of New Brunswick, Saint John

Saud Choudhry, Trent University

Louis Christofides, University of Guelph

Kam Hon Chu, Memorial University of Newfoundland

George Churchman, University of Manitoba

Avi J. Cohen, York University

Constantin Colonescu, Grant MacEwan University

Ryan A. Compton, University of Manitoba

Marilyn Cottrell, Brock University

Rosilyn Coulson, Douglas College

Brian Coulter, University College of the Fraser Valley

Stanya Cunningham, Concordia University College of Alberta

Douglas Curtis, Trent University

Garth Davies, Olds College

Ajit Dayanandan, University of Northern British Columbia

Carol Derksen, Red River College

David Desjardins, John Abbott College

Vaughan Dickson, University of New Brunswick (Fredericton)

Livio Di Matteo, Lakehead University

Mohammed Dore, Brock University

Torben Drewes, Trent University

Byron Eastman, Laurentian University

Fahira Eston, Humber College

Sigrid Ewender, Kwantlen Polytechnic University

Brian Ferguson, University of Guelph

Len Fitzpatrick, Carleton University

Peter Fortura, Algonquin College

Oliver Franke, Athabasca University

Bruno Fullone, George Brown College

Donald Garrie, Georgian College

Philippe Ghayad, Dawson College and Concordia University

David Gray, University of Ottawa

Sandra Hadersbeck, Okanagan College

Rod Hill, University of New Brunswick

Eric Kam, Ryerson University

Susan Kamp, University of Alberta

Cevat Burc Kayahan, University of Guelph

Peter Kennedy, Simon Fraser University

Harvey King, University of Regina

Patricia Koss, Concordia University

Robert Kunimoto, Mt. Royal University

David Johnson, Wilfrid Laurier University

Cliff Jutlah, York University, Glendon Campus

Michael G. Lanyi, University of Lethbridge

Eva Lau, University of Waterloo

Gordon Lee, University of Alberta

Byron Lew, Trent University

Anastasia M. Lintner, University of Guelph

Scott Lynch, Memorial University

Dan MacKay, SIAST

Leigh MacDonald, University of Western Ontario

Keith MacKinnon, York University

Mohammad Mahbobi, Thompson Rivers University

S. Manchouri, University of Alberta

Christian Marfels, Dalhousie University

Raimo Martalla, Malaspina University College

Perry Martens, University of Regina

Roberto Martínez-Espíneira, St. Francis Xavier University

Dennis McGuire, Okanagan University College

Rob Moir, University of New Brunswick, Saint John

Saeed Moshiri, University of Manitoba

Joseph Muldoon, Trent University

David Murrell, University of New Brunswick, Fredericton

Robin Neill, Carleton University

A. Gyasi Nimarko, Vanier College

Sonia Novkovic, Saint Mary's University

John O'Brien, Concordia University

Arne Paus-Jenssen, University of Saskatchewan

Andrea Podhorsky, York University

Derek Pyne, Memorial University of Newfoundland

Stephen Rakoczy, Humber College

Don Reddick, Kwantlen University College

June Riley, John Abbott College

E. Riser, Memorial University

Roberta Robb, Brock University

Nick Rowe, Carleton University

Michael Rushton, University of Regina
Balbir Sahni, Concordia University
Brian Scarfe, University of Regina
Marlyce Searcy, SIAST Palliser
Jim Sentance, University of Prince Edward Island
Lance Shandler, Kwantlen University College
Stan Shedd, University of Calgary
Chandan Shirvaikar, Red Deer College
Peter Sinclair, Wilfrid Laurier University
Ian Skaith, Fanshawe College
Scott Skjei, Acadia University
Judith Skuce, Georgian College
George Slasor, University of Toronto
Norman Smith, Georgian College
Bert Somers, John Abbott College
Lewis Soroka, Brock University

Glen Stirling, University of Western Ontario
Brennan Thompson, Ryerson University
Irene Trela, University of Western Ontario
Russell Uhler, University of British Columbia
Brian VanBlarcom, Acadia University
Marianne Vigneault, Bishop's University
Jane Waples, Memorial University of Newfoundland
Tony Ward, Brock University
Bruce Wilkinson, University of Alberta
Christopher Willmore, University of Victoria
Andrew Wong, Grant MacEwan University
Peter Wylie, University of British Columbia, Okanagan
Arthur Younger, Humber College Institute of Technology and Advanced Learning
Ayoub Yousefi, University of Western Ontario
Weiqiu Yu, University of New Brunswick, Fredericton

PARKIN ◆ BADE

MACROECONOMICS

CANADA IN THE GLOBAL ENVIRONMENT   TENTH EDITION

1

WHAT IS ECONOMICS?

After studying this chapter, you will be able to:

◆ Define economics and distinguish between microeconomics and macroeconomics

◆ Explain the two big questions of economics

◆ Explain the key ideas that define the economic way of thinking

◆ Explain how economists go about their work as social scientists and policy advisers

◆ Describe the jobs available to the graduates of a major in economics

Is economics about money: How people make it and spend it? Is it about business, government, and jobs? Is it about why some people and some nations are rich and others poor? Economics is about all these things. But its core is the study of *choices* and their *consequences*.

Your life will be shaped by the choices that you make and the challenges that you face. To face those challenges and seize the opportunities they present, you must understand the powerful forces at play. The economics that you're about to learn will become your most reliable guide. This chapter gets you started by describing the questions that economists try to answer and looking at how economists think as they search for the answers.

1

Definition of Economics

A fundamental fact dominates our lives: We want more than we can get. Our inability to get everything we want is called **scarcity**. Scarcity is universal. It confronts all living things. Even parrots face scarcity!

Not only do I want a cracker—we all want a cracker!

© The New Yorker Collection 1985
Frank Modell from cartoonbank.com. All Rights Reserved.

Think about the things that *you* want and the scarcity that *you* face. You want to go to a good school, college, or university. You want to live in a well-equipped, spacious, and comfortable home. You want the latest smartphone and the fastest Internet connection for your laptop or iPad. You want some sports and recreational gear—perhaps some new running shoes, or a new bike. You want much more time than is available to go to class, do your homework, play sports and games, read novels, go to the movies, listen to music, travel, and hang out with your friends. And you want to live a long and healthy life.

What you can afford to buy is limited by your income and by the prices you must pay. And your time is limited by the fact that your day has 24 hours.

You want some other things that only governments provide. You want to live in a safe neighbourhood in a peaceful and secure world, and enjoy the benefits of clean air, lakes, rivers, and oceans.

What governments can afford is limited by the taxes they collect. Taxes lower people's incomes and compete with the other things they want to buy.

What *everyone* can get—what *society* can get—is limited by the productive resources available. These resources are the gifts of nature, human labour and ingenuity, and all the previously produced tools and equipment.

Because we can't get everything we want, we must make *choices*. You can't afford *both* a laptop *and* an iPhone, so you must *choose* which one to buy. You can't spend tonight *both* studying for your next test *and* going to the movies, so again, you must *choose* which one to do. Governments can't spend a tax dollar on *both* national defence *and* environmental protection, so they must *choose* how to spend that dollar.

Your choices must somehow be made consistent with the choices of *others*. If you choose to buy a laptop, someone else must choose to sell it. Incentives reconcile choices. An **incentive** is a reward that encourages an action or a penalty that discourages one. Prices act as incentives. If the price of a laptop is too high, more will be offered for sale than people want to buy. And if the price is too low, fewer will be offered for sale than people want to buy. But there is a price at which choices to buy and sell are consistent.

Economics is the social science that studies the *choices* that individuals, businesses, governments, and entire societies make as they cope with *scarcity* and the *incentives* that influence and reconcile those choices.

The subject has two parts:

- Microeconomics
- Macroeconomics

Microeconomics is the study of the choices that individuals and businesses make, the way these choices interact in markets, and the influence of governments. Some examples of microeconomic questions are: Why are people downloading more movies? How would a tax on e-commerce affect eBay?

Macroeconomics is the study of the performance of the national economy and the global economy. Some examples of macroeconomic questions are: Why does the Canadian unemployment rate fluctuate? Can the Bank of Canada make the unemployment rate fall by keeping interest rates low?

REVIEW QUIZ

1 List some examples of the scarcity that you face.
2 Find examples of scarcity in today's headlines.
3 Find an example of the distinction between microeconomics and macroeconomics in today's headlines.

Work these questions in Study Plan 1.1 and get instant feedback. MyLab Economics

Two Big Economic Questions

Two big questions summarize the scope of economics:

- How do choices end up determining *what, how*, and *for whom* goods and services are produced?
- Do choices made in the pursuit of *self-interest* also promote the *social interest*?

What, How, and For Whom?

Goods and services are the objects that people value and produce to satisfy wants. *Goods* are physical objects such as cellphones and automobiles. *Services* are tasks performed for people such as cellphone service and auto-repair service.

What? *What* we produce varies across countries and changes over time. In Canada today, agriculture accounts for 2 percent of total production, manufactured goods for 28 percent, and services (retail and wholesale trade, healthcare, and education are the biggest ones) for 70 percent. In contrast, in China today, agriculture accounts for 8 percent of total production, manufactured goods for 41 percent, and services for 51 percent.

Figure 1.1 shows these numbers and also the percentages for China, which fall between those for the Canada and Ethiopia.

What determines these patterns of production? How do choices end up determining the quantities of cellphones, automobiles, cellphone service, auto-repair service, and the millions of other items that are produced in Canada and around the world?

How? *How* we produce is described by the technologies and resources that we use. The resources used to produce goods and services are called **factors of production**, which are grouped into four categories:

- Land
- Labour
- Capital
- Entrepreneurship

Land The "gifts of nature" that we use to produce goods and services are called **land**. In economics, *land* is what in everyday language we call *natural resources*. It includes land in the everyday sense

FIGURE 1.1   What Three Countries Produce

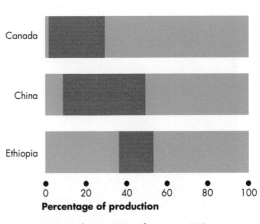

Percentage of production

■ Agriculture   ■ Manufacturing   ■ Services

Agriculture and manufacturing are small percentages of production in rich countries such as Canada and large percentages of production in poorer countries such as Ethiopia. Most of what is produced in Canada is services.

Source of data: CIA Factbook 2016, Central Intelligence Agency.

———— MyLab Economics Animation ————

together with minerals, oil, gas, coal, water, air, forests, and fish.

Our land surface and water resources are renewable, and some of our mineral resources can be recycled. But the resources that we use to create energy are nonrenewable—they can be used only once.

Labour The work time and work effort that people devote to producing goods and services is called **labour**. Labour includes the physical and mental efforts of all the people who work on farms and construction sites and in factories, shops, and offices.

The *quality* of labour depends on **human capital**, which is the knowledge and skill that people obtain from education, on-the-job training, and work experience. You are building your own human capital right now as you work on your economics course, and your human capital will continue to grow as you gain work experience.

Human capital expands over time. Today, 95 percent of the adult population of Canada have completed high school and 25 percent have a college or university degree. Figure 1.2 shows these measures of human capital in Canada and its growth over the past 41 years.

FIGURE 1.2   A Measure of Human Capital

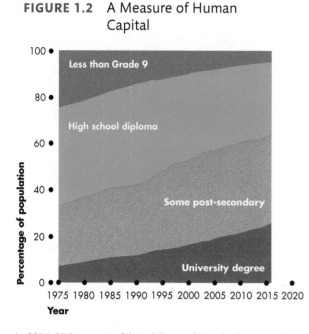

In 2016, 25.3 percent of the adult population had a university degree. A further 38.4 percent had some post-secondary education, and 94.8 percent had completed high school.

Source of data: Statistics Canada.

————————————— MyLab Economics Animation —————————

Capital The tools, instruments, machines, buildings, and other constructions that businesses use to produce goods and services are called **capital**.

In everyday language, we talk about money, stocks, and bonds as being "capital." These items are *financial capital*. Financial capital plays an important role in enabling businesses to borrow the funds that they use to buy physical capital. But financial capital is not used to produce goods and services and it is not a factor of production.

Entrepreneurship The human resource that organizes labour, land, and capital is called **entrepreneurship**. Entrepreneurs are the drivers of economic progress. They develop new ideas about what and how to produce, make business decisions, and bear the risks that arise from these decisions.

What determines how the factors of production are used to produce each good and service?

For Whom? *Who* consumes the goods and services that are produced depends on the incomes that people earn. People with large incomes can buy a wide range of goods and services. People with small incomes have fewer options and can afford a smaller range of goods and services.

People earn their incomes by selling the services of the factors of production they own:

- Land earns **rent**.
- Labour earns **wages**.
- Capital earns **interest**.
- Entrepreneurship earns **profit**.

Which factor of production earns the most income? The answer is labour. Wages and fringe benefits are around 70 percent of total income, and the incomes from land, capital, and entrepreneurship share the rest. These shares have been remarkably constant over time.

Knowing how income is shared among the factors of production doesn't tell us how it is shared among individuals. And the distribution of income among individuals is extremely unequal. You know of some people who earn very large incomes: Dwayne "The Rock" Johnson (Hercules) earned $64.5 million in 2016; and Canadian Shea Weber of the Montreal Canadiens earned $16 million in 2017.

You know of even more people who earn very small incomes. Servers at Tim Hortons, grocery store cashiers, cleaners, and janitors all earn the provincial minimum wage.

You probably know about other persistent differences in incomes. Men, on average, earn more than women; whites earn more than minorities; university graduates earn more than high school graduates.

We can get a good sense of who consumes the goods and services produced by looking at the percentages of total income earned by different groups of people. The 20 percent of people with the lowest incomes earn about 5 percent of total income, while the richest 20 percent earn close to 50 percent of total income. So on average, people in the richest 20 percent earn more than 10 times the incomes of those in the poorest 20 percent. There is even huge inequality within the richest 20 percent, and the top 1 percent earns almost 15 percent of total income.

Why is the distribution of income so unequal?

Economics provides some answers to all these questions about *what, how*, and *for whom* goods and services are produced and much of the rest of this book will help you to understand those answers.

We're now going to look at the second big question of economics: Do choices made in the pursuit of self-interest also promote the social interest?

Do Choices Made in the Pursuit of Self-Interest also Promote the Social Interest?

Every day, you and 35.4 million other Canadians, along with 7.2 billion people in the rest of the world, make economic choices that result in *what, how*, and *for whom* goods and services are produced. These choices are made by people who are pursuing their self-interest.

Self-Interest You make a choice in your **self-interest** if you think that choice is the best one available for you. All the choices that people make about how to use their time and other resources are made in the pursuit of self-interest. When you allocate your time or your budget, you do what makes the most sense to you. You might think about how your choices affect other people and take into account how you feel about that, but it is how *you* feel that influences your choice. You order a home-delivery pizza because you're hungry, not because the delivery person needs a job. And when the pizza delivery person shows up at your door, he's not doing you a favour. He's pursuing *his* self-interest and hoping for a tip and another call next week.

The big question is: Is it possible that all the choices that each one of us makes in the pursuit of self-interest could end up achieving an outcome that is best for everyone?

Social Interest An outcome is in the **social interest** if it is best for society as a whole. It is easy to see how you decide what is in *your* self-interest. But how do we decide if something is in the social interest? To help you answer this question, imagine a scene like that in *Economics in the News* on p. 6.

Ted, an entrepreneur, creates a new business. He hires a thousand workers and pays them $20 an hour, $1 an hour more than they earned in their old jobs. Ted's business is extremely profitable and his own earnings increase by $1 million per week.

You can see that Ted's decision to create the business is in his self-interest—he gains $1 million a week. You can also see that for Ted's employees, their decisions to work for Ted are in their self-interest—they gain $1 an hour (say $40 a week). And the decisions of Ted's customers must be in their self-interest, otherwise they wouldn't buy from him. But is this outcome in the social interest?

The economist's answer is "Yes." It is in the social interest because it makes everyone better off. There are no losers.

Efficiency and the Social Interest Economists use the everyday word "efficient" to describe a situation that can't be improved upon. Resource use is **efficient** if it is *not* possible to make someone better off without making someone else worse off. If it *is* possible to make someone better off without making anyone worse off, society can be made better off and the situation is not efficient.

In the Ted story everyone is better off, so it improves efficiency and the outcome is in the social interest. But notice that it would also have been efficient if the workers and customers had gained nothing and Ted had gained even more than $1 million a week. But would that efficient outcome be in the social interest?

Many people have trouble seeing the outcome in which Ted is the only winner as being in the social interest. They say that the social interest requires Ted to share some of his gain either with his workers in higher wages or with his customers in lower prices, or with both groups.

Fair Shares and the Social Interest The idea that the social interest requires "fair shares" is a deeply held one. Think about what you regard as a fair share. To help you, imagine the following game.

I put $100 on the table and tell someone you don't know and who doesn't know you to *propose* a share of the money between the two of you. If you *accept* the proposed share, you each get the agreed shares. If you don't accept the proposed share, you both get nothing.

It would be efficient—you would both be better off—if the proposer offered to take $99 and leave you with $1 and you accepted that offer.

But would you accept the $1? If you are like most people, the idea that the other person gets 99 times as much as you is just too much to stomach. "No way," you say and the $100 disappears. That outcome is inefficient. You have both given up something.

When the game I've just described is played in a classroom experiment, about half of the players reject offers of below $30.

So fair shares matter. But what is *fair*? There isn't a crisp definition of fairness to match that of efficiency. Reasonable people have a variety of views about it. Almost everyone agrees that too much inequality is unfair. But how much is too much? And inequality of what: income, wealth, or the *opportunity* to work, earn an income, and accumulate wealth?

You will examine efficiency again in Chapter 2 and efficiency and fairness in Chapter 5.

Questions about the social interest are hard ones to answer and they generate discussion, debate, and disagreement. Four issues in today's world put some flesh on these questions. The issues are:

- Globalization
- Information-age monopolies
- Climate change
- Economic instability

Globalization The term *globalization* means the expansion of international trade, borrowing and lending, and investment.

When Nike produces sports shoes, people in Malaysia get work; and when China Airlines buys new regional jets, Canadians who work at Bombardier build them. While globalization brings expanded production and job opportunities for some workers, it destroys many Canadian jobs. Workers across the manufacturing industries must learn new skills or take service jobs, which often pay less, or retire earlier than previously planned.

Globalization is in the self-interest of those consumers who buy low-cost goods and services produced in other countries; and it is in the self-interest of the multinational firms that produce in low-cost regions and sell in high-price regions. But is globalization in the self-interest of the low-wage worker in Malaysia who sews your new running shoes and the displaced shoemaker in Toronto? Is it in the social interest?

ECONOMICS IN THE NEWS

The Invisible Hand

From Brewer to Bio-Tech Entrepreneur

Kiran Mazumdar-Shaw trained to become a master brewer and learned about enzymes, the stuff from which bio-pharmaceuticals are made. Discovering it was impossible for a woman in India to become a master brewer, the 25-year-old Kiran decided to create a bio-pharmaceutical business.

Kiran's firm, Biocom, employed uneducated workers who loved their jobs and the living conditions made possible by their high wages. But when a labour union entered the scene and unionized the workers, a furious Kiran fired the workers, automated their jobs, and hired a smaller number of educated workers. Biocom continued to grow and today, Kiran's wealth exceeds $1 billion.

Kiran has become wealthy by developing and producing bio-pharmaceuticals that improve people's lives. But Kiran is sharing her wealth in creative ways. She has opened a cancer treatment centre to help thousands of patients who are too poor to pay and created a health insurance scheme.

Source: Ariel Levy, "Drug Test," *The New Yorker*, January 2, 2012.

THE QUESTIONS

- Whose decisions in the story were taken in self-interest?
- Whose decisions turned out to be in the social interest?
- Did any of the decisions harm the social interest?

THE ANSWERS

- All the decisions—Kiran's, the workers', the union's, and the firm's customers'—are taken in the pursuit of self-interest.
- Kiran's decisions serve the social interest: She creates jobs that benefit her workers and products that benefit her customers. And her charitable work brings yet further social benefits.
- The labour union's decision might have harmed the social interest because it destroyed the jobs of uneducated workers.

KIRAN MAZUMDAR-SHAW, FOUNDER AND CEO OF BIOCOM

Information-Age Monopolies The technological change of the past forty years has been called the *Information Revolution*. Bill Gates, a co-founder of Microsoft, held a privileged position in this revolution. For many years, Windows was the only available operating system for the PC. The PC and Mac competed, but the PC had a huge market share.

An absence of competition gave Microsoft the power to sell Windows at prices far above the cost of production. With lower prices, many more people would have been able to afford and buy a computer.

The information revolution has clearly served your self-interest: It has provided your cellphone, laptop, loads of handy applications, and the Internet. It has also served the self-interest of Bill Gates who has seen his wealth soar.

But did the information revolution best serve the social interest? Did Microsoft produce the best possible Windows operating system and sell it at a price that was in the social interest? Or was the quality too low and the price too high?

Climate Change Burning fossil fuels to generate electricity and to power airplanes, automobiles, and trucks pours a staggering 28 billion tonnes—4 tonnes per person—of carbon dioxide into the atmosphere each year. These carbon emissions, two-thirds of which come from the United States, China, the European Union, Russia, and India, bring global warming and climate change.

Every day, when you make self-interested choices to use electricity and gasoline, you leave your carbon footprint. You can lessen this footprint by walking, riding a bike, taking a cold shower, or planting a tree.

But can each one of us be relied upon to make decisions that affect the Earth's carbon-dioxide concentration in the social interest? Must governments change the incentives we face so that our self-interested choices are also in the social interest? How can governments change incentives? How can we

encourage the use of wind and solar power to replace the burning of fossil fuels that brings climate change?

Economic Instability In 2008, U.S. banks were in trouble. They had made loans that borrowers couldn't repay and they were holding securities the values of which had crashed.

Banks' choices to take deposits and make loans are made in self-interest, but does this lending and borrowing serve the social interest? Do banks lend too much in the pursuit of profit?

When U.S. banks got into trouble in 2008, the U.S. Federal Reserve (the Fed) bailed them out with big loans backed by taxpayer dollars. Did the Fed's bailout of troubled banks serve the social interest? Or might the Fed's rescue action encourage banks to repeat their dangerous lending in the future?

We've looked at four topics and asked many questions that illustrate the potential conflict between the pursuit of self-interest and the social interest. We've asked questions but not answered them because we've not yet explained the economic principles needed to do so. We answer these questions in future chapters.

⬥ **REVIEW QUIZ**

1 Describe the broad facts about *what*, *how*, and *for whom* goods and services are produced.

2 Use headlines from the recent news to illustrate the potential for conflict between self-interest and the social interest.

Work these questions in Study Plan 1.2 and get instant feedback.   MyLab Economics

◆ AT **ISSUE**

The Protest Against Market Capitalism

Market capitalism is an economic system in which individuals own land and capital and are free to buy and sell land, capital, and goods and services in markets. Markets for goods and services, along with markets for land and capital, coordinate billions of self-interested choices, which determine what, how, and for whom goods and services are produced. A few people earn enormous incomes, many times the average income. There is no supreme planner guiding the use of scarce resources, and the outcome is unintended and unforeseeable.

Centrally planned socialism is an economic system in which the government owns all the land and capital, directs workers to jobs, and decides what, how, and for whom to produce. The Soviet Union, several Eastern European countries, and China have used this system in the past but have now abandoned it. Only Cuba and North Korea use this system today. A few bureaucrats in positions of great power receive huge incomes, many times that of an average person.

Our economy today is a **mixed economy**, which is market capitalism with government regulation.

The Protest

The protest against market capitalism takes many forms. Historically, **Karl Marx** and other communist and socialist thinkers wanted to replace it with *socialism* and *central planning*. Today, thousands of people who feel let down by the economic system want less market capitalism and more government regulation. The **Occupy Wall Street** movement, with its focus on the large incomes of the top 1 percent, is a visible example of today's protest. Protesters say:

- Big corporations (especially big banks) have too much power and influence on governments.

- Democratically elected governments can do a better job of allocating resources and distributing income than uncoordinated markets.

- More regulation in the social interest is needed—to serve "human need, not corporate greed."

- In a market, for every winner, there is a loser.

- Big corporations are the winners. Workers and unemployed people are the losers.

The Economist's Response

Economists agree that market capitalism isn't perfect. But they argue that it is the best system available and while some government intervention and regulation can help, government attempts to serve the social interest often end up harming it.

Adam Smith (see p. 57), who gave the first systematic account of how market capitalism works, says:

- The self-interest of big corporations is *maximum profit*.

- But an *invisible hand* leads production decisions made in pursuit of self-interest to *unintentionally* promote the social interest.

- Politicians are ill-equipped to regulate corporations or to intervene in markets, and those who think they can improve on the market outcome are most likely wrong.

- In a market, buyers get what they want for less than they would be willing to pay and sellers earn a profit. Both buyers and sellers gain. A market transaction is a "win-win" event.

An Occupy Wall Street protester

"It is not from the benevolence of the butcher, the brewer, or the baker that we expect our dinner, but from their regard to their own interest."
The Wealth of Nations,
1776

Adam Smith

The Economic Way of Thinking

The questions that economics tries to answer tell us about the *scope of economics,* but they don't tell us how economists *think* and go about seeking answers to these questions. You're now going to see how economists go about their work.

We're going to look at six key ideas that define the *economic way of thinking.* These ideas are:

- A choice is a *tradeoff.*
- People make *rational choices* by comparing *benefits* and *costs.*
- *Benefit* is what you gain from something.
- *Cost* is what you *must give up* to get something.
- Most choices are "*how-much*" choices made at the *margin.*
- Choices respond to *incentives.*

A Choice Is a Tradeoff

Because we face scarcity, we must make choices. And when we make a choice, we select from the available alternatives. For example, you can spend Saturday night studying for your next test or having fun with your friends, but you can't do both of these activities at the same time. You must choose how much time to devote to each. Whatever choice you make, you could have chosen something else.

You can think about your choices as tradeoffs. A **tradeoff** is an exchange—giving up one thing to get something else. When you choose how to spend your Saturday night, you face a tradeoff between studying and hanging out with your friends.

Making a Rational Choice

Economists view the choices that people make as rational. A **rational choice** is one that compares costs and benefits and achieves the greatest benefit over cost for the person making the choice.

Only the wants of the person making a choice are relevant to determine its rationality. For example, you might like your coffee black and strong but your friend prefers his milky and sweet. So it is rational for you to choose espresso and for your friend to choose cappuccino.

The idea of rational choice provides an answer to the first question: *What* goods and services will be produced and in what quantities? The answer is those that people rationally choose to buy!

But how do people choose rationally? Why do more people choose an iPhone rather than a Black-Berry? Why don't CN and CPR build high-speed tracks so that VIA Rail can run Bombardier super-fast trains like those used in Europe? The answers turn on comparing benefits and costs.

Benefit: What You Gain

The **benefit** of something is the gain or pleasure that it brings and is determined by **preferences**—by what a person likes and dislikes and the intensity of those feelings. If you get a huge kick out of "Leagues of Legends," that video game brings you a large benefit. And if you have little interest in listening to Yo-Yo Ma playing a Vivaldi cello concerto, that activity brings you a small benefit.

Some benefits are large and easy to identify, such as the benefit that you get from being in school. A big piece of that benefit is the goods and services that you will be able to enjoy with the boost to your earning power when you graduate. Some benefits are small, such as the benefit you get from a slice of pizza.

Economists measure benefit as the most that a person is *willing to give up* to get something. You are willing to give up a lot to be in school. But you would give up only an iTunes download for a slice of pizza.

Cost: What You *Must* Give Up

The **opportunity cost** of something is the highest-valued alternative that must be given up to get it.

To make the idea of opportunity cost concrete, think about *your* opportunity cost of being in school. It has two components: the things you can't afford to buy and the things you can't do with your time.

Start with the things you can't afford to buy. You've spent all your income on tuition, residence fees, books, and a laptop. If you weren't in school, you would have spent this money on tickets to ball games and movies and all the other things that you enjoy. But that's only the start of your opportunity cost.

You've also given up the opportunity to get a job and earn an income. Suppose that the best job you could get if you weren't in school is working at CIBC as a teller earning $25,000 a year. Another part of your opportunity cost of being in school is all the things that you could buy with the extra $25,000 you would have.

As you well know, being a student eats up many hours in class time, doing homework assignments, preparing for tests, and so on. To do all these school activities, you must give up many hours of what would otherwise be leisure time spent with your friends.

So the opportunity cost of being in school is all the good things that you can't afford and don't have the spare time to enjoy. You might want to put a dollar value on that cost or you might just list all the items that make up the opportunity cost.

The examples of opportunity cost that we've just considered are all-or-nothing costs—you're either in school or not in school. Most situations are not like this one. They involve choosing *how much* of an activity to do.

How Much? Choosing at the Margin

You can allocate the next hour between studying and chatting online with your friends, but the choice is not all or nothing. You must decide how many minutes to allocate to each activity. To make this decision, you compare the benefit of a little bit more study time with its cost—you make your choice at the **margin**.

The benefit that arises from an increase in an activity is called **marginal benefit**. For example, your marginal benefit from one more night of study before a test is the boost it gives to your grade. Your marginal benefit doesn't include the grade you're already achieving without that extra night of work.

The *opportunity cost* of an *increase* in an activity is called **marginal cost**. For you, the marginal cost of studying one more night is the cost of not spending that night on your favourite leisure activity.

To make your decisions, you compare marginal benefit and marginal cost. If the marginal benefit from an extra night of study exceeds its marginal cost, you study the extra night. If the marginal cost exceeds the marginal benefit, you don't study the extra night.

Choices Respond to Incentives

Economists take human nature as given and view people as acting in their self-interest. All people— you, other consumers, producers, politicians, and public servants—pursue their self-interest.

Self-interested actions are not necessarily *selfish* actions. You might decide to use your resources in ways that bring pleasure to others as well as to yourself. But a self-interested act gets the most benefit for *you* based on *your* view about benefit.

The central idea of economics is that we can predict the self-interested choices that people make by looking at the *incentives* they face. People undertake those activities for which marginal benefit exceeds marginal cost; they reject options for which marginal cost exceeds marginal benefit.

For example, your economics instructor gives you a problem set and tells you these problems will be on the next test. Your marginal benefit from working these problems is large, so you diligently work them. In contrast, your math instructor gives you a problem set on a topic that she says will never be on a test. You get little marginal benefit from working these problems, so you decide to skip most of them.

Economists see incentives as the key to reconciling self-interest and social interest. When our choices are *not* in the social interest, it is because of the incentives we face. One of the challenges for economists is to figure out the incentives that result in self-interested choices being in the social interest.

Economists emphasize the crucial role that institutions play in influencing the incentives that people face as they pursue their self-interest. Laws that protect private property and markets that enable voluntary exchange are the fundamental institutions. You will learn as you progress with your study of economics that where these institutions exist, self-interest can indeed promote the social interest.

REVIEW QUIZ

1 Explain the idea of a tradeoff and think of three tradeoffs that you have made today.
2 Explain what economists mean by rational choice and think of three choices that you've made today that are rational.
3 Explain why opportunity cost is the best forgone alternative and provide examples of some opportunity costs that you have faced today.
4 Explain what it means to choose at the margin and illustrate with three choices at the margin that you have made today.
5 Explain why choices respond to incentives and think of three incentives to which you have responded today.

Work these questions in Study Plan 1.3 and get instant feedback.   MyLab Economics

◆ Economics as Social Science and Policy Tool

Economics is both a social science and a toolkit for advising on policy decisions.

Economist as Social Scientist

As social scientists, economists seek to discover how the economic world works. In pursuit of this goal, like all scientists, economists distinguish between positive and normative statements.

Positive Statements A *positive* statement is about what *is*. It says what is currently believed about the way the world operates. A positive statement might be right or wrong, but we can test it by checking it against the facts. "Our planet is warming because of the amount of coal that we're burning" is a positive statement. We can test whether it is right or wrong.

A central task of economists is to test positive statements about how the economic world works and to weed out those that are wrong. Economics first got off the ground in the late 1700s, so it is a young science compared with, for example, physics, and much remains to be discovered.

Normative Statements A *normative* statement is about what *ought to be*. It depends on values and cannot be tested. Policy goals are normative statements. For example, "We ought to cut our use of coal by 50 percent" is a normative policy statement. You may agree or disagree with it, but you can't test it. It doesn't assert a fact that can be checked.

Unscrambling Cause and Effect Economists are particularly interested in positive statements about cause and effect. Are computers getting cheaper because people are buying them in greater quantities? Or are people buying computers in greater quantities because they are getting cheaper? Or is some third factor causing both the price of a computer to fall and the quantity of computers bought to increase?

To answer such questions, economists create and test economic models. An **economic model** is a description of some aspect of the economic world that includes only those features that are needed for the purpose at hand. For example, an economic model of a cellphone network might include features such as the prices of calls, the number of cellphone users, and the volume of calls. But the model would ignore cellphone colours and ringtones.

A model is tested by comparing its predictions with the facts. But testing an economic model is difficult because we observe the outcomes of the simultaneous change of many factors. To cope with this problem, economists look for natural experiments (situations in the ordinary course of economic life in which the one factor of interest is different and other things are equal or similar); conduct statistical investigations to find correlations; and perform economic experiments by putting people in decision-making situations and varying the influence of one factor at a time to discover how they respond.

Economist as Policy Adviser

Economics is useful. It is a toolkit for advising governments and businesses and for making personal decisions. Some of the most famous economists work partly as policy advisers.

Many leading Canadian economists have advised governments and other organizations on a wide range of economic policy issues. Among them are David Laidler of the University of Western Ontario, Christopher Ragan of McGill University, and Angela Reddish of the University of British Columbia, all of whom have spent time advising the Bank of Canada and the Department of Finance.

All the policy questions on which economists provide advice involve a blend of the positive and the normative. Economics can't help with the normative part—the policy goal. But it can help to clarify the goal. And for a given goal, economics provides the tools for evaluating alternative solutions—comparing marginal benefits and marginal costs and finding the solution that makes the best use of the available resources.

◥ REVIEW QUIZ

1 Distinguish between a positive statement and a normative statement and provide examples.
2 What is a model? Can you think of a model that you might use in your everyday life?
3 How do economists try to disentangle cause and effect?
4 How is economics used as a policy tool?

Work these questions in Study Plan 1.4 and get instant feedback.   MyLab Economics

◆ Economists in the Economy

What are the jobs available to an economics major? Is the number of economics jobs expected to grow or shrink? How much do economics graduates earn? And what are the skills needed for an economics job?

Jobs for an Economics Major

A major in economics opens the door to the pursuit of a master's or Ph.D. and a career as an economist. Relatively few people take this path, but for those who do, the challenges are exciting and job satisfaction is high.

Economics majors work in a wide variety of jobs and situations. Some create and manage their own business, and others get jobs in private firms, government departments, think-tanks, and international organizations.

The economic way of thinking is a basic tool for running a successful business. Courtney Roofing Ltd. is an example. Jim Courtney started this business when he was a student at Western. He went on to graduate with an economics major in 1979, and today, Courtney Roofing is one of the London area's largest and most successful roofing firms.

The jobs of economics majors can generally be described as collecting and analyzing data on the production and use of resources, goods, and services; predicting future trends; and studying ways of using resources more efficiently.

Writing reports and giving talks are a big part of the job of an economist.

An economics major also opens the door to a range of jobs that have the word "analyst" in the title. Three of these jobs, that between them employ almost 1 million people, are market research analyst, financial analyst, and budget analyst.

A *market research analyst* works with data on buying patterns and tries to forecast the likely success of a product and the price that buyers are willing to pay for it.

A *financial analyst* studies trends and fluctuations in interest rates and stock and bond prices and tries to predict the cost of borrowing and the returns on investments.

A *budget analyst* keeps track of an organization's cash flow—its receipts and payments—and prepares budget plans that incorporate predictions of future cash flows.

Jim Courtney started his roofing business when he was an economics student at the University of Western Ontario.

Will Jobs for Economics Majors Grow?

The future is always uncertain and things rarely turn out as expected. But we can't avoid trying to peep into the future when we make choices that commit to a long-term plan. Economists at the U.S. Bureau of Labor Statistics (the BLS) have done their best to provide some forecasts for the U.S. economy.

The BLS forecasts that employment growth from 2014 to 2024 will be 7 percent—for every 100 jobs in 2014, there will be 107 in 2024.

Jobs for those with a Ph.D. in economics are forecasted to grow by 6 percent. This growth is a bit slower than for jobs on average because government jobs for economists are expected to shrink.

Budget analyst jobs are expected to grow by a slow 2 percent because this job is easy to replace with artificial intelligence. But jobs for financial analysts are expected to grow by 12 percent and for market research analysts by 19 percent.

Although these forecasts are for the U.S. economy, it is likely that the numbers in Canada will be similar. While there are no guarantees, these forecasts imply a bright future for people who choose to major in economics.

Earnings of Economics Majors

Earnings of economics majors vary a lot depending on the job and the level of qualifications. The Web resource payscale.com reports a pay range for its sample of economists from $44,441 to $127,500, with a median of $85,970.

A person who majors in economics and goes on to complete a Ph.D. and gets a job as an economist would expect to earn about $100,000 a year by mid-career. Economists working in finance, insurance, and government jobs earn more than the average.

Pay in "analyst" jobs are lower and range from an average of $62,000 a year for market research analysts to $80,000 a year for financial analysts.

These rates of pay put economics graduates at the top of the distribution, as you can see in Fig. 1.3. Graduates who major in political science, finance, engineering, applied math, and business earn less than economists in this sample of jobs.

Skills Needed for Economics Jobs

What are the skills that an employer looks for in a candidate for an economics-related job? Five skill requirments stand out. They are:

- Critical-thinking skills
- Analytical skills
- Math skills
- Writing skills
- Oral communication skills

Critical-Thinking Skills The ability to clarify and solve problems using logic and relevant evidence

Analytical Skills The use of economic ideas and tools to examine data, notice patterns, and reach a logical conclusion

Math Skills The ability to use mathematical and statistical tools to analyze data and reach valid conclusions

Writing Skills The ability to present ideas, conclusions, and reasons in succinct written reports appropriate for the target audience

Oral Communication Skills The ability to explain ideas, conclusions, and reasons to people with a limited background in economics

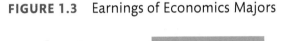

FIGURE 1.3   Earnings of Economics Majors

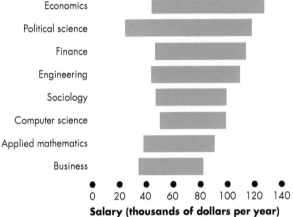

The bars show the range of earnings for eight majors in a sample of jobs monitored by the jobs survey firm PayScale. Economics graduates are the highest earners among the eight majors shown here.

Source of data: payscale.com

——————— MyLab Economics Animation ———————

You can see these skills at work (except the last one) in the forecasts of the BLS economists described earlier. These economists used their critical-thinking skills to focus on a manageable number of key features of jobs. They went on to gather relevant data on earnings and employment for a large number of jobs categories, analyzed the data using their math and economics tools, and predicted future jobs growth. They then presented their findings online at https://www.bls.gov/ooh. Round off this topic by taking a look at their work.

REVIEW QUIZ

1 What types of jobs do economists do?
2 What is the range and median level of economists' pay?
3 What are the skills needed for an economics job?

Work these questions in Study Plan 1.5 and get instant feedback.   MyLab Economics

◆ ECONOMICS IN THE NEWS

The Internet for Everyone

Mark Zuckerberg's Big Idea: The "Next 5 Billion"
Facebook founder Mark Zuckerberg wants to make it so that anyone, anywhere, can get online. To achieve this goal, he has created internet.org, "a global partnership between technology leaders, nonprofits, local communities, and experts who are working together to bring the Internet to the two-thirds of the world's population that don't have it."

Sources: CNN Money, August 21, 2013, and internet.org

THE DATA

- The figure shows that almost 80 percent of Americans and Canadians have Internet access compared to only 16 percent of Africans and 28 percent of Asians.

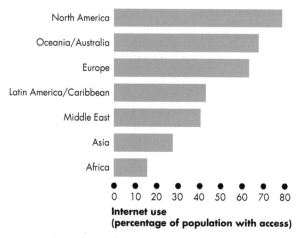

Internet use (percentage of population with access)

Internet Access by Region

- Of the 5 billion people who Mark Zuckerberg wants to have Internet access, 1 billion live in Africa and 2.8 billion live in Asia.
- To figure out what it would take for everyone to have Internet access, we must make an assumption about how many people share resources.
- If four people shared, it would cost about $285 billion for computers and $115 billion a year for Internet access for everyone to get online.
- Satisfying Mark Zuckerberg's want would cost the equivalent of 400 years of Facebook's 2012 profit, or 1,600 Boeing 787 Dreamliners, or 90 aircraft carriers, or 87 billion Big Macs.

THE QUESTIONS

- What is the fundamental economic problem and how does this news clip illustrate it?
- What are some of the things that might be forgone for more people to get online?
- Why don't more people make the tradeoffs needed to get online?
- Why might it be in Mark Zuckerberg's self-interest to get everyone online?
- Why might it not be in the social interest for everyone to get online?

In Africa, 4 in 5 people lack Internet access.

THE ANSWERS

- The fundamental economic problem is scarcity—the fact that wants exceed the resources available to satisfy them. The news clip illustrates scarcity because Mark Zuckerberg's want for everyone to get online *exceeds* the resources available to satisfy it.
- Some of the scarce resources that are used to produce airplanes, war ships, and Big Macs could be reallocated and used to produce more computers and Internet service.
- People don't make the tradeoffs needed to get online because for them the marginal cost of doing so would exceed the marginal benefit.
- It might be in Mark Zuckerberg's self-interest to get everyone online because that would increase the number of Facebook users and increase the firm's advertising revenues.
- It would not be in the social interest to get everyone online if the marginal cost of an Internet connection exceeded its marginal benefit.

SUMMARY

Key Points

Definition of Economics (p. 2)

- All economic questions arise from scarcity—from the fact that wants exceed the resources available to satisfy them.
- Economics is the social science that studies the choices that people make as they cope with scarcity.
- The subject divides into microeconomics and macroeconomics.

Working Problem 1 will give you a better understanding of the definition of economics.

Two Big Economic Questions (pp. 3–8)

- Two big questions summarize the scope of economics:

  1. How do choices end up determining *what, how,* and *for whom* goods and services are produced?
  2. When do choices made in the pursuit of *self-interest* also promote the *social interest*?

Working Problems 2 and 3 will give you a better understanding of the two big questions of economics.

The Economic Way of Thinking (pp. 9–10)

- Every choice is a tradeoff—exchanging more of something for less of something else.

- People make rational choices by comparing benefit and cost.
- Cost—*opportunity cost*—is what you must give up to get something.
- Most choices are "how much" choices made at the *margin* by comparing marginal benefit and marginal cost.
- Choices respond to incentives.

Working Problems 4 and 5 will give you a better understanding of the economic way of thinking.

Economics as Social Science and Policy Tool (p. 11)

- Economists distinguish between positive statements—what is—and normative statements—what ought to be.
- To explain the economic world, economists create and test economic models.
- Economics is a toolkit used to provide advice on government, business, and personal economic decisions.

Working Problem 6 will give you a better understanding of economics as social science and policy tool.

Economists in the Economy (pp. 12–14)

- Economics majors work in a wide range of jobs as economists and analysts.
- The job growth outlook for economics majors is good and pay is above average.

Key Terms

MyLab Economics Key Terms Quiz

Benefit, 9
Capital, 4
Economic model, 11
Economics, 2
Efficient, 5
Entrepreneurship, 4
Factors of production, 3
Goods and services, 3
Human capital, 3
Incentive, 2

Interest, 4
Labour, 3
Land, 3
Macroeconomics, 2
Margin, 10
Marginal benefit, 10
Marginal cost, 10
Microeconomics, 2
Opportunity cost, 9
Preferences, 9

Profit, 4
Rational choice, 9
Rent, 4
Scarcity, 2
Self-interest, 5
Social interest, 5
Tradeoff, 9
Wages, 4

STUDY PLAN PROBLEMS AND APPLICATIONS

MyLab Economics Work Problems 1 to 6 in Chapter 1 Study Plan and get instant feedback.

Definition of Economics (Study Plan 1.1)

1. Apple Inc. decides to make iTunes freely available in unlimited quantities.
    a. Does Apple's decision change the incentives that people face?
    b. Is Apple's decision an example of a microeconomic or a macroeconomic issue?

Two Big Economic Questions (Study Plan 1.2)

2. Which of the following pairs does not match?
    a. Labour and wages
    b. Land and rent
    c. Entrepreneurship and profit
    d. Capital and profit

3. Explain how the following news headlines concern self-interest and the social interest.
    a. Starbucks Expands in China
    b. McDonald's Moves into Online Ordering
    c. Food Must Be Labelled with Nutrition Data

The Economic Way of Thinking (Study Plan 1.3)

4. The night before an economics test, you decide to go to the movies instead of staying home and working your MyLab Study Plan. Your grade on the test was 50 percent, lower than your usual score of 70 percent.
    a. Did you face a tradeoff?
    b. What was the opportunity cost of your evening at the movies?

5. **Cost of Rio Olympics**
    Brazilian federal, state, and local governments spent R$2.8 billion and private sponsors spent R$4.2 billion on 17 new Olympic facilities, 10 of which will be used for sporting events after the Olympics.
    Source: *Financial Times*, August 6, 2016

    Was the opportunity cost of the Rio Olympics R$2.8 billion or R$7 billion? Explain your answer.

Economics as Social Science and Policy Tool (Study Plan 1.4)

6. Which of the following statements is positive, which is normative, and which can be tested?
    a. Canada should cut its imports.
    b. China is Canada's largest trading partner.
    c. If the price of gasoline rises, people will drive less and use less gasoline.

ADDITIONAL PROBLEMS AND APPLICATIONS

MyLab Economics Work these problems in Homework or Test if assigned by your instructor.

Definition of Economics

7. **Kanye West Offers Free Concert Tickets**
    Kayne West has teamed with Los Angeles inner-city schools to offer free passes for students!
    Source: consequenceofsound.net, November 27, 2016
    When Kayne West gave away tickets, what was free and what was scarce? Explain your answer.

Two Big Economic Questions

8. How does the creation of a successful movie influence *what*, *how*, and *for whom* goods and services are produced?

9. How does a successful movie illustrate self-interested choices that are also in the social interest?

The Economic Way of Thinking

10. Before starting in *Guardians of the Galaxy*, Chris Pratt had appeared in 11 movies that grossed an average of $7 million on the opening weekend. *Guardians of the Galaxy* grossed $94 million.
    a. How will the success of *Guardians of the Galaxy* influence the opportunity cost of hiring Chris Pratt?.
    b. How have the incentives for a movie producer to hire Chris Pratt changed?

11. What might be an incentive for you to take a class in summer school? List some of the benefits and costs involved in your decision. Would your choice be rational?

Economics as Social Science and Policy Tool

12. Look at today's *National Post*. What is the leading economic news story? Which big economic questions and tradeoffs does it discuss or imply?

13. Provide two microeconomic statements and two macroeconomic statements. Classify your statements as positive or normative. Explain why.

APPENDIX

Graphs in Economics

After studying this appendix, you will be able to:

◆ Make and interpret a scatter diagram

◆ Identify linear and nonlinear relationships and relationships that have a maximum and a minimum

◆ Define and calculate the slope of a line

◆ Graph relationships among more than two variables

◆ Graphing Data

A graph represents a quantity as a distance on a line. In Fig. A1.1, a distance on the horizontal line represents temperature, measured in degrees Celsius. A movement from left to right shows an increase in temperature. The point 0 represents zero degrees Celsius. To the right of 0, the temperature is positive. To the left of 0, the temperature is negative (as indicated by the minus sign). A distance on the vertical line represents height, measured in thousands of metres. The point 0 represents sea level. Points above 0 represent metres above sea level. Points below 0 represent metres below sea level (indicated by a minus sign).

In Fig. A1.1, the two scale lines are perpendicular to each other and are called *axes*. The vertical line is the *y*-axis, and the horizontal line is the *x*-axis. Each axis has a zero point, which is shared by the two axes and called the *origin*.

To make a two-variable graph, we need two pieces of information: the value of the variable *x* and the value of the variable *y*. For example, off the coast of British Columbia, the temperature is 10 degrees—the value of *x*. A fishing boat is located at 0 metres above sea level—the value of *y*. These two bits of information appear as point *A* in Fig. A1.1. A climber at the top of Mount McKinley on a cold day is 6,194 metres above sea level in a zero-degree gale. These two pieces of information appear as point *B*. On a warmer day, a climber might be at the peak of Mt. McKinley when the temperature is 10 degrees, at point *C*.

FIGURE A1.1   Making a Graph

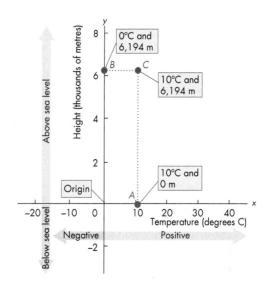

Graphs have axes that measure quantities as distances. Here, the horizontal axis (*x*-axis) measures temperature, and the vertical axis (*y*-axis) measures height. Point *A* represents a fishing boat at sea level (0 on the *y*-axis) on a day when the temperature is 10°C. Point *B* represents a climber at the top of Mt. McKinley, 6,194 metres above sea level, at a temperature of 0°C. Point *C* represents a climber at the top of Mt. McKinley, 6,194 metres above sea level, at a temperature of 10°C.

———— MyLab Economics Animation ————

We can draw two lines, called *coordinates*, from point *C*. One, called the *x*-coordinate, runs from *C* to the vertical axis. This line is called "the *x*-coordinate" because its length is the same as the value marked off on the *x*-axis. The other, called the *y*-coordinate, runs from *C* to the horizontal axis. This line is called "the *y*-coordinate" because its length is the same as the value marked off on the *y*-axis.

We describe a point on a graph by the values of its *x*-coordinate and its *y*-coordinate. For example, at point *C*, *x* is 10 degrees and *y* is 6,194 metres.

A graph like that in Fig. A1.1 can be made using any quantitative data on two variables. The graph can show just a few points, like Fig. A1.1, or many points. Before we look at graphs with many points, let's reinforce what you've just learned by looking at two graphs made with economic data.

Graphing Economic Data

Economists measure variables that describe *what, how,* and *for whom* goods and services are produced. These variables are quantities produced and consumed and their prices.

Figure A1.2 shows an example of an economics graph. This graph provides information about movies in 2016. The *x*-axis measures the quantity of movie tickets sold and the *y*-axis measures the average price of a ticket. Point *A* tells us what the quantity and price were. You can "read" this graph as telling you that in 2016, 1.3 billion movie tickets were sold at an average ticket price of $8.43.

The two graphs that you've just seen show you how to make a graph and how to read a data point on a graph, but they don't improve on the raw data. Graphs become interesting and revealing when they contain a number of data points because then you can visualize the data.

FIGURE A1.2   Making an Economics Graph

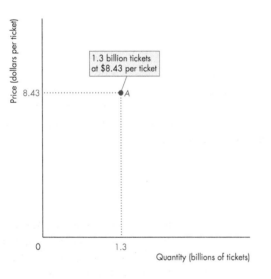

When you look at a graph, start by reading the axis labels. In this economics graph, the horizontal axis (*x*-axis) measures the quantity of movie tickets sold, and the vertical axis (*y*-axis) measures the average price of a ticket.

Once you are clear about what is being measured on the axes, look at the data graphed.

Here, there is just one point, A. It tells us the data for 2016. In that year, 1.3 billion tickets were sold at an average price of $8.43.

———————— MyLab Economics Animation ————————

Economists create graphs based on the principles in Figs. A1.1 and A1.2 to reveal, describe, and visualize the relationships among variables. We're now going to look at some examples. These graphs are called scatter diagrams.

Scatter Diagrams

A **scatter diagram** is a graph that plots the value of one variable against the value of another variable for a number of different values of each variable. Such a graph reveals whether a relationship exists between two variables and describes their relationship.

The table in Fig. A1.3 shows some data on two variables: the number of tickets sold at the box office and the worldwide box office revenue from the ticket sales for these movies.

What is the relationship between these two variables? Does a big production budget generate large ticket sales and box office revenue? Or does accurate forecasting of box office success lead to a big production budget? Or is there no connection between these two variables?

We can answer these questions by making a scatter diagram. We do so by graphing the data in the table. In the graph in Fig. A1.3, each point shows the production budget (the *x* variable) and the box office revenue (the *y* variable) of one of the movies. There are 10 movies, so there are 10 points "scattered" within the graph.

The point labelled *A* tells us that *Star Wars Episode VII: The Force Awakens* cost $306 million to produce and generated $2,059 million of box office revenue.

Star Wars was the second most costly movie to produce and brought in the second most revenue. Find the point in the graph for *Avatar*. Notice that it cost more to produce and brought in more revenue than *Star Wars*. These two points in the graph suggest that large box office sales and a big production budget are related. But look at the other eight points and a different picture emerges. There is no clear pattern formed by these data. If you want to predict a movie's box office success with any confidence, you need to know more than the movie's production budget.

Figure A1.4 shows two scatter diagrams of economic variables. Part (a) shows the relationship between income and expenditure, on average, from 2005 to 2015. Each point represents income and expenditure in a given year. For example, point *A* shows that in 2010, income was $40,000 and expenditure was $27,000. This graph shows that as income increases, so does expenditure, and the relationship is a close one.

FIGURE A1.3   A Scatter Diagram

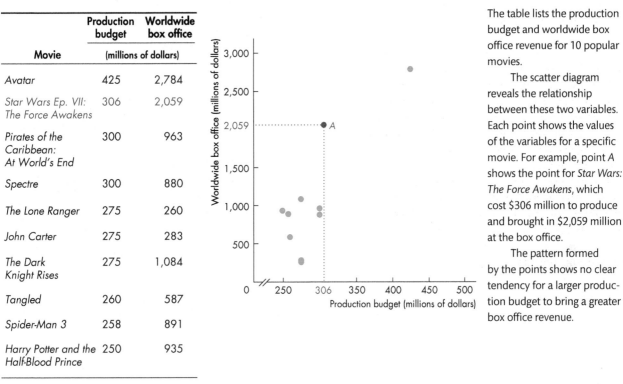

Movie	Production budget	Worldwide box office
	(millions of dollars)	
Avatar	425	2,784
Star Wars Ep. VII: The Force Awakens	306	2,059
Pirates of the Caribbean: At World's End	300	963
Spectre	300	880
The Lone Ranger	275	260
John Carter	275	283
The Dark Knight Rises	275	1,084
Tangled	260	587
Spider-Man 3	258	891
Harry Potter and the Half-Blood Prince	250	935

The table lists the production budget and worldwide box office revenue for 10 popular movies.

The scatter diagram reveals the relationship between these two variables. Each point shows the values of the variables for a specific movie. For example, point *A* shows the point for *Star Wars: The Force Awakens*, which cost $306 million to produce and brought in $2,059 million at the box office.

The pattern formed by the points shows no clear tendency for a larger production budget to bring a greater box office revenue.

MyLab Economics Animation

Figure A1.4(b) shows a scatter diagram of inflation and unemployment in Canada from 2006 to 2016. Here, the points show no relationship between the two variables. For example, when unemployment was high, the inflation rate was high in 2011 and low in 2009.

You can see that a scatter diagram conveys a wealth of information, and it does so in much less space than we have used to describe only some of its features. But you do have to "read" the graph to obtain all this information.

FIGURE A1.4   Two Economic Scatter Diagrams

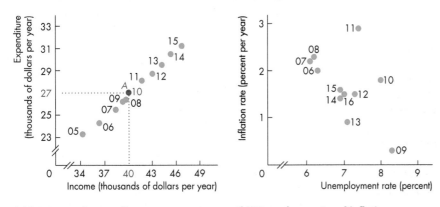

(a) Income and expenditure

(b) Unemployment and inflation

The scatter diagram in part (a) shows the relationship between income and expenditure from 2005 to 2015. Point *A* shows that in 2010, income was $40,000 on the *x*-axis and expenditure was $27,000 on the *y*-axis. This graph shows that as income rises, so does expenditure, and the relationship is a close one.

The scatter diagram in part (b) shows a weak relationship between unemployment and inflation in Canada during most of the years.

MyLab Economics Animation

Breaks in the Axes The graph in Fig. A1.4(a) has breaks in its axes, as shown by the small gaps. The breaks indicate that there are jumps from the origin, 0, to the first values recorded.

The breaks are used because the lowest value of income is $34,300 and the lowest value of expenditure exceeds $23,300. If we made this graph with no breaks in its axes, there would be a lot of empty space, the points would be crowded into the top right corner, and it would be difficult to see whether a relationship exists between these two variables. By breaking the axes, we are able to bring the relationship into view.

Putting a break in one or both axes is like using a zoom lens to bring the relationship into the centre of the graph and magnify it so that the relationship fills the graph.

Misleading Graphs Breaks can be used to highlight a relationship, but they can also be used to mislead—to make a graph that lies. The most common way of making a graph lie is to put a break in the axis and either to stretch or compress the scale. For example, suppose that in Fig. A1.4(a), the *y*-axis that measures expenditure ran from zero to $28,000 while the *x*-axis was the same as the one shown. The graph would now create the impression that despite a huge increase in income, expenditure had barely changed.

To avoid being misled, it is a good idea to get into the habit of always looking closely at the values and the labels on the axes of a graph before you start to interpret it.

Correlation and Causation A scatter diagram that shows a clear relationship between two variables, such as Fig. A1.4(a), tells us that the two variables have a high correlation. When a high correlation is present, we can predict the value of one variable from the value of the other variable. But correlation does not imply causation.

Sometimes a high correlation does arise from a causal relationship. It is likely that rising income causes rising expenditure (Fig. A1.4a). But a high correlation can mean that two variables have a common cause. For example, ice cream sales and pool drownings are correlated not because one causes the other, but because both are caused by hot weather.

You've now seen how we can use graphs in economics to show economic data and to reveal relationships. Next, we'll learn how economists use graphs to construct and display economic models.

◆ Graphs Used in Economic Models

The graphs used in economics are not always designed to show real-world data. Often they are used to show general relationships among the variables in an economic model.

An *economic model* is a stripped-down, simplified description of an economy or of a component of an economy such as a business or a household. It consists of statements about economic behaviour that can be expressed as equations or as curves in a graph. Economists use models to explore the effects of different policies or other influences on the economy in ways that are similar to the use of model airplanes in wind tunnels and models of the climate.

You will encounter many different kinds of graphs in economic models, but there are some repeating patterns. Once you've learned to recognize these patterns, you will instantly understand the meaning of a graph. Here, we'll look at the different types of curves that are used in economic models, and we'll see some everyday examples of each type of curve. The patterns to look for in graphs are the four cases in which:

- Variables move in the same direction.
- Variables move in opposite directions.
- Variables have a maximum or a minimum.
- Variables are unrelated.

Let's look at these four cases.

Variables That Move in the Same Direction

Figure A1.5 shows graphs of the relationships between two variables that move up and down together. A relationship between two variables that move in the same direction is called a **positive relationship** or a **direct relationship**. A line that slopes upward shows such a relationship.

Figure A1.5 shows three types of relationships: one that has a straight line and two that have curved lines. All the lines in these three graphs are called curves. Any line on a graph—no matter whether it is straight or curved—is called a *curve*.

A relationship shown by a straight line is called a **linear relationship**. Figure A1.5(a) shows a linear relationship between the number of kilometres travelled

FIGURE A1.5 Positive (Direct) Relationships

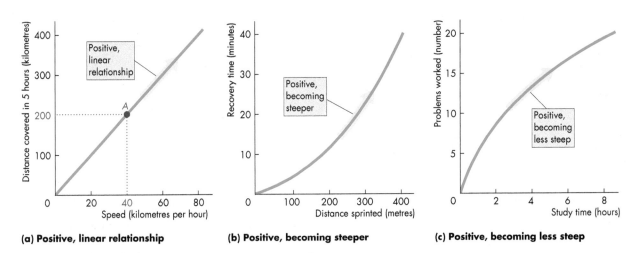

(a) Positive, linear relationship   **(b) Positive, becoming steeper**   **(c) Positive, becoming less steep**

Each part shows a positive (direct) relationship between two variables. That is, as the value of the variable measured on the *x*-axis increases, so does the value of the variable measured on the *y*-axis. Part (a) shows a linear positive relationship—as the two variables increase together, we move along a straight line.

Part (b) shows a positive relationship such that as the two variables increase together, we move along a curve that becomes steeper.

Part (c) shows a positive relationship such that as the two variables increase together, we move along a curve that becomes flatter.

MyLab Economics Animation

in 5 hours and speed. For example, point *A* shows that you will travel 200 kilometres in 5 hours if your speed is 40 kilometres an hour. If you double your speed to 80 kilometres an hour, you will travel 400 kilometres in 5 hours.

Figure A1.5(b) shows the relationship between distance sprinted and recovery time (the time it takes the heart rate to return to its normal resting rate). This relationship is an upward-sloping one that starts out quite flat but then becomes steeper as we move along the curve away from the origin. The reason this curve becomes steeper is that the additional recovery time needed from sprinting an additional 100 metres increases. It takes less than 5 minutes to recover from sprinting 100 metres but more than 10 minutes to recover from 200 metres.

Figure A1.5(c) shows the relationship between the number of problems worked by a student and the amount of study time. This relationship is an upward-sloping one that starts out quite steep and becomes flatter as we move along the curve away from the origin. Study time becomes less productive as the student spends more hours studying and becomes more tired.

Variables That Move in Opposite Directions

Figure A1.6 shows relationships between things that move in opposite directions. A relationship between variables that move in opposite directions is called a **negative relationship** or an **inverse relationship**.

Figure A1.6(a) shows the relationship between the hours spent playing squash and the hours spent playing tennis when the total time available is 5 hours. One extra hour spent playing tennis means one hour less spent playing squash and vice versa. This relationship is negative and linear.

Figure A1.6(b) shows the relationship between the cost per kilometre travelled and the length of a journey. The longer the journey, the lower is the cost per kilometre. But as the journey length increases, even though the cost per kilometre decreases, the fall in the cost per kilometre is smaller, the longer is the journey. This feature of the relationship is shown by the fact that the curve slopes downward, starting out steep at a short journey length and then becoming flatter as the journey length increases. This relationship arises because some of the costs are fixed, such as auto insurance, and the fixed costs are spread over a longer journey.

FIGURE A1.6 Negative (Inverse) Relationships

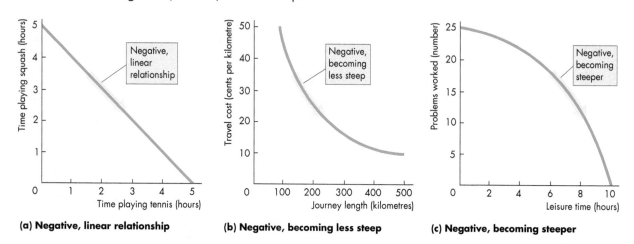

(a) Negative, linear relationship   **(b) Negative, becoming less steep**   **(c) Negative, becoming steeper**

Each part shows a negative (inverse) relationship between two variables. Part (a) shows a linear negative relationship. The total time spent playing tennis and squash is 5 hours. As the time spent playing tennis increases, the time spent playing squash decreases, and we move along a straight line.

Part (b) shows a negative relationship such that as the journey length increases, the travel cost decreases as we move along a curve that becomes less steep.

Part (c) shows a negative relationship such that as leisure time increases, the number of problems worked decreases as we move along a curve that becomes steeper.

MyLab Economics Animation

Figure A1.6(c) shows the relationship between the amount of leisure time and the number of problems worked by a student. Increasing leisure time produces an increasingly large reduction in the number of problems worked. This relationship is a negative one that starts out with a gentle slope at a small number of leisure hours and becomes steeper as the number of leisure hours increases. This relationship is a different view of the idea shown in Fig. A1.5(c).

Variables That Have a Maximum or a Minimum

Many relationships in economic models have a maximum or a minimum. For example, firms try to make the maximum possible profit and to produce at the lowest possible cost. Figure A1.7 shows relationships that have a maximum or a minimum.

Figure A1.7(a) shows the relationship between rainfall and wheat yield. When there is no rainfall, wheat will not grow, so the yield is zero. As the rainfall increases up to 10 days a month, the wheat yield increases. With 10 rainy days each month, the wheat

yield reaches its maximum at 2 tonnes per hectare (point *A*). Rain in excess of 10 days a month starts to lower the yield of wheat. If every day is rainy, the wheat suffers from a lack of sunshine and the yield decreases to zero. This relationship is one that starts out sloping upward, reaches a maximum, and then slopes downward.

Figure A1.7(b) shows the reverse case—a relationship that begins sloping downward, falls to a minimum, and then slopes upward. Most economic costs are like this relationship. An example is the relationship between the cost per kilometre and the speed of the car. At low speeds, the car is creeping in a traffic snarl-up. The number of kilometres per litre is low, so the gasoline cost per kilometre is high. At high speeds, the car is travelling faster than its efficient speed, using a large quantity of gasoline, and again the number of kilometres per litre is low and the gasoline cost per kilometre is high. At a speed of 100 kilometres an hour, the gasoline cost per kilometre is at its minimum (point *B*). This relationship is one that starts out sloping downward, reaches a minimum, and then slopes upward.

FIGURE A1.7   Maximum and Minimum Points

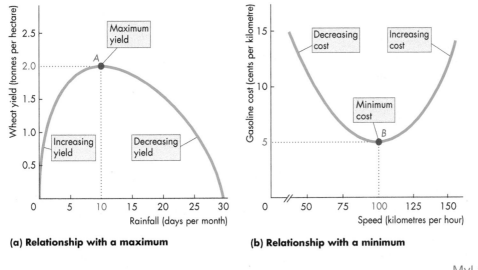

(a) Relationship with a maximum

(b) Relationship with a minimum

Part (a) shows a relationship that has a maximum point, A. The curve slopes upward as it rises to its maximum point, is flat at its maximum, and then slopes downward.

Part (b) shows a relationship with a minimum point, B. The curve slopes downward as it falls to its minimum, is flat at its minimum, and then slopes upward.

Variables That Are Unrelated

There are many situations in which no matter what happens to the value of one variable, the other variable remains constant. Sometimes we want to show the independence between two variables in a graph, and Fig. A1.8 shows two ways of achieving this.

In describing the graphs in Fig. A1.5 through Fig. A1.7, we have talked about curves that slope upward or slope downward and curves that become less steep or steeper. Let's spend a little time discussing exactly what we mean by *slope* and how we measure the slope of a curve.

FIGURE A1.8   Variables That Are Unrelated

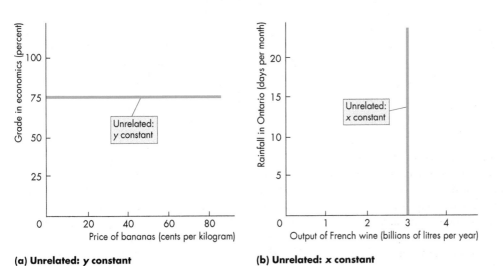

(a) Unrelated: *y* constant

(b) Unrelated: *x* constant

This figure shows how we can graph two variables that are unrelated. In part (a), a student's grade in economics is plotted at 75 percent on the *y*-axis regardless of the price of bananas on the *x*-axis. The curve is horizontal.

In part (b), the output of the vineyards of France on the *x*-axis does not vary with the rainfall in Ontario on the *y*-axis. The curve is vertical.

◆ The Slope of a Relationship

We can measure the influence of one variable on another by the slope of the relationship. The **slope** of a relationship is the change in the value of the variable measured on the y-axis divided by the change in the value of the variable measured on the x-axis. We use the Greek letter Δ (*delta*) to represent "change in." Thus Δy means the change in the value of the variable measured on the y-axis, and Δx means the change in the value of the variable measured on the x-axis. Therefore the slope of the relationship is

$$\text{Slope} = \frac{\Delta y}{\Delta x}.$$

If a large change in the variable measured on the y-axis (Δy) is associated with a small change in the variable measured on the x-axis (Δx), the slope is large and the curve is steep. If a small change in the variable measured on the y-axis (Δy) is associated with a large change in the variable measured on the x-axis (Δx), the slope is small and the curve is flat.

We can make the idea of slope clearer by doing some calculations.

The Slope of a Straight Line

The slope of a straight line is the same regardless of where on the line you calculate it. The slope of a straight line is constant. Let's calculate the slope of the positive relationship in Fig. A1.9.

FIGURE A1.9 The Slope of a Straight Line

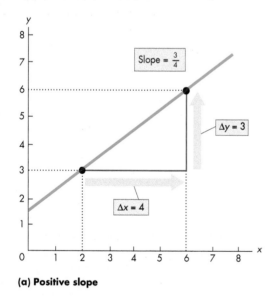

(a) Positive slope

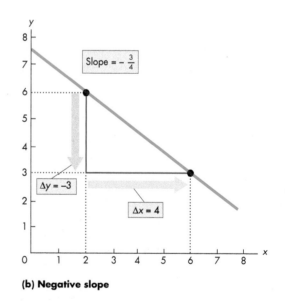

(b) Negative slope

To calculate the slope of a straight line, we divide the change in the value of the variable measured on the y-axis (Δy) by the change in the value of the variable measured on the x-axis (Δx) as we move along the line.

Part (a) shows the calculation of a positive slope. When x increases from 2 to 6, Δx equals 4. That change in

x brings about an increase in y from 3 to 6, so Δy equals 3. The slope (Δy/Δx) equals 3/4.

Part (b) shows the calculation of a negative slope. When x increases from 2 to 6, Δx equals 4. That increase in x brings about a decrease in y from 6 to 3, so Δy equals −3. The slope (Δy/Δx) equals −3/4.

In part (a), when x increases from 2 to 6, y increases from 3 to 6. The change in x is $+4$—that is, Δx is 4. The change in y is $+3$—that is, Δy is 3. The slope of that line is

$$\frac{\Delta y}{\Delta x} = \frac{3}{4}.$$

In part (b), when x increases from 2 to 6, y decreases from 6 to 3. The change in y is *minus* 3—that is, Δy is -3. The change in x is *plus* 4—that is, Δx is 4. The slope of the curve is

$$\frac{\Delta y}{\Delta x} = \frac{-3}{4}.$$

Notice that the two slopes have the same magnitude (3/4), but the slope of the line in part (a) is positive ($+3/+4 = 3/4$) while that in part (b) is negative ($-3/+4 = -3/4$). The slope of a positive relationship is positive; the slope of a negative relationship is negative.

The Slope of a Curved Line

The slope of a curved line is trickier. The slope of a curved line is not constant, so the slope depends on where on the curved line we calculate it. There are two ways to calculate the slope of a curved line: You can calculate the slope at a point, or you can calculate the slope across an arc of the curve. Let's look at the two alternatives.

Slope at a Point To calculate the slope at a point on a curve, you need to construct a straight line that has the same slope as the curve at the point in question. Figure A1.10 shows how this is done. Suppose you want to calculate the slope of the curve at point A. Place a ruler on the graph so that the ruler touches point A and no other point on the curve, then draw a straight line along the edge of the ruler. The straight red line is this line, and it is the tangent to the curve at point A. If the ruler touches the curve only at point A, then the slope of the curve at point A must be the same as the slope of the edge of the ruler. If the curve and the ruler do not have the same slope, the line along the edge of the ruler will cut the curve instead of just touching it.

Now that you have found a straight line with the same slope as the curve at point A, you can calculate the slope of the curve at point A by calculating the slope of the straight line. Along the straight

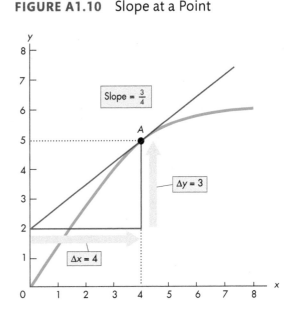

FIGURE A1.10   Slope at a Point

To calculate the slope of the curve at point A, draw the red line that just touches the curve at A–the tangent. The slope of this straight line is calculated by dividing the change in y by the change in x along the red line. When x increases from 0 to 4, Δx equals 4. That change in x is associated with an increase in y from 2 to 5, so Δy equals 3. The slope of the red line is 3/4, so the slope of the curve at point A is 3/4.

MyLab Economics Animation

line, as x increases from 0 to 4 (Δx is 4) y increases from 2 to 5 (Δy is 3). Therefore the slope of the straight line is

$$\frac{\Delta y}{\Delta x} = \frac{3}{4}.$$

So the slope of the curve at point A is 3/4.

Slope Across an Arc An arc of a curve is a piece of a curve. Figure A1.11 shows the same curve as in Fig. A1.10, but instead of calculating the slope at point A, we are now going to calculate the slope across the arc from point B to point C. You can see that the slope of the curve at point B is greater than at point C. When we calculate the slope across an arc, we are calculating the average slope between two points. As we move along the arc from B to C, x increases from 3 to 5 and y increases from 4.0 to 5.5. The change in x is 2 (Δx is 2), and the change in y is 1.5 (Δy is 1.5).

FIGURE A1.11 Slope Across an Arc

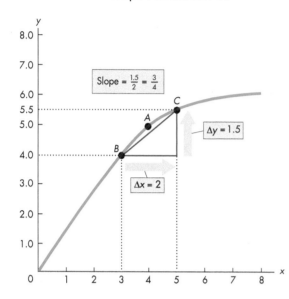

To calculate the average slope of the curve along the arc *BC*, draw a straight line from point *B* to point *C*. The slope of the line *BC* is calculated by dividing the change in *y* by the change in *x*. In moving from *B* to *C*, the increase in *x* is 2 (Δ*x* equals 2) and the change in *y* is 1.5 (Δ*y* equals 1.5). The slope of the line *BC* is 1.5 divided by 2, or 3/4. So the slope of the curve across the arc *BC* is 3/4.

—————— MyLab Economics Animation ——————

Therefore the slope is

$$\frac{\Delta y}{\Delta x} = \frac{1.5}{2} = \frac{3}{4}.$$

So the slope of the curve across the arc *BC* is 3/4.

This calculation gives us the slope of the curve between points *B* and *C*. The actual slope calculated is the slope of the straight line from *B* to *C*. This slope approximates the average slope of the curve along the arc *BC*. In this particular example, the slope across the arc *BC* is identical to the slope of the curve at point *A*, but the calculation of the slope of a curve does not always work out so neatly. You might have fun constructing some more examples and a few counter examples.

You now know how to make and interpret a graph. So far, we've limited our attention to graphs of two variables. We're now going to learn how to graph more than two variables.

Graphing Relationships Among More Than Two Variables

We have seen that we can graph the relationship between two variables as a point formed by the *x*- and *y*-coordinates in a two-dimensional graph. You might be thinking that although a two-dimensional graph is informative, most of the things in which you are likely to be interested involve relationships among many variables, not just two. For example, the amount of ice cream consumed depends on the price of ice cream and the temperature. If ice cream is expensive and the temperature is low, people eat much less ice cream than when ice cream is inexpensive and the temperature is high. For any given price of ice cream, the quantity consumed varies with the temperature; and for any given temperature, the quantity of ice cream consumed varies with its price.

Figure A1.12 shows a relationship among three variables. The table shows the number of litres of ice cream consumed each day at two different temperatures and at a number of different prices of ice cream. How can we graph these numbers?

To graph a relationship that involves more than two variables, we use the *ceteris paribus* assumption.

Ceteris Paribus

Ceteris paribus (often shortened to *cet par*) means "if all other relevant things remain the same." To isolate the relationship of interest in a laboratory experiment, a scientist holds everything constant except for the variable whose effect is being studied. Economists use the same method to graph a relationship that has more than two variables.

Figure A1.12 shows an example. There, you can see what happens to the quantity of ice cream consumed when the price of ice cream varies but the temperature is held constant.

The curve labelled 21°C shows the relationship between ice cream consumption and the price of ice cream if the temperature remains at 21°C. The numbers used to plot that curve are those in the first two columns of the table. For example, if the temperature is 21°C, 10 litres of ice cream are consumed when the price is $2.75 a scoop and 18 litres are consumed when the price is $2.25 a scoop.

The curve labelled 32°C shows the relationship between ice cream consumption and the price of ice cream if the temperature remains at 32°C. The numbers used to plot that curve are those in the first

FIGURE A1.12   Graphing a Relationship Among Three Variables

Price (dollars per scoop)	Ice cream consumption (litres per day)	
	21°C	32°C
2.00	25	50
2.25	18	36
2.50	13	26
2.75	**10**	**20**
3.00	7	14
3.25	5	10
3.50	3	6

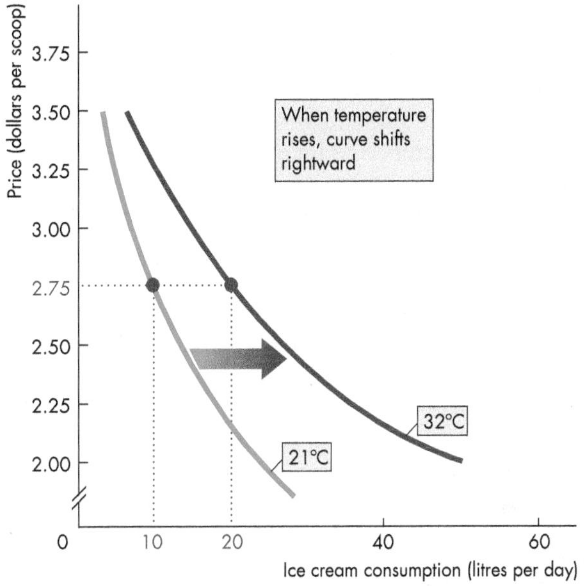

Ice cream consumption depends on its price and the temperature. The table tells us how many litres of ice cream are consumed each day at different prices and two different temperatures. For example, if the price is $2.75 a scoop and the temperature is 21°C, 10 litres of ice cream are consumed. But if the temperature is 32°C, 20 litres are consumed.

To graph a relationship among three variables, the value of one variable is held constant. The graph shows the relationship between price and consumption when the temperature is held constant. One curve holds the temperature at 21°C and the other holds it at 32°C.

A change in the price of ice cream brings a movement along one of the curves—along the blue curve at 21°C and along the red curve at 32°C.

When the temperature *rises* from 21°C to 32°C, the curve that shows the relationship between consumption and the price *shifts* rightward from the blue curve to the red curve.

MyLab Economics Animation

and third columns of the table. For example, if the temperature is 32°C, 20 litres are consumed when the price is $2.75 a scoop and 36 litres are consumed when the price is $2.25 a scoop.

When the price of ice cream changes but the temperature is constant, you can think of what happens in the graph as a movement along one of the curves. At 21°C there is a movement along the blue curve, and at 32°C there is a movement along the red curve.

When Other Things Change

The temperature is held constant along each of the curves in Fig. A1.12, but in reality the temperature changes. When that event occurs, you can think of

what happens in the graph as a shift of the curve. When the temperature rises from 21°C to 32°C, the curve that shows the relationship between ice cream consumption and the price of ice cream shifts rightward from the blue curve to the red curve.

You will encounter these ideas of movements along and shifts of curves at many points in your study of economics. Think carefully about what you've just learned and make up some examples (with assumed numbers) about other relationships.

With what you have learned about graphs, you can move forward with your study of economics. There are no graphs in this book that are more complicated than those that have been explained in this appendix.

MATHEMATICAL NOTE

Equations of Straight Lines

If a straight line in a graph describes the relationship between two variables, we call it a linear relationship. Figure 1 shows the *linear relationship* between a person's expenditure and income. This person spends $100 a week (by borrowing or spending previous savings) when income is zero. Out of each dollar earned, this person spends 50 cents (and saves 50 cents).

All linear relationships are described by the same general equation. We call the quantity that is measured on the horizontal axis (or *x*-axis) *x,* and we call the quantity that is measured on the vertical axis (or *y*-axis) *y.* In the case of Fig. 1, *x* is income and *y* is expenditure.

A Linear Equation

The equation that describes a straight-line relationship between *x* and *y* is

$$y = a + bx.$$

In this equation, *a* and *b* are fixed numbers and they are called *constants*. The values of *x* and *y* vary, so these numbers are called *variables*. Because the equation describes a straight line, the equation is called a *linear equation*.

The equation tells us that when the value of *x* is zero, the value of *y* is *a*. We call the constant *a* the *y*-axis intercept. The reason is that on the graph the straight line hits the *y*-axis at a value equal to *a*. Figure 1 illustrates the *y*-axis intercept.

For positive values of *x*, the value of *y* exceeds *a*. The constant *b* tells us by how much *y* increases above *a* as *x* increases. The constant *b* is the slope of the line.

Slope of the Line

As we explain in the appendix, the *slope* of a relationship is the change in the value of *y* divided by the change in the value of *x*. We use the Greek letter Δ (delta) to represent "change in." So Δy means the change in the value of the variable measured on the *y*-axis, and Δx means the change in the value of the variable measured on the *x*-axis. Therefore the slope of the relationship is

$$\text{Slope} = \frac{\Delta y}{\Delta x}.$$

To see why the slope is *b*, suppose that initially the value of *x* is x_1, or $200 in Fig. 2. The corresponding value of *y* is y_1, also $200 in Fig. 2. The equation of the line tells us that

$$y_1 = a + bx_1. \tag{1}$$

Now the value of *x* increases by Δx to $x_1 + \Delta x$ (or $400 in Fig. 2). And the value of *y* increases by Δy to $y_1 + \Delta y$ (or $300 in Fig. 2). The equation of the line now tells us that

$$y_1 + \Delta y = a + b(x_1 + \Delta x). \tag{2}$$

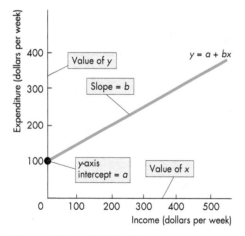

Figure 1 Linear Relationship

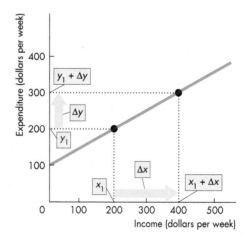

Figure 2 Calculating Slope

To calculate the slope of the line, subtract equation (1) from equation (2) to obtain

$$\Delta y = b \Delta x \qquad (3)$$

and now divide equation (3) by Δx to obtain

$$\Delta y / \Delta x = b.$$

So the slope of the line is b.

Position of the Line

The y-axis intercept determines the position of the line on the graph. Figure 3 illustrates the relationship between the y-axis intercept and the position of the line. In this graph, the y-axis measures saving and the x-axis measures income.

When the y-axis intercept, a, is positive, the line hits the y-axis at a positive value of y—as the blue line does. Its y-axis intercept is 100. When the y-axis intercept, a, is zero, the line hits the y-axis at the origin—as the purple line does. Its y-axis intercept is 0. When the y-axis intercept, a, is negative, the line hits the y-axis at a negative value of y—as the red line does. Its y-axis intercept is -100.

As the equations of the three lines show, the value of the y-axis intercept does not influence the slope of the line. All three lines have a slope equal to 0.5.

Positive Relationships

Figure 1 shows a positive relationship—the two variables x and y move in the same direction. All positive relationships have a slope that is positive. In the equation of the line, the constant b is positive. In this example, the y-axis intercept, a, is 100. The slope b equals $\Delta y / \Delta x$, which in Fig. 2 is 100/200 or 0.5. The equation of the line is

$$y = 100 + 0.5x.$$

Negative Relationships

Figure 4 shows a negative relationship—the two variables x and y move in the opposite direction. All negative relationships have a slope that is negative. In the equation of the line, the constant b is negative. In the example in Fig. 4, the y-axis intercept, a, is 30. The slope, b, equals $\Delta y / \Delta x$, which is $-20/2$ or -10. The equation of the line is

$$y = 30 + (-10)x$$

or

$$y = 30 - 10x.$$

Example

A straight line has a y-axis intercept of 50 and a slope of 2. What is the equation of this line?

The equation of a straight line is

$$y = a + bx$$

where a is the y-axis intercept and b is the slope. So the equation is

$$y = 50 + 2x.$$

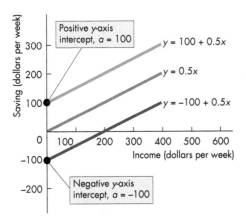

Figure 3 The *y*-Axis Intercept

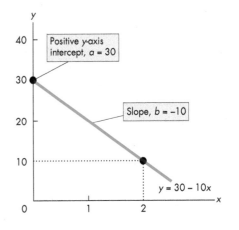

Figure 4 Negative Relationship

REVIEW QUIZ

1 Explain how we "read" the two graphs in Figs. A1.1 and A1.2.

2 Explain what scatter diagrams show and why we use them.

3 Explain how we "read" the three scatter diagrams in Figs. A1.3 and A1.4.

4 Draw a graph to show the relationship between two variables that move in the same direction.

5 Draw a graph to show the relationship between two variables that move in opposite directions.

6 Draw a graph of two variables whose relationship shows (a) a maximum and (b) a minimum.

7 Which of the relationships in Questions 4 and 5 is a positive relationship and which is a negative relationship?

8 What are the two ways of calculating the slope of a curved line?

9 How do we graph a relationship among more than two variables?

10 Explain what change will bring a *movement along* a curve.

11 Explain what change will bring a *shift* of a curve.

Work these questions in Study Plan 1A and get instant feedback.   MyLab Economics

SUMMARY

Key Points

Graphing Data (pp. 17–20)

■ A graph is made by plotting the values of two variables x and y at a point that corresponds to their values measured along the x-axis and the y-axis.

■ A scatter diagram is a graph that plots the values of two variables for a number of different values of each.

■ A scatter diagram shows the relationship between the two variables. It shows whether they are positively related, negatively related, or unrelated.

Graphs Used in Economic Models (pp. 20–23)

■ Graphs are used to show relationships among variables in economic models.

■ Relationships can be positive (an upward-sloping curve), negative (a downward-sloping curve), positive and then negative (have a maximum point), negative and then positive (have a minimum point), or unrelated (a horizontal or vertical curve).

The Slope of a Relationship (pp. 24–26)

■ The slope of a relationship is calculated as the change in the value of the variable measured on the y-axis divided by the change in the value of the variable measured on the x-axis—that is, $\Delta y/\Delta x$.

■ A straight line has a constant slope.

■ A curved line has a varying slope. To calculate the slope of a curved line, we calculate the slope at a point or across an arc.

Graphing Relationships Among More Than Two Variables (pp. 26–27)

■ To graph a relationship among more than two variables, we hold constant the values of all the variables except two.

■ We then plot the value of one of the variables against the value of another.

■ A *cet par* change in the value of a variable on an axis of a graph brings a movement along the curve.

■ A change in the value of a variable held constant along the curve brings a shift of the curve.

Key Terms

MyLab Economics Key Terms Quiz

Ceteris paribus, 26
Direct relationship, 20
Inverse relationship, 21

Linear relationship, 20
Negative relationship, 21
Positive relationship, 20

Scatter diagram, 18
Slope, 24

STUDY PLAN PROBLEMS AND APPLICATIONS

MyLab Economics Work Problems 1 to 11 in Chapter 1A Study Plan and get instant feedback.

Use the following spreadsheet to work Problems 1 to 3. The spreadsheet provides the economic data: Column A is the year, column B is the inflation rate, column C is the interest rate, column D is the growth rate, and column E is the unemployment rate.

	A	B	C	D	E
1	2006	2.5	4.9	2.7	4.6
2	2007	4.1	4.5	1.8	4.6
3	2008	0.1	1.4	−0.3	5.8
4	2009	2.7	0.2	−2.8	9.3
5	2010	1.5	0.1	2.5	9.6
6	2011	3.0	0.1	1.6	8.9
7	2012	1.7	0.1	2.2	8.1
8	2013	1.5	0.1	1.7	7.4
9	2014	0.8	0.0	2.4	6.2
10	2015	0.7	0.1	2.6	5.3
11	2016	2.1	0.3	1.6	4.9

1. Draw a scatter diagram of the inflation rate and the interest rate. Describe the relationship.
2. Draw a scatter diagram of the growth rate and the unemployment rate. Describe the relationship.
3. Draw a scatter diagram of the interest rate and the unemployment rate. Describe the relationship.

Use the following news clip to work Problems 4 to 6.

Kong Tops the Box Office

Movie	Theatres (number)	Revenue (dollars per theatre)
Kong: Skull Island	3,846	$15,867
Logan	4,071	$9,362
Get Out	3,143	$6,600
The Shack	2,888	$3,465

Source: boxofficemojo.com,
Data for weekend of February 10–12, 2017

4. Draw a graph of the relationship between the revenue per theatre on the *y*-axis and the number of theatres on the *x*-axis. Describe the relationship.
5. Calculate the slope of the relationship in Problem 4 between 3,846 and 4,071 theatres.
6. Calculate the slope of the relationship in Problem 4 between 4,071 and 3,143 theatres.

7. Calculate the slope of the following relationship.

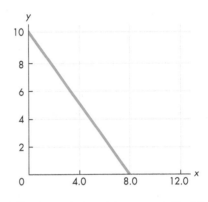

Use the following relationship to work Problems 8 and 9.

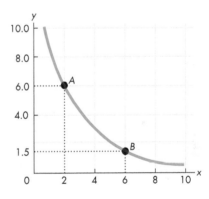

8. Calculate the slope of the relationship at point *A* and at point *B*.
9. Calculate the slope across the arc *AB*.

Use the following table to work Problems 10 and 11. The table gives the price of a balloon ride, the temperature, and the number of rides a day.

Price (dollars per ride)	Balloon rides (number per day)		
	10°C	20°C	30°C
5	32	40	50
10	27	32	40
15	18	27	32

10. Draw a graph to show the relationship between the price and the number of rides when the temperature is 20°C. Describe this relationship.
11. What happens in the graph in Problem 10 if the temperature rises to 30°C?

ADDITIONAL PROBLEMS AND APPLICATIONS

MyLab Economics You can work these problems in Homework or Test if assigned by your instructor.

Use the following spreadsheet to work Problems 12 to 14. The spreadsheet provides data on oil and gasoline: Column A is the year, column B is the price of oil (dollars per barrel), column C is the price of gasoline (cents per litre), column D is oil production, and column E is the quantity of gasoline refined (both in millions of barrels per day).

	A	B	C	D	E
1	2006	66	262	5.1	15.6
2	2007	72	284	5.1	15.4
3	2008	100	330	5.0	15.3
4	2009	62	241	5.4	14.8
5	2010	79	284	5.5	15.2
6	2011	95	358	5.6	15.1
7	2012	94	368	6.5	15.5
8	2013	98	358	7.5	15.2
9	2014	93	344	8.8	15.5
10	2015	49	252	9.4	16.6
11	2016	45	225	8.9	16.4

12. Draw a scatter diagram of the price of oil and the quantity of oil produced. Describe the relationship.

13. Draw a scatter diagram of the price of gasoline and the quantity of gasoline refined. Describe the relationship.

14. Draw a scatter diagram of the quantity of oil produced and the quantity of gasoline refined. Describe the relationship.

Use the following data to work Problems 15 to 17. Draw a graph that shows the relationship between the two variables x and y:

x	0	1	2	3	4	5
y	25	24	22	18	12	0

15. a. Is the relationship positive or negative?
    b. Does the slope of the relationship become steeper or flatter as the value of x increases?
    c. Think of some economic relationships that might be similar to this one.

16. Calculate the slope of the relationship between x and y when x equals 3.

17. Calculate the slope of the relationship across the arc as x increases from 4 to 5.

18. Calculate the slope of the curve in the figure in the next column at point A.

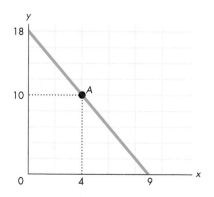

Use the following relationship to work Problems 19 and 20.

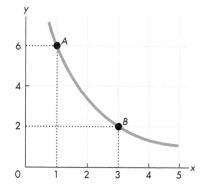

19. Calculate the slope at point A and at point B.
20. Calculate the slope across the arc AB.

Use the following table to work Problems 21 to 23. The table gives data about umbrellas: price, the number purchased, and rainfall in millimetres (mm).

Price	Umbrellas (number purchased per day)		
(dollars per umbrella)	0 mm	200 mm	400 mm
20	4	7	8
30	2	4	7
40	1	2	4

21. Draw a graph to show the relationship between the price and the number of umbrellas purchased, holding the amount of rainfall constant at 200 mm. Describe this relationship.

22. What happens in the graph in Problem 21 if the price rises and rainfall is constant?

23. What happens in the graph in Problem 21 if the rainfall increases from 200 mm to 400 mm?

THE ECONOMIC PROBLEM

After studying this chapter, you will be able to:

◆ Define the production possibilities frontier and use it to calculate opportunity cost

◆ Distinguish between production possibilities and preferences and describe an efficient allocation of resources

◆ Explain how specialization and trade expand production possibilities

◆ Explain how current production choices expand future production possibilities, change what we produce, and destroy and create jobs

◆ Describe the economic institutions that coordinate decisions

Canada has vast oil and natural gas resources and we produce much more energy than we consume. We are an energy-exporting nation. Should we produce and export even more oil and gas? How do we know when we are using our energy and other resources efficiently?

In this chapter, you study an economic model that answers questions about the efficiency of production and trade.

At the end of the chapter, in *Economics in the News*, we'll apply what you learn to explain why it is smart to export some of our oil and gas, and why it might not be smart to increase our gas exports.

◆ Production Possibilities and Opportunity Cost

Every working day, in mines, factories, shops, and offices and on farms and construction sites across Canada, 18 million people produce a vast variety of goods and services valued at $60 billion. But the quantities of goods and services that we can produce are limited by our available resources and by technology. And if we want to increase our production of one good, we must decrease our production of something else—we face a tradeoff. You are now going to study the limits to production.

The **production possibilities frontier** (*PPF*) is the boundary between those combinations of goods and services that can be produced and those that cannot. To illustrate the *PPF*, we look at a *model economy* in which the quantities produced of only two goods change, while the quantities produced of all the other goods and services remain the same.

Let's look at the production possibilities frontier for cola and pizza, which represent *any* pair of goods or services.

Production Possibilities Frontier

The *production possibilities frontier* for cola and pizza shows the limits to the production of these two goods, given the total resources and technology available to produce them. Figure 2.1 shows this production possibilities frontier. The table lists combinations of the quantities of pizza and cola that can be produced in a month and the figure graphs these combinations. The *x*-axis shows the quantity of pizzas produced, and the *y*-axis shows the quantity of cola produced.

The *PPF* illustrates *scarcity* because the points outside the frontier are *unattainable*. These points describe wants that can't be satisfied.

We can produce at any point *inside* the *PPF* or *on* the *PPF*. These points are *attainable*. For example, we can produce 4 million pizzas and 5 million cans of cola. Figure 2.1 shows this combination as point *E* in the graph and as possibility *E* in the table.

Moving along the *PPF* from point *E* to point *D* (possibility *D* in the table) we produce more cola and less pizza: 9 million cans of cola and 3 million pizzas. Or moving in the opposite direction from point *E* to point *F* (possibility *F* in the table), we produce more pizza and less cola: 5 million pizzas and no cola.

FIGURE 2.1 Production Possibilities Frontier

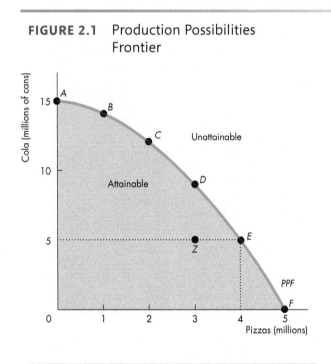

Possibility	Pizzas (millions)		Cola (millions of cans)
A	0	and	15
B	1	and	14
C	2	and	12
D	3	and	9
E	4	and	5
F	5	and	0

The table lists six production possibilities for cola and pizzas. Row *A* tells us that if we produce no pizzas, the maximum quantity of cola we can produce is 15 million cans. Points *A*, *B*, *C*, *D*, *E*, and *F* in the figure represent the rows of the table. The curve passing through these points is the production possibilities frontier (*PPF*).

The *PPF* separates the attainable from the unattainable. Production is possible at any point *inside* the orange area or *on* the frontier. Points outside the frontier are unattainable. Points inside the frontier, such as point *Z*, are inefficient because resources are wasted or misallocated. At such points, it is possible to use the available resources to produce more of either or both goods.

—— MyLab Economics Animation and Draw Graph ——

Production Efficiency

We achieve **production efficiency** if we produce goods and services at the lowest possible cost. This outcome occurs at all the points *on* the *PPF*. At points *inside* the *PPF*, production is inefficient because we are giving up more than necessary of one good to produce a given quantity of the other good.

For example, at point *Z* in Fig. 2.1, we produce 3 million pizzas and 5 million cans of cola, but we have enough resources to produce 3 million pizzas and 9 million cans of cola. Our pizzas cost more cola than necessary. We can get them for a lower cost. Only when we produce *on* the *PPF* do we incur the lowest possible cost of production.

Production inside the *PPF* is *inefficient* because resources are either *unused* or *misallocated* or both.

Resources are *unused* when they are idle but could be working. For example, we might leave some of the factories idle or some workers unemployed.

Resources are *misallocated* when they are assigned to tasks for which they are not the best match. For example, we might assign skilled pizza chefs to work in a cola factory and skilled cola workers to cook pizza in a pizzeria. We could get more pizzas *and* more cola if we reassigned these workers to the tasks that more closely match their skills.

Tradeoff Along the *PPF*

A choice *along* the *PPF* involves a *tradeoff*. Tradeoffs like that between cola and pizza arise in every imaginable real-world situation in which a choice must be made. At any given time, we have a fixed amount of labour, land, capital, and entrepreneurship and a given state of technology. We can employ these resources and technology to produce goods and services, but we are limited in what we can produce.

When doctors want to spend more on cancer research, they face a tradeoff: more medical research for less of some other things. When Parliament wants to spend more on education, it faces a tradeoff: more education for less national defence or border security. When an environmental group argues for less logging, it is suggesting a tradeoff: greater conservation of endangered wildlife for less paper. When you want a higher grade on your next test, you face a tradeoff: spend more time studying and less leisure or sleep time.

All the tradeoffs you've just considered involve a cost—an opportunity cost.

Opportunity Cost

The **opportunity cost** of an action is the highest-valued alternative forgone. The *PPF* makes this idea precise and enables us to calculate opportunity cost. Along the *PPF*, there are only two goods, so there is only one alternative forgone: some quantity of the other good. To produce more pizzas we must produce less cola. The opportunity cost of producing an additional pizza is the cola we *must* forgo. Similarly, the opportunity cost of producing an additional can of cola is the quantity of pizza we must forgo.

In Fig. 2.1, if we move from point *C* to point *D*, we produce an additional 1 million pizzas but 3 million fewer cans of cola. The additional 1 million pizzas *cost* 3 million cans of cola. Or 1 pizza costs 3 cans of cola. Similarly, if we move from *D* to *C*, we produce an additional 3 million cans of cola but 1 million fewer pizzas. The additional 3 million cans of cola *cost* 1 million pizzas. Or 1 can of cola costs 1/3 of a pizza.

Opportunity Cost Is a Ratio Opportunity cost is a ratio. It is the decrease in the quantity produced of one good divided by the increase in the quantity produced of another good as we move along the production possibilities frontier.

Because opportunity cost is a ratio, the opportunity cost of producing an additional can of cola is equal to the *inverse* of the opportunity cost of producing an additional pizza. Check this proposition by returning to the calculations we've just done. In the move from *C* to *D*, the opportunity cost of a pizza is 3 cans of cola. In the move from *D* to *C*, the opportunity cost of a can of cola is 1/3 of a pizza. So the opportunity cost of pizza is the inverse of the opportunity cost of cola.

Increasing Opportunity Cost The opportunity cost of a pizza increases as the quantity of pizzas produced increases. The outward-bowed shape of the *PPF* reflects increasing opportunity cost. When we produce a large quantity of cola and a small quantity of pizza—between points *A* and *B* in Fig. 2.1—the frontier has a gentle slope. An increase in the quantity of pizzas costs a small decrease in the quantity of cola—the opportunity cost of a pizza is a small quantity of cola.

When we produce a large quantity of pizzas and a small quantity of cola—between points *E* and *F* in Fig. 2.1—the frontier is steep. A given increase in the quantity of pizzas *costs* a large decrease in the quantity of cola, so the opportunity cost of a pizza is a large quantity of cola.

ECONOMICS IN THE NEWS

Opportunity Cost of Kale

Kale Popularity Puts Pressure on Seed Supply
With kale's surging popularity, kale farmers are taking pre-cautions to avoid wasting seeds. Kale sales are up more than 30 percent and the price has gone up 80 percent over the past three years.

Source: *CBS News*, January 18, 2016

THE QUESTIONS

■ How does the *PPF* illustrate (1) the limits to kale pro-duction; (2) the tradeoff we must make to increase kale production; and (3) the effect of increased kale consumption on the cost of producing kale?

THE ANSWERS

■ The figure shows the global *PPF* for kale and other goods and services. Point *A* on the *PPF* tells us that if 4 million tonnes of kale are produced, a maximum of 96 units of other goods and services can be produced.

■ The movement along the *PPF* from *A* to *B* shows the tradeoff we must make to increase kale production.

■ The slope of the *PPF* measures the opportunity cost of producing kale. If kale production increases from zero to 4 million tonnes, the production of other goods and services decreases from 100 units to 96 units. The opportunity cost of producing 1 tonne of kale is 1 unit of other goods and services.

■ But if kale production increases from 4 million tonnes

to 8 million tonnes, the production of other goods and services decreases from 96 units to 80 units. The opportunity cost of producing 1 tonne of kale is now 4 units of other goods and services.

■ As resources are moved into producing kale, labour, land, and capital less suited to the task of kale produc-tion are used and the cost of the additional kale pro-duced increases.

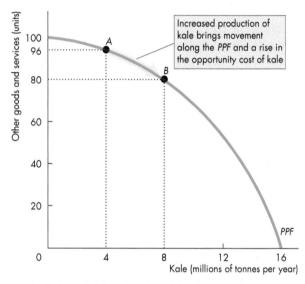

PPF for Kale and Other Goods and Services

MyLab Economics Economics in the News

The *PPF* is bowed outward because resources are not all equally productive in all activities. People with many years of experience working for PepsiCo are good at producing cola but not very good at making pizzas. So if we move some of these people from PepsiCo to Domino's, we get a small increase in the quantity of pizzas but a large decrease in the quantity of cola.

Similarly, people who have spent years working at Domino's are good at producing pizzas, but they have no idea how to produce cola. So if we move some peo-ple from Domino's to PepsiCo, we get a small increase in the quantity of cola but a large decrease in the quan-tity of pizzas. The more we produce of either good, the less productive are the additional resources we use and the larger is the opportunity cost of a unit of that good.

How do we choose among the points on the *PPF*? How do we know which point is the best?

REVIEW QUIZ

1 How does the production possibilities frontier illustrate scarcity?

2 How does the production possibilities frontier illustrate production efficiency?

3 How does the production possibilities frontier show that every choice involves a tradeoff?

4 How does the production possibilities frontier illustrate opportunity cost?

5 Why is opportunity cost a ratio?

6 Why does the *PPF* bow outward and what does that imply about the relationship between opportunity cost and the quantity produced?

Work these questions in Study Plan 2.1 and get instant feedback.   MyLab Economics

◆ Using Resources Efficiently

We achieve *production efficiency* at every point on the *PPF*, but which of these points is best? The answer is the point on the *PPF* at which goods and services are produced in the quantities that provide the greatest possible benefit. When goods and services are produced at the lowest possible cost and in the quantities that provide the greatest possible benefit, we have achieved **allocative efficiency**.

The questions that we raised when we reviewed the four big issues in Chapter 1 are questions about allocative efficiency. To answer such questions, we must measure and compare costs and benefits.

The *PPF* and Marginal Cost

The **marginal cost** of a good is the opportunity cost of producing one more unit of it. We calculate marginal cost from the slope of the *PPF*. As the quantity of pizzas produced increases, the *PPF* gets steeper and the marginal cost of a pizza increases. Figure 2.2 illustrates the calculation of the marginal cost of a pizza.

Begin by finding the opportunity cost of pizza in blocks of 1 million pizzas. The cost of the first million pizzas is 1 million cans of cola; the cost of the second million pizzas is 2 million cans of cola; the cost of the third million pizzas is 3 million cans of cola, and so on. The bars in part (a) illustrate these calculations.

The bars in part (b) show the cost of an average pizza in each of the 1 million pizza blocks. Focus on the third million pizzas—the move from *C* to *D* in part (a). Over this range, because 1 million pizzas cost 3 million cans of cola, one of these pizzas, on average, costs 3 cans of cola—the height of the bar in part (b).

Next, find the opportunity cost of each additional pizza—the marginal cost of a pizza. The marginal cost of a pizza increases as the quantity of pizzas produced increases. The marginal cost at point *C* is less than it is at point *D*. On average over the range from *C* to *D*, the marginal cost of a pizza is 3 cans of cola. But it exactly equals 3 cans of cola only in the middle of the range between *C* and *D*.

The red dot in part (b) indicates that the marginal cost of a pizza is 3 cans of cola when 2.5 million pizzas are produced. Each black dot in part (b) is interpreted in the same way. The red curve that passes through these dots, labelled *MC*, is the marginal cost curve. It shows the marginal cost of a pizza at each quantity of pizzas as we move along the *PPF*.

FIGURE 2.2   The *PPF* and Marginal Cost

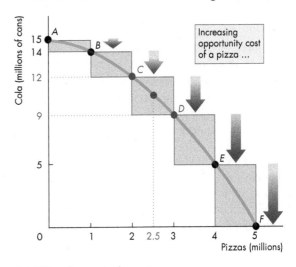

(a) *PPF* and opportunity cost

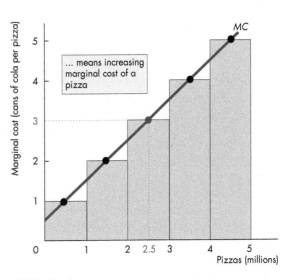

(b) Marginal cost

Marginal cost is calculated from the slope of the *PPF*. As the quantity of pizzas produced increases, the *PPF* gets steeper and the marginal cost of a pizza increases. The bars in part (a) show the opportunity cost of pizza in blocks of 1 million pizzas. The bars in part (b) show the cost of an average pizza in each of these 1 million blocks. The red curve, *MC*, shows the marginal cost of a pizza at each point along the *PPF*. This curve passes through the centre of each of the bars in part (b).

MyLab Economics Animation

Preferences and Marginal Benefit

The **marginal benefit** from a good or service is the benefit received from consuming one more unit of it. This benefit is subjective. It depends on people's **preferences**—people's likes and dislikes and the intensity of those feelings.

Marginal benefit and *preferences* stand in sharp contrast to *marginal cost* and *production possibilities*. Preferences describe what people like and want and the production possibilities describe the limits or constraints on what is feasible.

We need a concrete way of illustrating preferences that parallels the way we illustrate the limits to production using the *PPF*.

The device that we use to illustrate preferences is the **marginal benefit curve**, which is a curve that shows the relationship between the marginal benefit from a good and the quantity consumed of that good. Note that the *marginal benefit curve* is *unrelated* to the *PPF* and cannot be derived from it.

We measure the marginal benefit from a good or service by the most that people are *willing to pay* for an additional unit of it. The idea is that you are willing to pay less for a good than it is worth to you but you are not willing to pay more: The most you are willing to pay for something is its marginal benefit.

It is a general principle that the more we have of any good or service, the smaller is its marginal benefit and the less we are willing to pay for an additional unit of it. This tendency is so widespread and strong that we call it a principle—the *principle of decreasing marginal benefit*.

The basic reason why marginal benefit decreases is that we like variety. The more we consume of any one good or service, the more we tire of it and would prefer to switch to something else.

Think about your willingness to pay for a pizza. If pizza is hard to come by and you can buy only a few slices a year, you might be willing to pay a high price to get an additional slice. But if pizza is all you've eaten for the past few days, you are willing to pay almost nothing for another slice.

You've learned to think about cost as opportunity cost, not as a dollar cost. You can think about marginal benefit and willingness to pay in the same way. The marginal benefit, measured by what you are willing to pay for something, is the quantity of other goods and services that you are willing to forgo. Let's continue with the example of cola and pizza and illustrate preferences this way.

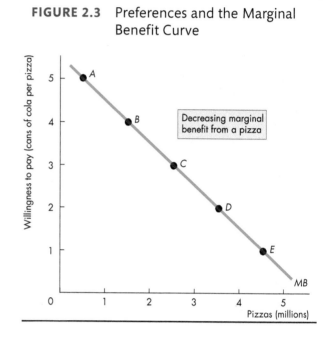

FIGURE 2.3 Preferences and the Marginal Benefit Curve

Possibility	Pizzas (millions)	Willingness to pay (cans of cola per pizza)
A	0.5	5
B	1.5	4
C	2.5	3
D	3.5	2
E	4.5	1

The smaller the quantity of pizzas available, the more cola people are willing to give up for an additional pizza. With 0.5 million pizzas available, people are willing to pay 5 cans of cola per pizza. But with 4.5 million pizzas, people are willing to pay only 1 can of cola per pizza. Willingness to pay measures marginal benefit. A universal feature of people's preferences is that marginal benefit decreases.

MyLab Economics Animation

Figure 2.3 illustrates preferences as the willingness to pay for pizza in terms of cola. In row *A*, with 0.5 million pizzas available, people are willing to pay 5 cans of cola per pizza. As the quantity of pizzas increases, the amount that people are willing to pay for a pizza falls. With 4.5 million pizzas available, people are willing to pay only 1 can of cola per pizza.

Let's now use the concepts of marginal cost and marginal benefit to describe allocative efficiency.

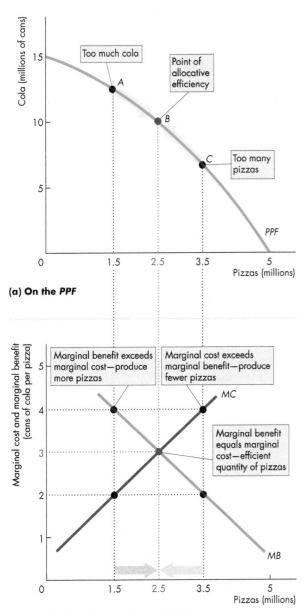

FIGURE 2.4   Efficient Use of Resources

(a) On the PPF

(b) Marginal benefit equals marginal cost

The greater the quantity of pizzas produced, the smaller is the marginal benefit (*MB*) from pizza—the less cola people are willing to give up to get an additional pizza. But the greater the quantity of pizzas produced, the greater is the marginal cost (*MC*) of a pizza—the more cola people must give up to get an additional pizza. When marginal benefit equals marginal cost, resources are being used efficiently.

MyLab Economics Animation

Allocative Efficiency

At *any* point on the *PPF*, we cannot produce more of one good without giving up some other good. At the *best* point on the *PPF*, we cannot produce more of one good without giving up some other good that provides greater benefit. We are producing at the point of allocative efficiency—the point on the *PPF* that we prefer above all other points.

Suppose in Fig. 2.4 we produce 1.5 million pizzas. In part (b), the marginal cost of a pizza is 2 cans of cola and the marginal benefit from a pizza is 4 cans of cola. Because someone values an additional pizza more highly than it costs to produce, we can get more value from our resources by moving some of them out of producing cola and into producing pizza.

Now suppose we produce 3.5 million pizzas. The marginal cost of producing a pizza is now 4 cans of cola, but the marginal benefit from a pizza is only 2 cans of cola. Because the additional pizza costs more than anyone thinks it is worth, we can get more value from our resources by moving some of them away from producing pizza and into producing cola.

Suppose we produce 2.5 million pizzas. Marginal cost and marginal benefit are now equal at 3 cans of cola. This allocation of resources between pizzas and cola is efficient. If more pizzas are produced, the forgone cola is worth more than the additional pizzas. If fewer pizzas are produced, the forgone pizzas are worth more than the additional cola.

REVIEW QUIZ

1 What is marginal cost? How is it measured?
2 What is marginal benefit? How is it measured?
3 How does the marginal benefit from a good change as the quantity produced of that good increases?
4 What is allocative efficiency and how does it relate to the production possibilities frontier?
5 What conditions must be satisfied if resources are used efficiently?

Work these questions in Study Plan 2.2 and get instant feedback.   *MyLab Economics*

You now understand the limits to production and the conditions under which resources are used efficiently. Your next task is to to see how both buyer and seller gain from specialization and trade.

◆ Gains from Trade

People can produce for themselves all the goods and services that they consume, or they can produce one good or a few goods and trade with others. Producing only one good or a few goods is called *specialization*. We are going to learn how people gain by specializing in the production of the good in which they have a *comparative advantage* and trading with others.

Comparative Advantage and Absolute Advantage

A person has a **comparative advantage** in an activity if that person can perform the activity at a lower opportunity cost than anyone else. Differences in opportunity costs arise from differences in individual abilities and from differences in the characteristics of other resources.

No one excels at everything. One person is an outstanding pitcher but a poor catcher; another person is a brilliant lawyer but a poor teacher. In almost all human endeavours, what one person does easily, someone else finds difficult. The same applies to land and capital. One plot of land is fertile but has no mineral deposits; another plot of land has outstanding views but is infertile. One machine has great precision but is difficult to operate; another is fast but often breaks down.

Although no one excels at everything, some people excel and can outperform others in a large number of activities—perhaps even in all activities. A person who is more productive than others has an **absolute advantage**.

Absolute advantage involves comparing productivities—production per hour—whereas comparative advantage involves comparing opportunity costs.

A person who has an absolute advantage does not have a *comparative* advantage in every activity. John Grisham is a better lawyer and a better author of fast-paced thrillers than most people. He has an absolute advantage in these two activities. But compared to others, he is a better writer than lawyer, so his *comparative* advantage is in writing.

Because ability and resources vary from one person to another, people have different opportunity costs of producing various goods. These differences in opportunity cost are the source of comparative advantage.

Let's explore the idea of comparative advantage by looking at two smoothie bars: one operated by Liz and the other operated by Joe.

Joe's Smoothie Bar Joe produces smoothies and salads in a small, low-tech bar. He has only one blender, and it's a slow, old machine that keeps stopping. Even if Joe uses all his resources to produce smoothies, he can produce only 6 an hour—see Table 2.1. But Joe is good at making salads, and if he uses all his resources in this activity, he can produce 30 salads an hour.

Joe's ability to make smoothies and salads is the same regardless of how he splits an hour between the two tasks. He can make a salad in 2 minutes or a smoothie in 10 minutes. For each additional smoothie Joe produces, he must decrease his production of salads by 5. And for each additional salad he produces, he must decrease his production of smoothies by 1/5 of a smoothie. So

> Joe's opportunity cost of producing 1 smoothie is 5 salads,

and

> Joe's opportunity cost of producing 1 salad is 1/5 of a smoothie.

Joe's customers buy smoothies and salads in equal quantities. So Joe spends 50 minutes of each hour making smoothies and 10 minutes of each hour making salads. With this division of his time, Joe produces 5 smoothies and 5 salads an hour.

Figure 2.5(a) illustrates the production possibilities at Joe's smoothie bar—Joe's *PPF*.

Joe's *PPF* is linear (not outward bowed) because his ability to produce salads and smoothies is the same no matter how he divides his time between the two activities. Joe's opportunity cost of a smoothie is constant—it is the same at all quantities of smoothies produced.

TABLE 2.1   Joe's Production Possibilities

Item	Minutes to produce 1	Quantity per hour
Smoothies	10	6
Salads	2	30

Liz's Smoothie Bar Liz also produces smoothies and salads but in a high-tech bar that is much more productive than Joe's. Liz can turn out either a smoothie or a salad every 2 minutes—see Table 2.2.

If Liz spends all her time making smoothies, she can produce 30 an hour. And if she spends all her time making salads, she can also produce 30 an hour.

Liz's ability to make smoothies and salads, like Joe's, is the same regardless of how she divides her time between the two tasks. She can make a salad in 2 minutes or a smoothie in 2 minutes. For each additional smoothie Liz produces, she must decrease her production of salads by 1. And for each additional salad she produces, she must decrease her production of smoothies by 1. So

> Liz's opportunity cost of producing 1 smoothie is 1 salad,

and

> Liz's opportunity cost of producing 1 salad is 1 smoothie.

TABLE 2.2 Liz's Production Possibilities

Item	Minutes to produce 1	Quantity per hour
Smoothies	2	30
Salads	2	30

Liz's customers buy smoothies and salads in equal quantities, so she splits her time equally between the two items and produces 15 smoothies and 15 salads an hour.

Figure 2.5(b) illustrates the production possibilities at Liz's smoothie bar—Liz's *PPF*.

Like Joe's, Liz's *PPF* is linear because her ability to produce salads and smoothies is the same no matter how she divides her time between the two activities. Liz's opportunity cost of a smoothie is 1 salad at all quantities of smoothies produced.

FIGURE 2.5 The Production Possibilities Frontiers

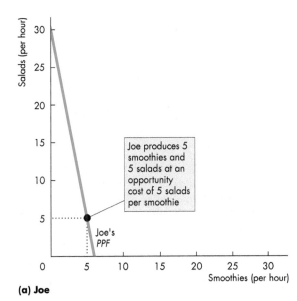

(a) Joe

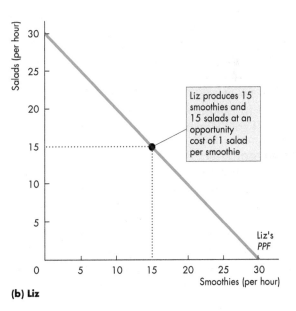

(b) Liz

Joe can produce 30 salads per hour, 1 every 2 minutes, if he produces no smoothies. Or, he can produce 6 smoothies per hour, 1 every 10 minutes, if he produces no salads. Joe's customers buy equal quantities of salads and smoothies, so Joe produces 5 of each. His opportunity cost of a smoothie is 5 salads.

Liz can produce 30 salads or 30 smoothies per hour, 1 of either item every 2 minutes. Liz's customers buy equal quantities of salads and smoothies, so she produces 15 of each. Liz's opportunity cost of a smoothie is 1 salad.

Joe's Comparative Advantage In which of the two activities does Joe have a comparative advantage? To answer this question, first recall the definition of comparative advantage. A person has a comparative advantage when that person's opportunity cost of producing a good is lower than another person's opportunity cost of producing that same good.

Joe's opportunity cost of producing a salad is only 1/5 of a smoothie, while Liz's opportunity cost of producing a salad is 1 smoothie. So Joe has a comparative advantage in producing salads.

Liz's Comparative Advantage If Joe has a comparative advantage in producing salads, Liz must have a comparative advantage in producing smoothies. Check the numbers. For Joe, a smoothie costs 5 salads, and for Liz, a smoothie costs only 1 salad. So Liz has a comparative advantage in making smoothies.

Achieving the Gains from Trade

Liz and Joe run into each other one evening in a singles bar. After a few minutes of getting acquainted, Liz tells Joe about her amazing smoothie business. Her only problem, she tells Joe, is that she would like to produce more because potential customers leave when her lines get too long.

Joe doesn't want to risk spoiling a potential relationship by telling Liz about his own struggling business, but he takes the risk. Joe explains to Liz that he spends 50 minutes of every hour making 5 smoothies and 10 minutes making 5 salads. Liz's eyes pop. "Have I got a deal for you!" she exclaims.

Liz's Proposal Here's the deal that Liz sketches on a paper napkin:

1. We'll both specialize in producing the good in which we have a comparative advantage.

2. Joe will stop making smoothies and allocate all his time to producing salads.

3. Liz will stop making salads and allocate all her time to producing smoothies.

4. Together we will produce 30 smoothies and 30 salads—see Table 2.3(b).

5. We will then trade. Joe will get smoothies from Liz, and Liz will get salads from Joe.

6. We must agree on a price at which to trade.

Agreeing on a Price Liz is buying salads from Joe, and Joe is buying smoothies from Liz. Normally, in

TABLE 2.3 Liz and Joe Gain from Trade

(a) Initially	Liz	Joe
Smoothies	15	5
Salads	15	5

(b) After specialization	Liz	Joe
Smoothies	30	0
Salads	0	30

(c) Trade	Liz	Joe
Smoothies	sell 10	buy 10
Salads	buy 20	sell 20

(d) After trade	Liz	Joe
Smoothies	20	10
Salads	20	10

(e) Gains from trade	Liz	Joe
Smoothies	+5	+5
Salads	+5	+5

a situation like this one, the trading partners will bargain about the price, with each person trying for the lowest price at which to buy and the highest price at which to sell.

But Liz and Joe like each other and quickly agree on a price that ends up sharing the gains from the new arrangement equally.

The price is not expressed in dollars but in salads per smoothie. They agree on a price of 2 salads per smoothie. For Liz, that is a good deal because she can produce a smoothie at a cost of 1 salad and sell it to Joe for 2 salads. It is also a good deal for Joe because he can produce a salad at a cost of 1/5 of a smoothie and sell it to Liz for 1/2 a smoothie.

Liz explains that any price above 1 salad per smoothie is good for her and any price below 5 salads per smoothie is good for Joe, so a price of 2 salads per smoothie lets them both gain, as she now describes.

At the proposed price of 2 salads per smoothie, Liz offers to sell Joe 10 smoothies in exchange for 20 salads. Equivalently, Joe sells Liz 20 salads in exchange for 10 smoothies—see Table 2.3(c).

FIGURE 2.6   The Gains from Trade

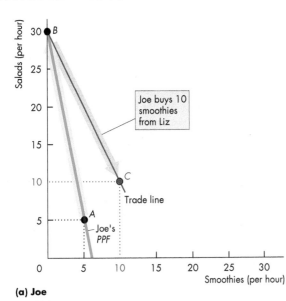

(a) Joe

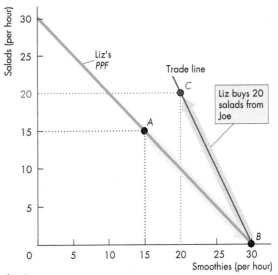

(b) Liz

Initially, Joe produces at point *A* on his *PPF* in part (a), and Liz produces at point *A* on her *PPF* in part (b). Joe's opportunity cost of producing a salad is less than Liz's, so Joe has a comparative advantage in producing salads. Liz's opportunity cost of producing a smoothie is less than Joe's, so Liz has a comparative advantage in producing smoothies.

If Joe specializes in making salads, he produces 30 salads and no smoothies at point *B* on his *PPF*. If Liz specializes in

making smoothies, she produces 30 smoothies and no salads at point *B* on her *PPF*. They exchange salads for smoothies along the red "Trade line." Liz buys salads from Joe for less than her opportunity cost of producing them. Joe buys smoothies from Liz for less than his opportunity cost of producing them. Each goes to point *C*—a point outside his or her *PPF*. With specialization and trade, Joe and Liz gain 5 smoothies and 5 salads each with no extra resources.

MyLab Economics Animation and Draw Graph

After this trade, Joe has 10 salads—the 30 salads he produces minus the 20 he sells to Liz. He also has the 10 smoothies that he buys from Liz. So Joe now has increased the quantities of smoothies and salads that he can sell to his customers—see Table 2.3(d).

Liz has 20 smoothies—the 30 she produces minus the 10 she sells to Joe. She also has the 20 salads that she buys from Joe. Liz has increased the quantities of smoothies and salads that she can sell to her customers—see Table 2.3(d). Both Liz and Joe gain 5 smoothies and 5 salads an hour—see Table 2.3(e).

Illustrating Liz's Idea To illustrate her idea, Liz grabs a fresh napkin and draws the graphs in Fig. 2.6. First, she sketches Joe's *PPF* in part (a) and shows the point at which he is producing before they meet. Recall that he is producing 5 smoothies and 5 salads an hour at point *A*.

She then sketches her own *PPF* in part (b), and marks the point *A* at which she is producing 15 smoothies and 15 salads an hour.

She then shows what happens when they each specialize in producing the good in which they have a comparative advantage. Joe specializes in producing salads and produces 30 salads and no smoothies at point *B* on his *PPF*. Liz specializes in producing smoothies and produces 30 smoothies and no salads at point *B* on her *PPF*.

They then trade smoothies and salads at a price of 2 salads per smoothie or 1/2 a smoothie per salad. The red "Trade line" that Liz draws on each part of the figure illustrates the tradeoff that each faces at the proposed price.

Liz now shows Joe the amazing outcome of her idea. After specializing and trading, Joe gets 10 smoothies and 10 salads at point *C*—a gain of 5 smoothies and 5 salads. He moves to a point *outside* his *PPF*. And Liz gets 20 smoothies and 20 salads at point *C*—also a gain of 5 smoothies and 5 salads—and moves to a point *outside* her *PPF*.

Despite Liz being more productive than Joe, both gain from specializing at producing the good in which they have a comparative advantage and trading.

The Liz–Joe Economy and Its *PPF*

With specialization and trade, Liz and Joe get outside their individual *PPF*s. But think about Liz and Joe as representing an entire economy. You know that it isn't possible to produce outside the economy's *PPF*. So, what's going on?

The answer is that although Liz and Joe get outside their individual *PPF*s with specialization, they produce on the economy's *PPF*.

Figure 2.7 illustrates the construction of the economy's *PPF*.

If both Liz and Joe produce only salads, the economy produces 60 salads per hour at point *A* in Fig. 2.7. Liz produces the first 30 at a cost of 1 salad per smoothie.

When Liz is using all her resources to produce smoothies, the economy is at point *B*. At this point, both are specializing in the good for which they have a comparative advantage.

If the economy is to produce more than 30 smoothies, Joe must join Liz in producing some. But the 31st smoothie, produced by Joe, costs 5 salads. If all its resources are used to produce smoothies, the economy produces 36 per hour at point *C*.

Outward-Bowed *PPF* The outward-kinked curve, *PPF*, is the Liz–Joe economy's production possibilities frontier. Despite Liz and Joe having constant opportunity costs—linear *PPF*s—along the economy's *PPF* opportunity cost is increasing. For the economy with only two people, the economy's *PPF* is kinked rather than bowed outward. But applying the same ideas that you've seen in the Liz–Joe economy to an economy with millions of people, the *PPF* is outward bowed.

Efficiency and Inefficiency When Liz and Joe specialize, they produce efficiently on the economy's *PPF*. They can also produce efficiently at any other point along their economy *PPF*. But without specialization and trade, they produce at an inefficient point inside the economy's *PPF*. You can see this fact in Fig. 2.7. If Liz and Joe produce their own smoothies and salads, they produce at point *D* inside the economy *PPF*. All the economy's resources are fully employed at point *D*, but they are misallocated.

FIGURE 2.7 The Liz–Joe Economy *PPF*

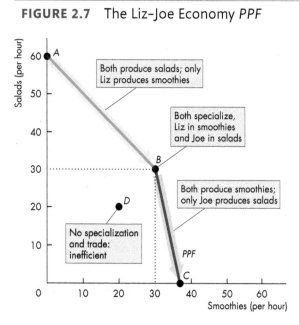

When the economy produces more than 30 salads per hour, both Liz and Joe produce salads but only Liz produces smoothies. When the economy produces more than 30 smoothies per hour, both Liz and Joe produce smoothies but only Joe produces salads.

When Liz and Joe specialize in their comparative advantage, the economy produces 30 salads and 30 smoothies at an efficient point on the economy's *PPF*.

Without specialization and trade, Liz and Joe produce at an inefficient point inside the economy's *PPF*.

MyLab Economics Animation and Draw Graph

REVIEW QUIZ

1 What gives a person a comparative advantage?
2 Distinguish between comparative advantage and absolute advantage.
3 Why do people specialize and trade?
4 What are the gains from specialization and trade?
5 What is the source of the gains from trade?
6 Why do specialization and the gains from trade make the economy's *PPF* bow outward?
7 Why is not specializing and reaping the gains from trade inefficient?

Work these questions in Study Plan 2.3 and get instant feedback.   MyLab Economics

◆ Economic Growth

During the past 30 years, production per person in Canada has doubled. The expansion of production possibilities is called **economic growth**. Economic growth increases our *standard of living,* but it doesn't overcome scarcity and avoid opportunity cost. To make our economy grow, we face a tradeoff—the faster we make production grow, the greater is the opportunity cost of economic growth.

The Cost of Economic Growth

Economic growth comes from technological change and capital accumulation. **Technological change** is the development of new goods and of better ways of producing goods and services. **Capital accumulation** is the growth of capital resources, including *human capital.*

Technological change and capital accumulation have vastly expanded our production possibilities. We can produce automobiles that provide us with more transportation than was available when we had only horses and carriages. We can produce satellites that provide global communications on a much larger scale than that available with the earlier cable technology. But if we use our resources to develop new technologies and produce capital, we must decrease our production of consumption goods and services. New technologies and new capital have an opportunity cost. Let's look at this opportunity cost.

Instead of studying the *PPF* of pizzas and cola, we'll hold the quantity of cola produced constant and examine the *PPF* for pizzas and pizza ovens. Figure 2.8 shows this *PPF* as the blue curve PPF_0. If we devote no resources to producing pizza ovens, we produce at point *A.* If we produce 3 million pizzas, we can produce 6 pizza ovens at point *B.* If we produce no pizza, we can produce 10 ovens at point *C.*

The amount by which our production possibilities expand depends on the resources we devote to technological change and capital accumulation. If we devote no resources to this activity (point *A*), our *PPF* remains the blue curve PPF_0 in Fig. 2.8. If we cut the current pizza production and produce 6 ovens (point *B*), then in the future, we'll have more capital and our *PPF* will rotate outward to the position shown by the red curve PPF_1.

By allocating fewer resources to producing pizza and more resources to producing ovens, the greater is the expansion of our future production possibilities.

FIGURE 2.8 Economic Growth

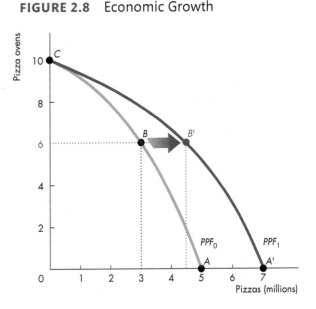

PPF_0 shows the limits to the production of pizzas and pizza ovens, with the production of all other goods and services remaining the same. If we devote no resources to producing pizza ovens and produce 5 million pizzas, our production possibilities will remain the same at PPF_0. But if we decrease pizza production to 3 million and produce 6 ovens, at point *B,* our production possibilities expand. After one period, the *PPF* rotates outward to PPF_1 and we can produce at point *B',* a point outside the original PPF_0. We can rotate the *PPF* outward, but we cannot avoid opportunity cost. The opportunity cost of producing more pizzas in the future is fewer pizzas today.

— MyLab Economics Animation and Draw Graph —

Economic growth brings enormous benefits in the form of increased consumption in the future, but economic growth is not free and it doesn't abolish scarcity.

In Fig. 2.8, to make economic growth happen, we must use some resources to produce new capital (ovens), which leaves fewer resources to produce pizzas. To move to *B'* in the future, we must move from *A* to *B* today. The opportunity cost of producing more pizzas in the future is fewer pizzas today. Also, on the new *PPF,* we still face a tradeoff and opportunity cost.

The ideas about economic growth that we have explored in the setting of the pizza industry also apply to nations. Hong Kong and Canada provide a striking case study.

ECONOMICS IN ACTION

Hong Kong Overtakes Canada

In 1966, the production possibilities per person in Canada were more than three times those in Hong Kong (see the figure). Canada devotes one-fifth of its resources to accumulating capital, and in 1966, Canada was at point A on its *PPF*. Hong Kong devotes one-third of its resources to accumulating capital, and in 1966, Hong Kong was at point A on its *PPF*.

Since 1966, both economies have experienced economic growth, but because Hong Kong devotes a bigger fraction of its resources to accumulating capital, its production possibilities have expanded more quickly.

By 2016, production possibilities per person in Hong Kong had *overtaken* those in Canada. If Hong Kong continues to devote more resources to accumulating capital (at point B on its 2016 *PPF*) than Canada does, Hong Kong will continue to grow more rapidly than Canada. But if Hong Kong decreases its capital accumulation (moving to point D on its 2016 *PPF*), then its rate of economic growth will slow.

Hong Kong is typical of the fast-growing Asian economies, which include Taiwan, Thailand, South Korea, China, and India. Production possibilities

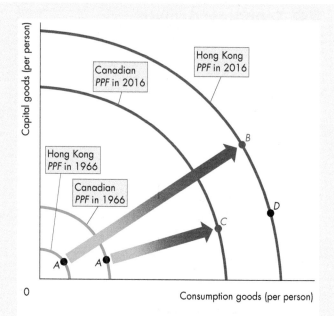

Economic Growth in Canada and Hong Kong

expand in these countries by between 5 percent and almost 10 percent a year.

If such high economic growth rates are maintained, these other Asian countries will continue to catch up with and eventually overtake Canada, as Hong Kong has done.

A Nation's Economic Growth

The experiences of Canada and Hong Kong make a striking example of the effects of our choices about consumption and capital accumulation on the rate of economic growth.

If an economy devotes all its factors of production to producing consumption goods and services and none to advancing technology and accumulating capital, its production possibilities in the future will be the same as they are today.

To expand production possibilities in the future, a nation or an economy must devote fewer resources to producing current consumption goods and services and allocate some resources to accumulating capital and developing new technologies. As production possibilities expand, consumption in the future can increase. The decrease in today's consumption is the opportunity cost of tomorrow's increase in consumption.

When production possibilities expand, the pattern of what is produced changes. Let's see how and why.

Changes in What We Produce

You saw in Chapter 1 that there are large differences in what is produced in a poor country like Ethiopia, and a middle-income country like China, and a rich country like Canada. Economic growth brings these changes, and the model that you've learned about in this chapter enables you to understand the differences in the patterns of production.

In a low-income country, just producing enough food is a high priority, and the marginal benefit from food is high. So in Ethiopia, agriculture accounts for a large percent of total production (36 percent).

As a country invests in capital and uses more advanced technologies, its production possibilities expand. The country can easily satisfy the want for food, so most of the increase in production is in industry (manufactured goods). In China, where production per person is 7 times that of Ethiopia, agriculture shrinks to 9 percent of total production and industry expands to 41 percent.

FIGURE 2.9   How Economic Growth Changes What We Produce

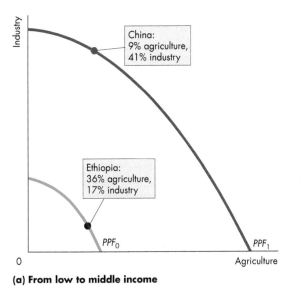

(a) From low to middle income

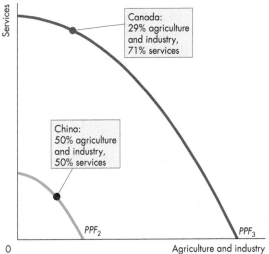

(b) From middle to high income

Ethiopia, a low-income country, has production possibilities per person on PPF_0. More than one-third of its production, 36 percent, is from agriculture and 17 percent from industry.

Investment in capital and more productive technology expands production possibilities to the middle-income level in China on PPF_1. Industry increases to 41 percent of production and agriculture shrinks to 9 percent.

In part (b), at China's level of production on PPF_2, production is divided equally between services and a combination of agriculture and industry.

When investment in capital and more productive technology expands production possibilities to the high-income level in Canada on PPF_3, most of the increase is in production of services, which increases to 80 percent.

MyLab Economics Animation and Draw Graph

If China invests even more in capital and advanced robot technologies, production possibilities will expand to Canada's level, which today is 4 times (per person) its level in China. Manufacturing is reaping most of the advances in technology, which means that industrial production is increasing, but the industrial labour force is shrinking. Labour released from industrial jobs, in turn, expands production possibilities in the services sector. It is the production of services that expands the most. The share of agriculture shrinks to 19 percent, and services expand to 80 percent.

Figure 2.9 illustrates the contrasts between Ethiopia and China in part (a) and China and Canada in part (b).

If the pace of industrial jobs loss and service jobs creation is rapid, as it has been in Canada over the past 40 years, serious problems arise for those workers whose jobs disappear. Many of these workers lack the skills needed for the new jobs, and they must be trained in new skills. Because most of the new jobs are in different places from those in which jobs are lost, people must relocate to get a new job. Job

training and relocating are costly and time-consuming activities, so a large number of people avoid those costs and remain unemployed, which places the economy inside its *PPF*.

REVIEW QUIZ

1 What generates economic growth?
2 How does economic growth influence the production possibilities frontier?
3 What is the opportunity cost of economic growth?
4 Explain why Hong Kong has experienced faster economic growth than Canada.
5 Does economic growth overcome scarcity?
6 How does economic growth change the patterns of production?
7 Why does economic growth destroy and create jobs?

Work these questions in Study Plan 2.4 and get instant feedback.   MyLab Economics

◆ Economic Coordination

For 7 billion people to specialize and produce millions of different goods and services, individual choices must somehow be coordinated. Two competing coordination systems have been used: central economic planning and markets (see *At Issue*, p. 8).

Central economic planning works badly because economic planners don't know people's production possibilities and preferences, so production ends up *inside* the *PPF* and the wrong things are produced.

Decentralized coordination works best, but to do so it needs four complementary social institutions. They are:

- Firms
- Markets
- Property rights
- Money

Firms

A **firm** is an economic unit that hires factors of production and organizes them to produce and sell goods and services.

Firms coordinate a huge amount of economic activity. For example, Loblaws buys or rents large buildings, equips them with storage shelves and checkout lanes, and hires labour. Loblaws directs the labour and decides what goods to buy and sell.

But Galen Weston would not have become one of the wealthiest people in Canada if Loblaws produced everything that it sells. He became rich by specializing in providing retail services and buying from other firms that specialize in producing goods (just as Liz and Joe did). This trade needs markets.

Markets

In ordinary speech, the word *market* means a place where people buy and sell goods such as fish, meat, fruits, and vegetables.

In economics, a **market** is any arrangement that enables buyers and sellers to get information and to do business with each other. An example is the world oil market, which is not a place but a network of producers, consumers, wholesalers, and brokers who buy and sell oil. In the world oil market, decision makers make deals by using the Internet. Enterprising individuals and firms, each pursuing their own self-interest, have profited by making markets—by standing ready to buy or sell items in which they specialize. But markets can work only when property rights exist.

Property Rights

The social arrangements that govern the ownership, use, and disposal of anything that people value are called **property rights**. *Real property* includes land and buildings—the things we call property in ordinary speech—and durable goods such as plant and equipment. *Financial property* includes stocks and bonds and money in the bank. *Intellectual property* is the intangible product of creative effort. This type of property includes books, music, computer programs, and inventions of all kinds and is protected by copyrights and patents.

Where property rights are enforced, people have the incentive to specialize and produce the goods and services in which they have a comparative advantage. Where people can steal the production of others, resources are devoted not to production but to protecting possessions.

Money

Money is any commodity or token that is generally acceptable as a means of payment. Liz and Joe don't need money. They can exchange salads and smoothies. In principle, trade in markets can exchange any item for any other item. But you can perhaps imagine how complicated life would be if we exchanged goods for other goods. The "invention" of money makes trading in markets much more efficient.

Circular Flows Through Markets

Trading in markets for goods and services and factors of production creates a circular flow of expenditures and incomes. Figure 2.10 shows the circular flows. Households specialize and choose the quantities of labour, land, capital, and entrepreneurial services to sell or rent to firms. Firms choose the quantities of factors of production to hire. These (red) flows go through the *factor markets*. Households choose the quantities of goods and services to buy, and firms choose the quantities to produce. These (red) flows go through the *goods markets*. Households receive incomes and make expenditures on goods and services (the green flows).

How do markets coordinate all these decisions?

FIGURE 2.10   Circular Flows in the Market Economy

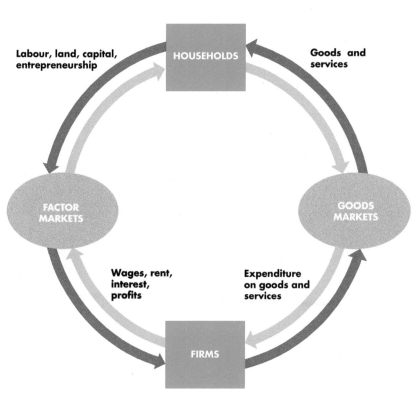

Households and firms make economic choices and markets coordinate these choices.

Households choose the quantities of labour, land, capital, and entrepreneurial services to sell or rent to firms in exchange for wages, rent, interest, and profits. Households also choose how to spend their incomes on the various types of goods and services available.

Firms choose the quantities of factors of production to hire and the quantities of goods and services to produce.

Goods markets and factor markets coordinate these choices of households and firms.

The counterclockwise red flows are real flows—the flow of factors of production from households to firms and the flow of goods and services from firms to households.

The clockwise green flows are the payments for the red flows. They are the flow of incomes from firms to households and the flow of expenditure on goods and services from households to firms.

MyLab Economics Animation

Coordinating Decisions

Markets coordinate decisions through price adjustments. Suppose that some people who want to buy hamburgers are not able to do so. To make buying and selling plans the same, either more hamburgers must be offered for sale or buyers must scale down their appetites (or both). A rise in the price of a hamburger produces this outcome. It encourages producers to offer more hamburgers for sale and encourages some people to change their lunch plans. When the price is right, buying plans and selling plans match.

Alternatively, suppose that more hamburgers are available than people want to buy. In this case, more hamburgers must be bought or fewer hamburgers must be offered for sale (or both). A fall in the price of a hamburger achieves this outcome. It encourages people to buy more hamburgers and it encourages firms to produce a smaller quantity of hamburgers.

◆ REVIEW QUIZ

1 Why are social institutions such as firms, markets, property rights, and money necessary?

2 What are the main functions of markets?

3 What are the flows in the market economy that go from firms to households and the flows from households to firms?

Work these questions in Study Plan 2.5 and get instant feedback.   MyLab Economics

◆ You have now begun to see how economists approach economic questions. You can see all around you the lessons you've learned in this chapter. *Economics in the News* on pp. 50–51 provides an opportunity to apply the *PPF* model to deepen your understanding of why Canada produces more liquified natural gas (LNG) than it consumes and exports the rest.

Expanding Production Possibilities

B.C. First Nation Gives Nod to Proposed LNG Export Facility

The Canadian Press
March 27, 2017

A First Nation on Vancouver Island has approved a proposed liquefied natural gas export facility on its traditional territories.

Leaders of the Huu-ay-aht First Nation and the CEO of Vancouver-based Steelhead LNG held a joint news conference in Vancouver on Monday to announce what Chief Robert Dennis said was the First Nation's "official entry into the international business world."

Members of the small First Nation voted Saturday to approve development of the LNG facility at Sarita Bay, on the west coast of Vancouver Island …

The company's plans could even include building a new pipeline linking Vancouver Island and the B.C. mainland …

The company planned to make a final investment decision on Sarita Bay by 2019 or 2020, with first production targeted for 2024, he said. …

John Jack, executive councillor with the Huu-ay-aht, said it's time the First Nation took its place within Canada and British Columbia.

"This is an example of a First Nation working with business and working with the people of B.C. and Canada in order to create value that fits both of our interests."

© The Canadian Press

ESSENCE OF THE STORY

- The Huu-ay-aht First Nation on Vancouver Island has approved a liquefied natural gas export facility on its traditional territories.

- Steelhead LNG will build and operate the facility.

- A new pipeline linking Vancouver Island and the B.C. mainland is a possible part of the plan.

- Production is targeted to start in 2024.

MyLab Economics Economics in the News

ECONOMIC ANALYSIS

- Steelhead LNG is one of Canada's hundreds of liquefied natural gas (LNG) producers.

- In 2017, Canada produced 426 million cubic metres of LNG per day, consumed 256 million, and exported 170 million.

- We can use the ideas you have learned in this chapter to explain Canada's LNG production, consumption, and exports as well as the effects of the deal reported in the news article.

- Figure 1 shows how building new LNG production and export facilities changes Canada's production possibilities.

- The blue curve PPF_0 shows what our production possibilities would be without the new facilities.

- The investment in new facilities expands our production possibilities and the PPF becomes the red PPF_{2017}. At each quantity of other goods and services (measured on the y-axis), Canada can produce more LNG (measured on the x-axis).

- Figure 2 shows the point on PPF_{2017} at which Canada produced in 2017. It produced 426 million cubic metres of LNG and 30 units of other goods and services a day at point A.

- The slope of the PPF at point A measures the opportunity cost of producing LNG—the units of other goods and services that must be forgone to get another million cubic metres of LNG per day.

- Canada can sell LNG to other countries and the terms on which that trade occurs is shown by the red "Trade line." This line is like that for trade between Joe and Liz in Fig. 2.6.

- In 2017, Canada consumed 256 million cubic metres of LNG a day at point B, and exported 170 million cubic metres a day, as shown by the blue arrow.

- Canada's consumption at point B is outside its PPF, which means that by exporting LNG, Canadians consume more other goods and services than could have been produced in Canada.

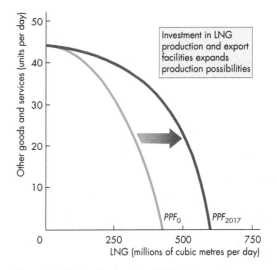

Figure 1 LNG Production Possibilities Expand

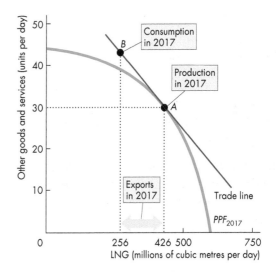

Figure 2 Production, Exports, and Consumption of LNG in 2017

◆ WORKED PROBLEM

MyLab Economics Work this problem in Chapter 2 Study Plan.

Leisure Island has 50 hours of labour a day that it can use to produce entertainment and good food. The table shows the maximum quantity of each good that it can produce with different quantities of labour.

Labour (hours)	Entertainment (shows per week)		Good food (meals per week)
0	0	or	0
10	2	or	5
20	4	or	9
30	6	or	12
40	8	or	14
50	10	or	15

Questions

1. Can Leisure Island produce 4 shows and 14 meals a week?

2. If Leisure Island produces 4 shows and 9 meals a week, is production efficient?

3. If Leisure Island produces 8 shows and 5 meals a week, do the people of Leisure Island face a tradeoff?

4. Suppose that Leisure Island produces 4 shows and 12 meals a week. Calculate the opportunity cost of producing 2 additional shows a week.

Solutions

1. To produce 4 shows it would use 20 hours and to produce 14 meals it would use 40 hours, so to produce 4 shows and 14 meals a week, Leisure Island would use 60 hours of labour. Leisure Island has only 50 hours of labour available, so it cannot produce 4 shows and 14 meals a week.

Key Point: Production is *unattainable* if it uses more resources than are available.

2. When Leisure Island produces 4 shows it uses 20 hours of labour and when it produces 9 meals it uses 20 hours. In total, it uses 40 hours, which is *less than* the 50 hours of labour available. So Leisure Island's production is not efficient.

Key Point: Production is *efficient* only if the economy uses all its resources.

3. When Leisure Island produces 8 shows and 5 meals, it uses 50 hours of labour. Leisure Island is using all its resources, so to produce more of either good it would face a tradeoff.

Key Point: An economy faces a *tradeoff* only when it uses all the available resources.

4. When Leisure Island produces 4 shows and 12 meals a week, it uses 50 hours of labour. To

produce 2 additional shows a week, Leisure Island faces a tradeoff and incurs an opportunity cost.

To produce 2 additional shows a week, Leisure Island moves 10 hours of labour from good food production, which decreases the quantity of meals from 12 to 9 a week—a decrease of 3 meals. That is, to get 2 additional shows a week Leisure Island *must give up* 3 meals a week. The opportunity cost of the 2 additional shows is 3 meals a week.

Key Point: When an economy is using all its resources and it decides to increase production of one good, it incurs an opportunity cost equal to the quantity of the good that it *must* forgo.

Key Figure

Each row of the following table sets out the combination of shows and meals that Leisure Island can produce in a week when it uses 50 hours of labour.

	Entertainment (shows per week)		Good food (meals per week)
A	0	and	15
B	2	and	14
C	4	and	12
D	6	and	9
E	8	and	5
F	10	and	0

Points *A* through *F* plot these combinations of shows and meals. The blue curve through these points is Leisure Island's *PPF*. Point *X* (4 shows and 14 meals in Question 1) is unattainable; Point *Y* (4 shows and 9 meals in Question 2) is inefficient. Point *E* (8 shows and 5 meals in Question 3) is on the *PPF* and the arrow illustrates the tradeoff and from it you can calculate the opportunity cost of 2 extra shows a week.

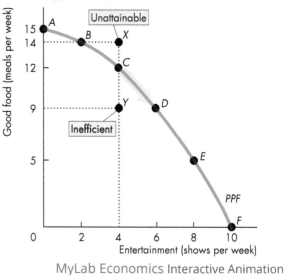

MyLab Economics Interactive Animation

SUMMARY

Key Points

Production Possibilities and Opportunity Cost
(pp. 34–36)

- The production possibilities frontier is the boundary between production levels that are attainable and those that are unattainable when all the available resources are used to their limits.
- Production efficiency occurs at points on the production possibilities frontier.
- Along the production possibilities frontier, the opportunity cost of producing more of one good is the amount of the other good that must be given up.
- The opportunity cost of all goods increases as the production of the good increases.

Working Problems 1 to 3 will give you a better understanding of production possibilities and opportunity cost.

Using Resources Efficiently (pp. 37–39)

- Allocative efficiency occurs when goods and services are produced at the least possible cost and in the quantities that bring the greatest possible benefit.
- The marginal cost of a good is the opportunity cost of producing one more unit of it.
- The marginal benefit from a good is the benefit received from consuming one more unit of it and is measured by the willingness to pay for it.
- The marginal benefit of a good decreases as the amount of the good available increases.
- Resources are used efficiently when the marginal cost of each good is equal to its marginal benefit.

Working Problems 4 to 6 will give you a better understanding of the efficient use of resources.

Gains from Trade (pp. 40–44)

- A person has a comparative advantage in producing a good if that person can produce the good at a lower opportunity cost than everyone else.
- People gain by specializing in the activity in which they have a comparative advantage and trading with others.

Working Problems 7 and 8 will give you a better understanding of the gains from trade.

Economic Growth (pp. 45–47)

- Economic growth, which is the expansion of production possibilities, results from capital accumulation and technological change.
- The opportunity cost of economic growth is forgone current consumption.
- The benefit of economic growth is increased future consumption.

Working Problem 9 will give you a better understanding of economic growth.

Economic Coordination (pp. 48–49)

- Firms coordinate a large amount of economic activity, but there is a limit to the efficient size of a firm.
- Markets coordinate the economic choices of people and firms.
- Markets can work efficiently only when property rights exist.
- Money makes trading in markets more efficient.

Working Problem 10 will give you a better understanding of economic coordination.

Key Terms

Absolute advantage, 40
Allocative efficiency, 37
Capital accumulation, 45
Comparative advantage, 40
Economic growth, 45
Firm, 48

Marginal benefit, 38
Marginal benefit curve, 38
Marginal cost, 37
Market, 48
Money, 48
Opportunity cost, 35

Preferences, 38
Production efficiency, 35
Production possibilities frontier, 34
Property rights, 48
Technological change, 45

STUDY PLAN PROBLEMS AND APPLICATIONS

MyLab Economics Work Problems 1 to 10 in Chapter 2 Study Plan and get instant feedback.

Production Possibilities and Opportunity Cost
(Study Plan 2.1)

Use the following data to work Problems 1 to 3.

Brazil produces ethanol from sugar, and the land used to grow sugar can be used to grow food crops. The table sets out Brazil's production possibilities for ethanol and food crops.

Ethanol (barrels per day)		Food crops (tonnes per day)
70	and	0
64	and	1
54	and	2
40	and	3
22	and	4
0	and	5

1. a. Draw a graph of Brazil's *PPF* and explain how your graph illustrates scarcity.

   b. If Brazil produces 40 barrels of ethanol a day, how much food must it produce to achieve production efficiency?

   c. Why does Brazil face a tradeoff on its *PPF*?

2. a. If Brazil increases ethanol production from 40 barrels per day to 54 barrels a day, what is the opportunity cost of the additional ethanol?

   b. If Brazil increases food production from 2 tonnes per day to 3 tonnes per day, what is the opportunity cost of the additional food?

   c. What is the relationship between your answers to parts (a) and (b)?

3. Does Brazil face an increasing opportunity cost of ethanol? What feature of Brazil's *PPF* illustrates increasing opportunity cost?

Using Resources Efficiently (Study Plan 2.2)

Use the table above to work Problems 4 and 5.

4. Define marginal cost and calculate Brazil's marginal cost of producing a tonne of food when the quantity produced is 2.5 tonnes per day.

5. Define marginal benefit. Explain how it is measured and why the data in the table do not enable you to calculate Brazil's marginal benefit from food.

6. Distinguish between *production efficiency* and *allocative efficiency*. Explain why many production possibilities achieve production efficiency but only one achieves allocative efficiency.

Gains from Trade (Study Plan 2.3)

Use the following data to work Problems 7 and 8.

In an hour, Sue can produce 40 caps or 4 jackets and Tessa can produce 80 caps or 4 jackets.

7. a. Calculate Sue's opportunity cost of producing a cap.

   b. Calculate Tessa's opportunity cost of producing a cap.

   c. Who has a comparative advantage in producing caps?

   d. If Sue and Tessa specialize in producing the good in which they have a comparative advantage and then trade 1 jacket for 15 caps, who gains from the specialization and trade?

8. Suppose that Tessa buys a new machine that enables her to make 20 jackets an hour. (She can still make only 80 caps per hour.)

   a. Who now has a comparative advantage in producing jackets?

   b. Can Sue and Tessa still gain from trade?

   c. Would Sue and Tessa still be willing to trade 1 jacket for 15 caps? Explain your answer.

Economic Growth (Study Plan 2.4)

9. A farm grows wheat and produces pork. The marginal cost of producing each of these products increases as more of it is produced.

   a. Make a graph that illustrates the farm's *PPF*.

   b. The farm adopts a new technology that allows it to use fewer resources to fatten pigs. On your graph, sketch the impact of the new technology on the farm's *PPF*.

   c. With the farm using the new technology in part (b), has the opportunity cost of producing a tonne of wheat changed? Explain and illustrate your answer.

   d. Is the farm more efficient with the new technology than it was with the old one? Why?

Economic Coordination (Study Plan 2.5)

10. For 50 years, Cuba has had a centrally planned economy in which the government makes the big decisions on how resources will be allocated.

    a. Why would you expect Cuba's production possibilities (per person) to be smaller than those of Canada?

    b. What are the social institutions that Cuba might lack that help Canada to achieve allocative efficiency?

ADDITIONAL PROBLEMS AND APPLICATIONS

MyLab Economics Work these problems in Homework or Test if assigned by your instructor.

Production Possibilities and Opportunity Cost

Use the following table to work Problems 11 and 12. Suppose that Yucatan's production possibilities are:

Food (kilograms per month)		Sunscreen (litres per month)
300	and	0
200	and	50
100	and	100
0	and	150

11. a. Draw a graph of Yucatan's *PPF* and explain how your graph illustrates a tradeoff.
    b. If Yucatan produces 150 kilograms of food per month, how much sunscreen must it produce if it achieves production efficiency?
    c. What is Yucatan's opportunity cost of producing (i) 1 kilogram of food and (ii) 1 litre of sunscreen?
    d. What is the relationship between your answers to part (c)?
12. What feature of a *PPF* illustrates increasing opportunity cost? Explain why Yucatan's opportunity cost does or does not increase.

Using Resources Efficiently

13. In Problem 11, what is the marginal cost of 1 kilogram of food in Yucatan when the quantity produced is 150 kilograms per day? What is special about the marginal cost of food in Yucatan?
14. The table describes the preferences in Yucatan.

Sunscreen (litres per month)	Willingness to pay (kilograms of food per litre)
25	3
75	2
125	1

    a. What is the marginal benefit from sunscreen and how is it measured?
    b. Using the table in Problem 11, what does Yucatan produce to achieve allocative efficiency?
15. **Macy's, Kmart, JCPenney: More Retailers Closing Brick-and-Mortar Stores**

    As more people choose online shopping over brick-and-mortar stores, Macy's, Kmart, JCPenney and others are closing stores.
    Source: *Springfield News-Sun*, March 24, 2017
    a. Draw the *PPF* curves for brick-and mortar retailers and online retailers before and after the Internet became available.
    b. Draw the marginal cost and marginal benefit curves for brick-and-mortar retailers and online retailers before and after the Internet became available.
    c. Explain how changes in production possibilities, preferences or both have changed the way in which goods are retailed.

Use the following news clip to work Problems 16 and 17.

Gates Doubles Down on Malaria Eradication

The End Malaria Council, convened by Bill Gates and Ray Chambers, seeks to mobilize resources to prevent and treat malaria. The current level of financing is too low to end malaria. Bruno Moonen, deputy director for malaria at the Gates Foundation, says that more resources, more leadership, and new technologies are needed to eradicate malaria in the current generation.
Source: Catherine Cheney, *Devex*, January 20, 2017

16. Is Bruno Moonen talking about *production efficiency* or *allocative efficiency* or both?
17. Make a graph with the percentage of malaria cases eliminated on the *x*-axis and the marginal cost and marginal benefit of driving down malaria cases on the *y*-axis. On your graph:
    (i) Draw a marginal cost curve and a marginal benefit curve that are consistent with Bruno Moonen's opinion.
    (ii) Identify the quantity of malaria eradicated that achieves allocative efficiency.

Gains from Trade

Use the following data to work Problems 18 and 19.

Kim can produce 40 pies or 400 cakes an hour. Liam can produce 100 pies or 200 cakes an hour.

18. a. Calculate Kim's opportunity cost of a pie and Liam's opportunity cost of a pie.
    b. If each spends 30 minutes of each hour producing pies and 30 minutes producing cakes, how many pies and cakes does each produce?
    c. Who has a comparative advantage in producing (i) pies and (ii) cakes?
19. a. Draw a graph of Kim's *PPF* and Liam's *PPF* and show the point at which each produces when each spends 30 minutes of each hour producing pies and 30 minutes producing cakes.

b. On your graph, show what Kim produces and what Liam produces when they specialize.

c. When they specialize and trade, what are the total gains from trade?

d. If Kim and Liam share the total gains equally, what trade takes place between them?

20. Tony and Patty produce skis and snowboards. The tables show their production possibilities. Each week, Tony produces 5 snowboards and 40 skis; Patty produces 10 snowboards and 5 skis.

Tony's Production Possibilities

Snowboards (units per week)		Skis (units per week)
25	and	0
20	and	10
15	and	20
10	and	30
5	and	40
0	and	50

Patty's Production Possibilities

Snowboards (units per week)		Skis (units per week)
20	and	0
10	and	5
0	and	10

a. Who has a comparative advantage in producing (i) snowboards and (ii) skis?

b. If Tony and Patty specialize and trade 1 snowboard for 1 ski, what are the gains from trade?

Economic Growth

21. Capital accumulation and technological change bring economic growth: Production that was unattainable yesterday becomes attainable today; production that is unattainable today will become attainable tomorrow. Why doesn't economic growth bring an end to scarcity?

Use the following data to work Problems 22 and 23.

SpaceX Plans to Send Two People Around the Moon

SpaceX CEO Elon Musk announced that SpaceX plans to send two citizens on a one-week, 350,000-mile trip around the moon in 2018.

Source: *The Verge*, February 27, 2017

22. What is the opportunity cost of creating the technology for trips around the moon?

23. Sketch SpaceX's *PPF* for trips around the moon and other goods and services and its planned production in 2018.

Economic Coordination

24. On a graph of the circular flows in the market economy, indicate the real and money flows in which the following items belong:

a. You buy an iPad from the Apple Store.

b. Apple Inc. pays the designers of the iPad.

c. Apple Inc. decides to expand and rents an adjacent building.

d. You buy a new e-book from Amazon.

e. Apple Inc. hires a student as an intern during the summer.

Economics in the News

25. After you have studied *Economics in the News* on pp. 50–51, answer the following questions.

a. How does investing in LNG production and export facilities change Canada's *PPF*?

b. How do technological advances in the production of other goods and services change Canada's *PPF*?

c. How will the deal between Huu-ay-aht First Nation and Steelhead LNG change Canada's opportunity cost of exporting LNG?

d. When technological advances in the production of other goods and services occur, how does the opportunity cost of producing LNG change? Does it increase or decrease?

26. **YouTube Launches Live TV in the U.S.**

Google has launched YouTube TV, a $35-a-month service that carries live streaming from all the major broadcast and sports networks as well as some cable networks and local sports and news channels. Users will be able to record an unlimited amount of content and multiple shows simultaneously, without using up any data space on mobile devices.

Source: *Mediatel*, March 1, 2017

a. How has live streaming changed the production possibilities of video entertainment and other goods and services?

b. Sketch a *PPF* for video entertainment and other goods and services before live streaming.

c. Show how the arrival of inexpensive live streaming has changed the *PPF*.

d. Sketch a marginal benefit curve and marginal cost curve for video entertainment before and after live streaming.

e. Explain how the efficient quantity of video entertainment has changed.

3 DEMAND AND SUPPLY

After studying this chapter, you will be able to:

◆ Describe a competitive market and think about a price as an opportunity cost

◆ Explain the influences on demand

◆ Explain the influences on supply

◆ Explain how demand and supply determine prices and quantities bought and sold

◆ Use the demand and supply model to make predictions about changes in prices and quantities

As more of us get breakfast on the go, we're drinking more smoothies and energy drinks and less orange juice. What is happening to the price of orange juice and the quantity of oranges harvested? The demand and supply model answers this question.

This model that you're about to study is the main tool of economics. It explains how prices are determined and how they guide the use of resources to influence *what*, *how*, and *for whom* goods and services are produced.

Economics in the News at the end of the chapter answers the questions about orange juice.

◆ Markets and Prices

When you need a new pair of running shoes, want a bagel and a latte, plan to upgrade your smartphone, or need to fly home for Thanksgiving, you must find a place where people sell those items or offer those services. The place in which you find them is a *market*. You learned in Chapter 2 (p. 48) that a market is any arrangement that enables buyers and sellers to get information and to do business with each other.

A market has two sides: buyers and sellers. There are markets for *goods* such as apples and hiking boots, for *services* such as haircuts and tennis lessons, for *factors of production* such as computer programmers and earthmovers, and for other manufactured *inputs* such as memory chips and auto parts. There are also markets for money such as Japanese yen and for financial securities such as Yahoo! stock. Only our imagination limits what can be traded in markets.

Some markets are physical places where buyers and sellers meet and where an auctioneer or a broker helps to determine the prices. Examples of this type of market are live car and house auctions and the wholesale fish, meat, and produce markets.

Some markets are groups of people spread around the world who never meet and know little about each other but are connected through the Internet or by telephone and fax. Examples are the e-commerce markets and the currency markets.

But most markets are unorganized collections of buyers and sellers. You do most of your trading in this type of market. An example is the market for basketball shoes. The buyers in this $3 billion-a-year market are the 45 million Canadians and Americans who play basketball (or who want to make a fashion statement). The sellers are the tens of thousands of retail sports equipment and footwear stores. Each buyer can visit several different stores, and each seller knows that the buyer has a choice of stores.

Markets vary in the intensity of competition that buyers and sellers face. In this chapter, we're going to study a **competitive market**—a market that has many buyers and many sellers, so no single buyer or seller can influence the price.

Producers offer items for sale only if the price is high enough to cover their opportunity cost. And consumers respond to changing opportunity cost by seeking cheaper alternatives to expensive items.

We are going to study how people respond to *prices* and the forces that determine prices. But to pursue these tasks, we need to understand the relationship between a price and an opportunity cost.

In everyday life, the *price* of an object is the number of dollars that must be given up in exchange for it. Economists refer to this price as the **money price**.

The *opportunity cost* of an action is the highest-valued alternative forgone. If, when you buy a cup of coffee, the highest-valued thing you forgo is some gum, then the opportunity cost of the coffee is the *quantity* of gum forgone. We can calculate the quantity of gum forgone from the money prices of the coffee and the gum.

If the money price of coffee is $1 a cup and the money price of gum is 50¢ a pack, then the opportunity cost of one cup of coffee is two packs of gum. To calculate this opportunity cost, we divide the price of a cup of coffee by the price of a pack of gum and find the *ratio* of one price to the other. The ratio of one price to another is called a **relative price**, and a *relative price is an opportunity cost.*

We can express the relative price of coffee in terms of gum or any other good. The normal way of expressing a relative price is in terms of a "basket" of all goods and services. To calculate this relative price, we divide the money price of a good by the money price of a "basket" of all goods (called a *price index*). The resulting relative price tells us the opportunity cost of the good in terms of how much of the "basket" we must give up to buy it.

The demand and supply model that we are about to study determines *relative prices,* and the word "price" means *relative* price. When we predict that a price will fall, we do not mean that its *money* price will fall—although it might. We mean that its *relative* price will fall. That is, its price will fall *relative* to the average price of other goods and services.

◆ REVIEW QUIZ

1 What is the distinction between a money price and a relative price?
2 Explain why a relative price is an opportunity cost.
3 Think of examples of goods whose relative price has risen or fallen by a large amount.

Work these questions in Study Plan 3.1 and get instant feedback.   MyLab Economics

Let's begin our study of demand and supply, starting with demand.

◆ Demand

If you demand something, then you:

1. Want it.
2. Can afford it.
3. Plan to buy it.

Wants are the unlimited desires or wishes that people have for goods and services. How many times have you thought that you would like something "if only you could afford it" or "if it weren't so expensive"? Scarcity guarantees that many—perhaps most—of our wants will never be satisfied. Demand reflects a decision about which wants to satisfy.

The **quantity demanded** of a good or service is the amount that consumers plan to buy during a given time period at a particular price. The quantity demanded is not necessarily the same as the quantity actually bought. Sometimes the quantity demanded exceeds the amount of goods available, so the quantity bought is less than the quantity demanded.

The quantity demanded is measured as an amount per unit of time. For example, suppose that you buy one cup of coffee a day. The quantity of coffee that you demand can be expressed as 1 cup per day, 7 cups per week, or 365 cups per year.

Many factors influence buying plans, and one of them is the price. We look first at the relationship between the quantity demanded of a good and its price. To study this relationship, we keep all other influences on buying plans the same and we ask: How, other things remaining the same, does the quantity demanded of a good change as its price changes?

The law of demand provides the answer.

The Law of Demand

The **law of demand** states:

> Other things remaining the same, the higher the price of a good, the smaller is the quantity demanded; and the lower the price of a good, the greater is the quantity demanded.

Why does a higher price reduce the quantity demanded? For two reasons:

- Substitution effect
- Income effect

Substitution Effect When the price of a good rises, other things remaining the same, its *relative* price— its opportunity cost—rises. Although each good is unique, it has *substitutes*—other goods that can be used in its place. As the opportunity cost of a good rises, the incentive to economize on its use and switch to a substitute becomes stronger.

Income Effect When a price rises, other things remaining the same, the price rises *relative* to income. Faced with a higher price and an unchanged income, people cannot afford to buy all the things they previously bought. They must decrease the quantities demanded of at least some goods and services. Normally, the good whose price has increased will be one of the goods that people buy less of.

To see the substitution effect and the income effect at work, think about the effects of a change in the price of an energy bar. Several different goods are substitutes for an energy bar. For example, an energy drink could be consumed instead of an energy bar.

Suppose that an energy bar initially sells for $3 and then its price falls to $1.50. People now substitute energy bars for energy drinks—the substitution effect. And with a budget that now has some slack from the lower price of an energy bar, people buy even more energy bars—the income effect. The quantity of energy bars demanded increases for these two reasons.

Now suppose that an energy bar initially sells for $3 and then the price doubles to $6. People now buy fewer energy bars and more energy drinks—the substitution effect. And faced with a tighter budget, people buy even fewer energy bars—the income effect. The quantity of energy bars demanded decreases for these two reasons.

Demand Curve and Demand Schedule

You are now about to study one of the two most used curves in economics: the demand curve. You are also going to encounter one of the most critical distinctions: the distinction between *demand* and *quantity demanded*.

The term **demand** refers to the entire relationship between the price of a good and the quantity demanded of that good. Demand is illustrated by the demand curve and the demand schedule. The term *quantity demanded* refers to a point on a demand curve—the quantity demanded at a particular price.

Figure 3.1 shows the demand curve for energy bars. A **demand curve** shows the relationship between the quantity demanded of a good and its price when all other influences on consumers' planned purchases remain the same.

The table in Fig. 3.1 is the demand schedule for energy bars. A *demand schedule* lists the quantities demanded at each price when all the other influences on consumers' planned purchases remain the same. For example, if the price of a bar is 50¢, the quantity demanded is 22 million a week. If the price is $2.50, the quantity demanded is 5 million a week. The other rows of the table show the quantities demanded at prices of $1.00, $1.50, and $2.00.

We graph the demand schedule as a demand curve with the quantity demanded on the *x*-axis and the price on the *y*-axis. The points on the demand curve labelled *A* through *E* correspond to the rows of the demand schedule. For example, point *A* on the graph shows a quantity demanded of 22 million energy bars a week at a price of 50¢ a bar.

Willingness and Ability to Pay Another way of looking at the demand curve is as a willingness-and-ability-to-pay curve. The willingness and ability to pay is a measure of *marginal benefit*.

If a small quantity is available, the highest price that someone is willing and able to pay for one more unit is high. But as the quantity available increases, the marginal benefit of each additional unit falls and the highest price that someone is willing and able to pay also falls along the demand curve.

In Fig. 3.1, if only 5 million energy bars are available each week, the highest price that someone is willing to pay for the 5 millionth bar is $2.50. But if 22 million energy bars are available each week, someone is willing to pay 50¢ for the last bar bought.

A Change in Demand

When any factor that influences buying plans changes, other than the price of the good, there is a **change in demand**. Figure 3.2 illustrates an increase in demand. When demand increases, the demand curve shifts rightward and the quantity demanded at each price is greater. For example, at $2.50 a bar, the quantity demanded on the original (blue) demand curve is 5 million energy bars a week. On the new (red) demand curve, at $2.50 a bar, the quantity demanded is 15 million bars a week. Look closely at the numbers in the table and check that the quantity demanded at each price is greater.

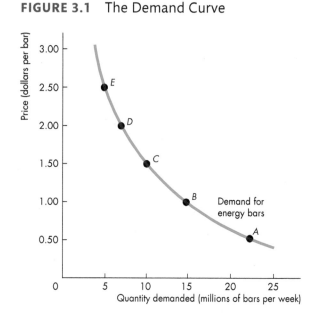

FIGURE 3.1 The Demand Curve

	Price (dollars per bar)	Quantity demanded (millions of bars per week)
A	0.50	22
B	1.00	15
C	1.50	10
D	2.00	7
E	2.50	5

The table shows a demand schedule for energy bars. At a price of 50¢ a bar, 22 million bars a week are demanded; at a price of $1.50 a bar, 10 million bars a week are demanded. The demand curve shows the relationship between quantity demanded and price, other things remaining the same. The demand curve slopes downward: As the price falls, the quantity demanded increases.

The demand curve can be read in two ways. For a given price, the demand curve tells us the quantity that people plan to buy. For example, at a price of $1.50 a bar, people plan to buy 10 million bars a week. For a given quantity, the demand curve tells us the maximum price that consumers are willing and able to pay for the last bar available. For example, the maximum price that consumers will pay for the 15 millionth bar is $1.00.

MyLab Economics Animation

FIGURE 3.2 An Increase in Demand

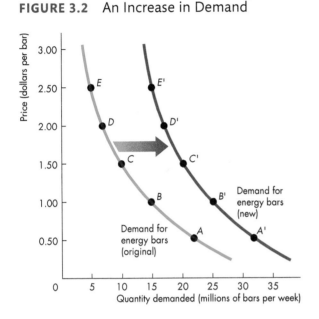

Original demand schedule			New demand schedule		
Original income			New higher income		
	Price (dollars per bar)	Quantity demanded (millions of bars per week)		Price (dollars per bar)	Quantity demanded (millions of bars per week)
A	0.50	22	A'	0.50	32
B	1.00	15	B'	1.00	25
C	1.50	10	C'	1.50	20
D	2.00	7	D'	2.00	17
E	2.50	5	E'	2.50	15

A change in any influence on buying plans other than the price of the good itself results in a new demand schedule and a shift of the demand curve. A change in income changes the demand for energy bars. At a price of $1.50 a bar, 10 million bars a week are demanded at the original income (row C of the table) and 20 million bars a week are demanded at the new higher income (row C'). A rise in income increases the demand for energy bars. The demand curve shifts *rightward*, as shown by the shift arrow and the resulting red curve.

Six main factors bring changes in demand. They are changes in:

- The prices of related goods
- Expected future prices
- Income
- Expected future income and credit
- Population
- Preferences

Prices of Related Goods The quantity of energy bars that consumers plan to buy depends in part on the prices of substitutes for energy bars. A **substitute** is a good that can be used in place of another good. For example, a bus ride is a substitute for a train ride; a hamburger is a substitute for a hot dog; and an energy drink is a substitute for an energy bar. If the price of a substitute for an energy bar rises, people buy less of the substitute and more energy bars. For example, if the price of an energy drink rises, people buy fewer energy drinks and more energy bars. The demand for energy bars increases.

The quantity of energy bars that people plan to buy also depends on the prices of complements with energy bars. A **complement** is a good that is used in conjunction with another good. Hamburgers and fries are complements, and so are energy bars and exercise. If the price of an hour at the gym falls, people buy more gym time *and more* energy bars.

Expected Future Prices If the expected future price of a good rises and if the good can be stored, the opportunity cost of obtaining the good for future use is lower today than it will be in the future when people expect the price to be higher. So people retime their purchases—they substitute over time. They buy more of the good now before its price is expected to rise (and less afterward), so the demand for the good today increases.

For example, suppose that a Florida frost damages the season's orange crop. You expect the price of orange juice to rise, so you fill your freezer with enough frozen juice to get you through the next six months. Your current demand for frozen orange juice has increased, and your future demand has decreased.

Similarly, if the expected future price of a good falls, the opportunity cost of buying the good today is high relative to what it is expected to be in the future. So again, people retime their purchases. They buy less of the good now before its price is expected to fall, so the demand for the good decreases today and increases in the future.

Computer prices are constantly falling, and this fact poses a dilemma. Will you buy a new computer now, in time for the start of the school year, or will you wait until the price has fallen some more? Because people expect computer prices to keep falling, the current demand for computers is less (and the future demand is greater) than it otherwise would be.

Income Consumers' income influences demand. When income increases, consumers buy more of most goods; and when income decreases, consumers buy less of most goods. Although an increase in income leads to an increase in the demand for *most* goods, it does not lead to an increase in the demand for *all* goods. A **normal good** is one for which demand increases as income increases. An **inferior good** is one for which demand decreases as income increases. As incomes increase, the demand for air travel (a normal good) increases and the demand for long-distance bus trips (an inferior good) decreases.

Expected Future Income and Credit When expected future income increases or credit becomes easier to get, demand for a good might increase now. For example, a salesperson gets the news that she will receive a big bonus at the end of the year, so she goes into debt and buys a new car right now, rather than waiting until she receives the bonus.

Population Demand also depends on the size and the age structure of the population. The larger the population, the greater is the demand for all goods and services; the smaller the population, the smaller is the demand for all goods and services.

For example, the demand for parking spaces, running shoes, movies, or just about anything that you can imagine is much greater in the Greater Toronto Area (population 6 million) than it is in Thunder Bay, Ontario (population 146,000).

Also, the larger the proportion of the population in an age group, the greater is the demand for the goods and services used by that group. For example, in 2010, there were 2.3 million 20- to 24-year-olds in Canada compared with 2.1 million in 2000. As a result, the demand for university places in 2010 was greater than in 2000. During this period, the number of Canadians aged 90 years more than doubled and the demand for nursing home services increased.

TABLE 3.1 The Demand for Energy Bars

The Law of Demand

The quantity of energy bars demanded

Decreases if:	Increases if:
■ The price of an energy bar rises	■ The price of an energy bar falls

Changes in Demand

The demand for energy bars

Decreases if:	Increases if:
■ The price of a substitute falls	■ The price of a substitute rises
■ The price of a complement rises	■ The price of a complement falls
■ The expected future price of an energy bar falls	■ The expected future price of an energy bar rises
■ Income falls*	■ Income rises*
■ Expected future income falls or credit becomes harder to get*	■ Expected future income rises or credit becomes easier to get*
■ The population decreases	■ The population increases

*An energy bar is a normal good.

Preferences Demand depends on preferences. *Preferences* determine the value that people place on each good and service. Preferences depend on such things as the weather, information, and fashion. For example, greater health and fitness awareness has shifted preferences in favour of energy bars, so the demand for energy bars has increased.

Table 3.1 summarizes the influences on demand and the direction of those influences.

A Change in the Quantity Demanded Versus a Change in Demand

Changes in the influences on buying plans bring either a change in the quantity demanded or a change in demand. Equivalently, they bring either a movement along the demand curve or a shift of the demand curve. The distinction between a change in the quantity demanded and a change in demand is the same as that between a movement along the demand curve and a shift of the demand curve.

A point on the demand curve shows the quantity demanded at a given price, so a movement along the demand curve shows a **change in the quantity demanded**. The entire demand curve shows demand, so a shift of the demand curve shows a *change in demand*. Figure 3.3 illustrates these distinctions.

Movement Along the Demand Curve If the price of the good changes but no other influence on buying plans changes, we illustrate the effect as a movement along the demand curve.

A fall in the price of a good increases the quantity demanded of it. In Fig. 3.3, we illustrate the effect of a fall in price as a movement down along the demand curve D_0.

A rise in the price of a good decreases the quantity demanded of it. In Fig. 3.3, we illustrate the effect of a rise in price as a movement up along the demand curve D_0.

A Shift of the Demand Curve If the price of a good remains constant but some other influence on buying plans changes, there is a change in demand for that good. We illustrate a change in demand as a shift of the demand curve. For example, if more people work out at the gym, consumers buy more energy bars regardless of the price of a bar. That is what a rightward shift of the demand curve shows—more energy bars are demanded at each price.

In Fig. 3.3, there is a *change in demand* and the demand curve shifts when any influence on buying plans changes, other than the price of the good. Demand *increases* and the demand curve *shifts rightward* (to the red demand curve D_1) if the price of a substitute rises, the price of a complement falls, the expected future price of the good rises, income increases (for a normal good), expected future income or credit increases, or the population increases. Demand *decreases* and the demand curve *shifts leftward* (to the red demand curve D_2) if the price of a substitute falls, the price of a complement rises, the expected future price of the good falls, income decreases (for a normal good), expected future income or credit decreases, or the population decreases. (For an inferior good, the effects of changes in income are in the opposite direction to those described above.)

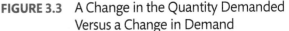

FIGURE 3.3 A Change in the Quantity Demanded Versus a Change in Demand

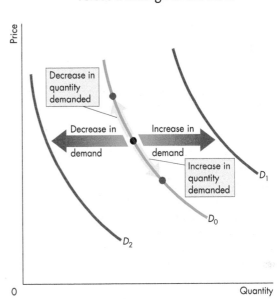

When the price of the good changes, there is a movement along the demand curve and *a change in the quantity demanded*, shown by the blue arrows on demand curve D_0. When any other influence on buying plans changes, there is a shift of the demand curve and a *change in demand*. An increase in demand shifts the demand curve rightward (from D_0 to D_1). A decrease in demand shifts the demand curve leftward (from D_0 to D_2).

——— MyLab Economics Animation and Draw Graph ———

◆ Supply

If a firm supplies a good or service, the firm:

1. Has the resources and technology to produce it.
2. Can profit from producing it.
3. Plans to produce it and sell it.

A supply is more than just having the *resources* and the *technology* to produce something. *Resources and technology* are the constraints that limit what is possible.

Many useful things can be produced, but they are not produced unless it is profitable to do so. Supply reflects a decision about which technologically feasible items to produce.

The **quantity supplied** of a good or service is the amount that producers plan to sell during a given time period at a particular price. The quantity supplied is not necessarily the same amount as the quantity actually sold. Sometimes the quantity supplied is greater than the quantity demanded, so the quantity sold is less than the quantity supplied.

Like the quantity demanded, the quantity supplied is measured as an amount per unit of time. For example, suppose that GM produces 1,000 cars a day. The quantity of cars supplied by GM can be expressed as 1,000 a day, 7,000 a week, or 365,000 a year. Without the time dimension, we cannot tell whether a particular quantity is large or small.

Many factors influence selling plans, and again one of them is the price of the good. We look first at the relationship between the quantity supplied of a good and its price. Just as we did when we studied demand, to isolate the relationship between the quantity supplied of a good and its price, we keep all other influences on selling plans the same and ask: How does the quantity supplied of a good change as its price changes when other things remain the same?

The law of supply provides the answer.

The Law of Supply

The **law of supply** states:

> Other things remaining the same, the higher the price of a good, the greater is the quantity supplied; and the lower the price of a good, the smaller is the quantity supplied.

Why does a higher price increase the quantity supplied? It is because *marginal cost increases*. As the quantity produced of any good increases, the marginal cost of producing the good increases. (See Chapter 2, p. 37, to review marginal cost.)

It is never worth producing a good if the price received for the good does not at least cover the marginal cost of producing it. When the price of a good rises, other things remaining the same, producers are willing to incur a higher marginal cost, so they increase production. The higher price brings forth an increase in the quantity supplied.

Let's now illustrate the law of supply with a supply curve and a supply schedule.

Supply Curve and Supply Schedule

You are now going to study the second of the two most used curves in economics: the supply curve. You're also going to learn about the critical distinction between *supply* and *quantity supplied*.

The term **supply** refers to the entire relationship between the price of a good and the quantity supplied of it. Supply is illustrated by the supply curve and the supply schedule. The term *quantity supplied* refers to a point on a supply curve—the quantity supplied at a particular price.

Figure 3.4 shows the supply curve of energy bars. A **supply curve** shows the relationship between the quantity supplied of a good and its price when all other influences on producers' planned sales remain the same. The supply curve is a graph of a supply schedule.

The table in Fig. 3.4 sets out the supply schedule for energy bars. A *supply schedule* lists the quantities supplied at each price when all the other influences on producers' planned sales remain the same. For example, if the price of an energy bar is 50¢, the quantity supplied is zero—in row *A* of the table. If the price of an energy bar is $1.00, the quantity supplied is 6 million energy bars a week—in row *B*. The other rows of the table show the quantities supplied at prices of $1.50, $2.00, and $2.50.

To make a supply curve, we graph the quantity supplied on the *x*-axis and the price on the *y*-axis. The points on the supply curve labelled *A* through *E* correspond to the rows of the supply schedule. For example, point *A* on the graph shows a quantity supplied of zero at a price of 50¢ an energy bar. Point *E* shows a quantity supplied of 15 million bars at $2.50 an energy bar.

FIGURE 3.4   The Supply Curve

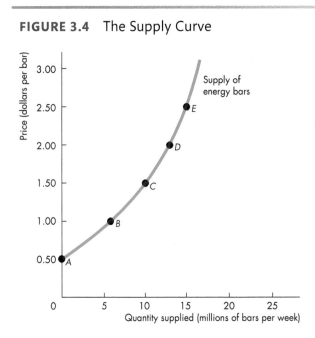

	Price (dollars per bar)	Quantity supplied (millions of bars per week)
A	0.50	0
B	1.00	6
C	1.50	10
D	2.00	13
E	2.50	15

The table shows the supply schedule of energy bars. For example, at a price of $1.00, 6 million bars a week are supplied; at a price of $2.50, 15 million bars a week are supplied. The supply curve shows the relationship between the quantity supplied and the price, other things remaining the same. The supply curve slopes upward: As the price of a good increases, the quantity supplied increases.

A supply curve can be read in two ways. For a given price, the supply curve tells us the quantity that producers plan to sell at that price. For example, at a price of $1.50 a bar, producers are planning to sell 10 million bars a week. For a given quantity, the supply curve tells us the minimum price at which producers are willing to sell one more bar. For example, if 15 million bars are produced each week, the lowest price at which a producer is willing to sell the 15 millionth bar is $2.50.

———— MyLab Economics Animation ————

Minimum Supply Price The supply curve can be interpreted as a minimum-supply-price curve—a curve that shows the lowest price at which someone is willing to sell. This lowest price is the *marginal cost*.

If a small quantity is produced, the lowest price at which someone is willing to sell one more unit is low. But as the quantity produced increases, the marginal cost of each additional unit rises, so the lowest price at which someone is willing to sell an additional unit rises along the supply curve.

In Fig. 3.4, if 15 million bars are produced each week, the lowest price at which someone is willing to sell the 15 millionth bar is $2.50. But if 10 million bars are produced each week, someone is willing to accept $1.50 for the last bar produced.

A Change in Supply

When any factor that influences selling plans other than the price of the good changes, there is a **change in supply**. Six main factors bring changes in supply. They are changes in:

- The prices of factors of production
- The prices of related goods produced
- Expected future prices
- The number of suppliers
- Technology
- The state of nature

Prices of Factors of Production The prices of the factors of production used to produce a good influence its supply. To see this influence, think about the supply curve as a minimum-supply-price curve. If the price of a factor of production rises, the lowest price that a producer is willing to accept for that good rises, so supply decreases. For example, during 2008, as the price of jet fuel increased, the supply of air travel decreased. Similarly, a rise in the minimum wage decreases the supply of hamburgers.

Prices of Related Goods Produced The prices of related goods that firms produce influence supply. For example, if the price of an energy drink rises, firms switch production from sugary drinks to energy drinks. The supply of sugary drinks decreases. Energy drinks and sugary drinks are *substitutes in production*—goods that can be produced by using the same resources. If the price of beef rises, the supply of cowhide increases. Beef and cowhide are *complements in production*—goods that must be produced together.

Expected Future Prices If the expected future price of a good rises, the return from selling the good in the future increases and is higher than it is today. So supply decreases today and increases in the future.

The Number of Suppliers The larger the number of firms that produce a good, the greater is the supply of the good. As new firms enter an industry, the supply in that industry increases. As firms leave an industry, the supply in that industry decreases.

Technology The term "technology" is used broadly to mean the way that factors of production are used to produce a good. A technology change occurs when a new method is discovered that lowers the cost of producing a good. For example, new methods used in the factories that produce computer chips have lowered the cost and increased the supply of chips.

The State of Nature The state of nature includes all the natural forces that influence production. It includes the state of the weather and, more broadly, the natural environment. Good weather can increase the supply of many agricultural products and bad weather can decrease their supply. Extreme natural events such as earthquakes, tornadoes, and hurricanes can also influence supply.

Figure 3.5 illustrates an increase in supply. When supply increases, the supply curve shifts rightward and the quantity supplied at each price is larger. For example, at $1.00 per bar, on the original (blue) supply curve, the quantity supplied is 6 million bars a week. On the new (red) supply curve, the quantity supplied is 15 million bars a week. Look closely at the numbers in the table in Fig. 3.5 and check that the quantity supplied is larger at each price.

Table 3.2 summarizes the influences on supply and the directions of those influences.

A Change in the Quantity Supplied Versus a Change in Supply

Changes in the influences on selling plans bring either a change in the quantity supplied or a change in supply. Equivalently, they bring either a movement along the supply curve or a shift of the supply curve.

A point on the supply curve shows the quantity supplied at a given price. A movement along the supply curve shows a **change in the quantity supplied**. The entire supply curve shows supply. A shift of the supply curve shows a *change in supply*.

FIGURE 3.5 An Increase in Supply

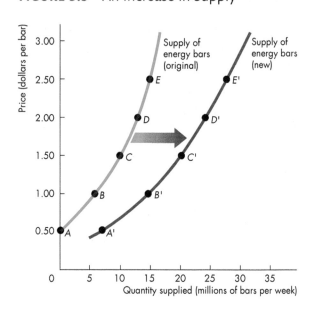

Original supply schedule Old technology		New supply schedule New technology	
Price (dollars per bar)	**Quantity supplied (millions of bars per week)**	**Price (dollars per bar)**	**Quantity supplied (millions of bars per week)**
A 0.50	0	A' 0.50	7
B 1.00	6	B' 1.00	15
C 1.50	10	C' 1.50	20
D 2.00	13	D' 2.00	25
E 2.50	15	E' 2.50	27

A change in any influence on selling plans other than the price of the good itself results in a new supply schedule and a shift of the supply curve. For example, a new, cost-saving technology for producing energy bars changes the supply of energy bars. At a price of $1.50 a bar, 10 million bars a week are supplied when producers use the old technology (row C of the table) and 20 million energy bars a week are supplied when producers use the new technology (row C'). An advance in technology *increases* the supply of energy bars. The supply curve shifts *rightward*, as shown by the shift arrow and the resulting red curve.

MyLab Economics Animation

Figure 3.6 illustrates and summarizes these distinctions. If the price of the good changes and other things remain the same, there is a *change in the quantity supplied* of that good. If the price of the good falls, the quantity supplied decreases and there is a movement down along the supply curve S_0. If the price of the good rises, the quantity supplied increases and there is a movement up along the supply curve S_0. When any other influence on selling plans changes, the supply curve shifts and there is a *change in supply*. If supply increases, the supply curve shifts rightward to S_1. If supply decreases, the supply curve shifts leftward to S_2.

TABLE 3.2   The Supply of Energy Bars

The Law of Supply

The quantity of energy bars supplied

Decreases if:	*Increases if:*
■ The price of an energy bar falls	■ The price of an energy bar rises

Changes in Supply

The supply of energy bars

Decreases if:	*Increases if:*
■ The price of a factor of production used to produce energy bars rises	■ The price of a factor of production used to produce energy bars falls
■ The price of a substitute in production rises	■ The price of a substitute in production falls
■ The price of a complement in production falls	■ The price of a complement in production rises
■ The expected future price of an energy bar rises	■ The expected future price of an energy bar falls
■ The number of suppliers of bars decreases	■ The number of suppliers of bars increases
■ A technology change decreases energy bar production	■ A technology change increases energy bar production
■ A natural event decreases energy bar production	■ A natural event increases energy bar production

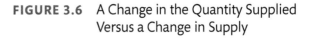

FIGURE 3.6   A Change in the Quantity Supplied Versus a Change in Supply

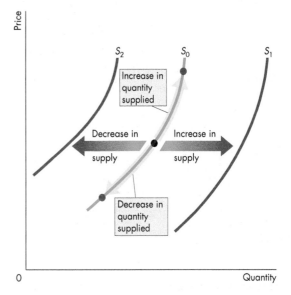

When the price of the good changes, there is a movement along the supply curve and a *change in the quantity supplied*, shown by the blue arrows along the supply curve S_0. When any other influence on selling plans changes, there is a shift of the supply curve and a *change in supply*. An increase in supply shifts the supply curve rightward (from S_0 to S_1), and a decrease in supply shifts the supply curve leftward (from S_0 to S_2).

—— MyLab Economics Animation and Draw Graph ——

◀ REVIEW QUIZ

1. Define the quantity supplied of a good or service.
2. What is the law of supply and how do we illustrate it?
3. What does the supply curve tell us about the producer's minimum supply price?
4. List all the influences on selling plans, and for each influence, say whether it changes supply.
5. What happens to the quantity of smartphones supplied and the supply of smartphones if the price of a smartphone falls?

Work these questions in Study Plan 3.3 and get instant feedback.   MyLab Economics

Now we're going to combine demand and supply and see how prices and quantities are determined.

Market Equilibrium

We have seen that when the price of a good rises, the quantity demanded *decreases* and the quantity supplied *increases*. We are now going to see how the price adjusts to coordinate buying plans and selling plans and achieve an equilibrium in the market.

An *equilibrium* is a situation in which opposing forces balance each other. Equilibrium in a market occurs when the price balances buying plans and selling plans. The **equilibrium price** is the price at which the quantity demanded equals the quantity supplied. The **equilibrium quantity** is the quantity bought and sold at the equilibrium price. A market moves toward its equilibrium because:

- Price regulates buying and selling plans.
- Price adjusts when plans don't match.

Price as a Regulator

The price of a good regulates the quantities demanded and supplied. If the price is too high, the quantity supplied exceeds the quantity demanded. If the price is too low, the quantity demanded exceeds the quantity supplied. There is one price at which the quantity demanded equals the quantity supplied. Let's work out what that price is.

Figure 3.7 shows the market for energy bars. The table shows the demand schedule (from Fig. 3.1) and the supply schedule (from Fig. 3.4). If the price is 50¢ a bar, the quantity demanded is 22 million bars a week but no bars are supplied. There is a shortage of 22 million bars a week. The final column of the table shows this shortage. At a price of $1.00 a bar, there is still a shortage but only of 9 million bars a week.

If the price is $2.50 a bar, the quantity supplied is 15 million bars a week but the quantity demanded is only 5 million bars. There is a surplus of 10 million bars a week.

The one price at which there is neither a shortage nor a surplus is $1.50 a bar. At that price, the quantity demanded equals the quantity supplied: 10 million bars a week. The equilibrium price is $1.50 a bar, and the equilibrium quantity is 10 million bars a week.

Figure 3.7 shows that the demand curve and the supply curve intersect at the equilibrium price of $1.50 a bar. At each price *above* $1.50 a bar, there is a surplus of bars. For example, at $2.00 a bar, the surplus is

FIGURE 3.7 Equilibrium

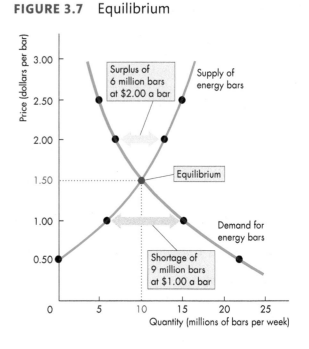

Price (dollars per bar)	Quantity demanded	Quantity supplied	Shortage (−) or surplus (+)
	(millions of bars per week)		
0.50	22	0	−22
1.00	15	6	−9
1.50	**10**	**10**	**0**
2.00	7	13	+6
2.50	5	15	+10

The table lists the quantity demanded and the quantity supplied as well as the shortage or surplus of bars at each price. If the price is $1.00 a bar, 15 million bars a week are demanded and 6 million bars are supplied. There is a shortage of 9 million bars a week, and the price rises.

If the price is $2.00 a bar, 7 million bars a week are demanded and 13 million bars are supplied. There is a surplus of 6 million bars a week, and the price falls.

If the price is $1.50 a bar, 10 million bars a week are demanded and 10 million bars are supplied. There is neither a shortage nor a surplus, and the price does not change. The price at which the quantity demanded equals the quantity supplied is the equilibrium price, and 10 million bars a week is the equilibrium quantity.

—— MyLab Economics Animation and Draw Graph ——

6 million bars a week, as shown by the blue arrow. At each price *below* $1.50 a bar, there is a shortage of bars. For example, at $1.00 a bar, the shortage is 9 million bars a week, as shown by the red arrow.

Price Adjustments

You've seen that if the price is below equilibrium there is a shortage, and that if the price is above equilibrium there is a surplus. But can we count on the price to change and eliminate a shortage or a surplus? We can, because such price changes are beneficial to both buyers and sellers. Let's see why the price changes when there is a shortage or a surplus.

A Shortage Forces the Price Up Suppose that the price of an energy bar is $1. Consumers plan to buy 15 million bars a week, and producers plan to sell 6 million bars a week. Consumers can't force producers to sell more than they plan, so the quantity that is actually offered for sale is 6 million bars a week. In this situation, powerful forces operate to increase the price and move it toward the equilibrium price. Some producers, noticing lines of unsatisfied consumers, raise the price. Some producers increase their output. As producers push the price up, the price rises toward its equilibrium. The rising price reduces the shortage because it decreases the quantity demanded and increases the quantity supplied. When the price has increased to the point at which there is no longer a shortage, the forces moving the price stop operating and the price comes to rest at its equilibrium.

A Surplus Forces the Price Down Suppose the price of a bar is $2. Producers plan to sell 13 million bars a week, and consumers plan to buy 7 million bars a week. Producers cannot force consumers to buy more than they plan, so the quantity that is actually bought is 7 million bars a week. In this situation, powerful forces operate to lower the price and move it toward the equilibrium price. Some producers, unable to sell the quantities of energy bars they planned to sell, cut their prices. In addition, some producers scale back production. As producers cut the price, the price falls toward its equilibrium. The falling price decreases the surplus because it increases the quantity demanded and decreases the quantity supplied. When the price has fallen to the point at which there is no longer a surplus, the forces moving the price stop operating and the price comes to rest at its equilibrium.

The Best Deal Available for Buyers and Sellers

When the price is below equilibrium, it is forced upward. Why don't buyers resist the increase and refuse to buy at the higher price? The answer is because they value the good more highly than its current price and they can't satisfy their demand at the current price. In some markets—for example, the markets that operate on eBay—the buyers might even be the ones who force the price up by offering to pay a higher price.

When the price is above equilibrium, it is bid downward. Why don't sellers resist this decrease and refuse to sell at the lower price? The answer is because their minimum supply price is below the current price and they cannot sell all they would like to at the current price. Sellers willingly lower the price to gain market share.

At the price at which the quantity demanded and the quantity supplied are equal, neither buyers nor sellers can do business at a better price. Buyers pay the highest price they are willing to pay for the last unit bought, and sellers receive the lowest price at which they are willing to supply the last unit sold.

When people freely make offers to buy and sell and when demanders try to buy at the lowest possible price and suppliers try to sell at the highest possible price, the price at which trade takes place is the equilibrium price—the price at which the quantity demanded equals the quantity supplied. The price coordinates the plans of buyers and sellers, and no one has an incentive to change it.

REVIEW QUIZ

1 What is the equilibrium price of a good or service?
2 Over what range of prices does a shortage arise? What happens to the price when there is a shortage?
3 Over what range of prices does a surplus arise? What happens to the price when there is a surplus?
4 Why is the price at which the quantity demanded equals the quantity supplied the equilibrium price?
5 Why is the equilibrium price the best deal available for both buyers and sellers?

Work these questions in Study Plan 3.4 and get instant feedback.   MyLab Economics

◆ Predicting Changes in Price and Quantity

The demand and supply model that we have just studied provides us with a powerful way of analyzing influences on prices and the quantities bought and sold. According to the model, a change in price stems from a change in demand, a change in supply, or a change in both demand and supply. Let's look first at the effects of a change in demand.

An Increase in Demand

If more people join health clubs, the demand for energy bars increases. The table in Fig. 3.8 shows the original and new demand schedules for energy bars as well as the supply schedule of energy bars.

The increase in demand creates a shortage at the original price, and to eliminate the shortage the price must rise.

Figure 3.8 shows what happens. The figure shows the original demand for and supply of energy bars. The original equilibrium price is $1.50 an energy bar, and the equilibrium quantity is 10 million energy bars a week. When demand increases, the demand curve shifts rightward. The equilibrium price rises to $2.50 an energy bar, and the quantity supplied increases to 15 million energy bars a week, as highlighted in the figure. There is an *increase in the quantity supplied* but *no change in supply*—a movement along, but no shift of, the supply curve.

A Decrease in Demand

We can reverse this change in demand. Start at a price of $2.50 a bar with 15 million energy bars a week being bought and sold, and then work out what happens if demand decreases to its original level. Such a decrease in demand might arise if people switch to energy drinks (a substitute for energy bars). The decrease in demand shifts the demand curve leftward. The equilibrium price falls to $1.50 a bar, the quantity supplied decreases, and the equilibrium quantity decreases to 10 million bars a week.

We can now make our first two predictions:

1. When demand increases, the price rises and the quantity increases.
2. When demand decreases, the price falls and the quantity decreases.

FIGURE 3.8 The Effects of a Change in Demand

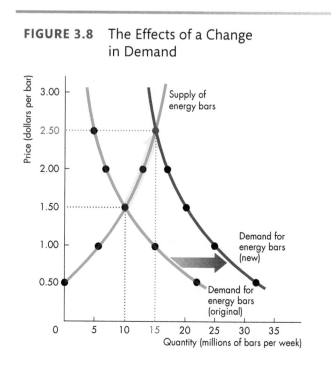

Price (dollars per bar)	Quantity demanded (millions of bars per week)		Quantity supplied (millions of bars per week)
	Original	New	
0.50	22	32	0
1.00	15	25	6
1.50	**10**	20	**10**
2.00	7	17	13
2.50	5	**15**	**15**

Initially, the demand for energy bars is the blue demand curve. The equilibrium price is $1.50 a bar, and the equilibrium quantity is 10 million bars a week. When more health-conscious people do more exercise, the demand for energy bars increases and the demand curve shifts rightward to become the red curve.

At $1.50 a bar, there is now a shortage of 10 million bars a week. The price of a bar rises to a new equilibrium of $2.50. As the price rises to $2.50, the quantity supplied increases—shown by the blue arrow on the supply curve—to the new equilibrium quantity of 15 million bars a week. Following an increase in demand, the quantity supplied increases but supply does not change—the supply curve does not shift.

—— MyLab Economics Animation and Draw Graph ——

◆ ECONOMICS IN THE NEWS

The Markets for Chocolate and Cocoa

World's Sweet Tooth Heats Up Cocoa

With rising incomes in China and other fast-growing economies, the consumption of chocolate and the cocoa from which it is made is soaring. And the price of cocoa is soaring too.

Source: *The Wall Street Journal*, February 3, 2014

THE DATA

Year	Quantity of Cocoa (millions of tonnes per year)	Price of Cocoa (dollars per tonne)
2010	4	1,500
2014	5	3,000

THE QUESTIONS

- What does the data table tell us?
- Why did the price of cocoa increase? Is it because the demand for cocoa changed or the supply changed, and in which direction?

THE ANSWERS

- The data table tells us that from 2010 to 2014, both the quantity of cocoa produced and the price of cocoa increased.
- An increase in demand brings an increase in the quantity and a rise in the price.
- An increase in supply brings an increase in the quantity and a fall in the price.
- Because both the quantity of cocoa and the price of cocoa increased, there must have been in increase in the demand for cocoa.
- The demand for cocoa increases if cocoa is a normal good and incomes increase.
- Cocoa is a normal good and the news clip says that incomes are rising fast in China and some other countries. These increases in income have brought an increase in the demand for cocoa.
- The figure illustrates the market for cocoa in 2010 and 2014. The supply curve *S* shows the supply of cocoa.

- In 2010, the demand curve was D_{2010}, the price was $1,500 per tonne, and the quantity of cocoa traded was 4 million tonnes.

- By 2014, the higher incomes in China and other countries had increased the demand for cocoa to D_{2014}. The price rose to $3,000 per tonne and the quantity traded increased to 5 million tonnes.

- The higher price brought an increase in the quantity of cocoa supplied, which is shown by the movement upward along the supply curve.

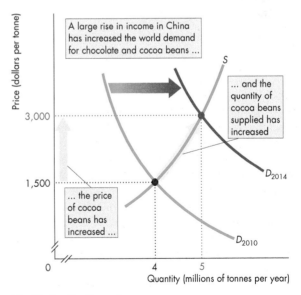

The Market for Cocoa Beans

An Increase in Supply

When Nestlé (the producer of PowerBar) and other energy bar producers switch to a new cost-saving technology, the supply of energy bars increases. Figure 3.9 shows the new supply schedule (the same one that was shown in Fig. 3.5). What are the new equilibrium price and quantity? The price falls to $1.00 a bar, and the quantity increases to 15 million bars a week. You can see why by looking at the quantities demanded and supplied at the old price of $1.50 a bar. The new quantity supplied at that price is 20 million bars a week, and there is a surplus. The price falls. Only when the price is $1.00 a bar does the quantity supplied equal the quantity demanded.

Figure 3.9 illustrates the effect of an increase in supply. It shows the demand curve for energy bars and the original and new supply curves. The initial equilibrium price is $1.50 a bar, and the equilibrium quantity is 10 million bars a week. When supply increases, the supply curve shifts rightward. The equilibrium price falls to $1.00 a bar, and the quantity demanded increases to 15 million bars a week, highlighted in the figure. There is an *increase in the quantity demanded* but *no change in demand*—a movement along, but no shift of, the demand curve.

A Decrease in Supply

Start out at a price of $1.00 a bar with 15 million bars a week being bought and sold. Then suppose that the cost of labour or raw materials rises and the supply of energy bars decreases. The decrease in supply shifts the supply curve leftward. The equilibrium price rises to $1.50 a bar, the quantity demanded decreases, and the equilibrium quantity decreases to 10 million bars a week.

We can now make two more predictions:

1. When supply increases, the price falls and the quantity increases.
2. When supply decreases, the price rises and the quantity decreases.

You've now seen what happens to the price and the quantity when either demand or supply changes while the other one remains unchanged. In real markets, both demand and supply can change together. When this happens, to predict the changes in price and quantity, we must combine the effects that you've just seen. That is your final task in this chapter.

FIGURE 3.9 The Effects of a Change in Supply

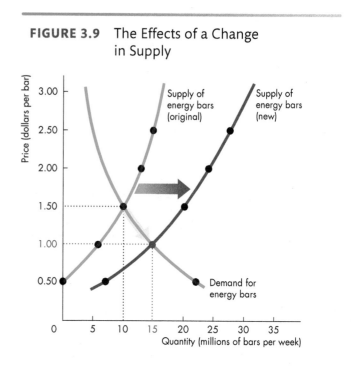

Price (dollars per bar)	Quantity demanded (millions of bars per week)	Quantity supplied (millions of bars per week)	
		Original	New
0.50	22	0	7
1.00	15	6	15
1.50	10	10	20
2.00	7	13	25
2.50	5	15	27

Initially, the supply of energy bars is shown by the blue supply curve. The equilibrium price is $1.50 a bar, and the equilibrium quantity is 10 million bars a week. When the new cost-saving technology is adopted, the supply of energy bars increases and the supply curve shifts rightward to become the red curve.

At $1.50 a bar, there is now a surplus of 10 million bars a week. The price of an energy bar falls to a new equilibrium of $1.00 a bar. As the price falls to $1.00, the quantity demanded increases—shown by the blue arrow on the demand curve—to the new equilibrium quantity of 15 million bars a week. Following an increase in supply, the quantity demanded increases but demand does not change—the demand curve does not shift.

—— MyLab Economics Animation and Draw Graph ——

ECONOMICS IN THE NEWS

The Market for Vanilla Bean

Price of Ice Cream Set to Spike
A poor harvest in Madagascar has exploded the price of vanilla bean, the flavouring in Canada's top ice cream.

Source: *The Toronto Star*, April 7, 2016

THE DATA

Year	Quantity of Vanilla Bean (billions of tonnes per year)	Price of Vanilla Bean (dollars per kilogram)
2015	7.6	70
2016	5.6	425

THE QUESTIONS

- What does the data table tell us?
- Why did the price of vanilla bean rise? Is it because demand changed or supply changed, and in which direction?

THE ANSWERS

- The data table tells us that during 2016, the quantity of vanilla bean produced increased and the price of vanilla bean increased sharply.
- An increase in demand brings an increase in the quantity and a rise in the price.
- A decrease in supply brings a decrease in the quantity and a rise in the price.
- Because the quantity of vanilla bean decreased and the price increased, there must have been a decrease in the supply of vanilla bean
- The supply of vanilla bean decreases if a poor harvest decreases production.
- The news clip says there was a poor harvest in Madagascar. This decrease in production brought a decrease in the supply of vanilla bean.
- The figure illustrates the market for vanilla bean in 2015 and 2016. The demand curve D shows the demand for vanilla bean.
- In 2015, the supply curve was S_{15}, the price was $70 per kilogram, and the quantity of vanilla bean traded was 7.6 billion tonnes.

- In 2016, the decreased production in Madagasscar decreased the supply of vanilla bean to S_{16}.
- The price increased to $425 per kilogram and the quantity traded decreased to 5.6 billion tonnes.
- The higher price brought a decrease in the quantity of vanilla bean demanded, which is shown by the movement along the demand curve.

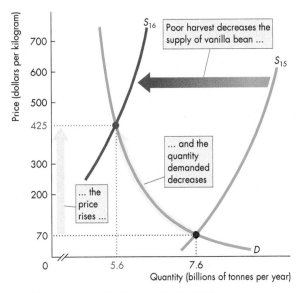

The Market for Vanilla Bean in 2015–2016

Changes in Both Demand and Supply

You now know how a change in demand or a change in supply changes the equilibrium price and quantity. But sometimes, events occur that change both demand and supply. When both demand and supply change, we find the resulting change in the equilibrium price and equilibrium quantity by combining the separate cases you've just studied.

Four cases need to be considered. Both demand and supply increase or decrease, or either demand or supply increases and the other decreases.

Demand and Supply Change in the Same Direction

When demand and supply change in the *same* direction, the equilibrium quantity changes in that same direction, but to predict whether the price rises or falls, we need to know the magnitudes of the changes in demand and supply.

If demand increases by more than supply increases, the price rises. But if supply increases by more than demand increases, the price falls.

Figure 3.10(a) shows the case when both demand and supply increase and by the same amount. The

equilibrium quantity increases. But because the increase in demand equals the increase in supply, neither a shortage nor a surplus arises so the price doesn't change. A bigger increase in demand would have created a shortage and a rise in the price; a bigger increase in supply would have created a surplus and a fall in the price.

Figure 3.10(b) shows the case when both demand and supply decrease by the same amount. Here the equilibrium quantity decreases and again the price might either rise or fall.

Demand and Supply Change in Opposite Directions

When demand and supply change in *opposite* directions, we can predict how the price changes, but we need to know the magnitudes of the changes in demand and supply to say whether the equilibrium quantity increases or decreases.

If demand changes by more than supply, the equilibrium quantity changes in the same direction as the change in demand. But if supply changes by more than demand, the equilibrium quantity changes in the same direction as the change in supply.

FIGURE 3.10 The Effects of Changes in Demand and Supply in the Same Direction

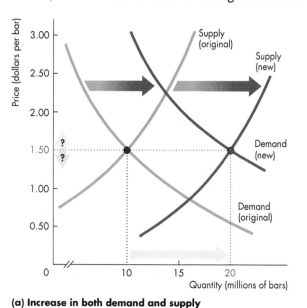

(a) Increase in both demand and supply

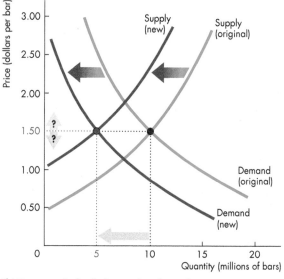

(b) Decrease in both demand and supply

An increase in demand shifts the demand curve rightward to become the red new demand curve and an increase in supply shifts the supply curve rightward to become the red new supply curve. The price might rise or fall, but the quantity increases.

A decrease in demand shifts the demand curve leftward to become the red new demand curve and a decrease in supply shifts the supply curve leftward to become the red new supply curve. The price might rise or fall, but the quantity decreases.

FIGURE 3.11   The Effects of Changes in Demand and Supply in Opposite Directions

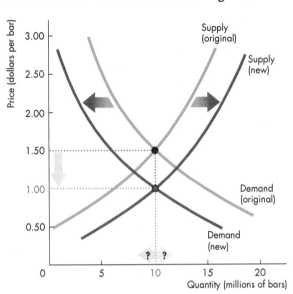

(a) Decrease in demand; increase in supply

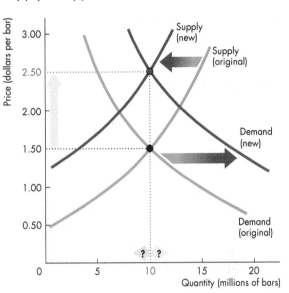

(b) Increase in demand; decrease in supply

A decrease in demand shifts the demand curve leftward to become the red new demand curve and an increase in supply shifts the supply curve rightward to become the red new supply curve. The price falls, but the quantity might increase or decrease.

An increase in demand shifts the demand curve rightward to become the red new demand curve and a decrease in supply shifts the supply curve leftward to become the red new supply curve. The price rises, but the quantity might increase or decrease.

MyLab Economics Animation

Figure 3.11(a) illustrates what happens when demand decreases and supply increases by the *same* amount. At the initial price, there is a surplus, so the price falls. A decrease in demand decreases the quantity and an increase in supply increases the quantity, so when these changes occur together, we can't say what happens to the quantity unless we know the magnitudes of the changes.

Figure 3.11(b) illustrates what happens when demand increases and supply decreases by the same amount. In this case, at the initial price, there is a shortage, so the price rises. An increase in demand increases the quantity and a decrease in supply decreases the quantity, so again, when these changes occur together, we can't say what happens to the quantity unless we know the magnitudes of the changes in demand and supply.

For all the cases in Figures 3.10 and 3.11 where you "can't say" what happens to price or quantity, draw some examples that go in each direction.

REVIEW QUIZ

What is the effect on the price and quantity of smartphones if:

1 The price of a music-streaming subscription falls or the price of a wireless plan rises? (Draw the diagrams!)

2 More firms produce smartphones or electronics workers' wages rise? (Draw the diagrams!)

3 Any two of the events in questions 1 and 2 occur together? (Draw the diagrams!)

Work these questions in Study Plan 3.5 and get instant feedback.   MyLab Economics

◆ To complete your study of demand and supply, take a look at *Economics in the News* on pp. 76–77, which explains what has happened in the market for frozen concentrated orange juice. Try to get into the habit of using the demand and supply model to understand the changes in prices in your everyday life.

Demand and Supply: The Market for Orange Juice

The Frozen Concentrated Orange-Juice Market Has Virtually Disappeared

The Wall Street Journal
August 28, 2016

The once-thriving market for frozen orange-juice concentrate is getting squeezed. ...

Americans drank less orange juice in 2015 than in any year since Nielsen began collecting data in 2002, as more exotic beverages like tropical smoothies and energy drinks take market share and fewer Americans sit down for breakfast.

When they do drink orange juice, they aren't drinking it from concentrate.

Frozen concentrated orange juice was invented in Florida in the 1940s, primarily as a way to provide juice for the military, readily storable, and easy to ship. But frozen juice has been losing favor for years.

Not-from-concentrate orange juice surpassed the concentrated orange-juice market in the 1980s. Now, the 1.4 million gallons of frozen concentrate that Americans drink each month pales in comparison to the 19.1 million gallons of fresh juice consumed each month, Nielsen said.

Louis Dreyfus Co. is scaling back the one citrus facility in Florida that is devoted entirely to concentrated orange juice. The commodities giant is laying off 59 of the plant's 94 workers as it sells the operation that packs frozen concentrated orange juice into cans for retail.

There are now seven orange-juice processors left in Florida, down from the four dozen that once called the state home. ...

A bacterial disease, citrus greening, ... has slashed the orange crop in half in recent years. ... Diseased trees are plucked out and replaced by new ones, which also catch the disease.

ESSENCE OF THE STORY

- Americans are drinking less frozen concentrated orange juice and more tropical smoothies, energy drinks, and not-from-concentrate orange juice.

- Today, Americans drink 1.4 million gallons of frozen concentrate each month compared to 19.1 million gallons of fresh juice consumed each month.

- Florida producers of concentrated orange juice are cutting production and laying off workers and dozens have gone out of business.

- In recent years, a bacterial disease, citrus greening, has halved the orange crop.

ECONOMIC ANALYSIS

- The quantity of frozen concentrated orange juice produced has been falling, and in 2016, the quantity produced was less than half that of 2008.

- Figure 1 shows the falling and fluctuating quantity produced.

- Figure 1 also shows the price of frozen concentrated orange juice, which has also trended downward.

- Look carefully at Fig. 1 and notice that from 2012 to 2014, the price and quantity moved in the same direction—they both fell; and from 2014 to 2015, the price and quantity moved in opposite directions—the quantity continued to fall but the price rose.

- The demand and supply model can be put to work to explain these changes in price and quantity.

- Figure 2 explains what occurred from 2012 to 2014.

- In 2012, the supply of frozen concentrated orange juice was S_0 and the demand was D_0. The price was $2.40 per can and the equilibrium quantity was 149 million boxes of cans of orange juice.

- By 2014, with unchanged supply, changing preferences decreased demand to D_1. The price fell to $2.14 per can and the equilibrium quantity decreased to 105 million boxes of cans.

- Figure 3 explains what happened in 2015.

- The bacterial disease citrus greening decreased the orange crop, which decreased the supply of frozen concentrated orange juice from S_0 to S_1. With demand unchanged at D_1, the price increased to $2.31 a can and the equilibrium quantity decreased to 97 million boxes.

- So, the demand and supply model explains the fall in the quantity of orange juice in 2014 as resulting from a decrease in demand, which brought a fall in price and a decrease in the quantity supplied.

- The demand and supply model also explains the fall in the quantity of orange juice in 2015 as resulting from a decrease in supply, which brought a rise in price and a decrease in the quantity demanded.

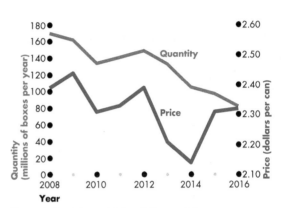

Figure 1 Quantity and Price of Orange Juice

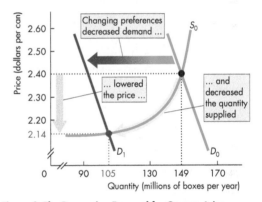

Figure 2 The Decreasing Demand for Orange Juice

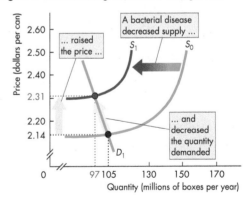

Figure 3 The Decrease in the Supply of Orange Juice

MATHEMATICAL NOTE

Demand, Supply, and Equilibrium

Demand Curve

The law of demand says that as the price of a good or service falls, the quantity demanded of that good or service increases. We can illustrate the law of demand by drawing a graph of the demand curve or writing down an equation. When the demand curve is a straight line, the following equation describes it:

$$P = a - bQ_D,$$

where P is the price and Q_D is the quantity demanded. The a and b are positive constants.

The demand equation tells us three things:

1. The price at which no one is willing to buy the good (Q_D is zero). That is, if the price is a, then the quantity demanded is zero. You can see the price a in Fig. 1. It is the price at which the demand curve hits the y-axis—what we call the demand curve's "y-intercept."

2. As the price falls, the quantity demanded increases. If Q_D is a positive number, then the price P must be less than a. As Q_D gets larger, the price P becomes smaller. That is, as the quantity increases, the maximum price that buyers are willing to pay for the last unit of the good falls.

3. The constant b tells us how fast the maximum price that someone is willing to pay for the good falls as the quantity increases. That is, the constant b tells us about the steepness of the demand curve. The equation tells us that the slope of the demand curve is $-b$.

Supply Curve

The law of supply says that as the price of a good or service rises, the quantity supplied of that good or service increases. We can illustrate the law of supply by drawing a graph of the supply curve or writing down an equation. When the supply curve is a straight line, the following equation describes it:

$$P = c + dQ_S,$$

where P is the price and Q_S is the quantity supplied. The c and d are positive constants.

The supply equation tells us three things:

1. The price at which sellers are not willing to supply the good (Q_S is zero). That is, if the price is c, then no one is willing to sell the good. You can see the price c in Fig. 2. It is the price at which the supply curve hits the y-axis—what we call the supply curve's "y-intercept."

2. As the price rises, the quantity supplied increases. If Q_S is a positive number, then the price P must be greater than c. As Q_S increases, the price P becomes larger. That is, as the quantity increases, the minimum price that sellers are willing to accept for the last unit rises.

3. The constant d tells us how fast the minimum price at which someone is willing to sell the good rises as the quantity increases. That is, the constant d tells us about the steepness of the supply curve. The equation tells us that the slope of the supply curve is d.

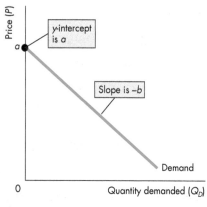

Figure 1 Demand Curve

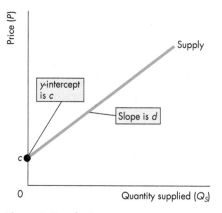

Figure 2 Supply Curve

Market Equilibrium

Demand and supply determine market equilibrium. Figure 3 shows the equilibrium price ($P*$) and equilibrium quantity ($Q*$) at the intersection of the demand curve and the supply curve.

We can use the equations to find the equilibrium price and equilibrium quantity. The price of a good adjusts until the quantity demanded Q_D equals the quantity supplied Q_S. So at the equilibrium price ($P*$) and equilibrium quantity ($Q*$),

$$Q_D = Q_S = Q*.$$

To find the equilibrium price and equilibrium quantity, substitute $Q*$ for Q_D in the demand equation and $Q*$ for Q_S in the supply equation. Then the price is the equilibrium price ($P*$), which gives

$$P* = a - bQ*$$

$$P* = c + dQ*.$$

Notice that

$$a - bQ* = c + dQ*.$$

Now solve for $Q*$:

$$a - c = bQ* + dQ*$$

$$a - c = (b + d)Q*$$

$$Q* = \frac{a - c}{b + d}.$$

To find the equilibrium price $P*$, substitute for $Q*$ in either the demand equation or the supply equation.

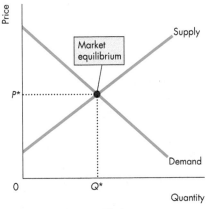

Figure 3 Market Equilibrium

Using the demand equation, we have

$$P* = a - b\left(\frac{a - c}{b + d}\right)$$

$$P* = \frac{a(b + d) - b(a - c)}{b + d}$$

$$P* = \frac{ad + bc}{b + d}.$$

Alternatively, using the supply equation, we have

$$P* = c + d\left(\frac{a - c}{b + d}\right)$$

$$P* = \frac{c(b + d) + d(a - c)}{b + d}$$

$$P* = \frac{ad + bc}{b + d}.$$

An Example

The demand for ice-cream cones is

$$P = 800 - 2Q_D.$$

The supply of ice-cream cones is

$$P = 200 + 1Q_S.$$

The price of a cone is expressed in cents, and the quantities are expressed in cones per day.

To find the equilibrium price ($P*$) and equilibrium quantity ($Q*$), substitute $Q*$ for Q_D and Q_S and $P*$ for P. That is,

$$P* = 800 - 2Q*$$

$$P* = 200 + 1Q*.$$

Now solve for $Q*$:

$$800 - 2Q* = 200 + 1Q*$$

$$600 = 3Q*$$

$$Q* = 200.$$

And

$$P* = 800 - 2(200)$$

$$= 400.$$

The equilibrium price is $4 a cone, and the equilibrium quantity is 200 cones per day.

WORKED PROBLEM

MyLab Economics Work this problem in Chapter 3 Study Plan.

The table sets out the demand and supply schedules for roses on a normal weekend.

Price (dollars per rose)	Quantity demanded	Quantity supplied
	(roses per week)	
6.00	150	60
7.00	100	100
8.00	70	130
9.00	50	150

Questions

1. If the price of a rose is $6, describe the situation in the rose market. Explain how the price adjusts.
2. If the price of a rose is $9, describe the situation in the rose market. Explain how the price adjusts.
3. What is the market equilibrium?
4. Rose sellers know that Mother's Day is next weekend and they expect the price to be higher, so they withhold 60 roses from the market this weekend. What is the price this weekend?
5. On Mother's Day, demand increases by 160 roses. What is the price of a rose on Mother's Day?

Solutions

1. At $6 a rose, the quantity demanded is 150 and the quantity supplied is 60. The quantity demanded exceeds the quantity supplied and there is a *shortage* of 90 roses. With people lining up and a shortage, the price rises above $6 a rose.

Key Point: When a shortage exists, the price rises.

2. At $9 a rose, the quantity demanded is 50 and the quantity supplied is 180. The quantity supplied exceeds the quantity demanded and there is a *surplus* of 130 roses. With slow sales of roses and a surplus, the price falls to below $9 a rose.

Key Point: When a surplus exists, the price falls.

3. Market equilibrium occurs at the price at which the quantity demanded *equals* the quantity supplied. That price is $7 a rose. The market equilibrium is a price of $7 a rose and 100 roses a week are bought and sold, Point *A* on the figure.

Key Point: At market equilibrium, there is no shortage or surplus.

4. Sellers expect a higher price next weekend, so they decrease the supply this weekend by 60 roses at each price. Create the new table:

Price (dollars per rose)	Quantity demanded	Quantity supplied
	(roses per week)	
6.00	150	0
7.00	**100**	**40**
8.00	70	70
9.00	50	90

At $7 a rose, there was a shortage of 60 roses, so the price rises to $8 a rose at which the quantity demanded equals the quantity supplied (Point *B*).

Key Point: When supply decreases, the price rises.

5. Demand increases by 160 roses. Sellers plan to increase the normal supply by the 60 roses withheld last weekend. Create the new table:

Price (dollars per rose)	Quantity demanded	Quantity supplied
	(roses per week)	
6.00	310	120
7.00	**260**	**160**
8.00	230	190
9.00	210	210

At $7 a rose, there is a shortage of 100 roses, so the price rises. It rises until at $9 a rose, the quantity demanded equals the quantity supplied. The price on Mother's Day is $9 a rose (Point *C*).

Key Point: When demand increases by more than supply, the price rises.

Key Figure

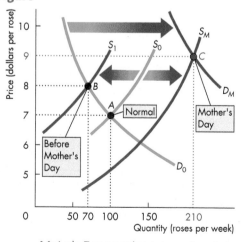

MyLab Economics Interactive Animation

SUMMARY

Key Points

Markets and Prices (p. 58)

- A competitive market is one that has so many buyers and sellers that no single buyer or seller can influence the price.
- Opportunity cost is a relative price.
- Demand and supply determine relative prices.

Working Problem 1 will give you a better understanding of markets and prices.

Demand (pp. 59–63)

- Demand is the relationship between the quantity demanded of a good and its price when all other influences on buying plans remain the same.
- The higher the price of a good, other things remaining the same, the smaller is the quantity demanded—the law of demand.
- Demand depends on the prices of related goods (substitutes and complements), expected future prices, income, expected future income and credit, the population, and preferences.

Working Problems 2 to 4 will give you a better understanding of demand.

Supply (pp. 64–67)

- Supply is the relationship between the quantity supplied of a good and its price when all other influences on selling plans remain the same.
- The higher the price of a good, other things remaining the same, the greater is the quantity supplied—the law of supply.

- Supply depends on the prices of factors of production used to produce a good, the prices of related goods produced, expected future prices, the number of suppliers, technology, and the state of nature.

Working Problems 5 and 6 will give you a better understanding of supply.

Market Equilibrium (pp. 68–69)

- At the equilibrium price, the quantity demanded equals the quantity supplied.
- At any price above the equilibrium price, there is a surplus and the price falls.
- At any price below the equilibrium price, there is a shortage and the price rises.

Working Problem 7 will give you a better understanding of market equilibrium.

Predicting Changes in Price and Quantity (pp. 70–75)

- An increase in demand brings a rise in the price and an increase in the quantity supplied. A decrease in demand brings a fall in the price and a decrease in the quantity supplied.
- An increase in supply brings a fall in the price and an increase in the quantity demanded. A decrease in supply brings a rise in the price and a decrease in the quantity demanded.
- An increase in demand and an increase in supply bring an increased quantity but an uncertain price change. An increase in demand and a decrease in supply bring a higher price but an uncertain change in quantity.

Working Problems 8 to 10 will give you a better understanding of predicting changes in price and quantity.

Key Terms

MyLab Economics Key Terms Quiz

Change in demand, 60	Demand curve, 60	Quantity demanded, 59
Change in supply, 65	Equilibrium price, 68	Quantity supplied, 64
Change in the quantity demanded, 63	Equilibrium quantity, 68	Relative price, 58
	Inferior good, 62	Substitute, 61
Change in the quantity supplied, 66	Law of demand, 59	Supply, 64
Competitive market, 58	Law of supply, 64	Supply curve, 64
Complement, 61	Money price, 58	
Demand, 59	Normal good, 62	

STUDY PLAN PROBLEMS AND APPLICATIONS

MyLab Economics Work Problems 1 to 10 in Chapter 3 Study Plan and get instant feedback.

Markets and Prices (Study Plan 3.1)

1. In April 2014, the money price of a litre of milk was $2.01 and the money price of a litre of gasoline was $1.30. Calculate the real price of a litre of gasoline in terms of milk.

Demand (Study Plan 3.2)

2. The price of food increased during the past year.
   a. Explain why the law of demand applies to food just as it does to other goods and services.
   b. Explain how the substitution effect influences food purchases when the price of food rises and other things remain the same.
   c. Explain how the income effect influences food purchases and provide some examples of the income effect.

3. Which of the following goods are likely substitutes and which are likely complements? (You may use an item more than once.)

   coal, oil, natural gas, wheat, corn, pasta, pizza, sausage, skateboard, roller blades, video game, laptop, iPad, smartphone, text message, email

4. As the average income in China continues to increase, explain how the following would change:
   a. The demand for beef
   b. The demand for rice

Supply (Study Plan 3.3)

5. In 2016, the price of corn fell and some corn farmers switched from growing corn in 2017 to growing soybeans.
   a. Does this fact illustrate the law of demand or the law of supply? Explain your answer.
   b. Why would a corn farmer grow soybeans?

6. Dairies make low-fat milk from full-cream milk, and in the process they produce cream, which is made into ice cream. The following events occur one at a time:
   (i)   The wage rate of dairy workers rises.
   (ii) The price of cream rises.
   (iii) The price of low-fat milk rises.
   (iv) With a drought forecasted, dairies raise their expected price of low-fat milk next year.
   (v)   New technology lowers the cost of producing ice cream.

   Explain the effect of each event on the supply of low-fat milk.

Market Equilibrium (Study Plan 3.4)

7. The demand and supply schedules for gum are:

Price (cents per pack)	Quantity demanded	Quantity supplied
	(millions of packs a week)	
20	180	60
40	140	100
60	100	140
80	60	180

   a. Suppose that the price of gum is 70¢ a pack. Describe the situation in the gum market and explain how the price adjusts.
   b. Suppose that the price of gum is 30¢ a pack. Describe the situation in the gum market and explain how the price adjusts.

Predicting Changes in Price and Quantity (Study Plan 3.5)

8. The following events occur one at a time:
   (i)   The price of crude oil rises.
   (ii) The price of a car rises.
   (iii) All speed limits on highways are abolished.
   (iv) Robots cut car production costs.

   Explain the effect of each of these events on the market for gasoline.

9. In Problem 7, a fire destroys some factories that produce gum and the quantity of gum supplied decreases by 40 million packs a week at each price.
   a. Explain what happens in the market for gum and draw a graph to illustrate the changes.
   b. Suppose that at the same time as the fire, the teenage population increases and the quantity of gum demanded increases by 40 million packs a week at each price. What is the new market equilibrium? Illustrate these changes on your graph.

10. **Singing the Blues: March Frost Destroys Blueberry Crop**
   Chris and Rhonda Luther had big plans for their small blueberry farm, but freezing temperatures killed these plans, reducing their usual output by about 95 percent. The freeze cut total production by 80 percent.

   Source: *Red and Black*, March 25, 2017

   Draw a graph to show the market for blueberries before and after the freeze in March.

ADDITIONAL PROBLEMS AND APPLICATIONS

Markets and Prices

11. What features of the world market for crude oil make it a competitive market?

12. The money price of a textbook is $90 and the money price of the Wii game *Super Mario Galaxy* is $45.

    a. What is the opportunity cost of a textbook in terms of the Wii game?

    b. What is the relative price of the Wii game in terms of textbooks?

Demand

13. The price of gasoline has increased during the past year.

    a. Explain why the law of demand applies to gasoline just as it does to all other goods and services.

    b. Explain how the substitution effect influences gasoline purchases and provide some examples of substitutions that people might make when the price of gasoline rises and other things remain the same.

    c. Explain how the income effect influences gasoline purchases and provide some examples of the income effects that might occur when the price of gasoline rises and other things remain the same.

14. Think about the demand for the three game consoles: Xbox One, PlayStation 4, and Wii U. Explain the effect of each of the following events on the demand for Xbox One games and the quantity of Xbox One games demanded, other things remaining the same. The events are:

    a. The price of an Xbox One falls.

    b. The prices of a PlayStation 4 and a Wii U fall.

    c. The number of people writing and producing Xbox One games increases.

    d. Consumers' incomes increase.

    e. Programmers who write code for Xbox One games become more costly to hire.

    f. The expected future price of an Xbox One game falls.

    g. A new game console that is a close substitute for Xbox One comes onto the market.

Supply

15. Classify the following pairs of goods and services as substitutes in production, complements in production, or neither.

    a. Bottled water and health club memberships

    b. French fries and baked potatoes

    c. Leather boots and leather shoes

    d. Hybrids and SUVs

    e. Diet Coke and regular Coke

16. When a timber mill makes logs from trees it also produces sawdust, which is used to make plywood.

    a. Explain how a rise in the price of sawdust influences the supply of logs.

    b. Explain how a rise in the price of sawdust influences the supply of plywood.

17. **New Maple Syrup Sap Method**
    With the new way to tap maple trees, farmers could produce 10 times as much maple syrup per acre.
    Source: cbc.ca, February 5, 2014

    Will the new method change the supply of maple syrup or the quantity supplied of maple syrup, other things remaining the same? Explain.

Market Equilibrium

Use the following figure to work Problems 18 and 19.

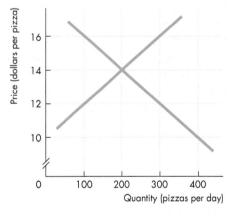

18. a. Label the curves. Which curve shows the willingness to pay for a pizza?

    b. If the price of a pizza is $16, is there a shortage or a surplus and does the price rise or fall?

c. Sellers want to receive the highest possible price, so why would they be willing to accept less than $16 a pizza?

19. a. If the price of a pizza is $12, is there a shortage or a surplus and does the price rise or fall?

    b. Buyers want to pay the lowest possible price, so why would they be willing to pay more than $12 for a pizza?

20. The demand and supply schedules for potato chips are:

Price	Quantity demanded	Quantity supplied
(cents per bag)	(millions of bags per week)	
50	160	130
60	150	140
70	140	150
80	130	160
90	120	170
100	110	180

    a. Draw a graph of the potato chip market and mark in the equilibrium price and quantity.

    b. If the price is 60¢ a bag, is there a shortage or a surplus, and how does the price adjust?

Predicting Changes in Price and Quantity

21. In Problem 20, a new dip increases the quantity of potato chips that people want to buy by 30 million bags per week at each price.

    a. Does the demand for chips change? Does the supply of chips change? Describe the change.

    b. How do the equilibrium price and equilibrium quantity of chips change?

22. In Problem 20, if a virus destroys potato crops and the quantity of potato chips produced decreases by 40 million bags a week at each price, how does the supply of chips change?

23. If the virus in Problem 22 hits just as the new dip in Problem 21 comes onto the market, how do the equilibrium price and equilibrium quantity of chips change?

24. **U.S. Craft Beer Bolsters U.K. Hop Production**

    U.K. hop farmers stepped up production in response to a rapid growth of U.S. craft beer production. U.S. craft beer makers prefer the subtle taste of U.K. hop varieties.

    Source: BBC, October 3, 2014

    a. Describe the changes in the market for U.S. craft beer.

    b. Explain whether the increase in U.K. hop production is a change in supply or a change in the quantity supplied.

    c. What could be the impact on the price of U.K. hops if U.S. farmers switched to U.K. hop varieties?

25. **Vietnamese Farmers Switch to Pepper as Coffee Prices Fall**

    The high pepper price and falling coffee price has made Vietnamese farmers replace coffee plants with pepper plants. Analysts fear farmers have used diseased pepper plants which could fail.

    Source: *VietNam News*, May 28, 2016

    a. Explain how the market for Vietnamese coffee will change as farmers switch to pepper.

    b. If pepper plants fail, what would happen to the price of pepper?

26. **Watch Out for Rising Dry-Cleaning Bills**

    The price of dry-cleaning solvent doubled and more than 4,000 dry cleaners disappeared as consumers cut back. The price of hangers used by dry cleaners is now expected to double.

    Source: CNN Money, June 4, 2012

    a. Explain the effect of rising solvent prices on the market for dry cleaning.

    b. Explain the effect of consumers becoming more budget conscious along with the rising price of solvent on the price of dry cleaning.

    c. If the price of hangers does rise this year, do you expect additional dry cleaners to disappear? Explain why or why not.

Economics in the News

27. After you have studied *Economics in the News* on pp. 76–77, answer the following questions.

    a. Would you classify frozen concentrated orange juice as a normal good or an inferior good? Why?

    b. What would happen to the price of orange juice if citrus greening wiped out the Florida orange crop?

    c. What are some of the substitutes for orange juice and what would happen to the demand, supply, price, and quantity in the markets for each of these items if citrus greening became more severe?

    d. What are some of the complements of orange juice and what would happen to the demand, supply, price, and quantity in the markets for each of these items if citrus greening became more severe?

Your Economic Revolution

UNDERSTANDING THE SCOPE OF ECONOMICS

Three periods in human history stand out as ones of economic revolution. The first, the *Agricultural Revolution*, occurred 10,000 years ago. In what is today Iraq, people learned to domesticate animals and plant crops. People stopped roaming in search of food and settled in villages, towns, and cities where they specialized in the activities in which they had a comparative advantage and developed markets in which to exchange their products. Wealth increased enormously.

Economics was born during the *Industrial Revolution,* which began in England during the 1760s. For the first time, people began to apply science and create new technologies for the manufacture of textiles and iron, to create steam engines, and to boost the output of farms.

You are studying economics at a time that future historians will call the *Information Revolution*. Over the entire world, people are embracing new information technologies and prospering on an unprecedented scale.

During all three economic revolutions, many have prospered but others have been left behind. It is the range of human progress that poses the greatest question for economics and the one that Adam Smith addressed in the first work of economic science: What causes the differences in wealth among nations?

Many people had written about economics before **Adam Smith***, but he made economics a science. Born in 1723 in Kirkcaldy, a small fishing town near Edinburgh, Scotland, Smith was the only child of the town's customs officer. Lured from his professorship (he was a full professor at 28) by a wealthy Scottish duke who gave him a pension of £300 a year—10 times the average income at that time—Smith devoted 10 years to writing his masterpiece:* An Inquiry into the Nature and Causes of the Wealth of Nations, *published in 1776.*

Why, Adam Smith asked, are some nations wealthy while others are poor? He was pondering these questions at the height of the Industrial Revolution, and he answered by emphasizing the power of the division of labour and free markets in raising labour productivity.

To illustrate his argument, Adam Smith described two pin factories. In the first, one person, using the hand tools available in the 1770s, could make 20 pins a day. In the other, by using those same hand tools but breaking the process into a number of individually small operations in which people specialize—by the division of labour—10 people could make a staggering 48,000 pins a day. One draws out the wire,

Every individual who intends only his own gain is led by an invisible hand to promote an end (the public good) which was no part of his intention.

ADAM SMITH
The Wealth of Nations

another straightens it, a third cuts it, a fourth points it, a fifth grinds it. Three specialists make the head, and a fourth attaches it. Finally, the pin is polished and packaged.

But a large market is needed to support the division of labour: One factory employing 10 workers would need to sell more than 15 million pins a year to stay in business!

ESTHER DUFLO is the Abdul Latif Jameel Professor of Poverty Alleviation and Development Economics at the Massachusetts Institute of Technology. Among her many honours are the 2010 John Bates Clark Medal for the best economist under 40 and the Financial Times and Goldman Sachs Business Book of the Year Award in 2011 for her book (with Abhijit Banerjee) *Poor Economics: A Radical Rethinking of the Way to Fight Global Poverty*. Professor Duflo's research seeks to advance our understanding of the economic choices of the extremely poor by conducting massive real-world experiments.

Professor Duflo was an undergraduate student of history and economics at École Normale Supérieure and completed a master's degree at DELTA in Paris before moving to the United States. She earned her Ph.D. in economics at MIT in 1999.

Michael Parkin and Robin Bade talked with her about her work, which advances our understanding of the economic choices and condition of the very poor.

Professor Duflo, what's the story about how you became an economist and in particular the architect of experiments designed to understand the economic choices of the very poor?

When I was a kid, I was exposed to many stories and images of poor children: through my mother's engagement as a doctor in a small NGO dealing with child victims of war and through books and stories about children living all around the world.

I remember asking myself how I could justify my luck of being born where I was. I had a very exaggerated idea of what it was to be poor, but this idea caused sufficient discomfort that I knew I had to do something about it, if I could. Quite by accident, I discovered that economics was the way in which I could actually be useful: While spending a year in Russia teaching French and studying history, I realized that academic economists have the ability to intervene in the world while keeping enough sanity to analyze it. I thought this would be ideal for me and I have never regretted it. I have the best job in the world.

> ... imagine living on under a dollar a day after your rent is paid in Seattle or Denver. Not easy!

The very poor who you study are people who live on $1 a day or $2 a day. ... Is $1 a day a true measure that includes everything these poor people consume?

For defining the poverty line, we don't include the cost of housing. The poor also get free goods, sometimes of bad quality (education, healthcare) and the value of those is also not included. Other than that, yes, it is everything.

Moreover, you have to realize this is everything, taking into account the fact that life is much cheaper in many poor countries because salaries are lower, so anything that is made and consumed locally (e.g., a haircut) is cheaper.

For example, in India, the purchasing power of a dollar (in terms of the real goods you can buy) is about 3 times what it is in the United States. So the poverty line we use for India is 33 cents per day, not a dollar.

All told, you really have to imagine living on under a dollar a day after your rent is paid in Seattle or Denver. Not easy!

*Read the full interview with Esther Duflo in MyLab Economics.

4 MONITORING THE VALUE OF PRODUCTION: GDP

After studying this chapter, you will be able to:

◆ Define GDP and explain why GDP equals aggregate expenditure and aggregate income

◆ Explain how Statistics Canada measures Canadian GDP and real GDP

◆ Explain the uses and limitations of real GDP as a measure of economic well-being

Will our economy expand more rapidly next year or will it sink into another recession? Many Canadian businesses want to know the answer to this question. To assess the state of the economy and to make big decisions about business expansion, firms such as Bombardier and Rogers Communications use forecasts of GDP. What exactly is GDP and what does it tell us about the state of the economy?

In this chapter, you will find out how Statistics Canada measures GDP. You will also learn about the uses and the limitations of GDP. In *Economics in the News* at the end of the chapter, we compare GDP in Canada and the United States and see which has had the faster growth in recent years.

Gross Domestic Product

What exactly is GDP, how is it calculated, what does it mean, and why do we care about it? You are going to discover the answers to these questions in this chapter. First, what *is* GDP?

GDP Defined

GDP, or **gross domestic product**, is the market value of the final goods and services produced within a country in a given time period. This definition has four parts:

- Market value
- Final goods and services
- Produced within a country
- In a given time period

We'll examine each in turn.

Market Value To measure total production, we must add together the production of apples and oranges, computers and popcorn. Just counting the items doesn't get us very far. For example, which is the greater total production: 100 apples and 50 oranges or 50 apples and 100 oranges?

GDP answers this question by valuing items at their *market values*—the prices at which items are traded in markets. If the price of an apple is 10¢, then the market value of 50 apples is $5. If the price of an orange is 20¢, then the market value of 100 oranges is $20. By using market prices to value production, we can add the apples and oranges together. The market value of 50 apples and 100 oranges is $5 plus $20, or $25.

Final Goods and Services To calculate GDP, we value the *final goods and services* produced. A **final good** (or service) is an item that is bought by its final user during a specified time period. It contrasts with an **intermediate good** (or service), which is an item that is produced by one firm, bought by another firm, and used as a component of a final good or service.

For example, a new Ford truck is a final good, but a Firestone tire on that truck is an intermediate good. Your new iPad is a final good, but the chip inside it is an intermediate good.

If we were to add the value of intermediate goods and services produced to the value of final goods and services, we would count the same thing many times—a problem called *double counting*. The value of a truck already includes the value of the tires, and the value of an iPad already includes the value of the chip inside it.

Some goods can be an intermediate good in some situations and a final good in other situations. For example, the ice cream that you buy on a hot summer day is a final good, but the ice cream that a restaurant buys and uses to make sundaes is an intermediate good. The sundae is the final good. So whether a good is an intermediate good or a final good depends on what it is used for, not what it is.

Some items that people buy are neither final goods nor intermediate goods and they are not part of GDP. Examples of such items include financial assets—stocks and bonds—and secondhand goods—used cars or existing homes. A secondhand good was part of GDP in the year in which it was produced, but not in GDP this year.

Produced Within a Country Only goods and services that are produced *within a country* count as part of that country's GDP. Roots, a Canadian firm, produces T-shirts in Taiwan, and the market value of those shirts is part of Taiwan's GDP, not part of Canada's GDP. Toyota, a Japanese firm, produces automobiles in Cambridge, Ontario, and the value of this production is part of Canada's GDP, not part of Japan's GDP.

In a Given Time Period GDP measures the value of production *in a given time period*—normally either a quarter of a year—called the quarterly GDP data—or a year—called the annual GDP data.

GDP measures not only the value of total production but also total income and total expenditure. The equality between the value of total production and total income is important because it shows the direct link between productivity and living standards. Our standard of living rises when our incomes rise and we can afford to buy more goods and services. But we must produce more goods and services if we are to be able to buy more goods and services.

Rising incomes and a rising value of production go together. They are two aspects of the same phenomenon: increasing productivity. To see why, we study the circular flow of expenditure and income.

GDP and the Circular Flow of Expenditure and Income

Figure 4.1 illustrates the circular flow of expenditure and income. The economy consists of households, firms, governments, and the rest of the world (the rectangles), which trade in factor markets and goods (and services) markets. We focus first on households and firms.

Households and Firms Households sell and firms buy the services of labour, capital, and land in factor markets. For these factor services, firms pay income to households: wages for labour services, interest for the use of capital, and rent for the use of land. A fourth factor of production, entrepreneurship, receives profit.

Firms' retained earnings—profits that are not distributed to households—are part of the household sector's income. You can think of retained earnings as being income that households save and lend back to firms. Figure 4.1 shows the total income—*aggregate income*—received by households, including retained earnings, as the blue flow labelled *Y*.

Firms sell and households buy consumer goods and services—such as inline skates and haircuts—in the goods market. The total payment for these goods and services is **consumption expenditure**, shown by the red flow labelled *C*.

Firms buy and sell new capital equipment—such as computer systems, airplanes, trucks, and assembly line equipment—in the goods market. Some of what firms produce is not sold but is added to inventory. For example, if GM produces 1,000 cars and sells 950 of them, the other 50 cars remain in GM's inventory of unsold cars, which increases by 50 cars. When a firm adds unsold output to inventory, we can think of the firm as buying goods from itself. The

---

FIGURE 4.1 The Circular Flow of Expenditure and Income

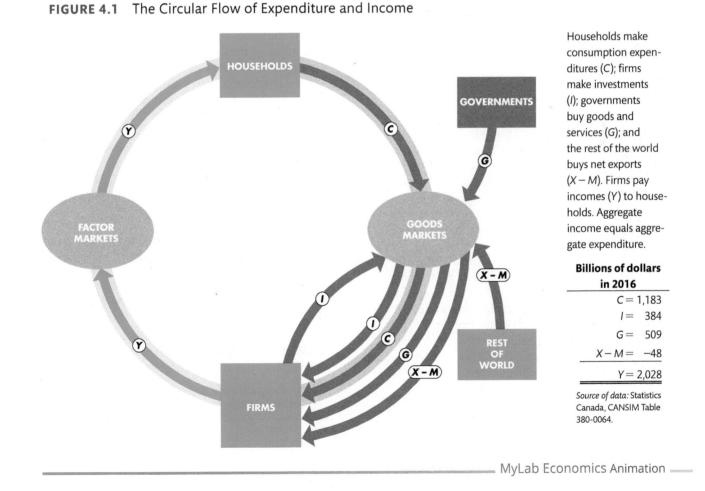

Households make consumption expenditures (*C*); firms make investments (*I*); governments buy goods and services (*G*); and the rest of the world buys net exports (*X − M*). Firms pay incomes (*Y*) to households. Aggregate income equals aggregate expenditure.

Billions of dollars in 2016	
C =	1,183
I =	384
G =	509
X − M =	−48
Y =	2,028

Source of data: Statistics Canada, CANSIM Table 380-0064.

MyLab Economics Animation

purchase of new plant, equipment, and buildings and the additions to inventories are **investment**, shown by the red flow labelled *I*.

Governments Governments buy goods and services from firms and their expenditure on goods and services is called **government expenditure**. In Fig. 4.1, government expenditure is shown as the red flow *G*.

Governments finance their expenditure with taxes. But taxes are not part of the circular flow of expenditure and income. Governments also make financial transfers to households, such as social security benefits and unemployment benefits, and pay subsidies to firms. These financial transfers, like taxes, are not part of the circular flow of expenditure and income.

Rest of the World Firms in Canada sell goods and services to the rest of the world—**exports**—and buy goods and services from the rest of the world—**imports**. The value of exports (*X*) minus the value of imports (*M*) is called **net exports** (*NX*), the red flow $X - M$ in Fig. 4.1. If net exports are positive, the net flow of goods and services is from Canadian firms to the rest of the world. If net exports are negative, the net flow of goods and services is from the rest of the world to Canadian firms.

GDP Equals Expenditure Equals Income Gross domestic product can be measured in two ways: by the total expenditure on goods and services or by the total income earned producing goods and services.

The total expenditure—*aggregate expenditure*—is the sum of the red flows in Fig. 4.1. Aggregate expenditure equals consumption expenditure plus investment plus government expenditure plus net exports.

Aggregate income is equal to the total amount paid for the services of the factors of production used to produce final goods and services—wages, interest, rent, and profit. The blue flow in Fig. 4.1 shows aggregate income. Because firms pay out as incomes (including retained profits) everything they receive from the sale of their output, aggregate income (the blue flow) equals aggregate expenditure (the sum of the red flows). That is,

$$Y = C + I + G + X - M$$

The table in Fig. 4.1 shows the values of the expenditures for 2016 and that their sum is $2,028 billion, which also equals aggregate income.

Because aggregate expenditure equals aggregate income, the two methods of measuring GDP give the same answer. So

GDP equals aggregate expenditure and equals aggregate income.

The circular flow model is the foundation on which the national economic accounts are built.

Why Is Domestic Product "Gross"?

"Gross" means before subtracting the depreciation of capital. The opposite of "gross" is "net," which means after subtracting the depreciation of capital.

Depreciation is the decrease in the value of a firm's capital that results from wear and tear and obsolescence. The total amount spent both buying new capital and replacing depreciated capital is called **gross investment**. The amount by which the value of capital increases is called **net investment**. Net investment equals gross investment minus depreciation.

For example, if an airline buys 5 new airplanes and retires 2 old airplanes from service, its gross investment is the value of the 5 new airplanes, depreciation is the value of the 2 old airplanes retired, and net investment is the value of 3 new airplanes.

Gross investment is one of the expenditures included in the expenditure approach to measuring GDP. So the resulting value of total product is a gross measure.

Gross profit, which is a firm's profit before subtracting depreciation, is one of the incomes included in the income approach to measuring GDP. So again, the resulting value of total product is a gross measure.

REVIEW QUIZ

1 Define GDP and distinguish between a final good and an intermediate good. Provide examples.
2 Why does GDP equal aggregate income and also equal aggregate expenditure?
3 What are the distinctions between domestic and national, and gross and net?

Work these questions in Study Plan 4.1 and get instant feedback.   MyLab Economics

Let's now see how the ideas that you've just studied are used in practice. We'll see how GDP and its components are measured in Canada today.

Measuring Canada's GDP

Statistics Canada uses the concepts in the circular flow model to measure GDP and its components in the *National Income and Expenditure Accounts*. Because the value of aggregate production equals aggregate expenditure and aggregate income, there are two approaches available for measuring GDP, and both are used. They are:

- The expenditure approach
- The income approach

The Expenditure Approach

The *expenditure approach* measures GDP as the sum of consumption expenditure (C), investment (I), government expenditure on goods and services (G), and net exports of goods and services ($X - M$). These expenditures correspond to the red flows through the goods markets in the circular flow model in Fig. 4.1. Table 4.1 shows these expenditures and the calculation of GDP for 2016.

Consumption expenditure is the expenditure by Canadian households on goods and services produced in Canada and in the rest of the world and is shown by the red flow C in Fig. 4.2. They include goods such as avocados and books and services such as banking and legal advice. They also include

TABLE 4.1 GDP: The Expenditure Approach

Item	Symbol	Amount in 2016 (billions of dollars)	Percentage of GDP
Consumption expenditure	C	1,183	58.3
Investment	I	384	19.0
Government expenditure on goods and services	G	509	25.1
Net exports of goods and services	X − M	− 48	− 2.4
Gross domestic product	**Y**	**2,028**	**100.0**

The expenditure approach measures GDP as the sum of consumption expenditure C, investment I, government expenditure on goods and services G, and net exports X − M. In 2016, GDP measured by the expenditure approach was $2,028 billion. Some 58 percent of aggregate expenditure is expenditure by Canadian households on consumption goods and services.

Source of data: Statistics Canada, CANSIM Table 380-0064.

the purchase of consumer durable goods, such as computers and microwave ovens. But they do *not* include the purchase of new homes, which Statistics Canada counts as part of investment.

Investment is the expenditure on capital equipment and buildings by firms and the additions to business inventories. It also includes expenditure on new homes by households. Investment is the red flow I in Fig. 4.2.

Government expenditure on goods and services is the expenditure by all levels of government on goods and services, such as national defence and garbage collection. It does *not* include *transfer payments*, such as unemployment benefits, because they are not expenditures on goods and services. Government expenditure is the red flow G in Fig. 4.2.

Net exports of goods and services are the value of exports minus the value of imports. This item includes telephone equipment that Nortel sells to AT&T (a Canadian export), and Japanese DVD players that Sears buys from Sony (a Canadian import) and is shown by the red flow $X - M$ in Fig. 4.2.

Table 4.1 shows the relative magnitudes of the four items of aggregate expenditure.

FIGURE 4.2 Aggregate Expenditure

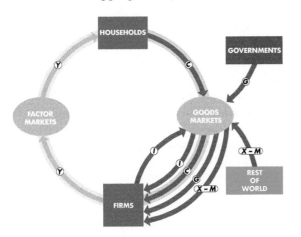

Aggregate expenditure is the sum of the red flows.

MyLab Economics Animation

The Income Approach

The *income approach* measures GDP by summing the incomes that firms pay households for the factors of production they hire—wages for labour, interest for capital, rent for land, and profit for entrepreneurship. These incomes sum to the blue flows through the factor markets in the circular flow model in Fig. 4.1. We divide the incomes in the *National Income and Expenditure Accounts* into two broad categories:

1. Wages, salaries, and supplementary labour income
2. Other factor incomes

Wages, salaries, and supplementary labour income is the payment for labour services. It includes gross wages plus benefits such as pension contributions and is shown by the blue flow *W* in Fig. 4.3.

Other factor incomes include corporate profits, interest, farmers' income, and income from non-farm unincorporated businesses. These incomes are a mixture of interest, rent, and profit and include some labour income from self-employment. They are included in the blue flow *OFI* in Fig. 4.3.

Table 4.2 shows these incomes and their relative magnitudes. They sum to net domestic income at factor cost.

An *indirect tax* is a tax paid by consumers when they buy goods and services. (In contrast, a *direct tax* is a tax on income.) An indirect tax makes the market price exceed factor cost. A *subsidy* is a payment by the government to a producer. With a

TABLE 4.2   GDP: The Income Approach

Item	Amount in 2016 (billions of dollars)	Percentage of GDP
Wages, salaries, and supplementary labour income	1,051	51.8
Other factor incomes	399	19.7
Net domestic income at factor cost	1,450	71.5
Indirect taxes *less* subsidies	227	11.2
Net domestic income at market prices	1,677	82.7
Depreciation	351	17.3
GDP (income approach)	**2,028**	**100.0**
Statistical discrepancy	0	0.0
GDP (expenditure approach)	**2,028**	**100.0**

The sum of factor incomes equals *net domestic income at factor cost*. GDP equals net domestic income at factor cost plus indirect taxes less subsidies plus depreciation.

In 2016, GDP measured by the income approach was $2,028 billion. This amount is equal to GDP measured by the expenditure approach. The statistical discrepancy was less than $0.5 billion, which rounds to $0 billion.

Wages, salaries, and supplementary labour income is by far the largest component of aggregate income.

Source of data: Statistics Canada, CANSIM Table 380-0063.

FIGURE 4.3   Aggregate Income

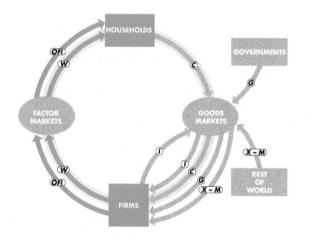

Aggregate income is the sum of the blue flows.

subsidy, factor cost exceeds market price. To get from factor cost to market price, we add indirect taxes and subtract subsidies. Making this adjustment brings us to *net domestic income at market prices*.

We still must get from a net to a gross measure. Total expenditure is a *gross* number because it includes *gross investment*. Net domestic income at market prices is a net income measure because corporate profits are measured *after deducting depreciation*. They are a net income measure. To get from net income to gross income, we must *add depreciation*.

We've now arrived at GDP using the income approach. This number is not exactly the same as GDP using the expenditure approach. The gap between the expenditure approach and the income approach is called the *statistical discrepancy* and it is calculated as the GDP expenditure total minus the GDP income total. The discrepancy is never large. In 2016, it was less than $0.5 billion, which rounds to $0 billion.

Nominal GDP and Real GDP

Often, we want to *compare* GDP in two periods, say 2000 and 2016. In 2000, GDP was $1,102 billion, and in 2016 it was $2,028 billion—84 percent higher than in 2000. This increase in GDP is a combination of an increase in production and a rise in prices. To isolate the increase in production from the rise in prices, we distinguish between *real* GDP and *nominal* GDP.

Real GDP is the value of final goods and services produced in a given year when *valued at the prices of a reference base year*. By comparing the value of production in the two years at the same prices, we reveal the change in production.

Currently, the reference base year is 2007 and we describe real GDP as measured in 2007 dollars—in terms of what the dollar would buy in 2007.

Nominal GDP is the value of final goods and services produced in a given year when valued at the prices of that year. Nominal GDP is just a more precise name for GDP.

Economists at Statistics Canada calculate real GDP using the method described in the Mathematical Note on pp. 104–105. Here, we'll explain the basic idea but not the technical details.

Calculating Real GDP

We'll calculate real GDP for an economy that produces one consumption good, one capital good, and one government service. Net exports are zero.

Table 4.3 shows the quantities produced and the prices in 2007 (the base year) and in 2016. In part (a), we calculate nominal GDP in 2007. For each item, we multiply the quantity produced in 2007 by its price in 2007 to find the total expenditure on the item. We sum the expenditures to find nominal GDP, which in 2007 is $100 million. Because 2007 is the base year, both real GDP and nominal GDP equal $100 million.

In Table 4.3(b), we calculate nominal GDP in 2016, which is $300 million. Nominal GDP in 2016 is three times its value in 2007. But by how much has production increased? Real GDP will tell us.

In Table 4.3(c), we calculate real GDP in 2016. The quantities of the goods and services produced are those of 2016, as in part (b). The prices are those in the reference base year—2007, as in part (a).

For each item, we multiply the quantity produced in 2016 by its price in 2007. We then sum these expenditures to find real GDP in 2016, which is $160 million. This number is what total expenditure

TABLE 4.3   Calculating Nominal GDP and Real GDP

Item	Quantity (millions)	Price (dollars)	Expenditure (millions of dollars)
(a) In 2007			
C T-shirts	10	5	50
I Computer chips	3	10	30
G Security services	1	20	20
Y Real GDP in 2007			100
(b) In 2016			
C T-shirts	4	5	20
I Computer chips	2	20	40
G Security services	6	40	240
Y Nominal GDP in 2016			300
(c) Quantities of 2016 valued at prices of 2007			
C T-shirts	4	5	20
I Computer chips	2	10	20
G Security services	6	20	120
Y Real GDP in 2016			160

In 2007, the reference base year, real GDP equals nominal GDP and was $100 million. In 2016, nominal GDP increased to $300 million, but real GDP, which is calculated by using the quantities in 2016 in part (b) and the prices in 2007 in part (a), was only $160 million—a 60 percent increase from 2007.

would have been in 2016 if prices had remained the same as they were in 2007.

Nominal GDP in 2016 is three times its value in 2007, but real GDP in 2016 is only 1.6 times its 2007 value—a 60 percent increase in production.

REVIEW QUIZ

1 What is the expenditure approach to measuring GDP?
2 What is the income approach to measuring GDP?
3 What adjustments must be made to total income to make it equal GDP?
4 What is the distinction between nominal GDP and real GDP?
5 How is real GDP calculated?

Work these questions in Study Plan 4.2 and get instant feedback.   MyLab Economics

◆ The Uses and Limitations of Real GDP

Economists use estimates of real GDP for two main purposes:

- To compare the standard of living over time
- To compare the standard of living across countries

The Standard of Living over Time

One method of comparing the standard of living over time is to calculate real GDP per person in different years. **Real GDP per person** is real GDP divided by the population. Real GDP per person tells us the value of goods and services that the average person can enjoy. By using *real* GDP, we remove any influence that rising prices and a rising cost of living might have had on our comparison.

We're interested in both the long-term trends and the shorter-term cycles in the standard of living.

Long-Term Trend A handy way of comparing real GDP per person over time is to express it as a ratio of some reference year. For example, in 1961, real GDP per person was $18,000, and in 2016 it was $50,000 (both rounded to the nearest thousand). So real GDP per person in 2016 was 2.8 times its 1961 level. To the extent that real GDP per person measures well-being, people were almost three times as well off in 2016 as their grandparents had been in 1961.

Figure 4.4 shows the path of Canadian real GDP per person from 1961 to 2016 and highlights two features of our expanding living standard:

- The growth of potential GDP per person
- Fluctuations of real GDP per person

The Growth of Potential GDP **Potential GDP** is the maximum quantity of real GDP that can be produced while avoiding shortages of labour, capital, land, and entrepreneurial ability that would bring rising inflation. Potential GDP per person, the smoother black line in Fig. 4.4, grows at a steady pace because the quantities of the factors of production and their productivities grow at a steady pace.

But potential GDP per person doesn't grow at a *constant* pace. During the 1960s, it grew at 3.4 percent per year but slowed to 2.4 percent per year during the 1970s. This slowdown might seem small, but it had big consequences, as you'll soon see.

FIGURE 4.4 Rising Standard of Living in Canada

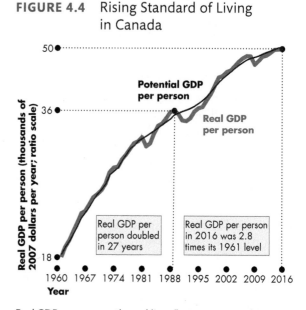

Real GDP per person, the red line, fluctuates around potential GDP per person, the black line. The black line becomes less steep after 1970, which indicates the slowdown in the potential GDP growth rate. (The y-axis is a ratio scale—see the Appendix, pp. 102–103.)

Sources of data: Statistics Canada, CANSIM Tables 380-0064 and 051-0001. International Monetary Fund World Economic Outlook output gap data used to calculate potential GDP.

—————— MyLab Economics Real-time data ——————

Fluctuations of Real GDP You can see that real GDP per person shown by the red line in Fig. 4.4 fluctuates around potential GDP per person, and sometimes real GDP per person shrinks.

Let's take a closer look at the two features of our expanding living standard that we've just outlined.

Productivity Growth Slowdown How costly was the slowdown in productivity growth after 1970? The answer is provided by the *Lucas wedge*, which is the dollar value of the accumulated gap between what real GDP per person would have been if the growth rate of the 1960s had persisted and what real GDP per person turned out to be. (Nobel Laureate Robert E. Lucas Jr. drew attention to this gap.)

Figure 4.5 illustrates the Lucas wedge. The wedge started out small during the 1970s, but by 2016 real GDP per person was $54,000 per year lower than it would have been with no growth slowdown, and the accumulated gap was an astonishing $790,000 per person.

FIGURE 4.5 The Cost of Slower Growth: The Lucas Wedge

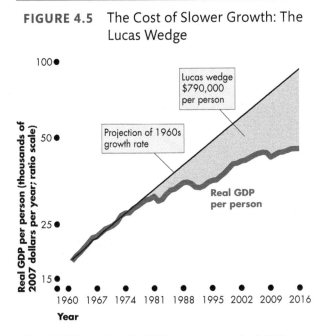

The black line projects the 1960s growth rate of real GDP per person to 2016. The Lucas wedge arises from the slowdown of productivity growth that began during the 1970s. The cost of the slowdown is $790,000 per person.

Sources of data: Statistics Canada, CANSIM Tables 380-0064 and 051-0001 and authors' calculations.

—————— MyLab Economics Real-time data ——————

Real GDP Fluctuations—The Business Cycle We call the fluctuations in the pace of expansion of real GDP the **business cycle**. The business cycle is a periodic but irregular up-and-down movement of total production and other measures of economic activity. The business cycle isn't a regular predictable cycle like the phases of the moon, but every cycle has two phases:

1. Expansion
2. Recession

and two turning points:

1. Peak
2. Trough

Figure 4.6 shows these features of the most recent Canadian business cycle.

An **expansion** is a period during which real GDP increases. In the early stage of an expansion real GDP returns to potential GDP, and as the expansion progresses potential GDP grows, and real GDP eventually exceeds potential GDP.

A common definition of **recession** is a period during which real GDP decreases—its growth rate is negative—for at least two successive quarters. A more general definition of recession and one used by the U.S. National Bureau of Economic Research is "a period of significant decline in total output, income, employment, and trade, usually lasting from six months to a year, and marked by contractions in many sectors of the economy."

An expansion ends and recession begins at a business cycle *peak*, which is the highest level that real GDP has attained up to that time. A recession ends at a *trough*, when real GDP reaches a temporary low point and from which the next expansion begins.

In 2008, Canada went into an unusually severe recession. Starting from a long way below potential GDP, a new expansion began in mid-2009. Real GDP returned to potential GDP in 2011, increased above potential in 2014 and 2015, and slipped below potential again in 2016.

FIGURE 4.6 The Most Recent Canadian Business Cycle

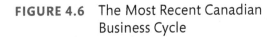
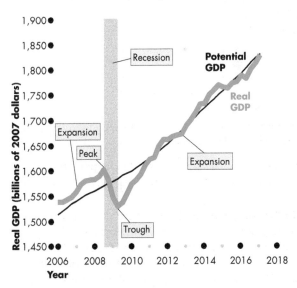

A recession began at a peak in the third quarter of 2008 and ended at a trough in the second quarter of 2009. Then a slow expansion began and real GDP remained below potential GDP until 2011. Real GDP then remained mainly above potential GDP until 2016.

Sources of data: Statistics Canada, CANSIM Table 380-0064 and Bank of Canada quarterly output gap data used to calculate potential GDP.

—————— MyLab Economics Real-time data ——————

The Standard of Living Across Countries

Two problems arise in using real GDP to compare living standards across countries. First, the real GDP of one country must be converted into the same currency units as the real GDP of the other country. Second, the goods and services in both countries must be valued at the same prices. Comparing China and the United States provides a striking example of these two problems.

China and the United States in U.S. Dollars In 2016, nominal GDP per person in the United States was $51,200 and in China it was 53,908 yuan. The yuan is the currency of China and the price at which the dollar and the yuan exchanged, the *market exchange rate*, was 6.64 yuan per $1 U.S. Using this exchange rate, 53,908 yuan converts to $8,119. On these numbers, GDP per person in the United States in 2016 was 6.3 times that in China.

The red line in Fig. 4.7 shows *real* GDP per person in China from 1980 to 2016 when the market exchange rate is used to convert yuan to U.S. dollars.

China and the United States at PPP Figure 4.7 shows a second estimate of China's real GDP per person that values China's production on the same terms as U.S. production. It uses *purchasing power parity* or *PPP* prices, which are the *same prices* for both countries.

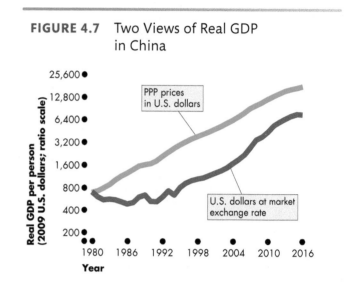

FIGURE 4.7   Two Views of Real GDP in China

Real GDP per person in China has grown rapidly. But how rapidly it has grown and to what level depends on how real GDP is valued. When GDP in 2016 is valued at the market exchange rate (the red curve), U.S. income per person is 6.3 times that in China. China looks like a poor, developing country. But the comparison is misleading. When GDP is valued at purchasing power parity prices (the green curve), U.S. income per person is only 3.8 times that in China.

Source of data: International Monetary Fund, *World Economic Outlook database*, April 2017.

—————— MyLab Economics Animation ——————

The prices of some goods are higher in the United States than in China, so these items get a smaller weight in the calculation of China's real GDP than they get in U.S. real GDP. An example is a Big Mac, which costs $5.30 in Chicago. In Shanghai, a Big Mac costs 19.40 yuan, which is the equivalent of $2.92. So in China's real GDP, a Big Mac gets about half the weight that it gets in U.S. real GDP.

Some prices in China are higher than in the United States but more prices are lower, so Chinese prices put a lower value on China's production than do U.S. prices.

According to the PPP comparisons (same prices in both countries), real GDP per person in the United States in 2016 was 3.8 times that of China, not 6.3 times.

You've seen how real GDP is used to make standard of living comparisons over time and across countries. But real GDP isn't a perfect measure of the standard of living, and we'll now examine its limitations.

In July 2016, a Big Mac cost $5.30 in Chicago and 19.40 yuan or $2.92 in Shanghai. To compare real GDP in China and the United States, we must value China's Big Macs at the $5.30 U.S. price—the PPP price.

Limitations of Real GDP

Real GDP measures the value of goods and services that are bought in markets. Some of the factors that influence the standard of living and that are not part of GDP are:

- Household production
- Underground economic activity
- Leisure time
- Environmental quality

Household Production Preparing meals, changing a light bulb, mowing a lawn, washing a car, and caring for a child are all examples of household production. Because these productive activities are not traded in markets, they are not included in GDP.

The omission of household production from GDP means that GDP *underestimates* total production. But it also means that the growth rate of GDP *overestimates* the growth rate of total production. The reason is that some of the growth rate of market production (included in GDP) is a replacement for home production. So part of the increase in GDP arises from a decrease in home production.

Underground Economic Activity The *underground economy* is economic activity hidden from the view of the government to avoid taxes and regulations or because the activity is illegal. Because underground economic activity is unreported, it is omitted from GDP. The Canadian underground economy is estimated to range between 5 and 15 percent of GDP ($100 billion to $300 billion).

Leisure Time Leisure time is an economic good that adds to our economic well-being and the standard of living. Other things remaining the same, the more leisure we have, the better off we are. Our working time is valued as part of GDP, but our leisure time is not. Yet that leisure time must be at least as valuable to us as the wage that we earn for the last hour worked. If it were not, we would work instead of taking leisure. Over the years, leisure time has steadily increased. The workweek has become shorter, more people take early retirement, and the number of vacation days has increased. These improvements in economic well-being are not reflected in real GDP.

Environmental Quality Economic activity directly influences the quality of the environment. The burning of hydrocarbon fuels is the most visible activity that damages our environment, but it is not the only example. The depletion of nonrenewable natural resources, the mass clearing of forests, and the pollution of lakes and rivers are other major environmental consequences of industrial production.

Resources used to protect the environment are valued as part of GDP. For example, the value of catalytic converters that protect the atmosphere from automobile emissions is part of GDP.

An industrial society might produce more atmospheric pollution than an agricultural society does, but pollution does not always increase as we become wealthier. Wealthy people value a clean environment and are willing to pay for one. Compare the pollution in China today with pollution in Canada. The air in Beijing is much more polluted than that of Toronto or Montreal.

Whose production is more valuable: the chef's whose work gets counted in GDP . . .

. . . or the busy mother's whose dinner preparation and child minding don't get counted?

AT **ISSUE**

Should GNNP Replace GDP?

The standard view of economists is that despite its limitations, GDP is a useful measure of the value of production and the overall level of economic activity in a country or region.

But a prominent economist, Joseph Stiglitz, has argued that GDP is dangerously misleading and needs to be replaced by a measure that he calls Green Net National Product (or GNNP).

Let's look at both sides of this issue.

Joe Stiglitz says...

- GDP has passed its use-by date.

- A *gross* measure is wrong because it ignores the depreciation of assets.

- A *domestic* measure is wrong because it ignores the incomes paid to foreigners who exploit a nation's resources.

- A *green* measure is needed to take account of the environmental damage that arises from production.

- GNNP subtracts from GDP incomes paid to foreigners, depreciation, the value of depleted natural resources, and the cost of a degraded environment.

- The existence of a market price for carbon emissions makes it possible to measure the cost of these emissions and subtract them from GDP.

- A bad accounting framework is likely to lead to bad decisions.

- America's "drain America first" energy policy is an example of a bad decision. It increases GDP but decreases GNNP and makes Americans poorer.

The Mainstream View

- As a measure of the value of market production in an economy, GDP does a good job.

- GDP is used to track the ups and downs of economic activity and it is a useful indicator for making macroeconomic stabilization policy decisions.

- GDP is *not* used to measure net national economic well-being nor to guide microeconomic resource allocation decisions.

- There is no disagreement that a *net national* measure is appropriate for measuring national economic well-being.

- There is no disagreement that "negative externalities" arising from carbon emissions and other pollution detract from economic well-being.

- The omissions from GDP of household production and underground production are *bigger* problems than those emphasized by Stiglitz.

- It isn't clear that depleting oil and coal resources is costly and misguided because advances in green energy technology will eventually make oil and coal of little value. The Stone Age didn't end because we ran out of stone, and the Carbon Age won't end because we run out of oil and coal!

Bad accounting frameworks are likely to lead to bad decisions. A government focused on GDP might be encouraged to give away mining or oil concessions; a focus on green NNP might make it realize that the country risks being worse off.

Joseph Stiglitz,
"Good Numbers Gone Bad,"
Fortune, September 25, 2006

When the Anglo-Australian company BHP Billiton mines copper in Papua New Guinea, the country's GDP rises, but profits go abroad and the 40,000 locals who live by a polluted river lose their means of earning a living. GNNP measures that loss.

ECONOMICS IN ACTION

A Broader Indicator of Economic Well-Being

The limitations of real GDP reviewed in this chapter affect the standard of living and general well-being of every country. So to make international comparisons of the general state of economic well-being, we must look at real GDP and other indicators.

The United Nations has constructed a broader measure called the Human Development Index (HDI), which combines real GDP, life expectancy and health, and education. Real GDP per person (measured on the PPP basis—the same prices in all countries) is a major component of the HDI so, as you can see in the figure, the two are strongly correlated.

The figure shows the data for 2015. In that year, Norway had the highest HDI, but Qatar had the highest real GDP per person. Canada ranked twentieth on real GDP per person and tenth on the HDI.

The HDI of Canada is lower than that of Norway and Australia mainly because the people of those countries have a longer life expectancy than do Canadians.

African nations have the lowest levels of economic well-being. The figure shows that Central African Republic had the lowest HDI and the lowest real GDP per person.

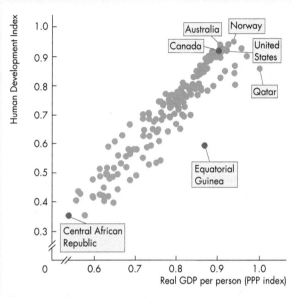

The Human Development Index

Source of data: United Nations hdr.undp.org/en/statistics/data

Equatorial Guinea is the biggest outlier, with a high, but unequally shared real GDP, and average HDI.

The Bottom Line Do we get the wrong message about the level and growth in economic well-being and the standard of living by looking at the growth of real GDP? The influences that are omitted from real GDP are probably large. Developing countries have a larger amount of household production than do developed countries, so the gap between their living standards is exaggerated. Also, as real GDP grows, part of the growth is a switch from home production to market production. This switch overstates the growth in economic well-being and the improvement in the standard of living.

It is possible to construct broader measures that combine the many influences that contribute to human happiness. The United Nations' Human Development Index or HDI (above) and Green Net National Product or GNNP (previous page) are two examples of dozens of other measures that have been proposed.

Despite all the alternatives, real GDP per person remains the most widely used indicator of economic well-being.

REVIEW QUIZ

1 Distinguish between real GDP and potential GDP and describe how each grows over time.

2 How does the growth rate of real GDP contribute to an improved standard of living?

3 What is a business cycle and what are its phases and turning points?

4 What is PPP and how does it help us to make valid international comparisons of real GDP?

5 Explain why real GDP might be an unreliable indicator of the standard of living.

Work these questions in Study Plan 4.3 and get instant feedback.   MyLab Economics

◆ You now know how economists measure GDP and what the GDP data tell us. *Economics in the News* on pp. 100–101 compares Canadian and U.S. real GDP in 2017 and through the recovery from the deep recession of 2008.

Comparing Canadian and U.S. Real GDP Growth

Canada's Economic Growth Triples U.S.'s

Statistics Canada reported that real GDP rose at a 3.7 percent annual pace in the first quarter of 2017. In comparison, real GDP in the United States grew at a 1.2 percent pace.

"Wasn't it America that was supposed to be made great again? And yet boring old Canada saw a first quarter pace of growth that more than tripled what was seen for the U.S.," commented TD Bank senior economist Brian DePratto to the *Huffington Post*.

DePratto noted that, with this quarter's results, Canada has seen the fastest pace of economic expansion since 2010, when the country was recovering from the global financial crisis.

The details behind the headline GDP number show that household consumption spending grew at a 4.3 percent annual rate. Transport was the largest contributor to increased household spending. But purchases of vehicles contributed to higher imports.

Growth in housing investment accelerated and was particularly strong in Ontario. Business non-residential investment rebounded following declines in four of the previous five quarters. Businesses accumulated $12.2 billion in inventories in the first quarter, following a draw-down of $2.8 billion in the previous quarter.

Exports edged down and imports rebounded.

With household spending growing faster than GDP, household saving decreased, and debt increased.

Sources: Based on Statistics Canada, *The Daily*, May 31, 2017; and Tencer, Daniel, "Canada's Economic Growth Triples U.S.'s," *Huffington Post Canada*, May 31, 2017.

ESSENCE OF THE STORY

- Canada's GDP grew at a 3.7 percent annual rate in the first quarter of 2017.

- This rate is more than three times that of the United States and Canada's fastest since 2010.

- Consumption expenditure, with strong auto sales, increased at a 4.3 percent annual rate.

- Business investment grew at a rapid pace.

- Exports decreased slightly.

MyLab Economics Economics in the News

ECONOMIC ANALYSIS

- In the first quarter of 2017, real GDP increased by $16 billion from $1,813 billion to $1,829 billion.

- This increase in real GDP is 0.88 percent ($16 is 0.88 percent of $1,813).

- If this growth rate is maintained for a full year, real GDP will be 3.7 percent higher at the end of the year. That is what the news article means when it reports that real GDP grew at a 3.7 percent pace.

- Figure 1 shows the increases in real GDP and its expenditure components for the first quarter of 2017. The figure also shows the same information for the U.S. economy.

- The red Canadian bars show stronger growth than the blue U.S. bars for GDP and all its expenditure components except net exports. And as the news article reports, Canada's real GDP grew at triple the rate of U.S. real GDP.

- Canadian consumption expenditure increased at a faster pace than the growth of GDP, as the news article notes. But investment grew fastest.

- The faster-growing Canadian economy is not a new phenomenon.

- Figure 2 compares the 2008 recession and subsequent expansion in Canada and the United States.

- To compare the two economies, with U.S. real GDP about 10 times Canada's, the graph measures all the variables as percentages of their levels in 2006.

- You can see that the Canadian recession started one quarter later than the U.S. recession and was less severe.

- You can also see that Canada's real GDP expanded more rapidly than U.S. real GDP, especially from 2010 to 2012.

- By 2012, Canada's real GDP had returned to potential GDP while U.S. real GDP remained well below potential.

- So although the U.S. economy has a large influence on Canada, the Canadian economy has performed better than the U.S. economy.

- One reason for Canada's better performance is the fact that Canada exports oil, gas, and mineral resources to a more rapidly growing Asia.

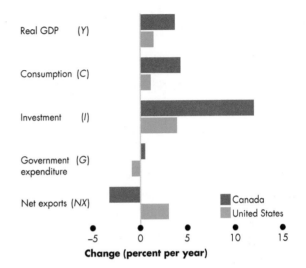

Figure 1 Canada and U.S. First Quarter 2017

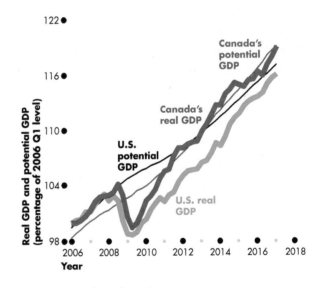

Figure 2 Canada and U.S. Expansions

- We examine the source of and other reasons for Canada's faster real GDP growth in Chapter 6.

APPENDIX

Graphs in Macroeconomics

After studying this appendix, you will be able to:

◆ Make and interpret a time-series graph

◆ Make and interpret a graph that uses a ratio scale

◢◆ The Time-Series Graph

In macroeconomics we study the fluctuations and trends in the key variables that describe macroeconomic performance and policy. These variables include GDP and its expenditure and income components that you've learned about in this chapter. They also include variables that describe the labour market and consumer prices, which you will study in Chapter 5.

Regardless of the variable of interest, we want to be able to compare its value today with that in the past; and we want to describe how the variable has changed over time. The most effective way to do these things is to make a time-series graph.

Making a Time-Series Graph

A **time-series graph** measures time (for example, years, quarters, or months) on the *x*-axis and the variable or variables in which we are interested on the *y*-axis. Figure A4.1 is an example of a time-series graph. It provides some information about unemployment in Canada since 1980. In this figure, we measure time in years starting in 1980. We measure the unemployment rate (the variable that we are interested in) on the *y*-axis.

A time-series graph enables us to visualize how a variable has changed over time and how its value in one period relates to its value in another period. It conveys an enormous amount of information quickly and easily.

Let's see how to "read" a time-series graph.

Reading a Time-Series Graph

To practise reading a time-series graph, take a close look at Fig. A4.1. The graph shows the level, change, and speed of change of the variable.

FIGURE A4.1   A Time-Series Graph

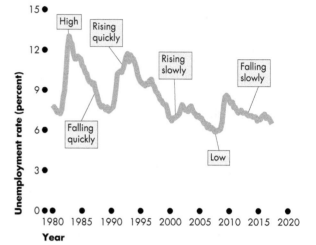

A time-series graph plots the level of a variable on the *y*-axis against time (here measured in years) on the *x*-axis. This graph shows the unemployment rate each year from 1980 to 2017. The graph shows when unemployment was high, when it was low, when it increased, when it decreased, and when it changed quickly and slowly.

——————— MyLab Economics Animation ———

■ The *level* of the variable: It tells us when unemployment is *high* and *low*. When the line is a long distance above the *x*-axis, the unemployment rate is high, as it was, for example, in 1983. When the line is close to the *x*-axis, the unemployment rate is low, as it was, for example, in 2007.

■ The *change* in the variable: It tells us how unemployment *changes*—whether it *increases* or *decreases*. When the line slopes upward, as it did in 2008 and 2009, the unemployment rate is rising. When the line slopes downward, as it did in 1984 and 1997, the unemployment rate is falling.

■ The *speed of change* in the variable: It tells us whether the unemployment rate is rising or falling *quickly* or *slowly*. If the line is very steep, then the unemployment rate increases or decreases quickly. If the line is not steep, the unemployment rate increases or decreases slowly. For example, the unemployment rate rose quickly in 1994 and slowly in 2003, and it fell quickly in 1987 and slowly in 2016.

Ratio Scale Reveals Trend

A time-series graph also reveals whether a variable has a **cycle**, which is a tendency for a variable to alternate between upward and downward movements, or a **trend**, which is a tendency for a variable to move in one general direction.

The unemployment rate in Fig. A4.1 has a cycle but no trend. When a trend is present, a special kind of time-series graph, one that uses a ratio scale on the *y*-axis, reveals the trend.

A Time-Series with a Trend

Many macroeconomics variables, among them GDP and the average level of prices, have an upward trend. Figure A4.2 shows an example of such a variable: the average prices paid by consumers.

In Fig. A4.2(a), Canadian consumer prices since 1970 are graphed on a normal scale. In 1970 the level is 100. In other years, the average level of prices is measured as a percentage of the 1970 level.

The graph clearly shows the upward trend of prices. But it doesn't tell us when prices were rising fastest or whether there was any change in the trend. Just looking at the upward-sloping line in Fig. A4.2(a) gives the impression that the pace of growth of consumer prices was constant.

Using a Ratio Scale

On a graph axis with a normal scale, the gap between 1 and 2 is the same as that between 3 and 4. On a graph axis with a ratio scale, the gap between 1 and 2 is the same as that between 2 and 4. The ratio 2 to 1 equals the ratio 4 to 2. By using a ratio scale, we can "see" when the growth rate (the percentage change per unit of time) changes.

Figure A4.2(b) shows an example of a ratio scale. Notice that the values on the *y*-axis get closer together but the gap between 400 and 200 equals the gap between 200 and 100: The ratio gaps are equal.

Graphing the data on a ratio scale reveals the trends. In the case of consumer prices, the trend is much steeper during the 1970s and early 1980s than in the later years. The steeper the line in the ratio-scale graph in part (b), the faster prices are rising. Prices rose rapidly during the 1970s and early 1980s and more slowly in the later 1980s and the 1990s. The ratio-scale graph reveals this fact. We use ratio-scale graphs extensively in macroeconomics.

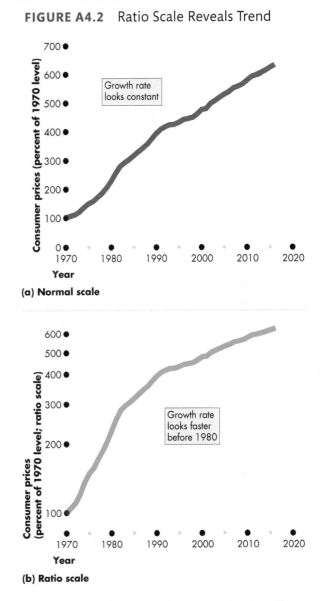

FIGURE A4.2 Ratio Scale Reveals Trend

The graph shows the average of consumer prices from 1970 to 2017. The level is 100 in 1970 and the value for other years are percentages of the 1970 level. Consumer prices normally rise each year, so the line slopes upward. In part (a), where the y-axis scale is normal, the rate of increase appears to be constant.

In part (b), where the y-axis is a ratio scale (the ratio of 400 to 200 equals the ratio 200 to 100), prices rose faster during the 1970s and early 1980s and slower in the later years. The ratio scale reveals this trend.

MyLab Economics Animation

MATHEMATICAL NOTE

Chained-Dollar Real GDP

In the real GDP calculation on p. 93, real GDP in 2016 is 1.6 times its value in 2007. But suppose that we use 2016 as the reference base year and value real GDP in 2007 at 2016 prices. If you do the math, you will see that real GDP in 2007 is $150 million at 2016 prices. GDP in 2016 is $300 million (in 2016 prices), so now the numbers say that real GDP has doubled. Which is correct: Did real GDP increase 1.6 times or double? Should we use the prices of 2007 or 2016? The answer is that we need to use *both* sets of prices.

Statistics Canada uses a measure of real GDP called *chained-dollar real GDP*. Three steps are needed to calculate this measure:

- Value production in the prices of adjacent years
- Find the average of two percentage changes
- Link (chain) to the base year

Value Production in Prices of Adjacent Years

The first step is to value production in *adjacent* years at the prices of *both* years. We'll make these calculations for 2016 and its preceding year, 2015.

Table 1 shows the quantities produced and prices in the two years. Part (a) shows the nominal GDP calculation for 2015—the quantities produced in 2015 valued at the prices of 2015. Nominal GDP in 2015 is $145 million. Part (b) shows the nominal GDP calculation for 2016—the quantities produced in 2016 valued at the prices of 2016. Nominal GDP in 2016 is $300 million. Part (c) shows the value of the quantities produced in 2016 at the prices of 2015. This total is $160 million. Finally, part (d) shows the value of the quantities produced in 2015 at the prices of 2016. This total is $275 million.

Find the Average of Two Percentage Changes

The second step is to find the percentage change in the value of production based on the prices in the two adjacent years. Table 2 summarizes these calculations.

Part (a) shows that, valued at the prices of 2015, production increased from $145 million in 2015 to $160 million in 2016, an increase of 10.3 percent.

TABLE 1 Real GDP Calculation Step 1: Value Production in Adjacent Years at Prices of Both Years

	Item	Quantity (millions)	Price (dollars)	Expenditure (millions of dollars)
(a) In 2015				
C	T-shirts	3	5	15
I	Computer chips	3	10	30
G	Security services	5	20	100
Y	Nominal GDP in 2015			**145**
(b) In 2016				
C	T-shirts	4	5	20
I	Computer chips	2	20	40
G	Security services	6	40	240
Y	Nominal GDP in 2016			**300**
(c) Quantities of 2016 valued at prices of 2015				
C	T-shirts	4	5	20
I	Computer chips	2	10	20
G	Security services	6	20	120
Y	2016 production at 2015 prices			**160**
(d) Quantities of 2015 valued at prices of 2016				
C	T-shirts	3	5	15
I	Computer chips	3	20	60
G	Security services	5	40	200
Y	2015 production at 2016 prices			**275**

Step 1 is to value the production of adjacent years at the prices of both years. Here, we value the production of 2015 and 2016 at the prices of both 2015 and 2016. The value of 2015 production at 2015 prices, in part (a), is nominal GDP in 2015. The value of 2016 production at 2016 prices, in part (b), is nominal GDP in 2016. Part (c) calculates the value of 2016 production at 2015 prices, and part (d) calculates the value of 2015 production at 2016 prices. We use these numbers in Step 2.

Part (b) shows that, valued at the prices of 2016, production increased from $275 million in 2015 to $300 million in 2016, an increase of 9.1 percent. Part (c) shows that the average of these two percentage changes in the value of production is 9.7. That is, $(10.3 + 9.1) \div 2 = 9.7$.

What we've just calculated is the *growth rate of real GDP* in 2016. But what is the *level* of real GDP? Finding the level of real GDP is what happens in Step 3 that we'll now describe.

TABLE 2   Real GDP Calculation Step 2:
Find Average of Two Percentage
Changes

Value of Production	Millions of dollars
(a) At 2015 prices	
Nominal GDP in 2015	145
2016 production at 2015 prices	160
Percentage change in production at 2015 prices	10.3
(b) At 2016 prices	
2015 production at 2016 prices	275
Nominal GDP in 2016	300
Percentage change in production at 2016 prices	9.1
(c) Average percentage change in 2016	**9.7**

Using the numbers calculated in Step 1, the change in production from 2015 to 2016 valued at 2015 prices is 10.3 percent, in part (a). The change in production from 2015 to 2016 valued at 2016 prices is 9.1 percent, in part (b). The average of these two percentage changes is 9.7 percent in part (c).

Link (Chain) to the Base Year

The third step is to measure real GDP in the prices of the *reference base year*. To do this, Statistics Canada selects a base year (currently 2007) in which, *by definition*, real GDP equals nominal GDP. Statistics

Canada performs calculations like the ones that you've just worked through for 2016 to find the percentage change in real GDP in each pair of adjacent years. Finally, it uses the percentage changes calculated in Step 2 to find real GDP in 2007 prices for each year.

Figure 1 illustrates these Step 3 calculations to chain link to the base year. In the reference base year, 2007, real GDP equals nominal GDP, which we'll assume is $110 million (highlighted in the chain). Using the same methods that we've just described for 2015 and 2016, we'll assume that the growth rate of real GDP from 2007 to 2008 is 7 percent (also shown in the chain). If real GDP in 2007 is $110 million and the growth rate in 2007 is 7 percent, then real GDP in 2008 is $118 million—7 percent higher than real GDP in 2007.

By repeating these calculations for each year, we obtain *chained-dollar real GDP* in 2007 dollars for each year. The growth rates shown in the figure for 2007 to 2016 take real GDP in 2015 to $182 million. That is, the 2015 *chained-dollar real GDP* in 2007 dollars is $182 million.

We've calculated the growth rate for 2016, which is highlighted in Fig. 1 as 9.7 percent. Applying this growth rate to the $182 million level of real GDP in 2015 gives real GDP in 2016 as $200 million.

Notice that the growth rates depend only on prices and quantities produced in adjacent years and do not depend on what the reference base year is. Changing the reference base year changes the *level* of real GDP in each year, but it does not change the *growth rates*.

Figure 1 Real GDP Calculation Step 3: Repeat Growth Rate Calculations and Chain Link

Exercise

The table provides data on the economy of Tropical Republic, which produces only bananas and coconuts. Use this data to calculate Tropical Republic's

1. Nominal GDP in 2015 and 2016

2. Chained-dollar real GDP in 2016 expressed in 2015 dollars.

Table

Quantities	2015	2016
Bananas	1,000 bunches	1,100 bunches
Coconuts	500 bunches	525 bunches

Prices	2015	2016
Bananas	$2 a bunch	$3 a bunch
Coconuts	$10 a bunch	$8 a bunch

WORKED PROBLEM

MyLab Economics Work this problem in Chapter 4 Study Plan.

Items in Dreamland's national accounts include:

- Government expenditure on goods and services: $600
- Consumption expenditure: $1,950
- Rent and interest: $400
- Indirect taxes less subsidies: $350
- Investment: $550
- Wages: $1,600
- Profit: $500
- Net exports: $200
- Depeciation: $450

Questions

1. Use the expenditure approach to calculate GDP.
2. Calculate net domestic income at factor cost.
3. Calculate net domestic income at market prices.
4. Use the income approach to calculate GDP.

Solutions

1. The expenditure approach sums the expenditure on final goods and services. That is, GDP is the sum of consumption expenditure, investment, government expenditure, and net exports. That is, GDP = $1,950 + $550 + $600 + $200 = $3,300.

Key Point: GDP equals aggregate expenditure on final goods produced in Dreamland, which equals $C + I + G + NX$. See the figure.

2. Net domestic income at factor cost is the sum of the incomes paid to factors of production (labour, land, capital, and entrepreneurship): wages, rent, interest, and profit.

Net domestic income at factor cost equals $1,600 + $400 + $500 = $2,500.

Key Point: The incomes earned by the factors of production sum to net domestic incomes at factor cost. See the figure.

3. Expenditure on goods and services equals the quantity bought multiplied by the market price. Incomes are total factor costs. The market price of a good or service equals the cost of the factors of production used to produce it if production is not subsidized and sale of the good is not taxed.

If the producer of a good receives a subsidy, then the market price of the good is less than the cost of producing it. If a tax is imposed on the sale of the good, then the market price exceeds the cost of producing it. That is,

Market price = Factor cost + Indirect taxes less subsidies.

Net domestic income at factor cost is $2,500, so net domestic income at market prices equals $2,500 + $350 = $2,850.

Key Point: To convert from factor cost to market prices, add indirect taxes less subsidies. See the figure.

4. GDP is a gross measure of total production at market prices while net domestic income at market prices is a net measure. So using the income approach to measuring GDP, depreciation must be added to net domestic income at market prices to convert it to GDP. That is, using the incomes approach, GDP = $2,850 + $450 = $3,300.

Key Point: To convert net domestic income at market prices into GDP, add depreciation. See the figure.

Key Figure

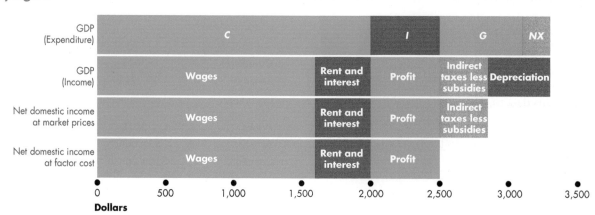

SUMMARY

Key Points

Gross Domestic Product (pp. 88–90)

- GDP, or gross domestic product, is the market value of all the final goods and services produced in a country during a given period.
- A final good is an item that is bought by its final user, and it contrasts with an intermediate good, which is a component of a final good.
- GDP is calculated by using either the expenditure or income totals in the circular flow model.
- Aggregate expenditure on goods and services equals aggregate income and GDP.

Working Problems 1 to 4 will give you a better understanding of gross domestic product.

Measuring Canada's GDP (pp. 91–93)

- Because aggregate expenditure, aggregate income, and the value of aggregate production are equal, we can measure GDP by using the expenditure approach or the income approach.
- The expenditure approach sums consumption expenditure, investment, government expenditure on goods and services, and net exports.
- The income approach sums wages, interest, rent, and profit (plus indirect taxes less subsidies plus depreciation).

- Real GDP is measured using a common set of prices to remove the effects of inflation from GDP.

Working Problems 5 to 8 will give you a better understanding of measuring Canada's GDP.

The Uses and Limitations of Real GDP (pp. 94–99)

- Real GDP is used to compare the standard of living over time and across countries.
- Real GDP per person grows and fluctuates around the more smoothly growing potential GDP.
- Incomes would be much higher today if the growth rate of real GDP per person had not slowed during the 1970s.
- International real GDP comparisons use PPP prices.
- Real GDP is not a perfect measure of the standard of living because it excludes household production, the underground economy, health and life expectancy, leisure time, security, environmental quality, and political freedom and social justice.

Working Problem 9 will give you a better understanding of the uses and limitations of real GDP.

Key Terms

MyLab Economics Key Terms Quiz

Business cycle, 95
Consumption expenditure, 89
Cycle, 103
Depreciation, 90
Expansion, 95
Exports, 90
Final good, 88
Government expenditure, 90

Gross domestic product (GDP), 88
Gross investment, 90
Imports, 90
Intermediate good, 88
Investment, 90
Net exports, 90
Net investment, 90
Nominal GDP, 93

Potential GDP, 94
Real GDP, 93
Real GDP per person, 94
Recession, 95
Time-series graph, 102
Trend, 103

STUDY PLAN PROBLEMS AND APPLICATIONS

MyLab Economics Work Problems 1 to 10 in Chapter 4 Study Plan and get instant feedback.

Gross Domestic Product (Study Plan 4.1)

1. Classify each of the following items as a final good or service or an intermediate good or service and identify each item as a component of consumption expenditure, investment, or government expenditure on goods and services:
   - Banking services bought by a student.
   - New cars bought by Hertz, the car rental firm.
   - Newsprint bought by the *National Post*.
   - A new limo bought for the prime minister.
   - A new house bought by Alanis Morissette.

2. Use the following figure, which illustrates the circular flow model.

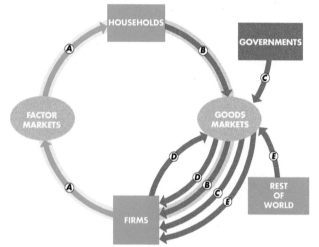

   During 2017, flow *A* was $13.0 billion, flow *B* was $9.1 billion, flow *D* was $3.3 billion, and flow *E* was –$0.8 billion. Calculate (i) GDP and (ii) government expenditure.

3. Use the following data to calculate aggregate expenditure and imports of goods and services:
   - Government expenditure: $20 billion
   - Aggregate income: $100 billion
   - Consumption expenditure: $67 billion
   - Investment: $21 billion
   - Exports of goods and services: $30 billion

4. **Canadian Economy in 2017 First Quarter**
   Real GDP grew 0.9 percent, business investment increased 2.9 percent, exports shrank 0.1 percent, and imports rose by 3.3 percent.
   Source: Statistics Canada, *The Daily*, May 31, 2017

   Use the flows in the figure in Problem 2 to identify each flow in the news clip. How can GDP have grown by 0.9 percent with investment and imports growing by more than 0.9 percent?

Measuring Canada's GDP (Study Plan 4.2)

Use the following data to work Problems 5 and 6. The table lists some data for Canada in 2008.

Item	Billions of dollars
Wages paid to labour	815
Consumption expenditure	885
Net domestic income at factor cost	1,210
Investment	304
Government expenditure	357
Net exports	32
Depreciation	202

5. Calculate Canada's GDP in 2008.

6. Explain the approach (expenditure or income) that you used to calculate GDP.

Use the following data to work Problems 7 and 8. Tropical Republic produces only bananas and coconuts. The base year is 2016.

Quantities	2016	2017
Bananas	800 bunches	900 bunches
Coconuts	400 bunches	500 bunches

Prices	2016	2017
Bananas	$2 a bunch	$4 a bunch
Coconuts	$10 a bunch	$5 a bunch

7. Calculate nominal GDP in 2016 and 2017.

8. Calculate real GDP in 2017 in base-year prices.

The Uses and Limitations of Real GDP (Study Plan 4.3)

9. Explain in which of the years Canada's standard of living (i) increased and (ii) decreased.

Year	Real GDP	Population
2007	$1,311 billion	32.9 million
2008	$1,320 billion	33.3 million
2009	$1,284 billion	33.7 million
2010	$1,325 billion	34.1 million

Mathematical Note (Study Plan 4.MN)

10. An island economy produces only fish and crabs.

Quantities	2016	2017
Fish	1,000 tonnes	1,100 tonnes
Crabs	500 tonnes	525 tonnes

Prices	2016	2017
Fish	$20 a tonne	$30 a tonne
Crabs	$10 a tonne	$8 a tonne

Calculate the island's chained-dollar real GDP in 2017 expressed in 2016 dollars.

ADDITIONAL PROBLEMS AND APPLICATIONS

Gross Domestic Product

11. Classify each of the following items as a final good or service or an intermediate good or service and identify which is a component of consumption expenditure, investment, or government expenditure on goods and services:
    - Banking services bought by Loblaws.
    - Security system bought by the TD Bank.
    - Coffee beans bought by Tim Hortons.
    - New coffee grinders bought by Second Cup.
    - Starbucks grande mocha frappuccino bought by a student at a campus coffee bar.
    - New helicopters bought by Canada's army.

Use the figure in Problem 2 to work Problems 12 and 13.

12. In 2016, flow *A* was $1,000 billion, flow *C* was $250 billion, flow *B* was $650 billion, and flow *E* was $50 billion. Calculate investment.

13. In 2017, flow *D* was $2 trillion, flow *E* was −$1 trillion, flow *A* was $10 trillion, and flow *C* was $4 trillion. Calculate consumption expenditure.

Use the following information to work Problems 14 and 15.

The components and robots for Toyota's auto assembly lines in Canada are built in Japan and Toyota assembles cars for the Canadian market in Ontario.

14. Explain where these activities appear in Canada's *National Income and Expenditure Accounts*.

15. Explain where these activities appear in Japan's *National Income and Expenditure Accounts*.

Use the following news clip to work Problems 16 and 17, and use the circular flow model to illustrate your answers.

Boeing Doubles Outsourcing From India

Three Indian firms are producing components for Boeing fighter jets F15 and F18 and for the Chinook heavy-lift helicopter in Bangalore, Hyderabad, and other places in India.

Source: *The Economic Times*, February 17, 2016

16. Explain how Boeing's activities and its transactions affect U.S. and Indian GDP.

17. Explain how the Indian firms' activities and its transactions affect U.S. and Indian GDP.

Measuring Canada's GDP

Use the following data to work Problems 18 and 19. The table lists some data for Xanadu in 2017.

Item	Billions of dollars
Wages paid to labour	800
Consumption expenditure	1,000
Profit, interest, and rents	340
Investment	150
Government expenditure	290
Net exports	−34

18. Calculate Xanadu's GDP in 2017.

19. Explain the approach (expenditure or income) that you used to calculate GDP.

Use the following data to work Problems 20 and 21.

An economy produces only apples and oranges. The base year is 2016, and the table gives the quantities produced and the prices.

Quantities	2016	2017
Apples	60	160
Oranges	80	220
Prices	**2016**	**2017**
Apples	$0.50	$1.00
Oranges	$0.25	$2.00

20. Calculate nominal GDP in 2016 and 2017.

21. Calculate real GDP in 2016 and 2017 expressed in base-year prices.

Use the following news clip to work Problems 22 and 23.

China's Economy Accelerates as Retail, Investment Pick Up

China's real GDP increased 6.9 percent in the first quarter of 2017 from a year earlier. Investment grew by 9.2 percent and retail sales by 10.9 percent. In current prices, GDP increased by 11.8 percent from a year earlier.

Source: *Bloomberg News*, April 17, 2017

22. Explain how China's real GDP can grow at a 6.9 percent rate when consumption and investment grew faster than 6.9 percent.

23. Explain why the growth rate of GDP in current prices does not provide information about how quickly the economy is really growing.

The Uses and Limitations of Real GDP

24. The United Nations' Human Development Index (HDI) is based on real GDP per person, life expectancy at birth, and indicators of the quality and quantity of education.
    a. Explain why the HDI might be better than real GDP as a measure of economic welfare.
    b. Which items in the HDI are part of real GDP and which items are not in real GDP?
    c. Do you think the HDI should be expanded to include items such as pollution, resource depletion, and political freedom? Explain.
    d. What other influences on economic welfare should be included in a comprehensive measure?

Use the following information to work Problems 25 and 26.

Comparing Real GDP per Person

The International Monetary Fund reported the following data on gross domestic product per capita, meaured in U.S. dollars at market exchange rates in 2016: Canada $42,210, China $8,113, United Kingdom $40,096, and United States $57,436.

> Source: International Monetary Fund, *World Economic Outlook Database*, April 2017

25. Explain the special complications involved with attempting to compare the economic welfare in China and the United States by using the GDP for each country.

26. Explain why the data reported here might be a poor indicator of the differences in economic welfare among Canada, the United Kingdom, and the United States, but nevertheless provide the correct ranking of the countries.

27. **India to Be Home to 437,000 Millionaires by 2018**

    India, with the world's largest population of poor people, is creating millionaires at a rapid pace and by 2008 is projected to have 437,000 millionaires measured in U.S. dollars. That is 1 millionaire for about 1,600 people living on less than $2 a day.

    > Source: *The Times of India*, July 8, 2015

    a. Why might real GDP per person misrepresent the standard of living of the average Indian?

    b. Why might $2 a day underestimate the standard of living of the poorest Indians?

Economics in the News

28. After you have studied *Economics in the News* on pp. 100–101, answer the following questions.
    a. Which economy—the Canadian or the U.S.—had the longer and deeper recession in 2008–2009?
    b. Which economy—the Canadian or the U.S.—had the lower estimated growth rate of potential GDP?
    c. What features of the Canadian economy might have contributed to its faster growth in 2010–2012?
    d. What features of the Canadian economy provide some immunity from U.S. economic ills?

29. **Five Measures of Growth That Are Better Than GDP**

    Speaking at the World Economic Forum, Stewart Wallis, a self-described advocate of a new economic system, suggested five economic indicators that he says are better than GDP. His five are: Good jobs, Well-being, Environment, Fairness, and Health.

    > Source: World Economic Forum, April 19, 2016

    a. Explain the factors that the news clip identifies as limiting the usefulness of GDP as a measure of economic welfare.
    b. What are the challenges involved in trying to incorporate measurements of those factors in an effort to better measure economic welfare?
    c. Explain whether the UN Human Development Index captures any of the five indicators.
    d. Explain which of the five indicators are included in GDP and likely to result in a high correlation between GDP and the other indicators of economic welfare.

Mathematical Note

30. Use the information in Problem 20 to calculate the chained-dollar real GDP in 2017 expressed in 2016 dollars.

 # MONITORING JOBS AND INFLATION

After studying this chapter, you will be able to:

◆ Explain why unemployment is a problem and how we measure the unemployment rate and other labour market indicators

◆ Explain why unemployment occurs and why it is present even at full employment

◆ Explain why inflation is a problem and how we measure the inflation rate

Each month, we chart the course of unemployment and inflation as measures of Canadian economic health. How do we measure the unemployment rate and the inflation rate and are they reliable vital signs?

As the Canadian economy slowly expanded after a recession in 2008 and 2009, job growth was weak and questions about the health of the labour market became of vital importance to millions of Canadian families. *Economics in the News*, at the end of this chapter, compares the Canadian and U.S. labour markets through the recession and a long return to full employment.

◆ Employment and Unemployment

What kind of job market will you enter when you graduate? Will there be plenty of good jobs to choose among, or will jobs be so hard to find that you end up taking one that doesn't use your education and pays a low wage? The answer depends, to a large degree, on the total number of jobs available and on the number of people competing for them.

The class of 2017 had a tough time in the jobs market. In June 2017, seven years after a recession, 1.3 million Canadians wanted a job but couldn't find one, and another 700,000 had given up the search for a job or had reluctantly settled for a part-time job.

Despite the high unemployment, the Canadian economy is an incredible job-creating machine. Even in 2009 at the depths of recession, 16.8 million people had jobs—5 million more than in 1989. But in recent years, population growth has outstripped jobs growth, so unemployment is a persistent problem.

Why Unemployment Is a Problem

Unemployment is a serious personal and social economic problem for two main reasons. It results in:

- Lost incomes and production
- Lost human capital

Lost Incomes and Production The loss of a job brings a loss of income and lost production. These losses are devastating for the people who bear them and they make unemployment a frightening prospect for everyone. Unemployment benefits create a safety net, but they don't fully replace lost earnings.

Lost production means lower consumption and a lower investment in capital, which lowers the living standard in both the present and the future.

Lost Human Capital Prolonged unemployment permanently damages a person's job prospects by destroying human capital.

ECONOMICS IN ACTION

What Kept Ben Bernanke Awake at Night

The Great Depression began in October 1929, when the U.S. stock market crashed. It reached its deepest point in 1933, when 25 percent of the labour force was unemployed, and lasted until 1941, when the United States entered World War II. The Depression quickly spread globally to envelop most nations.

The 1930s were and remain the longest and worst period of high unemployment in history. Failed banks, shops, farms, and factories left millions of Americans and Canadians without jobs, homes, and food. Without the support of government and charities, millions would have starved.

The Great Depression was an enormous political event: It fostered the rise of the German and Japanese militarism that was to bring the most devastating war humans have ever fought. It also led to a "New Deal" proposed first by President Franklin D. Roosevelt and then by Prime Minister R. B. Bennett, which expanded government intervention in markets and questioned the efficiency and equity of the market economy.

The Great Depression also brought a revolution in economics. British economist John Maynard Keynes published his *General Theory of Employment, Interest, and Money* and created what we now call macroeconomics.

Many economists have studied the Great Depression and tried to determine why what started out as an ordinary recession became so devastating. Among them is Ben Bernanke, the former chairman of the U.S. Federal Reserve.

One of the reasons the U.S. Federal Reserve was so aggressive in 2008–2009 in cutting interest rates and saving banks from going under is that Ben Bernanke is so vividly aware of the horrors of total economic collapse and was determined to avoid any risk of a repeat of the Great Depression.

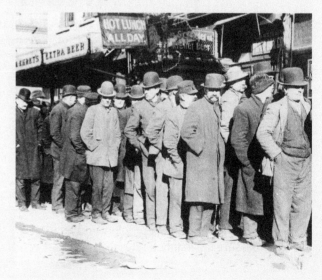

Think about a manager who loses his job when his employer downsizes. The only work he can find is driving a taxi. After a year in this work, he discovers that he can't compete with new MBA graduates. Eventually, he gets hired as a manager but in a small firm and at a lower wage than before. He has lost some of his human capital. The cost of lost human capital is particularly acute for older workers.

Governments make strenuous efforts to measure unemployment accurately and to adopt policies to moderate its level and ease its pain. Let's see how the Canadian government monitors unemployment.

Labour Force Survey

Every month, Statistics Canada conducts a *Labour Force Survey* in which it asks 54,000 households a series of questions about the age and job market status of the members of each household during a previous week called the *reference week*.

Figure 5.1 shows the population categories used by Statistics Canada and the relationships among the categories.

The population divides into two broad groups: the working-age population and others who are too young to work or who live in institutions and are unable to work. The **working-age population** is the total number of people aged 15 years and over. The working-age population is also divided into two groups: those in the labour force and those not in the labour force, such as retirees. Members of the labour force are either employed or unemployed. So the **labour force** is the sum of the employed and the unemployed. The employed are either full-time or part-time workers; and part-time workers either want part-time work (voluntary part time) or want full-time work (involuntary part time).

To be counted as employed in the Labour Force Survey, a person must have either a full-time job or a part-time job. To be counted as unemployed, a person must be *available for work* and must be in one of three categories:

1. On temporary layoff with an expectation of recall
2. Without work but has looked for work in the past four weeks
3. Has a new job to start within four weeks

People who satisfy one of these three criteria are counted as unemployed. People in the working-age population who are neither employed nor unemployed are classified as *not in the labour force*.

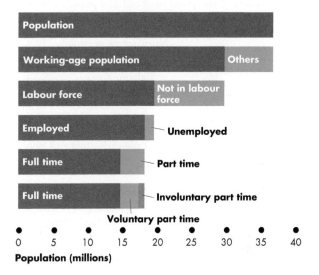

FIGURE 5.1 Population Labour Force Categories

Population (millions)

The total population is divided into the working-age population and others. The working-age population is divided into those in the labour force and those not in the labour force. The labour force is divided into the employed and the unemployed. And the employed are either full time or part time, and the part-time employed are either voluntary or involuntary part time.

Source of data: Statistics Canada, CANSIM Tables 051-0005, 282-0002, and 282-0014.

—— MyLab Economics Animation ——

In 2017, the population of Canada was 36.6 million; the working-age population was 29.88 million. Of this number, 10.20 million were not in the labour force. Most of these people were in school full time or had retired from work. The remaining 19.68 million people made up the Canadian labour force. Of these, 18.41 million were employed and 1.27 million were unemployed. Of the 18.41 million employed, 3.54 million had part-time jobs, and 0.87 million of them wanted a full-time job but couldn't find one.

Four Labour Market Indicators

Statistics Canada calculates four indicators of the state of the labour market. They are:

- The unemployment rate
- The involuntary part-time rate
- The labour force participation rate
- The employment rate

The Unemployment Rate The amount of unemployment is an indicator of the extent to which people who want jobs can't find them. The **unemployment rate** is the percentage of the people in the labour force who are unemployed. That is,

$$\text{Unemployment rate} = \frac{\text{Number of people unemployed}}{\text{Labour force}} \times 100.$$

People in the labour force are either employed or unemployed, so

$$\text{Labour force} = \frac{\text{Number of people employed}}{} + \frac{\text{Number of people unemployed}}{}$$

In June 2017, the number of people employed was 18.41 million and the number unemployed was 1.27 million. By using the above equations, you can verify that the labour force was 19.68 million (18.41 million plus 1.27 million) and the unemployment rate was 6.5 percent (1.27 million divided by 19.68 million, multiplied by 100).

Figure 5.2 shows the unemployment rate from 1960 to 2017. The average during this period is 7.6 percent. The unemployment rate fluctuates over the business cycle. It increases as a recession deepens, reaches a peak value after a recession ends, and decreases as the expansion gets underway.

The Involuntary Part-Time Rate Many part-time workers want part-time jobs, but some want full-time work and the *involuntary part-time rate* is the percentage of the people in the labour force who work part time but want full-time jobs.

$$\text{Involuntary part-time rate} = \frac{\text{Number of involuntary part-time workers}}{\text{Labour force}} \times 100.$$

In 2017, with 865,400 involuntary part-time workers and a labour force of 19.68 million, the involuntary part-time rate was 4.4 percent.

The Labour Force Participation Rate Statistics Canada measures the **labour force participation rate** as the percentage of the working-age population who are members of the labour force. That is,

$$\text{Labour force participation rate} = \frac{\text{Labour force}}{\text{Working-age population}} \times 100.$$

In June 2017, the labour force was 19.68 million and the working-age population was 29.88 million. By using the above equation, you can verify that the labour force participation rate was 65.9 percent (19.68 million divided by 29.88 million, multiplied by 100).

FIGURE 5.2 The Unemployment Rate: 1960–2017

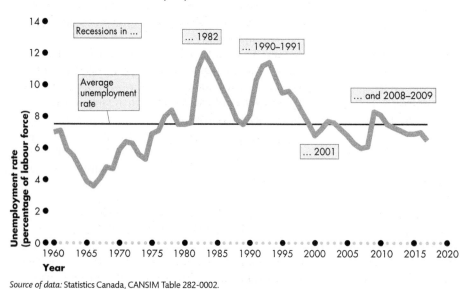

The average unemployment rate from 1960 to 2017 was 7.5 percent. The unemployment rate increases in a recession, peaks after the recession ends, and decreases in an expansion. The unemployment rate was unusually high following the recessions of 1982 and 1990–1991. The unemployment rate following the recession of 2008–2009 was less severe than that following the two earlier recessions.

Source of data: Statistics Canada, CANSIM Table 282-0002.

FIGURE 5.3   Labour Force Participation and Employment: 1960–2017

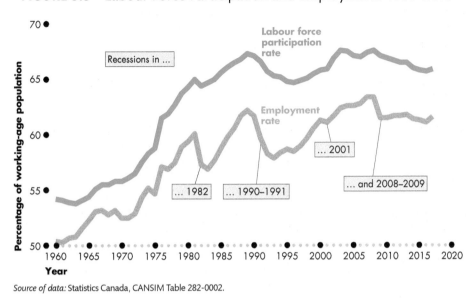

The labour force participation rate and the employment rate increased rapidly before 1990 and slowly after 1990. Both fluctuate with the business cycle.

The employment rate fluctuates more than the labour force participation rate and reflects cyclical fluctuations in the unemployment rate.

Source of data: Statistics Canada, CANSIM Table 282-0002.

MyLab Economics Real-time data

The Employment Rate The number of people of working age who have jobs is an indicator of the availability of jobs and the match of skills to jobs. The **employment rate** is the percentage of people of working age who have jobs. That is,

$$\text{Employment rate} = \frac{\text{Number of people employed}}{\text{Working-age population}} \times 100.$$

In June 2017, the number of people employed was 18.41 million and the working-age population was 29.88 million. By using the above equation, you can verify that the employment rate was 61.6 percent (18.41 million divided by 29.88 million, multiplied by 100).

Figure 5.3 shows the labour force participation rate and the employment rate. These indicators follow an upward trend before 1990 and then flatten off. The increase before 1990 means that the Canadian economy created jobs at a faster rate than the working-age population grew.

The employment rate fluctuates with the business cycle: It falls in a recession and rises in an expansion. The labour force participation rate has milder business cycle swings that reflect movements into and out of the labour force.

Other Definitions of Unemployment

You've seen that to be counted as unemployed, a person must be available for work and either be on temporary layoff with an expectation of recall; or be without work and have looked for work in the past four weeks; or have a new job to start within four weeks. Some people without a job might want one but not meet the strict criteria for being counted as unemployed. Also, people who have part-time jobs but want to work full time might be regarded as part-time unemployed.

Statistics Canada believes that the official definition of unemployment is the correct measure, but recognizes other wider definitions that bring in three types of *underemployed* labour excluded from the official measure. They are:

- Discouraged searchers
- Long-term future starts
- Involuntary part-timers

Discouraged Searchers A person who currently is neither working nor looking for work but has indicated that he or she wants a job, is available for work, and has looked for work sometime in the recent past but has stopped looking because of repeated failure is called a **discouraged searcher**. The official unemployment measure excludes discouraged searchers because they haven't made specific efforts to find a job within the past four weeks. In all other respects, they are unemployed.

Long-Term Future Starts Someone with a job that starts more than four weeks in the future is classified as not in the labour force. The economic difference between someone who starts a new job within four weeks and someone who starts farther in the future is slight and is a potential source of underestimating the true amount of unemployment.

Involuntary Part-Timers Part-time workers who would like full-time jobs and can't find them are part-time unemployed but not counted as such in the official statistics.

Most Costly Unemployment

All unemployment is costly, but the most costly is long-term unemployment that results from job loss.

People who are unemployed for a few weeks and then find another job bear some costs of unemployment. But these costs are low compared to those borne by people who remain unemployed for many weeks. The unemployment rate doesn't distinguish among the different lengths of unemployment spells. If most unemployment is long term, the situation is worse than if most are short-term job searchers.

Alternative Measures of Unemployment

To provide information about the aspects of unemployment that we've just discussed, Statistics Canada reports eight alternative measures of the unemployment rate: three that are narrower than the official rate and four that are broader. The narrower measures focus on the personal cost of unemployment and the broader measures focus on assessing the full amount of underemployed labour resources.

Figure 5.4 shows these measures from 1996 (the first year for which all eight are available) to 2016. R4 is the official rate and R3 is comparable to the official U.S. rate. Long-term unemployment (R1) is a small part of total unemployment. Short-term unemployment (R2) is more than double that of long term. Adding discouraged searchers (R5) makes very little difference to the unemployment rate, but adding long-term future starts (R6) makes a bigger difference and adding involuntary part-timers (R7) makes a big difference. R8 is the total *underemployment rate*.

FIGURE 5.4 Eight Alternative Measures of Unemployment

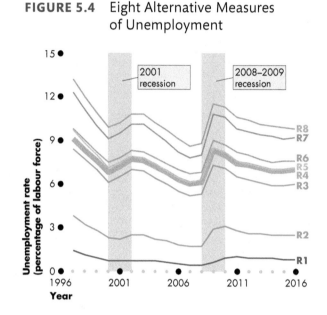

R1 are those unemployed for 1 year or more, and R2 are those unemployed for 3 months or less. R3 is comparable to the official U.S. rate. R4 is Canada's official rate. R5 adds discouraged searchers, R6 adds long-term future starts, and R7 adds involuntary part-timers to R4. R8 adds all three groups added separately in R5, R6, and R7. Fluctuations in all alternative measures are similar to those in the official rate, R4.

Source of data: Statistics Canada, CANSIM Table 282-0086.

———— MyLab Economics Real-time data ————

REVIEW QUIZ

1 What distinguishes an unemployed person from one who is not in the labour force?
2 Describe the trends and fluctuations in the Canadian unemployment rate since 1960.
3 Describe the trends and fluctuations in the Canadian employment rate and labour force participation rate since 1960.
4 Describe the alternative measures of unemployment.

Work these questions in Study Plan 5.1 and get instant feedback. MyLab Economics

You've seen how we measure employment and unemployment. Your next task is to see what we mean by full employment and how unemployment and real GDP fluctuate over the business cycle.

◆ Unemployment and Full Employment

There is always someone without a job who is searching for one, so there is always some unemployment. The key reason is that the economy is a complex mechanism that is always changing—it experiences frictions, structural change, and cycles.

Frictional Unemployment

There is an unending flow of people into and out of the labour force as people move through the stages of life—from being in school to finding a job, to working, perhaps to becoming unhappy with a job and looking for a new one, and finally, to retiring from full-time work.

There is also an unending process of job creation and job destruction as new firms are born, firms expand or contract, and some firms fail and go out of business.

The flows into and out of the labour force and the processes of job creation and job destruction create the need for people to search for jobs and for businesses to search for workers. Businesses don't usually hire the first person who applies for a job, and unemployed people don't usually take the first job that comes their way. Instead, both firms and workers spend time searching for what they believe will be the best available match. By this process of search, people can match their own skills and interests with the available jobs and find a satisfying job and a good income.

The unemployment that arises from the normal labour turnover we've just described—from people entering and leaving the labour force and from the ongoing creation and destruction of jobs—is called **frictional unemployment**. Frictional unemployment is a permanent and healthy phenomenon in a dynamic, growing economy.

Structural Unemployment

The unemployment that arises when changes in technology or international competition change the skills needed to perform jobs or change the locations of jobs is called **structural unemployment**. Structural unemployment usually lasts longer than frictional unemployment because workers must retrain and possibly relocate to find a job. When a steel plant in Hamilton, Ontario, is automated, some jobs in

that city disappear. Meanwhile, new jobs for security guards, retail clerks, and life-insurance salespeople are created in Toronto and Vancouver. The unemployed former steelworkers remain unemployed for several months until they move, retrain, and get new jobs. Structural unemployment is painful, especially for older workers for whom the best available option might be to retire early or take a lower-skilled, lower-paying job.

Cyclical Unemployment

The higher-than-normal unemployment at a business cycle trough and the lower-than-normal unemployment at a business cycle peak is called **cyclical unemployment**. A worker who is laid off because the economy is in a recession and who gets rehired some months later when the expansion begins has experienced cyclical unemployment.

"Natural" Unemployment

Natural unemployment is the unemployment that arises from frictions and structural change when there is no cyclical unemployment—when all the unemployment is frictional and structural. Natural unemployment as a percentage of the labour force is called the **natural unemployment rate**.

Full employment is defined as a situation in which the unemployment rate equals the natural unemployment rate.

What determines the natural unemployment rate? Is it constant or does it change over time?

The natural unemployment rate is influenced by many factors but the most important ones are:

- The age distribution of the population
- The scale of structural change
- The real wage rate
- Unemployment benefits

The Age Distribution of the Population An economy with a young population has a large number of new job seekers every year and has a high level of frictional unemployment. An economy with an aging population has fewer new job seekers and a low level of frictional unemployment.

The Scale of Structural Change The scale of structural change is sometimes small. The same jobs using the same machines remain in place for many years. But sometimes there is a technological upheaval and the old ways are swept aside. Millions of jobs are lost and the skill to perform them loses value.

The amount of structural unemployment fluctuates with the pace and volume of technological change and the change driven by fierce international competition, especially from fast-changing Asian economies. A high level of structural unemployment is present in many parts of Canada today (as you can see in *Economics in Action*).

The Real Wage Rate The natural unemployment rate is influenced by the real wage rate. If the government sets a high minimum wage, or if firms pay a wage above the average wage to attract the most productive workers, the real wage rate is above the level that balances the supply and demand in the labour market. In this situation, more people want jobs than firms want to hire, so persistent unemployment arises.

Unemployment Benefits Unemployment benefits increase the natural unemployment rate by lowering the opportunity cost of job search. Canada and European countries have more generous unemployment benefits and higher natural unemployment rates than the United States. Extending unemployment benefits raises the natural unemployment rate.

There is no controversy about the existence of a natural unemployment rate. Nor is there disagreement that the natural unemployment rate changes. But economists don't know the exact size of the natural unemployment rate or the extent to which it fluctuates. Canada has no official estimates of the natural unemployment rate, but a reasonable guess is that it is 7 percent—a bit more than the 2017 unemployment rate.

Real GDP and Unemployment over the Cycle

The quantity of real GDP at full employment is *potential GDP* (Chapter 4, p. 94). Over the business cycle, real GDP fluctuates around potential GDP. The gap between real GDP and potential GDP is called the **output gap**. As the output gap fluctuates over the business cycle, the unemployment rate fluctuates around the natural unemployment rate.

Figure 5.5 illustrates these fluctuations in Canada between 1980 and 2017—the output gap in part (a) and the unemployment rate and natural unemployment rate in part (b).

When the economy is at full employment, the unemployment rate equals the natural

ECONOMICS IN ACTION
Structural Unemployment in Canada

If all unemployment were frictional, arising from the ongoing flow of people into and out of the labour force and creation and destruction of firms and jobs, we would expect all Canada's provinces to exhibit similar unemployment rates. They wouldn't be exactly equal, but the ranking of provinces would change randomly over time. But that is not what the data say.

Provincial unemployment rates are extremely unequal, and the ranking of provinces is persistent.

In 2017, provincial unemployment rates ranged from 14.9 percent in Newfoundland and Labrador to 5.1 percent in British Columbia. All the provinces west of Ontario, except Alberta, had unemployment rates below the national average, Ontario and Quebec were close to but a bit below the national average, and the Maritime provinces were above the national average.

This range of unemployment rates across the provinces can only be accounted for by structural features of the Canadian economy.

The West is growing more rapidly. The Maritimes and to a lesser extent Quebec and Ontario are growing more slowly. People must leave the eastern provinces and move westward to find work. A reluctuance to uproot keeps the unemployment rates widely dispersed.

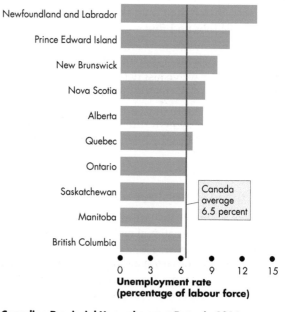

Canadian Provincial Unemployment Rates in 2016

Source of data: Statistics Canada, CANSIM Table 282–0087.

FIGURE 5.5   The Output Gap and the
Unemployment Rate

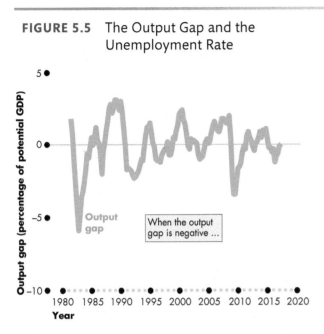

(a) Output gap

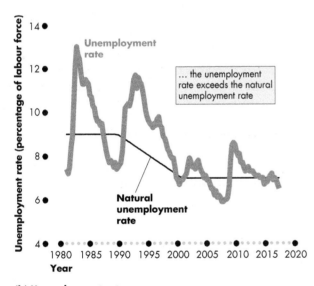

(b) Unemployment rate

As real GDP fluctuates around potential GDP in part (a), the
unemployment rate fluctuates around the natural employment rate in part (b). In recessions, cyclical unemployment
increases and the output gap becomes negative. At business
cycle peaks, the unemployment rate falls below the natural
unemployment rate and the output gap becomes positive.
The natural unemployment rate decreased during the 1990s.

Sources of data: Statistics Canada, CANSIM Table 282-0087 and Bank
of Canada output gap estimates. The natural unemployment rate is the
authors' estimate.

——————— MyLab Economics Real-time data ———————

unemployment rate and real GDP equals potential
GDP, so the output gap is zero. When the unemployment rate is below the natural unemployment
rate, real GDP exceeds potential GDP and the output gap is positive. And when the unemployment
rate is greater than the natural unemployment rate,
real GDP is less than potential GDP and the output
gap is negative.

The Changing Natural Unemployment Rate

Figure 5.5(b) shows our estimate of the natural
unemployment rate since 1980. This estimate puts
the natural unemployment rate at 9 percent of
the labour force during the 1980s, falling steadily
through the 1990s to 7 percent by around 2000, and
remaining at around 7 percent since 2000. This view
of the natural unemployment rate is consistent with
the Bank of Canada's estimate of the output gap in
Fig. 5.5(a).

REVIEW QUIZ

1 Why does unemployment arise and what makes
   some unemployment unavoidable?
2 Define frictional unemployment, structural
   unemployment, and cyclical unemployment.
   Give examples of each type of unemployment.
3 What is the natural unemployment rate?
4 How does the natural unemployment rate
   change and what factors might make it change?
5 Why is the unemployment rate never zero, even
   at full employment?
6 What is the output gap? How does it change
   when the economy goes into recession?
7 How does the unemployment rate fluctuate
   over the business cycle?

Work these questions in Study Plan 5.2 and
get instant feedback.   MyLab Economics

Your next task is to see how we monitor the price
level and its changes—inflation and deflation. You
will learn about the Consumer Price Index (CPI),
which is monitored every month. You will also learn
about other measures of the price level and how to
calculate the inflation rate.

◆ The Price Level, Inflation, and Deflation

What will it *really* cost you to pay off your student loan? What will your parents' life savings buy when they retire? The answers depend on what happens to the **price level**, the average level of prices, and the value of money. A persistently rising price level is called **inflation**; a persistently falling price level is called **deflation**.

We are interested in the price level, inflation, and deflation for two main reasons. First, we want to measure the annual percentage change of the price level—the inflation rate or deflation rate. Second, we want to distinguish between the money values and real values of economic variables such as your student loan and your parents' savings.

We begin by explaining why inflation and deflation are problems. Then we'll look at how we measure the price level and the inflation rate. Finally, we'll return to the task of distinguishing real values from money values.

Why Inflation and Deflation Are Problems

Low, steady, and anticipated inflation or deflation isn't a problem, but an unexpected burst of inflation or period of deflation brings big problems and costs. An unexpected inflation or deflation:

- Redistributes income
- Redistributes wealth
- Lowers real GDP and employment
- Diverts resources from production

Redistributes Income Workers and employers sign wage contracts that last for a year or more. An unexpected burst of inflation raises prices but doesn't immediately raise wages. Workers are worse off because their wages buy less than they bargained for and employers are better off because their profits rise.

An unexpected period of deflation has the opposite effect. Wage rates don't fall but prices fall. Workers are better off because their fixed wages buy more than they bargained for and employers are worse off with lower profits.

Redistributes Wealth People enter into loan contracts that are fixed in money terms and that pay an interest rate agreed as a percentage of the money borrowed and lent. With an unexpected burst of inflation, the money that the borrower repays to the lender buys less than the money originally loaned. The borrower wins and the lender loses. The interest paid on the loan doesn't compensate the lender for the loss in the value of the money loaned. With an unexpected deflation, the money that the borrower repays to the lender buys *more* than the money originally loaned. The borrower loses and the lender wins.

Lowers Real GDP and Employment Unexpected inflation that raises firms' profits brings a rise in investment and a boom in production and employment. Real GDP rises above potential GDP and the unemployment rate falls below the natural rate. But this situation is *temporary*. Profitable investment dries up, spending falls, real GDP falls below potential GDP, and the unemployment rate rises. Avoiding these swings in production and jobs means avoiding unexpected swings in the inflation rate.

An unexpected deflation has even greater consequences for real GDP and jobs. Businesses and households that are in debt (borrowers) are worse off and they cut their spending. A fall in total spending brings a recession and rising unemployment.

Diverts Resources from Production Unpredictable inflation or deflation turns the economy into a casino and diverts resources from productive activities to forecasting inflation. It can become more profitable to forecast the inflation rate or deflation rate correctly than to invent a new product. Doctors, lawyers, accountants, farmers—just about everyone—can make themselves better off, not by specializing in the profession for which they have been trained but by spending more of their time dabbling as amateur economists and inflation forecasters and managing their investments.

From a social perspective, the diversion of talent that results from unpredictable inflation is like throwing scarce resources onto a pile of garbage. This waste of resources is a cost of inflation.

At its worst, inflation becomes **hyperinflation**—an inflation rate of 50 percent a month or higher that grinds the economy to a halt and causes a society to collapse. Hyperinflation is rare, but Zimbabwe in recent years and several European and Latin American countries have experienced it.

We pay close attention to the inflation rate, even when its rate is low, to avoid its consequences. We monitor the price level every month and devote considerable resources to measuring it accurately. You're now going to see how we do this.

The Consumer Price Index

Every month, Statistics Canada measures the price level by calculating the **Consumer Price Index (CPI)**, which is a measure of the average of the prices paid by urban consumers for a fixed basket of consumer goods and services. What you learn here will help you to make sense of the CPI and relate it to your own economic life. The CPI tells you about the *value* of the money in your pocket.

Reading the CPI Numbers

The CPI is defined to equal 100 for a period called the *reference base period*. Currently, the reference base period is 2002. That is, the average CPI of the 12 months of 2002 is defined to be equal to 100.

In June 2017, the CPI was 130.4. This number tells us that the average of the prices paid by urban consumers for a fixed market basket of consumer goods and services was 30.4 percent *higher* in June 2017 than it was on average during 2002.

Constructing the CPI

Constructing the CPI involves three stages:

- Selecting the CPI basket
- Conducting the monthly price survey
- Calculating the CPI

The CPI Basket The first stage in constructing the CPI is to select what is called the *CPI basket*. This basket contains the goods and services represented in the index, each weighted by its relative importance. The idea is to make the relative importance of the items in the CPI basket the same as that in the budget of an average urban household. For example, because people spend more on housing than on bus rides, the CPI places more weight on the price of housing than on the price of a bus ride.

To determine the CPI basket, Statistics Canada conducts a survey of consumer expenditures. Today's CPI basket is based on data gathered in a 2015 survey valued at the prices in January 2017.

Figure 5.6 shows the CPI basket. As you look at the relative importance of the items in the CPI basket, remember that it applies to the *average* household. *Individual* household's baskets are spread around the average. Think about what you buy and compare *your* basket with the CPI basket.

FIGURE 5.6 The CPI Basket

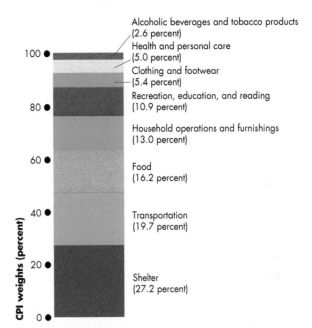

The CPI basket consists of the items that an average urban household buys. The figure shows the percentages.

Sources of data: Statistics Canada, CANSIM Table 326-0031. The basket is for 2015.

MyLab Economics Animation

The Monthly Price Survey Each month, Statistics Canada employees check the prices of the goods and services in the CPI basket in the major cities. Because the CPI aims to measure price *changes*, it is important that the prices recorded each month refer to exactly the same item. For example, suppose the price of a box of jelly beans has increased but a box now contains more beans. Has the price of jelly beans increased? Statistics Canada employees must record the details of changes in quality or packaging so that price changes can be isolated from other changes.

Once the raw price data are in hand, the next task is to calculate the CPI.

Calculating the CPI To calculate the CPI, we:

1. Find the cost of the CPI basket at base-period prices.
2. Find the cost of the CPI basket at current-period prices.
3. Calculate the CPI for the base period and the current period.

We'll work through these three steps for the simple artificial economy in Table 5.1, in which the base year is 2015 and the current year is 2018. The table shows the quantities in the CPI basket and the prices in these two years.

Part (a) contains the data for the base period. In that period, consumers bought 10 oranges at $1 each and 5 haircuts at $8 each. To find the cost of the CPI basket in the base-period prices, multiply the quantities in the CPI basket by the base-period prices. The cost of oranges is $10 (10 at $1 each), and the cost of haircuts is $40 (5 at $8 each). So the total cost of the CPI basket in the base period at base-period prices is $50 ($10 + $40).

Part (b) contains the price data for the current period. The price of an orange increased from $1 to $2, which is a 100 percent increase—($1 ÷ $1) × 100 = 100. The price of a haircut increased from $8 to $10, which is a 25 percent increase—($2 ÷ $8) × 100 = 25.

The CPI provides a way of averaging these price increases by comparing the cost of the basket rather than the price of each item. To find the cost of the CPI basket in the current period, 2018, multiply the quantities in the basket by their 2018 prices. The cost of

oranges is $20 (10 at $2 each), and the cost of haircuts is $50 (5 at $10 each). So total cost of the fixed CPI basket at current-period prices is $70 ($20 + $50).

You've now taken the first two steps toward calculating the CPI: calculating the cost of the CPI basket in the base period and the current period. The third step uses the numbers you've just calculated to find the CPI for 2015 and 2018.

The formula for the CPI is

$$\text{CPI} = \frac{\begin{array}{c}\text{Cost of CPI basket}\\ \text{at current-period prices}\end{array}}{\begin{array}{c}\text{Cost of CPI basket}\\ \text{at base-period prices}\end{array}} \times 100.$$

In Table 5.1, you established that in 2015 (the base period), the cost of the CPI basket was $50 and in 2018, it was $70. If we use these numbers in the CPI formula, we can find the CPI for 2015 and 2018. For 2015, the CPI is

$$\text{CPI in 2015} = \frac{\$50}{\$50} \times 100 = 100.$$

For 2018, the CPI is

$$\text{CPI in 2018} = \frac{\$70}{\$50} \times 100 = 140.$$

The principles that you've applied in this simplified CPI calculation apply to the more complex calculations performed every month by Statistics Canada.

Measuring the Inflation Rate

A major purpose of the CPI is to measure changes in the cost of living and in the value of money. To measure these changes, we calculate the *inflation rate* as the annual percentage change in the CPI. To calculate the inflation rate, we use the formula:

$$\frac{\text{Inflation}}{\text{rate}} = \frac{\text{CPI this year} - \text{CPI last year}}{\text{CPI last year}} \times 100.$$

We can use this formula to calculate the inflation rate in 2017. The CPI in June 2016 was 129.1, and the CPI in June 2017 was 130.4. So the inflation rate during the 12 months to June 2017 was

$$\frac{\text{Inflation}}{\text{rate}} = \frac{(130.4 - 129.1)}{129.1} \times 100 = 1.0\%.$$

TABLE 5.1   The CPI:
A Simplified Calculation

(a) The cost of the CPI basket at base-period prices: 2015

CPI basket			Cost of
Item	Quantity	Price	CPI Basket
Oranges	10	$1	$10
Haircuts	5	$8	$40
Cost of CPI basket at base-period prices			$50

(b) The cost of the CPI basket at current-period prices: 2018

CPI basket			Cost of
Item	Quantity	Price	CPI Basket
Oranges	10	$2	$20
Haircuts	5	$10	$50
Cost of CPI basket at current-period prices			$70

Distinguishing High Inflation from a High Price Level

Figure 5.7 shows the CPI and the inflation rate in Canada between 1970 and 2017. The two parts of the figure are related and emphasize the distinction between high inflation and high prices.

When the price level in part (a) *rises rapidly*, (1970 through 1982), the inflation rate in part (b) is *high*. When the price level in part (a) *rises slowly*, (after 1982), the inflation rate in part (b) is *low*.

A high inflation rate means that the price level is rising rapidly. A high price level means that there has been a sustained period of rising prices.

When the price level in part (a) *falls* (2009), the inflation rate in part (b) is negative—deflation.

The CPI is not a perfect measure of the price level and changes in the CPI probably overstate the inflation rate. Let's look at the sources of bias.

The Biased CPI

The main sources of bias in the CPI are:

- New goods bias
- Quality change bias
- Commodity substitution bias
- Outlet substitution bias

New Goods Bias If you want to compare the price level in 2017 with that in 1970, you must somehow compare the price of a computer today with that of a typewriter in 1970. Because a PC is more expensive than a typewriter was, the arrival of the PC puts an upward bias into the CPI and its inflation rate.

Quality Change Bias Cars and many other goods get better every year. Part of the rise in the prices of these goods is a payment for improved quality and is not inflation. But the CPI counts the entire price rise as inflation and so overstates inflation.

Commodity Substitution Bias Changes in relative prices lead consumers to change the items they buy. For example, if the price of beef rises and the price of chicken remains unchanged, people buy more chicken and less beef. This switch from beef to chicken might provide the same amount of meat and the same enjoyment as before and expenditure is the same as before. The price of meat has not changed. But because the CPI ignores the substitution of chicken for beef, it says the price of meat has increased.

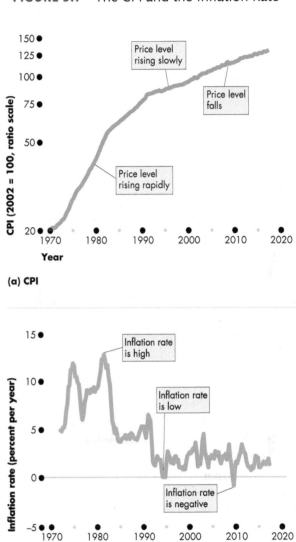

FIGURE 5.7 The CPI and the Inflation Rate

(a) CPI

(b) Inflation rate

When the price level rises rapidly, the inflation rate is high; and when the price level rises slowly, the inflation rate is low. When the price level falls, the inflation rate is negative.

From 1970 through 1982, the price level increased rapidly in part (a) and the inflation rate was high in part (b). After 1982, the price level rose slowly in part (a) and the inflation rate was low in part (b). In 2009, the price level fell and the inflation rate was negative—there was deflation.

Source of data: Statistics Canada, CANSIM Table 326-0020.

Outlet Substitution Bias When confronted with higher prices, people use discount stores more frequently and convenience stores less frequently. This phenomenon is called *outlet substitution*. The CPI surveys do not monitor outlet substitutions.

The Magnitude of the Bias

You've reviewed the sources of bias in the CPI. But how big is the bias? This question is addressed periodically and the most recent estimate is provided in a study by Bank of Canada economist James Rossiter at about 0.6 percent per year.

Some Consequences of the Bias

The bias in the CPI distorts private contracts and increases government outlays. Many private agreements, such as wage contracts, are linked to the CPI. For example, a firm and its workers might agree to a three-year wage deal that increases the wage rate by 2 percent a year plus the percentage increase in the CPI. Such a deal ends up giving the workers more real income than the firm intended.

Close to a third of federal government outlays are linked directly to the CPI. And while a bias of 0.6 percent a year seems small, accumulated over a decade it adds up to several billion dollars of additional expenditures.

Alternative Price Indexes

The CPI is just one of many alternative price level index numbers, and because of the bias in the CPI other measures are used for some purposes. We'll describe two alternatives to the CPI and explain when and why they might be preferred to the CPI. The alternatives are:

- GDP deflator
- Chained price index for consumption

GDP Deflator The *GDP deflator* is an index of the prices of all the items included in GDP and is the ratio of nominal GDP to real GDP. That is,

$$\text{GDP deflator} = \frac{\text{Nominal GDP}}{\text{Real GDP}} \times 100.$$

Because real GDP includes consumption expenditure, investment, government expenditure, and net exports, the GDP deflator is an index of the prices of all these items.

Real GDP is calculated using the chained-dollar method (see Chapter 4, pp. 104–105), which means that the weights attached to each item in the GDP deflator are the components of GDP in both the current year and the preceding year.

Because it uses current period and previous period quantities rather than fixed quantities from an earlier period, a chained-dollar price index incorporates substitution effects and new goods and overcomes the sources of bias in the CPI.

Over the period 2000 to 2016, the GDP deflator has increased at an average rate of 1.9 percent per year, which is 0.3 percentage points *below* the CPI inflation rate.

The GDP deflator is appropriate for macroeconomics because, like GDP, it is a comprehensive measure of the cost of the real GDP basket of goods and services. But as a measure of the cost of living, it is too broad—it includes items that consumers don't buy.

Chained Price Index for Consumption The *chained price index for consumption (CPIC)* is an index of the prices of all the items included in consumption expenditure in GDP and is the ratio of nominal consumption expenditure to real consumption expenditure. That is,

$$\text{CPIC} = \frac{\text{Nominal consumption expenditure}}{\text{Real consumption expenditure}} \times 100.$$

Like the GDP deflator, because the CPIC uses current-period and previous-period quantities rather than fixed quantities from an earlier period, it incorporates substitution effects and new goods and overcomes the sources of bias in the CPI.

Over the period 2000 to 2016, the CPIC has increased at an average rate of 1.8 percent per year, which is 0.4 percentage points *below* the CPI inflation rate.

Core Inflation

No matter whether we calculate the inflation rate using the CPI, the GDP deflator, or the CPIC, the number bounces around a good deal from month to month or quarter to quarter. To determine whether the inflation rate is trending upward or downward, we need to strip the raw numbers of their volatility. The **core inflation rate**, which is the inflation rate excluding volatile elements, attempts to do just that and reveal the underlying inflation trend.

The Bank of Canada monitors several measures of core inflation to enable it to see the trend CPI inflation rate. The Bank's first core inflation measure was the percentage change in the CPI excluding food and fuel, two items with the most volatile prices. But this measure gave a misleading view of the trend inflation rate when food and fuel got cheaper relative to other items. So, the Bank now monitors three measures of core inflation that avoid this problem. The measures are CPI-trim, CPI-median, and CPI-common.

The items in the CPI basket change at a wide distribution of rates and the CPI measures the average or mean rate of price change. CPI-trim excludes or trims the top and bottom 20 percent most extreme price changes. CPI-median measures inflation as the percentage change of the middle items in the basket. CPI-common uses a statistical method to reveal the most common price changes.

Figure 5.8 shows the CPI and CPI-trim core inflation rates from 1984 to 2017.

The Real Variables in Macroeconomics

You saw in Chapter 3 the distinction between a money price and a relative price (see p. 58). Another name for a money price is a nominal price. In macroeconomics, we often want to distinguish between a real variable and its corresponding nominal variable. We want to distinguish a real price from its corresponding nominal price because a real price is an opportunity cost that influences choices. And we want to distinguish a real quantity (like real GDP) from a nominal quantity (like nominal GDP) because we want to see what is "really" happening to variables that influence the standard of living.

You've seen in this chapter how we view real GDP as nominal GDP deflated by the GDP deflator. Viewing real GDP in this way opens up the idea of using the same method to calculate other real variables. By using the GDP deflator, we can deflate any nominal variable and find its corresponding real values. An important example is the wage rate, which is the price of labour. We measure the economy's real wage rate as the nominal wage rate divided by the GDP deflator.

There is one variable that is a bit different—an interest rate. A real interest rate is not a nominal interest rate divided by the price level. You'll learn how to adjust interest rates for inflation to find a real interest rate in Chapter 8. But all the other real variables of macroeconomics are calculated by dividing a nominal variable by the price level.

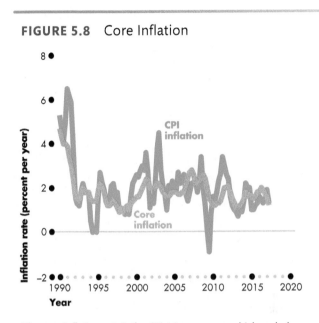

FIGURE 5.8 Core Inflation

The core inflation rate is the CPI-trim measure, which excludes the top and bottom 20 percent of the most extreme price changes. The core inflation rate removes most of the wide swings in the CPI inflation rate because it removes the most volatile price changes.

Source of data: Statistics Canada, CANSIM Table 326-0020 and 0023.

——— MyLab Economics Real-time data ———

REVIEW QUIZ

1 What is the price level?
2 What is the CPI and how is it calculated?
3 How do we calculate the inflation rate and what is its relationship with the CPI?
4 What are the four main ways in which the CPI is an upward-biased measure of the price level?
5 What problems arise from the CPI bias?
6 What are the alternative measures of the price level and how do they address the problem of bias in the CPI?

Work these questions in Study Plan 5.3 and get instant feedback.　　MyLab Economics

◆ You've now completed your study of the measurement of macroeconomic performance. Your next task is to learn what determines that performance and how policy actions might improve it. But first, compare the Canadian and U.S. labour markets in *Economics in the News* on pp. 126–127.

Comparing Jobs Growth in Canada and the United States

Jobs Data Highlights Divergence Between Canada, U.S.

July 2017

Jobs reports from Statistics Canada and the U.S. Bureau of Labor Statistics for June 2017 highlight a divergence between the labour markets of the two economies.

Statistics Canada's Labour Force Survey reported an increase in employment of 45,000 in June, and compared with June 2016, an increase of 351,000, or 1.9 percent. Most of the employment increase was in full-time work. The pace of increase was also rising. During the second quarter of 2017, employment increased by 103,000 in what was the fourth consecutive quarter of strong employment growth and the largest quarterly increase since 2010.

Despite Canada's strong pace of jobs growth, the unemployment rate was stubbornly high, barely changing at 6.5 percent, down only 0.1 percentage points from the May figure.

Job gains were not spread evenly across the country, and the strongest job-creating provinces were Quebec and British Columbia.

The Bureau of Labor Statistics reported that the U.S. economy created 222,000 jobs in June 2017, consolidating the gain of the preceding 24 months. But jobs growth in the year to June 2017, at 2.1 million, or 1.4 percent, was down from a peak growth of 1.7 percent in 2015.

The U.S. unemployment rate was unchanged in June at 4.4 percent, but down from 5.3 percent two years earlier and at a nine-year low.

Sources: Based on Statistics Canada, *The Daily*, July 7, 2017; and the U.S. Department of Labor, Bureau of Labor Statistics, News Release, July 7, 2017.

ESSENCE OF THE STORY

- Quebec and British Columbia were the strongest job-creating provinces in 2017.

- Canada created 351,000 jobs in the year to June 2017 and had the largest quarterly increase since 2010.

- The Canadian unemployment rate in June 2017 was 6.5 percent, down from 6.6 percent a month earlier.

- The United States created 2.1 million jobs in the year to June 2017.

- The U.S. unemployment rate was 4.4 percent, a nine-year low.

ECONOMIC ANALYSIS

- This news article reports some Canadian and U.S. labour market data and says that the United States is creating jobs at a faster pace than Canada and that Canada has the higher unemployment rate.

- The global recession of 2008–2009 had a bigger effect on the U.S. economy than on the Canadian economy, and the recovery during 2010 and 2011 was weaker in the United States than in Canada.

- The three figures compare the two economies during 2008–2017.

- Figure 1 shows the two output gaps and two key facts: The U.S. recession was double the depth of Canada's, and Canada had returned to full employment by 2011 while the U.S. output gap remained large.

- Canada's relatively stronger performance during 2010 and 2011 is driven by the strength of the Asian economies—China and India in particular—and Canada's resource exports to these economies.

- Figure 1 also shows that while the United States has been returning to full employment, Canada has been fluctuating around full employment.

- Figure 2 shows the two unemployment rates. Before the recession and in 2014, Canada had a higher unemployment rate than the United States.

- But during 2008, the U.S. unemployment rate climbed steeply, and by the end of 2008 the U.S. unemployment rate was above the Canadian rate, where it remained until 2014.

- Since 2014, the U.S. unemployment rate continued to fall while Canada's unemployment rate barely changed. These facts suggest that the U.S. natural unemployment rate is lower than Canada's.

- Figure 3 shows the two employment rates and that the U.S. employment rate fell more steeply than Canada's during the recession.

- Figure 3 also shows that the Canadian employment rate increased through 2013 before starting to fall.

- A steep fall in the world price of oil weakened the Canadian job market in Alberta and is a likely source of Canada's falling employment rate and higher natural unemployment rate.

Figure 1 The Output Gaps

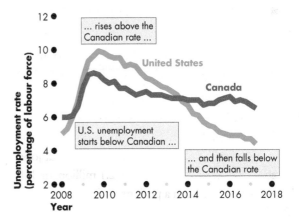

Figure 2 The Unemployment Rates

Figure 3 The Employment Rates

WORKED PROBLEM

MyLab Economics Work this problem in Chapter 5 Study Plan.

Statistics Canada's Labour Force Survey (LFS) reported the following situations in July 2014:

- Sarah works 10 hours a week at McDonald's. She is available to work more hours but hasn't looked for extra work.
- Kevin spent the first six months of 2014 actively searching for a job but he didn't get hired. He believes there are no jobs, so he has given up looking.
- Pat quit the job he had for the past two years and is actively looking for a better-paying job. He is available to work and is still searching for a job.
- Mary is a new graduate who was hired while she was a student to start a job in August.
- Johnnie quit his band in June, has no job in July, and is not looking for work.

Questions

1. Who does the LFS classify as being unemployed, a part-time worker, an employed person, a discouraged searcher, and not in the labour force? Explain your classification.
2. How will the labour force change if Sarah starts a second job, Pat finds a good job and is hired, and Mary takes a job at McDonald's while she waits to start her new job?
3. How will the unemployment rate change if Sarah quits and starts to search for a full-time job?
4. How will the labour force participation rate change if Kevin starts creating football apps in his garage and they turn out to be very popular?

Solutions

1. Sarah is a part-time worker, so the LFS classifies her as employed. She doesn't need to be looking for extra work.

   Kevin is a discouraged searcher. In the past he searched for a job but now he has given up. He is not unemployed because he didn't look for work in July, is not laid off, and is not waiting to start a new job within four weeks. The labour force includes only those employed and those unemployed, so Kevin is not in the labour force.

   Pat is unemployed. He has no job, is available to work, and has looked for work during July.

   Mary doesn't have a job, but she is available for work and will start a job within four weeks, so she is classified as unemployed.

Johnnie is not in the labour force. When he played in the band he was employed, but now he is not employed. He is not unemployed because he is not looking for a job.

Key Point: To be counted in the labour force a person must be either employed or unemployed. To be counted as employed, a person must have a job. To be counted as unemployed, a person must have looked for a job in the last four weeks and be available for work or be starting one within four weeks.

2. The labour force consists of the people who are counted by the LFS as employed or unemployed.

   Sarah is already counted as employed, so when she starts a second job the labour force does not change.

   Pat is currently unemployed, so when he is hired he transfers from being unemployed to being employed. So his change of status does not change the labour force.

   Mary is currently counted as unemployed, so taking on a part-time job at McDonald's while she waits to start the new job does not change the labour force.

Key Point: The labour force will change if working-age people not currently in the labour force start to look for work and become unemployed or start a job and become employed.

3. The unemployment rate is the percentage of the labour force who are classified as unemployed. If Sarah quits her job and searches for a full-time job, she becomes unemployed. The labour force doesn't change, so the unemployment rate rises.

Key Point: The unemployment rate rises when people quit their jobs and start searching for new ones.

4. The labour force participation rate is the percentage of the working-age population who are in the labour force. Kevin is currently not in the labour force because he is a discouraged searcher. When Kevin starts creating football apps in his garage and they turn out to be very popular, Kevin has created a job and is counted as employed. He is now in the labour force, so the labour force participation rate rises.

Key Point: The labour force participation rate changes as working-age people enter and exit the labour force.

SUMMARY

Key Points

Employment and Unemployment (pp. 112–116)

- Unemployment is a serious personal, social, and economic problem because it results in lost output and income and a loss of human capital.

- The unemployment rate averaged 7.6 percent between 1960 and 2014. It increases in recessions and decreases in expansions.

- The labour force participation rate and the employment rate have an upward trend and fluctuate with the business cycle.

- Two alternative measures of unemployment, narrower than the official measure, include the long-term unemployed and short-term unemployed.

- Three alternative measures of unemployment, broader than the official measure, include discouraged searchers, long-term future starts, and part-time workers who want full-time jobs.

Working Problems 1 to 5 will give you a better understanding of employment and unemployment.

Unemployment and Full Employment (pp. 117–119)

- Some unemployment is unavoidable because people are constantly entering and leaving the labour force and losing or quitting jobs; also, firms that create jobs are constantly being born, expanding, contracting, and dying.

- Unemployment can be frictional, structural, or cyclical.

- When all unemployment is frictional and structural, the unemployment rate equals the natural unemployment rate, the economy is at full employment, and real GDP equals potential GDP.

- Over the business cycle, real GDP fluctuates around potential GDP and the unemployment rate fluctuates around the natural unemployment rate.

Working Problems 6 and 7 will give you a better understanding of unemployment and full employment.

The Price Level, Inflation, and Deflation (pp. 120–125)

- Inflation and deflation that are unexpected redistribute income and wealth and divert resources from production.

- The Consumer Price Index (CPI) is a measure of the average of the prices paid by urban consumers for a fixed basket of consumer goods and services.

- The CPI is defined to equal 100 for a reference base period—currently 2002.

- The inflation rate is the percentage change in the CPI from one period to the next.

- Changes in the CPI probably overstate the inflation rate because of the bias that arises from new goods, quality changes, commodity substitution, and outlet substitution.

- The bias in the CPI distorts private contracts and increases government outlays.

- Alternative price level measures such as the GDP deflator and the CPIC avoid the bias of the CPI but do not make a large difference to the measured inflation rate.

- Real economic variables (except the real interest rate) are calculated by dividing nominal variables by the price level.

Working Problems 8 to 11 will give you a better understanding of the price level, inflation, and deflation.

Key Terms

MyLab Economics Key Terms Quiz

Consumer Price Index (CPI), 121
Core inflation rate, 124
Cyclical unemployment, 117
Deflation, 120
Discouraged searcher, 115
Employment rate, 115

Frictional unemployment, 117
Full employment, 117
Hyperinflation, 120
Inflation, 120
Labour force, 113
Labour force participation rate, 114

Natural unemployment rate, 117
Output gap, 118
Price level, 120
Structural unemployment, 117
Unemployment rate, 114
Working-age population, 113

STUDY PLAN PROBLEMS AND APPLICATIONS

MyLab Economics Work Problems 1 to 11 in Chapter 5 Study Plan and get instant feedback.
Problems marked ⊕ update with real-time data.

Employment and Unemployment (Study Plan 5.1)

1. Statistics Canada reported the following data for 2016:

   Labour force: 19.4 million
   Employment: 18.1 million
   Working-age population: 29.6 million

   Calculate the:

   a. Unemployment rate

   b. Labour force participation rate

   c. Employment rate

2. In July 2017, in the economy of Sandy Island, 10,000 people were employed, 1,000 were unemployed, and 5,000 were not in the labour force. During August 2017, 80 people lost their jobs and didn't look for new ones, 20 people quit their jobs and retired, 150 unemployed people were hired, 50 people quit the labour force, and 40 people entered the labour force to look for work. Calculate for July 2017:

   a. The unemployment rate

   b. The employment rate

   And calculate for the end of August 2017

   c. The number of people unemployed, the number employed, and the unemployment rate

Use the following data to work Problems 3 and 4.
In March 2016, Canada's unemployment rate was 7.7 percent. In November 2016, it was 6.3 percent.

3. If the labour force was constant during 2016, explain what happened to unemployment.

4. If unemployment was constant during 2016, explain what happened to the labour force.

5. **Canada Adds 67,200 Jobs but Unemployment Rate Unchanged**

   Despite two months of employment growth and a rising labour force participation rate, Canada's unemployment rate was unchanged at 7 percent. Bank of Canada senior deputy governor Carolyn Wilkins said that there is excess capacity in the labour market, which is indicated by a high number of discouraged searchers.

   Source: *The Toronto Star*, October 8, 2016

   Explain the facts reported in the news clip and how discouraged searchers influence the official unemployment rate and the R5 unemployment rate.

Unemployment and Full Employment (Study Plan 5.2)

Use the following news clip to work Problems 6 and 7.

High-Tech Sector Looks to Federal Budget to Spark Innovation Boom, Deliver Skilled Workforce

High-tech firms are struggling to find enough skilled workers. It is estimated that by 2020, the high-tech sector will have a shortage of 220,000 workers. Yet 40 percent of existing jobs are expected to disappear during the 2020s. Craig Alexander of the Conference Board of Canada says: "So we have a situation where we have people without jobs, and we have jobs without people." The finance minister wants to "help Canadians get the skills they need in a challenging economic environment."

Source: CBC News, March 20, 2017

6. How do the facts, estimates, and projections in the news clip influence the unemployment rate and the natural unemployment rate?

7. How would a government-funded skills training program influence frictional, structural, and cyclical unemployment?

The Price Level, Inflation, and Deflation (Study Plan 5.3)

Use the following data to work Problems 8 and 9.
The people on Coral Island buy only juice and cloth. The CPI basket contains the quantities bought in 2013. The average household spent $60 on juice and $30 on cloth in 2013 when juice was $2 a bottle and cloth was $5 a metre. In 2014, juice is $4 a bottle and cloth is $6 a metre.

8. Calculate the CPI basket and the percentage of the household's budget spent on juice in 2013.

9. Calculate the CPI and the inflation rate in 2014.

Use the following data to work Problems 10 and 11.
Statistics Canada reported the following CPI data:

   December 2014 125.5
   December 2015 127.5
   December 2016 129.4

10. Calculate the inflation rates for the years ended December 2015 and December 2016. How did the inflation rate change in 2016?

11. Why might these CPI numbers be biased? How can alternative price indexes avoid this bias?

ADDITIONAL PROBLEMS AND APPLICATIONS

MyLab Economics You can work these problems in Homework or Test if assigned by your instructor. Problems marked ⬤ update with real-time data.

Employment and Unemployment

12. What is the unemployment rate supposed to measure and why is it an imperfect measure?

⬤ 13. Statistics Canada reported the following data for July 2016:

    Labour force participation rate: 66.6 percent
    Working-age population: 29.6 million
    Employment rate: 61.8

    Calculate the:

    a. Labour force

    b. Employment

    c. Unemployment rate

14. **Jobs Report for May Expected to Hit a Positive Note**

    When Statistics Canada releases its May Labour Force Survey, economists expect employment to be up 11,000 and the unemployment rate to nudge up from 6.5 percent to 6.6 percent. They expect the labour force participation rate will rise.

    Source: *The Globe and Mail*, June 5, 2017

    Explain how the labour force and unemployment would have changed if the only change were that:

    a. All the newly hired people had been unemployed in April.

    b. More people started searching for a job.

15. In Canada between June and July in 2016, the number of full-time jobs increased by 63,200 while part-time jobs fell by 108,800. The unemployment rate increased from 6.4 percent to 7.2 percent. The labour force participation rate increased from 66.5 percent to 66.6 percent.

    a. Explain the link between the rise in the participation rate and the rise in the unemployment rate.

    b. If all the workers who entered the job market were discouraged searchers, explain how the R5 unemployment would have changed.

16. A high unemployment rate tells us that a large percentage of the labour force is unemployed but not why the unemployment rate is high. What unemployment measure tells us if (i) people are searching longer than usual to find a job, (ii) more people are involuntary part-time workers, or (iii) more unemployed people are discouraged searchers?

17. With about 1.3 million Canadians looking for work, some employers are swamped with job applicants while other can't hire enough workers. The job market has changed. During the recession, millions of middle-skill, middle-wage jobs disappeared. Now with the recovery, these people can't find the skilled jobs that they seek and must adjust to lower-skilled work with less pay.

    Why might the unemployment rate underestimate the underutilization of labour resources?

Unemployment and Full Employment

Use the following data to work Problems 18 to 20. The IMF *World Economic Outlook* reports the following unemployment rates:

Region	2015	2016
United States	5.3	4.9
Spain	22.1	19.6
Venezuela	7.4	21.2
Singapore	1.9	2.1

18. What do these numbers tell you about the phase of the business cycle in the four countries in 2016?

19. What do these numbers tell us about the relative size of their natural unemployment rates?

20. Do these numbers tell us anything about the relative size of their labour force participation rates and employment rates?

Use the following news clip to work Problems 21 to 23.

Economic Conditions at the Cycle Bottom

Employment rebounded by 0.1 percent in August 2008, its first gain in four months. All of the increase was in full-time jobs. The unemployment rate in August 2008 was unchanged at 6.1 percent.

    Source: *Canadian Economic Observer*, September 2008

21. How did the unemployment rate in August 2008 compare to the unemployment rate during the recessions of the early 1980s and early 1990s?

22. How can the unemployment rate not change when employment rises?

23. Compare the unemployment rate in August 2008 to the estimated natural unemployment rate. What does this imply about the relationship between real GDP and potential GDP at this time?

24. CNN reported that for the first six months of 2008, the U.S. economy lost 438,000 jobs. The job losses in June were concentrated in manufacturing and construction, two sectors that have been badly battered in the recession.
    a. Based on the report, what might be the main source of increased unemployment?
    b. Based on the report, what might be the main type of increased unemployment?

25. **Retraining**

    Many people graduate with a bachelor's degree that doesn't open job doors. Aquiring a skill provides a way of getting a decent paycheque. But aquring a skill isn't a one-time event: It is an ongoing process. A skill doesn't last for decades and retraining is required. Government-funded job training is a promising way to help individual workers, employers, and the country as a whole.

    Source: *The New York Times*, February 26, 2017

    a. What is the main type of unemployment that retraining programs seek to avoid? Explain.
    b. How might government-funded retraining influence the natural unemployment rate? Explain.

The Price Level, Inflation, and Deflation

26. A typical family on Sandy Island consumes only juice and cloth. Last year, which was the base year, the family spent $40 on juice and $25 on cloth. In the base year, juice was $4 a bottle and cloth was $5 a length. This year, juice is $4 a bottle and cloth is $6 a length. Calculate:
    a. The CPI basket
    b. The CPI in the current year
    c. The inflation rate in the current year

27. A firm agreed to pay its workers $20 an hour in 2016 and $22 an hour in 2017. The price level for these years was 241 in 2016 and 245 in 2017. Calculate the real wage rate in each year. What is the real wage increase received by these workers in 2017?

28. **News Release**

    Real consumption expenditure in 2007 chained dollars was $1,002.3 billion in 2015 and $1,026.2 billion in 2016. In current dollars, it was $1,115.6 billion in 2015 and $1,153.5 billion in 2016.

    Source: Statistics Canada

    a. Calculate the chained price index for consumption (CPIC) for 2015 and 2016.
    b. Calculate the CPIC inflation rate for 2016.
    c. Why might the CPIC inflation rate be preferred to the CPI inflation rate?
    d. Did real consumption expenditure increase by more or by less than nominal consumption expenditure? Why?

Economics in the News

29. After you have studied *Economics in the News* on pp. 126–127, answer the following questions.
    a. Describe the key differences in the U.S. and Canadian output gaps during 2008–2017.
    b. Describe the key differences in performance of the U.S. and Canadian job markets during 2008–2017.
    c. Why might the U.S. job market have been so much weaker than the Canadian job market during 2008–2009?
    d. Do you think the differences between the U.S. and Canadian job markets in 2008–2017 were frictional, structural, or cyclical unemployment?

30. **Older Workers Struggle to Find Jobs**

    In August 2016, 151,000 new jobs were created. But 2.5 million workers over 55 were either unemployed, in part-time jobs but wanting full time, or had given up on seeking work. Age discrimination is illegal but hiring discrimination is hard to prove and economists at the University of California at Irvine and Tulane University say they have found evidence of age discrimination in hiring, particularly for older women.

    Source: *Fortune*, September 8, 2016

    a. What type of unemployment might older workers be more prone to experience?
    b. Explain how the unemployment rate of older workers is influenced by the business cycle.
    c. Why might older unemployed workers become marginally attached or discouraged searchers?

The Big Picture

MONITORING MACROECONOMIC PERFORMANCE

Macroeconomics is a large and controversial subject that is interlaced with political ideological disputes. And it is a field in which charlatans as well as serious thinkers have much to say.

You have just learned in Chapters 4 and 5 how we monitor and measure the main macroeconomic variables. We use real GDP to calculate the rate of economic growth and business cycle fluctuations. And we use the CPI and other measures of the price level to calculate the inflation rate and to "deflate" nominal values to find *real* values.

In the chapters that lie ahead, you will learn the theories that economists have developed to explain economic growth, fluctuations, and inflation.

First, in Chapters 6 to 9, you will study the long-term trends. This material is central to the oldest question in macroeconomics that Adam Smith tried to answer: What are the causes of the wealth of nations? You will also study three other old questions that Adam Smith's contemporary and friend David Hume first addressed: What causes inflation? What causes international deficits and surpluses? And why do exchange rates fluctuate?

In Chapters 10 to 12, you will study macroeconomic fluctuations.

Finally, in Chapters 13 and 14, you will study the policies that the federal government and the Bank of Canada might adopt to make the economy perform well.

David Hume, *a Scot who lived from 1711 to 1776, did not call himself an economist. "Philosophy and general learning" is how he described the subject of his life's work. Hume was an extraordinary thinker and writer. Published in 1742, his* Essays, Moral and Political, *range across economics, political science, moral philosophy, history, literature, ethics, and religion and explore such topics as love, marriage, divorce, suicide, death, and the immortality of the soul!*

His economic essays provide astonishing insights into the forces that cause inflation, business cycle fluctuations, balance of payments deficits, and interest rate fluctuations; and they explain the effects of taxes and government deficits and debts.

Data were scarce in Hume's day, so he was not able to draw on detailed evidence to support his analysis. But he was empirical. He repeatedly appealed to experience and observation as the ultimate judge of the validity of an argument. Hume's fundamentally empirical approach dominates macroeconomics today.

"… in every kingdom into which money begins to flow in greater abundance than formerly, everything takes a new face: labour and industry gain life; the merchant becomes more enterprising, the manufacturer more diligent and skillful, and even the farmer follows his plow with greater alacrity and attention."

DAVID HUME
Essays, Moral and Political

The ... most difficult thing that empirical economists try to do is infer a causal relationship.

DAVID CARD is Class of 1950 Professor of Economics and Director of the Center for Labor Economics at the University of California, Berkeley, and Faculty Research Associate at the National Bureau of Economic Research.

Born in Canada, Professor Card obtained his B.A. at Queen's University, Kingston, Ontario, and his Ph.D. at Princeton University. He has received many honours, the most notable of which is the American Economic Association's John Bates Clark Prize, awarded to the best economist under 40.

Professor Card's research on labour markets and the effects of public policies on earnings, jobs, and the distribution of income is published in more than 100 articles and several books. His most recent books include two volumes of the *Handbook of Labor Economics* (co-edited with Orley Ashenfelter). An earlier book (co-authored with Alan B. Krueger), *Myth and Measurement: The New Economics of the Minimum Wage* (Princeton, NJ: Princeton University Press, 1995), made a big splash and upset one of the most fundamental beliefs about the effects of minimum wages.

Michael Parkin and Robin Bade talked with David Card about his work and the progress that economists have made in understanding how public policies can influence the distribution of income and economic well-being.

Almost all your work is grounded in data. You are an empirical economist. How do you go about your work, where do your data come from, and how do you use data?

The data I use come from many different sources. I have collected my own data from surveys; transcribed data from historical sources and government publications; and used computerized data files based on records from censuses and surveys in the United States, Canada, Britain, and other countries.

An economist can do three things with data. The first is to develop simple statistics on basic questions such as "What fraction of families live in poverty?" For this, one needs to understand how the data were collected and processed and how the questions were asked. For example, the poverty rate depends on how you define a "family." If a single mother and her child live with the mother's parents, the income of the mother and the grandparents is counted as "family income."

The second thing economists do with data is develop descriptive comparisons. For example, I have compared the wage differences between male and female workers. Again, the details are important. For example, the male–female wage differential is much bigger if you look at annual earnings than at earnings per hour, because women work fewer hours per year.

Once you've established some simple facts, you start to get ideas for possible explanations. You can also rule out a lot of other ideas.

The third and most difficult thing that empirical economists try to do is infer a causal relationship. In rare instances, we have a true experiment in which a random subgroup of volunteers is enrolled in a "treatment group" and the remainder become the "control group."...

*Read the full interview with David Card in MyLab Economics.

6

ECONOMIC GROWTH

After studying this chapter, you will be able to:

◆ Define and calculate the economic growth rate and explain the implications of sustained growth

◆ Describe the economic growth trends in Canada and other countries and regions

◆ Explain what makes potential GDP grow

◆ Explain the sources of labour productivity growth

◆ Explain the theories of economic growth and policies to increase its rate

Canadian real GDP per person and the standard of living tripled between 1966 and 2016. We see even more dramatic change in China, where incomes have tripled not in 50 years but in the 13 years from 2003 to 2016. But Canadian real GDP growth has been slower since 2000 than it was in the 1990s, and slower in the 1990s than in the 1960s.

In this chapter, we study the forces that make real GDP grow; and in *Economics in the News* at the end of the chapter, we look at lessons we can learn from comparing the Canadian growth rate with that of the United States.

◆ The Basics of Economic Growth

Economic growth is the expansion of production possibilities. A rapid pace of economic growth maintained over a number of years can transform a poor nation into a rich one. Such have been the stories of Hong Kong, South Korea, and some other Asian economies. Slow economic growth or the absence of growth can condemn a nation to devastating poverty. Such has been the fate of Sierra Leone, Somalia, Zambia, and much of the rest of Africa.

The goal of this chapter is to help you understand why some economies expand rapidly and others stagnate. We'll begin by learning how to calculate a growth rate, by distinguishing between economic growth and a business cycle expansion, and by discovering the magic of sustained growth.

Calculating Growth Rates

We express a **growth rate** as the annual percentage change of a variable—the change in the level expressed as a percentage of the initial level. The growth rate of real GDP, for example, is calculated as:

$$\text{Real GDP growth rate} = \frac{\text{Real GDP in current year} - \text{Real GDP in previous year}}{\text{Real GDP in previous year}} \times 100.$$

Using some numbers, if real GDP in the current year is $1,650 billion and if real GDP in the previous year was $1,500 billion, then the economic growth rate is 10 percent.

The growth rate of real GDP tells us how rapidly the *total* economy is expanding. This measure is useful for telling us about potential changes in the balance of economic power among nations. But it does not tell us about changes in the standard of living.

The standard of living depends on **real GDP per person** (also called *per capita* real GDP), which is real GDP divided by the population. So the contribution of real GDP growth to the change in the standard of living depends on the growth rate of real GDP per person. We use the above formula to calculate this growth rate, replacing real GDP with real GDP per person.

Suppose, for example, that in the current year, when real GDP is $1,650 billion, the population is 30.3 million. Then real GDP per person is $1,650 billion divided by 30.3 million, which equals $54,455. And suppose that in the previous year,

when real GDP was $1,500 billion, the population was 30 million. Then real GDP per person in that year was $1,500 billion divided by 30 million, which equals $50,000.

Use these two values of real GDP per person with the growth formula above to calculate the growth rate of real GDP per person. That is,

$$\text{Real GDP per person growth rate} = \frac{\$54,455 - \$50,000}{\$50,000} \times 100 = 8.9 \text{ percent.}$$

The growth rate of real GDP per person can also be calculated (approximately) by subtracting the population growth rate from the real GDP growth rate. In the example you've just worked through, the growth rate of real GDP is 10 percent. The population changes from 30 million to 30.3 million, so the population growth rate is 1 percent. The growth rate of real GDP per person is approximately equal to 10 percent minus 1 percent, which equals 9 percent.

Real GDP per person grows only if real GDP grows faster than the population grows. If the growth rate of the population exceeds the growth of real GDP, then real GDP per person falls.

Economic Growth Versus Business Cycle Expansion

Real GDP can increase for two distinct reasons: The economy might be returning to full employment in an expansion phase of the business cycle or *potential* GDP might be increasing.

The return to full employment in an expansion phase of the business cycle isn't economic growth. It is just taking up the slack that resulted from the previous recession. The expansion of potential GDP is economic growth.

Figure 6.1 illustrates this distinction using the production possibilities frontier (the *PPF* that you studied in Chapter 2, p. 34). A return to full employment in a business cycle expansion is a movement from *inside* the *PPF* at a point such as *A* to a point *on* the *PPF* such as *B*.

Economic growth is the expansion of production possibilities. It is an outward movement of the *PPF* such as the shift from PPF_0 to PPF_1 and the movement from point *B* on PPF_0 to point *C* on PPF_1.

The growth rate of potential GDP measures the pace of expansion of production possibilities and smooths out the business cycle fluctuations in the growth rate of real GDP.

FIGURE 6.1 Economic Growth and a
Business Cycle Expansion

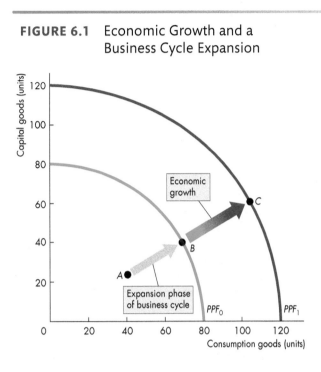

The increase in aggregate production in the move from point
A inside PPF_0 to point B on PPF_0 is an expansion phase of the
business cycle and it occurs with no change in production
possibilities. Such an expansion is not economic growth. The
increase in aggregate production in the move from point B
on PPF_0 to point C on PPF_1 is economic growth—an expansion of production possibilities shown by an outward shift of
the PPF.

—————— MyLab Economics Animation ——————

FIGURE 6.2 Growth Rates of Real GDP
and Potential GDP

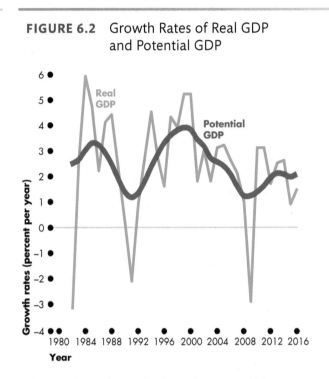

The annual growth rate of real GDP fluctuates widely over
the business cycle and masks changes in the underlying
trend growth rate. The annual growth rate of potential GDP
provides information about changes in the trend growth rate.
Both the growth rate of potential GDP and the trend growth
rate of real GDP have fallen since 2000.

Sources of data: Statistics Canada, CANSIM Table 282-0002 and Bank of Canada
output gap estimates used to calculate the growth rate of potential GDP.

—————— MyLab Economics Real-time data ——————

Figure 6.2 shows how the growth rate of potential
GDP (red curve) smoothes the more erratic fluctuations in the growth rate of real GDP. Business cycle
fluctuations in the real GDP growth rate mask the
underlying *trend* growth rate revealed by the growth
rate of *potential* GDP.

The Magic of Sustained Growth

Sustained growth of real GDP per person can
transform a poor society into a wealthy one. The
reason is that economic growth is like compound
interest.

Compound Interest Suppose that you put $100
in the bank and earn 5 percent a year interest on
it. After one year, you have $105. If you leave

that $105 in the bank for another year, you earn
5 percent interest on the original $100 *and on the
$5 interest that you earned last year*. You are now earn-
ing interest on interest! The next year, things get
even better. Then you earn 5 percent on the original $100 and on the interest earned in the first year
and the second year. You are even earning interest
on the interest that you earned on the interest of
the first year.

Your money in the bank is growing at a rate of
5 percent a year. Before too many years have passed,
your initial deposit of $100 will have grown to $200.
But after how many years?

The answer is provided by a formula called the **Rule
of 70**, which states that the number of years it takes
for the level of any variable to double is approximately

FIGURE 6.3 The Rule of 70

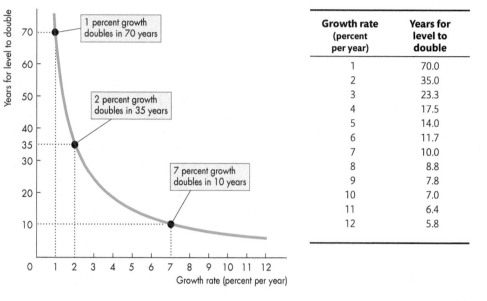

Growth rate (percent per year)	Years for level to double
1	70.0
2	35.0
3	23.3
4	17.5
5	14.0
6	11.7
7	10.0
8	8.8
9	7.8
10	7.0
11	6.4
12	5.8

The number of years it takes for the level of a variable to double is approximately 70 divided by the annual percentage growth rate of the variable.

MyLab Economics Animation

70 divided by the annual percentage growth rate of the variable. Using the Rule of 70, you can now calculate how many years it takes your $100 to become $200. It is 70 divided by 5, which is 14 years.

Applying the Rule of 70

The Rule of 70 applies to any variable, so it applies to real GDP per person. Figure 6.3 shows the doubling time for growth rates of 1 percent per year to 12 percent per year.

You can see that real GDP per person doubles in 70 years (70 divided by 1)—an average human life span—if the growth rate is 1 percent a year. It doubles in 35 years if the growth rate is 2 percent a year and in just 10 years if the growth rate is 7 percent a year.

We can use the Rule of 70 to answer other questions about economic growth. For example, in 2014, Canadian real GDP per person was approximately 4 times that of China. China's recent growth rate of real GDP per person was 10 percent a year. If this growth rate were maintained, how long would it take China's real GDP per person to reach that of Canada in 2014? The answer, provided by the Rule of 70, is 14 years. China's real GDP per person doubles in 7 years

(70 divided by 10). It doubles again to 4 times its current level in another 7 years. So after 14 years of growth at 10 percent a year, China's real GDP per person is 4 times its current level and equals that of Canada in 2014. Of course, after 14 years, Canadian real GDP per person would have increased, so China would still not have caught up to Canada. But at the current growth rates, China's real GDP per person will equal that of Canada by the late 2020s.

REVIEW QUIZ

1 What is economic growth and how do we calculate its rate?

2 What is the relationship between the growth rate of real GDP and the growth rate of real GDP per person?

3 Use the Rule of 70 to calculate the growth rate that leads to a doubling of real GDP per person in 20 years.

Work these questions in Study Plan 6.1 and get instant feedback.   MyLab Economics

◆ Long-Term Growth Trends

You have just seen the power of economic growth to increase incomes. At a 1 percent growth rate, it takes a human life span to double the standard of living. But at a 7 percent growth rate, the standard of living doubles every decade. How fast has our economy grown over the long term? How fast are other economies growing? Are poor countries catching up to rich ones, or do the gaps between the rich and poor persist or even widen? Let's answer these questions.

Long-Term Growth in Canada

Figure 6.4 shows *real GDP per person* in Canada for the 90 years from 1926 to 2016. The average growth rate over this period was 2 percent a year.

The earliest years in the graph are dominated by two extraordinary events: the Great Depression of the 1930s and World War II in the 1940s. The fall in real GDP during the Depression and the bulge during the war obscure the changes in the long-term growth trend that occurred within these years. Averaging out the Depression and the war, the long-term growth rate was close to its 90-year average of 2 percent a year.

The 1950s had slow growth but then, during the 1960s, the growth rate speeded up and averaged 3.3 percent a year. The 1970s growth rate slowed to 2.0 percent a year, and in the late 1980s the growth rate slowed to a crawl of 0.5 percent a year. In the 1990s the growth rate increased again to 1.8 percent a year, but after 1996 it slowed to 0.9 percent a year.

A major goal of this chapter is to explain why our economy grows and why the long-term growth rate varies. Why did growth speed up during the 1960s, slow through the 1970s and 1980s, and then speed up again during the late 1990s? Another goal is to explain variations in the growth rate across countries.

Let's look at some facts about the growth rates of other nations and compare them with Canada's growth rates.

FIGURE 6.4   Economic Growth in Canada: 1926–2016

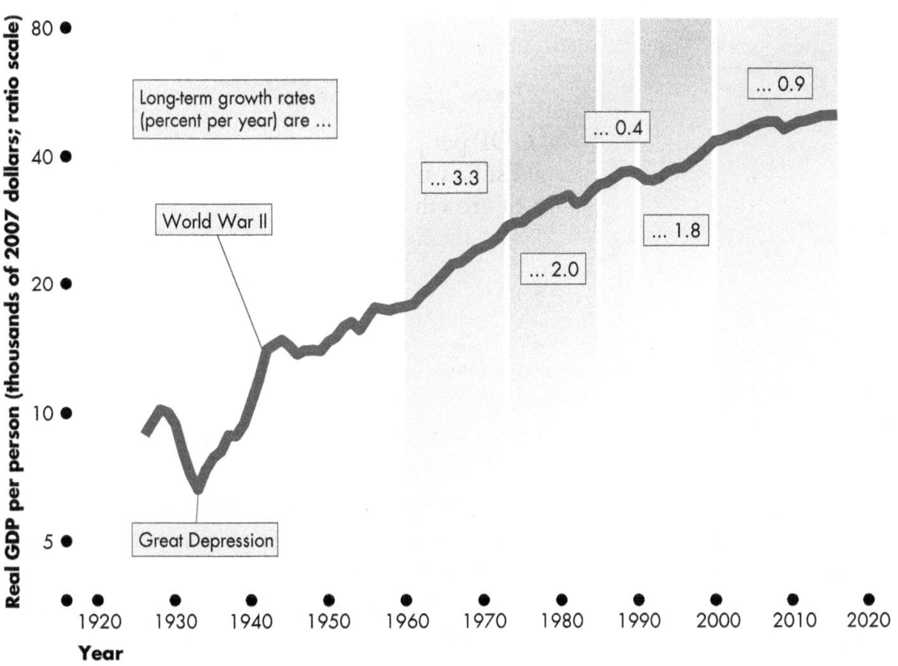

During the 90 years from 1926 to 2016, real GDP per person in Canada grew by 2 percent a year, on average. The growth rate was most rapid during the 1960s and slowest during the 1980s.

Sources of data: F. H. Leacy (ed.), *Historical Statistics of Canada*, 2nd edition, catalogue 11-516, series A1, F32, F55, Statistics Canada, Ottawa, 1983. Statistics Canada, Tables 380-0002 and 051-0005

Real GDP Growth in the World Economy

Figure 6.5 shows real GDP per person in the United States and in other countries between 1980 and 2016. Part (a) looks at the seven richest countries—known as the G7 nations. Among these nations, the United States has the highest real GDP per person. In 2016, Canada had the second-highest real GDP per person, ahead of France, Germany, Italy, and the United Kingdom (collectively the Europe Big 4), and Japan.

During the 36 years shown here, the gaps between the United States, Canada, and the Europe Big 4 have been almost constant. But starting from a long way below, Japan grew fastest. It caught up to Europe in 1990 and to Canada in 1991. But during the 1990s, Japan's economy stagnated.

Many other countries are growing more slowly than, and falling farther behind. Figure 6.5(b) looks at some of these countries.

Real GDP per person in Mexico was 48 percent of the Canadian level in 1980. But it grew more slowly than Canada and fell to 41 percent of the Canadian level by 2016.

Russia's data on real GDP per person start in 1992, when it stood at 55 percent of the Canadian level. After six years of shrinking, the Russian economy enjoyed a decade of more rapid growth, but it has stagnated since 2008 and in 2016 its real GDP per person was 57 percent of the Canadian level.

Nigeria's data also start in 1992 and show that it has grown slightly more quickly than Canada to go from 10 percent of the Canadian level in 1992 to 13 percent in 2016.

FIGURE 6.5   Economic Growth Around the World: Catch-Up or Not?

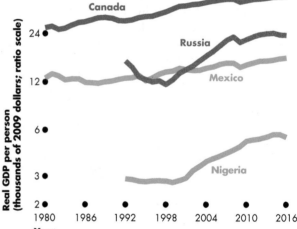

(a) Catch-up?

(b) No catch-up?

Real GDP per person has grown throughout the world. Among the rich industrial countries in part (a), real GDP per person has grown slightly faster in the United States than in Canada and the four big countries of Europe (France, Germany, Italy, and the United Kingdom). Japan had the fastest growth rate before 1990 but then growth slowed and Japan's economy stagnated during the 1990s.

In part (b), Mexico's growth rate has been lower than that of Canada, and the growth rates of Russia and Nigeria slightly faster. So, the gap between the real GDP per person in Canada and Mexico has widened, while the gaps for Russia and Nigeria have narrowed slightly.

Source of data: World Economic Outlook Database, International Monetary Fund, April 2017.

ECONOMICS IN ACTION

Fast Trains on the Same Track

Five Asian economies, Hong Kong, Korea, Singapore, Taiwan, and China, have experienced spectacular growth, which you can see in the figure. In 1980, real GDP per person ranged from 3 percent (China) to 77 percent (Singapore) of that in Canada. In 2016, real GDP per person in Singapore, Hong Kong, and Taiwan exceded that of Canada and China had climbed to 33 percent of the Canadian level.

The Asian economies shown here are like fast trains running on the same track at similar speeds and with a roughly constant gap between them. Singapore is the lead train, which runs about 15 years ahead of Hong Kong, 21 years ahead of Taiwan, 24 years ahead of Korea and 50 years ahead of China.

Real GDP per person in Korea in 2016 was similar to that in Hong Kong in 2006, and real GDP in China in 2016 was similar to that of Hong Kong in 1980. Between 1980 and 2016, Hong Kong transformed itself from a middle-income economy into one of the richest economies in the world.

The rest of China is now doing what Hong Kong has done. China has a population almost 200 times that of Hong Kong and more than 4 times that of the United States. So if China continues its rapid growth, the world economy will change dramatically.

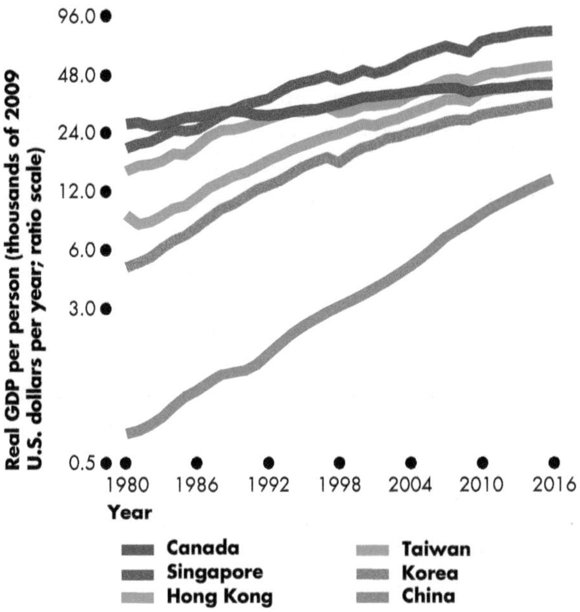

Closing the Gap

Source of data: World Economic Outlook Database, International Monetary Fund, April 2017

As these fast-growing Asian economies catch up with and overtake Canada, we can expect their growth rates to slow. But it will be surprising if China's growth rate slows to that of Canada before the gap has narrowed or perhaps even reversed.

Even modest differences in growth rates sustained over a number of years bring big differences in the standard of living. So the facts about economic growth raise some big questions.

What are the preconditions for economic growth? What sustains economic growth once it gets going? How can we identify the sources of economic growth and measure the contribution that each source makes? What can we do to increase the sustainable rate of economic growth?

We're now going to address these questions and discover the causes of economic growth. We start by seeing how potential GDP is determined and what makes it grow.

You will see that labour productivity growth is the key to the rising living standards that economic growth brings and go on to explore the sources of this growth.

REVIEW QUIZ

1. What has been the average growth rate of Canadian real GDP per person over the past 86 years? In which periods was growth most rapid and in which periods was it slowest?
2. Describe the gaps between real GDP per person in Canada and in other countries. For which countries is the gap narrowing? For which is it widening? For which is it the same?
3. Compare the growth rates in Hong Kong, Korea, Singapore, Taiwan, China, and Canada. In terms of real GDP per person, how far is China behind these others?

Work these questions in Study Plan 6.2 and get instant feedback. MyLab Economics

How Potential GDP Grows

Economic growth occurs when real GDP increases. But a one-shot rise in real GDP or a recovery from recession isn't economic growth. Economic growth is a sustained, year-after-year increase in *potential GDP*.

So what determines potential GDP and what are the forces that make it grow?

What Determines Potential GDP?

Labour, capital, land, and entrepreneurship produce real GDP, and the productivity of the factors of production determines the quantity of real GDP that can be produced.

The quantity of land is fixed, and on any given day the quantities of entrepreneurial ability and capital are also fixed and their productivities are given. The quantity of labour employed is the only *variable* factor of production. Potential GDP is the level of real GDP when the quantity of labour employed is the full-employment quantity.

To determine potential GDP, we use a model with two components:

■ An aggregate production function
■ An aggregate labour market

Aggregate Production Function When you studied the limits to production in Chapter 2 (see p. 34), you learned that the *production possibilities frontier* is the boundary between the combinations of goods and services that can be produced and those that cannot. We're now going to think about the production possibilities frontier for two special "goods": real GDP and the quantity of leisure time.

Think of real GDP as a number of big shopping carts. Each cart contains some of each kind of different goods and services produced, and one cartload of items costs $1 billion. To say that real GDP is $1,800 billion means that it is 1,800 very big shopping carts of goods and services.

The quantity of leisure time is the number of hours spent not working. Each leisure hour could be spent working. If we spent all our time taking leisure, we would do no work and produce nothing. Real GDP would be zero. The more leisure we forgo, the greater is the quantity of labour we supply and the greater is the quantity of real GDP produced.

But labour hours are not all equally productive. We use our most productive hours first, and as more

hours are worked, these hours are increasingly less productive. So for each additional hour of leisure forgone (each additional hour of labour), real GDP increases but by successively smaller amounts.

The **aggregate production function** is the relationship that tells us how real GDP changes as the quantity of labour changes when all other influences on production remain the same. Figure 6.6 shows this relationship—the curve labelled *PF*. An increase in the quantity of labour (and a corresponding decrease in leisure hours) brings a movement along the production function and an increase in real GDP.

Aggregate Labour Market In macroeconomics, we pretend that there is one large labour market that determines the quantity of labour employed and the quantity of real GDP produced. To see how this aggregate labour market works, we study the demand for labour, the supply of labour, and labour market equilibrium.

The Demand for Labour The *demand for labour* is the relationship between the quantity of labour demanded and the real wage rate. The quantity of labour demanded is the number of labour hours hired by all the firms in the economy during a given

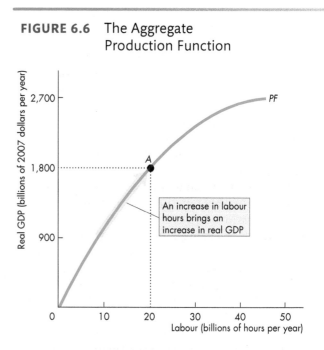

FIGURE 6.6 The Aggregate Production Function

At point *A* on the aggregate production function *PF*, 20 billion hours of labour produce $1,800 billion of real GDP.

MyLab Economics Animation

period. This quantity depends on the price of labour, which is the real wage rate.

The **real wage rate** is the money wage rate divided by the price level. The real wage rate is the quantity of goods and services that an hour of labour earns. It contrasts with the money wage rate, which is the number of dollars that an hour of labour earns.

The *real* wage rate influences the quantity of labour demanded because what matters to firms is not the number of dollars they pay (money wage rate) but how much output they must sell to earn those dollars.

The quantity of labour demanded *increases* as the real wage rate *decreases*—the demand for labour curve slopes downward. Why? The answer lies in the shape of the production function.

You've seen that along the production function, each additional hour of labour increases real GDP by successively smaller amounts. This tendency has a name: the *law of diminishing returns*. Because of diminishing returns, firms will hire more labour only if the real wage rate falls to match the fall in the extra output produced by that labour.

The Supply of Labour The *supply of labour* is the relationship between the quantity of labour supplied and the real wage rate. The quantity of labour supplied is the number of labour hours that all the households in the economy plan to work during a given period. This quantity depends on the real wage rate.

The *real* wage rate influences the quantity of labour supplied because what matters to households is not the number of dollars they earn (money wage rate) but what they can buy with those dollars.

The quantity of labour supplied *increases* as the real wage rate *increases*—the supply of labour curve slopes upward. At a higher real wage rate, more people choose to work and more people choose to work longer hours if they can earn more per hour.

Labour Market Equilibrium The price of labour is the real wage rate. The forces of supply and demand operate in labour markets just as they do in the markets for goods and services to eliminate a shortage or a surplus. But a shortage or a surplus of labour brings only a gradual change in the real wage rate. If there is a shortage of labour, the real wage rate rises to eliminate it; and if there is a surplus of labour, the real wage rate eventually falls to eliminate it. When there is neither a shortage nor a surplus, the labour market is in equilibrium—a full-employment equilibrium.

FIGURE 6.7 Labour Market Equilibrium

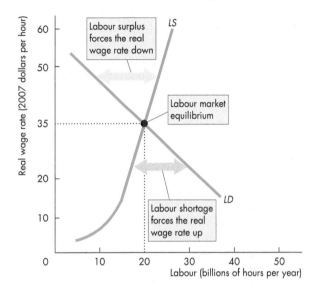

Labour market equilibrium occurs when the quantity of labour demanded equals the quantity of labour supplied. The equilibrium real wage rate is $35 an hour, and equilibrium employment is 20 billion hours per year.

At a wage rate above $35 an hour, there is a surplus of labour and the real wage rate falls to eliminate the surplus. At a wage rate below $35 an hour, there is a shortage of labour and the real wage rate rises to eliminate the shortage.

————— MyLab Economics Animation —————

Figure 6.7 illustrates labour market equilibrium. The demand for labour curve is *LD* and the supply of labour curve is *LS*. This labour market is in equilibrium at a real wage rate of $35 an hour and 20 billion hours a year are employed.

If the real wage rate exceeds $35 an hour, the quantity of labour supplied exceeds the quantity demanded and there is a surplus of labour. When there is a surplus of labour, the real wage rate falls toward the equilibrium real wage rate where the surplus is eliminated.

If the real wage rate is less than $35 an hour, the quantity of labour demanded exceeds the quantity supplied and there is a shortage of labour. When there is a shortage of labour, the real wage rate rises toward the equilibrium real wage rate where the shortage is eliminated.

If the real wage rate is $35 an hour, the quantity of labour demanded equals the quantity supplied and there is neither a shortage nor a surplus of labour. In this situation, there is no pressure in either direction on the real wage rate. So the real wage rate remains constant and the market is in equilibrium. At this equilibrium real wage rate and level of employment, the economy is at *full employment*.

Potential GDP   You've seen that the production function tells us the quantity of real GDP that a given amount of labour can produce—see Fig. 6.6. The quantity of real GDP produced increases as the quantity of labour increases. At the equilibrium quantity of labour, the economy is at full employment. The quantity of real GDP when the economy is at full employment is potential GDP, so the full-employment quantity of labour produces potential GDP.

Figure 6.8 illustrates the determination of potential GDP. Part (a) shows labour market equilibrium. At the equilibrium real wage rate, equilibrium employment is 20 billion hours. Part (b) shows the production function. With 20 billion hours of labour, the economy can produce a real GDP of $1,800 billion. This amount is potential GDP.

What Makes Potential GDP Grow?

We can divide all the forces that make potential GDP grow into two categories:

■ Growth of the supply of labour
■ Growth of labour productivity

Growth of the Supply of Labour   When the supply of labour grows, the supply of labour curve shifts rightward. The quantity of labour at a given real wage rate increases.

The quantity of labour is the number of workers employed multiplied by average hours per worker. The number employed equals the employment-to-population ratio multiplied by the working-age population, divided by 100 (Chapter 5, p. 115). So the quantity of labour changes as a result of changes in:

1. Average hours per worker
2. The employment-to-population ratio
3. The working-age population

Average hours per worker have decreased as the workweek has become shorter, and the employment-to-population ratio has increased as more women have entered the labour force. The combined effect of

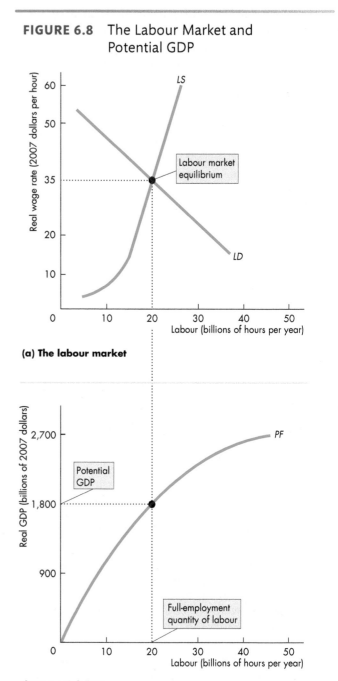

FIGURE 6.8   The Labour Market and Potential GDP

(a) The labour market

(b) Potential GDP

The economy is at full employment when the quantity of labour demanded equals the quantity of labour supplied, in part (a). The real wage rate is $35 an hour, and employment is 20 billion hours a year. Part (b) shows potential GDP. It is the quantity of real GDP determined by the production function at the full-employment quantity of labour.

——— MyLab Economics Animation and Draw Graph ———

these two factors has kept the average hours per working-age person (approximately) constant.

Growth in the supply of labour has come from growth in the working-age population. In the long run, the working-age population grows at the same rate as the total population.

The Effects of Population Growth Population growth brings growth in the supply of labour, but it does not change the demand for labour or the production function. The economy can produce more output by using more labour, but there is no change in the quantity of real GDP that a given quantity of labour can produce.

With an increase in the supply of labour and no change in the demand for labour, the real wage rate falls and the equilibrium quantity of labour increases. The increased quantity of labour produces more output and potential GDP increases.

Illustrating the Effects of Population Growth Figure 6.9 illustrates the effects of an increase in the population. In Fig. 6.9(a), the demand for labour curve is LD and initially the supply of labour curve is LS_0. The equilibrium real wage rate is $35 an hour and the quantity of labour is 20 billion hours a year. In Fig. 6.9(b), the production function (PF) shows that with 20 billion hours of labour employed, potential GDP is $1,800 billion at point A.

An increase in the population increases the supply of labour and the supply of labour curve shifts rightward to LS_1. At a real wage rate of $35 an hour, there is now a surplus of labour, so the real wage rate falls. In this example, the real wage rate will fall until it reaches $25 an hour. At $25 an hour, the quantity of labour demanded equals the quantity of labour supplied. The equilibrium quantity of labour increases to 30 billion hours a year.

Figure 6.9(b) shows the effect on real GDP. As the equilibrium quantity of labour increases from 20 billion to 30 billion hours, potential GDP increases along the production function from $1,800 billion to $2,250 billion at point B.

So an increase in the population increases the full-employment quantity of labour and potential GDP and lowers the real wage rate. But the population increase *decreases* potential GDP per hour of labour. Initially, it was $90 ($1,800 billion divided by 20 billion). With the population increase, potential GDP per hour of labour is $75 ($2,250 billion divided by 30 billion). Diminishing returns are the source of the decrease in potential GDP per hour of labour.

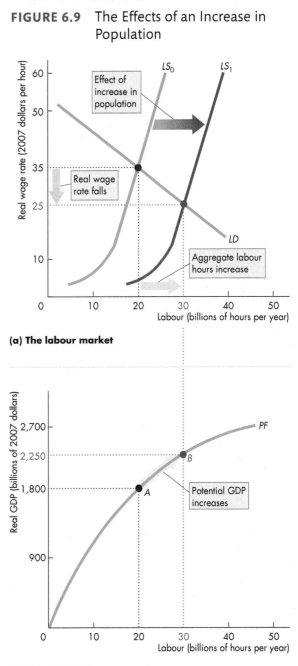

FIGURE 6.9 The Effects of an Increase in Population

(a) The labour market

(b) Potential GDP

An increase in the population increases the supply of labour. In part (a), the supply of labour curve shifts rightward. The real wage rate falls and aggregate labour hours increase. In part (b), the increase in aggregate labour hours brings an increase in potential GDP. But diminishing returns bring a decrease in potential GDP per hour of labour.

MyLab Economics Animation

Growth of Labour Productivity **Labour productivity** is the quantity of real GDP produced by an hour of labour. It is calculated by dividing real GDP by aggregate labour hours. For example, if real GDP is $1,800 billion and aggregate hours are 20 billion, labour productivity is $90 per hour.

When labour productivity grows, real GDP per person grows and brings a rising standard of living. Let's see how an increase in labour productivity changes potential GDP.

Effects of an Increase in Labour Productivity If labour productivity increases, production possibilities expand. The quantity of real GDP that any given quantity of labour can produce increases. If labour is more productive, firms are willing to pay more for a given number of hours of labour so the demand for labour also increases.

With an increase in the demand for labour and *no change in the supply of labour*, the real wage rate rises and the quantity of labour supplied increases. The equilibrium quantity of labour also increases.

So an increase in labour productivity increases potential GDP for two reasons: Labour is more productive and more labour is employed.

Illustrating the Effects of an Increase in Labour Productivity Figure 6.10 illustrates the effects of an increase in labour productivity.

In part (a), the production function initially is PF_0. With 20 billion hours of labour employed, potential GDP is $1,800 billion at point A.

In part (b), the demand for labour curve is LD_0 and the supply of labour curve is LS. The real wage rate is $35 an hour, and the equilibrium quantity of labour is 20 billion hours a year.

Now labour productivity increases. In Fig. 6.10(a), the increase in labour productivity shifts the production function upward to PF_1. At each quantity of labour, more real GDP can be produced. For example, at 20 billion hours, the economy can now produce $2,500 billion of real GDP at point B.

In Fig. 6.10(b), the increase in labour productivity increases the demand for labour and the demand for labour curve shifts rightward to LD_1. At the initial real wage rate of $35 an hour, there is now a shortage of labour. The real wage rate rises. In this example, the real wage rate will rise until it reaches $45 an hour. At $45 an hour, the quantity of labour demanded equals the quantity of labour supplied. The equilibrium quantity of labour is 22.5 billion hours a year.

FIGURE 6.10 The Effects of an Increase in Labour Productivity

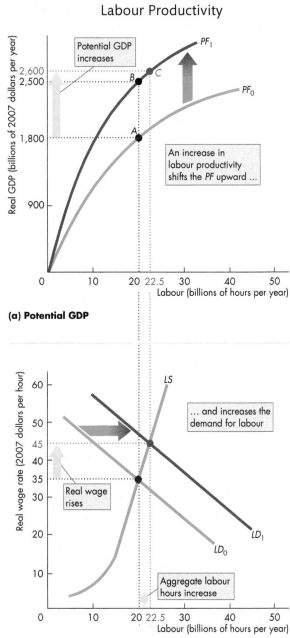

(a) Potential GDP

(b) The labour market

An increase in labour productivity shifts the production function upward from PF_0 to PF_1 in part (a) and shifts the demand for labour curve rightward from LD_0 to LD_1 in part (b). The real wage rate rises to $45 an hour, and aggregate labour hours increase from 20 billion to 22.5 billion. Potential GDP increases from $1,800 billion to $2,600 billion.

MyLab Economics Animation and Draw Graph

Figure 6.10(a) shows the effects of the increase in labour productivity on potential GDP. There are two effects. At the initial quantity of labour, real GDP increases to point *B* on the new production function. But as the equilibrium quantity of labour increases from 20 billion to 22.5 billion hours, potential GDP increases to $2,600 billion at point *C*.

Potential GDP per hour of labour also increases. Initially, it was $90 ($1,800 billion divided by 20 billion). With the increase in labour productivity, potential GDP per hour of labour increased to $115.56 ($2,600 billion divided by 22.5 billion).

The increase in aggregate labour hours that you have just seen is a consequence of an increase in labour productivity. This increase in aggregate labour hours and labour productivity is an example of the interaction effects that economists seek to identify in their search for the ultimate *causes* of economic growth. In the case that we've just studied, aggregate labour hours increase but that increase is a *consequence*, not a cause, of the growth of potential GDP. The source of the increase in potential GDP is an increase in labour productivity.

Labour productivity is the key to increasing output per hour of labour and raising living standards. But what brings an increase in labour productivity? The next section answers this question.

REVIEW QUIZ

1 What is the aggregate production function?

2 What determines the demand for labour, the supply of labour, and labour market equilibrium?

3 What determines potential GDP?

4 What are the two broad sources of potential GDP growth?

5 What are the effects of an increase in the population on potential GDP, the quantity of labour, the real wage rate, and potential GDP per hour of labour?

6 What are the effects of an increase in labour productivity on potential GDP, the quantity of labour, the real wage rate, and potential GDP per hour of labour?

Work these questions in Study Plan 6.3 and get instant feedback.   MyLab Economics

Why Labour Productivity Grows

You've seen that labour productivity growth makes potential GDP grow; and you've seen that labour productivity growth is essential if real GDP per person and the standard of living are to grow. But why does labour productivity grow? What are the preconditions that make labour productivity growth possible and what are the forces that make it grow? Why does labour productivity grow faster at some times and in some places than others?

Preconditions for Labour Productivity Growth

The fundamental precondition for labour productivity growth is the *incentive* system created by firms, markets, property rights, and money. These four social institutions are the same as those described in Chapter 2 (see pp. 48–49) that enable people to gain by specializing and trading.

It was the presence of secure property rights in Britain in the middle 1700s that got the Industrial Revolution going (see *Economics in Action* on p. 148). And it is their absence in some parts of Africa today that is keeping labour productivity stagnant.

With the preconditions for labour productivity growth in place, three things influence its pace:

- Physical capital growth
- Human capital growth
- Technological advances

Physical Capital Growth

As the amount of capital per worker increases, labour productivity also increases. Production processes that use hand tools can create beautiful objects, but production methods that use large amounts of capital per worker are much more productive. The accumulation of capital on farms, in textile factories, in iron foundries and steel mills, in coal mines, on building sites, in chemical plants, in auto plants, in banks and insurance companies, and in shopping malls has added incredibly to the labour productivity of our economy. The next time you see a movie that is set in the Old West or colonial times, look carefully at the small amount of capital around. Try to imagine how productive you would be in such circumstances compared with your productivity today.

ECONOMICS IN ACTION

Intellectual Property Rights Propel Growth

In 1760, when what is now Canada and the United States of America were developing agricultural economies, England was on the cusp of an economic revolution, the *Industrial Revolution*.

For 70 dazzling years, technological advances in the use of steam power; the manufacture of cotton, wool, iron, and steel; and in transportation, accompanied by massive capital investment associated with these technologies, transformed the economy of England. Incomes rose and brought an explosion in an increasingly urbanized population.

By 1825, advances in steam technology had reached a level of sophistication that enabled Robert Stevenson to build the world's first steam-powered rail engine (the Rocket pictured here in the Science Museum, London) and the birth of the world's first railroad.

Why did the Industrial Revolution happen? Why did it start in 1760? And why in England?

Economic historians say that intellectual property rights—England's patent system—provides the answer.

England's patent system began with the Statute of Monopolies of 1624, which gave inventors a monopoly to use their idea for a term of 14 years. For about 100 years, the system was used to reward friends of

the royal court rather than true inventors. But from around 1720 onward, the system started to work well. To be granted a 14-year monopoly, an inventor only had to pay the required £100 fee (about $22,000 in today's money) and register his or her invention. The inventor was not required to describe the invention in too much detail, so registering and getting a patent didn't mean sharing the invention with competitors.

This patent system, which is essentially the same as today's, aligned the self-interest of entrepreneurial inventors with the social interest and unleashed a flood of inventions, the most transformative of which was steam power and, by 1825, the steam locomotive.

Human Capital Growth

Human capital—the accumulated skill and knowledge of human beings—is the fundamental source of labour productivity growth. Human capital grows when a new discovery is made and it grows as more and more people learn how to use past discoveries.

The development of one of the most basic human skills—writing—was the source of some of the earliest major gains in productivity. The ability to keep written records made it possible to reap ever-larger gains from specialization and trade. Imagine how hard it would be to do any kind of business if all the accounts, invoices, and agreements existed only in people's memories.

Later, the development of mathematics laid the foundation for the eventual extension of knowledge about physical forces and chemical and biological processes. This base of scientific knowledge was the foundation for the technological advances of the Industrial Revolution and of today's Information Revolution.

But a lot of human capital that is extremely productive is much more humble. It takes the form

of millions of individuals learning and becoming remarkably more productive by repetitively doing simple production tasks. One much-studied example of this type of human capital growth occurred in World War II. With no change in physical capital, thousands of workers and managers in U.S. shipyards learned from experience and accumulated human capital that more than doubled their productivity in less than two years.

Technological Advances

The accumulation of physical capital and human capital has made large contributions to labour productivity growth. But technologial change—the discovery and the application of new technologies—has made an even greater contribution.

Labour is many times more productive today than it was 100 years ago but not because we have more steam engines and more horse-drawn carriages per person. Rather, it is because we have transportation equipment that uses technologies that were unknown

FIGURE 6.11   The Sources of Economic Growth

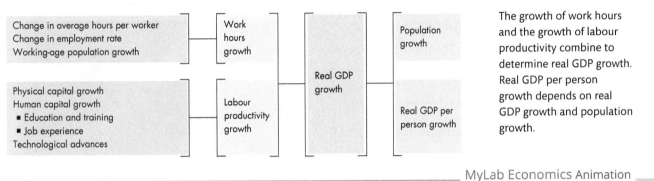

The growth of work hours and the growth of labour productivity combine to determine real GDP growth. Real GDP per person growth depends on real GDP growth and population growth.

MyLab Economics Animation

ECONOMICS IN ACTION

The Source of Canada's Growth Slowdown

You saw in Fig. 6.4 that real GDP per person grew at around 3 percent a year during the 1960s and then slowed. What was the source of the growth slowdown?

Figure 6.11 above identifies two major sources of real GDP growth, work hours and labour productivity, and the figure below shows how the sources changed over the past almost six decades.

Labour productivity growth was most rapid during the 1960s and the dot.com revolution of the 1990s. The growth in work hours was greatest during the 1970s and 1980s, two decades of growth in the employment rate: first as the baby-boomer generation entered the labour force and second, and most persistently, as the female labour force participation rate increased. During the 1990s, work hours contributed nothing to the growth of real GDP and during the 2000s, the growth rate of labour productivity had slowed to barely 1 percent a year.

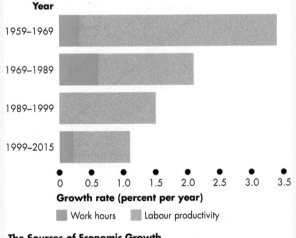

The Sources of Economic Growth

100 years ago and that are more productive than the old technologies were.

Technological advance arises from formal research and development programs and from informal trial and error, and it involves discovering new ways of getting more out of our resources.

To reap the benefits of technological change, capital must increase. Some of the most powerful and far-reaching fundamental technologies are embodied in human capital—for example, language, writing, and mathematics. But most technologies are embodied in physical capital. For example, to reap the benefits of the internal combustion engine, millions of horse-drawn carriages had to be replaced with automobiles; and to reap the benefits of digital music, millions of Discmans had to be replaced by iPods.

Figure 6.11 summarizes the sources of labour productivity growth and, more broadly, of real GDP growth. The figure also emphasizes that for real GDP per person to grow, real GDP must grow faster than the population.

Economics in the News on p. 150 provides an example of today's labour productivity growth arising from the spread of robot technologies.

REVIEW QUIZ

1 What are the preconditions for labour productivity growth?
2 Describe the sources of economic growth and identify the source of Canada's growth slowdown.
3 Explain the influences on the pace of labour productivity growth.

Work these questions in Study Plan 6.4 and get instant feedback.   MyLab Economics

◆ ECONOMICS IN THE NEWS

Robots Raise Labour Productivity

Thousands of Robots Improve Human Efficiency at an Amazon Facility

Thousands of robots move pallets of goods at Amazon's distribution centres and perform other tasks that make workers more productive.

Source: bizjournals.com, July 24, 2017

SOME FACTS

"The Robot Report" (www.therobotreport.com) says the auto industry has been the main customer for industrial robots but the scene is changing. Robot manufacturers are creating equipment tailored to the requirements of firms like Amazon and producers of a wide range of items, just a few of which are metals, food and drink, glass, pharmaceuticals, medical devices, and solar panels.

Around 600 firms worldwide specialize in the design and production of robots and hundreds of start-up companies enter this industry each year. More than 2,000 firms have some connection with industrial robots.

THE QUESTIONS

- How will the adoption of industrial robots change employment, the real wage rate, and potential GDP?
- Do robots kill jobs and create unemployment?

THE ANSWERS

- Robots make workers more productive. One person working with a robot can produce as much as hundreds of workers with non-robot technology.
- Robots replace some workers but create a demand for other workers to design, produce, install, and maintain robots.
- In aggregate, robots increase the productivity of labour. The production function shifts upward and the demand for labour curve shifts rightward.
- The equilibrium real wage rate rises, employment increases, and potential GDP increases.
- As robot production technologies spread, many jobs will disappear, but many new jobs will be created.
- Some displaced workers will take new jobs with lower wages. Others will take jobs as skilled robot technicians and producers with higher wages. Average wages will rise.

A robot moves goods around a warehouse.

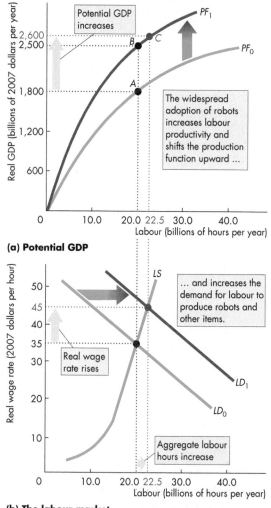

(a) Potential GDP

(b) The labour market

The Effects of Robots on Employment and GDP

◆ Is Economic Growth Sustainable? Theories, Evidence, and Policies

You've seen how population growth and labour productivity growth make potential GDP grow. You've also seen that the growth of physical capital and human capital and technological advances make labour productivity grow. But what *causes* economic growth? Why do growth rates vary? How do population growth, capital accumulation, and technoloical change interact to determine the economic growth rate? What can we say about the future of economic growth? Is growth sustainable? Will the rich economies and the economies of the developing world keep growing, or will growth end to be followed by stagnation or even a falling standard of living?

Economists have wrestled with these questions for the past 250 years and made progress in answering them. We're now going to look at the evolution of ideas about the sustainability of economic growth and the policies that might achieve faster growth.

We start by studying the three main theories about the process of economic growth:

- Classical growth theory
- Neoclassical growth theory
- New growth theory

Classical Growth Theory

Classical growth theory is the view that the growth of real GDP per person is temporary and that when it rises above the subsistence level, a population explosion eventually brings it back to the subsistence level. Adam Smith, Thomas Robert Malthus, and David Ricardo—the leading economists of the late eighteenth and early nineteenth centuries—proposed this theory, but the view is most closely associated with the name of Malthus and is sometimes called the *Malthusian theory.* Charles Darwin's ideas about evolution by natural selection were inspired by the insights of Malthus.

Modern-Day Malthusians Many people today are Malthusians. They say that if today's global population of 7.2 billion explodes to 11 billion by 2050 and perhaps 35 billion by 2300, we will run out of resources, real GDP per person will decline, and we will return to a primitive standard of living. We must, say Malthusians, contain population growth.

Modern-day Malthusians also point to global warming and climate change as reasons to believe that, eventually, real GDP per person will decrease.

Neoclassical Growth Theory

Neoclassical growth theory is the proposition that real GDP per person grows because technological change induces saving and investment that make capital per hour of labour grow. Growth ends if technological change stops because of diminishing marginal returns to both labour and capital. Robert Solow of MIT suggested the most popular version of this growth theory in the 1950s.

Neoclassical growth theory's big break with its classical predecessor is its view about population growth.

Neoclassical Theory of Population Growth The population explosion of eighteenth-century Europe that created the classical theory of population growth eventually ended. The birth rate fell, and while the population continued to increase, its rate of increase moderated.

The key economic influence that slows the population growth rate is the opportunity cost of a woman's time. As women's wage rates increase and their job opportunities expand, the opportunity cost of having children increases. Faced with a higher opportunity cost, families choose to have fewer children and the birth rate falls.

Technological advances that bring higher incomes also bring advances in healthcare that extend lives. So as incomes increase, both the birth rate and the death rate decrease. These opposing forces offset each other and result in a slowly rising population.

This modern view of population growth and the historical trends that support it contradict the views of the classical economists. They also call into question the modern doomsday view that the planet will be swamped with more people than it can support.

Technological Change and Diminishing Returns In neoclassical growth theory, the pace of technological change influences the economic growth rate but economic growth does not influence the pace of technological change. It is assumed that technological change results from chance. When we're lucky, we have rapid technological change, and when bad luck strikes, the pace of technological advance slows.

To understand neoclassical growth theory, imagine the world of the mid-1950s, when Robert Solow is explaining his idea. Income per person is around $12,000 a year in today's money. The population is growing at about 1 percent a year. Saving and investment are about 20 percent of GDP, enough to keep the quantity of capital per hour of labour constant. Income per person is growing but not very fast.

Then technology begins to advance at a more rapid pace across a range of activities. The transistor revolutionizes an emerging electronics industry. New plastics revolutionize the manufacture of household appliances. The interstate highway system revolutionizes road transportation. Jet airliners start to replace piston-engine airplanes and speed air transportation.

These technological advances bring new profit opportunities. Businesses expand, and new businesses are created to exploit the newly available profitable technologies. Investment and saving increase. The economy enjoys new levels of prosperity and growth. But will the prosperity last? And will the growth last? Neoclassical growth theory says that the *prosperity* will last but the *growth* will not last unless technology keeps advancing.

According to neoclassical growth theory, the prosperity will persist because there is no classical population growth to induce the wage rate to fall. So the gains in income per person are permanent.

But growth will eventually stop if technology stops advancing because of diminishing marginal returns to capital. The high profit rates that result from technological change bring increased saving and capital accumulation. But as more capital is accumulated, more and more projects are undertaken that have lower rates of return—diminishing marginal returns. As the return on capital falls, the incentive to keep investing weakens. With weaker incentives to save and invest, saving decreases and the rate of capital accumulation slows. Eventually, the pace at which capital is accumulated slows so that capital accumulation is only keeping up with population growth. Capital per worker remains constant.

A Problem with Neoclassical Growth Theory All economies have access to the same technologies, and capital is free to roam the globe, seeking the highest available real interest rate. Capital will flow until rates of return are equal, and rates of return will be equal when capital per hour of labour is equal across regions. Real GDP growth rates and income levels per person around the world will converge. Figure 6.5 on p. 140 shows that while there is some sign of convergence among the rich countries in part (a), convergence is slow, and part (b) shows that it does not appear to be imminent for all countries. New growth theory overcomes this shortcoming of neoclassical growth theory. It also explains what determines the pace of technological change.

New Growth Theory

New growth theory holds that real GDP per person grows because of the choices people make in the pursuit of profit and that growth will persist indefinitely. Paul Romer of Stanford University developed this theory during the 1980s, based on ideas of Joseph Schumpeter during the 1930s and 1940s.

According to the new growth theory, the pace at which new discoveries are made—and at which technology advances—is not determined by chance. It depends on how many people are looking for a new technology and how intensively they are looking. The search for new technologies is driven by incentives.

Profit is the spur to technological change. The forces of competition squeeze profits, so to increase profit, people constantly seek either lower-cost methods of production or new and better products for which people are willing to pay a higher price. Inventors can maintain a profit for several years by taking out a patent or a copyright, but eventually, a new discovery is copied, and profits disappear. So more research and development is undertaken in the hope of creating a new burst of profitable investment and growth.

Two facts about discoveries and technological knowledge play a key role in the new growth theory: Discoveries are (at least eventually) a public capital good; and knowledge is capital that is not subject to diminishing marginal returns.

Economists call a good a *public good* when no one can be excluded from using it and when one person's use does not prevent others from using it. National defence is the classic example of a public good. The programming language used to write apps for the iPhone is another.

Because knowledge is a public good, as the benefits of a new discovery spread, free resources become available. Nothing is given up when they are used: They have a zero opportunity cost. When a student in Waterloo writes a new iPhone app, his use of the programming language doesn't prevent another student in Calgary from using it.

Knowledge is even more special because it is *not* subject to diminishing returns. But increasing the stock of knowledge makes both labour and machines more productive. Knowledge capital does not bring diminishing returns. Biotech knowledge illustrates this idea well. Biologists have spent a lot of time developing DNA sequencing technology. As more has been discovered, the productivity of this knowledge capital has relentlessly increased. In 1990, it cost about $50 to sequence one DNA base pair. That cost had fallen to $1 by 2000 and to 1/10,000th of a penny by 2010.

The implication of this simple and appealing observation is astonishing. Unlike the other two theories, new growth theory has no growth-stopping mechanism. As physical capital accumulates, the return to capital—the real interest rate—falls. But the incentive to innovate and earn a higher profit becomes stronger. So innovation occurs, capital becomes more productive, the demand for capital increases, and the real interest rate rises again.

Labour productivity grows indefinitely as people discover new technologies that yield a higher real interest rate. The growth rate depends only on people's incentives and ability to innovate.

A Perpetual Motion Economy New growth theory sees the economy as a perpetual motion machine, which Fig. 6.12 illustrates.

No matter how rich we become, our wants exceed our ability to satisfy them. We always want a higher standard of living. In the pursuit of a higher standard of living, human societies have developed incentive systems—markets, property rights, and money—that enable people to profit from innovation. Innovation leads to the development of new and better techniques of production and new and better products. To take advantage of new techniques and to produce new products, new firms start up and old firms go out of business—firms are born and die. As old firms die and new firms are born, some jobs are destroyed and others are created. The new jobs created are better than the old ones and they pay higher real wage rates. Also, with higher wage rates and more productive techniques, leisure increases. New and better jobs and new and better products lead to more consumption goods and services and, combined with increased leisure, bring a higher standard of living.

But our insatiable wants are still there, so the process continues: Wants and incentives create innovation, new and better products, and a yet higher standard of living.

FIGURE 6.12   A Perpetual Motion Machine

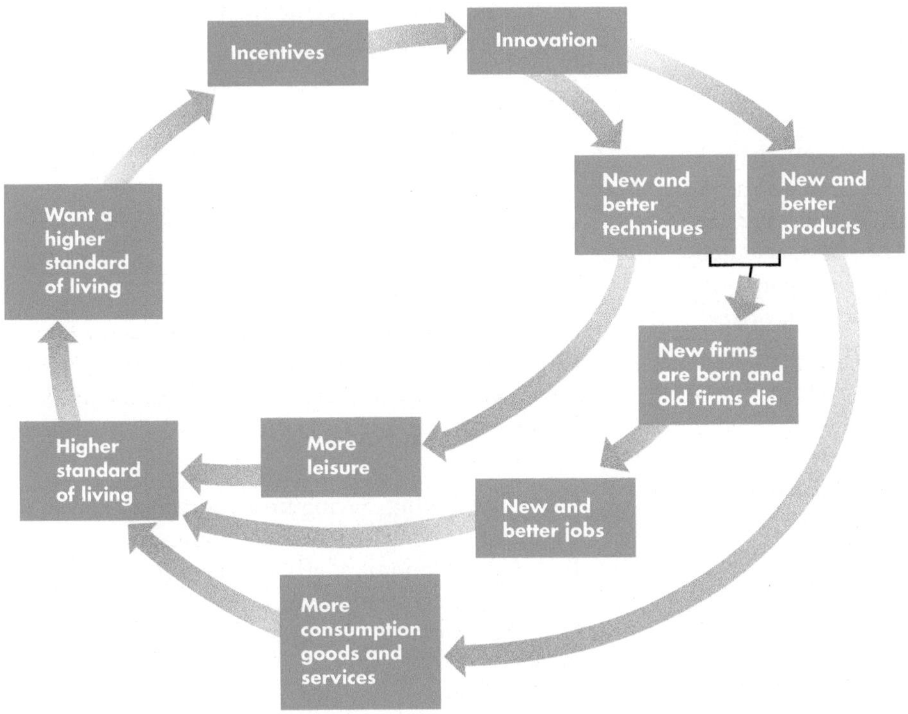

People want a higher standard of living and are spurred by profit incentives to make the innovations that lead to new and better techniques and new and better products.

These new and better techniques and products, in turn, lead to the birth of new firms and the death of some old firms, new and better jobs, and more leisure and more consumption goods and services.

The result is a higher standard of living, but people want a still higher standard of living, and the growth process continues.

Source: Based on a similar figure in *These Are the Good Old Days: A Report on U.S. Living Standards*, Federal Reserve Bank of Dallas 1993 Annual Report.

New Growth Theory Versus Malthusian Theory

The contrast between the Malthusian theory and new growth theory couldn't be more sharp. Malthusians see the end of prosperity as we know it today and new growth theorists see unending plenty. The contrast becomes clearest by thinking about the differing views about population growth.

To a Malthusian, population growth is part of the problem. To a new growth theorist, population growth is part of the solution. People are the ultimate economic resource. A larger population brings forth more wants, but it also brings a greater amount of scientific discovery and technological advance. So rather than being the source of falling real GDP per person, population growth generates faster labour productivity growth and rising real GDP per person. Resources are limited, but the human imagination and ability to increase productivity are unlimited.

Sorting Out the Theories

Which theory is correct? None of them tells us the whole story, but each teaches us something of value.

Classical growth theory reminds us that our physical resources are limited and that without advances in technology, we must eventually hit diminishing returns.

Neoclassical growth theory reaches the same conclusion but not because of a population explosion. Instead, it emphasizes diminishing returns to capital and reminds us that we cannot keep growth going just by accumulating physical capital. We must also advance technology and accumulate human capital. We must become more creative in our use of scarce resources.

New growth theory emphasizes the capacity of human resources to innovate at a pace that offsets diminishing returns. New growth theory fits the facts of today's world more closely than do either of the other two theories.

The Empirical Evidence on the Causes of Economic Growth

Economics makes progress by the interplay between theory and empirical evidence. A theory makes predictions about what we will observe if the theory is correct. Empirical evidence, the data generated by history and the natural experiments that it performs, provide the data for testing the theory.

Economists have done an enormous amount of research confronting theories of growth with the empirical evidence. The way in which this research has been conducted has changed over the years.

In 1776, when Adam Smith wrote about "the nature and causes of the Wealth of Nations" in his celebrated book, empirical evidence took the form of carefully selected facts described in words and stories. Today, large databases, sophisticated statistical methods, and fast computers provide numerical measurements of the causes of economic growth.

Economists have looked at the growth rate data for more than 100 countries for the period since 1960 and explored the correlations between the growth rate and more than 60 possible influences on it. The conclusion of this data crunching is that most of these possible influences have variable and unpredictable effects, but a few of them have strong and clear effects. Table 6.1 summarizes these more robust influences. They are arranged in order of difficulty (or in the case of region, impossibility) of changing. Political and economic systems are hard to change, but market distortions, investment, and openness to international trade are features of a nation's economy that can be influenced by policy.

Let's now look at growth policies.

Policies for Achieving Faster Growth

Growth theory supported by empirical evidence tells us that to achieve faster economic growth, we must increase the growth rate of physical capital, the pace of technological advance, or the growth rate of human capital and openness to international trade.

The main suggestions for achieving these objectives are:

- Stimulate saving
- Stimulate research and development
- Improve the quality of education
- Provide international aid to developing nations
- Encourage international trade

Stimulate Saving Saving finances investment, so stimulating saving increases economic growth. The East Asian economies have the highest growth rates and the highest saving rates. Some African economies have the lowest growth rates and the lowest saving rates.

Tax incentives can increase saving. Registered Retirement Savings Plans (RRSPs) are a tax incentive to save. Economists claim that a tax on consumption rather than income provides the best saving incentive.

TABLE 6.1 The Influences on Economic Growth

Influence	Good for Economic Growth	Bad for Economic Growth
Region	▪ Far from equator	▪ Sub-Saharan Africa
Politics	▪ Rule of law	▪ Revolutions
	▪ Civil liberties	▪ Military coups
		▪ Wars
Economic system	▪ Capitalist	
Market distortions		▪ Exchange rate distortions
		▪ Price controls and black markets
Investment	▪ Human capital	
	▪ Physical capital	
International trade	▪ Open to trade	

Source of data: Xavier Sala-i-Martin, "I Just Ran Two Million Regressions," *The American Economic Review*, Vol. 87, No. 2 (May 1997), pp. 178–183.

Stimulate Research and Development Everyone can use the fruits of *basic* research and development efforts. For example, all biotechnology firms can use advances in gene-splicing technology. Because basic inventions can be copied, the inventor's profit is limited and the market allocates too few resources to this activity. Governments can direct public funds toward financing basic research, but this solution is not foolproof. It requires a mechanism for allocating the public funds to their highest-valued use.

Improve the Quality of Education The free market produces too little education because it brings benefits beyond those valued by the people who receive the education. By funding basic education and by ensuring high standards in basic skills such as language, mathematics, and science, governments can contribute to a nation's growth potential. Education can also be stimulated and improved by using tax incentives to encourage improved private provision.

Provide International Aid to Developing Nations It seems obvious that if rich countries give financial aid to developing countries, investment and growth will increase in the recipient countries. Unfortunately, the obvious does not routinely happen. A large amount of data-driven research on the effects of aid on growth has turned up a zero and even negative effect. Aid often gets diverted and spent on consumption.

Encourage International Trade Trade, not aid, stimulates economic growth. It works by extracting the available gains from specialization and trade. The fastest-growing nations are those most open to trade. If the rich nations truly want to aid economic development, they will lower their trade barriers against developing nations, especially in farm products. The World Trade Organization's efforts to achieve more open trade are being resisted by the richer nations.

REVIEW QUIZ

1 What is the key idea of classical growth theory that leads to the dismal outcome?

2 What, according to neoclassical growth theory, is the fundamental cause of economic growth?

3 What is the key proposition of new growth theory that makes economic growth persist?

Work these questions in Study Plan 6.5 and get instant feedback. MyLab Economics

◆ To complete your study of economic growth, take a look at *Economics in the News* on pp. 156–157, which compares the growth performance of Canada and the United States.

North American Economic Growth

Canada's Economic Growth Triples U.S.'s

The first quarter of 2017 was a strong one for the Canadian economy, with GDP growing at an annualized rate of 3.7 percent, according to data from Statistics Canada. In comparison, the U.S. economy grew at only 1.2 percent.

According to TD Economics, this marks the fastest pace of expansion since 2011 and puts Canada at the top of the leaderboard among G7 countries when it comes to economic growth. TD Economics also noted that 2017 is expected to be the first year since 2014 that all major sectors of the economy have contributed positively to economic growth. Consumer spending, housing, and auto sales were strong drivers of first quarter growth.

BMO Financial Group chief economist Douglas Porter, quoted in *The Financial Post*, said that "even with some expected cooldown in the next few months, this still leaves the Canadian economy expanding at an underlying pace well above any other major economy at this point." Porter sees Canadian GDP outpacing U.S. GDP in 2017. "Quite the dramatic turnabout from the past two years," he said.

Beyond Canada, global growth is expected to continue at its current pace and, according to *The Huffington Post*, provided the United States doesn't enact protectionist trade policies, U.S. growth will be the fastest among the G7 in 2017.

Sources: Based on Daniel Tencer, "Canada's Economic Growth Triples U.S.'s," *Huffington Post*, May 31, 2017; *The Financial Post*, May 31, 2017, *The Daily*, Statistics Canada, May 31, 2017, TD Bank, Quarterly Economic Forecast, June 15, 2017.

ESSENCE OF THE STORY

- At an annual rate of 3.7 percent, Canada's GDP grew at triple the U.S. growth rate in the first quarter of 2017.

- Canada's real GDP growth was its fastest since 2011—during the recovery from recession.

- U.S. growth is predicted to be the fastest of the G7 countries in 2017.

- Increased U.S. protectionism could slow global growth.

MyLab Economics Economics in the News

ECONOMIC ANALYSIS

- Canada's real GDP growth rate was triple that of the United States in the first quarter of 2017.

- But a single quarter's growth of real GDP doesn't tell us about the pace of economic growth. It combines economic growth, business cycle expansion, and random events.

- To measure and compare economic growth rates, we need to look at a longer period.

- To compare U.S. and Canadian economic growth, we will look at the levels of real GDP in 2017 relative to their levels before the 2008–2009 recession.

- Figure 1 shows real GDP in Canada and the United States from 2006 to 2017, where each country is compared with its 2006 level.

- You can see that real GDP in Canada has grown more quickly than in the United States, but not much more quickly. Over the 11-year period, Canada's real GDP expanded by 19 percent and U.S. real GDP expanded by 16 percent.

- Why did real GDP grow faster in Canada? To answer this question, we need to look at the sources of growth set out in Fig. 6.11.

- The growth rate of real GDP equals labour supply growth plus labour productivity growth. And labour supply growth equals population growth plus the growth rate of work hours per person.

- Figure 2 shows the data on the sources of real GDP growth from 2006 to 2015, the most recent year for which the data are available. Over this 9-year period, Canada's real GDP expanded by 14 percent and U.S. real GDP expanded by 12 percent.

- The data in Fig. 2 show that Canada's growth rate of real GDP exceeded the U.S. growth rate because Canada's population growth rate exceeded that of the United States.

- The growth rate of real GDP per person was higher in the United States.

- The data in Fig. 2 show why: U.S. output per work hour—labour productivity—grew faster than Canada's.

- And the data also show that U.S. workers took some of the productivity gain in fewer work hours per person.

- Figure 3 illustrates how the production function is changing in the two economies. It is shifting upward at a more rapid pace in the United States than in Canada.

- The United States is outpacing Canada in labour productivity growth because it is adopting more productive technologies at a faster pace than Canada.

Sources of data: U.S. real GDP, Bureau of Economic Analysis; Canada real GDP, Statistics Canada; Productivity data, Center for the Study of Living Standards.

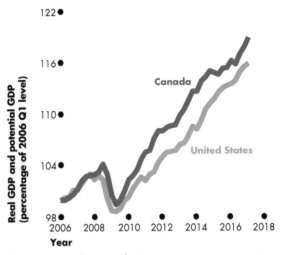

Figure 1 Canada Expands Faster

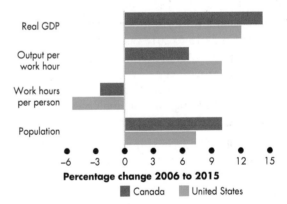

Figure 2 U.S. Productivity Grows Faster

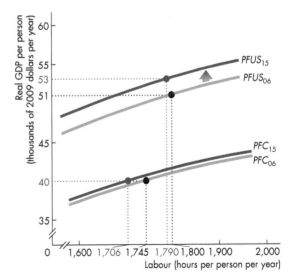

Figure 3 Labour Productivity Growth

157

WORKED PROBLEM

MyLab Economics Work this problem in Chapter 6 Study Plan.

The *World Economic Outlook* reports the following information:

- China's real GDP was 69.9 trillion yuan in 2015 and 74.6 trillion yuan in 2016.
- China's population was 1,375 million in 2015 and 1,383 million in 2016.

Questions

1. Calculate China's real GDP growth rate and its population growth rate during 2017.
2. Calculate the growth rate of China's standard of living during 2017.
3. If the growth rate of China's standard of living during 2017 is maintained, how many years will it take to double?

Solutions

1. The growth of a variable equals the change in the value from 2015 to 2016 calculated as a percentage of the value in 2015.

   China's growth rate of real GDP during 2016 equals (74.6 trillion yuan − 69.9 trillion yuan) divided by 69.9 trillion yuan, multiplied by 100. That is, China's real GDP growth rate equals:

   $$(4.7 \div 69.9) \times 100 = 6.7 \text{ percent.}$$

   China's population growth rate equals (1,383 million − 1,375 million) divided by 1,375 million, multiplied by 100. That is, China's population growth rate equals:

   $$(8 \div 1,375) \times 100 = 0.6 \text{ percent.}$$

Key Point: The growth rate of a variable equals the annual percentage change in the value of the variable.

2. Real GDP per person measures the standard of living.

   In 2015, real GDP per person was 69.9 trillion yuan divided by 1,375 million, which equals 50,836 yuan.

   In 2016, real GDP per person was 74.6 trillion yuan divided by 1,383 million, which equals 53,941 yuan.

   The growth rate of real GDP per person equals (53,941 yuan − 50,836 yuan) ÷ 50,836 yuan, multiplied by 100.

   The growth rate of real GDP per person equals (3,105 ÷ 50,836) × 100, which is 6.1 percent.

   So during 2016, China's standard of living increased by 6.1 percent.

   An alternative way of calculating the growth rate of the standard of living is to compare the growth rates of real GDP and the population.

   Notice that a higher real GDP growth rate increases the growth rate of real GDP per person, but a higher population growth rate lowers the growth rate of real GDP per person.

   So when real GDP grows by 6.1 percent and the population doesn't change, the standard of living grows by 6.1 percent.

   When the population grows by 0.6 percent and real GDP doesn't change, the standard of living falls by 0.6 percent.

   That is, the growth rate of China's standard of living during 2016 is approximately equal to the growth rate of real GDP minus the population growth rate, which equals 6.7 percent minus 0.6 percent, or 6.1 percent.

Key Point: The growth rate of the standard of living equals the growth rate of real GDP minus the growth rate of the population.

3. The number of years it will take for the standard of living to double its 2015 level is given by the Rule of 70.

   China's standard of living is growing at 6.1 percent a year. The Rule of 70 says that if this growth rate is sustained, China's standard of living will double in 70 years divided by 6.1, which equals 11.5 years.

   China's standard of living will be twice what it was in 2015 sometime during 2027.

Key Point: The time it takes for the standard of living to double equals 70 years divided by the sustained growth rate of the standard of living.

SUMMARY

Key Points

The Basics of Economic Growth (pp. 136–138)

- Economic growth is the sustained expansion of production possibilities and is measured as the annual percentage rate of change of real GDP.
- The Rule of 70 tells us the number of years in which real GDP doubles—70 divided by the annual percentage growth rate.

Working Problems 1 to 3 will give you a better understanding of the basics of economic growth.

Long-Term Growth Trends (pp. 139–141)

- Real GDP per person in Canada grows at an average rate of 2 percent a year. Growth was most rapid during the 1960s and the 1990s.
- The gap in real GDP per person between Canada and Central and South America has persisted. The gaps between Canada and Hong Kong, Korea, and China have narrowed. The gap between Canada and Africa has widened.

Working Problem 4 will give you a better understanding of long-term growth trends.

How Potential GDP Grows (pp. 142–147)

- The aggregate production function and equilibrium in the aggregate labour market determine potential GDP.
- Potential GDP grows if the labour supply grows or if labour productivity grows.

- Only labour productivity growth makes real GDP per person and the standard of living grow.

Working Problems 5 to 7 will give you a better understanding of how potential GDP grows.

Why Labour Productivity Grows (pp. 147–150)

- Labour productivity growth requires an incentive system created by firms, markets, property rights, and money.
- The sources of labour productivity growth are growth of physical capital and human capital and advances in technology.

Working Problem 8 will give you a better understanding of why labour productivity grows.

Is Economic Growth Sustainable? Theories, Evidence, and Policies (pp. 151–155)

- In classical theory, real GDP per person keeps returning to the subsistence level.
- In neoclassical growth theory, diminishing returns to capital limit economic growth.
- In new growth theory, economic growth persists indefinitely at a rate determined by decisions that lead to innovation and technological change.
- Policies for achieving faster growth include stimulating saving and research and development, encouraging international trade, and improving the quality of education.

Working Problem 9 will give you a better understanding of growth theories, evidence, and policies.

Key Terms

MyLab Economics Key Terms Quiz

STUDY PLAN PROBLEMS AND APPLICATIONS

MyLab Economics Work Problems 1 to 9 in Chapter 6 Study Plan and get instant feedback.

The Basics of Economic Growth (Study Plan 6.1)

1. Mexico's real GDP was 14,461 billion pesos in 2016 and 14,702 billion pesos in 2017. Mexico's population was 121 million in 2016 and 122 million in 2017. Calculate:

   a. The growth rate of real GDP

   b. The growth rate of real GDP per person

   c. The approximate number of years it takes for real GDP per person in Mexico to double if the 2017 growth rate of real GDP and the population growth rate are maintained

2. The IMF projects that China's real GDP per person will be 57,163 yuan in 2017 and 60,334 yuan in 2018 and that India's real GDP per person will be 98,028 rupees in 2017 and 104,191 rupees in 2018. By maintaining their current growth rates, which country will be first to double its standard of living and when will that happen?

3. The Asian Development Bank reported that Myanmar's GDP growth accelerated to 7.5% in 2013 from 7.3% in 2012. Growth was supported by rising investment, improved business confidence, commodity exports, and buoyant tourism. Is this expansion more likely to be a business cycle expansion or economic growth? Explain your answer.

Long-Term Growth Trends (Study Plan 6.2)

4. China was the largest economy for centuries because everyone had the same type of economy—subsistence—and so the country with the most people would be economically biggest. Then the Industrial Revolution sent the West on a more prosperous path. Now the world is returning to a common economy, this time technology- and information-based, so once again population triumphs.

   a. Why was China the world's largest economy until 1890?

   b. Why did the United States surpass China in 1890 to become the world's largest economy?

How Potential GDP Grows (Study Plan 6.3)

Use the tables in the next column to work Problems 5 to 7.

The tables describe an economy's labour market and its production function in 2017.

Real wage rate (dollars per hour)	Labour hours supplied	Labour hours demanded
80	45	5
70	40	10
60	35	15
50	30	20
40	25	25
30	20	30
20	15	35

Labour (hours)	Real GDP (2007 dollars)
5	425
10	800
15	1,125
20	1,400
25	1,625
30	1,800
35	1,925
40	2,000

5. In 2017, what are the equilibrium real wage rate, the quantity of labour employed, labour productivity, and potential GDP?

6. In 2018, the population increases and labour hours supplied increases by 10 at each real wage rate. What are the equilibrium real wage rate, labour productivity, and potential GDP in 2018?

7. In 2018, the population increases and labour hours supplied increase by 10 at each real wage rate. Does the standard of living in this economy increase in 2018? Explain why or why not.

Why Labour Productivity Grows (Study Plan 6.4)

8. For three years, there was no technological change in Longland but capital per hour of labour increased from $10 to $20 to $30 and real GDP per hour of labour increased from $3.80 to $5.70 to $7.13. Then, in the fourth year, capital per hour of labour remained constant, but real GDP per hour of labour increased to $10. Does Longland experience diminishing returns? Explain why or why not.

Is Economic Growth Sustainable? Theories, Evidence, and Policies (Study Plan 6.5)

9. Explain the processes that will bring the growth of real GDP per person to a stop according to the classical, neoclassical, and new growth theories.

ADDITIONAL PROBLEMS AND APPLICATIONS

MyLab Economics You can work these problems in Homework or Test if assigned by your instructor.

The Basics of Economic Growth

10. In 2018 Brazil's real GDP is growing at 1.7 percent a year and its population is growing at 0.7 percent a year. If these growth rates continue, in what year will Brazil's real GDP per person be twice what it is in 2018?

11. The IMF forecasted Canada's real GDP at $1,830 billion in 2017 and $1,866 billion in 2018, and Canada's population at 36.7 million in 2017 and 37.1 million in 2018. Calculate:
    a. The growth rate of real GDP
    b. The growth rate of real GDP per person
    c. The approximate number of years it will take for real GDP per person in Canada to double if the 2018 growth rate of real GDP and the population growth rate are maintained

12. The IMF forecasted Australia's real GDP at $A1,730 billion in 2017 and $A1,782 billion in 2018, and Australia's population at 24.6 million in 2017 and 25.0 million in 2018. Calculate:
    a. The growth rate of real GDP
    b. The growth rate of real GDP per person
    c. The approximate number of years it will take for real GDP per person in Australia to double if the current growth rate of real GDP is maintained

Long-Term Growth Trends

13. **A Shifting Global Economic Landscape**
    Global growth for 2016 is estimated at 3.1 percent. Advanced economies are projected to grow by 1.9 percent in 2017 and 2.0 percent in 2018. The primary factor underlying the strengthening global outlook over 2017–18 is the projected pickup in developing economy's growth estimated at 4.1 percent in 2016, and projected to reach 4.5 percent for 2017. A further pickup in growth to 4.8 percent is projected for 2018. Notably, the growth forecast for 2017 was revised up for China to 6.5 percent.
    Source: International Monetary Fund, January 2017

    Do the growth rates projected by the IMF indicate that gaps in real GDP per person around the world are shrinking, growing, or staying the same? Explain.

How Potential GDP Grows

14. If a large increase in investment increases labour productivity, explain what happens to:
    a. Potential GDP
    b. Employment
    c. The real wage rate

15. If a severe drought decreases labour productivity, explain what happens to:
    a. Potential GDP
    b. Employment
    c. The real wage rate

Use the following tables to work Problems 16 to 18. The first table describes an economy's labour market in 2017 and the second table describes its production function in 2017.

Real wage rate (dollars per hour)	Labour hours supplied	Labour hours demanded
80	55	15
70	50	20
60	45	25
50	40	30
40	35	35
30	30	40
20	25	45

Labour (hours)	Real GDP (2007 dollars)
15	1,425
20	1,800
25	2,125
30	2,400
35	2,625
40	2,800
45	2,925
50	3,000

16. What are the equilibrium real wage rate and the quantity of labour employed in 2017?

17. What are labour productivity and potential GDP in 2017?

18. Suppose that labour productivity increases in 2018. What effect will the increased labour productivity have on the demand for labour, the supply of labour, potential GDP, and real GDP per person?

Why Labour Productivity Grows

19. **India's Economy Hits the Wall**

    Just six months ago, India was looking good. Annual growth was 9 percent, consumer demand was huge, and foreign investment was growing. But now most economic forecasts expect growth to slow to 7 percent—a big drop for a country that needs to accelerate growth. India needs urgently to upgrade its infrastructure and education and healthcare facilities. Agriculture is unproductive and needs better technology. The legal system needs to be strengthened with more judges and courtrooms.

    Source: *BusinessWeek*, July 1, 2008

    Explain five potential sources for faster economic growth in India suggested in this news clip.

Is Economic Growth Sustainable? Theories, Evidence, and Policies

20. **The Productivity Watch**

    According to former Federal Reserve chairman Alan Greenspan, IT investments in the 1990s boosted productivity, which boosted corporate profits, which led to more IT investments, and so on, leading to a nirvana of high growth.

    Source: *Fortune*, September 4, 2006

    Which of the growth theories that you've studied in this chapter best corresponds to the explanation given by Mr. Greenspan?

21. Is faster economic growth always a good thing? Argue the case for faster growth and the case for slower growth. Then reach a conclusion on whether growth should be increased or slowed.

22. **Why Canada's Industry Leaders Need to Embrace the Technology Mindset**

    We are at a tipping point where technology—from software to hardware and everything in between—is weaving its way into all that we do

and is about to touch every industry. Every day, we are reminded how quickly things are changing, from connected cars, to wearable devices, to manufacturing. Just look at the rapid advance in China's economy and standard of living driven in large part by an innovative spirit unleashed in the late 1990s.

    Source: *Financial Post*, July 11, 2014

    Explain which growth theory best describes the news clip.

23. What is the fundamental fact that drives the new growth theory perpetual motion machine and keeps it in motion?

24. Describe the components of the new growth theory perpetual motion machine and explain the role played by incentives in keeping the machine in motion.

25. Why and how does new growth theory imply that technological change, even robots and artificial intelligence, will create as many jobs as it will destroy?

Economics in the News

26. After you have studied *Economics in the News* on pp. 156–157, answer the following questions.

    a. How do the real GDP growth rates of Canada and the United States compare since 2006?

    b. How do the real GDP-per-person growth rates of Canada and the United States compare since 2006?

    c. How do we measure labour productivity?

    d. Why might work hours per person have decreased in both the United States and Canada, and why might the U.S. decrease be greater than the Canadian decrease?

    e. Explain why productivity is growing faster in the United States than in Canada. What must Canada do to replicate the U.S. productivity growth rate?

7
FINANCE, SAVING, AND INVESTMENT

After studying this chapter, you will be able to:

◆ Describe the flows of funds in financial markets

◆ Explain how saving and investment decisions are made and how they interact in financial markets

◆ Explain how governments influence financial markets

The financial markets and financial institutions that you learn about in this chapter are often in the headlines. But behind the headlines and drama they create, these markets and institutions play a crucial, mostly unseen, role funnelling funds from savers and lenders to investors and borrowers.

The past ten years have not been normal in financial markets. Governments, businesses, and households have been able to borrow at unusually low rates. This chapter explains how financial markets work, and *Economics in the News* at the end of the chapter looks at the forces at work during 2016 that led to yet lower interest rates.

◆ Financial Markets and Financial Institutions

The financial markets and institutions that we study in this chapter play a crucial role in the economy. They provide the channels through which saving flows to finance the investment in new capital that makes the economy grow.

In studying the economics of financial institutions and markets, we distinguish between:

- Finance and money
- Physical capital and financial capital

Finance and Money

In economics, we use the term *finance* to describe the activity of providing the funds that finance expenditures on capital. The study of finance looks at how households and firms obtain and use financial resources and how they cope with the risks that arise in this activity.

Money is what we use to pay for goods and services and factors of production and to make financial transactions. The study of money looks at how households and firms use it, how much of it they hold, how banks create and manage it, and how its quantity influences the economy.

In the economic lives of individuals and businesses, finance and money are closely interrelated. And some of the main financial institutions, such as banks, provide both financial services and monetary services. Nevertheless, by distinguishing between *finance* and *money* and studying them separately, we will better understand our financial and monetary markets and institutions.

For the rest of this chapter, we study finance. Money is the topic of the next chapter.

Physical Capital and Financial Capital

Economists distinguish between physical capital and financial capital. *Physical capital* is the tools, instruments, machines, buildings, and other items that have been produced in the past and that are used today to produce goods and services. Inventories of raw materials, semifinished goods, and components are part of physical capital. When economists use the term capital, they mean *physical* capital. The funds that firms use to buy physical capital are called **financial capital**.

Along the *aggregate production function* in Chapter 6 (see p. 142), the quantity of capital is fixed. An increase in the quantity of capital increases production possibilities and shifts the aggregate production function upward. You're going to see, in this chapter, how investment, saving, borrowing, and lending decisions influence the quantity of capital and make it grow and, as a consequence, make real GDP grow.

We begin by describing the links between capital and investment and between wealth and saving.

Capital and Investment

The quantity of capital changes because of investment and depreciation. *Investment* increases the quantity of capital and *depreciation* decreases it (see Chapter 4, p. 90). The total amount spent on new capital is called **gross investment**. The change in the value of capital is called **net investment**. Net investment equals gross investment minus depreciation.

Figure 7.1 illustrates these terms. On January 1, 2018, Ace Bottling Inc. had machines worth $30,000—Ace's initial capital. During 2018, the market value of Ace's machines fell by 67 percent—$20,000. After this depreciation, Ace's machines were valued at $10,000. During 2018, Ace spent $30,000 on new machines. This amount is Ace's gross investment. By December 31, 2018, Ace Bottling had capital valued at $40,000, so its capital had increased by $10,000. This amount is Ace's net investment. Ace's net investment equals its gross investment of $30,000 minus depreciation of its initial capital of $20,000.

Wealth and Saving

Wealth is the value of all the things that people own. What people own is related to what they earn, but it is not the same thing. People earn an *income*, which is the amount they receive during a given time period from supplying the services of the resources they own. **Saving** is the amount of income that is not paid in taxes or spent on consumption goods and services. Saving increases wealth. Wealth also increases when the market value of assets rises—called *capital gains*—and decreases when the market value of assets falls—called *capital losses*.

For example, if at the end of the school year you have $250 in the bank and a coin collection worth $300, then your wealth is $550. During the summer,

FIGURE 7.1   Capital and Investment

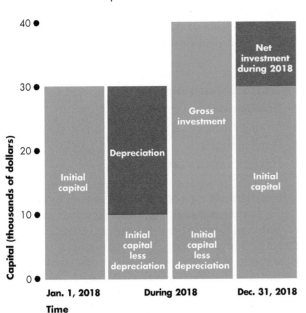

On January 1, 2018, Ace Bottling had capital worth $30,000. During the year, the value of Ace's capital fell by $20,000—depreciation—and it spent $30,000 on new capital—gross investment. Ace's net investment was $10,000 ($30,000 gross investment minus $20,000 depreciation) so that at the end of 2018, Ace had capital worth $40,000.

———— MyLab Economics Animation ————

suppose that you earn $5,000 (net of taxes) and spend $1,000 on consumption goods and services, so your saving is $4,000. Your bank account increases to $4,250 and your wealth becomes $4,550. The $4,000 increase in wealth equals saving. If coins rise in value and your coin collection is now worth $500, you have a capital gain of $200, which is also added to your wealth.

National wealth and national saving work like this personal example. The wealth of a nation at the end of a year equals its wealth at the start of the year plus its saving during the year, which equals income minus consumption expenditure.

To make real GDP grow, saving and wealth must be transformed into investment and capital. This transformation takes place in the markets for financial capital and through the activities of financial institutions. We're now going to describe these markets and institutions.

Financial Capital Markets

Saving is the source of the funds that are used to finance investment, and these funds are supplied and demanded in three types of financial markets:

- Loan markets
- Bond markets
- Stock markets

Loan Markets Businesses often want short-term finance to buy inventories or to extend credit to their customers. Sometimes they get this finance in the form of a loan from a bank. Households often want finance to purchase big-ticket items, such as automobiles or household furnishings and appliances. They get this finance as bank loans, often in the form of outstanding credit card balances.

Households also get finance to buy new homes. (Expenditure on new homes is counted as part of investment.) These funds are usually obtained as a loan that is secured by a **mortgage**—a legal contract that gives ownership of a home to the lender in the event that the borrower fails to meet the agreed loan payments (repayments and interest). In 2007–2008, U.S. mortgages were at the centre of a global credit crisis.

Financing these types of purchases takes place in loan markets.

Bond Markets When Walmart expands its business and opens new stores, it gets the finance it needs by selling bonds. Governments—federal, provincial, and municipal—also raise finance by issuing bonds.

A **bond** is a promise to make specified payments on specified dates. For example, you can buy a McDonald's Corporation bond that promises to pay $3.50 every year until 2020 and then to make a final payment of $100 on July 15, 2020.

The buyer of a bond from McDonald's makes a loan to the company and is entitled to the payments promised by the bond. When a person buys a newly issued bond, he or she may hold the bond until the borrower has repaid the amount borrowed or sell it to someone else. Bonds issued by corporations and governments are traded in the **bond market**.

The term of a bond might be long (decades) or short (just a month or two). Corporations often issue very short-term bonds as a way of getting paid for their sales before the buyer is able to pay. For example, suppose that Bombardier sells $100 million of railway locomotives to VIA Rail. Bombardier wants to be paid when the items are shipped, but VIA Rail doesn't want to pay until the locomotives are earning an income. So VIA Rail promises to pay Bombardier $101 million three months in the future. A bank is willing to buy Bombardier's promise for (say) $100 million. Bombardier gets $100 million immediately and the bank gets $101 million in three months when VIA Rail honours its promise. The Government of Canada issues promises of this type, called Treasury bills.

Another type of bond is a **mortgage-backed security**, which entitles its holder to the income from a package of mortgages. Mortgage lenders create mortgage-backed securities. They make mortgage loans to home buyers and then create securities that they sell to obtain more funds to make more mortgage loans. The holder of a mortgage-backed security is entitled to receive payments that derive from the payments received by the mortgage lender from the home buyer–borrower.

Mortgage-backed securities created in the United States were at the centre of the storm in the financial markets in 2007–2008 that brought a global financial crisis.

Stock Markets When Petro-Canada wants finance to expand its business, it issues stock. A **stock** is a certificate of ownership and claim to the firm's profits. Petro-Canada has issued 484 million shares of its stock. So if you owned 484 Petro-Canada shares, you would own one-millionth of the firm and be entitled to receive one-millionth of its profits.

Unlike a stockholder, a bondholder does not own part of the firm that issued the bond.

A **stock market** is a financial market in which shares of stocks of corporations are traded. The Toronto Stock Exchange, the New York Stock Exchange, the London Stock Exchange (in England), and the Tokyo Stock Exchange (in Japan) are all examples of stock markets.

Financial Institutions

Financial markets are highly competitive because of the role played by financial institutions in those markets. A **financial institution** is a firm that operates on both sides of the markets for financial capital. The financial institution is a borrower in one market and a lender in another.

Financial institutions also stand ready to trade so that households with funds to lend and firms or households seeking funds can always find someone on the other side of the market with whom to trade. The key Canadian financial institutions are:

- Banks
- Trust and loan companies
- Credit unions and caisses populaires
- Mutual funds
- Pension funds
- Insurance companies

Banks Banks accept deposits and use the funds to buy government bonds and other securities and to make loans. Canada has 14 domestic banks, and a further 33 foreign banks operate in Canada. These banks hold more than 70 percent of the total assets of the Canadian financial services sector. Economists distinguish banks from other financial institutions because bank deposits are money. We'll return to these institutions in Chapter 8, where we study the role of money in our economy.

Trust and Loan Companies Trust and loan companies provide similar services to banks and the largest of them are owned by banks. They accept deposits and make personal loans and mortgage loans. They also administer estates, trusts, and pension plans.

Credit Unions and Caisses Populaires Credit unions and caisses populaires are banks that are owned and controlled by their depositors and borrowers, are regulated by provincial rules, and operate only inside their own provincial boundaries. These institutions are large in number but small in size.

Mutual Funds Mutual funds are financial institutions that buy assets using funds provided by individual savers. Mutual funds vary in the assets that they hold—some specializing in bonds, some in stocks, and some holding both. In December 2016, Canadian mutual funds held assets valued at $1.4 trillion and managed financial assets for one-third of Canadian households.

Pension Funds Pension funds are financial institutions that receive the pension contributions of firms and workers. They use these funds to buy a diversified portfolio of bonds and stocks that they expect to generate an income that balances risk and return. The income is used to pay pension benefits.

Pension funds can be very large and play an active role in the firms whose stock they hold.

Insurance Companies Insurance companies provide risk-sharing services. They enter into agreements with households and firms to provide compensation in the event of accident, theft, fire, and a host of other misfortunes. They receive premiums from their customers and make payments against claims.

Insurance companies use the funds they have received but not paid out as claims to buy bonds and stocks on which they earn interest income.

Some insurance companies also insure corporate bonds and other risky financial assets. They provide insurance that pays out if a firm fails and cannot meet its bond obligations. Some insurance companies insure other insurers in a complex network of reinsurance.

In normal times, insurance companies have a steady flow of funds coming in from premiums and interest on the financial assets they hold and a steady, but smaller, flow of funds paying claims. Their profit is the gap between the two flows. But in unusual times, when large and widespread losses are being incurred, insurance companies can run into difficulty in meeting their obligations. Such a situation arose in 2008 for one of the world's biggest insurers, AIG, and the firm was taken into public ownership.

Canadian insurance companies have very large international operations and earn 70 percent of their income outside Canada.

All financial institutions face risk, which poses two problems: solvency and liquidity problems.

Insolvency and Illiquidity

A financial institution's **net worth** is the market value of what it has lent minus the market value of what it has borrowed. If net worth is positive, the institution is *solvent*. But if net worth is negative, the institution is *insolvent*. An insolvent business cannot pay its debts and must go out of business. The owners of an insolvent financial institution—usually its stockholders—bear the loss but the firms and individuals who are owed payments by an insolvent firm also incur losses.

A financial institution both borrows and lends, so it is exposed to the risk that its net worth might become negative. To limit that risk, financial institutions are regulated and a minimum amount of their lending must be backed by their net worth.

Sometimes, a financial institution is solvent but illiquid. A firm is *illiquid* if it has made long-term loans with borrowed funds and is faced with a sudden demand to repay more of what it has borrowed than its available cash. In normal times, a financial institution that is illiquid can borrow from another institution. But if all the financial institutions are short of cash, the market for loans among financial institutions dries up.

Both insolvency and illiquidity were at the core of the financial meltdown of 2007–2008. When a large financial institution becomes insolvent, its consequences spread to the entire financial system.

Interest Rates and Asset Prices

Stocks, bonds, short-term securities, and loans are collectively called *financial assets*. The interest rate on a financial asset is the interest received expressed as a percentage of the price of the asset.

Because the interest rate is a percentage of the price of an asset, if the asset price rises, other things remaining the same, the interest rate falls. Conversely, if the asset price falls, other things remaining the same, the interest rate rises.

To see this inverse relationship between an asset price and the interest rate, let's look at an example. We'll consider a bond that promises to pay its holder $5 a year forever. What is the rate of return—the interest rate—on this bond? The answer depends on the price of the bond. If you could buy this bond for $50, the interest rate would be 10 percent per year:

Interest rate = ($5 ÷ $50) × 100 = 10 percent.

But if the price of this bond increased to $200, its rate of return or interest rate would be only 2.5 percent per year. That is,

Interest rate = ($5 ÷ $200) × 100 = 2.5 percent.

This relationship means that the price of an asset and the interest rate on that asset are determined simultaneously—one implies the other.

This relationship also means that if the interest rate on the asset rises, the price of the asset falls, debts become harder to pay, and the net worth of the financial institution falls. Insolvency can arise from a previously unexpected large rise in the interest rate.

In the next part of this chapter, we learn how interest rates and asset prices are determined in the financial markets.

Funds that Finance Investment

The circular flow model of Chapter 4 (see p. 89) can be extended to include flows in the loanable funds market that finance investment (Fig. 7.2). They come from three sources:

1. Household saving
2. Government budget surplus
3. Borrowing from the rest of the world

Households' income, Y, is spent on consumption goods and services, C, saved, S, or paid in net taxes, T. **Net taxes** are the taxes paid to governments minus the cash transfers received from governments (such as social security and unemployment benefits). So income is equal to the sum of consumption expenditure, saving, and net taxes:

$$Y = C + S + T$$

You saw in Chapter 4 (p. 90) that Y also equals the sum of the items of aggregate expenditure: consumption expenditure, C, investment, I, government expenditure, G, and exports, X, minus imports, M. That is:

$$Y = C + I + G + X - M$$

By using these two equations, you can see that

$$I + G + X = S + T + M$$

Subtract G and X from both sides of the last equation to obtain:

$$I = S + (T - G) + (M - X)$$

This equation tells us that investment, I, is financed by household saving, S, the government

---

FIGURE 7.2 Financial Flows and the Circular Flow of Expenditure and Income

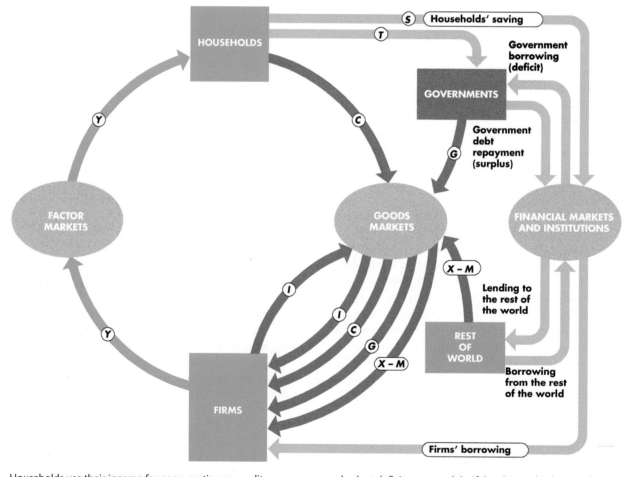

Households use their income for consumption expenditure (C), saving (S), and net taxes (T). Firms borrow to finance their investment expenditure. Governments borrow to finance a budget deficit or repay debt if they have a budget surplus. The rest of the world borrows to finance its deficit or lends its surplus.

budget surplus, $(T - G)$, and borrowing from the rest of the world, $(M - X)$.

The sum of private saving, S, and government saving, $(T - G)$, is called **national saving**.

National saving and foreign borrowing finance investment. In 2017, Canadian investment was $384 billion. Governments (federal, provincial, and local combined) had a deficit of $26 billion. This total of $410 billion was financed by private saving of $362 billion and borrowing from the rest of the world (negative net exports) of $48 billion.

In the rest of this chapter, we focus on the influences on national saving and the effects of a government budget deficit (or surplus) in the loanable funds market. We broaden our view to examine the influences on and the effects of borrowing from the rest of the world in Chapter 9. You can think of this chapter as an account of the Canadian loanable funds market when exports equal imports ($X = M$), or as an account of the global loanable funds market.

You're going to see how investment and saving and the flows of loanable funds—all measured in constant 2007 dollars—are determined. The price in the loanable funds market that achieves equilibrium is an interest rate, which we also measure in real terms as the *real* interest rate. In the loanable funds market, there is just one interest rate, which is an average of the interest rates on all the different types of financial securities that we described earlier. Let's see what we mean by the real interest rate.

The Real Interest Rate

The **nominal interest rate** is the number of dollars that a borrower pays and a lender receives in interest in a year expressed as a percentage of the number of dollars borrowed and lent. For example, if you lend a friend $100 and get repaid $105 a year later, the nominal interest rate is 5 percent per year

The **real interest rate** is the nominal interest rate adjusted to remove the effects of inflation on the buying power of money, and is approximately equal to the nominal interest rate minus the inflation rate.

To see why, think about what your $105 in the above example will buy if the inflation rate is 2 percent per year. You need $102 to buy what $100 would have bought when you made the loan. You've got $105, so you've really earned only $3 or 3 percent. So the real interest rate equals the nominal interest rate of 5 percent minus the 2 percent inflation rate.

The real interest rate is the opportunity cost of loanable funds. The real interest *paid* on borrowed

ECONOMICS IN ACTION
Nominal and Real Interest Rates

Nominal and real interest rates were extremely high during the 1980s. They have trended downward for the past 30 years. Where will they go next? See *Economics in the News* on pp. 176–177.

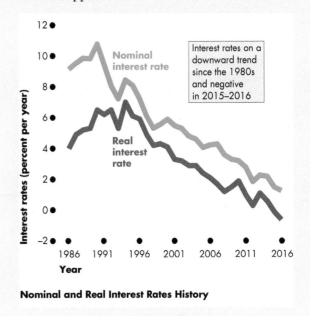

Nominal and Real Interest Rates History

funds is the opportunity cost of borrowing. And the real interest rate *forgone* when funds are used either to buy consumption goods and services or to invest in new capital goods is the opportunity cost of not saving or not lending those funds.

REVIEW QUIZ

1 Distinguish between physical capital and financial capital and give two examples of each.
2 What is the distinction between gross investment and net investment?
3 What are the three main types of markets for financial capital?
4 Explain the connection between the price of a financial asset and its interest rate.
5 Why is the real interest rate the opportunity cost of loanable funds?

Work these questions in Study Plan 7.1 and get instant feedback.   MyLab Economics

The Loanable Funds Market

In macroeconomics, we group all the financial markets that we described in the previous section into a single loanable funds market. The **loanable funds market** is the aggregate of all the individual financial markets.

We're now going to see how the loanable funds market determines the real interest rate, the quantity of funds loaned, saving, and investment. In the rest of this section, we will ignore the government and the rest of the world and focus on households and firms in the loanable funds market. We will study:

- The demand for loanable funds
- The supply of loanable funds
- Equilibrium in the loanable funds market

The Demand for Loanable Funds

The *quantity of loanable funds demanded* is the total quantity of funds demanded to finance investment, the government budget deficit, and international investment or lending during a given period. Our focus here is on investment. We'll bring the budget deficit into the picture later in this chapter.

What determines investment and the demand for loanable funds to finance it? Many details influence this decision, but we can summarize them in two factors:

1. The real interest rate
2. Expected profit

Firms invest in capital only if they expect to earn a profit, and fewer projects are profitable at a high real interest rate than at a low real interest rate, so:

> Other things remaining the same, the higher the real interest rate, the smaller is the quantity of loanable funds demanded; and the lower the real interest rate, the greater the quantity of loanable funds demanded.

Demand for Loanable Funds Curve The **demand for loanable funds** is the relationship between the quantity of loanable funds demanded and the real interest rate, when all other influences on borrowing plans remain the same. The demand curve *DLF* in Fig. 7.3 is a demand for loanable funds curve.

To understand the demand for loanable funds, think about Amazon.com's decision to borrow $100 million to build some new warehouses. If

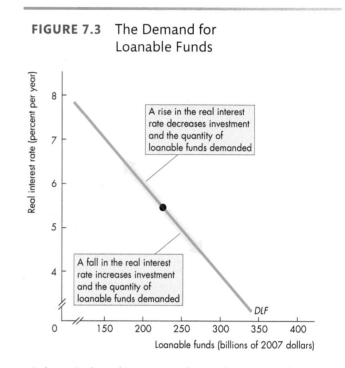

FIGURE 7.3 The Demand for Loanable Funds

A rise in the real interest rate decreases investment and the quantity of loanable funds demanded

A fall in the real interest rate increases investment and the quantity of loanable funds demanded

A change in the real interest rate changes the quantity of loanable funds demanded and brings a movement along the demand for loanable funds curve.

——— MyLab Economics Animation ———

Amazon expects to get a return of $5 million a year from this investment before paying interest costs and the interest rate is less than 5 percent a year, Amazon would make a profit, so it builds the warehouses. But if the interest rate is more than 5 percent a year, Amazon would incur a loss, so it doesn't build the warehouses. The quantity of loanable funds demanded is greater the lower is the real interest rate.

Changes in the Demand for Loanable Funds When the expected profit changes, the demand for loanable funds changes. Other things remaining the same, the greater the expected profit from new capital, the greater is the amount of investment and the greater the demand for loanable funds.

The Supply of Loanable Funds

The *quantity of loanable funds supplied* is the total funds available from private saving, the government budget surplus, and international borrowing during a given period. Our focus here is on saving. We'll bring the other two items into the picture later.

How do you decide how much of your income to save and supply in the loanable funds market? Your decision is influenced by many factors, but chief among them are:

1. The real interest rate
2. Disposable income
3. Expected future income
4. Wealth
5. Default risk

We begin by focusing on the real interest rate.

> Other things remaining the same, the higher the real interest rate, the greater is the quantity of loanable funds supplied; and the lower the real interest rate, the smaller is the quantity of loanable funds supplied.

The Supply of Loanable Funds Curve The **supply of loanable funds** is the relationship between the quantity of loanable funds supplied and the real interest rate when all other influences on lending plans remain the same. The curve *SLF* in Fig. 7.4 is a supply of loanable funds curve.

Think about a student's decision to save some of what she earns from her summer job. With a real interest rate of 2 percent a year, she decides that it is not worth saving much—better to spend the income and take a student loan if funds run out during the semester. But if the real interest rate jumped to 10 percent a year, the payoff from saving would be high enough to encourage her to cut back on spending and increase the amount she saves.

Changes in the Supply of Loanable Funds A change in disposable income, expected future income, wealth, or default risk changes the supply of loanable funds.

Disposable Income A household's *disposable income* is the income earned minus net taxes. When disposable income increases, other things remaining the same, consumption expenditure increases but by less than the increase in income. Some of the increase in income is saved. So the greater a household's disposable income, other things remaining the same, the greater is its saving.

Expected Future Income The higher a household's expected future income, other things remaining the same, the smaller is its saving today.

Wealth The higher a household's wealth, other things remaining the same, the smaller is its saving. If a

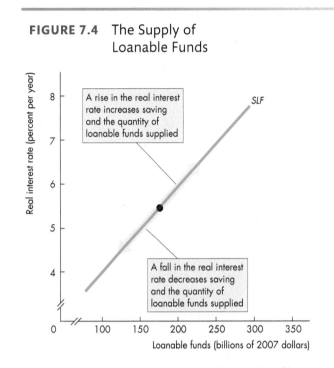

FIGURE 7.4   The Supply of Loanable Funds

A rise in the real interest rate increases saving and the quantity of loanable funds supplied

A fall in the real interest rate decreases saving and the quantity of loanable funds supplied

A change in the real interest rate changes the quantity of loanable funds supplied and brings a movement along the supply of loanable funds curve.

MyLab Economics Animation

person's wealth increases because of a capital gain, the person sees less need to save. For example, from 2002 through 2006, when house prices were rising rapidly, wealth increased despite the fact that personal saving decreased.

Default Risk The risk that a loan will not be repaid is called **default risk**. The greater that risk, the higher is the interest rate needed to induce a person to lend and the smaller is the supply of loanable funds.

Shifts of the Supply of Loanable Funds Curve When any of the four influences on the supply of loanable funds changes, the supply of loanable funds changes and the supply curve shifts. An increase in disposable income, a decrease in expected future income, a decrease in wealth, or a fall in default risk increases saving and increases the supply of loanable funds.

Equilibrium in the Loanable Funds Market

You've seen that, other things remaining the same, the higher the real interest rate, the greater is the quantity of loanable funds supplied and the smaller

ECONOMICS IN ACTION

The Total Quantities Supplied and Demanded

Around $7,300 billion of loanable funds have been supplied and demanded, and the figure shows who supplies and who demands. About 40 percent of the funds get supplied to banks and other financial institutions.

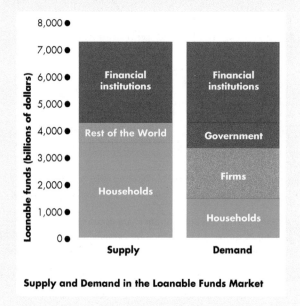

Supply and Demand in the Loanable Funds Market

FIGURE 7.5 Equilibrium in the Loanable Funds Market

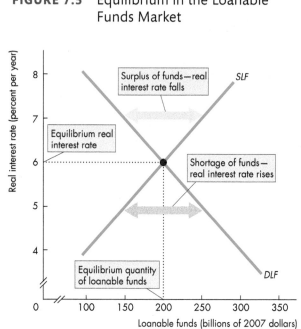

A surplus of funds lowers the real interest rate and a shortage of funds raises it. At an interest rate of 6 percent a year, the quantity of funds demanded equals the quantity supplied and the market is in equilibrium.

────── MyLab Economics Animation and Draw Graph ──────

is the quantity of loanable funds demanded. There is one real interest rate—the equilibrium real interest rate—at which the quantities of loanable funds demanded and supplied are equal.

Figure 7.5 shows how the demand for and supply of loanable funds determine the real interest rate. The *DLF* curve is the demand curve and the *SLF* curve is the supply curve. If the real interest rate exceeds 6 percent a year, the quantity of loanable funds supplied exceeds the quantity demanded—a surplus of funds. Borrowers find it easy to get funds, but lenders are unable to lend all the funds they have available. The real interest rate falls and continues to fall until the quantity of funds supplied equals the quantity of funds demanded.

If the real interest rate is less than 6 percent a year, the quantity of loanable funds supplied is less than the quantity demanded—a shortage of funds. Borrowers can't get the funds they want, but lenders are able to lend all the funds they have. So the real interest rate rises until the quantity of funds supplied equals the quantity demanded.

Regardless of whether there is a surplus or a shortage of loanable funds, the real interest rate changes and is pulled toward an equilibrium level. In Fig. 7.5, the equilibrium real interest rate is 6 percent a year. At this interest rate, there is neither a surplus nor a shortage of loanable funds. Borrowers can get the funds they want, and lenders can lend all the funds they have available. The investment plans of borrowers and the saving plans of lenders are consistent with each other.

Changes in Demand and Supply

Financial markets are highly volatile in the short run but remarkably stable in the long run. Volatility in the market comes from fluctuations in either the demand for loanable funds or the supply of loanable funds. These fluctuations bring fluctuations in the real interest rate and in the equilibrium quantity of funds lent and borrowed. They also bring fluctuations in asset prices.

Here we'll illustrate the effects of *increases* in demand and supply in the loanable funds market.

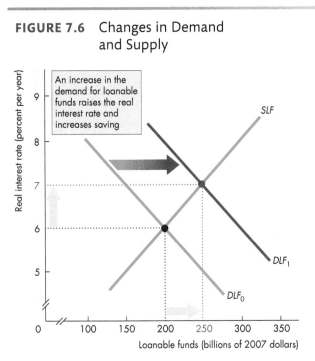

FIGURE 7.6 Changes in Demand and Supply

An increase in the demand for loanable funds raises the real interest rate and increases saving

(a) An increase in demand

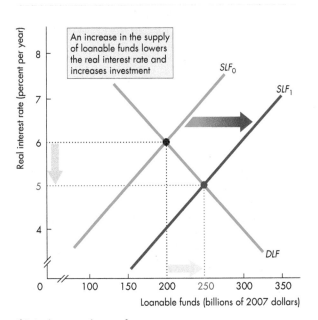

An increase in the supply of loanable funds lowers the real interest rate and increases investment

(b) An increase in supply

In part (a), the demand for loanable funds increases and supply doesn't change. The real interest rate rises (financial asset prices fall) and the quantity of funds increases. In part (b), the supply of loanable funds increases and demand doesn't change. The real interest rate falls (financial asset prices rise) and the quantity of funds increases.

MyLab Economics Animation and Draw Graph

An Increase in Demand If the profits that firms expect to earn increase, they increase their planned investment and increase their demand for loanable funds to finance that investment. With an increase in the demand for loanable funds, but no change in the supply of loanable funds, there is a shortage of funds. As borrowers compete for funds, the interest rate rises and lenders increase the quantity of funds supplied.

Figure 7.6(a) illustrates these changes. An increase in the demand for loanable funds shifts the demand curve rightward from DLF_0 to DLF_1. With no change in the supply of loanable funds, there is a shortage of funds at a real interest rate of 6 percent a year. The real interest rate rises until it is 7 percent a year. Equilibrium is restored and the equilibrium quantity of funds has increased.

An Increase in Supply If one of the influences on saving plans changes and increases saving, the supply of loanable funds increases. With no change in the demand for loanable funds, the market is flush with loanable funds. Borrowers find bargains and lenders find themselves accepting a lower interest rate. At the lower interest rate, borrowers find additional investment projects profitable and increase the quantity of loanable funds that they borrow.

Figure 7.6(b) illustrates these changes. An increase in supply shifts the supply curve rightward from SLF_0 to SLF_1. With no change in demand, there is a surplus of funds at a real interest rate of 6 percent a year. The real interest rate falls until it is 5 percent a year. Equilibrium is restored and the equilibrium quantity of funds has increased.

REVIEW QUIZ

1 What is the loanable funds market?
2 How do firms make investment decisions?
3 What determines the demand for loanable funds and what makes it change?
4 How do households make saving decisions?
5 What determines the supply of loanable funds and what makes it change?
6 How do changes in the demand for and supply of loanable funds change the real interest rate and quantity of loanable funds?

Work these questions in Study Plan 7.2 and get instant feedback. MyLab Economics

Government in the Loanable Funds Market

Government enters the loanable funds market when it has a budget surplus or budget deficit. A government budget surplus increases the supply of loanable funds and contributes to financing investment; a government budget deficit increases the demand for loanable funds and competes with businesses for funds. Let's study the effects of government on the loanable funds market.

A Government Budget Surplus

A government budget surplus increases the supply of loanable funds. The real interest rate falls, which decreases household saving and decreases the quantity of private funds supplied. The lower real interest rate increases the quantity of loanable funds demanded and increases investment.

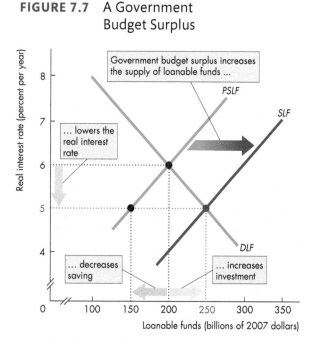

FIGURE 7.7 A Government Budget Surplus

A government budget surplus of $100 billion adds to private saving and the private supply of loanable funds curve, *PSLF*, to determine the supply of loanable funds curve, *SLF*. The real interest rate falls to 5 percent a year, private saving decreases, but investment increases to $250 billion.

MyLab Economics Animation

Figure 7.7 shows these effects of a government budget surplus. The private supply of loanable funds curve is *PSLF*. The supply of loanable funds curve, *SLF*, shows the sum of private supply and the government budget surplus. Here, the government budget surplus is $100 billion, so at each real interest rate the *SLF* curve lies $100 billion to the right of the *PSLF* curve. That is, the horizontal distance between the *PSLF* curve and the *SLF* curve equals the government budget surplus.

With no government surplus, the real interest rate is 6 percent a year, the quantity of loanable funds is $200 billion a year, and investment is $200 billion a year. But with the government surplus of $100 billion a year, the equilibrium real interest rate falls to 5 percent a year and the equilibrium quantity of loanable funds increases to $250 billion a year.

The fall in the interest rate decreases private saving to $150 billion, but investment increases to $250 billion, which is financed by private saving plus the government budget surplus (government saving).

A Government Budget Deficit

A government budget deficit increases the demand for loanable funds. The real interest rate rises, which increases household saving and increases the quantity of private funds supplied. But the higher real interest rate decreases investment and the quantity of loanable funds demanded by firms to finance investment.

Figure 7.8 shows these effects of a government budget deficit. The private demand for loanable funds curve is *PDLF*. The demand for loanable funds curve, *DLF*, shows the sum of private demand and the government budget deficit. Here, the government budget deficit is $100 billion, so at each real interest rate the *DLF* curve lies $100 billion to the right of the *PDLF* curve. That is, the horizontal distance between the *PDLF* curve and the *DLF* curve equals the government budget deficit.

With no government deficit, the real interest rate is 6 percent a year, the quantity of loanable funds is $200 billion a year, and investment is $200 billion a year. But with the government budget deficit of $100 billion a year, the equilibrium real interest rate rises to 7 percent a year and the equilibrium quantity of loanable funds increases to $250 billion a year.

The rise in the real interest rate increases private saving to $250 billion, but investment decreases to $150 billion because $100 billion of private saving must finance the government budget deficit.

FIGURE 7.8 A Government Budget Deficit

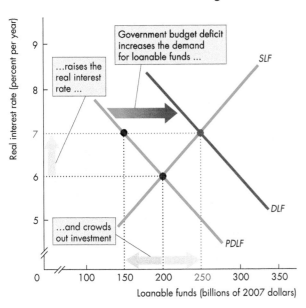

A government budget deficit adds to the private demand for loanable funds curve, *PDLF*, to determine the demand for loanable funds curve, *DLF*. The real interest rate rises, saving increases, but investment decreases—a crowding-out effect.

———— MyLab Economics Animation ————

The Crowding-Out Effect The tendency for a government budget deficit to raise the real interest rate and decrease investment is called the **crowding-out effect**. The crowding-out effect does not decrease investment by the full amount of the government budget deficit because a higher real interest rate induces an increase in private saving that partly contributes toward financing the deficit.

The Ricardo-Barro Effect First suggested by the English economist David Ricardo in the eighteenth century and refined by Robert J. Barro of Harvard University, the Ricardo-Barro effect holds that both of the effects we've just shown are wrong and the government budget has no effect on either the real interest rate or investment.

Barro says that taxpayers are rational and can see that a budget deficit today means that future taxes must be higher and future disposable incomes smaller. With smaller expected future disposable incomes, saving increases today. The private supply of loanable funds increases to match the quantity of loanable funds demanded by the government. So the budget deficit has no effect on either the real interest rate or investment. Figure 7.9 shows this outcome.

FIGURE 7.9 The Ricardo-Barro Effect

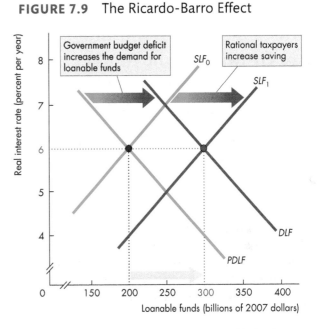

A budget deficit increases the demand for loanable funds. Rational taxpayers increase saving, which shifts the supply of loanable funds curve from *SLF*₀ to *SLF*₁. Crowding out is avoided: Increased saving finances the budget deficit.

———— MyLab Economics Animation ————

Most economists regard the Ricardo-Barro view as extreme. But there might be some change in private saving that goes in the direction suggested by the Ricardo-Barro effect that lessens the crowding-out effect.

REVIEW QUIZ

1 How does a government budget surplus or deficit influence the loanable funds market?

2 What is the crowding-out effect and how does it work?

3 What is the Ricardo-Barro effect and how does it modify the crowding-out effect?

Work these questions in Study Plan 7.3 and get instant feedback. MyLab Economics

◆ To complete your study of financial markets, take a look at *Economics in the News* on pp. 176–177 and see how you can use the model of the loanable funds market to understand why interest rates fell in 2016.

Interest Rates Low but Fall

After a Summer Bond Binge, Signs of Angst Are Growing in the Market

Bondholders make the largest returns when interest rates are low and falling. In those conditions, bond prices are high and rising. Bondholders make the smallest returns, and incur losses, when interest rates rise and bond prices fall.

So, whether bond interest rates have bottomed and bond prices have peaked is a big question for bondholders.

It's a question that *Bloomberg News* addressed in mid-2017. Looking for evidence of a market poised to run out of steam, it noted that high-grade U.S. companies had already sold almost $1 trillion of bonds in the year to July 2017, and less safe companies had issued a record volume of junk bonds, whose yields had fallen to 5.8 percent. As an example, despite the firm's failure to earn a profit, electric carmaker Tesla was able to unload $1.8 billion of bonds at a rock bottom interest rate.

But there were signs of an end to the low and falling interest rates and the 18-month-long rally in junk bonds.

These signs were laid out by Michael Heise, writing in the *Financial Times*. He notes that the expansion of China is boosting global trade, debt has been rising since 2014, the debt-to-income ratio has been rising, and in the major economies, firms are producing at full capacity and will need to increase investment in new capital to sustain expansion.

If Michael Heise is correct, interest rates will start to rise and the bond rally will end.

Sources: Based on *Bloomberg News*, August 14, 2017, and *Financial Times*, September 26, 2017

ESSENCE OF THE STORY

- U.S. high-grade companies sold almost $1 trillion of bonds in the first half of 2017.

- Tesla Inc., an unprofitable electric carmaker, sold $1.8 billion in bonds at a low interest rate.

- American businesses had issued a record volume of risky (junk) bonds at an average interest rate of 5.8 percent.

- There were signs that an 18-month-long rally in junk bonds was about to end.

ECONOMIC ANALYSIS

- The news article reports that the bond component of the loanable funds market was booming through 2016 and the first half of 2017 and interest rates were low.

- Even the bonds issued by risky businesses (and in the case of Tesla, a loss-incurring firm), called junk bonds, could be sold for a price that made the interest rate low.

- But the news article says that the booming bond issues and low interest rates are coming to an end.

- You can understand why the interest rate was low and why it might start to rise with what you have learned in this chapter.

- We begin by looking at some interest rate data.

- Figure 1 shows the interest rate on corporate bonds from 2010 to mid-2017 (both the nominal rate and the real rate.) This interest rate is the average of that on high-grade and junk bonds.

- The striking feature of this graph is that the interest rate was both low *and falling* through 2016 and the first half of 2017.

- Recall that there is an inverse relationship between the interest rate and the price of a bond. When the interest rate is high, the bond price is low, and when the interest rate is low, the bond price is high.

- But also, when the interest rate is rising, the bond price is falling, and when the interest rate is *falling*, the bond price is *rising*.

- A rising bond price increases the return on bonds and makes them more attractive to hold.

- Figure 2 illustrates why the real interest rate was falling. The demand for loanable funds was *DLF*. We will assume that demand did not change. In the first quarter of 2016, the supply of loanable funds was SLF_{Q1-16}. The equilibrium real interest rate was 2.9 percent per year.

- During 2016, bondholders expected interest rates to remain low for longer and expected the bond prices to rise. The expected rising bond prices increased the supply of loanable funds and by the first quarter of 2017, supply had increased to SLF_{Q1-17}.

- The increased supply lowered the real interest rate to 1.7 percent.

- Firms like Tesla issued bonds to take advantage of higher bond prices and lower interest rates. The bonds issued

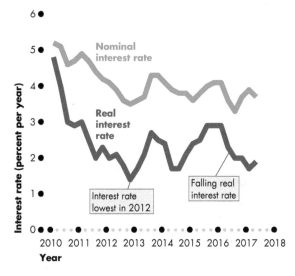

Figure 1 Interest Rate 2010 to 2017

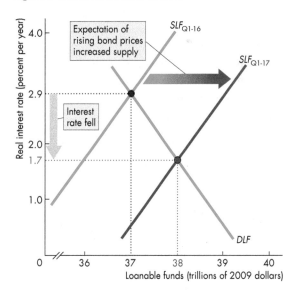

Figure 2 The Loanable Funds Market in 2016 and 2017

increased the quantity of loanable funds demanded—a movement down the demand curve—by $1 trillion from $37 trillion to $38 trillion.

- When bond prices are no longer expected to rise, the supply of bonds will decrease, interest rates will rise, and bond prices will start to fall.

WORKED PROBLEM

MyLab Economics Work this problem in Chapter 7 Study Plan.

Some facts about an economy are:

- In 2005, the nominal interest rate on bonds was 5 percent a year and the real interest rate was 2 percent a year. Investment was $2.7 billion and the government budget deficit was $0.5 billion.
- By 2009, the real interest rate had increased to 5 percent a year, but the nominal interest rate was unchanged at 5 percent a year. Investment had crashed to $1.8 billion and the government budget deficit had climbed to $1.8 billion.

Assume that the private demand for and private supply of loanable funds did not change between 2005 and 2009.

Questions

1. What was the inflation rate in 2005 and 2009? How do you know?
2. What happened to the price of a bond between 2005 and 2009? How do you know?
3. What happened to the demand for loanable funds between 2005 and 2009? How do you know?
4. Did the change in the government budget deficit crowd out some investment?
5. What happened to the quantity of saving and investment?

Solutions

1. The real interest rate equals the nominal interest rate minus the inflation rate. So the inflation rate equals the nominal interest rate minus the real interest rate. In 2005, the inflation rate was 3 percent a year, and in 2009 the inflation rate was zero.

Key Point: The nominal interest rate minus the real interest rate equals the inflation rate.

2. The price of a bond is inversely related to the nominal interest rate. Between 2005 and 2009, the nominal interest rate did not change—it remained at 5 percent a year. With the nominal interest rate unchanged, the price of a bond was also unchanged.

Key Point: The price of a bond is inversely related to the nominal interest rate.

3. The demand for loanable funds is the relationship between the quantity of loanable funds demanded and the real interest rate.

An increase in the government budget deficit increases the demand for loanable funds. Between 2005 and 2009, the government budget deficit increased from $0.5 billion to $1.8 billion, so the demand for loanable funds increased.

Key Point: An increase in the government budget deficit increases the demand for loanable funds.

4. The increase in the government budget deficit increased the demand for loanable funds. With no change in the supply of loanable funds, the real interest rate increases.

Between 2005 and 2009, the real interest rate increased from 2 percent a year to 5 percent a year. As the real interest rate increased, the quantity of loanable funds demanded by firms decreased from $2.7 billion to $1.8 billion. Crowding out occurred.

Key Point: Given the supply of loanable funds, an increase in the government budget deficit increases the real interest rate and crowds out investment.

5. Saving and investment plans depend on the real interest rate. Between 2005 and 2009, the real interest rate increased, which increased saving and decreased investment. The increase in saving increased the quantity supplied of loanable funds. The decrease in investment decreased the quantity demanded of loanable funds.

Key Point: A change in the real interest rate does not change the supply of or demand for loanable funds: It changes the quantities supplied and demanded.

Key Figure

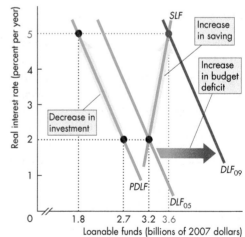

MyLab Economics Interactive Animation

SUMMARY

Key Points

Financial Markets and Financial Institutions
(pp. 164–169)

- Capital (*physical capital*) is a real productive resource; financial capital is the funds used to buy capital.
- Gross investment increases the quantity of capital and depreciation decreases it. Saving increases wealth.
- The markets for financial capital are the markets for loans, bonds, and stocks.
- Financial institutions ensure that borrowers and lenders can always find someone with whom to trade.

Working Problems 1 to 4 will give you a better understanding of financial institutions and financial markets.

The Loanable Funds Market (pp. 170–173)

- Investment in capital is financed by household saving, a government budget surplus, and funds from the rest of the world.
- The quantity of loanable funds demanded depends negatively on the real interest rate and the demand for loanable funds changes when profit expectations change.

- The quantity of loanable funds supplied depends positively on the real interest rate and the supply of loanable funds changes when disposable income, expected future income, wealth, and default risk change.
- Equilibrium in the loanable funds market determines the real interest rate and quantity of funds.

Working Problems 5 to 7 will give you a better understanding of the loanable funds market.

Government in the Loanable Funds Market
(pp. 174–175)

- A government budget surplus increases the supply of loanable funds, lowers the real interest rate, and increases investment and the equilibrium quantity of loanable funds.
- A government budget deficit increases the demand for loanable funds, raises the real interest rate, and increases the equilibrium quantity of loanable funds, but decreases investment in a crowding-out effect.
- The Ricardo-Barro effect is the response of rational taxpayers to a budget deficit: Private saving increases to finance the budget deficit. The real interest rate remains constant and the crowding-out effect is avoided.

Working Problems 8 to 11 will give you a better understanding of government in the loanable funds market.

Key Terms

MyLab Economics Key Terms Quiz

Bond, 165
Bond market, 165
Crowding-out effect, 175
Default risk, 171
Demand for loanable funds, 170
Financial capital, 164
Financial institution, 166
Gross investment, 164

Loanable funds market, 170
Mortgage, 165
Mortgage-backed security, 166
National saving, 169
Net investment, 164
Net taxes, 168
Net worth, 167
Nominal interest rate, 169

Real interest rate, 169
Saving, 164
Stock, 166
Stock market, 166
Supply of loanable funds, 171
Wealth, 164

STUDY PLAN PROBLEMS AND APPLICATIONS

MyLab Economics Work Problems 1 to 11 in Chapter 7 Study Plan and get instant feedback.

Financial Markets and Financial Institutions
(Study Plan 7.1)

Use the following data to work Problems 1 and 2.

Michael is an Internet service provider. On December 31, 2017, he bought an existing business with servers and a building worth $400,000. During 2018, his business grew and he bought new servers for $500,000. The market value of some of his older servers fell by $100,000.

1. What was Michael's gross investment, depreciation, and net investment during 2018?

2. What is the value of Michael's capital at the end of 2018?

3. Lori is a student who teaches golf on Saturdays. In a year, she earns $20,000 after paying her taxes. At the beginning of 2017, Lori owned $1,000 worth of books, DVDs, and golf clubs and she had $5,000 in a savings account at the bank. During 2017, the interest on her savings account was $300 and she spent a total of $15,300 on consumption goods and services. There was no change in the market values of her books, DVDs, and golf clubs.

   a. How much did Lori save in 2017?

   b. What was her wealth at the end of 2017?

4. **Funds to Avoid as Interest Rates Rise**

   Some of the funds popular with investment advisors are heading for a period of underperformance as interest rates rise.

   Source: *FT Adviser*, August 27, 2012

   What does the news clip mean by "underperformance"? Why might it be smart to avoid some bonds if interest rates are about to rise?

The Loanable Funds Market (Study Plan 7.2)

Use the following data to work Problems 5 and 6.

First Call, Inc., a smartphone company, plans to build an assembly plant—one that costs $10 million if the real interest rate is 6 percent a year; a larger plant that costs $12 million if the real interest rate is 5 percent a year; or a smaller plant that costs $8 million if the real interest rate is 7 percent a year.

5. Draw a graph of First Call's demand for loanable funds curve.

6. First Call expects its profit to double next year. Explain how this increase in expected profit influences First Call's demand for loanable funds.

7. The table sets out the data for an economy when the government's budget is balanced.

Real interest rate	Loanable funds demanded	Loanable funds supplied
(percent per year)	(billions of 2007 dollars)	
4	8.5	5.5
5	8.0	6.0
6	7.5	6.5
7	7.0	7.0
8	6.5	7.5
9	6.0	8.0
10	5.5	8.5

   a. Calculate the equilibrium real interest rate, investment, and private saving.

   b. If planned saving increases by $0.5 billion at each real interest rate, explain the change in the real interest rate.

   c. If planned investment increases by $1 billion at each real interest rate, explain the change in saving and the real interest rate.

Government in the Loanable Funds Market
(Study Plan 7.3)

Use the data in Problem 7 to work Problems 8 and 9.

8. If the government's budget becomes a deficit of $1 billion, what are the real interest rate and investment? Does crowding out occur?

9. If the government's budget becomes a deficit of $1 billion and the Ricardo-Barro effect occurs, what are the real interest rate and investment?

Use the table in Problem 7 and the following data to work Problems 10 and 11.

The quantity of loanable funds demanded increases by $1 billion at each real interest rate and the quantity of loanable funds supplied increases by $2 billion at each interest rate.

10. If the government budget remains balanced, what are the real interest rate, investment, and private saving? Does any crowding out occur?

11. If the government's budget becomes a deficit of $1 billion, what are the real interest rate, investment, and private saving? Does any crowding out occur?

ADDITIONAL PROBLEMS AND APPLICATIONS

MyLab Economics You can work these problems in Homework or Test if assigned by your instructor.

Financial Markets and Financial Institutions

12. On January 1, 2017, Terry's Towing Service owned 4 tow trucks valued at $300,000. During 2017, Terry's bought 2 new trucks for a total of $180,000. At the end of 2017, the market value of all of the firm's trucks was $400,000. What was Terry's gross investment? Calculate Terry's depreciation and net investment.

Use the following information to work Problems 13 and 14.

An economy's capital stock was $46.3 billion at the end of 2016, $46.6 billion at the end of 2017, and $47.0 billion at the end of 2018. Depreciation in 2017 was $2.4 billion, and gross investment during 2018 was $2.8 billion (all in 2007 dollars).

13. Calculate net investment and gross investment during 2017.

14. Calculate depreciation and net investment during 2018.

15. Annie runs a fitness centre. On December 31, 2017, she bought an existing business with exercise equipment and a building worth $300,000. During 2018, business improved and she bought some new equipment for $50,000. At the end of 2018, her equipment and buildings were worth $325,000. Calculate Annie's gross investment, depreciation, and net investment during 2018.

16. Karrie is a golf pro, and after she paid taxes, her income from golf and interest from financial assets was $1,500,000 in 2017. At the beginning of 2017, she owned $900,000 worth of financial assets. At the end of 2017, Karrie's financial assets were worth $1,900,000.

    a. How much did Karrie save during 2017?

    b. How much did she spend on consumption goods and services?

The Loanable Funds Market

17. **Canadians Saving More**

    Canadians are saving more, even as the returns on their savings have dwindled, which is not what standard economic theory predicts. In the second quarter of 2016, Canada's household savings rate was 4.2 percent, close to its average

since the end of the Great Recession and more than double the average rate for the five years preceding the crisis. Yet interest rates were much lower after the recession.

Source: *The Globe and Mail*, October 8, 2016

a. Is the news clip talking about the quantity of loanable funds supplied or the supply of loanable funds? Explain your answer.

b. Explain why an increase in saving accompanied by a fall in interest rates is not contrary to what economic theory predicts.

18. Draw a graph to illustrate the effect of an increase in the demand for loanable funds and an even larger increase in the supply of loanable funds on the real interest rate and the equilibrium quantity of loanable funds.

19. Draw a graph to illustrate how an increase in the supply of loanable funds and a decrease in the demand for loanable funds can lower the real interest rate and leave the equilibrium quantity of loanable funds unchanged.

Use the following data to work Problems 20 and 21.

In 2015, the Lee family had disposable income of $80,000, wealth of $140,000, and an expected future income of $80,000 a year. At a real interest rate of 4 percent a year, the Lee family saves $15,000 a year; at a real interest rate of 6 percent a year, they save $20,000 a year; and at a real interest rate of 8 percent, they save $25,000 a year.

20. Draw a graph of the Lee family's supply of loanable funds curve.

21. In 2016, suppose that the stock market crashes and the default risk increases. Explain how this increase in default risk influences the Lee family's supply of loanable funds curve.

22. **TransCanada Deal with U.S. Carrier Worth $13 Billion**

    TransCanada working with Columbia Pipeline Group aims to create a giant natural gas transmission business. The deal will create a 91,000-kilometre natural gas pipeline system.

    Source: *The Toronto Star*, March 18, 2016

    Show on a graph the effect of TransCanada going to the loanable funds market to finance the deal with Columbia. Explain the effect on the real interest rate, private saving, and investment.

23. The table sets out the data for an economy when the government's budget is balanced.

Real interest rate	Loanable funds demanded	Loanable funds supplied
(percent per year)	(billions of 2007 dollars)	
2	8.0	4.0
3	7.0	5.0
4	6.0	6.0
5	5.0	7.0
6	4.0	8.0
7	3.0	9.0
8	2.0	10.0

a. Calculate the equilibrium real interest rate, investment, and private saving.

b. If planned saving decreases by $1 billion at each real interest rate, explain the change in the real interest rate and investment.

c. If planned investment decreases by $1 billion at each real interest rate, explain the change in saving and the real interest rate.

Government in the Loanable Funds Market

Use the following information to work Problems 24, 25, and 26.

India's Budget Seeks Fiscal Restraint

The government of India set a budget deficit target of 3 percent of GDP for 2017–2018, down from 3.5 percent in 2016–2017. Economists predict the 3 percent target will be missed. India's public debt is the highest in Asia.

Source: CNBC, January 30, 2017

24. If the Indian government reduces its deficit and achieves its target, how will the demand for or supply of loanable funds in India change?

25. If the Indian government misses its deficit target, how will the demand for or supply of loanable funds in India change?

26. If India's economic growth slows and incomes grow more slowly, and if other things remain the same, how will the demand for or supply of loanable funds in India change?

27. **Canadian Budget in Persistent Deficit**

The projected deficit in 2017 is $28.5 billion and there is no timeline for a return to surplus.

Source: *The Globe and Mail*, March 23, 2017

a. Explain the effect of the ongoing budget deficit on the loanable funds market.

b. What effect does the budget deficit have on the real interest rate, private saving, and investment?

Economics in the News

28. After you have studied *Economics in the News* on pp. 176–177, answer the following questions.

a. Why do bond prices and interest rates move in opposite directions?

b. Looking at Fig. 1 on p. 177, what must have happened to either the demand for or the supply of loanable funds during 2011, 2012, 2013, 2014, and 2015?

c. If the assumption in Fig. 2 on p. 177, that the demand for bonds did not change, is wrong and the demand for bonds increased during 2016, how does that change the story about how the supply of bonds changed?

d. If an economic expansion gets going in 2018, what will happen to the demand for loanable funds and the real interest rate?

29. **E.U. Announces the G20 Will Miss 2018 Growth Targets**

The 2014 G20 meeting committed the 20 countries to boost investment, create new jobs, and boost world income by $2 trillion over 5 years. The E.U. says the 2018 target will be missed.

Source: *World Finance*, April 10, 2017

a. Explain the effect of the 2014 increase in planned investment on the demand for or supply of loanable funds.

b. If G20 countries had succeeded in increasing global income, how would the world real interest rate, saving, and investment have been different from the 2018 outcome? Explain your answer.

c. On a graph of the global loanable funds market, illustrate your answer to part (b).

8 MONEY, THE PRICE LEVEL, AND INFLATION

After studying this chapter, you will be able to:

◆ Define money and describe its functions

◆ Explain the economic functions of banks

◆ Describe the structure and functions of the Bank of Canada

◆ Explain how the banking system creates money

◆ Explain what determines the quantity of money and the nominal interest rate

◆ Explain how the quantity of money influences the price level and the inflation rate

Money, like fire and the wheel, has been around for a long time, and it has taken many forms. It was beads made from shells for North American Indians and tobacco for early American colonists. Today, we use dollar bills or swipe a card or, in some places, tap a cellphone. Are all these things money?

In this chapter, we study money, its functions, how it gets created, how the Bank of Canada regulates its quantity, and what happens when its quantity changes. In *Economics in the News* at the end of the chapter, we look at a suggestion that the Bank of Canada should create more money to stimulate economic expansion.

What Is Money?

What do beads, tobacco, and nickels and dimes have in common? They are all examples of **money**, which is defined as any commodity or token that is generally acceptable as a means of payment. A **means of payment** is a method of settling a debt. When a payment has been made, there is no remaining obligation between the parties to a transaction. So what beads, tobacco, and nickels and dimes have in common is that they have served (or still do serve) as the means of payment. Money serves three other functions:

- Medium of exchange
- Unit of account
- Store of value

Medium of Exchange

A *medium of exchange* is any object that is generally accepted in exchange for goods and services. Without a medium of exchange, goods and services must be exchanged directly for other goods and services—an exchange called *barter*. Barter requires a *double coincidence of wants*, a situation that rarely occurs. For example, if you want a hamburger, you might offer a DVD in exchange for it. But you must find someone who is selling hamburgers and wants your DVD.

A medium of exchange overcomes the need for a double coincidence of wants. Money acts as a medium of exchange because people with something to sell will always accept money in exchange for it. But money isn't the only medium of exchange. You can buy with a credit card, but a credit card isn't money. It doesn't make a final payment, and the debt it creates must eventually be settled by using money.

Unit of Account

A *unit of account* is an agreed-upon measure for stating the prices of goods and services. To get the most out of your budget, you have to figure out whether seeing one more movie is worth its opportunity cost. But that cost is not dollars and cents. It is the number of ice-cream cones, sodas, or cups of coffee that you must give up. It's easy to do such calculations when all these goods have prices in terms of dollars and cents (see Table 8.1). If the price of a movie is $8 and the price of a cappuccino is $4, you know right

TABLE 8.1 The Unit of Account Function of Money Simplifies Price Comparisons

Good	Price in money units	Price in units of another good
Movie	$8.00 each	2 cappuccinos
Cappuccino	$4.00 each	2 ice-cream cones
Ice cream	$2.00 per cone	2 packs of jelly beans
Jelly beans	$1.00 per pack	2 sticks of gum
Gum	$0.50 per stick	

Money as a unit of account: The price of a movie is $8 and the price of a stick of gum is 50¢, so the opportunity cost of a movie is 16 sticks of gum ($8.00 ÷ 50¢ = 16).

No unit of account: You go to a movie theatre and learn that the cost of seeing a movie is 2 cappuccinos. You go to a grocery store and learn that a pack of jelly beans costs 2 sticks of gum. But how many sticks of gum does seeing a movie cost you? To answer that question, you go to the coffee shop and find that a cappuccino costs 2 ice-cream cones. Now you head for the ice-cream shop, where an ice-cream cone costs 2 packs of jelly beans. Now you get out your pocket calculator: 1 movie costs 2 cappuccinos, or 4 ice-cream cones, or 8 packs of jelly beans, or 16 sticks of gum!

away that seeing one movie costs you 2 cappuccinos. If jelly beans are $1 a pack, one movie costs 8 packs of jelly beans. You need only one calculation to figure out the opportunity cost of any pair of goods and services.

Imagine how troublesome it would be if your local movie theatre posted its price as 2 cappuccinos, the coffee shop posted the price of a cappuccino as 2 ice-cream cones, the ice-cream shop posted the price of an ice-cream cone as 2 packs of jelly beans, and the grocery store priced a pack of jelly beans as 2 sticks of gum! Now how much running around and calculating will you have to do to find out how much that movie is going to cost you in terms of the cappuccinos, ice-cream cones, jelly beans, or gum that you must give up to see it? You get the answer for cappuccinos right away from the sign posted on the movie theatre. But for all the other goods, you're going to have to visit many different stores to establish the price of each good in terms of another and then calculate the prices in units that are relevant for your own decision. The hassle of doing all this research might be enough to make a person swear off movies! You can see how much simpler it is if all the prices are expressed in dollars and cents.

Store of Value

Money is a *store of value* in the sense that it can be held and exchanged later for goods and services. If money were not a store of value, it could not serve as a means of payment.

Money is not alone in acting as a store of value. A house, a car, and a work of art are other examples.

The more stable the value of a commodity or token, the better it can act as a store of value and the more useful it is as money. No store of value has a completely stable value. The value of a house, a car, or a work of art fluctuates over time. The values of the commodities and tokens that are used as money also fluctuate over time.

Inflation lowers the value of money and the values of other commodities and tokens that are used as money. To make money as useful as possible as a store of value, a low inflation rate is needed.

Money in Canada Today

In Canada today, money consists of:

- Currency
- Deposits at banks and other depository institutions

Currency The notes and coins held by individuals and businesses are known as **currency**. Notes are money because the government declares them so with the words "Ce billet a cours légal—this note is legal tender." Notes and coins inside banks are not counted as currency because they are not held by individuals and businesses. Currency is convenient for settling small debts and buying low-priced items.

Deposits Deposits of individuals and businesses at banks and other depository institutions, such as trust and mortgage companies, credit unions, and caisses populaires, are also counted as money. Deposits are money because the owners of the deposits can use them to make payments. Deposits owned by the Government of Canada are not counted as money because they are not held by individuals and businesses.

Official Measures of Money Two official measures of money in Canada today are known as M1 and M2. **M1** consists of currency held by individuals and businesses plus chequable deposits owned by individuals and businesses. **M2** consists of M1 plus all other deposits—non-chequable deposits and fixed term deposits—held by individuals and businesses.

ECONOMICS IN ACTION

Official Measures of Canadian Money

The figure shows the relative magnitudes of the items that make up M1 and M2. Notice that currency is a small part of our money.

	$ billions in May 2017
M2	**1,556**
Comprises all in M1, plus...	
Fixed term deposits	326
Non-chequable deposits, non-personal	51
Non-chequable deposits, personal	329
M1	850
Chequable deposits, non-personal	489
Chequable deposits, personal	281
Currency outside banks	80

Two Official Measures of Money

M1	■ Currency held by individuals and businesses
	■ Personal chequable deposits
	■ Non-personal chequable deposits
M2	■ M1
	■ Personal non-chequable deposits
	■ Non-personal non-chequable deposits
	■ Fixed term deposits

Source of data: Statistics Canada, CANSIM Table 176-0020. M1 is M1+ (gross), and M2 is M2 (gross). The data are for May 2017.

Are M1 and M2 Really Money? Money is the means of payment. So the test of whether an asset is money is whether it serves as a means of payment. Currency passes the test. But what about deposits? Chequable deposits are money because they can be transferred from one person to another by writing a cheque or using a debit card. Such a transfer of ownership is equivalent to handing over currency. Because M1 consists of currency plus chequable deposits and each of these is a means of payment, *M1 is money*.

But what about M2? Some of the savings deposits in M2 are just as much a means of payment as the chequable deposits in M1. You can use an ATM to get funds from your savings account to pay for your purchase at the grocery store or the gas station. But some savings deposits are not means of payment. They are known as liquid assets. *Liquidity* is the property of being easily convertible into a means of payment without loss in value. Because the deposits in M2 that are not means of payment are quickly and easily converted into a means of payment—currency or chequable deposits—they are counted as money.

Deposits Are Money but Cheques and Debit Cards Are Not We count deposits as money, but we don't count cheques or debit cards as money. Why are deposits money and cheques and debit cards not?

To see why deposits are money but cheques are not, think about what happens when Colleen buys some roller-blades for $100 from Rocky's Rollers. When Colleen goes to Rocky's shop, she has $500 in her deposit account at the Laser Bank. Rocky has $1,000 in his deposit account—at the same bank, as it happens. The deposits of these two people total $1,500. Colleen writes a cheque for $100, or swipes her debit card. Rocky takes the cheque to the bank, or when the debit card is swiped, Rocky's bank balance rises from $1,000 to $1,100, and Colleen's balance falls from $500 to $400. The deposits of Colleen and Rocky still total $1,500. Rocky now has $100 more than before, and Colleen has $100 less.

This transaction has transferred money from Colleen to Rocky, but the cheque or the debit card was not money. There wasn't an extra $100 of money while the cheque was in circulation. The cheque or the card swipe instructs the bank to transfer money from Colleen to Rocky.

If Colleen and Rocky use different banks, there is an extra step. Rocky's bank credits $100 to Rocky's account and then takes the cheque to a cheque-clearing centre. The cheque is then sent to Colleen's bank, which pays Rocky's bank $100 and then debits Colleen's account $100. This process can take a few days, but the principles are the same as when two people use the same bank.

Credit Cards Are Not Money You've just seen that cheques and debit cards are not money, but what about credit cards? Isn't having a credit card in your wallet and presenting it to pay for your roller-blades the same thing as using money? Why aren't credit cards somehow valued and counted as part of the quantity of money?

When you pay by cheque, you are frequently asked to show your driver's licence. It would never occur to you to think of your driver's licence as money. It's just an ID card. A credit card is also an ID card, but one that lets you take out a loan at the instant you buy something. When you swipe your credit card and key in your pin, you are saying, "I agree to pay for these goods when the credit card company bills me." Once you get your statement from the credit card company, you must make at least the minimum payment due. To make that payment, you need money—you need to have currency or a chequable deposit to pay the credit card company. So although you use a credit card when you buy something, the credit card is not the *means of payment* and it is not money.

REVIEW QUIZ

1 What makes something money? What functions does money perform? Why do you think packs of chewing gum don't serve as money?

2 What are the problems that arise when a commodity is used as money?

3 What are the main components of money in Canada today?

4 What are the official measures of money? Are all the measures really money?

5 Why are cheques, debit cards, and credit cards not money?

Work these questions in Study Plan 8.1 and get instant feedback.   MyLab Economics

We've seen that the main component of money in Canada is deposits held by individuals and businesses at banks and other depository institutions. Let's take a closer look at these institutions.

◆ Depository Institutions

A **depository institution** is a financial firm that takes deposits from households and firms. These deposits are components of M1 and M2. You will learn what these institutions are, what they do, the economic benefits they bring, how they are regulated, and how they innovate and create new financial products.

Types of Depository Institutions

The deposits of three types of depository institution make up Canada's money. They are:

- Chartered banks
- Credit unions and caisses populaires
- Trust and mortgage loan companies

Chartered Banks A **chartered bank** is a private firm chartered under the Bank Act of 1991 to receive deposits and make loans. The chartered banks are by far the largest institutions in the banking system and conduct all types of banking and financial business. In 2017, 30 Canadian-owned banks (including the Royal Bank of Canada, CIBC, Bank of Montreal, Bank of Nova Scotia, National Bank of Canada, and TD Canada Trust) and 24 foreign-owned banks had the bulk of the deposits in M1 and M2.

Credit Unions and Caisses Populaires A *credit union* is a cooperative organization that operates under the Cooperative Credit Associations Act of 1991 and that receives deposits from and makes loans to its members. A caisse populaire is a similar type of institution that operates in Quebec.

Trust and Mortgage Loan Companies A trust and mortgage loan company is a privately owned depository institution that operates under the Trust and Loan Companies Act of 1991. These institutions receive deposits, make loans, and act as trustee for pension funds and for estates.

All Banks Now Historically, Canada has made a sharp legal distinction between banks and other depository institutions. But the economic functions of all depository institutions have grown increasingly similar. This fact is recognized in laws governing these institutions that became effective in 1991. Because they all perform the same essential economic functions, we'll call all these institutions banks unless we need to distinguish among them.

What Depository Institutions Do

Depository institutions provide services such as cheque clearing, account management, credit cards, and Internet banking, all of which provide an income from service fees.

But depository institutions earn most of their income by using the funds they receive from depositors to make loans and buy securities that earn a higher interest rate than that paid to depositors. In this activity, a depository institution must perform a balance return against risk. To see this balancing act, we'll focus on the chartered banks.

A chartered bank puts the funds it receives from depositors and other funds that it borrows into four types of assets:

- Reserves
- Liquid assets
- Securities
- Loans

Reserves A depository institution's **reserves** are notes and coins in its vault or its deposit account at the Bank of Canada. (We study the Bank of Canada later in this chapter.) These funds are used to meet depositors' currency withdrawals and to make payments to other banks. In normal times, a bank keeps about a half of 1 percent of deposits as reserves.

Liquid Assets Liquid assets are Government of Canada Treasury bills and commercial bills. These assets are the banks' first line of defence if they need reserves. Liquid assets can be sold and instantly converted into reserves with virtually no risk of loss. Because they have a low risk, they also earn a low interest rate.

Securities Securities are Government of Canada bonds and other bonds such as mortgage-backed securities. These assets can be converted into reserves but at prices that fluctuate. Because their prices fluctuate, these assets are riskier than liquid assets, but they also have a higher interest rate.

Loans Loans are commitments of funds for an agreed-upon period of time. Banks make loans to corporations to finance the purchase of capital. They also make mortgage loans to finance the purchase of homes, and personal loans to finance consumer durable goods, such as cars or boats. The outstanding balances on credit card accounts are also bank loans.

Loans are the riskiest assets of a bank. They cannot be converted into reserves until they are due to be repaid. Also, some borrowers default and never repay. These assets earn the highest interest rate.

Table 8.2 provides a snapshot of the sources and uses of funds of all the chartered banks in April 2017.

Economic Benefits Provided by Depository Institutions

You've seen that a depository institution earns part of its profit because it pays a lower interest rate on deposits than what it receives on loans. What benefits do these institutions provide that make depositors willing to put up with a low interest rate and borrowers willing to pay a higher one?

Depository institutions provide four benefits:

- Create liquidity
- Pool risk
- Lower the cost of borrowing
- Lower the cost of monitoring borrowers

Create Liquidity Depository institutions create liquidity by borrowing short and lending long—taking deposits and standing ready to repay them on short notice or on demand and making loan commitments that run for terms of many years.

TABLE 8.2   Chartered Banks: Sources and Uses of Funds

	$ billions April 2017	Percentage of deposits
Total funds	2,723	122.1
Sources		
Deposits	2,241	100.0
Borrowing	108	4.8
Own capital	385	17.2
Uses		
Reserves	6	0.3
Liquid assets	240	10.7
Securities	357	16.0
Loans	2,127	95.3

Chartered banks get most of their funds from depositors and use most of them to make loans. They hold less than 1 percent of deposits as reserves but hold almost 11 percent of deposits as liquid assets.

Source of data: Statistics Canada, CANSIM Table 176-0011.

Pool Risk A loan might not be repaid—a default. If you lend to one person who defaults, you lose the entire amount loaned. If you lend to 1,000 people (through a bank) and one person defaults, you lose almost nothing. Depository institutions pool risk.

Lower the Cost of Borrowing Imagine a firm is looking for $1 million to buy a new factory and there are no depository institutions. The firm hunts around for several dozen people from whom to borrow the funds. Depository institutions lower the cost of this search. The firm gets its $1 million from a single institution that gets deposits from a large number of people but spreads the cost of this activity over many borrowers.

Lower the Cost of Monitoring Borrowers By monitoring borrowers, a lender can encourage good decisions that prevent defaults. But this activity is costly. Imagine how costly it would be if each household that lent money to a firm incurred the costs of monitoring that firm directly. Depository institutions can perform this task at a much lower cost.

How Depository Institutions Are Regulated

Responsibility for financial regulation in Canada is shared by the Department of Finance, the Bank of Canada, the Office of the Superintendent of Financial Institutions, the Canada Deposit Insurance Corporation, and provincial agencies. The goal of financial regulation is to identify, evaluate, and lessen the consequences of financial risk.

The Department of Finance bears the ultimate responsibility for regulation but delegates the day-to-day details to the other agencies.

The Bank of Canada ensures that the banks and other depository institutions have adequate liquidity and provides general guidance and advice to government.

The Office of the Superintendent of Financial Institutions supervises the banks and other depository institutions and ensures that their balance sheets have a high-enough capital ratio and their assets are sufficiently liquid to withstand stress.

The Canada Deposit Insurance Corporation operates a system of deposit insurance that insures deposits held at Canadian banks up to $100,000 in case of a bank failure.

Provincial government agencies regulate credit unions and caisses populaires.

Canadian financial regulation has successfully avoided major failures at times when U.S. banks have failed.

◆ AT **ISSUE**

Fractional-Reserve Banking Versus 100 Percent Reserve Banking

Fractional-reserve banking, a system in which banks keep a fraction of their depositors' funds as a cash reserve and lend the rest, was invented by goldsmiths in sixteenth-century Europe and is the only system in use today.

This system contrasts with **100 percent reserve banking**, a system in which banks keep the full amount of their depositors' funds as a cash reserve.

The 2008 global financial crisis raises the question: Should banks be required to keep 100 percent cash reserves to prevent them from failing and bringing recession?

Yes

- The most unrelenting advocates of 100 percent reserve banking are a group of economists known as the *Austrian School*, who say that fractional-reserve banking violates property rights.

- Because a deposit is owned by the depositor and not the bank, the bank has no legal right to lend the deposit to someone else.

- Mainstream economists Irving Fisher in the 1930s and Milton Friedman in the 1950s advocated 100 percent reserve banking.

- They said it enables the central bank to exercise more precise control over the quantity of money, and it eliminates the risk of a bank running out of cash.

Irving Fisher of Yale University supported 100 percent reserve banking.

No

- The requirement to hold 100 percent reserves would prevent the banks making loans and lower their profits.

- Lower bank profits weaken rather than strengthen the banks.

- The demand for loans would be met by a supply from unregulated institutions, and they might be riskier than the current fractional-reserve banks.

- Nonetheless, banks do need to be regulated.

- The Financial Stability Board, based in Basel, Switzerland, has drawn up rules, called Basel III, that are designed to eliminate the risk that a major bank will fail.

- Mark Carney, Chairman of the Financial Stability Board and Governor of the Bank of England, wants all banks to adopt the Basel III principles, which increase the amount of a bank's own capital that must be held as a buffer against a fall in asset values.

Mark Carney, Chairman of the Financial Stability Board and Governor of the Bank of England.

"Our destination should be one where financial institutions and markets play critical—and complementary—roles to support long-term economic prosperity. This requires institutions that are adequately capitalized, with sufficient liquidity buffers to manage shocks."

Mark Carney, remarks at the Institute of International Finance, Washington, D.C., September 25, 2011.

ECONOMICS IN ACTION

Canadian and U.S. Banks Compared

The figure compares the sources and uses of funds (sources are liabilities and uses are assets) of Canadian and U.S. banks in 2008 and in 2017.

The data are measured as percentages of deposits in 2008, so they enable us to compare the growth and changes in composition in both economies.

The overall growth in the size of banks is larger in Canada, and the Canadian economy grew by more than the U.S. economy.

There are big differences in the composition of the sources and uses of funds. The banks' own capital resources increased much more in Canada than in the United States. And the banks' reserves have increased more in the United States than in Canada.

Bank borrowing decreased in both economies, but by much more in Canada.

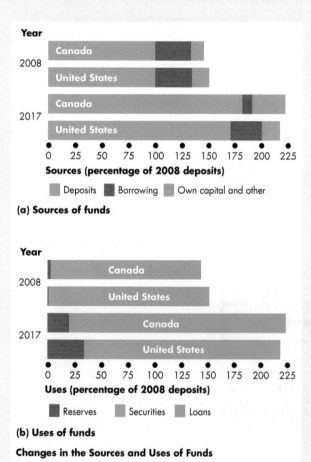

(a) Sources of funds

(b) Uses of funds

Changes in the Sources and Uses of Funds

Source of data: Statistics Canada.

Financial Innovation

In the pursuit of larger profits, depository institutions are constantly seeking ways to improve their products in a process called *financial innovation*.

During the late 1970s, a high inflation rate sent the interest rate on home-purchase loans to 15 percent a year. Traditional fixed interest rate mortgages became unprofitable, and variable interest rate mortgages were introduced.

During the 2000s, when interest rates were low and depository institutions were flush with funds, sub-prime mortgages were developed. To avoid the risk of carrying these mortgages, mortgage-backed securities were developed. The original lending institution sold these securities, lowered their own exposure to risk, and obtained funds to make more loans.

The development of low-cost computing and communication brought financial innovations such as credit cards and daily-interest deposit accounts.

Financial innovation has made little difference to the *composition* of money. Comparing 1989 and 2017, and expressed as percentages of M2, chequable deposits have changed from 48 percent to 49 percent. Non-chequable deposits have increased from 22 percent to 24 percent, and fixed term deposits have shrunk from 25 percent to 21 percent. Perhaps surprisingly, the use of currency has been rock steady at 5 percent of M2.

REVIEW QUIZ

1 What are depository institutions?
2 What are the functions of depository institutions?
3 How do depository institutions balance risk and return?
4 How do depository institutions create liquidity, pool risks, and lower the cost of borrowing?
5 How have depository institutions made innovations that have influenced the composition of money?

Work these questions in Study Plan 8.2 and get instant feedback.   MyLab Economics

You now know what money is. Your next task is to learn about the Bank of Canada and the ways in which it can influence the quantity of money.

The Bank of Canada

The Bank of Canada is Canada's **central bank**, a public authority that supervises other banks and financial institutions, financial markets, and the payments system, and conducts monetary policy.

The Bank of Canada is a bank. And like all banks, it accepts deposits, makes loans, and holds investment securities. But the Bank of Canada is special in three important ways. It is the:

- Banker to banks and government
- Lender of last resort
- Sole issuer of bank notes

Banker to Banks and Government

The Bank of Canada has a restricted list of customers. They are the chartered banks, credit unions and caisses populaires, and trust and mortgage loan companies that make up the banking system; the Government of Canada; and the central banks of other countries.

The Bank of Canada accepts deposits from these customers. The deposits of depository institutions are part of their reserves.

Lender of Last Resort

The Bank of Canada makes loans to banks. It is the **lender of last resort**, which means that it stands ready to make loans when the banking system as a whole is short of reserves. If some banks are short of reserves while others have surplus reserves, the overnight loan market moves the funds from one bank to another.

Sole Issuer of Bank Notes

The Bank of Canada is the only bank that is permitted to issue bank notes. You might think that such a monopoly is natural, but it isn't. In some banking systems—those of Ireland and Scotland are examples—private banks also issue bank notes. But in Canada and most other countries, the central bank has a monopoly on this activity.

The Bank of Canada's Balance Sheet

The Bank of Canada influences the economy by changing interest rates. You'll learn the details of the Bank's monetary policy strategy in Chapter 14 when you've studied all the tools needed to understand monetary policy. But to influence interest rates, the Bank must change the quantity of money

---

FIGURE 8.1   The Bank of Canada Home Page

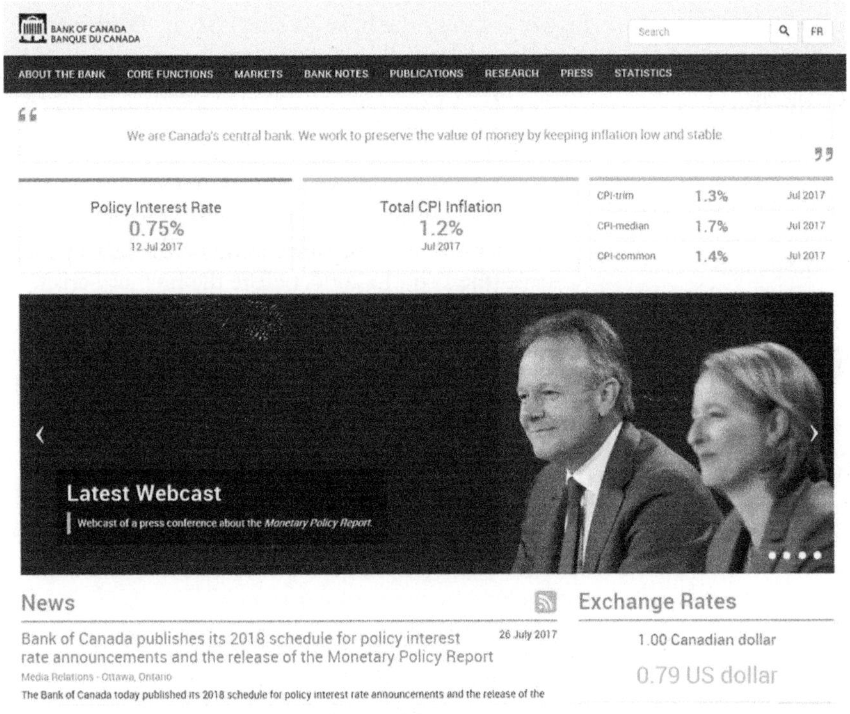

The Bank of Canada is located in Ottawa. Its governor, is Stephen S. Poloz, pictured here alongside senior deputy governor Carolyn Wilkins. Its Web site (Home Page shown here) is packed with useful information and data on the Bank's actions and the performance of the economy.

Source: Bank of Canada. Used by permission of Bank of Canada.

in the economy. This quantity depends on the size and composition of the Bank of Canada's balance sheet—its assets and liabilities. Let's look at the Bank of Canada's balance sheet, starting with its assets.

The Bank of Canada's Assets The Bank of Canada has two main assets:

1. Government securities
2. Loans to depository institutions

The Bank of Canada holds Government of Canada securities—Treasury bills—that it buys in the bills market. The Bank of Canada makes loans to depository institutions. When these institutions in aggregate are short of reserves, they can borrow from the Bank of Canada. In normal times this item is small, or zero, as it was in 2017 (see Table 8.3).

The Bank of Canada's Liabilities The Bank of Canada has two liabilities:

1. Bank of Canada notes
2. Depository institution deposits

Bank of Canada notes are the dollar bills that we use in our daily transactions. Some of these notes are held by individuals and businesses; others are in the tills and vaults of banks and other depository institutions. Depository institution deposits at the Bank of Canada are part of the reserves of these institutions (see p. 187).

The Monetary Base The Bank of Canada's liabilities together with coins issued by the Royal Canadian Mint (coins are not liabilities of the Bank of Canada) make up the monetary base. That is, the **monetary base** is the sum of Bank of Canada notes, coins, and depository institution deposits at the Bank of Canada. The monetary base is so named because it acts like a base that supports the nation's money. Table 8.3 provides a snapshot of the sources and uses of the monetary base in June 2017.

The Bank of Canada's Policy Tools

The Bank of Canada has two main policy tools:

- Open market operation
- Bank rate

Open Market Operation To change the monetary base, the Bank of Canada conducts an **open market operation**, which is the purchase or sale of government securities by the Bank of Canada in the

TABLE 8.3 The Sources and Uses of the Monetary Base

Sources (billions of dollars)		Uses (billions of dollars)	
Government of Canada securities	87.5	Notes	87.0
Loans to depository institutions	0	Reserves of depository institutions	0.5
Monetary base	87.5	Monetary base	87.5

Source of data: Statistics Canada. The data are for June 2017.

loanable funds market. Let's see how an open market operation works and what it does.

An Open Market Purchase An open market operation changes bank reserves, which changes the monetary base. To see how, suppose the Bank of Canada buys $100 million of government securities from CIBC.

ECONOMICS IN ACTION
A Tale of Two Central Banks

Figure 1 shows the balance sheet of the Bank of Canada. Almost all its assets (sources of monetary base) in part (a) are government securities. Almost all of its liabilities (uses of monetary base) in part (b) are notes and coins. The monetary base grew between 2007, the last year before a global financial crisis, and 2017 at an average annual rate of 6.2 percent.

Figure 2 shows the balance sheet of the U.S. Federal Reserve (the Fed). In 2007, before the financial crisis, this balance sheet looked like Canada's. Almost all its assets in part (a) were government securities and almost all of its liabilities in part (b) were notes and coins.

But through the financial crisis and still in place in mid-2017 and expected to be in place well into 2018, the Fed loaned billions of dollars to banks and other troubled institutions and created almost $4 trillion of monetary base—an increase of 460 percent or 17 percent per year on average. Most of this new monetary base is held by the banks as reserves.

When, and how quickly, the Fed unwinds this large increase in the monetary base and bank reserves will have a major influence on the U.S. and Canadian economies.

When the Bank of Canada makes this transaction, two things happen:

1. CIBC has $100 million less securities. The Bank of Canada has $100 million more securities.

2. The Bank of Canada pays for the securities by placing $100 million in CIBC's reserve deposit at the Bank of Canada.

Figure 8.2 shows the effects of these actions on the balance sheets of the Bank of Canada and CIBC. Ownership of the securities passes from CIBC to the Bank of Canada, so CIBC's assets decrease by $100 million and the Bank of Canada's assets increase by $100 million, as shown by the blue arrow running from CIBC to the Bank of Canada.

The Bank of Canada pays for the securities by placing $100 million in CIBC's reserve deposit at the Bank of Canada, as shown by the green arrow running from the Bank of Canada to CIBC.

The Bank of Canada's assets increase by $100 million and its liabilities increase by $100 million. The CIBC's total assets are unchanged: It sold securities to increase its reserves.

FIGURE 8.2 The Bank of Canada Buys Securities in the Open Market

The Bank of Canada

Assets (millions)		Liabilities (millions)	
Securities	+$100	Reserves of CIBC	+$100

The Bank of Canada buys securities from a bank ...   ... and pays for the securities by increasing the reserves of the bank

CIBC

Assets (millions)		Liabilities (millions)
Securities	–$100	
Reserves	+$100	

When the Bank of Canada buys securities in the open market, it creates bank reserves. The Bank of Canada's assets and liabilities increase, and CIBC exchanges securities for reserves.

MyLab Economics Animation

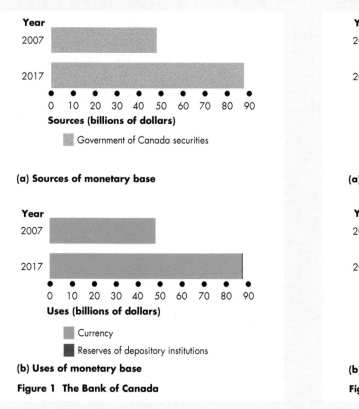

(a) Sources of monetary base

(b) Uses of monetary base

Figure 1 The Bank of Canada

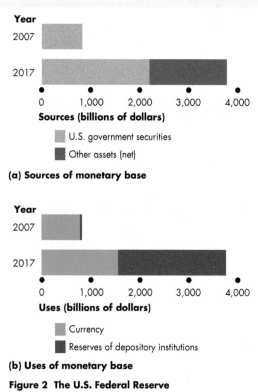

(a) Sources of monetary base

(b) Uses of monetary base

Figure 2 The U.S. Federal Reserve

An Open Market Sale If the Bank of Canada sells $100 million of government securities to CIBC:

1. CIBC has $100 million more securities and the Bank of Canada has $100 million less securities.
2. CIBC pays for the securities by using $100 million of its reserve deposit at the Bank of Canada.

You can follow the effects of these actions by reversing the arrows and the plus and minus signs in Fig. 8.2. Ownership of the securities passes from the Bank of Canada to CIBC, so the Bank of Canada's assets decrease by $100 million and CIBC's assets increase by $100 million.

CIBC uses $100 million of its reserves to pay for the securities.

The Bank of Canada's assets and liabilities decrease by $100 million. CIBC's total assets are unchanged: It has used reserves to buy securities.

Bank Rate   The Bank of Canada makes short-term, typically one-day, loans to major depository institutions when the banking system is temporarily short of reserves, and the interest rate that the Bank charges on these loans is called the **bank rate**.

The bank rate acts like an anchor for other short-term interest rates and is closely related to the Bank's target for the overnight loans rate among banks, which it targets to keep inflation in check.

You will study the Bank's monetary policy in Chapter 14.

REVIEW QUIZ

1 What is the central bank in Canada and what functions does it perform?
2 What is the monetary base and how does it relate to the Bank of Canada's balance sheet?
3 What are the Bank of Canada's two main policy tools?
4 How does an open market operation change the monetary base?

Work these questions in Study Plan 8.3 and get instant feedback.   MyLab Economics

Next, we're going to see how the banking system—the banks and the Bank of Canada—creates money and how the quantity of money changes when the Bank of Canada changes the monetary base.

How Banks Create Money

Banks create money. But this doesn't mean that they have smoke-filled back rooms in which counterfeiters are busily working. Remember, money is both currency and bank deposits. What banks create is deposits, and they do so by making loans.

Creating Deposits by Making Loans

The easiest way to see that banks create deposits is to think about what happens when Andy, who has a Visa card issued by CIBC, uses his card to buy a tank of gas from Shell. When Andy swipes his card, two financial transactions occur. First, Andy takes a loan from CIBC and obligates himself to repay the loan at a later date. Second, a message is transmitted to Shell's bank and the bank credits Shell's account with the amount of Andy's purchase (minus the bank's commission).

For now, let's assume that Shell, like Andy, banks at CIBC so that the two transactions we've just described both occur at the one bank.

You can see that these transactions have created a bank deposit and a loan. Andy has increased the size of his loan (his credit card balance), and Shell has increased the size of its bank deposit. Because bank deposits are money, CIBC has created money.

If, as we've just assumed, Andy and Shell use the same bank, no further transactions take place. But if two banks are involved, there is another transaction. To see this additional transaction and its effects, assume that Shell's bank is Royal Bank of Canada. To fully settle the payment for Andy's gas purchase, CIBC must pay Royal Bank of Canada.

To make this payment, CIBC uses its reserves. CIBC's reserves decrease by the amount of its loan to Andy; Royal Bank of Canada's reserves increase by the amount that Shell's deposit increases. All payments like this one between the banks are made at the end of the business day. So, at the end of the business day the banking system as a whole has an increase in loans and deposits but no change in reserves.

Three factors limit the quantity of loans and deposits that the banking system can create through transactions like Andy's. They are:

- The monetary base
- Desired reserves
- Desired currency holding

The Monetary Base You've seen that the *monetary base* is the sum of Bank of Canada notes and banks' deposits at the Bank of Canada. The size of the monetary base limits the total quantity of money that the banking system can create. This limit arises because banks have a desired quantity of reserves, households and firms have a desired holding of currency, and both of these desired holdings of the monetary base depend on the quantity of deposits.

Desired Reserves A bank's *desired reserves* are the reserves that it *plans* to hold. They contrast with a bank's *required reserves*, which is the minimum quantity of reserves that a bank *must* hold.

The quantity of desired reserves depends on the level of deposits and is determined by the **desired reserve ratio**—the ratio of reserves to deposits that the banks *plan* to hold. The *desired* reserve ratio exceeds the *required* reserve ratio by an amount that the banks determine to be prudent on the basis of their daily business requirements and in the light of the current outlook in financial markets.

Desired Currency Holding The proportions of money held as currency and bank deposits—the ratio of currency to deposits—depend on how households and firms choose to make payments: whether they plan to use currency or debit cards and cheques.

Choices about how to make payments change slowly, so the ratio of desired currency to deposits also changes slowly, and at any given time this ratio is fixed. If bank deposits increase, desired currency holding also increases. For this reason, when banks make loans that increase deposits, some currency leaves the banks—the banking system leaks reserves. We call the leakage of bank reserves into currency the *currency drain*, and we call the ratio of currency to deposits the **currency drain ratio**.

We've sketched the way that a loan creates a deposit and described the three factors that limit the amount of loans and deposits that can be created. We're now going to examine the money creation process more closely and discover a money multiplier.

The Money Creation Process

The money creation process begins with an increase in the monetary base, which occurs if the Bank of Canada conducts an open market operation in which it buys securities from banks and other institutions.

The Bank of Canada pays for the securities it buys with newly created bank reserves.

When the Bank of Canada buys securities from a bank, the bank's reserves increase but its deposits don't change. So the bank has excess reserves. A bank's **excess reserves** are its actual reserves minus its desired reserves.

When a bank has excess reserves, it makes loans and creates deposits. When the entire banking system has excess reserves, total loans and deposits increase and the quantity of money increases.

One bank can make a loan and get rid of excess reserves. But the banking system as a whole can't get rid of excess reserves so easily. When the banks make loans and create deposits, the extra deposits lower excess reserves for two reasons. First, the increase in deposits increases desired reserves. Second, a currency drain decreases total reserves. But excess reserves don't completely disappear. So the banks lend some more and the process repeats.

As the process of making loans and increasing deposits repeats, desired reserves increase, total reserves decrease through the currency drain, and eventually enough new deposits have been created to use all the new monetary base.

Figure 8.3 summarizes one round in the process we've just described. The sequence has the following eight steps:

1. Banks have excess reserves.
2. Banks lend excess reserves.
3. The quantity of money increases.
4. New money is used to make payments.
5. Some of the new money remains on deposit.
6. Some of the new money is a *currency drain*.
7. Desired reserves increase because deposits have increased.
8. Excess reserves decrease.

If the Bank of Canada *sells* securities in an open market operation, then banks have negative excess reserves—they are short of reserves. When the banks are short of reserves, loans and deposits decrease and the process we've described above works in a downward direction until desired reserves plus desired currency holding have decreased by an amount equal to the decrease in monetary base.

A money multiplier determines the change in the quantity of money that results from a change in the monetary base.

FIGURE 8.3   How the Banking System Creates Money by Making Loans

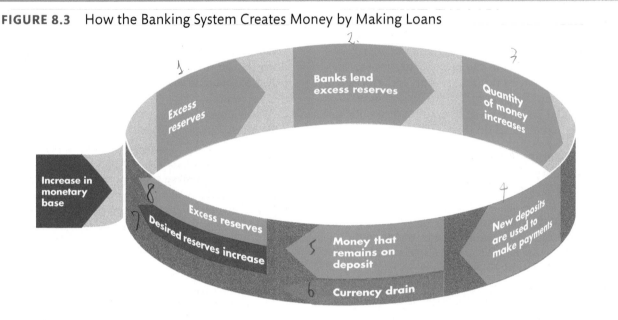

The Bank of Canada increases the monetary base, which increases bank reserves and creates excess reserves. Banks lend the excess reserves, which creates new deposits. The quantity of money increases. New deposits are used to make payments. Some of the new money remains on deposit at banks and some leaves the banks in a currency drain. The increase in bank deposits increases banks' desired reserves. But the banks still have excess reserves, though less than before. The process repeats until excess reserves have been eliminated.

MyLab Economics Animation

ECONOMICS IN ACTION

The Variable Money Multipliers

We can measure the money multiplier, other things remaining the same, as the ratio of the quantity of money to the monetary base. Because there are two definitions of money, M1 and M2, there are two money multipliers. These money multipliers, it turns out, are not constant.

In 1990, the M1 multiplier—the ratio of M1 to the monetary base—was about 5.5; and the M2 multiplier—the ratio of M2 to the monetary base—was about 16. Through the 1990s and 2000s, the currency drain ratio gradually decreased and so did the desired reserve ratio of the banks. Because these two uses of monetary base decreased relative to deposits, the money multipliers increased.

By 2017, the M1 multiplier was 9.7, almost double its 1990 value, and the M2 multiplier was 17.8.

Because the money multipliers have increased over time, the quantity of monetary base has grown more slowly than the quantities of M1 and M2.

The Money Multiplier

The **money multiplier** is the ratio of the change in the quantity of money to the change in monetary base. For example, if a $1 million increase in the monetary base increases the quantity of money by $2.5 million, then the money multiplier is 2.5.

The smaller the banks' desired reserve ratio and the smaller the currency drain ratio, the larger is the money multiplier. (See the Mathematical Note on pp. 206–207 for details on the money multiplier.)

REVIEW QUIZ

1 How do banks create money?
2 What limits the quantity of money that the banking system can create?
3 A bank manager tells you that she doesn't create money. She just lends the money that people deposit. Explain why she's wrong.

Work these questions in Study Plan 8.4 and get instant feedback.   MyLab Economics

ECONOMICS IN THE NEWS

A Massive Open Market Operation

QE2 Is No Silver Bullet

The U.S. Federal Reserve's $600 billion bond-buying program initiated last year, known as the second round of quantitative easing or QE2, will end on schedule this month with a mixed legacy, having proved to be neither the economy's needed elixir nor the scourge that critics describe.

Source: *The Wall Street Journal*, June 22, 2011

THE QUESTIONS

- What is *quantitative easing*? What transactions did the U.S. Fed undertake?
- How did QE2 affect the quantity of reserves, loans, and deposits of the U.S. banks?
- Why was QE2 neither "elixir" nor "scourge"?

THE ANSWERS

- *Quantitative easing*, or QE, is an open market purchase of securities by the Fed. QE2 was the purchase of $600 billion of long-term securities from businesses, pension funds, and other holders.
- The purchase was an open market operation similar to that described in Fig. 8.2 on p. 193 but with one more step because the Fed buys the securities from holders who are not banks.
- The figure illustrates the QE2 open market operation and the extra step in the chain of transactions.
- When the Fed buys securities, its assets increase. Its liabilities also increase because it creates monetary base to pay for the securities.
- For the businesses that sell bonds, their assets change: Securities decrease and bank deposits increase.
- For the U.S. banks, deposit liabilities increase and reserves, an asset, also increase.
- You saw on pp. 192–193 that the U.S banks are flush with reserves. They held on to the increase in reserves created by QE2. There was no multiplier effect on loans and deposits.
- QE2 would have been an "elixir" if it had resulted in a boost to bank lending, business investment, and economic expansion, and a "scourge" if it had caused inflation.

The New York Fed building where U.S. open market operations are conducted.

Federal Reserve Bank of New York

Assets (billions)	Liabilities (billions)
Securities +$600	Reserves of banks +$600

The Federal Reserve Bank of New York buys securities

Businesses, Pension Funds, and Other Bond Holders

Assets (billions)	Liabilities (billions)
Securities −$600	
Bank deposits +$600	

The Federal Reserve Bank of New York pays with electronic funds transfer

Commercial Banks

Assets (billions)	Liabilities (billions)
Reserves +$600	Bank deposits +$600

Commercial banks credit customers' deposit accounts and collect payment from the Federal Reserve

The QE2 Transactions

- QE2 had neither of these effects because the banks held on to the newly created reserves and neither loans nor the quantity of money increased.

The Money Market

There is no limit to the amount of money we would like to *receive* in payment for our labour or as interest on our savings. But there *is* a limit to how big an inventory of money we would like to *hold* and neither spend nor use to buy assets that generate an income. The *quantity of money demanded* is the inventory of money that people plan to hold on any given day. It is the quantity of money in our wallets and in our deposit accounts at banks. The quantity of money held must equal the quantity supplied, and the forces that bring about this equality in the money market have powerful effects on the economy, as you will see in the rest of this chapter.

But first, we need to explain what determines the amount of money that people plan to hold.

The Influences on Money Holding

The quantity of money that people plan to hold depends on four main factors:

- The price level
- The *nominal* interest rate
- Real GDP *check*
- Financial innovation

The Price Level The quantity of money measured in dollars is *nominal money*. The quantity of nominal money demanded is proportional to the price level, other things remaining the same. If the price level rises by 10 percent, people hold 10 percent more nominal money than before, other things remaining the same. If you hold $20 to buy your weekly movies and soda, you will increase your money holding to $22 if the prices of movies and soda—and your wage rate—increase by 10 percent.

The quantity of money measured in constant dollars (for example, in 2007 dollars) is real money. *Real money* is equal to nominal money divided by the price level and is the quantity of money measured in terms of what it will buy. In the above example, when the price level rises by 10 percent and you increase your money holding by 10 percent, your *real* money holding is constant. Your $22 at the new price level buys the same quantity of goods and is the same quantity of *real money* as your $20 at the original price level. The quantity of real money demanded is independent of the price level.

The *Nominal* Interest Rate A fundamental principle of economics is that as the opportunity cost of something increases, people try to find substitutes for it. Money is no exception. The higher the opportunity cost of holding money, other things remaining the same, the smaller is the quantity of real money demanded. The nominal interest rate on other assets minus the nominal interest rate on money is the opportunity cost of holding money.

The interest rate that you earn on currency and chequable deposits is zero. So the opportunity cost of holding these items is the nominal interest rate on other assets such as a savings bond or Treasury bill. By holding money instead, you forgo the interest that you otherwise would have received.

Money loses value because of inflation, so why isn't the inflation rate part of the cost of holding money? It is. Other things remaining the same, the higher the expected inflation rate, the higher is the nominal interest rate.

Real GDP The quantity of money that households and firms plan to hold depends on the amount they are spending. The quantity of money demanded in the economy as a whole depends on aggregate expenditure—real GDP.

Again, suppose that you hold an average of $20 to finance your weekly purchases of movies and soda. Now imagine that the prices of these goods and of all other goods remain constant but that your income increases. As a consequence, you now buy more goods and services and you also keep a larger amount of money on hand to finance your higher volume of expenditure.

Financial Innovation Technological change and the arrival of new financial products influence the quantity of money held. Financial innovations include:

1. Daily interest chequable deposits
2. Automatic transfers between chequable and saving deposits
3. Automatic teller machines
4. Credit cards and debit cards
5. Internet banking and bill paying

These innovations have occurred because of the development of computing power that has lowered the cost of calculations and record keeping.

We summarize the effects of the influences on money holding by using a demand for money curve.

The Demand for Money

The **demand for money** is the relationship between the quantity of real money demanded and the nominal interest rate when all other influences on the amount of money that people wish to hold remain the same.

Figure 8.4 shows a demand for money curve, *MD*. When the interest rate rises, other things remaining the same, the opportunity cost of holding money rises and the quantity of real money demanded decreases—there is a movement up along the demand for money curve. Similarly, when the interest rate falls, the opportunity cost of holding money falls, and the quantity of real money demanded increases—there is a movement down along the demand for money curve.

When any influence on money holding other than the interest rate changes, there is a change in the demand for money and the demand for money curve shifts. Let's study these shifts.

Shifts in the Demand for Money Curve

A change in real GDP or financial innovation changes the demand for money and shifts the demand for money curve.

Figure 8.5 illustrates the change in the demand for money. A decrease in real GDP decreases the demand for money and shifts the demand for money curve leftward from MD_0 to MD_1. An increase in real GDP has the opposite effect: It increases the demand for money and shifts the demand for money curve rightward from MD_0 to MD_2.

The influence of financial innovation on the demand for money curve is more complicated. It decreases the demand for currency and might increase the demand for some types of deposits and decrease the demand for others. But generally, financial innovation decreases the demand for money.

Changes in real GDP and financial innovation have brought large shifts in the demand for money in Canada.

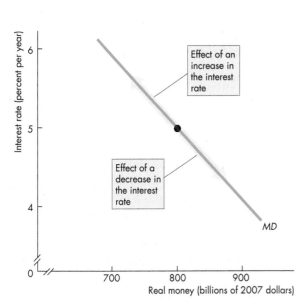

FIGURE 8.4   The Demand for Money

The demand for money curve, *MD*, shows the relationship between the quantity of real money that people plan to hold and the nominal interest rate, other things remaining the same. The interest rate is the opportunity cost of holding money. A change in the interest rate brings a movement along the demand for money curve.

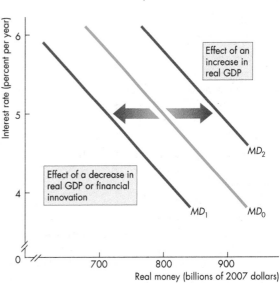

FIGURE 8.5   Changes in the Demand for Money

A decrease in real GDP decreases the demand for money. The demand for money curve shifts leftward from MD_0 to MD_1. An increase in real GDP increases the demand for money. The demand for money curve shifts rightward from MD_0 to MD_2. Financial innovation generally decreases the demand for money.

Money Market Equilibrium

You now know what determines the demand for money, and you've seen how the banking system creates money. Let's now see how the money market reaches an equilibrium.

Money market equilibrium occurs when the quantity of money demanded equals the quantity of money supplied. The adjustments that occur to bring money market equilibrium are fundamentally different in the short run and the long run.

Short-Run Equilibrium The quantity of money supplied is determined by the actions of the banks and the Bank of Canada. As the Bank of Canada adjusts the quantity of money, the interest rate changes.

In Fig. 8.6, the Bank of Canada uses open market operations to make the quantity of real money supplied equal to $800 billion and the supply of money curve is *MS*. With demand for money curve *MD*, the equilibrium interest rate is 5 percent a year.

If the interest rate were 4 percent a year, people would want to hold more money than is available.

FIGURE 8.6 Money Market Equilibrium

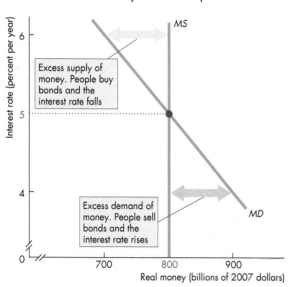

Money market equilibrium occurs when the quantity of money demanded equals the quantity supplied. In the short run, real GDP determines the demand for money curve, *MD*, and the Bank of Canada determines the quantity of real money supplied and the supply of money curve, *MS*. The interest rate adjusts to achieve equilibrium, here 5 percent a year.

—— MyLab Economics Animation and Draw Graph ——

They would sell bonds, bid down their price, and the interest rate would rise. If the interest rate were 6 percent a year, people would want to hold less money than is available. They would buy bonds, bid up their price, and the interest rate would fall.

The Short-Run Effect of a Change in the Quantity of Money Starting from a short-run equilibrium, if the Bank of Canada increases the quantity of money, people find themselves holding more money than the quantity demanded. With a surplus of money holding, people enter the loanable funds market and buy bonds. The increase in demand for bonds raises the price of a bond and lowers the interest rate (refresh your memory by looking at Chapter 7, p. 167).

If the Bank of Canada decreases the quantity of money, people find themselves holding less money than the quantity demanded. They now enter the loanable funds market to sell bonds. The decrease in the demand for bonds lowers their price and raises the interest rate.

Figure 8.7 illustrates the effects of the changes in the quantity of money that we've just described. When the supply of money curve shifts rightward from MS_0 to MS_1, the interest rate falls to 4 percent a year; when the supply of money curve shifts leftward to MS_2, the interest rate rises to 6 percent a year.

Long-Run Equilibrium You've just seen how the nominal interest rate is determined in the money market at the level that makes the quantity of money demanded equal the quantity supplied by the Bank of Canada. You learned in Chapter 7 (on pp. 171–172) that the real interest rate is determined in the loanable funds market at the level that makes the quantity of loanable funds demanded equal the quantity of loanable funds supplied. You also learned in Chapter 7 (on p. 169) that the real interest rate equals the nominal interest rate minus the inflation rate.

When the inflation rate equals the expected (or forecasted) inflation rate and when real GDP equals potential GDP, the money market, the loanable funds market, the goods market, and the labour market are in long-run equilibrium—the economy is in long-run equilibrium.

An increase in the quantity of money starting and ending in long-run equilibrium returns all the real variables to their original levels. But something does change: the price level. The price level rises by the same percentage as the rise in the quantity of money. Why does this outcome occur in the long run?

FIGURE 8.7   A Change in the Quantity of Money

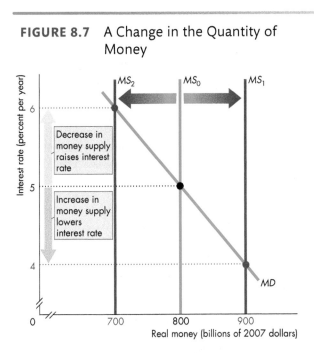

An increase in the quantity of money shifts the supply of money curve from MS_0 to MS_1 and the interest rate falls. A decrease in the quantity of money shifts the supply of money curve from MS_0 to MS_2 and the interest rate rises.

—— MyLab Economics Animation and Draw Graph ——

The reason is that real GDP and employment are determined by the demand for labour, the supply of labour, and the production function—the real forces described in Chapter 6 (pp. 142–144); and the real interest rate is determined by the demand for and supply of (real) loanable funds—the real forces described in Chapter 7 (pp. 171–172). The only variable that is free to respond to a change in the supply of money in the long run is the price level. The price level adjusts to make the quantity of real money supplied equal to the quantity demanded.

So when the nominal quantity of money changes, in the long run the price level changes by a percentage equal to the percentage change in the quantity of nominal money. In the long run, the change in price level is proportional to the change in the quantity of money.

The Transition from the Short Run to the Long Run
How does the economy move from the first short-run response to an increase in the quantity of money to the long-run response?

The adjustment process is lengthy and complex. Here, we'll only provide a sketch of the process. A more thorough account must wait until you've studied Chapter 10.

We start out in long-run equilibrium and the Bank of Canada increases the quantity of money by 10 percent. Here are the steps in what happens next.

First, the nominal interest rate falls (just like you saw on p. 199 and in Fig. 8.7). The real interest rate falls too, as people try to get rid of their excess money holdings and buy bonds.

With a lower real interest rate, people want to borrow and spend more. Firms want to borrow to invest and households want to borrow to invest in bigger homes or to buy more consumer goods.

The increase in the demand for goods cannot be met by an increase in supply because the economy is already at full employment. So there is a general shortage of all kinds of goods and services.

The shortage of goods and services forces the price level to rise.

As the price level rises, the real quantity of money decreases. The decrease in the quantity of real money raises the nominal interest rate and the real interest rate. As the interest rate rises, spending plans are cut back, and eventually the original full-employment equilibrium is restored. At the new long-run equilibrium, the price level has risen by 10 percent and nothing real has changed.

REVIEW QUIZ

1 What are the main influences on the quantity of real money that people and businesses plan to hold?
2 Show the effects of a change in the nominal interest rate and a change in real GDP using the demand for money curve.
3 How is money market equilibrium determined in the short run?
4 How does a change in the supply of money change the interest rate in the short run?
5 How does a change in the supply of money change the interest rate in the long run?

Work these questions in Study Plan 8.5 and get instant feedback.   MyLab Economics

Let's explore the long-run link between money and the price level a bit further.

◆ The Quantity Theory of Money

In the long run, the price level adjusts to make the quantity of real money demanded equal the quantity supplied. A special theory of the price level and inflation—the quantity theory of money—explains this long-run adjustment of the price level.

The **quantity theory of money** is the proposition that, in the long run, an increase in the quantity of money brings an equal percentage increase in the price level. To explain the quantity theory of money, we first need to define *the velocity of circulation*.

The **velocity of circulation** is the average number of times a dollar of money is used annually to buy the goods and services that make up GDP. But you know that GDP equals the price level (P) multiplied by *real* GDP (Y). That is,

$$GDP = PY.$$

Call the quantity of money M. The velocity of circulation, V, is determined by the equation:

$$V = PY/M.$$

For example, if GDP is \$1,000 billion (PY equals \$1,000 billion) and the quantity of money is \$250 billion, then the velocity of circulation is 4.

From the definition of the velocity of circulation, the *equation of exchange* tells us how M, V, P, and Y are connected. This equation is:

$$MV = PY.$$

Given the definition of the velocity of circulation, the equation of exchange is always true—it is true by definition. It becomes the quantity theory of money if the quantity of money does not influence the velocity of circulation or real GDP. In this case, the equation of exchange tells us that in the long run, the price level is determined by the quantity of money. That is,

$$P = M(V/Y),$$

where (V/Y) is independent of M. So a change in M brings a proportional change in P.

We can also express the equation of exchange in growth rates,[1] in which form it states that

$$\begin{array}{c} \text{Money} \\ \text{growth rate} \end{array} + \begin{array}{c} \text{Rate of} \\ \text{velocity} \\ \text{change} \end{array} = \begin{array}{c} \text{Inflation} \\ \text{rate} \end{array} + \begin{array}{c} \text{Real GDP} \\ \text{growth rate} \end{array}$$

ECONOMICS IN ACTION

Does the Quantity Theory Work?

On average, as predicted by the quantity theory of money, the inflation rate fluctuates in line with fluctuations in the money growth rate minus the real GDP growth rate. Figure 1 shows the relationship between money growth (M2 definition) and inflation in Canada. You can see a clear but inexact relationship between the two variables.

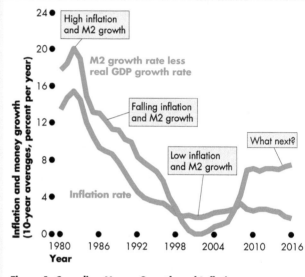

Figure 1 Canadian Money Growth and Inflation

Sources of data: Statistics Canada, CANSIM Tables 176-0020 and 380-0002.

Solving this equation for the inflation rate gives:

$$\begin{array}{c} \text{Inflation} \\ \text{rate} \end{array} = \begin{array}{c} \text{Money} \\ \text{growth rate} \end{array} + \begin{array}{c} \text{Rate of} \\ \text{velocity} \\ \text{change} \end{array} - \begin{array}{c} \text{Real GDP} \\ \text{growth rate} \end{array}$$

In the long run, the rate of velocity change is not influenced by the money growth rate. More

---

[1] To obtain this equation, begin with

$$MV = PY.$$

Then changes in these variables are related by the equation

$$V\Delta M + M\Delta V = Y\Delta P + P\Delta Y.$$

Divide this equation by the equation of exchange to obtain

$$\Delta M/M + \Delta V/V = \Delta P/P + \Delta Y/Y.$$

The term $\Delta M/M$ is the money growth rate, $\Delta V/V$ is the rate of velocity change, $\Delta P/P$ is the inflation rate, and $\Delta Y/Y$ is the real GDP growth rate.

International data also support the quantity theory. Figure 2 shows a scatter diagram of the inflation rate and the money growth rate in 174 countries, and Fig. 3 shows the inflation rate and money growth rate in countries with inflation rates below 20 percent a year. You can see a general tendency for money growth and inflation to be correlated, but the quantity theory (the red line) does not predict inflation precisely.

The correlation between money growth and inflation isn't perfect, and the correlation does not tell us that money growth *causes* inflation. Money growth might cause inflation; inflation might cause money growth; or some third variable might cause both inflation and money growth. Other evidence does confirm, though, that causation runs from money growth to inflation.

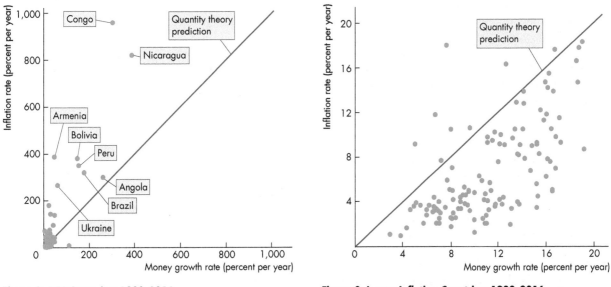

Figure 2 174 Countries: 1980–2016   **Figure 3 Lower-Inflation Countries: 1980–2016**

Sources of data: International Financial Statistics Yearbook, 2017, and International Monetary Fund, World Economic Outlook, April 2017.

strongly, in the long run, the rate of velocity change is approximately zero. With this assumption, the inflation rate in the long run is determined as

$$\text{Inflation rate} = \text{Money growth rate} - \text{Real GDP growth rate}$$

In the long run, fluctuations in the money growth rate minus the real GDP growth rate bring equal fluctuations in the inflation rate.

Also, in the long run, with the economy at full employment, real GDP equals potential GDP, so the real GDP growth rate equals the potential GDP growth rate. This growth rate might be influenced by inflation, but the influence is most likely small and the quantity theory assumes that it is zero. So the real GDP growth rate is given and doesn't change when the money growth rate changes—inflation is correlated with money growth.

REVIEW QUIZ

1 What is the quantity theory of money?
2 How is the velocity of circulation calculated?
3 What is the equation of exchange?
4 Does the quantity theory correctly predict the effects of money growth on inflation?

Work these questions in Study Plan 8.6 and get instant feedback.   MyLab Economics

◆ You now know what money is, how the banks create it, and why the quantity of money is important. *Economics in the News* on pp. 204–205 looks at a suggestion that the Bank of Canada should increase the quantity of money by a larger amount.

Money and the Economy

Poloz's Best Option: Increase the Money Supply

The C.D. Howe Institute, Media Release
November 3, 2016

Expanding the money supply is the best option for the Bank of Canada in a low interest rate environment, states a new report from the C.D. Howe Institute. In "Putting Money to Work: Monetary Policy in a Low Interest Rate Environment," author Steve Ambler suggests that the Bank of Canada should use quantitative easing (QE) to increase the broad money supply, on a longer term rather than a temporary basis, to encourage spending on goods and services by individuals and firms. . . .

QE involves open market purchases of government securities from banks or from the private sector. Buying securities from banks increases the cash balances they hold at the Bank. Banks can then use these balances to expand lending, which increases deposits held by their customers and thereby expands broader measures of the money supply. Purchases of securities from the private sector expand bank deposits and broad money directly. These in turn encourage increased spending on goods and services without necessarily having to lower interest rates.

According to Ambler, "the Bank of Canada should aim to provide monetary stimulus through open market operations or through direct purchase of securities from the private sector." However, this may require some rethinking of the way monetary policy is currently conducted. Currently, the Bank's operating procedures, particularly the goal of achieving close to zero net settlement balances each day, seem almost designed to eliminate the possibility of permanent increases in the monetary base via open market operations. . . .

"Increases in the money supply can have powerful real effects even at very low interest rates," concludes Ambler.

Courtesy of C.D. Howe Institute

ESSENCE OF THE STORY

- "Putting Money to Work: Monetary Policy in a Low Interest Rate Environment" is a research paper by Queen's University economics professor Steve Ambler, published by the C.D. Howe Institute.

- Ambler says the Bank of Canada should expand the money supply.

- It should use open market operations to buy government securities from the private sector to increase the broad money supply.

- Increasing the money supply on a permanent basis will stimulate spending, even at low interest rates.

MyLab Economics Economics in the News

ECONOMIC ANALYSIS

- To understand why Steve Ambler wants the Bank of Canada to increase the quantity of M2, we need to look at the past decade of Canadian monetary history.

- A global financial crisis started quietly in the summer of 2007, when the interest rate on Government of Canada 3-month Treasury bills was a bit more than 4 percent per year, and the quantity of M2 money was a bit below 50 percent of GDP.

- To keep the economy well supplied with cheap money, the Bank of Canada cut the interest rate to almost zero in 2009. In mid-2017, the rate was 0.75 percent.

- With the interest rate falling and then remaining low, the quantity of M2 money increased and by mid-2017 it stood at 72 percent of GDP.

- You've learned in this chapter that the quantity of money demanded depends inversely on the interest rate. So it is to be expected that a falling interest rate would bring an increasing quantity of money.

- Figure 1 shows this inverse relationship in the period 2007 to 2017. The demand for money is influenced by GDP, so the graph removes the influence of GDP by measuring the quantity of M2 as a percentage of GDP.

- The red dots are the data for each quarter between 2007 and 2017. The curve MD is the demand for money curve. The red data points don't all lie on the curve because other influences change the demand for money, but the points show a clear inverse relationship.

- Figures 2 and 3 focus on Steve Ambler's concern and shows what has been happening to M2 growth, real GDP growth, and the inflation rate.

- The burst of money growth in 2009 occurred because of the fall in the interest rate and the increase in the quantity of M2 demanded. During this time, the velocity of circulation of M2 decreased.

- Ambler's suggestion is that M2 growth should be maintained at a higher rate.

- After 2016, the time when Steve Ambler was writing, the M2 growth rate did increase. And the growth rate of real GDP and the inflation rate also increased.

- Looking at Figs. 2 and 3, there is no tendency for the real GDP growth rate and the inflation rate to be aligned with the money growth rate.

- The lag between money growth, real GDP growth, and inflation is long (and variable), and this lag could portend future inflation.

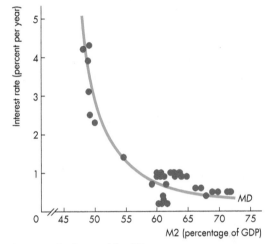

Figure 1 The Demand for M2

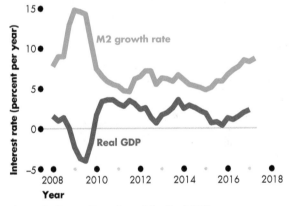

Figure 2 Money Growth and the Real GDP

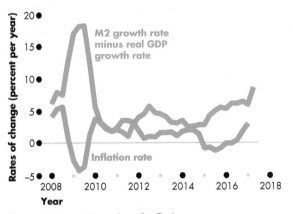

Figure 3 Money Growth and Inflation

205

MATHEMATICAL NOTE

The Money Multiplier

This note explains the basic math of the money multiplier and shows how the value of the multiplier depends on the banks' desired reserve ratio and the currency drain ratio.

To make the process of money creation concrete, we work through an example for a banking system in which each bank has a desired reserve ratio of 10 percent of deposits and the currency drain ratio is 50 percent of deposits. (Although these ratios are larger than the ones in the Canadian economy, they make the process end more quickly and enable you to see more clearly the principles at work.)

The figure keeps track of the numbers. Before the process begins, all the banks have no excess reserves. Then the monetary base increases by $100,000 and one bank has excess reserves of this amount.

The bank lends the $100,000 of excess reserves. When this loan is made, new money increases by $100,000.

Some of the new money will be held as currency and some as deposits. With a currency drain ratio of 50 percent of deposits, one-third of the new money will be held as currency and two-thirds will be held as deposits. That is, $33,333 drains out of the banks as currency and $66,667 remains in the banks as deposits. The increase in the quantity of money of $100,000 equals the increase in deposits plus the increase in currency holdings.

The increased bank deposits of $66,667 generate an increase in desired reserves of 10 percent of that amount, which is $6,667. Actual reserves have increased by the same amount as the increase in deposits: $66,667. So the banks now have excess reserves of $60,000.

The process we've just described repeats but begins with excess reserves of $60,000. The figure shows the next two rounds. At the end of the process, the quantity of money has increased by a multiple of the increase in the monetary base. In this case, the increase is $250,000, which is 2.5 times the increase in the monetary base.

The sequence in the figure shows the first stages of the process that finally reaches the total shown in the final row of the "money" column.

To calculate what happens at the later stages in the process and the final increase in the quantity of

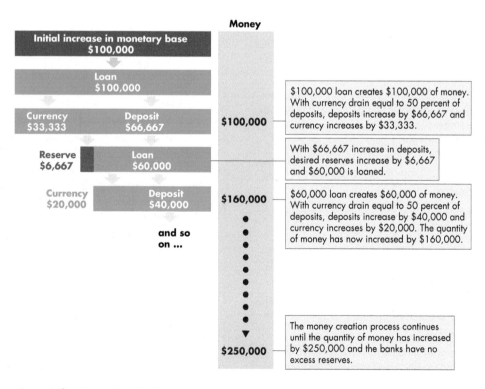

Figure 1 The Money Creation Process

money, look closely at the numbers in the figure. The initial increase in reserves is $100,000 (call it A). At each stage, the loan is 60 percent (0.6) of the previous loan and the quantity of money increases by 0.6 of the previous increase. Call that proportion L, then ($L = 0.6$). We can write down the complete sequence for the increase in the quantity of money as

$$A + AL + AL^2 + AL^3 + AL^4 + AL^5 + \dots .$$

Remember, L is a fraction, so at each stage in this sequence, the amount of new loans and new money gets smaller. The total value of loans made and money created at the end of the process is the sum of the sequence,[2] which is

$$A/(1 - L).$$

If we use the numbers from the example, the total increase in the quantity of money is

$$\$100,000 + 60,000 + 36,000 + \dots$$

$$= \$100,000 \ (1 + 0.6 + 0.36 + \dots)$$

$$= \$100,000 \ (1 + 0.6 + 0.6^2 + \dots)$$

$$= \$100,000 \times 1/(1 - 0.6)$$

$$= \$100,000 \times 1/(0.4)$$

$$= \$100,000 \times 2.5$$

$$= \$250,000.$$

The magnitude of the money multiplier depends on the desired reserve ratio and the currency drain ratio. Let's explore this relationship.

The money multiplier is the ratio of money to the monetary base. Call the money multiplier mm, the quantity of money M, and the monetary base MB.

---

[2]The sequence of values is called a convergent geometric series. To find the sum of a series such as this, begin by calling the sum S. Then write the sum as

$$S = A + AL + AL^2 + AL^3 + AL^4 + AL^5 + \dots$$

Multiply by L to get

$$LS = AL + AL^2 + AL^3 + AL^4 + AL^5 + \dots$$

and then subtract the second equation from the first to get

$$S(1 - L) = A$$

or

$$S = A/(1 - L).$$

Then

$$mm = M/MB.$$

Next recall that money, M, is the sum of deposits and currency. Call deposits D and currency C. Then

$$M = D + C.$$

The monetary base, MB, is the sum of banks' reserves and currency. Call banks' reserves R. Then

$$MB = R + C.$$

Use the equations for M and MB in the mm equation to give

$$mm = M/MB = (D + C)/(R + C).$$

Now divide all the variables on the right side of the equation by D to give

$$mm = M/MB = (1 + C/D)/(R/D) + C/D).$$

In this equation, C/D is the currency drain ratio and R/D is the banks' reserve ratio. If we use the values in the example on the previous page, C/D is 0.5 and R/D is 0.1, and

$$mm = (1 + 0.5)/(0.1 + 0.5).$$

$$= 1.5/0.6 = 2.5.$$

The Canadian Money Multiplier

The money multiplier in Canada can be found by using the formula above along with the values of C/D and R/D in the Canadian economy. Because we have two definitions of money, M1 and M2, we have two money multipliers. Call the M1 deposits $D1$ and call the M2 deposits $D2$.

The numbers for M1 in 2014 are $C/D1 = 0.1061$ and $R/D1 = 0.0003$. So

$$M1 \text{ multiplier} = (1 + 0.1061)/(0.0003 + 0.1061)$$

$$= 10.4.$$

The numbers for M2 in 2014 are $C/D2 = 0.0539$ and $R/D2 = 0.0002$, so

$$M2 \text{ multiplier} = (1 + 0.0539)/(0.0002 + 0.0539)$$

$$= 19.5.$$

WORKED PROBLEM

MyLab Economics You can work this problem in Chapter 8 Study Plan.

In June 2014, individuals and businesses held:

- $50 billion in currency
- $1,000 billion in chequable deposits
- $5,000 billion in non-chequable deposits
- $750 billion in fixed term deposits and other deposits.

In June 2014, banks held:

- $450 billion in notes and coins
- $100 billion in reserves at the central bank
- $800 billion in loans to households and businesses

Questions

1. Calculate the M1 and M2 measures of money.
2. Calculate the monetary base.
3. What are the currency drain ratio and the banks' reserve ratio?
4. What are the M1 and M2 money multipliers?
5. How is the money multiplier influenced by the banks' reserve ratio?

Solutions

1. M1 is the quantity of money held by individuals and businesses in the form of chequable deposits and currency.

   M1 = $1,000 billion + $50 billion, which equals $1,050 billion.

   M2 is M1 plus non-chequable deposits held by individuals and businesses, fixed term deposits, and other deposits.

   M2 = $1,050 billion + $5,000 billion + $750 billion, which equals $6,800 billion.

Key Point: M1 is a narrow measure of money that consists of chequable deposits and currency held by individuals and businesses.

   M2 is a broad measure of money that consists of M1 plus non-chequable deposits, term deposits, and other deposits of individuals and businesses.

2. Monetary base is the sum of bank reserves held at the central bank and notes and coins outside the central bank.

   Notes and coins outside the central bank are the notes and coins held by individuals, businesses, and banks.

Monetary base = $100 billion + $450 billion + $50 billion = $600 billion

Key Point: Monetary base equals the central bank's liabilities—bank reserves held at the central bank and notes issued by the central bank—plus coins outside the central bank.

3. Currency drain ratio = (Currency held by individuals and businesses ÷ Chequable deposits) × 100.

   Currency drain ratio = ($50 billion ÷ $1,000 billion) × 100, which equals 5 percent.

   Banks' reserve ratio = (Bank reserves ÷ Chequable deposits) × 100.

   Bank reserves = Notes and coins held by banks + reserves at the central bank.

   Bank reserves = $450 billion + $100 billion, which equals $550 billion.

   The banks' reserve ratio = ($550 billion ÷ $1,000 billion) × 100, which equals 55 percent.

Key Point: The currency drain ratio is the ratio of currency to chequable deposits held by individuals and businesses, expressed as a percentage. The banks' reserve ratio is the ratio of bank reserves to bank deposits, expressed as a percentage.

4. M1 Money multiplier = M1 ÷ Monetary base = $1,050 billion ÷ $600 billion = 1.75.

   M2 Money multiplier = M2 ÷ Monetary base = $6,800 billion ÷ $600 billion = 11.33.

Key Point: The money multiplier is the number by which the monetary base is multiplied to equal the quantity of money.

5. Money M is the sum of deposits D and currency C held by individuals and businesses.

   Monetary base MB is the sum of reserves R and currency C.

   Money multiplier = $(D + C) \div (R + C)$

   An increase in the banks' reserves R with no change in D increases the banks' reserves ratio and decreases the money multiplier.

Key Point: The money multiplier equals

   $(1 + C/D) \div (R/D + C/D)$, where C/D is the currency drain ratio and R/D is the banks' reserve ratio. An increase in the banks' reserve ratio decreases the money multiplier.

SUMMARY

Key Points

What Is Money? (pp. 184–186)

- Money is the means of payment. It functions as a medium of exchange, a unit of account, and a store of value.
- Today, money consists of currency and deposits.

Working Problems 1 and 2 will give you a better understanding of what money is.

Depository Institutions (pp. 187–190)

- Chartered banks, credit unions and caisses populaires, and trust and mortgage loan companies are depository institutions whose deposits are money.
- Depository institutions provide four main economic services: They create liquidity, minimize the cost of obtaining funds, minimize the cost of monitoring borrowers, and pool risks.

Working Problem 3 will give you a better understanding of depository institutions.

The Bank of Canada (pp. 191–194)

- The Bank of Canada is the central bank of Canada.
- The Bank of Canada has two main policy tools: open market operations and the bank rate.
- When the Bank buys securities in an open market operation, the monetary base increases; when the Bank sells securities, the monetary base decreases.

Working Problem 4 will give you a better understanding of the Bank of Canada.

How Banks Create Money (pp. 194–197)

- Banks create money by making loans.
- The total quantity of money that can be created depends on the monetary base, the desired reserve ratio, and the currency drain ratio.

Working Problems 5 and 6 will give you a better understanding of how banks create money.

The Money Market (pp. 198–201)

- The quantity of money demanded is the amount of money that people plan to hold.
- The quantity of real money equals the quantity of nominal money divided by the price level.
- The quantity of real money demanded depends on the nominal interest rate, real GDP, and financial innovation.
- The nominal interest rate makes the quantity of money demanded equal the quantity supplied.
- When the Bank of Canada increases the quantity of money, the nominal interest rate falls (the short-run effect).
- In the long run, when the Bank of Canada increases the quantity of money, the price level rises and the nominal interest rate returns to its initial level.

Working Problem 7 will give you a better understanding of the money market.

The Quantity Theory of Money (pp. 202–203)

- The quantity theory of money is the proposition that money growth and inflation move up and down together in the long run.

Working Problem 8 will give you a better understanding of the quantity theory of money.

Key Terms

MyLab Economics Key Terms Quiz

Bank rate, 194
Central bank, 191
Chartered bank, 187
Currency, 185
Currency drain ratio, 195
Demand for money, 199
Depository institution, 187

Desired reserve ratio, 195
Excess reserves, 195
Lender of last resort, 191
M1, 185
M2, 185
Means of payment, 184
Monetary base, 192

Money, 184
Money multiplier, 196
Open market operation, 192
Quantity theory of money, 202
Reserves, 187
Velocity of circulation, 202

STUDY PLAN PROBLEMS AND APPLICATIONS

MyLab Economics Work Problems 1 to 9 in Chapter 8 Study Plan and get instant feedback.

What Is Money? (Study Plan 8.1)

1. Money in Canada today includes which of the following items? Cash in CIBC's cash machines; Bank of Canada dollar bills in your wallet; your Visa card; your loan to pay for school fees.

2. In May 2014, currency held by individuals and businesses was $67 billion; chequable deposits owned by individuals were $244 billion and owned by businesses were $361 billion; non-chequable personal deposits were $238 billion; non-chequable business deposits were $39 billion; and term deposits and other deposits were $312 billion. Calculate M1 and M2 in May 2014.

Depository Institutions (Study Plan 8.2)

3. **Banks Ordered to Hold More Capital**

   U.K. banks must hold more capital as their holdings of consumer debt soars.

   Source: *The Guardian*, June 27, 2017

   What is the "capital" referred to in the news clip? How might the requirement to hold more capital make banks safer?

The Bank of Canada (Study Plan 8.3)

4. The Bank of Canada sells $20 million of securities to the Bank of Nova Scotia. Enter the transactions that take place to show the changes in the following balance sheets:

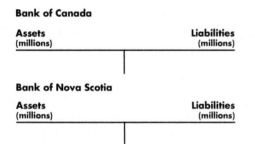

Bank of Canada

Assets (millions)	Liabilities (millions)

Bank of Nova Scotia

Assets (millions)	Liabilities (millions)

How Banks Create Money (Study Plan 8.4)

5. In the economy of Nocoin, bank deposits are $300 billion, bank reserves are $15 billion of which two-thirds are deposits with the central bank. Households and firms hold $30 billion in bank notes. There are no coins. Calculate:

   a. The monetary base and quantity of money.

   b. The banks' desired reserve ratio and the currency drain ratio (as percentages).

6. **China Cuts Banks' Reserve Ratios**

   The People's Bank of China announced it will cut the required reserve ratio for five big banks.

   Source: Reuters, January 20, 2017

   Explain how lowering the required reserve ratio will affect the money creation process.

The Money Market (Study Plan 8.5)

7. The spreadsheet provides data about the demand for money in Minland. Columns A and B show the demand for money schedule when real GDP (Y_0) is $10 billion, and Columns A and C show the demand for money schedule when real GDP (Y_1) is $20 billion. The quantity of money is $3 billion.

	A	B	C
1	r	Y_0	Y_1
2	7	1.0	1.5
3	6	1.5	2.0
4	5	2.0	2.5
5	4	2.5	3.0
6	3	3.0	3.5
7	2	3.5	4.0
8	1	4.0	4.5

   What is the interest rate when real GDP is $10 billion? Explain what happens in the money market in the short run if real GDP increases to $20 billion.

The Quantity Theory of Money (Study Plan 8.6)

8. In year 1, the economy is at full employment and real GDP is $400 million, the GDP deflator is 200 (the price level is 2), and the velocity of circulation is 20. In year 2, the quantity of money increases by 20 percent. If the quantity theory of money holds, calculate the quantity of money, the GDP deflator, real GDP, and the velocity of circulation in year 2.

Mathematical Note (Study Plan 8.MN)

9. In Problem 5, the banks have no excess reserves. Suppose that the central bank in Nocoin increases bank reserves by $0.5 billion.

   a. Explain why the change in the quantity of money is not equal to the change in the monetary base.

   b. Calculate the money multiplier.

ADDITIONAL PROBLEMS AND APPLICATIONS

MyLab Economics You can work these problems in Homework or Test if assigned by your instructor.

What Is Money?

10. Sara withdraws $1,000 from her savings account at the TD Bank, keeps $50 in cash, and deposits the balance in her chequable account at the TD Bank. What is the immediate change in M1 and M2?

11. Rapid inflation in Brazil in the early 1990s caused the cruzeiro to lose its ability to function as money. Which of the following commodities would most likely have taken the place of the cruzeiro in the Brazilian economy? Explain why.
    a. Tractor parts
    b. Packs of cigarettes
    c. Loaves of bread
    d. Impressionist paintings
    e. Baseball trading cards

12. **How to Pay for Everything with Your Smartphone**

    Many people stopped using cash in the early 2000s because they found debit cards were more convenient. Smartphones are now doing to plastic what cards did to cash.

    Source: *USA Today*, July 24, 2016

    If people can use their smartphone to make payments, will currency disappear? How will the components of M1 change?

Depository Institutions

Use the following news clip to work Problems 13 and 14.

Millennials Should Shop Around for Banks

Banks are in business to make money for their shareholders, not to put the interests of customers first. This key fact should not be overlooked. Banks sell financial services and compete hard for business. They want to be seen as the friend of students and offer no-cost accounts. But banks are not equal. By shopping around, you can get the deal that's best for you.

    Source: *The Globe and Mail*, September 19, 2016

13. Explain how this news clip illustrates the attempts by banks to maximize profits.

14. Why would banks want to be seen as friends of students and offer student accounts with no charges?

15. How does financial regulation in Canada help minimize the cost of bank failure? Does it bring more stability to the banking system?

The Bank of Canada

16. Explain the distinction between a central bank and a chartered bank.

17. If the Bank of Canada makes an open market sale of $1 million of securities to a bank, what initial changes occur in the economy?

18. Set out the transactions that the Bank of Canada undertakes to increase the quantity of money.

19. Describe the Bank of Canada's assets and liabilities. What is the monetary base and how does it relate to the Bank of Canada's balance sheet?

20. **Federal Reserve Wants to Start Unwinding the $4.5 Trillion in Bonds on Its Balance Sheet This Year**

    The Federal Reserve bought Treasury bonds and mortgage-backed securities during three rounds of quantitative easing following the financial crisis. Chair Janet Yellen said the Fed will soon start the process of selling the $4.5 trillion in bonds on its balance sheet. Shrinking the Fed's balance sheet will impact markets in a similar way to a rise in the interest rate.

    Source: CNBC, April 5, 2017

    a. What would the U.S. Federal Reserve do to shrink its balance sheet?

    b. How would the monetary base change, and how would bank reserves change?

How Banks Create Money

21. Banks in New Transylvania have a desired reserve ratio of 10 percent of deposits and no excess reserves. The currency drain ratio is 50 percent of deposits. Now suppose that the central bank increases the monetary base by $1,200 billion.
    a. How much do the banks lend in the first round of the money creation process?
    b. How much of the initial amount loaned flows back to the banking system as new deposits?
    c. How much of the initial amount loaned does not return to the banks but is held as currency?
    d. Why does a second round of lending occur?

The Money Market

22. Explain the change in the nominal interest rate in the short run if:
    a. Real GDP increases.
    b. The Bank of Canada increases the quantity of money.
    c. The price level rises.

23. The figure shows an economy's demand for money curve.

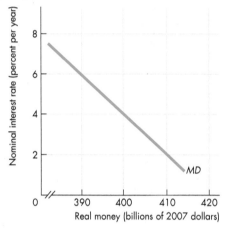

    If the central bank decreases the quantity of real money from $400 billion to $390 billion, explain how the price of a bond will change.

24. Use the data in Problem 7 to work this problem.

    The interest rate is 4 percent a year. Suppose that real GDP decreases from $20 billion to $10 billion and the quantity of money remains unchanged. Do people buy bonds or sell bonds? Explain how the interest rate changes.

The Quantity Theory of Money

25. The table provides some data for the United States in the first decade following the Civil War.

	1869	1879
Quantity of money	$1.3 billion	$1.7 billion
Real GDP (1929 dollars)	$7.4 billion	Z
Price level (1929 = 100)	X	54
Velocity of circulation	4.50	4.61

Source of data: Milton Friedman and Anna J. Schwartz, *A Monetary History of the United States 1867–1960.*

    a. Calculate the value of X in 1869.
    b. Calculate the value of Z in 1879.

c. Are the data consistent with the quantity theory of money? Explain your answer.

26. When he was the U.S. Federal Reserve chairman, Ben Bernanke said that financial innovation and the spread of U.S. currency throughout the world had broken down the relationships between money, inflation, and output growth, which made monetary aggregates less useful gauges for policymakers. Some other central banks use monetary aggregates as a guide to policy decisions, but Bernanke believed reliance on monetary aggregates would be unwise. He said that there are differences between the United States and Europe in terms of the stability of money demand.
    a. Explain how the debate surrounding the quantity theory of money could make "monetary gauges a less useful tool for policymakers."
    b. What do Ben Bernanke's statements reveal about his view on the accuracy of the quantity theory of money?

Economics in the News

27. After you have studied *Economics in the News* on pp. 204–205, answer the following questions.
    a. What changes in the interest rate and the quantity of M2 occurred between 2007 and 2017?
    b. When the interest rate fell, why did the quantity of M2 demanded increase?
    c. How would you interpret the growth of M2 and the inflation rate during the years 2009–2017 using the quantity theory of money?
    d. Why does Steve Ambler want the Bank of Canada to increase M2 at a higher rate?
    e. Why might faster M2 growth eventually bring higher inflation?

Mathematical Note

28. In the United Kingdom, the currency drain ratio is 38 percent of deposits and the reserve ratio is 2 percent of deposits. In Australia, the quantity of money is $150 billion, the currency drain ratio is 33 percent of deposits, and the reserve ratio is 8 percent of deposits.
    a. Calculate the U.K. money multiplier.
    b. Calculate the monetary base in Australia.

9

THE EXCHANGE RATE AND THE BALANCE OF PAYMENTS

After studying this chapter, you will be able to:

◆ Explain how the exchange rate is determined

◆ Explain interest rate parity and purchasing power parity

◆ Describe the alternative exchange rate policies and explain their effects

◆ Describe the balance of payments accounts and explain what causes an international deficit

The Canadian dollar–the loonie–is one of more than 100 different monies. Most international payments are made using the U.S. dollar ($), the euro (€), and the Japanese yen (¥). The Canadian dollar fluctuates against these monies. Why?

Sometimes we borrow from foreigners and at other times we repay our international debts. Why? What causes international deficits and surpluses?

In this chapter, you're going to discover the answers to these questions. In *Economics in the News* at the end of the chapter, we'll look at President Trump's proposal to lower the U.S. international deficit by renegotiating NAFTA.

◆ The Foreign Exchange Market

When Canadian Tire imports snow blowers from China, it pays for them using Chinese yuan. And when China Airlines buys an airplane from Bombardier, it pays using Canadian dollars.

Whenever people buy things from another country, they use the currency of that country to make the transaction. It doesn't make any difference what the item is that is being traded internationally. It might be a Blu-ray player, an airplane, insurance or banking services, real estate, the shares and bonds of a government or corporation, or even an entire business.

Foreign money is just like Canadian money. It consists of notes and coins issued by a central bank and mint and deposits in banks and other depository institutions. When we described Canadian money in Chapter 8, we distinguished between currency (notes and coins) and deposits. But when we talk about foreign money, we refer to it as foreign currency. **Foreign currency** is the money of other countries regardless of whether that money is in the form of notes, coins, or bank deposits.

We buy these foreign currencies and foreigners buy Canadian dollars in the foreign exchange market.

Trading Currencies

The currency of one country is exchanged for the currency of another in the **foreign exchange market**. The foreign exchange market is not a place like a downtown flea market or a fruit and vegetable market. The foreign exchange market is made up of thousands of people—importers and exporters, banks, international investors and speculators, international travellers, and specialist traders called *foreign exchange brokers*.

The foreign exchange market opens on Monday morning in Sydney, Australia, and Hong Kong, which is still Sunday evening in Toronto. As the day advances, markets open in Singapore, Tokyo, Bahrain, Frankfurt, London, New York, Toronto, Chicago, and San Francisco. As the West Coast markets close, Sydney is only an hour away from opening for the next day of business. The sun barely sets in the foreign exchange market. Dealers around the world are in continual Internet contact, and on a typical day in 2014, $5.3 trillion (of all currencies) were traded in the foreign exchange market—that's $6 million every second.

Exchange Rates

An **exchange rate** is the price at which one currency exchanges for another currency in the foreign exchange market. For example, on August 25, 2017, one Canadian dollar would buy 87 Japanese yen or 67 euro cents. So the exchange rate was 87 yen per dollar or, equivalently, 67 euro cents per dollar.

The exchange rate fluctuates. Sometimes it rises and sometimes it falls. A rise in the exchange rate is called an *appreciation* of the dollar, and a fall in the exchange rate is called a *depreciation* of the dollar. For example, when the exchange rate rises from 87 yen to 90 yen per dollar, the dollar appreciates against the yen; when the exchange rate falls from 87 yen to 84 yen per dollar, the dollar depreciates against the yen.

Economics in Action on p. 215 shows the fluctuations of the Canadian dollar against three currencies.

Questions About the Canadian Dollar Exchange Rate

The performance of the Canadian dollar in the foreign exchange market raises a number of questions that we address in this chapter.

First, how is the exchange rate determined? Why does the Canadian dollar sometimes appreciate and at other times depreciate?

Second, how do the Bank of Canada and other central banks operate in the foreign exchange market? In particular, how was the exchange rate between the U.S. dollar and the Chinese yuan fixed and why did it remain constant for many years?

Third, how do exchange rate fluctuations influence our international trade and international payments? In particular, could we influence our international deficit by changing the exchange rate? Would an appreciation of the yuan change the balance of trade and payments between China and the rest of the world?

We begin by learning how trading in the foreign exchange market determines the exchange rate.

An Exchange Rate Is a Price

An exchange rate is a price—the price of one currency in terms of another. And like all prices, an exchange rate is determined in a market—the *foreign exchange market*.

The Canadian dollar trades in the foreign exchange market and is supplied and demanded by tens of thousands of traders every hour of every

ECONOMICS IN ACTION

The Canadian Dollar: More Up than Down

The figure shows the Canadian dollar exchange rate against the three currencies that feature prominently in Canada's imports—the U.S. dollar, the European euro, and the Japanese yen—between 2000 and 2017.

The Canadian dollar has fallen in value—depreciated—against the other three currencies during the past two years. But over a longer period it has fluctuated in both directions. And compared with 2000, its 2017 value was 8 percent higher against the U.S. dollar and 12 percent higher against the Japanese yen.

Against the euro, the Canadian dollar has fluctuated around an average of 69 euro cents and its 2017 value was down 3 percent on its value in 2000.

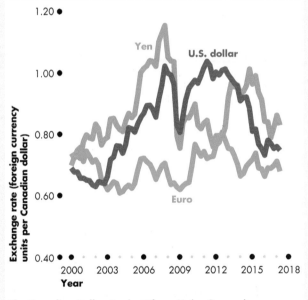

The Canadian Dollar Against Three Major Currencies

Source of data: Pacific Exchange Rate Service.

business day. Because it has many traders and no restrictions on who may trade, the foreign exchange market is a *competitive market.*

In a competitive market, demand and supply determine the price. So to understand the forces that determine the exchange rate, we need to study the factors that influence demand and supply in the foreign exchange market. But there is a feature of the foreign exchange market that makes it special.

The Demand for One Money Is the Supply of Another Money

When people who are holding the money of another country want to exchange it for Canadian dollars, they demand Canadian dollars and supply that other country's money. And when people who are holding Canadian dollars want to exchange them for the money of some other country, they supply Canadian dollars and demand that other country's money.

So the factors that influence the demand for Canadian dollars also influence the supply of euros, or yen, or yuan. And the factors that influence the demand for another country's money also influence the supply of Canadian dollars.

We'll first look at the influences on the demand for Canadian dollars in the foreign exchange market.

Demand in the Foreign Exchange Market

People buy Canadian dollars so that they can buy Canadian-produced goods and services—Canadian exports—or so they can buy Canadian assets such as bonds, stocks, businesses, and real estate or so that they can keep part of their money holding in a Canadian dollar bank account.

The quantity of Canadian dollars demanded in the foreign exchange market is the amount that traders plan to buy during a given time period at a given exchange rate. This quantity depends on many factors, but the main ones are:

1. The exchange rate
2. World demand for Canadian exports
3. Interest rates in the United States and other countries   *Canada*
4. The expected future exchange rate

We look first at the relationship between the quantity of Canadian dollars demanded in the foreign exchange market and the exchange rate when the other three influences remain the same.

The Law of Demand for Foreign Exchange The law of demand applies to Canadian dollars just as it does to anything else that people value. Other things remaining the same, the higher the exchange rate, the smaller is the quantity of Canadian dollars demanded in the foreign exchange market. For example, if the market price of the Canadian dollar rises from 100 yen to 120 yen but nothing else changes, the quantity of Canadian dollars that people plan to buy in the foreign exchange market decreases.

The exchange rate influences the quantity of Canadian dollars demanded for two reasons:

- Exports effect
- Expected profit effect

Exports Effect The larger the value of Canadian exports, the larger is the quantity of Canadian dollars demanded by the buyers of Canadian exports in the foreign exchange market. But the value of Canadian exports depends on the prices of Canadian-produced goods and services *expressed in the currency of the foreign buyer*. And these prices depend on the exchange rate. The lower the exchange rate, other things remaining the same, the lower are the prices of Canadian-produced goods and services to foreigners and the greater is the volume of Canadian exports. So if the exchange rate falls (and other influences remain the same), the quantity of Canadian dollars demanded in the foreign exchange market increases.

To see the exports effect at work, think about orders for Bombardier's regional jet. If the price of this airplane is $8 million and the exchange rate is 75 euro cents per Canadian dollar, its price to KLM, a European airline, is €6 million. KLM decides that this price is too high, so it doesn't buy the airplane. If the exchange rate falls to 60 euro cents, the price of a regional jet falls to €4.8 million, KLM decides to buy the plane and buys Canadian dollars in the foreign exchange market.

Expected Profit Effect The larger the expected profit from holding Canadian dollars, the greater is the quantity of Canadian dollars demanded in the foreign exchange market. But expected profit depends on the exchange rate. For a given expected future exchange rate, the lower the exchange rate today, the larger is the expected profit from buying Canadian dollars today and holding them, so the greater is the quantity of Canadian dollars demanded in the foreign exchange market today. Let's look at an example.

Suppose that Mitsubishi Bank, a Japanese bank, expects the exchange rate to be 120 yen per Canadian dollar at the end of the year. If today's exchange rate is also 120 yen per Canadian dollar, Mitsubishi Bank expects no profit from buying Canadian dollars and holding them until the end of the year. But if today's exchange rate is 100 yen per Canadian dollar and

Mitsubishi Bank buys Canadian dollars, it expects to sell those dollars at the end of the year for 120 yen per dollar and make a profit of 20 yen on each Canadian dollar bought.

The lower the exchange rate today, other things remaining the same, the greater is the expected profit from holding Canadian dollars, so the greater is the quantity of Canadian dollars demanded in the foreign exchange market today.

Demand Curve for Canadian Dollars

Figure 9.1 shows the demand curve for Canadian dollars in the foreign exchange market. A change in the exchange rate, other things remaining the same, brings a change in the quantity of Canadian dollars demanded and a movement along the demand curve. The arrows show such movements.

We will look at the factors that *change* demand in the next section. Before doing that, let's see what determines the supply of Canadian dollars.

FIGURE 9.1 The Demand for Canadian Dollars

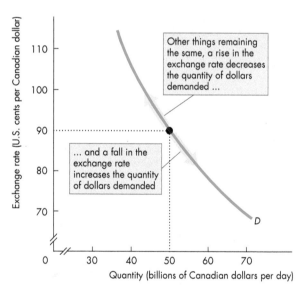

The quantity of Canadian dollars demanded depends on the exchange rate. Other things remaining the same, if the exchange rate rises, the quantity of Canadian dollars demanded decreases and there is a movement up along the demand curve. If the exchange rate falls, the quantity of Canadian dollars demanded increases and there is a movement down along the demand curve.

MyLab Economics Animation

Supply in the Foreign Exchange Market

People and businesses sell Canadian dollars and buy other currencies so that they can buy foreign-produced goods and services—Canadian imports—or so that they can buy foreign assets such as bonds, stocks, businesses, and real estate or so that they can hold part of their money in bank deposits denominated in a foreign currency.

The quantity of Canadian dollars supplied in the foreign exchange market is the amount that traders plan to sell during a given time period at a given exchange rate. This quantity depends on many factors, but the main ones are:

1. The exchange rate
2. Canadian demand for imports
3. Interest rates in the United States and other countries   *Canada*
4. The expected future exchange rate

Let's look at the law of supply in the foreign exchange market—the relationship between the quantity of Canadian dollars supplied in the foreign exchange market and the exchange rate when the other three influences remain the same.

The Law of Supply of Foreign Exchange Other things remaining the same, the higher the exchange rate, the greater is the quantity of Canadian dollars supplied in the foreign exchange market. For example, if the exchange rate rises from 100 yen to 120 yen per Canadian dollar and other things remain the same, the quantity of Canadian dollars that people plan to sell in the foreign exchange market increases.

The exchange rate influences the quantity of dollars supplied for two reasons:

- Imports effect
- Expected profit effect

Imports Effect The larger the value of Canadian imports, the larger is the quantity of Canadian dollars supplied in the foreign exchange market. But the value of Canadian imports depends on the prices of foreign-produced goods and services *expressed in Canadian dollars*. These prices depend on the exchange rate. The higher the exchange rate, other things remaining the same, the lower are the prices of foreign-produced goods and services to Americans and the greater is the volume of Canadian imports. So if the exchange rate rises (and other influences

remain the same), the quantity of Canadian dollars supplied in the foreign exchange market increases.

Expected Profit Effect This effect works just like that on the demand for the Canadian dollar but in the opposite direction. The higher the exchange rate today, other things remaining the same, the larger is the expected profit from selling Canadian dollars today and holding foreign currencies, so the greater is the quantity of Canadian dollars supplied in the foreign exchange market.

Supply Curve for Canadian Dollars

Figure 9.2 shows the supply curve of Canadian dollars in the foreign exchange market. A change in the exchange rate, other things remaining the same, brings a change in the quantity of Canadian dollars supplied and a movement along the supply curve. The arrows show such movements.

FIGURE 9.2   The Supply of Canadian Dollars

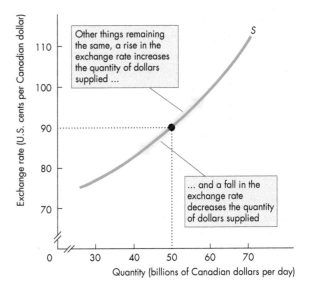

The quantity of Canadian dollars supplied depends on the exchange rate. Other things remaining the same, if the exchange rate rises, the quantity of Canadian dollars supplied increases and there is a movement up along the supply curve. If the exchange rate falls, the quantity of Canadian dollars supplied decreases and there is a movement down along the supply curve.

MyLab Economics Animation

Market Equilibrium

Equilibrium in the foreign exchange market depends on how the Bank of Canada and other central banks behave. Here, we will study the foreign exchange market with no central bank actions.

Figure 9.3 shows the demand curve for Canadian dollars, *D*, from Fig. 9.1, the supply curve of Canadian dollars, *S*, from Fig. 9.2, and the equilibrium exchange rate. The exchange rate acts as a regulator of the quantities demanded and supplied. If the exchange rate is too high, there is a surplus of dollars. For example, in Fig. 9.3, if the exchange rate is 100 U.S. cents per Canadian dollar, there is a surplus of Canadian dollars. If the exchange rate is too low, there is a shortage of dollars. For example, if the exchange rate is 80 U.S. cents per Canadian dollar, there is a shortage of Canadian dollars.

At the equilibrium exchange rate, there is neither a shortage nor a surplus—the quantity supplied equals the quantity demanded. In Fig. 9.3, the equilibrium exchange rate is 90 U.S. cents per Canadian dollar. At this exchange rate, the quantity demanded and the quantity supplied are each $50 billion a day.

The foreign exchange market is constantly pulled to its equilibrium by foreign exchange traders who are constantly looking for the best price they can get. If they are selling, they want the highest price available. If they are buying, they want the lowest price available. Information flows from trader to trader through a worldwide computer network, and the price adjusts minute by minute to keep the exchange rate at its equilibrium.

But as you've seen (in *Economics in Action* on p. 215), the Canadian dollar fluctuates a lot against other currencies. Changes in the demand for Canadian dollars or the supply of Canadian dollars bring these exchange rate fluctuations. We'll now look at the factors that make demand and supply change, starting with the demand side of the market.

Changes in the Demand for Canadian Dollars

The demand for Canadian dollars in the foreign exchange market changes when there is a change in:

- World demand for Canadian exports
- Canadian interest rate relative to the foreign interest rate
- The expected future exchange rate

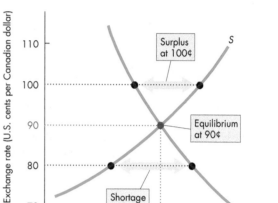

FIGURE 9.3   Equilibrium Exchange Rate

The demand curve for Canadian dollars is *D*, and the supply curve of Canadian dollars is *S*. If the exchange rate is 100 U.S. cents per Canadian dollar, there is a surplus of Canadian dollars and the exchange rate falls. If the exchange rate is 80 U.S. cents per Canadian dollar, there is a shortage of Canadian dollars and the exchange rate rises. If the exchange rate is 90 U.S. cents per Canadian dollar, there is neither a shortage nor a surplus of Canadian dollars and the exchange rate remains constant. The foreign exchange market is in equilibrium.

——— MyLab Economics Animation and Draw Graph ———

World Demand for Canadian Exports An increase in world demand for Canadian exports increases the demand for Canadian dollars. To see this effect, think about Bombardier's airplane sales. An increase in demand for air travel in Australia sends that country's airlines on a global shopping spree. They decide that Bombardier has the ideal plane, so they order some. The demand for Canadian dollars now increases.

Canadian Interest Rate Relative to the Foreign Interest Rate People and businesses buy financial assets to make a return. The higher the interest rate that people can make on Canadian assets compared with foreign assets, the more Canadian assets they buy.

What matters is not the *level* of the Canadian interest rate, but the Canadian interest rate relative to the foreign interest rate—the Canadian interest rate minus the foreign interest rate, which is called

When Supply > Demand ⇒ <AD depreciate.
D > S ⇒ Appreciate.

The Foreign Exchange Market   **219**

the **Canadian interest rate differential**. If the Canadian interest rate rises and the foreign interest rate remains constant, the Canadian interest rate differential increases. The larger the Canadian interest rate differential, the greater is the demand for Canadian assets and the greater is the demand for Canadian dollars in the foreign exchange market.

The Expected Future Exchange Rate For a given current exchange rate, other things remaining the same, a rise in the expected future exchange rate increases the profit that people expect to make by holding Canadian dollars, so the demand for Canadian dollars increases today.

Figure 9.4 summarizes the influences on the demand for Canadian dollars. An increase in the demand for Canadian exports, a rise in the Canadian interest rate differential, or a rise in the expected future exchange rate increases the demand for Canadian dollars today and shifts the demand curve rightward from D_0 to D_1. A decrease in the demand for Canadian exports, a fall in the Canadian interest rate differential, or a fall in the expected future exchange rate decreases the demand for Canadian dollars today and shifts the demand curve leftward from D_0 to D_2.

Changes in the Supply of Canadian Dollars

The supply of Canadian dollars in the foreign exchange market changes when there is a change in:

- Canadian demand for imports
- Canadian interest rate relative to the foreign interest rate
- The expected future exchange rate

Canadian Demand for Imports An increase in the Canadian demand for imports increases the supply of Canadian dollars in the foreign exchange market. To see why, think about Canadian Tire's purchase of snow blowers. An increase in the demand for snow blowers sends Canadian Tire shopping in China, and the supply of Canadian dollars increases as Canadian Tire buys Chinese yuan.

Canadian Interest Rate Relative to the Foreign Interest Rate The effect of the Canadian interest rate differential on the supply of Canadian dollars is the opposite of its effect on the demand for Canadian dollars. The larger the Canadian interest

↓ bigger #

FIGURE 9.4 Changes in the Demand for Canadian Dollars

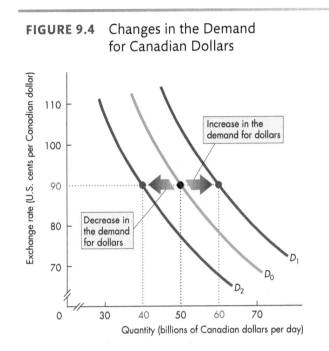

A change in any influence on the quantity of Canadian dollars that people plan to buy, other than the exchange rate, brings a change in the demand for Canadian dollars.

The demand for Canadian dollars

Increases if:	Decreases if:
■ World demand for Canadian exports increases	■ World demand for Canadian exports decreases
■ The Canadian interest rate differential rises	■ The Canadian interest rate differential falls
■ The expected future exchange rate rises	■ The expected future exchange rate falls

MyLab Economics Animation

---

rate differential, the *smaller* is the supply of Canadian dollars.

With a higher Canadian interest rate differential, people decide to keep more of their funds in Canadian dollar assets and less in foreign currency assets. They buy a smaller quantity of foreign currency and sell a smaller quantity of Canadian dollars.

So, a rise in the Canadian interest rate, other things remaining the same, decreases the supply of Canadian dollars in the foreign exchange market.

The Expected Future Exchange Rate For a given current exchange rate, other things remaining the same, a fall in the expected future exchange rate decreases the profit that can be made by holding Canadian dollars and decreases the quantity of Canadian dollars that people want to hold. To reduce their holdings of Canadian dollar assets, people must sell Canadian dollars. When they do so, the supply of Canadian dollars in the foreign exchange market increases.

Figure 9.5 summarizes the influences on the supply of Canadian dollars. If the supply of Canadian dollars increases, the supply curve shifts rightward from S_0 to S_1. If the supply of Canadian dollars decreases, the supply curve shifts leftward to S_2.

FIGURE 9.5 Changes in the Supply of Canadian Dollars

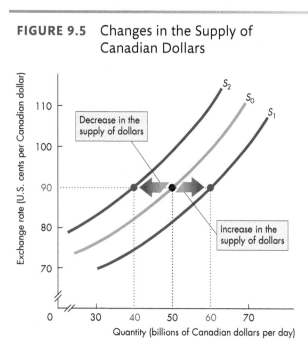

A change in any influence on the quantity of Canadian dollars that people plan to sell, other than the exchange rate, brings a change in the supply of dollars.

The supply of Canadian dollars

Increases if:

- Canadian import demand increases
- The Canadian interest rate differential falls
- The expected future exchange rate falls

Decreases if:

- Canadian import demand decreases
- The Canadian interest rate differential rises
- The expected future exchange rate rises

—— MyLab Economics Animation ——

Changes in the Exchange Rate

The exchange rate changes when either the demand for dollars or the supply of dollars changes.

An increase in the demand for Canadian dollars raises the exchange rate; and a decrease in the demand for Canadian dollars lowers the exchange rate. Similarly, a decrease in the supply of Canadian dollars raises the exchange rate; and an increase in the supply of Canadian dollars lowers the exchange rate.

These predictions are the same as those for any other market. Two episodes in the life of the Canadian dollar (next page) illustrate these predictions.

Two of the influences on demand and supply—the Canadian interest rate differential and the expected future exchange rate—change both sides of the foreign exchange market simultaneously. A rise in the Canadian interest rate differential or a rise in the expected future exchange rate increases demand, decreases supply, and raises the exchange rate. Similarly, a fall in the Canadian interest rate differential or a fall in the expected future exchange rate decreases demand, increases supply, and lowers the exchange rate.

We take a closer look at the interest rate differential and expectations in the next section.

REVIEW QUIZ

1 What are the influences on the demand for Canadian dollars in the foreign exchange market?
2 What are the influences on the supply of Canadian dollars in the foreign exchange market?
3 How is the equilibrium exchange rate determined?
4 What happens if there is a shortage or a surplus of Canadian dollars in the foreign exchange market?
5 What makes the demand for Canadian dollars change?
6 What makes the supply of Canadian dollars change?
7 What makes the Canadian dollar exchange rate fluctuate?

Work these questions in Study Plan 9.1 and get instant feedback.   MyLab Economics

ECONOMICS IN ACTION

The U.S. Dollar on a Roller Coaster

The foreign exchange market is a striking example of a competitive market. The expectations of thousands of traders around the world influence this market minute by minute throughout the 24-hour global trading day.

Demand and supply rarely stand still and their fluctuations bring a fluctuating exchange rate. Two episodes in the life of the U.S. dollar illustrate these fluctuations: 2007–2012, when the dollar depreciated and 2012–2014, when the dollar appreciated.

A Depreciating U.S. Dollar: 2007–2012 Between July 2007 and August 2012, the U.S. dollar depreciated against the yen. It fell from 120 yen to 77 yen per U.S. dollar. Part (a) of the figure provides a possible explanation for this depreciation.

In 2007, the demand and supply curves were those labelled D_{07} and S_{07}. The exchange rate was 120 yen per U.S. dollar.

During the last quarter of 2007 and the first three quarters of 2008, the U.S. economy entered a severe credit crisis. The Federal Reserve cut the interest rate in the United States, but the Bank of Japan kept the interest rate unchanged in Japan. With a narrowing of the U.S. interest rate differential, funds flowed out of the United States. Also, currency traders expected the U.S.

dollar to depreciate against the yen. The demand for U.S. dollars decreased and the supply of U.S. dollars increased.

In part (a) of the figure, the demand curve shifted leftward from D_{07} to D_{12}, the supply curve shifted rightward from S_{07} to S_{12}, and the exchange rate fell to 77 yen per U.S. dollar.

An Appreciating U.S. Dollar: 2012–2015 Between January 2012 and July 2015, the U.S. dollar appreciated against the yen. It rose from 77 yen to 121 yen per U.S. dollar. Part (b) of the figure provides an explanation for this appreciation. The demand and supply curves labelled D_{12} and S_{12} are the same as in part (a).

During 2012–2015, the Federal Reserve kept the U.S. interest rate low, but traders began to expect a future interest rate rise. Interest rates in Japan were even lower than in the United States, and the Bank of Japan, the central bank, embarked on a policy of expanding the Japanese money supply. With an expected future increase in U.S. interest rates and a lessened prospect of a rise in Japanese interest rates, the U.S. interest rate differential was expected to increase, so the dollar was expected to appreciate. The demand for U.S. dollars increased, and the supply of U.S. dollars decreased.

In the figure, the demand curve shifted rightward from D_{12} to D_{15}, the supply curve shifted leftward from S_{12} to S_{15}, and the exchange rate rose to 121 yen per U.S. dollar.

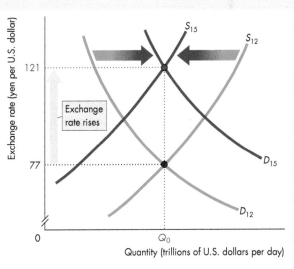

(a) 2007–2012

(b) 2012–2015

The Falling and Rising U.S. Dollar

◆ Arbitrage, Speculation, and Market Fundamentals

You've just seen how an exchange rate is determined. In our example, we used the Canadian dollar–U.S. dollar exchange rate, but exchange rates between the Canadian dollar and all other currencies are determined in a similar way. So are the exchange rates *among* the other currencies such as that of the European euro and U.K. pound. Exchange rates are kept in alignment with each other by a process called *arbitrage*.

Arbitrage

Arbitrage is the practice of seeking to profit by buying in one market and selling for a higher price in another related market. Arbitrage in the foreign exchange market and international loans markets and goods markets achieves three outcomes:

- The law of one price
- No round-trip profit
- Interest rate parity
- Purchasing power parity

The Law of One Price The *law of one price* states that if an item is traded in more than one place, the price will be the same in all locations. An example of this law is that the exchange rate between the Canadian dollar and the U.K. pound is the same in Toronto as it is in London.

You can see why arbitrage brings about this outcome by imagining that the exchange rate in London is 0.60 U.K. pounds per dollar and the price in Toronto is 0.61 U.K. pounds per dollar. In this imaginary sitiuation, a trader who buys dollars in London and sells them in Toronto makes a profit of 0.01 U.K. pounds on every dollar traded. A trade of 1 million dollars brings a profit of 10,000 U.K. pounds.

Within a few seconds, the demand for U.K. pounds increases in London and the supply of U.K. pounds increases in Toronto. These changes in demand and supply raise the exchange rate in London and lower it in Toronto and make it equal in both markets—removing the profit opportunity.

No Round-Trip Profit A round trip is using currency *A* to buy currency *B*, and then using *B* to buy *A*. A round trip might involve more stages, using *B* to buy *C* and then using *C* to buy *A*.

Arbitrage removes profit from all transactions of this type. Any fleeting profit is taken, and the changes in supply and demand induced by the momentarily available profit snap the exchange rates back to levels that remove the profit.

Interest Rate Parity Borrowers and lenders must choose the currency in which to denominate their assets and debts. **Interest rate parity**, which means equal rates of return across currencies, means that for risk-free transactions, there is no gain from choosing one currency over another.

To see why interest rate parity always prevails, suppose a Brazilian real bank deposit in Rio de Janeiro earns 10 percent a year and a Canadian dollar bank deposit in Toronto earns 1 percent a year. Why wouldn't people move their funds from Toronto to Rio?

The answer begins with the fact that to earn 10 percent in Rio, funds must be converted from Canadian dollars to reais at the beginning of the year and from reais back to dollars at the end of the year. This transaction can be done without risk by selling reais for Canadian dollars today for delivery one year from today at an exchange rate agreed on today. Such a transaction is called a *future* or *forward* transaction and it takes place at the *one-year forward exchange rate*.

Suppose that today's exchange rate is 2.30 reais per dollar, and you convert $100 to 230 reais. In one year, you will have 253 reais—your deposit of 230 reais plus interest of 23 reais. If the one-year forward exchange rate is 2.50 reais per Canadian dollar, you can contract today to sell 253 reais for $101 for delivery in one year. But that is exactly the amount you can earn by putting your $100 in the Toronto bank and earning 1 percent a year.

If, for a few seconds, interest rate parity did not hold and it was possible to profit from buying and holding Brazilian reais, traders would flock to the profit opportunity, supply dollars and demand reais, and drive the exchange rate to its interest rate parity level.

Purchasing Power Parity Suppose a camera costs 10,000 yen in Tokyo and $100 in Toronto. If the exchange rate is 100 yen per dollar, the two monies have the same value. You can buy the camera in either Tokyo or Toronto for the same price. You can express that price as either 10,000 yen or $100, but the price is the same in the two currencies.

The situation we've just described is called **purchasing power parity** (or PPP), which means *equal value of money*. PPP is an example of the law of one price, and if it does not prevail, arbitrage forces go to work. To see these forces, suppose that the price of the camera in Toronto is $120, but in Tokyo it remains at 10,000 yen and the exchange rate remains at 100 yen per dollar. In this case, the camera in Tokyo still costs 10,000 yen or $100, but in Toronto, it costs $120 or 12,000 yen. Money buys more in Japan than in Canada: Its value is *not* equal in the two countries.

Arbitrage now kicks in. With the camera cheaper in Toyko than in Toronto, the demand for cameras increases in Tokyo and the supply of cameras increases in Toronto. The Toronto price falls and the Tokyo price rises to eliminate the price difference and restore purchasing power parity.

If most goods and services cost more in one country than another, the currency of the first country is said to be *overvalued*: A depreciation of the currency would restore PPP. Similarly, the currency of the country with the lower prices is said to be *undervalued*: An appreciation of that currency would restore PPP. When goods and services cost the same in two countries, their currencies are said to be at their PPP levels.

Determining whether a currency is overvalued or undervalued based on PPP is not easy, and testing PPP by looking at individual prices requires care to ensure that the goods compared are identical. What is identical isn't always immediately obvious (see *Economics in Action* below).

Speculation

Speculation is trading on the *expectation* of making a profit. Speculation contrasts with arbitrage, which is trading on the certainty of making a profit. Most foreign exchange transactions are based on speculation, which explains why the expected future exchange rate plays such a central role in the foreign exchange market.

The expected future exchange rate influences both supply and demand, so it influences the current equilibrium exchange rate. But what determines the expected future exchange rate?

The Expected Future Exchange Rate An expectation is a forecast. Exchange rate forecasts, like weather forecasts, are made over horizons that run from a few hours to many months and perhaps years. Also, like weather forecasters, exchange rate forecasters use scientific models and data to make their predictions.

But exchange rate forecasting differs from weather forecasting in three ways. First, exchange rate forecasts are hedged with a lot of uncertainty; second, there are many divergent forecasts; and third, the forecasts influence the outcome.

The dependence of today's exchange rate on forecasts of tomorrow's exchange rate can give rise to exchange rate volatility in the short run.

ECONOMICS IN ACTION

A Big Mac Index

Because a Big Mac is the same in Chicago as in Beijing, *The Economist* magazine wondered if its price in these cities might tell us how far China's yuan is from its PPP level. In July 2017, the price of a Big Mac was $5.30 in America and 19.80 yuan or $2.92 in China. Does this dollar price difference mean that the yuan is undervalued?

The Big Mac price comparison doesn't answer this question. A Big Mac *looks* the same in all places but most of its value is in its *service*, not its *appearance*.

The figure shows the price of a Big Mac as a percentage of the U.S. price in July 2017. It shows that the price is above the U.S. price in a few rich countries and below the U.S. price in lower-income countries.

The price differences arise from different relative prices of services that arise from different costs of labour, not from over- or undervalued currencies.

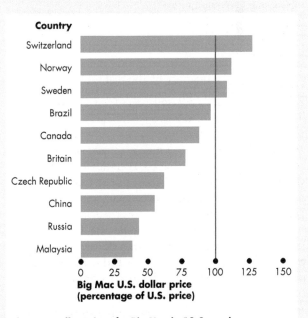

The U.S. Dollar Price of a Big Mac in 10 Countries

Source of data: www.economist.com/content/big-mac-index, July 2017.

Exchange Rate Volatility An exchange rate might rise one day and fall the next, as news about the influences on the exchange rate change the expected future exchange rate. For example, news that the Bank of Canada is going to start to raise interest rates next month brings an immediate increase in the demand for Canadian dollars, decrease in the supply of Canadian dollars, and appreciation of the Canadian dollar. As the news is digested and its expected consequences revised, expectations are revised sometimes upward and sometimes downward, bringing further changes in the exchange rate.

The influences of expectations and the constant arrival of news about the influences on supply and demand make day-to-day and week-to-week changes in the exchange rate impossible to predict. But exchange rate trends are more predictable and depend on market fundamentals.

Market Fundamentals

The market fundamentals that influence the exchange rate are world demand for Canadian exports, Canadian demand for imports, and the Canadian interest rate differential. But how these forces influence the exchange rate is different in the short run and the long run. The short-run influences are those described on pp. 215–217. To understand the long run, we need to define and understand the role played by the real exchange rate.

The Real Exchange Rate The **real exchange rate** is the relative price of Canadian-produced goods and services to foreign-produced goods and services. It is a measure of the quantity of the real GDP of other countries that a unit of Canadian real GDP buys. For example, the real Japanese yen exchange rate, RER, is given by:

$$RER = (E \times P) \div P^*,$$

where E is the exchange rate (yen per Canadian dollar), P is the Canadian price level, and P^* is the Japanese price level.

To understand the real exchange rate, suppose that the exchange rate E is 100 yen per dollar. Canada produces only computer chips priced at $150 each, so P equals $150 and $E \times P$ equals 15,000 yen. Japan produces only iPods priced at 5,000 yen each, so P^* equals 5,000 yen. Then the real Japanese yen exchange rate equals:

$$RER = (100 \times 150) \div 5,000 = 3 \text{ iPods per chip.}$$

Exchange Rate × Canada Price Level ÷ Japan Price Level

If Japan and Canada produced identical goods, the real exchange rate would equal 1 unit of Canadian real GDP per unit of Japanese real GDP.

In reality, Canadian real GDP is a different bundle of goods and services from Japanese real GDP. So the real exchange rate is not 1 and it changes over time. The forces of demand and supply in the markets for the millions of goods and services that make up real GDP determine the relative price of Japanese and Canadian real GDP and the real exchange rate.

Price Levels and Money We can turn the real exchange rate equation around and determine the exchange rate as:

$$E = (RER \times P^*) \div P.$$

This equation says that the exchange rate equals the real exchange rate multiplied by the foreign price level, divided by the domestic price level.

In the long run, the quantity of money determines the price level. But the quantity theory of money applies to all countries, so the quantity of money in Japan determines the price level in Japan, and the quantity of money in Canada determines the price level in Canada.

For a given real exchange rate, a change in the quantity of money brings a change in the price level *and* a change in the exchange rate.

The market fundamentals that determine the exchange rate in the long run are the real exchange rate and the quantities of money in each economy.

REVIEW QUIZ

1. What is arbitrage and what are its effects in the foreign exchange market?
2. What is interest rate parity and what happens when this condition doesn't hold?
3. What makes an exchange rate hard to predict?
4. What is purchasing power parity and what happens when this condition doesn't hold?
5. What determines the real exchange rate and the nominal exchange rate in the short run?
6. What determines the real exchange rate and the nominal exchange rate in the long run?

Work these questions in Study Plan 9.2 and get instant feedback. MyLab Economics

Exchange Rate Policy

Because the exchange rate is the price of a country's money in terms of another country's money, governments and central banks must have a policy toward the exchange rate. Three possible exchange rate policies are:

- Flexible exchange rate
- Fixed exchange rate
- Crawling peg

Flexible Exchange Rate

A **flexible exchange rate** is an exchange rate that is determined by demand and supply in the foreign exchange market with no direct intervention by the central bank.

Most countries, including Canada, operate a flexible exchange rate, and the foreign exchange market that we have studied so far in this chapter is an example of a flexible exchange rate regime.

But even a flexible exchange rate is influenced by central bank actions. If the Bank of Canada raises the Canadian interest rate and other countries keep their interest rates unchanged, the demand for Canadian dollars increases, the supply of Canadian dollars decreases, and the exchange rate rises. (Similarly, if the Bank of Canada lowers the Canadian interest rate, the demand for Canadian dollars decreases, the supply increases, and the exchange rate falls.)

In a flexible exchange rate regime, when the central bank changes the interest rate, its purpose is not usually to influence the exchange rate, but to achieve some other monetary policy objective. (We return to this topic at length in Chapter 14.)

Fixed Exchange Rate

A **fixed exchange rate** is an exchange rate that is determined by a decision of the government or the central bank and is achieved by central bank intervention in the foreign exchange market to block the unregulated forces of demand and supply.

The world economy operated a fixed exchange rate regime from the end of World War II to the early 1970s. China had a fixed exchange rate until recently. Hong Kong has had a fixed exchange rate for many years and continues with that policy today.

Active intervention in the foreign exchange market is required to achieve a fixed exchange rate.

If the Bank of Canada wanted to fix the Canadian dollar exchange rate against the U.S. dollar, it would have to sell Canadian dollars to prevent the exchange rate from rising above the target value and buy Canadian dollars to prevent the exchange rate from falling below the target value.

There is no limit to the quantity of Canadian dollars that the Bank of Canada can *sell* because it creates Canadian dollars. But there is a limit to the quantity of Canadian dollars the Bank of Canada can *buy*, which is set by Canadian official foreign currency reserves. Intervention to buy Canadian dollars would have to stop when Canadian official foreign currency reserves run out.

Let's look at the foreign exchange interventions that the Bank of Canada can make.

Suppose the Bank of Canada wants the exchange rate to be steady at 90 U.S. cents per Canadian dollar. If the exchange rate rises above 90 U.S. cents, the Bank of Canada sells dollars. If the exchange rate falls below 90 U.S. cents, the Bank of Canada buys dollars. By these actions, the Bank of Canada keeps the exchange rate close to its target rate of 90 U.S. cents per Canadian dollar.

Figure 9.6 shows the Bank of Canada's intervention in the foreign exchange market. The supply of dollars is S and initially the demand for dollars is D_0. The equilibrium exchange rate is 90 U.S. cents per dollar. This exchange rate is also the target exchange rate, shown by the horizontal red line.

When the demand for Canadian dollars increases and the demand curve shifts rightward to D_1, the Bank sells $10 billion. This action prevents the exchange rate from rising. When the demand for Canadian dollars decreases and the demand curve shifts leftward to D_2, the Bank buys $10 billion. This action prevents the exchange rate from falling.

If the demand for Canadian dollars fluctuates between D_1 and D_2 and on average is D_0, the Bank of Canada can repeatedly intervene in the way we've just seen. Sometimes the Bank of Canada buys and sometimes it sells but, on average, it neither buys nor sells.

But suppose the demand for Canadian dollars *increases permanently* from D_0 to D_1. To maintain the exchange rate at 90 U.S. cents per Canadian dollar, the Bank of Canada must sell dollars and buy foreign currency, so Canadian official foreign currency reserves would be increasing. At some point, the Bank of Canada would abandon the exchange rate of 90 U.S. cents per Canadian dollar and stop piling up foreign currency reserves.

FIGURE 9.6 Foreign Exchange Market Intervention

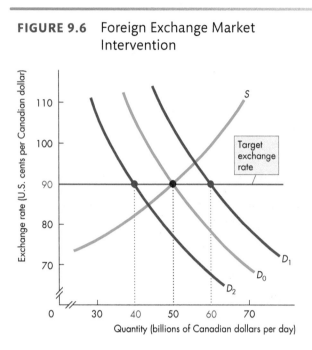

Initially, the demand for Canadian dollars is D_0, the supply of Canadian dollars is S, and the exchange rate is 90 U.S. cents per Canadian dollar. The Bank of Canada can intervene in the foreign exchange market to keep the exchange rate close to its target rate (90 U.S. cents). If the demand for Canadian dollars increases and the demand curve shifts from D_0 to D_1, the Bank of Canada sells Canadian dollars. If the demand for Canadian dollars decreases and the demand curve shifts from D_0 to D_2, the Bank of Canada buys Canadian dollars. Persistent intervention on one side of the market cannot be sustained.

———— MyLab Economics Animation ————

Now suppose the demand for Canadian dollars *decreases permanently* from D_0 to D_2. In this situation, the Bank of Canada *cannot* maintain the exchange rate at 90 U.S. cents per Canadian dollar indefinitely. To hold it at 90 U.S. cents, the Bank of Canada must *buy* Canadian dollars using Canada's official foreign currency reserves. So the Bank of Canada's action decreases its foreign currency reserves. Eventually, the Bank of Canada would run out of foreign currency and would then have to abandon the target exchange rate of 90 U.S. cents per Canadian dollar.

Crawling Peg

A **crawling peg** is an exchange rate that follows a path determined by a decision of the government or the central bank and is achieved in a similar way to a

ECONOMICS IN ACTION

The People's Bank of China in the Foreign Exchange Market

The exchange rate between the U.S. dollar and the Chinese yuan was constant for several years before 2005. The reason for this constant exchange rate is that China's central bank, the People's Bank of China, intervened to operate a *fixed exchange rate policy*. From 1997 until 2005, the yuan was pegged at 8.28 yuan per U.S. dollar. Since 2005, the yuan has appreciated slightly, but it has not been permitted to fluctuate freely. Since 2005, the yuan has been on a crawling peg.

How China Manages Its Exchange Rate The People's Bank manages the exchange rate between the yuan and the U.S. dollar by intervening in the foreign exchange market, buying or selling U.S. dollars. When it buys U.S. dollars, its reserves increase, and when it sells U.S. dollars, its reserves decrease.

Part (a) of the figure shows the changes in reserves that resulted from China's intervention in the foreign exchange market. You can see that China's reserves increased in most years, and by a record $510 billion in 2013.

The demand and supply curves in part (b) of the figure illustrate what happened in 2013 in the market for U.S. dollars and explains why China's reserves increased. The demand curve D_{13} and supply curve S_{13} intersect at 5 yuan per U.S. dollar. If the People's Bank of China takes no actions in the market, this exchange rate is the equilibrium rate (an assumed value). To keep the exchange rate at 6.20 yuan per dollar, the People's Bank bought $510 billion.

The demand and supply curves in part (c) of the figure illustrate what happened in 2015 in the market

fixed exchange rate by central bank intervention in the foreign exchange market. A crawling peg works like a fixed exchange rate except that the target value changes. The target might change at fixed intervals (daily, weekly, monthly) or at random intervals.

The Bank of Canada has never operated a crawling peg, but some countries do. When China abandoned its fixed exchange rate, it replaced it with a crawling peg. Developing countries might use a crawling peg as a method of trying to control inflation.

The ideal crawling peg sets a target for the exchange rate equal to the equilibrium exchange rate for U.S. dollars and explains why China's reserves *decreased* in that year. The demand curve D_{15} and supply curve S_{15} intersect at 7 yuan per U.S. dollar. If the People's Bank of China takes no actions in the market, this exchange rate is the equilibrium rate (an assumed value). To keep the exchange rate at 6.40 yuan per dollar, the People's Bank sold $512 billion.

The consequence of the fixed (and crawling peg) yuan exchange rate is that China's foreign exchange reserves fluctuate. Between 2000 and 2014, China's official foreign currency reserves grew by $3.7 trillion! Then, in 2015 and 2016, when the People's Bank sold dollars, its reserves fell by $830 billion.

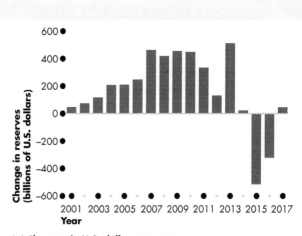

(a) Changes in U.S. dollar reserves

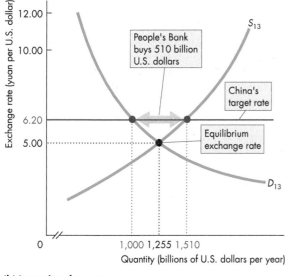

(b) Lowering the yuan

China's Foreign Exchange Market Intervention

Source of data: The People's Bank of China.

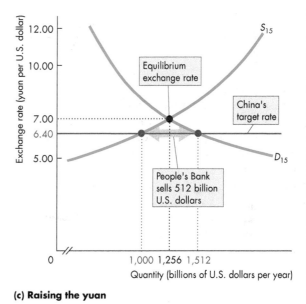

(c) Raising the yuan

on average. The peg seeks only to prevent large swings in the expected future exchange rate that change demand and supply and make the exchange rate fluctuate too wildly.

A crawling peg departs from the ideal if, as often happens with a fixed exchange rate, the target rate departs from the equilibrium exchange rate for too long. When this happens, the country either runs out of reserves or piles up reserves.

In the final part of this chapter, we explain how the balance of international payments is determined.

REVIEW QUIZ

1 What is a flexible exchange rate and how does it work?
2 What is a fixed exchange rate and how is its value fixed?
3 What is a crawling peg and how does it work?
4 How has China operated in the foreign exchange market, why, and with what effect?

Work these questions in Study Plan 9.3 and get instant feedback.   MyLab Economics

Financing International Trade

You now know how the exchange rate is determined, but what is the effect of the exchange rate? How does currency depreciation or currency appreciation influence our international trade and payments? We're going to lay the foundation for addressing these questions by looking at the scale of international trading, borrowing, and lending and at the way in which we keep our records of international transactions. These records are called the *balance of payments accounts*.

Balance of Payments Accounts

A country's **balance of payments accounts** records its international trading, borrowing, and lending in three accounts:

1. Current account
2. Capital and financial account
3. Official settlements account

The **current account** records receipts from exports of goods and services sold abroad, payments for imports of goods and services from abroad, net interest income paid abroad, and net transfers abroad (such as foreign aid payments). The *current account balance* equals the sum of exports minus imports, net interest income, and net transfers.

The **capital and financial account** records foreign investment in Canada minus Canadian investment abroad. (This account also has a statistical discrepancy that arises from errors and omissions in measuring international capital transactions.)

The **official settlements account** records the change in **Canadian official reserves**, which are the government's holdings of foreign currency. If Canadian official reserves *increase*, the official settlements account balance is *negative*. The reason is that holding foreign money is like investing abroad. Canadian investment abroad is a minus item in the capital and financial account and in the official settlements account.

The sum of the balances on the three accounts *always* equals zero. That is, to pay for our current account deficit, we must either borrow more from abroad than we lend abroad or use our official reserves to cover the shortfall.

Table 9.1 shows the Canadian balance of payments accounts in 2016. Items in the current account and the capital and financial account that provide foreign currency to Canada have a plus sign; items that cost Canada foreign currency have a minus sign. The table shows that in 2016, Canadian imports exceeded Canadian exports and the current account had a deficit of $67 billion. How do we pay for imports that exceed the value of our exports? That is, how do we pay for our current account deficit?

We pay for our current account deficit by borrowing from the rest of the world. The capital and financial account tells us by how much. We borrowed from the rest of the world (foreign investment in Canada) and we lent to the rest of the world (Canadian investment abroad). Our *net* foreign borrowing was $74 billion. There is almost always a statistical discrepancy between the capital and financial account and current account transactions, and in 2016, the discrepancy was close to zero, so the capital and financial account balance was $74 billion.

The capital and financial account balance plus the current account balance equals the change in

TABLE 9.1 Canadian Balance of Payments Accounts in 2016

Current account	Billions of dollars
Exports of goods and services	+629
Imports of goods and services	−677
Net interest income	−16
Net transfers	−3
Current account balance	−67

Capital and financial account	
Net foreign investment in Canada	+74
Statistical discrepancy	0
Capital and financial account balance	+74

Official settlements account	0
Offical settlements account balance	−7

Source of data: Statistics Canada, CANSIM Tables 376-0101 and 376-0104.

Canadian official reserves. In 2016, the capital and financial account balance of $74 billion plus the current account balance of −$67 billion equalled $7 billion. Canadian official reserves *increased* in 2016 by $7 billion. Holding more foreign reserves is like lending to the rest of the world, so this amount appears in the official settlements account as −$7 billion in Table 9.1. The sum of the balances on the three balance of payments accounts equals zero.

To see more clearly what the nation's balance of payments accounts mean, think about your own balance of payments accounts. They are similar to the nation's accounts.

An Individual's Balance of Payments Accounts An individual's current account records the income from supplying the services of factors of production and the expenditure on goods and services. Consider Jackie, for example. She worked in 2014 and earned an income of $25,000. Jackie has $10,000 worth of investments that earned her an interest income of $1,000. Jackie's current account shows an income of $26,000. Jackie spent $18,000 buying consumption goods and services. She also bought a new house, which cost her $60,000. So Jackie's total expenditure was $78,000. Jackie's expenditure minus her income is $52,000 ($78,000 minus $26,000). This amount is Jackie's current account deficit.

ECONOMICS IN ACTION

Three Decades of Deficits

The numbers that you reviewed in Table 9.1 give a snapshot of the balance of payments accounts in 2016. The figure below puts that snapshot into perspective by showing the balance of payments between 1982 and the first half of 2016.

Because the economy grows and the price level rises, changes in the dollar value of the balance of payments do not convey much information. To remove the influences of economic growth and inflation, the figure shows the balance of payments expressed as a percentage of nominal GDP.

As you can see, a large current account deficit emerged during the 1980s and declined during the 1990s and moved into surplus in the 2000s before returning to deficit after 2008.

The capital and financial account balance is almost a mirror image of the current account balance. The official settlements balance is very small in comparison with the balances on the other two accounts.

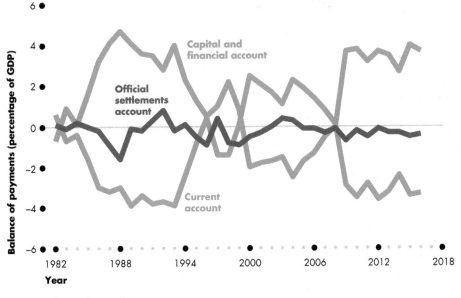

The Canadian Balance of Payments

Source of data: Statistics Canada, CANSIM Tables 376-0101 and 376-0104.

To pay for expenditure of $52,000 in excess of her income, Jackie must either use the money that she has in the bank or take out a loan. Suppose that Jackie took out a loan of $50,000 to help buy her house and that this loan was the only borrowing that she did. Borrowing is an *inflow* in the capital account, so Jackie's capital account *surplus* was $50,000. With a current account deficit of $52,000 and a capital account surplus of $50,000, Jackie was still $2,000 short. She got that $2,000 from her own bank account. Her cash holdings decreased by $2,000.

Jackie's income from her work is like a country's income from its exports. Her income from her investments is like a country's interest income from foreigners. Her purchases of goods and services, including her purchase of a house, are like a country's imports. Jackie's loan—borrowing from someone else—is like a country's borrowing from the rest of the world. The change in Jackie's bank account is like the change in the country's official reserves.

Borrowers and Lenders

A country that is borrowing more from the rest of the world than it is lending to the rest of the world is called a **net borrower**. Similarly, a **net lender** is a country that is lending more to the rest of the world than it is borrowing from the rest of the world.

Canada was a net borrower between 2009 and 2016 and a net lender between 1999 and 2008. Through most of the 1980s and 1990s, Canada was a net borrower.

The world's largest net borrower is the United States. Since the early 1980s, with the exception of only a single year, 1991, the United States has been a net borrower from the rest of the world. And during the years between 1992 and 2008, the scale of U.S. borrowing mushroomed. It has shrunk slightly since 2008.

Most countries are net borrowers like Canada and the United States. But a few countries, including China, Japan, and oil-rich Saudi Arabia, are net lenders. In 2014, when the United States borrowed $397 billion from the rest of the world, China alone lent more than $200 billion.

International borrowing and lending takes place in the global market for loanable funds. You studied the loanable funds market in Chapter 7, but there, we didn't take explicit account of the effects of the balance of payments and international borrowing and lending on the market. That's what we will now do.

The Global Loanable Funds Market

Figure 9.7(a) illustrates the demand for loanable funds, DLF_W, and the supply of loanable funds, SLF_W, in the global loanable funds market. The world equilibrium real interest rate makes the quantity of funds supplied in the world as a whole equal to the quantity demanded. In this example, the equilibrium real interest rate is 5 percent a year and the quantity of funds is $10 trillion.

An International Borrower Figure 9.7(b) shows the loanable funds market in a country that borrows from the rest of the world. The country's demand for loanable funds, DLF_D, is part of the world demand in Fig. 9.7(a). The country's supply of loanable funds, SLF_D, is part of the world supply.

If this country were isolated from the global market, the real interest rate would be 6 percent a year (where the DLF_D and SLF_D curves intersect). But if the country is integrated into the global economy, with an interest rate of 6 percent a year, funds would *flood into* it. With a real interest rate of 5 percent a year in the global market, suppliers of loanable funds would seek the higher return in this country. In effect, the country faces the supply of loanable funds curve, SLF, which is horizontal at the world equilibrium real interest rate.

The country's demand for loanable funds and the world interest rate determine the equilibrium quantity of loanable funds—$2.5 billion in Fig. 9.7(b).

An International Lender Figure 9.7(c) shows the situation in a country that lends to the rest of the world. As before, the country's demand for loanable funds, DLF_D, is part of the world demand and the country's supply of loanable funds, SLF_D, is part of the world supply in Fig. 9.7(a).

If this country were isolated from the global market, the real interest rate would be 4 percent a year (where the DLF_D and SLF_D curves intersect). But if this country is integrated into the global economy, with an interest rate of 4 percent a year, funds would quickly *flow out* of it. With a real interest rate of 5 percent a year in the rest of the world, domestic suppliers of loanable funds would seek the higher return in other countries. Again, the country faces the supply of loanable funds curve, SLF, which is horizontal at the world equilibrium real interest rate.

The country's demand for loanable funds and the world interest rate determine the equilibrium quantity of loanable funds—$1.5 billion in Fig. 9.7(c).

FIGURE 9.7   Borrowing and Lending in the Global Loanable Funds Market

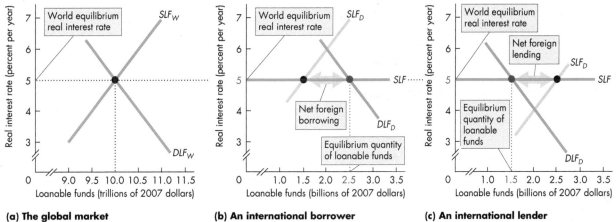

(a) The global market   **(b) An international borrower**   **(c) An international lender**

In the global loanable funds market in part (a), the demand for loanable funds curve, DLF_W, and the supply of funds curve, SLF_W, determine the world real interest rate. Each country can get funds at the world real interest rate and faces the (horizontal) supply curve SLF in parts (b) and (c).

At the world real interest rate, borrowers in part (b) want more funds than the quantity supplied by domestic lenders,

$1.5 billion on the domestic supply curve SLF_D. The shortage is made up by net foreign borrowing.

Domestic suppliers of funds in part (c) want to lend more than domestic borrowers demand, 1.5 billion on DLF_D. The excess quantity supplied goes to foreign borrowers.

MyLab Economics Animation

Debtors and Creditors

A net borrower might be decreasing its net assets held in the rest of the world, or it might be going deeper into debt. A nation's total stock of foreign investment determines whether it is a debtor or a creditor. A **debtor nation** is a country that during its entire history has borrowed more from the rest of the world than it has lent to it. It has a stock of outstanding debt to the rest of the world that exceeds the stock of its own claims on the rest of the world. A **creditor nation** is a country that during its entire history has invested more in the rest of the world than other countries have invested in it.

Canada is a debtor nation. Throughout the nineteenth century Canada borrowed from Europe to finance its westward expansion, railroads, and industrialization. The capital-hungry developing countries (such as Canada was during the nineteenth century) are among the largest debtor nations in the world. The international debt of these countries grew from less than a third to more than a half of their gross domestic product during the 1980s and created what was called the "Third World debt crisis."

But the United States is the largest debtor nation. Since 1986, the total stock of U.S. borrowing from

the rest of the world has exceeded U.S. lending to the rest of the world by $11.9 trillion (more than five times Canada's gross domestic product).

Should we be concerned that Canada is a net borrower and a debtor? The answer depends on whether the borrowing is financing investment that in turn is generating economic growth and higher income, or financing consumption expenditure. If the borrowed money is used to finance consumption, it will eventually have to be reduced, and the longer it goes on, the greater is the reduction in consumption that will eventually be necessary.

Is Canadian Borrowing for Consumption?

In 2016, Canada borrowed $74 billion from abroad. In that year, private investment in buildings, plant, and equipment was $466 billion and government investment in defence equipment and social projects was $79 billion. All this investment added to Canada's capital and increased productivity. The government also spends on education and healthcare services, which increase *human capital*. Canadian international borrowing is financing private and public investment, not consumption.

Current Account Balance

What determines a country's current account balance and net foreign borrowing? You've seen that net exports (NX) is the main item in the current account. We can define the current account balance (CAB) as:

$$CAB = NX + \text{Net interest income} + \text{Net transfers}.$$

We can study the current account balance by looking at what determines net exports because the other two items are small and do not fluctuate much.

Net Exports

Net exports are determined by the government budget and private saving and investment. To see how net exports are determined, we need to recall some of the things that we learned in Chapter 7 about the flows of funds that finance investment. Table 9.2 refreshes your memory and summarizes some calculations.

Part (a) lists the national income variables that are needed, with their symbols. Part (b) defines three balances: net exports, the government sector balance, and the private sector balance.

Net exports is exports of goods and services minus imports of goods and services.

The **government sector balance** is equal to net taxes minus government expenditure on goods and services. If that number is positive, a government sector surplus is lent to other sectors; if that number is negative, a government deficit must be financed by borrowing from other sectors. The government sector deficit is the sum of the deficits of the Bank of Canada, provincial, and local governments.

The **private sector balance** is saving minus investment. If saving exceeds investment, a private sector surplus is lent to other sectors. If investment exceeds saving, a private sector deficit is financed by borrowing from other sectors.

Part (b) also shows the values of these balances for Canada in 2016. As you can see, net exports were −$48 billion, a deficit of $48 billion. The government sector's revenue from *net* taxes was $471 billion and its expenditure was $509 billion, so the government sector balance was −$38 billion—a deficit of $38 billion. The private sector saved $375 billion and invested $385 billion, so its balance was −$10 billion—a deficit of $10 billion.

Part (c) shows the relationship among the three balances. From the national income and expenditure accounts, we know that real GDP, Y, is the sum of

---

TABLE 9.2   Net Exports, the Government Budget, Saving, and Investment

	Symbols and equations	Canada in 2016 (billions of dollars)
(a) Variables		
Exports*	X	629
Imports*	M	677
Government expenditure	G	509
Net taxes	T	471
Investment	I	385
Saving	S	375

(b) Balances		
Net exports	$X - M$	$629 - 677 = -48$
Government sector	$T - G$	$471 - 509 = -38$
Private sector	$S - I$	$375 - 385 = -10$

(c) Relationship among balances

National accounts	$Y = C + I + G + X - M$	
	$= C + S + T$	
Rearranging:	$X - M = S - I + T - G$	
Net exports equals:	$X - M$	−48
Government sector plus	$T - G$	−38
Private sector	$S - I$	−10

Source of data: Statistics Canada, CANSIM Tables 380-0002 and 380-0064.

* The national income and expenditure accounts measures of exports and imports are slightly different from the balance of payments accounts measures in Table 9.1 on p. 228.

---

consumption expenditure (C), investment (I), government expenditure (G), and net exports ($X - M$). Real GDP also equals the sum of consumption expenditure (C), saving (S), and net taxes (T). Rearranging these equations tells us that net exports is the sum of the government sector balance and the private sector balance. In Canada in 2016, the government sector balance was −$38 billion; the private

ECONOMICS IN ACTION

The Three Sector Balances

You've seen that net exports equal the sum of the government sector balance and the private sector balance. How do these three sector balances fluctuate over time?

The figure answers this question. It shows the government sector balance (the red line), net exports (the blue line), and the private sector balance (the green line).

The private sector balance and the government sector balance move in opposite directions. When the government sector deficit increased during the early 1980s and early 1990s, the private sector surplus increased. And when the government sector deficit decreased during the late 1990s and became a surplus from 2000 to 2008, the private sector's surplus decreased.

After 2008, when the government balance became a deficit again, the private sector balance also became a surplus, and net exports became negative.

Sometimes the government sector deficit and the net export surplus are correlated, but the net export balance does not follow the government sector balance closely. Rather, net exports respond to the sum of the government sector and private sector balances. When

the private sector surplus exceeds the government sector deficit, net exports are positive. When the government sector deficit exceeds the private sector surplus, net exports are negative.

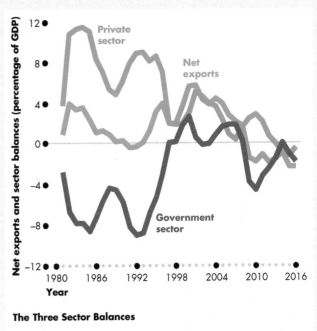

The Three Sector Balances

Source of data: Statistics Canada, CANSIM Tables 380-0002 and 380-0064.

sector balance was −$10 billion; and the sum of these sector balances equalled net exports of −$48 billion.

Where Is the Exchange Rate?

We haven't mentioned the exchange rate while discussing the balance of payments. Doesn't it play a role? The answer is that in the short run it does but in the long run it doesn't.

In the short run, a fall in the dollar lowers the real exchange rate, which makes Canadian imports more costly and Canadian exports more competitive. A higher price of imported consumption goods and services might induce a decrease in consumption expenditure and an increase in saving. A higher price of imported capital goods might induce a decrease in investment. Other things remaining the same, an increase in saving or a decrease in investment decreases the private sector deficit and decreases the current account deficit.

But in the long run, a change in the nominal exchange rate leaves the real exchange rate unchanged and has no effect on the current account balance.

REVIEW QUIZ

1 What are the transactions that the balance of payments accounts record?
2 Is Canada a net borrower or a net lender? Is it a debtor or a creditor nation?
3 How are net exports and the government sector balance linked?

Work these questions in Study Plan 9.4 and get instant feedback.   MyLab Economics

◆ *Economics in the News* on pp. 234–235 looks at the Trump administration's ideas about the U.S. trade balance, NAFTA, and currency manipulation.

NAFTA Trade Balances

Trump to Prioritize Cutting U.S.'s NAFTA Trade Deficits

The Financial Times

July 18, 2017

The Trump administration declared reducing U.S. trade deficits with Canada and Mexico as the top priority for its renegotiation of the North American Free Trade Agreement as Donald Trump renewed his promise to bring back manufacturing jobs by embracing a new era of American protectionism.

The focus on the deficits came in a rundown of NAFTA negotiating priorities sent to Congress on Monday and sets the stage for tough negotiations expected to begin as soon as next month. It sat alongside a reminder that Mr Trump—who is now considering new tariffs on steel imports in a move many fear could trigger a trade war—remains convinced of the value of protectionism.

"For most of our nation's history . . . American presidents have understood that in order to protect our economy and our security, we must protect our industry. And much of that comes at the border," Mr Trump told a White House event to celebrate "Made in America Week" featuring cowboy hats, baseball bats, and fire trucks among other nostalgic American products. . . .

Besides promising to reduce the U.S. trade deficit in goods with both Canada ($11bn in 2016) and Mexico ($64.3bn in 2016) the administration also pledged to ban countries from manipulating their currencies to gain competitive advantage, both important issues for economic nationalists in the administration. . . .

Shawn Donnan, Published July 17 2017, *Financial Times*

ESSENCE OF THE STORY

- The Trump administration intends to renegotiate the North American Free Trade Agreement (NAFTA).
- Reducing U.S. trade deficits with Canada and Mexico is its top priority.
- President Trump believes that manufacturing jobs can return to America by placing tariffs on imports.
- The administration also pledged to ban countries from manipulating their currencies to gain competitive advantage.

MyLab Economics Economics in the News

ECONOMIC ANALYSIS

- Let's begin with some facts about U.S. trade with Mexico and Canada in 2016.

- The United States had a trade deficit with Mexico of $63 billion. The deficit in goods was larger but there was a services trade *surplus* of $7.5 billion.

- With Canada, the trade balance was a *surplus* of $7.7 billion. A surplus of $24 billion in services trade more than wiped out a small deficit in goods trade.

- The overall NAFTA balance of trade in goods and services was a deficit of $55 billion.

- To put that deficit in perspective, it represents 0.3 percent of GDP.

- The NAFTA deficit also represents about 10 percent of the U.S. total international trade deficit.

- The figures show the U.S. trade volumes (total exports and imports) and balances since 1999, all as percentages of GDP.

- In Fig. 1, you can see that NAFTA trade has grown, but not by as much as trade with the rest of the world. The dip in trade in 2008 was an effect of a global financial crisis that year.

- In Fig. 2, you can see that the NAFTA trade deficit has been a small fraction of the deficit with the rest of the world, and the deficit has been very small since 2008.

- Why does the United States have an international trade deficit? U.S. imports exceed U.S. exports because the surplus of private saving over investment is too small to cover the large government sector deficit.

- The equation, $X - M = (T - G) + (S - I)$, determines the trade balance.

- How would a renegotiated NAFTA with tariffs on imports from Mexico and Canada influence the trade balance? The international deficit would decrease by the amount that tariff revenue reduces the government budget deficit. But if the tariff revenue were spent, the international deficit would not change.

- How would a renegotiated NAFTA with tariffs on imports from Mexico and Canada influence the trade volumes—total imports and total exports? It would lower the volume of both imports and exports by similar amounts.

- A tariff on imports would raise their prices in the United States and Americans would spend less on Mexican- and Canadian-produced goods and services.

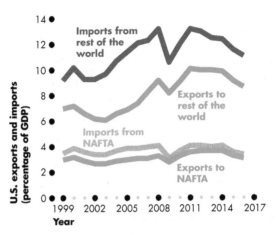

Figure 1 U.S. Exports and Imports

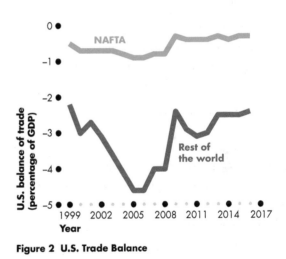

Figure 2 U.S. Trade Balance

- Mexicans and Canadians would earn less and spend less on U.S.-produced goods and services.

- Mexicans, Canadians, *and* Americans would be worse off because everyone would be paying more for the things they consume.

- So, tariffs are a bad idea. What about tackling currency manipulators, the other Trump idea?

- It is easy to target the market exchange rate but, as you learned on p. 233, it is only possible to target (manipulate) the real exchange rate in the short run. In the long run, prices respond to the exchange rate and the real exchange rate and trade balance are driven by the fundamental equation: $X - M = (T - G) + (S - I)$.

WORKED PROBLEM

MyLab Economics Work this problem in Chapter 9 Study Plan.

On June 1, 2015, the exchange rate was 101 yen per Canadian dollar. During that day, the Bank of Canada made a surprise announcement that it would raise the interest rate next month by 1 percentage point. At the same moment, the Bank of Japan announced that it would lower the interest rate next month.

On June 2, 2015, the exchange rate was 99 yen per Canadian dollar.

Questions

1. Explain the effect of the Bank of Canada's announcement on the demand for and supply of Canadian dollars.
2. Explain the effect of the Bank of Japan's announcement on the demand for and supply of Canadian dollars.
3. Explain the effect of the two announcements on the Canadian dollar–yen exchange rate: Would the Canadian dollar appreciate or depreciate?
4. Could the change in the exchange rate on June 2 have resulted from the two announcements, or must some other influence have changed too? If so, what might that influence have been?

Solutions

1. The Bank of Canada's announcement of a 1 percentage point rise in the Canadian interest rate next month means that, other interest rates remaining the same, the Canadian interest rate differential will increase next month.

   An increase in the Canadian interest rate differential next month will increase the demand for Canadian dollars and decrease the supply of Canadian dollars next month. The exchange rate next month will increase.

   With the increase in the exchange rate expected next month, the demand for Canadian dollars will increase and the supply of Canadian dollars will decrease on June 2.

Key Point: An expected *future* rise in the interest rate differential increases the demand for Canadian dollars and decreases the supply of Canadian dollars immediately through its effect on the expected future exchange rate.

2. The Bank of Japan's announcement that it will lower the interest rate in Japan next month has the same effect on the Canadian interest rate differential as a rise in the Canadian interest rate.

   So the effect of a Japanese interest rate cut reinforces that of a Canadian interest rate increase.

   The even-larger increase in the interest rate differential next month will bring a larger increase in the demand for Canadian dollars and decrease in the supply of Canadian dollars next month, and a larger increase in the exchange rate.

   The larger increase in the exchange rate expected next month will bring a larger increase in the demand for Canadian dollars and a decrease in the supply of Canadian dollars on June 2.

Key Point: A fall in the foreign interest rate has the same effects on the demand for and supply of Canadian dollars as a rise in the Canadian interest rate.

3. The two interest rate announcements have the same effect: They increase the demand for and decrease the supply of Canadian dollars.

   An increase in the demand for Canadian dollars raises the exchange rate and a decrease in the supply of Canadian dollars raises the exchange rate, so the announcements would make the dollar appreciate.

Key Point: An increase in demand and a decrease in supply have the same effect on price: They raise the price. The exchange rate is a price.

4. When the Canadian dollar fell from 101 yen on June 1 to 99 yen on June 2, the Canadian dollar depreciated. Other things remaining the same, the two central bank announcements would have appreciated the Canadian dollar.

   Because the exchange rate fell—the Canadian dollar depreciated—either the demand for Canadian dollars must have decreased or the supply of Canadian dollars must have increased.

   The influences on demand and supply that might have changed are Canadian exports or Canadian imports.

   A decrease in Canadian exports would have decreased the demand for Canadian dollars. An increase in Canadian imports would have increased the supply of Canadian dollars.

Key Point: When the Canadian dollar–yen exchange rate falls, either the demand for Canadian dollars has decreased or the supply of Canadian dollars has increased or both have occurred.

SUMMARY

Key Points

The Foreign Exchange Market (pp. 214–221)

- Foreign currency is obtained in exchange for domestic currency in the foreign exchange market.
- Demand and supply in the foreign exchange market determine the exchange rate.
- The higher the exchange rate, the smaller is the quantity of Canadian dollars demanded and the greater is the quantity of Canadian dollars supplied.
- At the equilibrium exchange rate, the quantity of Canadian dollars demanded equals the quantity of Canadian dollars supplied.
- A change in the demand for Canadian exports changes the demand for Canadian dollars, and a change in the Canadian demand for imports changes the supply of Canadian dollars.
- A change in the Canadian interest rate differential or the expected future exchange rate change *both* the demand for and supply of Canadian dollars, but in opposite directions.

Working Problems 1 to 5 will give you a better understanding of the foreign exchange market.

Arbitrage, Speculation, and Market Fundamentals (pp. 222–224)

- Arbitrage in the foreign exchange market achieves interest rate parity and purchasing power parity.

- Speculation in the foreign exchange market can bring excess volatility to the exchange rate.
- In the long run, the exchange rate is determined by the real exchange rate and the relative quantities of money.

Working Problems 6 to 8 will give you a better understanding of arbitrage, speculation, and market fundamentals.

Exchange Rate Policy (pp. 225–227)

- An exchange rate can be flexible, fixed, or a crawling peg.
- To achieve a fixed or a crawling exchange rate, a central bank must either buy or sell foreign currency in the foreign exchange market.

Working Problem 9 will give you a better understanding of exchange rate policy.

Financing International Trade (pp. 228–233)

- A country's international transactions are recorded in its current account, capital account, and official settlements account.
- The current account balance is similar to net exports and is determined by the government sector balance plus the private sector balance.
- International borrowing and lending take place in the global loanable funds market.

Working Problem 10 will give you a better understanding of financing international trade.

Key Terms

MyLab Economics Key Terms Quiz

Arbitrage, 222
Balance of payments accounts, 228
Canadian interest rate differential, 219
Canadian official reserves, 228
Capital and financial account, 228
Crawling peg, 226
Creditor nation, 231

Current account, 228
Debtor nation, 231
Exchange rate, 214
Fixed exchange rate, 225
Flexible exchange rate, 225
Foreign currency, 214
Foreign exchange market, 214
Government sector balance, 232

Interest rate parity, 222
Net borrower, 230
Net exports, 232
Net lender, 230
Official settlements account, 228
Private sector balance, 232
Purchasing power parity, 222
Real exchange rate, 224

STUDY PLAN PROBLEMS AND APPLICATIONS

MyLab Economics Work Problems 1 to 10 in Chapter 9 Study Plan and get instant feedback.

The Foreign Exchange Market (Study Plan 9.1)

Use the following data to work Problems 1 to 3.

The U.S. dollar exchange rate increased from $1.24 Canadian in June 2015 to $1.29 Canadian in June 2016, and it decreased from 121 Japanese yen in June 2015 to 108 yen in June 2016.

1. Did the U.S. dollar appreciate or depreciate against the Canadian dollar? Did the U.S. dollar appreciate or depreciate against the yen?

2. What was the value of the Canadian dollar in terms of U.S. dollars in June 2015 and June 2016? Did the Canadian dollar appreciate or depreciate against the U.S. dollar over the year June 2015 to June 2016?

3. What was the value of 100 yen in terms of U.S. dollars in June 2015 and June 2016? Did the yen appreciate or depreciate against the U.S. dollar over the year June 2015 to June 2016?

4. On June 23, 2016, the U.S. dollar was trading at 0.68 U.K. pounds per U.S. dollar on the foreign exchange market. On June 25, the U.S. dollar was trading at 0.76 U.K. pounds per U.S. dollar.

    a. What events could have brought this change in the value of the U.S. dollar?

    b. Did the events you've described change the demand for U.S. dollars, the supply of U.S. dollars, or both demand and supply in the foreign exchange market?

5. Colombia is the world's biggest producer of roses. The global demand for roses increases and at the same time Colombia's central bank increases the interest rate. In the foreign exchange market for Colombian pesos, what happens to:

    a. The demand for pesos?

    b. The supply of pesos?

    c. The quantity of pesos demanded?

    d. The quantity of pesos supplied?

    e. The peso–Canadian dollar exchange rate?

Arbitrage, Speculation, and Market Fundamentals (Study Plan 9.2)

6. If a euro deposit in France earns 4 percent a year and a yen deposit in Japan earns 0.5 percent a year, all other things remaining the same, what is the exchange rate expectation of the Japanese yen against the EU euro?

7. The U.K. pound is trading at 1.54 Canadian dollars per U.K. pound and purchasing power parity holds. The Canadian interest rate is 2 percent a year and the U.K. interest rate is 4 percent a year.

    a. Calculate the Canadian interest rate differential.

    b. What is the U.K. pound expected to be worth in terms of Canadian dollars one year from now?

    c. Which country more likely has the lower inflation rate? How can you tell?

8. The Canadian price level is 106.3, the Japanese price level is 95.4, and the real exchange rate is 103.6 Japanese real GDP per unit of Canadian real GDP. What is the nominal exchange rate?

Exchange Rate Policy (Study Plan 9.3)

9. With the strengthening of the yen against other currencies, Japan's central bank did not take any action. A Japanese politician called on the central bank to take actions to weaken the yen, saying it will help exporters in the short run and have no long-run effects.

    a. What is Japan's current exchange rate policy?

    b. What does the politician want the exchange rate policy to be in the short run? Why would such a policy have no effect on the exchange rate in the long run?

Financing International Trade (Study Plan 9.4)

10. The table gives some information about Canada's international transactions in 2013.

Item	Billions of dollars
Imports of goods and services	598
Net foreign investment in Canada	65
Exports of goods and services	566
Net interest income	26
Net transfers	−2
Statistical discrepancy	0

    a. Calculate the balance on the three balance of payments accounts.

    b. Was Canada a net borrower or a net lender in 2013? Explain your answer.

ADDITIONAL PROBLEMS AND APPLICATIONS

MyLab Economics You can work these problems in Homework or Test if assigned by your instructor.
Problems marked 🌐 update with real-time data.

The Foreign Exchange Market

11. Suppose that yesterday the Canadian dollar was trading on the foreign exchange market at 0.75 euros per Canadian dollar and today the Canadian dollar is trading at 0.80 euros per Canadian dollar. Which of the two currencies (the Canadian dollar or the euro) has appreciated and which has depreciated today?

12. Suppose that the exchange rate fell from 80 yen per Canadian dollar to 70 yen per Canadian dollar. What is the effect of this change on the quantity of Canadian dollars that people plan to buy in the foreign exchange market?

13. Suppose that the exchange rate rose from 80 yen per Canadian dollar to 90 yen per Canadian dollar. What is the effect of this change on the quantity of Canadian dollars that people plan to sell in the foreign exchange market?

14. Today's exchange rate between the yuan and the U.S. dollar is 6.40 yuan per dollar, and the central bank of China is buying U.S. dollars in the foreign exchange market. If the central bank of China did not purchase U.S. dollars would there be excess demand or excess supply of U.S. dollars in the foreign exchange market? Would the exchange rate remain at 6.40 yuan per U.S. dollar? If not, which currency would appreciate?

15. Yesterday, the current exchange rate was $1.05 Canadian per U.S. dollar and traders expected the exchange rate to remain unchanged for the next month. Today, with new information, traders now expect the exchange rate next month to fall to $1 Canadian per U.S. dollar. Explain how the revised expected future exchange rate influences the demand for U.S. dollars, or the supply of U.S. dollars, or both in the foreign exchange market.

16. In 2011, the exchange rate changed from 94 yen per U.S. dollar in January to 84 yen per U.S. dollar in June, and back to 94 yen per dollar in December. What information would you need to determine the factors that caused these changes in the exchange rate? Which factors would change *both* demand and supply?

17. Canada produces natural resources (coal, natural gas, and others), the demand for which has increased rapidly as China and other emerging economies expand.

a. Explain how growth in the demand for Canada's natural resources would affect the demand for Canadian dollars in the foreign exchange market.

b. Explain how the supply of Canadian dollars would change.

c. Explain how the value of the Canadian dollar would change.

d. Illustrate your answer with a graphical analysis.

Arbitrage, Speculation, and Market Fundamentals

Use the following news clip to work Problems 18 and 19.

Brexit Vote Could Mean U.S. Real Estate Boom

Property investors are looking outside London in the uncertain climate created by the U.K. vote to leave the European Union—Brexit. New York could gain from this changed outlook, but that's not all good news. It could add further upward momentum to an already overheated U.S. property market. A fall in the U.K. pound might moderate some of these predictions.

Based on an article in *The Guardian*, July 2, 2016

18. Explain why property investors are expected to sell in London and buy in New York and why a fall in the pound might make this predicted effect of Brexit less likely.

19. Explain what will happen if the expectation of rising prices on New York and falling prices in London becomes widespread. Might expectations become self-fulfilling?

Use the following information to work Problems 20 and 21.

Is the Loonie Going Up or Down?

The price of a Big Mac is $C6.00 in Toronto and $US5.30 in New York. The exchange rate is $C1.28 per U.S. dollar. The 3-month interest rate is 0.72 percent in Canada and 1.00 percent in the United States.

Source: *The Economist*, The Federal Reserve System, and the Bank of Canada, July 2017

20. Does purchasing power parity hold? If not, does PPP predict that the $C (loonie) will appreciate or depreciate against the U.S. dollar? Explain.

21. Does interest rate parity hold? If not, why not? Will the $C appreciate further or depreciate against the U.S. dollar if the Fed raises the interest rate while the Canadian interest rate remains at 0.72 percent a year?

22. **Over- or Undervalued?**

    The Economist magazine uses the price of a Big Mac to determine whether a currency is undervalued or overvalued. In July 2017, the price of a Big Mac was $5.30 in New York, 19.80 yuan in Beijing, and 6.50 Swiss francs in Geneva. The exchange rates were 6.79 yuan per U.S. dollar and 0.96 Swiss francs per U.S. dollar.

    Source: www.economist.com/content/big-mac-index July 2017

    a. Was the yuan undervalued or overvalued relative to purchasing power parity?

    b. Was the Swiss franc undervalued or overvalued relative to purchasing power parity?

    c. Do Big Mac prices in different countries provide a valid test of purchasing power parity?

Exchange Rate Policy

Use the following news clip to work Problems 23 to 25.

Calling Out China's Tricks

In 2016, the U.S. trade deficit with China hit an ever rising $350 billion, the largest deficit with any U.S. trading partner. Chinese currency, the yuan, has risen in value by 24 percent against the U.S. dollar since the Chinese government loosened its currency system in July 2005. However, U.S. manufacturers contend the yuan is still undervalued, making Chinese goods more competitive in this country and U.S. goods more expensive in China. China buys U.S. dollar-denominated securities to maintain the value of the yuan in terms of the U.S. dollar.

Source: *The New York Times*, April 12, 2017

23. What was the exchange rate policy adopted by China until July 2005? Explain how it worked. Draw a graph to illustrate your answer.

24. What was the exchange rate policy adopted by China after July 2005? Explain how it works.

25. Explain how fixed and crawling peg exchange rates can be used to manipulate trade balances in the short run, but not the long run.

26. **Concern in Denmark as Crown's Peg to Euro Is Strained**

    Since 1982, Denmark has pegged the exchange rate for the crown against first the German mark and later against the euro. In recent weeks the fixed exchange-rate regime has come under strain as the euro has fallen sharply, leading to speculation that Denmark's currency peg to the euro will break.

    Source: *The New York Times*, February 13, 2015

    a. What is Denmark's exchange rate policy? Explain why expectations about a possible break in the link of the crown and euro might put the crown under strain.

    b. To avoid a break in the link between the crown and the euro, what action must the central bank of Denmark take?

Financing International Trade

Use the following table to work Problems 27 and 28. The table gives some data about the U.K. economy:

Item	Billions of U.K. pounds
Consumption expenditure	721
Exports of goods and services	277
Government expenditures	230
Net taxes	217
Investment	181
Saving	162

27. Calculate the private sector and government sector balances.

28. What is the relationship between the government sector balance and net exports?

Economics in the News

29. After you have studied *Economics in the News* on pp. 234–235, answer the following questions.

    a. What are the U.S. trade balances with Mexico and Canada and how have those balances changed since 2000?

    b. What are the concerns of the Trump administration about these balances?

    c. What action does the Trump administration propose taking to change these balances?

    d. What is the source of the international trade balance of the United States? Explain the fundamental equation that determines the balance.

    e. What effect will the Trump administration's proposed action have on the balances of trade with Mexico and Canada?

    f. What other effects will the proposed actions have on trade with Mexico and Canada?

Expanding the Frontier

Economics is about how we cope with scarcity. We cope as individuals by making choices that balance marginal benefits and marginal costs so that we use our scarce resources efficiently. We cope as societies by creating incentive systems and social institutions that encourage specialization and exchange.

These choices and the incentive systems that guide them determine what we specialize in; how much work we do; how hard we work at school to learn the mental skills that form our human capital and that determine the kinds of jobs we get and the incomes we earn; how much we save for future big-ticket expenditures; how much businesses and governments spend on new capital—on auto assembly lines, computers and fibre cables for improved Internet services, shopping malls, highways, bridges, and tunnels; how intensively existing capital and natural resources are used and how quickly they wear out or are used up; and the problems that scientists, engineers, and other inventors work on to develop new technologies.

All the choices we've just described combine to determine the standard of living and the rate at which it improves—the economic growth rate.

Money that makes specialization and exchange in markets possible is a huge contributor to economic growth. But too much money brings a rising cost of living with no improvement in the standard of living.

Joseph Schumpeter, *the son of a textile factory owner, was born in Austria in 1883. He moved from Austria to Germany during the tumultuous 1920s when those two countries experienced hyperinflation. In 1932, in the depths of the Great Depression, he came to the United States and became a professor of economics at Harvard University.*

This creative economic thinker wrote about economic growth and development, business cycles, political systems, and economic biography. He was a person of strong opinions who expressed them forcefully and delighted in verbal battles.

Schumpeter saw the development and diffusion of new technologies by profit-seeking entrepreneurs as the source of economic progress. But he saw economic progress as a process of creative destruction—the creation of new profit opportunities and the destruction of currently profitable businesses. For Schumpeter, economic growth and the business cycle were a single phenomenon.

"Economic progress, in capitalist society, means turmoil."

JOSEPH SCHUMPETER
Capitalism, Socialism, and Democracy

XAVIER SALA-I-MARTIN is Professor of Economics at Columbia University. He is also a Research Associate at the National Bureau of Economic Research, Senior Economic Advisor to the World Economic Forum, Associate Editor of the *Journal of Economic Growth*, founder and CEO of Umbele Foundation: A Future for Africa, and President of the Economic Commission of the Barcelona Football Club.

Professor Sala-i-Martin was an undergraduate at Universitat Autonoma de Barcelona and a graduate student at Harvard University, where he obtained his Ph.D. in 1990.

In 2004, he was awarded the Premio Juan Carlos I de Economía, a biannual prize given by the Bank of Spain to the best economist in Spain and Latin America. With Robert Barro, he is the author of *Economic Growth*, Second Edition (MIT Press, 2003), the definitive graduate-level text on this topic.

Michael Parkin and Robin Bade talked with Xavier Sala-i-Martin about his work and the progress that economists have made in understanding economic growth.

How did economic growth become your major field of research?

I studied economics. I liked it. I studied mathematical economics. I liked it too, and I went to graduate school. In my second year at Harvard, Jeffrey Sachs hired me to go to Bolivia. I saw poor people for the first time in my life. I was shocked. I decided I should try to answer the question "Why are these people so poor and why are we so rich, and what can we do to turn their state into our state?" We live in a bubble world in the United States and Europe, and we don't realize how poor people really are. When you see poverty first hand, it is very hard to think about something else. So I decided to study economic growth. Coincidentally, when I returned from Bolivia, I was assigned to be Robert Barro's teaching assistant. He was teaching economic growth, so I studied with him and eventually wrote books and articles with him.

> If there's no investment, there's no growth. . . . Incentives are important.

What do we know today about the nature and causes of the wealth of nations that Adam Smith didn't know?

Actually, even though over the last 200 years some of the best minds have looked at the question, we know surprisingly little. We have some general principles that are not very easy to apply in practice. We know, for example, that markets are good. We know that for the economy to work, we need property rights to be guaranteed. If there are thieves—government or private thieves—that can steal the proceeds of the investment, there's no investment and there's no growth. We know that the incentives are very important.

These are general principles. Because we know these principles we should ask: How come Africa is still poor? The answer is, it is very hard to translate "Markets are good" and "Property rights work" into practical actions. We know that Zimbabwe has to guarantee property rights. With the government it has, that's not going to work. The U.S. constitution works in the United States. If you try to copy the constitution and impose the system in Zimbabwe, it's not going to work.

*You can read the full interview with Xavier Sala-i-Martin in MyLab Economics.

10 AGGREGATE SUPPLY AND AGGREGATE DEMAND

After studying this chapter, you will be able to:

◆ Explain what determines aggregate supply in the long run and in the short run

◆ Explain what determines aggregate demand

◆ Explain how real GDP and the price level are determined and what causes growth, inflation, and cycles

◆ Describe the main schools of thought in macroeconomics today

Real GDP grew by 3.7 percent in the first quarter of 2017, the fastest growth rate for 10 years. The inflation rate also edged upward in 2017. Why do real GDP and inflation fluctuate?

This chapter explains the economic fluctuations that we call the business cycle. You will study the *aggregate supply-aggregate demand model* or *AS-AD model*—a model of real GDP and the price level. And in *Economics in the News* at the end of the chapter, you will use that model to interpret and explain the state of the Canadian economy in 2017.

◆ Aggregate Supply

The purpose of the aggregate supply–aggregate demand model that you study in this chapter is to explain how real GDP and the price level are determined and how they interact. The model uses similar ideas to those that you encountered in Chapter 3 when you learned how the quantity and price in a competitive market are determined. But the *aggregate supply–aggregate* demand model (*AS-AD* model) isn't just an application of the competitive market model. Some differences arise because the *AS-AD* model is a model of an imaginary market for the total of all the final goods and services that make up real GDP. The quantity in this "market" is real GDP and the price is the price level measured by the GDP deflator.

One thing that the *AS-AD* model shares with the competitive market model is that both distinguish between *supply* and the *quantity supplied*. We begin by explaining what we mean by the quantity of real GDP supplied.

Quantity Supplied and Supply

The *quantity of real GDP supplied* is the total quantity of goods and services, valued in constant base-year (2007) dollars, that firms plan to produce during a given period. This quantity depends on the quantity of labour employed, the quantity of physical and human capital, and the state of technology.

At any given time, the quantity of capital and the state of technology are fixed. They depend on decisions that were made in the past. The population is also fixed. But the quantity of labour is not fixed. It depends on decisions made by households and firms about the supply of and demand for labour.

The labour market can be in any one of three states: at full employment, above full employment, or below full employment. At full employment, the quantity of real GDP supplied is *potential GDP*, which depends on the full-employment quantity of labour (see Chapter 6, pp. 143–144). Over the business cycle, employment fluctuates around full employment and the quantity of real GDP supplied fluctuates around potential GDP.

Aggregate supply is the relationship between the quantity of real GDP supplied and the price level. This relationship is different in the long run than in the short run and to study aggregate supply, we distinguish between two time frames:

- Long-run aggregate supply
- Short-run aggregate supply

Long-Run Aggregate Supply

Long-run aggregate supply is the relationship between the quantity of real GDP supplied and the price level when the money wage rate changes in step with the price level to maintain full employment. The quantity of real GDP supplied at full employment equals potential GDP, and this quantity is the same regardless of the price level.

The long-run aggregate supply curve in Fig. 10.1 illustrates long-run aggregate supply as the vertical line at potential GDP labelled *LAS*. Along the long-run aggregate supply curve, as the price level changes, the money wage rate also changes so that the real wage rate remains at the full-employment equilibrium level and real GDP remains at potential GDP. The long-run aggregate supply curve is always vertical and is always located at potential GDP.

The long-run aggregate supply curve is vertical because potential GDP is independent of the price level. The reason for this independence is that a movement along the *LAS* curve is accompanied by a change in *two* sets of prices: the prices of goods and services—the price level—and the prices of the factors of production, most notably, the money wage rate. A 10 percent increase in the prices of goods and services is matched by a 10 percent increase in the money wage rate. Because the price level and the money wage rate change by the same percentage, the *real wage rate* remains unchanged at its full-employment equilibrium level. So when the price level changes and the real wage rate remains constant, employment remains constant and real GDP remains constant at potential GDP.

Production at a Pepsi Plant You can see more clearly why real GDP is unchanged when all prices change by the same percentage by thinking about production decisions at a Pepsi bottling plant. How does the quantity of Pepsi supplied change if the price of Pepsi changes and the wage rate of the workers and prices of all the other resources used vary by the same percentage? The answer is that the quantity supplied doesn't change. The firm produces the quantity that maximizes profit. That quantity depends on the price of Pepsi relative to the cost of producing it. With no change in price *relative to cost*, production doesn't change.

Short-Run Aggregate Supply

Short-run aggregate supply is the relationship between the quantity of real GDP supplied and the price level *when the money wage rate, the prices of other resources, and potential GDP remain constant.* Figure 10.1 illustrates this relationship as the short-run aggregate supply curve *SAS* and the short-run aggregate supply schedule. Each point on the *SAS* curve corresponds to a row of the short-run aggregate supply schedule. For example, point *A* on the *SAS* curve and row *A* of the schedule tell us that if the price level is 100, the quantity of real GDP supplied is $1.6 trillion. In the short run, a rise in the price level brings an increase in the quantity of real GDP supplied. The short-run aggregate supply curve slopes upward.

With a given money wage rate, there is one price level at which the real wage rate is at its full-employment equilibrium level. At this price level, the quantity of real GDP supplied equals potential GDP and the *SAS* curve intersects the *LAS* curve. In this example, that price level is 110. If the price level rises above 110, the quantity of real GDP supplied increases along the *SAS* curve and exceeds potential GDP; if the price level falls below 110, the quantity of real GDP supplied decreases along the *SAS* curve and is less than potential GDP.

Back at the Pepsi Plant You can see why the short-run aggregate supply curve slopes upward by returning to the Pepsi bottling plant. If production increases, marginal cost rises; and if production decreases, marginal cost falls (see Chapter 2, p. 37).

If the price of Pepsi rises with no change in the money wage rate and other costs, Pepsi can increase profit by increasing production. Pepsi is in business to maximize its profit, so it increases production.

Similarly, if the price of Pepsi falls while the money wage rate and other costs remain constant, Pepsi can avoid a loss by decreasing production. The lower price weakens the incentive to produce, so Pepsi decreases production.

What's true for Pepsi bottlers is true for the producers of all goods and services. When all prices rise, the *price level rises.* If the price level rises and the money wage rate and other factor prices remain constant, all firms increase production and the quantity of real GDP supplied increases. A fall in the price level has the opposite effect and decreases the quantity of real GDP supplied.

FIGURE 10.1 Long-Run and Short-Run Aggregate Supply

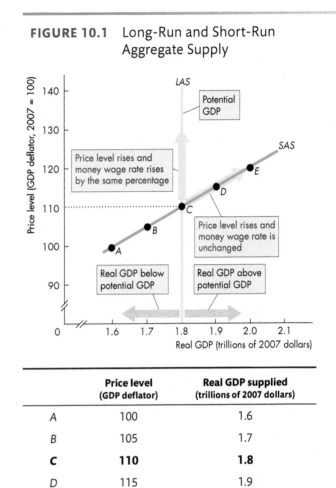

	Price level (GDP deflator)	**Real GDP supplied** (trillions of 2007 dollars)
A	100	1.6
B	105	1.7
C	**110**	**1.8**
D	115	1.9
E	120	2.0

In the long run, the quantity of real GDP supplied is potential GDP and the *LAS* curve is vertical at potential GDP. In the short run, the quantity of real GDP supplied increases if the price level rises, while all other influences on supply plans remain the same.

The short-run aggregate supply curve, *SAS*, slopes upward. The short-run aggregate supply curve is based on the aggregate supply schedule in the table. Each point *A* through *E* on the curve corresponds to the row in the table identified by the same letter.

When the price level is 110, the quantity of real GDP supplied is $1.8 trillion, which is potential GDP. If the price level rises above 110, the quantity of real GDP supplied increases and exceeds potential GDP; if the price level falls below 110, the quantity of real GDP supplied decreases below potential GDP.

——— MyLab Economics Animation and Draw Graph ———

Changes in Aggregate Supply

A change in the price level changes the quantity of real GDP supplied, which is illustrated by a movement along the short-run aggregate supply curve. It does not change aggregate supply. Aggregate supply changes when an influence on production plans other than the price level changes. These other influences include changes in potential GDP and changes in the money wage rate. Let's begin by looking at a change in potential GDP.

Changes in Potential GDP When potential GDP changes, aggregate supply changes. An increase in potential GDP increases both long-run aggregate supply and short-run aggregate supply.

Figure 10.2 shows the effects of an increase in potential GDP. Initially, potential GDP is $1.8 trillion, the long-run aggregate supply curve is LAS_0, and the short-run aggregate supply curve is SAS_0. If potential GDP increases to $2.0 trillion, the long-run aggregate supply curve shifts rightward to LAS_1. As long-run aggregate supply increases, so too does short-run aggregate supply. The short-run aggregate supply curve shifts rightward to SAS_1. The two supply curves shift by the same amount only if the full-employment price level remains constant, which we will assume to be the case.

Potential GDP can increase for any of three reasons:

- An increase in the full-employment quantity of labour
- An increase in the quantity of capital
- An advance in technology

Let's look at these influences on potential GDP and the aggregate supply curves.

An Increase in the Full-Employment Quantity of Labour A Pepsi bottling plant that employs 100 workers bottles more Pepsi than does an otherwise identical plant that employs 10 workers. The same is true for the economy as a whole. The larger the quantity of labour employed, the greater is real GDP.

Over time, potential GDP increases because the labour force increases. But (with constant capital and technology) *potential* GDP increases only if the full-employment quantity of labour increases. Fluctuations in employment over the business cycle bring fluctuations in real GDP. But these changes in real GDP are fluctuations around potential GDP.

FIGURE 10.2 A Change in Potential GDP

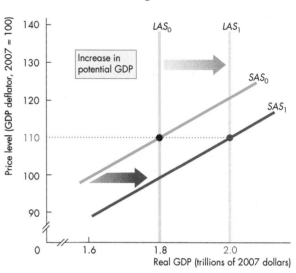

An increase in potential GDP increases both long-run aggregate supply and short-run aggregate supply. The long-run aggregate supply curve shifts rightward from LAS_0 to LAS_1, and the short-run aggregate supply curve shifts from SAS_0 to SAS_1.

— MyLab Economics Animation —

They are not changes in potential GDP and long-run aggregate supply.

An Increase in the Quantity of Capital A Pepsi bottling plant with two production lines bottles more Pepsi than does an otherwise identical plant that has only one production line. For the economy, the larger the quantity of capital, the more productive is the labour force and the greater is its potential GDP. Potential GDP per person in capital-rich Canada is vastly greater than that in capital-poor China or Russia.

Capital includes *human capital*. One Pepsi plant is managed by an economics major with an MBA and has a labour force with an average of 10 years of experience. This plant produces a larger output than does an otherwise identical plant that is managed by someone with no business training or experience and that has a young labour force that is new to bottling. The first plant has a greater amount of human capital than the second. For the economy as a whole, the larger the quantity of *human capital*—the skills that people have acquired in school and through on-the-job training—the greater is potential GDP.

An Advance in Technology A Pepsi plant that has machines with pre-computer technology produces less than one that uses the latest robot technology. Technological change enables firms to produce more from any given amount of factors of production. So even with fixed quantities of labour and capital, improvements in technology increase potential GDP.

Technological advances are by far the most important source of increased production over the past two centuries. As a result of technological advances, one farmer in Canada today can feed 100 people and in a year one autoworker can produce almost 14 cars and trucks.

Let's now look at the effects of changes in the money wage rate.

Changes in the Money Wage Rate When the money wage rate (or the money price of any other factor of production such as oil) changes, short-run aggregate supply changes but long-run aggregate supply does not change.

Figure 10.3 shows the effect of an increase in the money wage rate. Initially, the short-run aggregate supply curve is SAS_0. A rise in the money wage rate *decreases* short-run aggregate supply and shifts the short-run aggregate supply curve leftward to SAS_2.

A rise in the money wage rate decreases short-run aggregate supply because it increases firms' costs. With increased costs, the quantity that firms are willing to supply at each price level decreases, which is shown by a leftward shift of the SAS curve.

A change in the money wage rate does not change long-run aggregate supply because on the LAS curve, the change in the money wage rate is accompanied by an equal percentage change in the price level. With no change in *relative* prices, firms have no incentive to change production, so real GDP remains constant at potential GDP. With no change in potential GDP, the long-run aggregate supply curve LAS does not shift.

What Makes the Money Wage Rate Change? The money wage rate can change for two reasons: departures from full employment and expectations about inflation. Unemployment above the natural rate puts downward pressure on the money wage rate, and unemployment below the natural rate puts upward pressure on it. An expected rise in the inflation rate makes the money wage rate rise faster, and an expected fall in the inflation rate slows the rate at which the money wage rate rises.

FIGURE 10.3 A Change in the Money Wage Rate

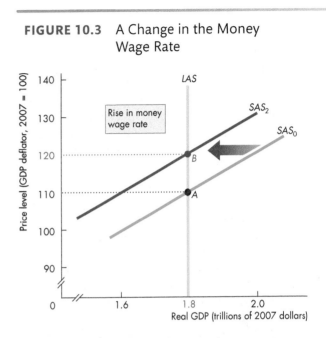

A rise in the money wage rate decreases short-run aggregate supply and shifts the short-run aggregate supply curve leftward from SAS_0 to SAS_2. A rise in the money wage rate does not change potential GDP, so the long-run aggregate supply curve does not shift.

MyLab Economics Animation

◄ REVIEW QUIZ

1 If the price level and the money wage rate rise by the same percentage, what happens to the quantity of real GDP supplied? Along which aggregate supply curve does the economy move?

2 If the price level rises and the money wage rate remains constant, what happens to the quantity of real GDP supplied? Along which aggregate supply curve does the economy move?

3 If potential GDP increases, what happens to aggregate supply? Does the LAS curve shift or is there a movement along the LAS curve? Does the SAS curve shift or is there a movement along the SAS curve?

4 If the money wage rate rises and potential GDP remains the same, does the LAS curve or the SAS curve shift or is there a movement along the LAS curve or the SAS curve?

Work these questions in Study Plan 10.1 and get instant feedback. MyLab Economics

 Aggregate Demand

The quantity of real GDP demanded (Y) is the sum of real consumption expenditure (C), investment (I), government expenditure (G), and exports (X) minus imports (M). That is,

$$Y = C + I + G + X - M$$

The *quantity of real GDP demanded* is the total amount of final goods and services produced in Canada that people, businesses, governments, and foreigners plan to buy.

These buying plans depend on many factors. Some of the main ones are:

1. The price level
2. Expectations
3. Fiscal policy and monetary policy
4. The world economy

We first focus on the relationship between the quantity of real GDP demanded and the price level. To study this relationship, we keep all other influences on buying plans the same and ask: How does the quantity of real GDP demanded vary as the price level varies?

The Aggregate Demand Curve

Other things remaining the same, the higher the price level, the smaller is the quantity of real GDP demanded. This relationship between the quantity of real GDP demanded and the price level is called **aggregate demand**. Aggregate demand is described by an *aggregate demand schedule* and an *aggregate demand curve*.

Figure 10.4 shows an aggregate demand curve (AD) and an aggregate demand schedule. Each point on the AD curve corresponds to a row of the schedule. For example, point C' on the AD curve and row C' of the schedule tell us that if the price level is 110, the quantity of real GDP demanded is $1.8 trillion.

The aggregate demand curve slopes downward for two reasons:

- Wealth effect
- Substitution effects

Wealth Effect When the price level rises but other things remain the same, *real* wealth decreases. Real

FIGURE 10.4 Aggregate Demand

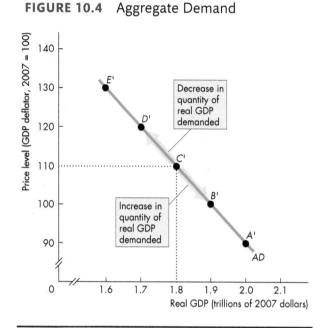

	Price level (GDP deflator)	Real GDP demanded (trillions of 2007 dollars)
A'	90	2.0
B'	100	1.9
C'	**110**	**1.8**
D'	120	1.7
E'	130	1.6

The aggregate demand curve (AD) shows the relationship between the quantity of real GDP demanded and the price level. The aggregate demand curve is based on the aggregate demand schedule in the table. Each point A' through E' on the curve corresponds to the row in the table identified by the same letter. When the price level is 110, the quantity of real GDP demanded is $1.8 trillion, as shown by point C' in the figure. A change in the price level, when all other influences on aggregate buying plans remain the same, brings a change in the quantity of real GDP demanded and a movement along the AD curve.

——— MyLab Economics Animation ———

wealth is the amount of money in the bank, bonds, shares, and other assets that people own, measured not in dollars but in terms of the goods and services that the money, bonds, and shares will buy.

People save and hold money, bonds, and shares for many reasons. One reason is to build up funds for education expenses. Another reason is to build up enough funds to meet home renovation expenses or other big bills. But the biggest reason is to build up enough funds to provide a retirement income.

If the price level rises, real wealth decreases. People then try to restore their wealth. To do so, they must increase saving and, equivalently, decrease current consumption. Such a decrease in consumption is a decrease in aggregate demand.

Maria's Wealth Effect You can see how the wealth effect works by thinking about Maria's buying plans. Maria lives in Moscow, Russia. She has worked hard all summer and saved 20,000 rubles (the ruble is the currency of Russia), which she plans to spend attending graduate school when she has finished her economics degree. So Maria's wealth is 20,000 rubles. Maria has a part-time job, and her income from this job pays her current expenses. The price level in Russia rises by 100 percent, and now Maria needs 40,000 rubles to buy what 20,000 once bought. To try to make up some of the fall in value of her savings, Maria saves even more and cuts her current spending to the bare minimum.

Substitution Effects When the price level rises and other things remain the same, interest rates rise. The reason is related to the wealth effect that you've just studied. A rise in the price level decreases the real value of the money in people's pockets and bank accounts. With a smaller amount of real money around, banks and other lenders can get a higher interest rate on loans. But faced with a higher interest rate, people and businesses delay plans to buy new capital and consumer durable goods and cut back on spending.

This substitution effect involves changing the timing of purchases of capital and consumer durable goods and is called an *intertemporal* substitution effect—a substitution across time. Saving increases to increase future consumption.

To see this intertemporal substitution effect more clearly, think about your own plan to buy a new computer. At an interest rate of 5 percent a year, you might borrow $1,000 and buy the new computer. But at an interest rate of 10 percent a year, you might decide that the payments would be too high. You don't abandon your plan to buy the computer, but you decide to delay your purchase.

A second substitution effect works through international prices. When the Canadian price level rises and other things remain the same, Canadian-made goods and services become more expensive relative to foreign-made goods and services. This change in *relative prices* encourages people to spend less on Canadian-made items and more on foreign-made items. For example, if the Canadian price level rises relative to the Japanese price level, Japanese buy fewer Canadian-made cars (Canadian exports decrease) and Canadians buy more Japanese-made cars (Canadian imports increase). Canadian GDP decreases.

Maria's Substitution Effects In Moscow, Russia, Maria makes some substitutions. She was planning to trade in her old motor scooter and get a new one. But with a higher price level and a higher interest rate, she decides to make her old scooter last one more year. Also, with the prices of Russian goods sharply increasing, Maria substitutes a low-cost dress made in Malaysia for the Russian-made dress she had originally planned to buy.

Changes in the Quantity of Real GDP Demanded
When the price level rises and other things remain the same, the quantity of real GDP demanded decreases—a movement up along the *AD* curve as shown by the arrow in Fig. 10.4. When the price level falls and other things remain the same, the quantity of real GDP demanded increases—a movement down along the *AD* curve.

We've now seen how the quantity of real GDP demanded changes when the price level changes. How do other influences on buying plans affect aggregate demand?

Changes in Aggregate Demand

A change in any factor that influences buying plans other than the price level brings a change in aggregate demand. The main factors are:

- Expectations
- Fiscal policy and monetary policy
- The world economy

Expectations An increase in expected future income increases the amount of consumption goods (especially expensive items such as cars) that people plan to buy today and increases aggregate demand today.

An increase in the expected future inflation rate increases aggregate demand today because people decide to buy more goods and services at today's relatively lower prices.

An increase in expected future profits increases the investment that firms plan to undertake today and increases aggregate demand today.

Fiscal Policy and Monetary Policy The government's attempt to influence the economy by setting and changing taxes, making transfer payments, and purchasing goods and services is called **fiscal policy**. A tax cut or an increase in transfer payments—for example, unemployment benefits or welfare payments—increases aggregate demand. Both of these influences operate by increasing households' *disposable* income. **Disposable income** is aggregate income minus taxes plus transfer payments. The greater the disposable income, the greater is the quantity of consumption goods and services that households plan to buy and the greater is aggregate demand.

Government expenditure on goods and services is one component of aggregate demand. So if the government spends more on spy satellites, schools, and highways, aggregate demand increases.

The Bank of Canada's attempt to influence the economy by changing interest rates and the quantity of money is called **monetary policy**. The Bank influences the quantity of money and interest rates by using the tools and methods described in Chapter 8.

An increase in the quantity of money increases aggregate demand through two main channels: It lowers interest rates and makes it easier to get a loan.

With lower interest rates, businesses plan greater investment in new capital and households plan greater expenditure on new homes, on home improvements, on automobiles, and a host of other consumer durable goods. Banks and others eager to lend lower their standards for making loans and more people are able to get home loans and other consumer loans.

A decrease in the quantity of money has the opposite effects and lowers aggregate demand.

The World Economy Two main influences that the world economy has on aggregate demand are the exchange rate and foreign income. The *exchange rate* is the amount of a foreign currency that you can buy with a Canadian dollar. Other things remaining the same, a rise in the exchange rate decreases aggregate

ECONOMICS IN ACTION

Central Banks Fight Recession

The global financial crisis of 2008 sent the global economy into a deep recession from which recovery was slow. Even nine years later, in 2017, the major economies were still returning to full employment. But the Canadian economy was leading the charge with the fastest growth and first back to full employment.

Starting in the fall of 2008, the Bank of Canada, in concert with the U.S. Federal Reserve, the European

Central Bank, and the Bank of England, cut the interest rate and took other measures to ease credit and encourage banks and other financial institutions to increase their lending.

The goal of these central bank actions was to restore business and consumer confidence and provide low-cost financing that might boost investment and consumer spending and increase aggregate demand.

Low interest rate policies helped to avoid a deeper recession, but they had limited success in bringing recovery and were still being pursued in 2017.

Bank of Canada, Ottawa   Federal Reserve, Washington, DC   European Central Bank, Frankfurt, Germany

FIGURE 10.5   Changes in Aggregate Demand

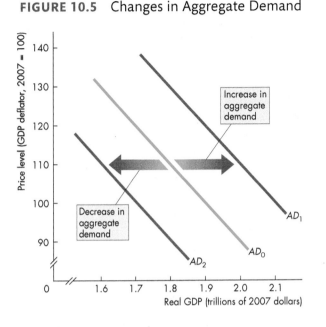

Aggregate demand

Decreases if:

■ Expected future income, inflation, or profit decreases

■ Fiscal policy decreases government expenditure, increases taxes, or decreases transfer payments

■ Monetary policy decreases the quantity of money and increases interest rates

■ The exchange rate increases or foreign income decreases

Increases if:

■ Expected future income, inflation, or profit increases

■ Fiscal policy increases government expenditure, decreases taxes, or increases transfer payments

■ Monetary policy increases the quantity of money and decreases interest rates

■ The exchange rate decreases or foreign income increases

——— MyLab Economics Animation ———

demand. To see how the exchange rate influences aggregate demand, suppose that the exchange rate is 1.20 euros per Canadian dollar. An Airbus plane made in France costs 120 million euros, and an equivalent Bombardier airplane made in Canada costs $110 million. In Canadian dollars, the Airbus

plane costs $100 million, so airlines both in Canada and around the world buy the cheaper airplane from France. Now suppose the exchange rate falls to 1 euro per Canadian dollar. The Airbus airplane now costs $120 million and is more expensive than the Bombardier airplane. Airlines will switch from the Airbus to Bombardier. Canadian exports will increase and Canadian imports will decrease, so Canadian aggregate demand will increase.

An increase in foreign income increases Canadian exports and increases Canadian aggregate demand. For example, an increase in income in China and the United States increases Chinese and U.S. consumers' and producers' planned expenditures on Canadian-produced goods and services.

Shifts of the Aggregate Demand Curve When aggregate demand changes, the aggregate demand curve shifts. Figure 10.5 shows two changes in aggregate demand and summarizes the factors that bring about such changes.

Aggregate demand increases and the AD curve shifts rightward from AD_0 to AD_1 when expected future income, inflation, or profit increases; government expenditure on goods and services increases; taxes are cut; transfer payments increase; the quantity of money increases and the interest rate falls; the exchange rate falls; or foreign income increases.

Aggregate demand decreases and the AD curve shifts leftward from AD_0 to AD_2 when expected future income, inflation, or profit decreases; government expenditure on goods and services decreases; taxes increase; transfer payments decrease; the quantity of money decreases and the interest rate rises; the exchange rate rises; or foreign income decreases.

◢ REVIEW QUIZ

1 What does the aggregate demand curve show? What factors change and what factors remain the same when there is a movement along the aggregate demand curve?

2 Why does the aggregate demand curve slope downward?

3 How do changes in expectations, fiscal policy and monetary policy, and the world economy change aggregate demand and the aggregate demand curve?

Work these questions in Study Plan 10.2 and get instant feedback.   MyLab Economics

Explaining Macroeconomic Trends and Fluctuations

The purpose of the *AS-AD* model is to explain changes in real GDP and the price level. The model's main purpose is to explain business cycle fluctuations in these variables. But the model also aids our understanding of economic growth and inflation trends. We begin by combining aggregate supply and aggregate demand to determine real GDP and the price level in equilibrium. Just as there are two time frames for aggregate supply, there are two time frames for macroeconomic equilibrium: a long-run equilibrium and a short-run equilibrium. We'll first look at short-run equilibrium.

Short-Run Macroeconomic Equilibrium

The aggregate demand curve tells us the quantity of real GDP demanded at each price level, and the short-run aggregate supply curve tells us the quantity of real GDP supplied at each price level. **Short-run macroeconomic equilibrium** occurs when the quantity of real GDP demanded equals the quantity of real GDP supplied. That is, short-run macroeconomic equilibrium occurs at the point of intersection of the *AD* curve and the *SAS* curve.

Figure 10.6 shows such an equilibrium at a price level of 110 and real GDP of $1.8 trillion (points *C* and *C'*).

To see why this position is the equilibrium, think about what happens if the price level is something other than 110. Suppose, for example, that the price level is 120 and that real GDP is $2.0 trillion (at point *E* on the *SAS* curve). The quantity of real GDP demanded is less than $2.0 trillion, so firms are unable to sell all their output. Unwanted inventories pile up, and firms cut both production and prices. Production and prices are cut until firms can sell all their output. This situation occurs only when real GDP is $1.8 trillion and the price level is 110.

Now suppose the price level is 100 and real GDP is $1.6 trillion (at point *A* on the *SAS* curve). The quantity of real GDP demanded exceeds $1.6 trillion, so firms are unable to meet the demand for their output. Inventories decrease, and customers clamour for goods and services, so firms increase production and raise prices. Production and prices increase until firms can meet the demand for their output. This situation occurs only when real GDP is $1.8 trillion and the price level is 110.

FIGURE 10.6 Short-Run Equilibrium

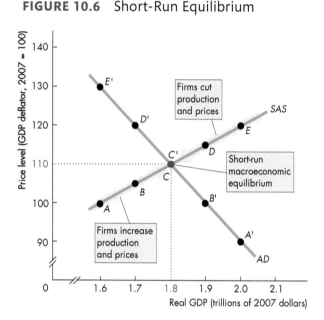

Short-run macroeconomic equilibrium occurs when real GDP demanded equals real GDP supplied—at the intersection of the aggregate demand curve (*AD*) and the short-run aggregate supply curve (*SAS*).

— MyLab Economics Animation and Draw Graph —

In the short run, the money wage rate is fixed. It does not adjust to move the economy to full employment. So in the short run, real GDP can be greater than or less than potential GDP. But in the long run, the money wage rate adjusts and real GDP moves toward potential GDP. Let's look at the long-run equilibrium and see how we get there.

Long-Run Macroeconomic Equilibrium

Long-run macroeconomic equilibrium occurs when real GDP equals potential GDP—equivalently, when the economy is on its *LAS* curve.

When the economy is away from long-run equilibrium, the money wage rate adjusts. If the money wage rate is too high, short-run equilibrium is below potential GDP and the unemployment rate is above the natural rate. With an excess supply of labour, the money wage rate falls. If the money wage rate is too low, short-run equilibrium is above potential GDP and the unemployment rate is below the natural rate.

With an excess demand for labour, the money wage rate rises.

Figure 10.7 shows the long-run equilibrium and how it comes about. If the short-run aggregate supply curve is SAS_1, the money wage rate is too high to achieve full employment. A fall in the money wage rate shifts the SAS curve to SAS^* and brings full employment. If the short-run aggregate supply curve is SAS_2, the money wage rate is too low to achieve full employment. Now, a rise in the money wage rate shifts the SAS curve to SAS^* and brings full employment.

In long-run equilibrium, potential GDP determines real GDP, and potential GDP and aggregate demand together determine the price level. The money wage rate adjusts until the SAS curve passes through the long-run equilibrium point.

Let's now see how the $AS\text{-}AD$ model helps us to understand economic growth and inflation.

Economic Growth and Inflation in the *AS-AD* Model

Economic growth results from a growing supply of labour and increasing labour productivity, which together make potential GDP grow (Chapter 6, pp. 143–147). Inflation results from a growing quantity of money that outpaces the growth of potential GDP (Chapter 8, pp. 202–203).

The $AS\text{-}AD$ model explains and illustrates economic growth and inflation. It explains economic growth as increasing long-run aggregate supply and it explains inflation as a persistent increase in aggregate demand at a faster pace than that of the increase in potential GDP.

ECONOMICS IN ACTION
Canadian Economic Growth and Inflation

The figure is a *scatter diagram* of Canadian real GDP and the price level. The graph has the same axes as those of the $AS\text{-}AD$ model. Each dot represents a year between 1961 and 2016. The three red dots are recession years. The pattern formed by the dots shows the combination of economic growth and inflation. Economic growth was fastest during the 1960s, and inflation was fastest during the 1970s.

The $AS\text{-}AD$ model interprets each dot as being at the intersection of the SAS and AD curves.

FIGURE 10.7 Long-Run Equilibrium

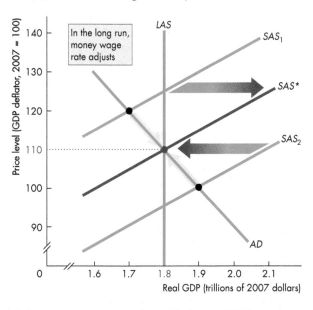

In long-run macroeconomic equilibrium, real GDP equals potential GDP. So long-run equilibrium occurs where the aggregate demand curve, *AD*, intersects the long-run aggregate supply curve, *LAS*. In the long run, aggregate demand determines the price level and has no effect on real GDP. The money wage rate adjusts in the long run, so that the *SAS* curve intersects the *LAS* curve at the long-run equilibrium price level.

___ MyLab Economics Animation and Draw Graph ___

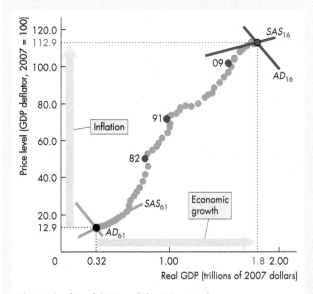

The Path of Real GDP and the Price Level

Source of data: Statistics Canada, CANSIM Table 380-0064.

Figure 10.8 illustrates this explanation in terms of the shifting *LAS* and *AD* curves.

When the *LAS* curve shifts rightward from LAS_0 to LAS_1, potential GDP grows from $1.8 trillion to $2.0 trillion. And in long-run equilibrium, real GDP also grows to $2.0 trillion.

When the *AD* curve shifts rightward from AD_0 to AD_1 and the growth of aggregate demand outpaces the growth of potential GDP, the price level rises from 110 to 120.

If aggregate demand were to increase at the same pace as long-run aggregate supply, real GDP would grow with no inflation.

Our economy experiences periods of growth and inflation, like those shown in Fig. 10.8, but it does not experience *steady* growth and *steady* inflation. Real GDP fluctuates around potential GDP in a business cycle. When we study the business cycle, we ignore economic growth and focus on the fluctuations around the trend growth rate. By doing so, we see the business cycle more clearly. Let's now see how the *AS-AD* model explains the business cycle.

The Business Cycle in the *AS-AD* Model

The business cycle occurs because aggregate demand and short-run aggregate supply fluctuate but the money wage rate does not adjust quickly enough to keep real GDP at potential GDP. Figure 10.9 shows three types of short-run equilibrium.

Figure 10.9(a) shows an above full-employment equilibrium. An **above full-employment equilibrium** is an equilibrium in which real GDP exceeds potential GDP. Real GDP minus potential GDP is the **output gap**. When real GDP exceeds potential GDP, the output gap is called an **inflationary gap**.

The above full-employment equilibrium shown in Fig. 10.9(a) occurs where the aggregate demand curve AD_0 intersects the short-run aggregate supply curve SAS_0 at a real GDP of $1.84 trillion. There is an inflationary gap of $0.04 trillion.

FIGURE 10.8 Economic Growth and Inflation

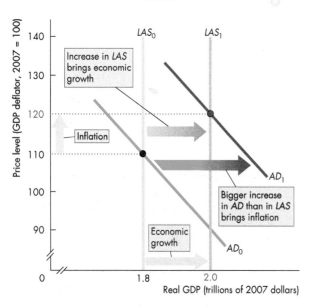

Economic growth results from a persistent increase in potential GDP—a rightward shift of the *LAS* curve. Inflation results from persistent growth in the quantity of money that shifts the *AD* curve rightward at a faster pace than the real GDP growth rate.

——— MyLab Economics Animation and Draw Graph ———

ECONOMICS IN ACTION

The Canadian Business Cycle

The Canadian economy had an inflationary gap in 2000 (at *A* in the figure), full employment in 2008 (at *B*), and a recessionary gap in 2009 (at *C*). The fluctuating output gap in the figure is the real-world version of Fig. 10.9(d) and is generated by fluctuations in aggregate demand and short-run aggregate supply.

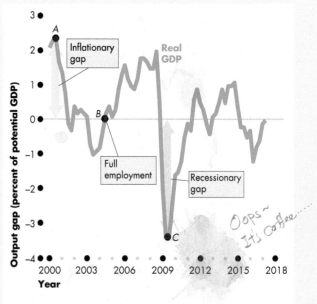

The Canadian Output Gap

Sources of data: Bank of Canada output gap, www.bankofcanada.ca/en/rates/indinf/product_data_en.html.

In Fig. 10.9(b), real GDP equals potential GDP and there is a **full-employment equilibrium**. In this example, the equilibrium occurs where the aggregate demand curve AD_1 intersects the short-run aggregate supply curve SAS_1 at a real GDP and potential GDP of $1.80 trillion.

In part (c), there is a below full-employment equilibrium. A **below full-employment equilibrium** is an equilibrium in which potential GDP exceeds real GDP. When potential GDP exceeds real GDP, the output gap is called a **recessionary gap**.

The below full-employment equilibrium shown in Fig. 10.9(c) occurs where the aggregate demand

curve AD_2 intersects the short-run aggregate supply curve SAS_2 at a real GDP of $1.76 trillion. Potential GDP is $1.80 trillion, so there is a recessionary gap of $0.04 trillion.

The economy moves from one type of macroeconomic equilibrium to another as a result of fluctuations in aggregate demand and in short-run aggregate supply. These fluctuations produce fluctuations in real GDP. Figure 10.9(d) shows how real GDP fluctuates around potential GDP.

Let's now look at some of the sources of these fluctuations around potential GDP.

FIGURE 10.9   The Business Cycle

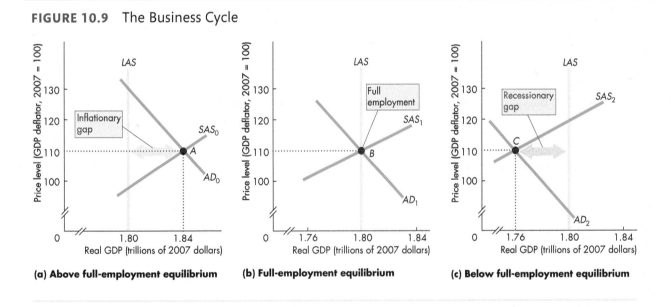

(a) Above full-employment equilibrium   **(b) Full-employment equilibrium**   **(c) Below full-employment equilibrium**

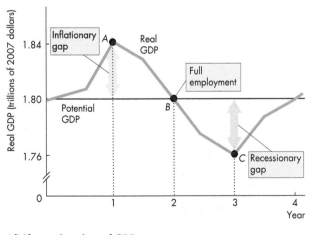

(d) Fluctuations in real GDP

Part (a) shows an above full-employment equilibrium in year 1; part (b) shows a full-employment equilibrium in year 2; and part (c) shows a below full-employment equilibrium in year 3. Part (d) shows how real GDP fluctuates around potential GDP in a business cycle during year 1, year 2, and year 3.

In year 1, an inflationary gap exists and the economy is at point A in parts (a) and (d). In year 2, the economy is at full employment and the economy is at point B in parts (b) and (d). In year 3, a recessionary gap exists and the economy is at point C in parts (c) and (d).

Fluctuations in Aggregate Demand

One reason real GDP fluctuates around potential GDP is that aggregate demand fluctuates. Let's see what happens when aggregate demand increases.

Figure 10.10(a) shows an economy at full employment. The aggregate demand curve is AD_0, the short-run aggregate supply curve is SAS_0, and the long-run aggregate supply curve is LAS. Real GDP equals potential GDP at $1.8 trillion, and the price level is 110.

Now suppose that the world economy expands and that the demand for Canadian-produced goods increases in Asia and Europe. The increase in Canadian exports increases aggregate demand in Canada, and the aggregate demand curve shifts rightward from AD_0 to AD_1 in Fig. 10.10(a).

Faced with an increase in demand, firms increase production and raise prices. Real GDP increases to $1.9 trillion, and the price level rises to 115. The economy is now in an above full-employment equilibrium. Real GDP exceeds potential GDP, and there is an inflationary gap.

The increase in aggregate demand has increased the prices of all goods and services. Faced with higher prices, firms increased their output rates. At this stage, prices of goods and services have increased but the money wage rate has not changed. (Recall that as we move along the SAS curve, the money wage rate is constant.)

The economy cannot produce in excess of potential GDP forever. Why not? What are the forces at work that bring real GDP back to potential GDP?

Because the price level has increased and the money wage rate is unchanged, workers have experienced a fall in the buying power of their wages and firms' profits have increased. Under these circumstances, workers demand higher wages and firms, anxious to maintain their employment and output levels, meet those demands. If firms do not raise the money wage rate, they will either lose workers or have to hire less productive ones.

As the money wage rate rises, the short-run aggregate supply begins to decrease. In Fig. 10.10(b), the short-run aggregate supply curve begins to shift from

---

FIGURE 10.10 An Increase in Aggregate Demand

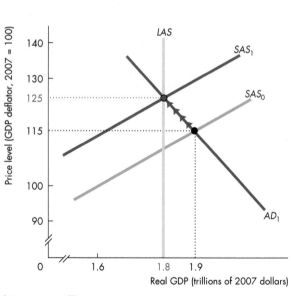

(a) Short-run effect

(b) Long-run effect

An increase in aggregate demand shifts the aggregate demand curve from AD_0 to AD_1. In short-run equilibrium, real GDP increases to $1.9 trillion and the price level rises to 115. In this situation, an inflationary gap exists. In the long run in part (b), the money wage rate starts to rise and short-run aggregate

supply starts to decrease. The SAS curve gradually shifts from SAS_0 toward SAS_1, intersecting the aggregate demand curve AD_1 at higher price levels and real GDP decreases. Eventually, the price level has risen to 125 and real GDP has decreased to $1.8 trillion—potential GDP.

SAS_0 toward SAS_1. The rise in the money wage rate and the shift in the SAS curve produce a sequence of new equilibrium positions. Along the adjustment path, real GDP decreases and the price level rises. The economy moves up along its aggregate demand curve as shown by the arrows in the figure.

Eventually, the money wage rate rises by the same percentage as the price level. At this time, the aggregate demand curve AD_1 intersects SAS_1 at a new full-employment equilibrium. The price level has risen to 125, and real GDP is back where it started, at potential GDP.

A decrease in aggregate demand has effects similar, but opposite, to those of an increase in aggregate demand. That is, a decrease in aggregate demand shifts the aggregate demand curve leftward. Real GDP decreases to less than potential GDP, and a recessionary gap emerges. Firms cut prices. The lower price level increases the purchasing power of wages and increases firms' costs relative to their output prices because the money wage rate is unchanged. Eventually, the money wage rate falls and the short-run aggregate supply increases.

Let's now work out how real GDP and the price level change when aggregate supply changes.

Fluctuations in Aggregate Supply

Fluctuations in short-run aggregate supply can bring fluctuations in real GDP around potential GDP. Suppose that initially real GDP equals potential GDP. Then there is a large but temporary rise in the price of oil. What happens to real GDP and the price level?

Figure 10.11 answers this question. The aggregate demand curve is AD_0, the short-run aggregate supply curve is SAS_0, and the long-run aggregate supply curve is LAS. Real GDP is $1.8 trillion, which equals potential GDP, and the price level is 110. Then the price of oil rises. Faced with higher energy and transportation costs, firms decrease production. Short-run aggregate supply decreases, and the short-run aggregate supply curve shifts leftward to SAS_1. The price level rises to 120, and real GDP decreases to $1.7 trillion. Because real GDP decreases, the economy experiences recession. Because the price level increases, the economy experiences inflation. A combination of recession and inflation is called **stagflation**. Canada experienced stagflation in the mid-1970s and early 1980s, but events like this are not common.

When the price of oil returns to its original level, the economy returns to full employment.

FIGURE 10.11   A Decrease in Aggregate Supply

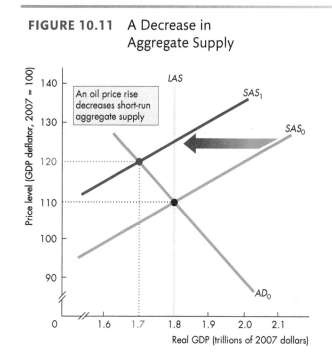

An increase in the price of oil decreases short-run aggregate supply and shifts the short-run aggregate supply curve from SAS_0 to SAS_1. Real GDP decreases from $1.8 trillion to $1.7 trillion, and the price level rises from 110 to 120. The economy experiences stagflation.

——————— MyLab Economics Animation ———————

REVIEW QUIZ

1 Does economic growth result from increases in aggregate demand, short-run aggregate supply, or long-run aggregate supply?

2 Does inflation result from increases in aggregate demand, short-run aggregate supply, or long-run aggregate supply?

3 Describe three types of short-run macroeconomic equilibrium.

4 How do fluctuations in aggregate demand and short-run aggregate supply bring fluctuations in real GDP around potential GDP?

Work these questions in Study Plan 10.3 and get instant feedback.   MyLab Economics

We can use the *AS-AD* model to explain and illustrate the views of the alternative schools of thought in macroeconomics. That is your next task.

Macroeconomic Schools of Thought

Macroeconomics is an active field of research, and much remains to be learned about the forces that make our economy grow and fluctuate. There is a greater degree of consensus and certainty about economic growth and inflation—the longer-term trends in real GDP and the price level—than there is about the business cycle—the short-term fluctuations in these variables. Here, we'll look only at differences of view about short-term fluctuations.

The *AS-AD* model that you've studied in this chapter provides a good foundation for understanding the range of views that macroeconomists hold about this topic. But what you will learn here is just a glimpse at the scientific controversy and debate. We'll return to these issues at various points later in the text and deepen your appreciation of the alternative views.

Classification usually requires simplification, and classifying macroeconomists is no exception to this general rule. The classification that we'll use here is simple, but it is not misleading. We're going to divide macroeconomists into three broad schools of thought and examine the views of each group in turn. The groups are:

■ Classical

■ Keynesian

■ Monetarist

The Classical View

A **classical** macroeconomist believes that the economy is self-regulating and always at full employment. The term "classical" derives from the name of the founding school of economics that includes Adam Smith, David Ricardo, and John Stuart Mill.

A **new classical** view is that business cycle fluctuations are the efficient responses of a well-functioning market economy that is bombarded by shocks that arise from the uneven pace of technological change.

The classical view can be understood in terms of beliefs about aggregate demand and aggregate supply.

Aggregate Demand Fluctuations In the classical view, technological change is the most significant influence on both aggregate demand and aggregate supply. For this reason, classical macroeconomists don't use the *AS-AD* framework. But their views can be interpreted in this framework. A technological change that increases the productivity of capital brings an increase in aggregate demand because firms increase their expenditure on new plant and equipment. A technological change that lengthens the useful life of existing capital decreases the demand for new capital, which decreases aggregate demand.

Aggregate Supply Response In the classical view, the money wage rate that lies behind the short-run aggregate supply curve is instantly and completely flexible. The money wage rate adjusts so quickly to maintain equilibrium in the labour market that real GDP always adjusts to equal potential GDP.

Potential GDP itself fluctuates for the same reasons that aggregate demand fluctuates: technological change. When the pace of technological change is rapid, potential GDP increases quickly and so does real GDP. And when the pace of technological change slows, so does the growth rate of potential GDP.

Classical Policy The classical view of policy emphasizes the potential for taxes to stunt incentives and create inefficiency. By minimizing the disincentive effects of taxes, employment, investment, and technological advance are at their efficient levels and the economy expands at an appropriate and rapid pace.

The Keynesian View

A **Keynesian** macroeconomist believes that, left alone, the economy would rarely operate at full employment and that to achieve and maintain full employment, active help from fiscal policy and monetary policy is required.

The term "Keynesian" derives from the name of one of the twentieth century's most famous economists, John Maynard Keynes (see p. 321).

The Keynesian view is based on beliefs about the forces that determine aggregate demand and short-run aggregate supply.

Aggregate Demand Fluctuations In the Keynesian view, *expectations* are the most significant influence on aggregate demand. Those expectations are based on herd instinct, or what Keynes himself called "animal spirits." A wave of pessimism about future profit prospects can lead to a fall in aggregate demand and plunge the economy into recession.

Aggregate Supply Response In the Keynesian view, the money wage rate that lies behind the short-run aggregate supply curve is extremely sticky in the downward direction. Basically, the money wage rate doesn't fall. So if there is a recessionary gap, there is no automatic mechanism for getting rid of it. If it were to happen, a fall in the money wage rate would increase short-run aggregate supply and restore full employment. But the money wage rate doesn't fall, so the economy remains stuck in recession.

A modern version of the Keynesian view, known as the **new Keynesian** view, holds not only that the money wage rate is sticky but also that prices of goods and services are sticky. With a sticky price level, the short-run aggregate supply curve is horizontal at a fixed price level.

Policy Response Needed The Keynesian view calls for fiscal policy and monetary policy to actively offset changes in aggregate demand that bring recession.

By stimulating aggregate demand in a recession, full employment can be restored.

The Monetarist View

A **monetarist** is a macroeconomist who believes that the economy is self-regulating and that it will normally operate at full employment, provided that monetary policy is not erratic and that the pace of money growth is kept steady.

The term "monetarist" was coined by an outstanding twentieth-century economist, Karl Brunner, to describe his own views and those of Milton Friedman (see p. 393).

The monetarist view can be interpreted in terms of beliefs about the forces that determine aggregate demand and short-run aggregate supply.

Aggregate Demand Fluctuations In the monetarist view, *the quantity of money* is the most significant influence on aggregate demand. The quantity of money is determined by the Bank of Canada. If the Bank of Canada keeps money growing at a steady pace, aggregate demand fluctuations will be minimized and the economy will operate close to full employment. But if the Bank of Canada decreases the quantity of money or even just slows its growth rate too abruptly, the economy will go into recession. In the monetarist view, all recessions result from inappropriate monetary policy.

Aggregate Supply Response The monetarist view of short-run aggregate supply is the same as the Keynesian view: The money wage rate is sticky. If the economy is in recession, it will take an unnecessarily long time for it to return unaided to full employment.

Monetarist Policy The monetarist view of policy is the same as the classical view on fiscal policy. Taxes should be kept low to avoid disincentive effects that decrease potential GDP. Provided that the quantity of money is kept on a steady growth path, no active stabilization is needed to offset changes in aggregate demand.

The Way Ahead

In the chapters that follow, you're going to encounter Keynesian, classical, and monetarist views again. In the next chapter, we study the original Keynesian model of aggregate demand. This model remains useful today because it explains how expenditure fluctuations are magnified and bring changes in aggregate demand that are larger than the changes in expenditure. We then go on to apply the *AS-AD* model to a deeper look at Canadian inflation and business cycle.

Our attention then turns to short-run macroeconomic policy—the fiscal policy of the government and the monetary policy of the Bank of Canada.

◆ REVIEW QUIZ

1 What are the defining features of classical macroeconomics and what policies do classical macroeconomists recommend?
2 What are the defining features of Keynesian macroeconomics and what policies do Keynesian macroeconomists recommend?
3 What are the defining features of monetarist macroeconomics and what policies do monetarist macroeconomists recommend?

Work these questions in Study Plan 10.4 and get instant feedback. MyLab Economics

◆ To complete your study of the *AS-AD* model, *Economics in the News* on pp. 260–261 looks at the Canadian economy in 2017 through the eyes of this model.

Aggregate Supply and Aggregate Demand in Action

Canada's Economy Grew at 3.7% Pace in First Quarter of 2017

CBC News
May 31, 2017

Canada's economy expanded at an annual pace of nearly four percent in the first quarter, more than three times the growth seen in the U.S. in the same period.

According to Statistics Canada, the total value of all goods and services sold in Canada grew in absolute terms by 0.9 percent from the level seen at the end of 2016. But that's an annualized pace of 3.7 percent. . . .

Domestic demand led the way in terms of growth, while exports were lower.

After falling in four of the previous five quarters, investment in machinery and equipment advanced 5.8 percent. Household final consumption increased 1.1 percent, led by vehicle purchases, the data agency said. . . .

But part of the reason the economy was booming to open up 2017 was the disproportionate impact of Canada's booming housing market.

Business investment in residential structures was a 3.7 percent boost to GDP, new construction increased 3.9 percent and renovation activity increased 2.1 percent.

"The Canadian economy continues to outperform against relatively modest expectations, but remains far too reliant on the housing sector to power growth," Cambridge Global Payments foreign exchange strategist Karl Schamotta said of the data.

Economist Frances Donald at Manulife Asset Management shares the concern that economic expansion so heavily tied to the housing market can't go on forever. . . .

TD Bank economist Brian DePratto . . . [said] . . . "it is again unlikely that the pace of first quarter growth . . . can be maintained, and the credit-fuelled nature of recent spending growth remains concerning." . . .

© CBC Licensing with files from Canadian Press

ESSENCE OF THE STORY

- Canada's real GDP grew at an annualized rate of 3.7 percent during the first quarter of 2017.

- Investment in machinery and equipment, investment in residential structures, and household consumption were the fastest growing components of aggregate expenditure growth.

- Economists were concerned that the growth was too heavily tied to the housing market, credit-fuelled, and unsustainable.

ECONOMIC ANALYSIS

- "Canada's economy" in the news story means real GDP.

- Canadian real GDP grew at an annual rate of 3.7 percent during the first quarter of 2017—the fastest growth rate in almost 10 years.

- In the first quarter of 2017, real GDP was estimated to be $1,829 billion. The price level was 116 (up 16 percent since 2007).

- A year earlier, in the first quarter of 2016, real GDP was $1,789 billion and the price level was 112.

- Figure 1 illustrates the situation in the first quarter of 2016. The aggregate demand curve was AD_{16} and the short-run aggregate supply curve was SAS_{16}. Real GDP ($1,789 billion) and the price level (112) are at the intersection of these curves.

- The Bank of Canada estimated that the output gap in the first quarter of 2016 was –0.3 percent, which implies that *potential* GDP in 2016 was $1,794 billion, so the long-run aggregate supply curve in 2016 was LAS_{16} in Fig. 1.

- Figure 1 shows the output gap in 2016, which was a recessionary gap of $5 billion.

- During the year from March 2016 to March 2017, the labour force increased, the capital stock increased, and labour productivity increased. Potential GDP increased to an estimated $1,831 billion.

- In Fig. 2, the LAS curve shifted rightward to LAS_{17}.

- Also during the year from March 2016 to March 2017, a combination of low interest rates and easy credit increased investment in machinery and equipment, investment in residential structures, and household consumption, all of which increased Canadian aggregate demand.

- The increase in aggregate demand exceeded the increase in long-run aggregate supply, and the AD curve shifted rightward to AD_{17}.

- Two forces act on short-run aggregate supply: The increase in potential GDP shifts the SAS curve rightward and a rise in the money wage rate and other factor prices shifts the SAS curve leftward.

- Because potential GDP didn't increase by much, short-run aggregate supply probably didn't change by much, and here we assume it didn't change at all. The SAS curve in 2017, SAS_{17}, was the same as SAS_{16}.

- Real GDP increased to $1,829 billion, the price level increased to 116, and the output gap shrank to –0.1 percent of potential GDP..

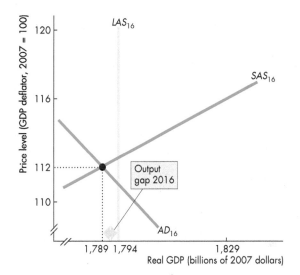

Figure 1 *AS-AD in First Quarter of 2016*

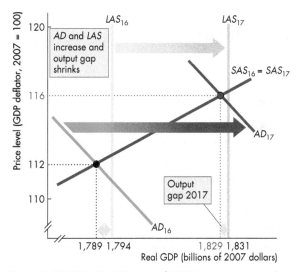

Figure 2 *AS-AD in First Quarter of 2017*

- As real GDP gets closer to potential GDP, increases in aggregate demand have a smaller effect on real GDP and a larger effect on the price level.

- It is the limits to the growth rate of potential GDP, not the fact that the recent growth was heavily in housing and credit-fuelled that make the growth rate of the first quarter of 2017 unsustainable.

WORKED PROBLEM

MyLab Economics Work this problem in Chapter 10 Study Plan.

The table shows the aggregate demand and short-run aggregate supply schedules of Lizard Island in which potential GDP is $600 billion.

Price level	Real GDP demanded	Real GDP supplied in the short run
	(billions of 2007 dollars)	
100	600	550
110	575	575
120	550	600
130	525	625

Questions

1. Calculate equilibrium real GDP and price level in the short run.
2. Does the country have an inflationary gap or a recessionary gap and what is its magnitude?
3. If aggregate demand increases by $50 billion, what is the new short-run macroeconomic equilibrium and the output gap?

Solutions

1. Short-run macroeconomic equilibrium occurs at the price level at which the quantity of real GDP demanded equals the quantity of real GDP supplied.

   At a price level of 110, the quantity of real GDP demanded is $575 billion and the quantity of real GDP supplied is $575 billion, so equilibrium real GDP is $575 billion and the price level is 110. See the equilibrium in the figure.

Key Point: Aggregate demand and aggregate supply determine the short-run macroeconomic equilibrium.

2. The output gap is the gap between equilibrium real GDP and potential GDP. Equilibrium real GDP is $575 billion and potential GDP is $600 billion, so the output gap is $25 billion. Because potential GDP exceeds equilibrium real GDP, the economy is in a below full-employment equilibrium and the output gap is a recessionary gap.

Key Point: A recessionary gap occurs when the economy is in a below full-employment equilibrium. When the economy is in an above full-employment equilibrium, the output gap is an inflationary gap.

3. The table below shows the new aggregate demand schedule when aggregate demand increases by $50 billion.

Price level	Real GDP demanded	Real GDP supplied in the short run
	(billions of 2007 dollars)	
100	650	550
110	625	575
120	600	600
130	575	675

At a price level of 110, the quantity of real GDP demanded ($625 billion) exceeds the quantity of real GDP supplied ($575 billion). Firms are unable to meet the demand for their output, so inventories start to decline. As people clamour for goods and services, firms increase production and start to raise their prices. Production and prices will continue to increase until a new short-run equilibrium is reached.

At the new equilibrium, real GDP is $600 billion and the price level is 120. Because equilibrium real GDP equals potential GDP of $600 billion, the economy is at full employment and there is no output gap. See the new short-run equilibrium in the figure.

Key Point: An increase in aggregate demand with no change in aggregate supply increases the price level and increases equilibrium real GDP.

Key Figure

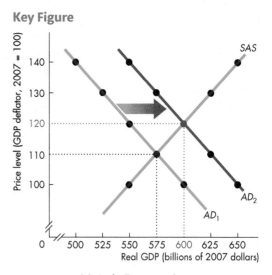

MyLab Economics Interactive Animation

SUMMARY

Key Points

Aggregate Supply (pp. 244–247)

- In the long run, the quantity of real GDP supplied is potential GDP.
- In the short run, a rise in the price level increases the quantity of real GDP supplied.
- A change in potential GDP changes long-run and short-run aggregate supply. A change in the money wage rate changes only short-run aggregate supply.

Working Problems 1 and 2 will give you a better understanding of aggregate supply.

Aggregate Demand (pp. 248–251)

- A rise in the price level decreases the quantity of real GDP demanded.
- Changes in expected future income, inflation, and profits; in fiscal policy and monetary policy; and in foreign income and the exchange rate change aggregate demand.

Working Problems 3 to 5 will give you a better understanding of aggregate demand.

Explaining Macroeconomic Trends and Fluctuations (pp. 252–257)

- Aggregate demand and short-run aggregate supply determine real GDP and the price level.
- In the long run, real GDP equals potential GDP and aggregate demand determines the price level.
- The business cycle occurs because aggregate demand and aggregate supply fluctuate.

Working Problems 6 to 8 will give you a better understanding of macroeconomic trends and fluctuations.

Macroeconomic Schools of Thought (pp. 258–259)

- Classical economists believe that the economy is self-regulating and always at full employment.
- Keynesian economists believe that full employment can be achieved only with active policy.
- Monetarist economists believe that recessions result from inappropriate monetary policy.

Working Problem 9 will give you a better understanding of the macroeconomic schools of thought.

Key Terms

MyLab Economics Key Terms Quiz

Above full-employment equilibrium, 254
Aggregate demand, 248
Below full-employment equilibrium, 255
Classical, 258
Disposable income, 250
Fiscal policy, 250

Full-employment equilibrium, 255
Inflationary gap, 254
Keynesian, 258
Long-run aggregate supply, 244
Long-run macroeconomic equilibrium, 252
Monetarist, 259
Monetary policy, 250

New classical, 258
New Keynesian, 259
Output gap, 254
Recessionary gap, 255
Short-run aggregate supply, 245
Short-run macroeconomic equilibrium, 252
Stagflation, 257

STUDY PLAN PROBLEMS AND APPLICATIONS

MyLab Economics Work Problems 1 to 9 in Chapter 10 Study Plan and get instant feedback.

Aggregate Supply (Study Plan 10.1)

1. Explain the influence of each of the following events on the quantity of real GDP supplied and aggregate supply in India and use a graph to illustrate.
   - Canadian firms move their call handling, IT, and data functions to India.
   - Fuel prices rise.
   - Walmart and Starbucks open in India.
   - Universities in India increase the number of engineering graduates.
   - The money wage rate rises.
   - The price level in India increases.

2. Labour productivity is rising at a rapid rate in China and wages are rising at a similar rate. Explain how a rise in labour productivity and wages in China will influence the quantity of real GDP supplied and aggregate supply in China.

Aggregate Demand (Study Plan 10.2)

3. Canada trades with the United States. Explain the effect of each of the following events on Canada's aggregate demand.
   - The government of Canada cuts income taxes.
   - The United States experiences strong economic growth.
   - Canada sets new environmental standards that require power utilities to upgrade their production facilities.

4. The Bank of Canada cuts the quantity of money and all other things remain the same. Explain the effect of the cut in the quantity of money on aggregate demand in the short run.

5. **Gross Domestic Product for the First Quarter of 2017**

   The increase in real GDP in the first quarter of 2017 primarily reflected changes in personal consumption expenditure (+1.1%), exports (−0.1%), and investment (+2.9%). Imports of goods and services increased by 3.3%.

   Source: Statistics Canada, May 31, 2017

   Explain how the items in the news clip influence Canada's aggregate demand.

Explaining Macroeconomic Trends and Fluctuations (Study Plan 10.3)

Use the following graph to work Problems 6 to 8. Initially, the short-run aggregate supply curve is SAS_0 and the aggregate demand curve is AD_0.

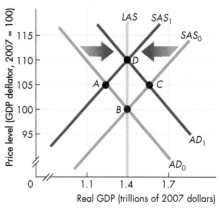

6. Some events change aggregate demand from AD_0 to AD_1. Describe two events that could have created this change in aggregate demand. What is the equilibrium after aggregate demand changed? If potential GDP is unchanged, the economy is at what type of macroeconomic equilibrium?

7. Some events change aggregate supply from SAS_0 to SAS_1. Describe two events that could have created this change in aggregate supply. What is the equilibrium after short-run aggregate supply changed? If potential GDP is unchanged, does the economy have an inflationary gap, a recessionary gap, or no output gap?

8. Some events change aggregate demand from AD_0 to AD_1 and aggregate supply from SAS_0 to SAS_1. What is the new macroeconomic equilibrium?

Macroeconomic Schools of Thought (Study Plan 10.4)

9. Describe the policy change that a classical macroeconomist, a Keynesian, and a monetarist would recommend for Canadian policymakers to adopt in response to each of the following events:
   a. Growth in the world economy slows.
   b. The world price of oil rises.
   c. Canadian labour productivity declines.

MyLab Economics You can work these problems in Homework or Test if assigned by your instructor.

ADDITIONAL PROBLEMS AND APPLICATIONS

Aggregate Supply

10. Explain for each event whether it changes the quantity of real GDP supplied, short-run aggregate supply, long-run aggregate supply, or a combination of them.
    - Automotive firms in Canada switch to a new technology that raises productivity.
    - Toyota and Honda build additional plants in Canada.
    - The prices of auto parts imported from China rise.
    - Autoworkers agree to a lower money wage rate.
    - The Canadian price level rises.

Aggregate Demand

11. Explain for each event whether it changes the quantity of real GDP demanded or aggregate demand in Canada.
    - Canada's exports to the European Union boom.
    - Canadian firms build new pipelines across the nation.
    - Foreign exchange dealers expect the Canadian dollar next year to appreciate against all currencies.

12. **Inventories Build Up**

    When real GDP increased in the first quarter of 2017, businesses accumulated $12.2 billion in inventories, following a decrease of $2.8 billion in the previous quarter.

    Source: Statistics Canada, May 31, 2017

    Explain how a fall in business inventories influences aggregate demand.

13. **Exports and Imports Increase**

    Real exports of goods and services decreased 0.1 percent in the first quarter of 2017, after rising 0.2 percent in the previous quarter. Real imports of goods and services increased 3.3 percent, after falling 3.0 percent in the previous quarter.

    Source: Statistics Canada, May 31, 2017

    Explain how the changes in exports and imports reported here influence the quantity of real GDP demanded and aggregate demand. In which of the two quarters did exports and imports contribute more to the change in aggregate demand?

Explaining Macroeconomic Trends and Fluctuations

Use the following information to work Problems 14 to 16.

The following events have occurred at times in the history of Canada:
- The world economy goes into an expansion.
- Canadian businesses expect future profits to rise.
- The government increases its expenditure on goods and services in a time of increased international tension.

14. Explain for each event whether it changes short-run aggregate supply, long-run aggregate supply, aggregate demand, or some combination of them.

15. Explain the separate effects of each event on Canadian real GDP and the price level, starting from a position of long-run equilibrium.

16. Explain the combined effects of these events on Canadian real GDP and the price level, starting from a position of long-run equilibrium.

Use the following information to work Problems 17 and 18.

In Japan, potential GDP is 600 trillion yen. The table shows Japan's aggregate demand and short-run aggregate supply schedules.

Price level	Real GDP demanded	Real GDP supplied in the short run
	(trillions of 2007 yen)	
75	600	400
85	550	450
95	500	500
105	450	550
115	400	600
125	350	650
135	300	700

17. a. Draw a graph of the aggregate demand curve and the short-run aggregate supply curve.

    b. What is the short-run equilibrium real GDP and price level?

18. Does Japan have an inflationary gap or a recessionary gap and what is its magnitude?

Use the following news clip to work Problems 19 and 20.

Millennials Are Starting to Spend More

Millennials, who spend an average of $85 a day, are expected to spend at a higher rate in the next 15 years. Only 37 percent of Americans report higher spending today than a year ago, while 42 percent of millennials say they are spending more. Millennials are spending more on rent or mortgages and leisure activities than they were spending a year ago.

Source: *Business Journal*, May 25, 2016

19. Explain the effect of a rise in expenditure by millenials on real GDP and the price level in the short run.

20. Describe the macroeconomic equilibrium after the change in spending by millenials:
    a. If the economy had been operating below full-employment equilibrium,
    b. If the economy had been operating at a full-employment equilibrium, and
    c. Explain and draw a graph to illustrate how the economy adjusts in the two situations described in parts a and b.

21. Suppose that the E.U. economy goes into an expansion. Explain the effect of the expansion on Canadian real GDP and unemployment in the short run.

22. Explain why changes in consumer spending and business investment play a large role in the business cycle.

23. **Fed Raises Rates as Job Gains, Firming Inflation Stoke Confidence**

    The U.S. Federal Reserve raised interest rates on Wednesday. The rate rise was the second in three months. This second rise comes in an economy that is growing faster and creating jobs at a more rapid pace. These gains are accompanied by a rising inflation rate.

    Source: Reuters, March 15, 2017

    a. Describe the process by which the Fed's action reported in the news clip flows through the economy.
    b. Draw a graph to illustrate the state of the economy that prompted the Fed to take the action described in the news clip.
    c. Draw a graph to illustrate the Fed's action and its effect.

Macroeconomic Schools of Thought

24. **Cut Taxes and Boost Spending? Raise Taxes and Cut Spending? Cut Taxes and Cut Spending?**

    This headline expresses three views about what to do to get an economy growing more rapidly and contribute to closing the recessionary gap.

    Economists from which macroeconomic school of thought would recommend pursuing policies described by each of these views?

Economics in the News

25. After you have studied *Economics in the News* on pp. 260–261, answer the following questions.
    a. Describe the main features of the Canadian economy in the first quarter of 2017.
    b. Did Canada have a recessionary gap or an inflationary gap in 2017? How do you know?
    c. Use the *AS-AD* model to show the changes in aggregate demand and aggregate supply that occurred in 2016 and 2017 that brought the economy to its situation in early 2017.
    d. Use the *AS-AD* model to show the changes in aggregate demand and aggregate supply that will have occurred when full employment is restored.
    e. Use the *AS-AD* model to show the changes in aggregate demand and aggregate supply that would occur if the government increased its expenditure on goods and services or cut taxes by enough to restore full employment.
    f. Use the *AS-AD* model to show the changes in aggregate demand and aggregate supply that would occur if the economy moved into an inflationary gap. Show the short-run and the long-run effects.

26. **Brazil's Worst Recession: 8 Consecutive Quarters of Contraction**

    Brazil is experiencing a collapse in business investment, rising unemployment, and falling consumer spending. Business and consumer confidence are low.

    Source: CNNMoney, March 7, 2017

    a. Explain and draw a graph to illustrate the state of Brazil's economy.
    b. Explain how business and consumer confidence influence aggregate demand.

11

EXPENDITURE MULTIPLIERS

After studying this chapter, you will be able to:

◆ Explain how expenditure plans are determined when the price level is fixed

◆ Explain how real GDP is determined when the price level is fixed

◆ Explain the expenditure multiplier

◆ Explain the relationship between aggregate expenditure and aggregate demand

Investment and inventories fluctuate like the volume of a rock singer's voice and the uneven surface of a pot-holed road. How does the economy react to those fluctuations? Does it behave like an amplifier, blowing up the fluctuations and spreading them out to affect the many millions of participants in an economic rock concert? Or does it react like a limousine, absorbing the shocks and providing a smooth ride for the economy's passengers?

You will explore these questions in this chapter, and in *Economics in the News* at the end of the chapter you will see the role played by inventory investment during 2017 as the economy expanded.

Fixed Prices and Expenditure Plans

In the model that we study in this chapter, all the firms are like your grocery store: They set their prices and sell the quantities their customers are willing to buy. If they persistently sell more than they plan to and keep running out of inventory, they eventually raise their prices. And if they persistently sell less than they plan to and have inventories piling up, they eventually cut their prices. But on any given day, their prices are fixed and the quantities they sell depend on demand, not supply.

Because each firm's prices are fixed, for the economy as a whole:

1. The *price level* is fixed, and
2. *Aggregate demand* determines real GDP.

We call this model the *Keynesian model* because it was first suggested by John Maynard Keynes (see p. 321) as a model of persistent depression.

We begin by identifying the forces that determine expenditure plans.

Expenditure Plans

Aggregate expenditure has four components: consumption expenditure, investment, government expenditure on goods and services, and net exports (exports *minus* imports). These four components sum to real GDP (see Chapter 4, pp. 89–90).

Aggregate planned expenditure is equal to the sum of the *planned* levels of consumption expenditure, investment, government expenditure on goods and services, and exports minus imports. Two of these components of planned expenditure, consumption expenditure and imports, change when income changes and so they depend on real GDP.

A Two-Way Link Between Aggregate Expenditure and Real GDP
There is a two-way link between aggregate expenditure and real GDP. Other things remaining the same:

- An increase in real GDP increases aggregate expenditure, and
- An increase in aggregate expenditure increases real GDP.

You are now going to study this two-way link.

Consumption and Saving Plans

Several factors influence consumption expenditure and saving plans. The more important ones are:

1. Disposable income
2. Real interest rate
3. Wealth
4. Expected future income

Disposable income is aggregate income minus taxes plus transfer payments. Aggregate income equals real GDP, so disposable income depends on real GDP. To explore the two-way link between real GDP and planned consumption expenditure, we focus on the relationship between consumption expenditure and disposable income when the other three factors listed above are constant.

Consumption Expenditure and Saving The table in Fig. 11.1 lists the consumption expenditure and the saving that people plan at each level of disposable income. Households can only spend their disposable income on consumption or save it, so planned consumption expenditure plus planned saving *always* equals disposable income.

The relationship between consumption expenditure and disposable income, other things remaining the same, is called the **consumption function**. The relationship between saving and disposable income, other things remaining the same, is called the **saving function**.

Consumption Function Figure 11.1(a) shows a consumption function. The *y*-axis measures consumption expenditure, and the *x*-axis measures disposable income. Along the consumption function, the points labelled *A* through *F* correspond to the rows of the table. For example, point *E* shows that when disposable income is $800 billion, consumption expenditure is $750 billion. As disposable income increases, consumption expenditure also increases.

At point *A* on the consumption function, consumption expenditure is $150 billion even though disposable income is zero. This consumption expenditure is called *autonomous consumption*, and it is the amount of consumption expenditure that would take place in the short run even if people had no current income. Consumption expenditure in excess of this amount is called *induced consumption*, which is the consumption expenditure that is induced by an increase in disposable income.

45° Line Figure 11.1(a) also contains a 45° line, the height of which measures disposable income. At each point on this line, consumption expenditure equals disposable income. Between points *A* and *D* consumption expenditure exceeds disposable income, between points *D* and *F* consumption expenditure is less than disposable income, and at point *D* consumption expenditure equals disposable income.

Saving Function Figure 11.1(b) shows a saving function. Again, the points *A* through *F* correspond to the rows of the table. For example, point *E* shows that when disposable income is $800 billion, saving is $50 billion. As disposable income increases, saving increases. Notice that when consumption expenditure exceeds disposable income in part (a), saving is negative, called *dissaving*, in part (b).

FIGURE 11.1   Consumption Function and Saving Function

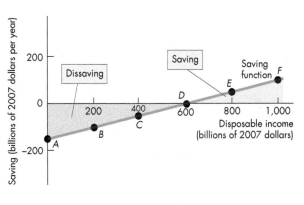

(a) **Consumption function**

(b) **Saving function**

	Disposable income	Planned consumption expenditure	Planned saving
		(billions of 2007 dollars)	
A	0	150	−150
B	200	300	−100
C	400	450	−50
D	600	600	0
E	800	750	50
F	1,000	900	100

The table shows consumption expenditure and saving plans at various levels of disposable income. Part (a) of the figure shows the relationship between consumption expenditure and disposable income (the consumption function). The height of the consumption function measures consumption expenditure at each level of disposable income. Part (b) shows the relationship between saving and disposable income (the saving function). The height of the saving function measures saving at each level of disposable income. Points *A* through *F* on the consumption and saving functions correspond to the rows in the table.

The height of the 45° line in part (a) measures disposable income. So along the 45° line, consumption expenditure equals disposable income. Consumption expenditure plus saving equals disposable income. When the consumption function is above the 45° line, saving is negative (dissaving occurs). When the consumption function is below the 45° line, saving is positive. At the point where the consumption function intersects the 45° line, all disposable income is spent on consumption and saving is zero.

Marginal Propensities to Consume and Save

The **marginal propensity to consume** (*MPC*) is the fraction of a *change* in disposable income that is spent on consumption. It is calculated as the *change* in consumption expenditure (ΔC) divided by the *change* in disposable income (ΔYD). The formula is

$$MPC = \frac{\Delta C}{\Delta YD}.$$

In the table in Fig. 11.1, when disposable income increases by \$200 billion, consumption expenditure increases by \$150 billion. The *MPC* is \$150 billion divided by \$200 billion, which equals 0.75.

The **marginal propensity to save** (*MPS*) is the fraction of a *change* in disposable income that is saved. It is calculated as the *change* in saving (ΔS) divided by the *change* in disposable income (ΔYD). The formula is

$$MPS = \frac{\Delta S}{\Delta YD}.$$

In the table in Fig. 11.1, when disposable income increases by \$200 billion, saving increases by \$50 billion. The *MPS* is \$50 billion divided by \$200 billion, which equals 0.25.

Because an increase in disposable income is either spent on consumption or saved, the marginal propensity to consume plus the marginal propensity to save equals 1. You can see why by using the equation

$$\Delta C + \Delta S = \Delta YD.$$

Divide both sides of the equation by the change in disposable income to obtain

$$\frac{\Delta C}{\Delta YD} + \frac{\Delta S}{\Delta YD} = 1.$$

$\Delta C/\Delta YD$ is the marginal propensity to consume (*MPC*), and $\Delta S/\Delta YD$ is the marginal propensity to save (*MPS*), so

$$MPC + MPS = 1.$$

Slopes and Marginal Propensities

The slope of the consumption function is the marginal propensity to consume, and the slope of the saving function is the marginal propensity to save.

Figure 11.2(a) shows the *MPC* as the slope of the consumption function. An increase in disposable income of \$200 billion is the base of the red triangle. The increase in consumption expenditure that results from this increase in disposable income is \$150 billion and is the height of the triangle. The slope of the consumption function is given by the formula "slope equals rise over run" and is \$150 billion divided by \$200 billion, which equals 0.75—the *MPC*.

Figure 11.2(b) shows the *MPS* as the slope of the saving function. An increase in disposable income of \$200 billion (the base of the red triangle) increases saving by \$50 billion (the height of the triangle). The slope of the saving function is \$50 billion divided by \$200 billion, which equals 0.25—the *MPS*.

FIGURE 11.2 The Marginal Propensities to Consume and Save

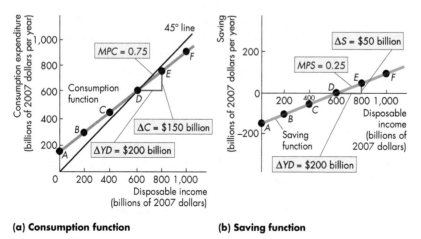

(a) Consumption function **(b) Saving function**

The marginal propensity to consume, *MPC*, is equal to the change in consumption expenditure divided by the change in disposable income, other things remaining the same. It is measured by the slope of the consumption function. In part (a), the *MPC* is 0.75.

The marginal propensity to save, *MPS*, is equal to the change in saving divided by the change in disposable income, other things remaining the same. It is measured by the slope of the saving function. In part (b), the *MPS* is 0.25.

MyLab Economics Animation

ECONOMICS IN ACTION

The Canadian Consumption Function

The figure shows the Canadian consumption function. Each point identified by a blue dot represents consumption expenditure and disposable income for a particular year. (The dots are for the years 1981 to 2016, and the dots for five of those years are identified in the figure.)

The Canadian consumption function is CF_{81} in 1981 and CF_{16} in 2016.

The slope of the consumption function in the figure is 0.8, which means that a $1 increase in disposable income increases consumption expenditure by 80 cents. This slope, which is an estimate of the marginal propensity to consume, is an assumption that is at the upper end of the range of values that economists have estimated for the marginal propensity to consume.

The consumption function shifts upward over time as other influences on consumption expenditure change. Of these other influences, the real interest rate and wealth fluctuate and so bring upward and downward shifts in the consumption function.

But increasing wealth and increasing expected future income bring a steady upward shift in the consumption function. As the consumption function shifts upward, autonomous consumption increases.

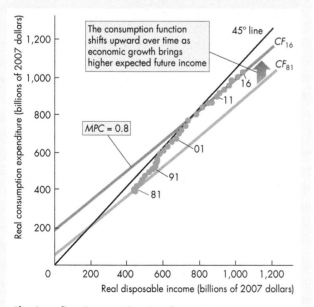

The Canadian Consumption Function

Source of data: Statistics Canada, CANSIM Tables 380-0002 and 380-0004.

Consumption as a Function of Real GDP

Consumption expenditure changes when disposable income changes, and disposable income changes when real GDP changes. So consumption expenditure depends not only on disposable income but also on real GDP. We use this link between consumption expenditure and real GDP to determine equilibrium expenditure. But before we do so, we need to look at one further component of aggregate expenditure: imports. Like consumption expenditure, imports are influenced by real GDP.

Import Function

Of the many influences on Canadian imports in the short run, Canadian real GDP is the main influence. Other things remaining the same, an increase in Canadian real GDP increases the quantity of Canadian imports.

The relationship between imports and real GDP is determined by the **marginal propensity to import**, which is the fraction of an increase in real GDP that is spent on imports. It is calculated as the change in imports divided by the change in real GDP, other things remaining the same. For example, if an increase in real GDP of $100 billion increases imports by $25 billion, the marginal propensity to import is 0.25.

REVIEW QUIZ

1. Which components of aggregate expenditure are influenced by real GDP?
2. Define and explain how we calculate the marginal propensity to consume and the marginal propensity to save.
3. How do we calculate the effects of real GDP on consumption expenditure and imports by using the marginal propensity to consume and the marginal propensity to import?

Work these questions in Study Plan 11.1 and get instant feedback.　　　MyLab Economics

Real GDP influences consumption expenditure and imports, which in turn influence real GDP. Your next task is to study this second piece of the two-way link between aggregate expenditure and real GDP and see how all the components of aggregate planned expenditure interact to determine real GDP.

◆ Real GDP with a Fixed Price Level

You are now going to see how, at a given price level, aggregate expenditure plans determine real GDP. We start by looking at the relationship between aggregate planned expenditure and real GDP. This relationship can be described by an aggregate expenditure schedule or an aggregate expenditure curve. The *aggregate expenditure schedule* lists aggregate planned expenditure generated at each level of real GDP. The *aggregate expenditure curve* is a graph of the aggregate expenditure schedule.

Aggregate Planned Expenditure

The table in Fig. 11.3 sets out an aggregate expenditure schedule. To calculate aggregate planned expenditure at a given real GDP, we add the expenditure components together. The first column of the table shows real GDP, and the second column shows the planned consumption at each level of real GDP. A $100 billion increase in real GDP increases consumption expenditure by $70 billion—the *MPC* is 0.7.

The next two columns show investment and government expenditure on goods and services, both of which are independent of the level of real GDP. Investment depends on the real interest rate and the expected profit (see Chapter 7, p. 170). At a given point in time, these factors generate a given level of investment. Suppose this level of investment is $290 billion. Also, suppose that government expenditure is $270 billion.

The next two columns show exports and imports. Exports are influenced by events in the rest of the world, prices of foreign-produced goods and services relative to the prices of similar Canadian-produced goods and services, and exchange rates. But they are not directly affected by Canadian real GDP. Exports are a constant $340 billion. Imports increase as Canadian real GDP increases. A $100 billion increase in Canadian real GDP generates a $20 billion increase in imports—the marginal propensity to import is 0.2.

The final column shows aggregate planned expenditure—the sum of planned consumption expenditure, investment, government expenditure on goods and services, and exports minus imports.

Figure 11.3 plots an aggregate expenditure curve. Real GDP is shown on the *x*-axis, and aggregate planned expenditure is shown on the *y*-axis. The aggregate expenditure curve is the red line *AE*.

Points *A* through *F* on that curve correspond to the rows of the table. The *AE* curve is a graph of aggregate planned expenditure (the last column) plotted against real GDP (the first column).

Figure 11.3 also shows the components of aggregate expenditure. The constant components—investment (*I*), government expenditure on goods and services (*G*), and exports (*X*)—are shown by the horizontal lines in the figure. Consumption expenditure (*C*) is the vertical gap between the lines labelled $I+G+X$ and $I+G+X+C$.

To construct the *AE* curve, subtract imports (*M*) from the $I+G+X+C$ line. Aggregate expenditure is expenditure on Canadian-produced goods and services. But the components of aggregate expenditure—*C, I,* and *G*—include expenditure on imported goods and services. For example, if you buy a new smartphone, your expenditure is part of consumption expenditure. But if the smartphone is a Samsung made in Korea, your expenditure on it must be subtracted from consumption expenditure to find out how much is spent on goods and services produced in Canada—Canadian real GDP. Money paid to Samsung for smartphone imports from Korea does not add to aggregate expenditure in Canada.

Because imports are only a part of aggregate expenditure, when we subtract imports from the other components of aggregate expenditure, aggregate planned expenditure still increases as real GDP increases, as you can see in Fig. 11.3.

Consumption expenditure minus imports, which varies with real GDP, is called **induced expenditure**. The sum of investment, government expenditure, and exports, which does not vary with real GDP, is called **autonomous expenditure**. Consumption expenditure and imports can also have an autonomous component—a component that does not vary with real GDP. Another way of thinking about autonomous expenditure is that it would be the level of aggregate planned expenditure if real GDP were zero.

In Fig. 11.3, autonomous expenditure is $900 billion—aggregate planned expenditure when real GDP is zero (point *A*). For each $100 billion increase in real GDP, induced expenditure increases by $50 billion.

The aggregate expenditure curve summarizes the relationship between aggregate *planned* expenditure and real GDP. But what determines the point on the aggregate expenditure curve at which the economy operates? What determines *actual* aggregate expenditure?

FIGURE 11.3   Aggregate Planned Expenditure: The *AE* Curve

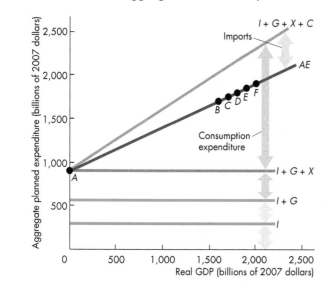

Aggregate planned expenditure is the sum of planned consumption expenditure, investment, government expenditure on goods and services, and exports minus imports. For example, in row C of the table, when real GDP is $1,700 billion, planned consumption expenditure is $1,190 billion, planned investment is $290 billion, planned government expenditure is $270 billion, planned exports are $340 billion, and planned imports are $340 billion. So when real GDP is $1,700 billion, aggregate planned expenditure is $1,750 billion ($1,190 + $290 + $270 + $340 − $340).

The schedule shows that aggregate planned expenditure increases as real GDP increases. This relationship is graphed as the aggregate expenditure curve *AE*. The components of aggregate expenditure that increase with real GDP are consumption expenditure and imports. The other components—investment, government expenditure, and exports—do not vary with real GDP.

	Real GDP (Y)	Consumption expenditure (C)	Investment (I)	Government expenditure (G)	Exports (X)	Imports (M)	Aggregate planned expenditure (AE = C + I + G + X − M)
				(billions of 2007 dollars)			
A	0	0	290	270	340	0	900
B	1,600	1,120	290	270	340	320	1,700
C	1,700	1,190	290	270	340	340	1,750
D	1,800	1,260	290	270	340	360	1,800
E	1,900	1,330	290	270	340	380	1,850
F	2,000	1,400	290	270	340	400	1,900

MyLab Economics Animation

Actual Expenditure, Planned Expenditure, and Real GDP

Actual aggregate expenditure is always equal to real GDP, as we saw in Chapter 4 (p. 90). But aggregate *planned* expenditure is not always equal to actual aggregate expenditure and therefore is not always equal to real GDP. How can actual expenditure and planned expenditure differ? The answer is that firms can end up with inventories that are greater or smaller than planned. People carry out their consumption

expenditure plans, the government implements its planned expenditure on goods and services, and net exports are as planned. Firms carry out their plans to purchase new buildings, plant, and equipment. But one component of investment is the change in firms' inventories. If aggregate planned expenditure is less than real GDP, firms sell less than they planned to sell and end up with unplanned inventories. If aggregate planned expenditure exceeds real GDP, firms sell more than they planned to sell and end up with inventories being too low.

Equilibrium Expenditure

Equilibrium expenditure is the level of aggregate expenditure that occurs when aggregate *planned* expenditure equals real GDP. Equilibrium expenditure is a level of aggregate expenditure and real GDP at which spending plans are fulfilled. At a given price level, equilibrium expenditure determines real GDP. When aggregate planned expenditure and actual aggregate expenditure are unequal, a process of convergence toward equilibrium expenditure occurs. Throughout this process, real GDP adjusts. Let's examine equilibrium expenditure and the process that brings it about.

Figure 11.4(a) illustrates equilibrium expenditure. The table sets out aggregate planned expenditure at various levels of real GDP. These values are plotted

---

FIGURE 11.4 Equilibrium Expenditure

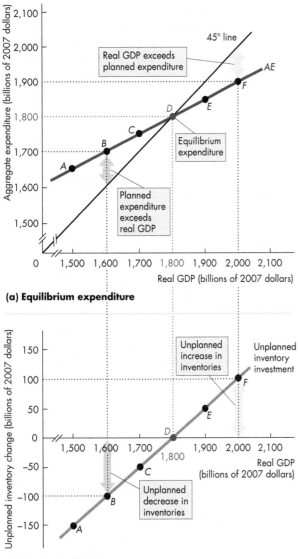

(a) Equilibrium expenditure

(b) Unplanned inventory changes

	Real GDP (Y)	Aggregate planned expenditure (AE)	Unplanned inventory change (Y − AE)
		(billions of 2007 dollars)	
A	1,500	1,650	−150
B	1,600	1,700	−100
C	1,700	1,750	−50
D	1,800	1,800	0
E	1,900	1,850	50
F	2,000	1,900	100

The table shows expenditure plans at different levels of real GDP. When real GDP is $1,800 billion, aggregate planned expenditure equals real GDP.

Part (a) of the figure illustrates equilibrium expenditure, which occurs when aggregate planned expenditure equals real GDP at the intersection of the 45° line and the *AE* curve. Part (b) of the figure shows the forces that bring about equilibrium expenditure.

When aggregate planned expenditure exceeds real GDP, inventories decrease—for example, at point *B* in both parts of the figure. So, firms increase production and real GDP increases.

When aggregate planned expenditure is less than real GDP, inventories increase—for example, at point *F* in both parts of the figure. So, firms cut production and real GDP decreases.

When aggregate planned expenditure equals real GDP, there are no unplanned inventory changes and real GDP remains constant at equilibrium expenditure.

MyLab Economics Animation and Draw Graph

as points *A* through *F* along the *AE* curve. The 45° line shows all the points at which aggregate planned expenditure equals real GDP. So where the *AE* curve lies above the 45° line, aggregate planned expenditure exceeds real GDP; where the *AE* curve lies below the 45° line, aggregate planned expenditure is less than real GDP; and where the *AE* curve intersects the 45° line, aggregate planned expenditure equals real GDP. Point *D* illustrates equilibrium expenditure. At this point, real GDP is $1,800 billion.

Convergence to Equilibrium

What are the forces that move aggregate expenditure toward its equilibrium level? To answer this question, we must look at a situation in which aggregate expenditure is away from its equilibrium level.

From Below Equilibrium Suppose that in Fig. 11.4, real GDP is $1,600 billion. With real GDP at $1,600 billion, actual aggregate expenditure is also $1,600 billion, but aggregate *planned* expenditure is $1,700 billion, point *B* in Fig. 11.4(a). Aggregate planned expenditure exceeds *actual* expenditure. When firms produce goods and services worth $1,600 billion and people spend $1,700 billion, firms' inventories decrease by $100 billion, point *B* in Fig. 11.4(b). Because the change in inventories is part of investment, *actual* investment is $100 billion less than *planned* investment. Actual expenditure is $16 billion.

Real GDP doesn't remain at $1,600 billion for very long. Firms have inventory targets based on their sales. When inventories fall below target, firms increase production to restore inventories to the target level.

To increase inventories, firms hire additional labour and increase production. Suppose that they increase production in the next period by $100 billion. Real GDP increases by $100 billion to $1,700 billion. But again, aggregate planned expenditure exceeds real GDP. When real GDP is $1,700 billion, aggregate planned expenditure is $1,750 billion, point *C* in Fig. 11.4(a). Again, inventories decrease, but this time by less than before. With real GDP of $1,700 billion and aggregate planned expenditure of $1,750 billion, inventories decrease by $50 billion, point *C* in Fig. 11.4(b). Again, firms hire additional labour and production increases; real GDP increases yet further.

The process that we've just described—planned expenditure exceeds real GDP, inventories decrease, and production increases to restore inventories—ends when real GDP has reached $1,800 billion. At this real

GDP, there is equilibrium expenditure. Unplanned inventory changes are zero. Firms do not change their production.

From Above Equilibrium If in Fig. 11.4 real GDP is $2,000 billion, the process that we've just described works in reverse. With real GDP at $2,000 billion, actual aggregate expenditure is also $2,000 billion, but aggregate planned expenditure is $1,900 billion, point *F* in Fig. 11.4(a). Actual expenditure exceeds planned expenditure. When firms produce goods and services worth $2,000 billion and people spend $1,900 billion, firms' inventories increase by $100 billion, point *F* in Fig. 11.4(b). Firms respond by cutting production and real GDP begins to decrease. As long as actual expenditure exceeds planned expenditure, inventories increase and production decreases. Again, the process ends when real GDP has reached $1,800 billion, the equilibrium at which unplanned inventory changes are zero and firms do not change their production.

REVIEW QUIZ

1 What is the relationship between aggregate planned expenditure and real GDP at equilibrium expenditure?

2 How does equilibrium expenditure come about? What adjusts to achieve equilibrium?

3 If real GDP and aggregate expenditure are less than equilibrium expenditure, what happens to firms' inventories? How do firms change their production? And what happens to real GDP?

4 If real GDP and aggregate expenditure are greater than equilibrium expenditure, what happens to firms' inventories? How do firms change their production? And what happens to real GDP?

Work these questions in Study Plan 11.2 and get instant feedback.   MyLab Economics

We've learned that when the price level is fixed, real GDP is determined by equilibrium expenditure. And we have seen how unplanned changes in inventories and the production response they generate bring a convergence toward equilibrium expenditure. We're now going to study *changes* in equilibrium expenditure and discover an economic amplifier called the *multiplier.*

◆ The Multiplier

Investment and exports can change for many reasons. A fall in the real interest rate might induce firms to increase their planned investment. A wave of innovation, such as occurred with the spread of multimedia computers in the 1990s, might increase expected future profits and lead firms to increase their planned investment. An economic boom in the United States, the European Union, and Japan might lead to a large increase in their expenditure on Canadian-produced goods and services—on Canadian exports. These are all examples of increases in autonomous expenditure.

When autonomous expenditure increases, aggregate expenditure increases and so does equilibrium expenditure and real GDP. But the increase in real GDP is *larger* than the change in autonomous expenditure. The **multiplier** is the amount by which a change in autonomous expenditure is magnified or multiplied to determine the change in equilibrium expenditure and real GDP.

To get the basic idea of the multiplier, we'll work with an example economy in which there are no income taxes and no imports. So we'll first assume that these factors are absent. Then, when you understand the basic idea, we'll bring these factors back into play and see what difference they make to the multiplier.

The Basic Idea of the Multiplier

Suppose that investment increases. The additional expenditure by businesses means that aggregate expenditure and real GDP increase. The increase in real GDP increases disposable income and, with no income taxes, real GDP and disposable income increase by the same amount. The increase in disposable income brings an increase in consumption expenditure. And the increased consumption expenditure adds even more to aggregate expenditure. Real GDP and disposable income increase further, and so does consumption expenditure.

The initial increase in investment brings an even bigger increase in aggregate expenditure because it induces an increase in consumption expenditure. The magnitude of the increase in aggregate expenditure that results from an increase in autonomous expenditure is determined by the *multiplier*.

The table in Fig. 11.5 sets out an aggregate planned expenditure schedule. Initially, when real GDP is $1,700 billion, aggregate planned expenditure is $1,725 billion. For each $100 billion increase in real GDP, aggregate planned expenditure increases by $75 billion. This aggregate expenditure schedule is shown in the figure as the aggregate expenditure curve AE_0. Initially, equilibrium expenditure is $1,800 billion. You can see this equilibrium in row B of the table and in the figure where the curve AE_0 intersects the 45° line at the point marked B.

Now suppose that autonomous expenditure increases by $50 billion. What happens to equilibrium expenditure? You can see the answer in Fig. 11.5. When this increase in autonomous expenditure is added to the original aggregate planned expenditure, aggregate planned expenditure increases by $50 billion at each level of real GDP. The new aggregate expenditure curve is AE_1. The new equilibrium expenditure, highlighted in the table (row D'), occurs where AE_1 intersects the 45° line and is $2,000 billion (point D'). At this real GDP, aggregate planned expenditure equals real GDP.

The Multiplier Effect

In Fig. 11.5, the increase in autonomous expenditure of $50 billion increases equilibrium expenditure by $200 billion. That is, the change in autonomous expenditure leads, like a rock singer's electronic equipment, to an amplified change in equilibrium expenditure. This amplified change is the *multiplier effect*—equilibrium expenditure increases by *more than* the increase in autonomous expenditure. The multiplier is greater than 1.

Initially, when autonomous expenditure increases, aggregate planned expenditure exceeds real GDP. As a result, inventories decrease. Firms respond by increasing production so as to restore their inventories to the target level. As production increases, so does real GDP. With a higher level of real GDP, *induced expenditure* increases. Equilibrium expenditure increases by the sum of the initial increase in autonomous expenditure and the increase in induced expenditure. In this example, equilibrium expenditure increases by $200 billion following the increase in autonomous expenditure of $50 billion, so induced expenditure increases by $150 billion.

Although we have just analyzed the effects of an *increase* in autonomous expenditure, this analysis also applies to a decrease in autonomous expenditure. If initially the aggregate expenditure curve is AE_1, equilibrium expenditure and real GDP are $2,000 billion. A decrease in autonomous expenditure of $50 billion shifts the aggregate expenditure curve downward by

FIGURE 11.5   The Multiplier

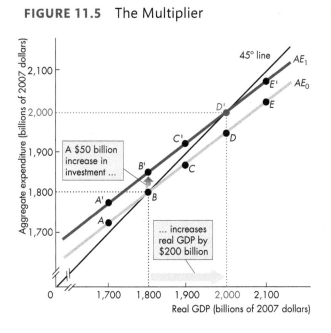

Real GDP (Y)	Aggregate planned expenditure			
	Original (AE₀)		New (AE₁)	
	(billions of 2007 dollars)			
1,700	A	1,725	A'	1,775
1,800	**B**	**1,800**	**B'**	**1,850**
1,900	C	1,875	C'	1,925
2,000	D	1,950	D'	2,000
2,100	E	2,025	E'	2,075

An increase in autonomous expenditure of $50 billion shifts the AE curve upward by $50 billion from AE_0 to AE_1. Equilibrium expenditure increases by $200 billion from $1,800 billion to $2,000 billion. The increase in equilibrium expenditure is 4 times the increase in autonomous expenditure, so the multiplier is 4.

_____ MyLab Economics Animation and Draw Graph _____

$50 billion to AE_0. Equilibrium expenditure decreases from $2,000 billion to $1,800 billion. The decrease in equilibrium expenditure ($200 billion) is larger than the decrease in autonomous expenditure that brought it about ($50 billion).

Why Is the Multiplier Greater Than 1?

We've seen that equilibrium expenditure increases by more than the increase in autonomous expenditure. This makes the multiplier greater than 1. Why does equilibrium expenditure increase by more than the increase in autonomous expenditure?

The multiplier is greater than 1 because induced expenditure increases—an increase in autonomous expenditure *induces* further increases in expenditure. For example, TransCanada will spend $5 billion to build the Prince Rupert Gas Transmission Project. This expenditure adds $5 billion directly to real GDP. But that is not the end of the story. Engineers and construction workers now have more income, and they spend part of the extra income on goods and services. Real GDP now increases by the initial $5 billion plus the extra consumption expenditure induced by the $5 billion increase in income. The producers of cars, TVs, vacation cruises, and other goods and services now have increased incomes, and they, in turn, spend part of the increase in their incomes on consumption goods and services. Additional income induces additional consumption expenditure, which creates additional income.

How big is the multiplier effect?

The Size of the Multiplier

Suppose that the economy is in a recession. Profit prospects start to look better, and firms are planning a large increase in investment. The world economy is also heading toward expansion. The question on everyone's lips is: How strong will the expansion be? This is a hard question to answer, but an important ingredient in the answer is the size of the multiplier.

The *multiplier* is the amount by which a change in autonomous expenditure is multiplied to determine the change in equilibrium expenditure that it generates. To calculate the multiplier, we divide the change in equilibrium expenditure by the change in autonomous expenditure.

Let's calculate the multiplier for the example in Fig. 11.5. Initially, equilibrium expenditure is $1,800 billion. Then autonomous expenditure increases by $50 billion, and equilibrium expenditure increases by $200 billion to $2,000 billion. Then

$$\text{Multiplier} = \frac{\text{Change in equilibrium expenditure}}{\text{Change in autonomous expenditure}}$$

$$\text{Multiplier} = \frac{\$200 \text{ billion}}{\$50 \text{ billion}} = 4.$$

The Multiplier and the Slope of the *AE* Curve

The magnitude of the multiplier depends on the slope of the *AE* curve. In Fig. 11.6, the *AE* curve in part (a) is steeper than the *AE* curve in part (b), and the multiplier is larger in part (a) than in part (b). To see why, let's do a calculation.

Aggregate expenditure and real GDP change because induced expenditure and autonomous expenditure change. The change in real GDP (ΔY) equals the change in induced expenditure (ΔN) plus the change in autonomous expenditure (ΔA). That is,

$$\Delta Y = \Delta N + \Delta A.$$

But the change in induced expenditure is determined by the change in real GDP and the slope of the *AE* curve. To see why, begin with the fact that the slope of the *AE* curve equals the "rise," ΔN, divided by the "run," ΔY. That is,

$$\text{Slope of } AE \text{ curve} = \Delta N \div \Delta Y.$$

So,

$$\Delta N = \text{Slope of } AE \text{ curve} \times \Delta Y.$$

Now, use this equation to replace ΔN in the first equation above to give

$$\Delta Y = \text{Slope of } AE \text{ curve} \times \Delta Y + \Delta A.$$

To solve for ΔY,

$$(1 - \text{Slope of } AE \text{ curve}) \times \Delta Y = \Delta A.$$

Now rearrange the equation to give

$$\Delta Y = \frac{\Delta A}{1 - \text{Slope of } AE \text{ curve}}.$$

Finally, divide both sides of this equation by ΔA to give

$$\text{Multiplier} = \frac{\Delta Y}{\Delta A} = \frac{1}{1 - \text{Slope of } AE \text{ curve}}.$$

If we use the example in Fig. 11.5, the slope of the *AE* curve is 0.75, so,

$$\text{Multiplier} = \frac{1}{1 - 0.75} = \frac{1}{0.25} = 4.$$

Where there are no income taxes and no imports, the slope of the *AE* curve equals the marginal propensity to consume (*MPC*). So,

$$\text{Multiplier} = \frac{1}{1 - MPC}.$$

But $(1 - MPC)$ equals *MPS*. So another formula is

$$\text{Multiplier} = \frac{1}{MPS}.$$

Again using the numbers in Fig. 11.5, we have

$$\text{Multiplier} = \frac{1}{0.25} = 4.$$

Because the marginal propensity to save (*MPS*) is a fraction—a number between 0 and 1—the multiplier is greater than 1.

FIGURE 11.6   The Multiplier and the Slope of the *AE* Curve

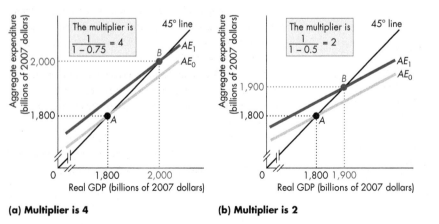

(a) Multiplier is 4

(b) Multiplier is 2

Imports and income taxes make the *AE* curve less steep and reduce the value of the multiplier. In part (a), with no imports and no income taxes, the slope of the *AE* curve is 0.75 (the marginal propensity to consume) and the multiplier is 4.

But with imports and income taxes, the slope of the *AE* curve is less than the marginal propensity to consume. In part (b), the slope of the *AE* curve is 0.5. In this case, the multiplier is 2.

MyLab Economics Animation

Imports and Income Taxes

Imports and income taxes influence the size of the multiplier and make it smaller than it otherwise would be.

To see why imports make the multiplier smaller, think about what happens following an increase in investment. The increase in investment increases real GDP, which in turn increases consumption expenditure. But part of the increase in expenditure is on imported goods and services. Only expenditure on Canadian-produced goods and services increases Canadian real GDP. The larger the marginal propensity to import, the smaller is the change in Canadian real GDP. The Mathematical Note on pp. 288–291 shows the effects of imports and income taxes on the multiplier.

Income taxes also make the multiplier smaller than it otherwise would be. Again, think about what happens following an increase in investment. The increase in investment increases real GDP. Income tax payments increase, so disposable income increases by less than the increase in real GDP and consumption expenditure increases by less than it would if taxes had not changed. The larger the income tax rate, the smaller is the change in real GDP.

The marginal propensity to import and the income tax rate together with the marginal propensity to consume determine the multiplier. And their combined influence determines the slope of the *AE* curve.

Over time, the value of the multiplier changes as tax rates change and as the marginal propensity to consume and the marginal propensity to import change. These ongoing changes make the multiplier hard to predict. But they do not change the fundamental fact that an initial change in autonomous expenditure leads to a magnified change in aggregate expenditure and real GDP.

The Multiplier Process

The multiplier effect isn't a one-shot event. It is a process that plays out over a few months. Figure 11.7 illustrates the multiplier process. Autonomous expenditure increases by $50 billion and real GDP increases by $50 billion (the green bar in round 1). This increase in real GDP increases induced expenditure in round 2. With the slope of the *AE* curve equal to 0.75, induced expenditure increases by 0.75 times the increase in real GDP, so the increase in real GDP of $50 billion induces a further

increase in expenditure of $37.5 billion. This change in induced expenditure (the green bar in round 2) when added to the previous increase in expenditure (the blue bar in round 2) increases real GDP by $87.5 billion. The round 2 increase in real GDP induces a round 3 increase in induced expenditure. The process repeats through successive rounds. Each increase in real GDP is 0.75 times the previous increase and eventually real GDP increases by $200 billion.

FIGURE 11.7   The Multiplier Process

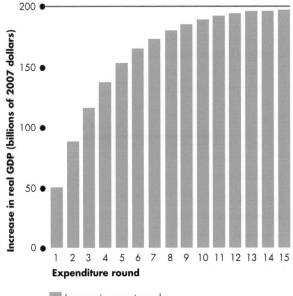

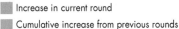

■ Increase in current round
■ Cumulative increase from previous rounds

Autonomous expenditure increases by $50 billion. In round 1, real GDP increases by the same amount. With the slope of the *AE* curve equal to 0.75, each additional dollar of real GDP induces an additional 0.75 of a dollar of induced expenditure. The increase in real GDP in round 1 increases induced expenditure by $37.5 billion in round 2. At the end of round 2, real GDP has increased by $87.5 billion.

The extra $37.5 billion of real GDP in round 2 brings a further increase in induced expenditure of $28.1 billion in round 3. At the end of round 3, real GDP has increased by $115.6 billion.

This process continues with real GDP increasing by ever-smaller amounts. When the process comes to an end, real GDP has increased by a total of $200 billion.

ECONOMICS IN ACTION

The Multiplier in the Great Depression

The aggregate expenditure model and its multiplier were developed during the 1930s by John Maynard Keynes to understand the most traumatic event in economic history, the *Great Depression*.

In 1929, the Canadian and global economies were booming. Canadian real GDP and real GDP per person had never been higher. By 1933, real GDP had fallen to 67 percent of its 1929 level and more than a quarter of the labour force was unemployed.

The table below shows the GDP numbers and components of aggregate expenditure in 1929 and 1933.

Autonomous expenditure collapsed as investment fell from $17 billion to $3 billion and exports fell by $3 billion. Government expenditure held steady.

The figure uses the *AE* model to illustrate the Great Depression. In 1929, with autonomous expenditure of $63 billion, the *AE* curve was AE_{29}. Equilibrium expenditure and real GDP were $104 billion.

By 1933, autonomous expenditure had fallen by $17 billion to $46 billion and the *AE* curve had shifted downward to AE_{33}. Equilibrium expenditure and real GDP had fallen to $76 billion.

The decrease in autonomous expenditure of $17 billion brought a decrease in real GDP of $28 billion. The multiplier was $28/$17 = 1.6. The slope of the *AE* curve is 0.39—the fall in induced expenditure, $11 billion, divided by the fall in real GDP, $28 billion. The multiplier formula, 1/(1 − Slope of *AE* curve), delivers a multiplier equal to 1.6.

	1929	1933
	(billions of 1929 dollars)	
Induced consumption	47	34
Induced imports	−6	−4
Induced expenditure	41	30
Autonomous consumption	30	30
Investment	17	3
Government expenditure	10	10
Exports	6	3
Autonomous expenditure	63	46
GDP	**104**	**76**

Source of data: Bureau of Economic Analysis.

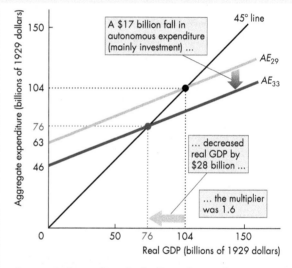

Aggregate Expenditure in the Great Depression

Business Cycle Turning Points

At business cycle turning points, the economy moves from expansion to recession or from recession to expansion. Economists understand these turning points as seismologists understand earthquakes. They know quite a lot about the forces and mechanisms that produce them, but they can't predict them. The forces that bring business cycle turning points are the swings in autonomous expenditure, such as investment and exports. The multiplier that you've just studied is the mechanism that gives momentum to the economy's new direction.

◆ REVIEW QUIZ

1 What is the multiplier? What does it determine? Why does it matter?
2 How do the marginal propensity to consume, the marginal propensity to import, and the income tax rate influence the multiplier?
3 How do fluctuations in autonomous expenditure influence real GDP?

Work these questions in Study Plan 11.3 and get instant feedback.   MyLab Economics

The Multiplier and the Price Level

We have just considered adjustments in spending that occur in the very short run when the price level is fixed. In this time frame, the economy's cobblestones, which are changes in investment and exports, are not smoothed by shock absorbers like those on a limousine. Instead, they are amplified like a rock singer's voice. But these outcomes occur only when the price level is fixed. We now investigate what happens after a long enough time lapse for the price level to change.

Adjusting Quantities and Prices

When firms can't keep up with sales and their inventories fall below target, they increase production, but at some point, they raise their prices. Similarly, when firms find unwanted inventories piling up, they decrease production, but eventually they cut their prices. So far, we've studied the macroeconomic consequences of firms changing their production levels when their sales change, but we haven't looked at the effects of price changes. When individual firms change their prices, the economy's price level changes.

To study the simultaneous determination of real GDP and the price level, we use the *AS-AD model*, which is explained in Chapter 10. But to understand how aggregate demand adjusts, we need to work out the connection between the *AS-AD* model and the aggregate expenditure model that we've used in this chapter. The key to understanding the relationship between these two models is the distinction between aggregate *expenditure* and aggregate *demand* and the related distinction between the aggregate *expenditure curve* and the aggregate *demand curve*.

Aggregate Expenditure and Aggregate Demand

The aggregate expenditure curve is the relationship between the aggregate planned expenditure and real GDP, all other influences on aggregate planned expenditure remaining the same. The aggregate demand curve is the relationship between the aggregate quantity of goods and services demanded and the price level, all other influences on aggregate demand remaining the same. Let's explore the links between these two relationships.

Deriving the Aggregate Demand Curve

When the price level changes, aggregate planned expenditure changes and the quantity of real GDP demanded changes. The aggregate demand curve slopes downward. Why? There are two main reasons:

- Wealth effect
- Substitution effects

Wealth Effect Other things remaining the same, the higher the price level, the smaller is the purchasing power of wealth. For example, suppose you have $100 in the bank and the price level is 105. If the price level rises to 125, your $100 buys fewer goods and services. You are less wealthy. With less wealth, you will probably want to try to spend a bit less and save a bit more. The higher the price level, other things remaining the same, the lower is aggregate planned expenditure.

Substitution Effects For a given expected future price level, a rise in the price level today makes current goods and services more expensive relative to future goods and services and results in a delay in purchases—an *intertemporal substitution*. A rise in the Canadian price level, other things remaining the same, makes Canadian-produced goods and services more expensive relative to foreign-produced goods and services. As a result, Canadian imports increase and Canadian exports decrease—an *international substitution*.

When the price level rises, each of these effects reduces aggregate planned expenditure at each level of real GDP. As a result, when the price level *rises*, the aggregate expenditure curve shifts *downward*. A fall in the price level has the opposite effect. When the price level *falls*, the aggregate expenditure curve shifts *upward*.

Figure 11.8(a) shows the shifts of the *AE* curve. When the price level is 110, the aggregate expenditure curve is AE_0, which intersects the 45° line at point *B*. Equilibrium expenditure is $1,800 billion. If the price level *rises* to 130, the aggregate expenditure curve shifts *downward* to AE_1, which intersects the 45° line at point *A*. Equilibrium expenditure decreases to $1,700 billion. If the price level *falls* to 90, the aggregate expenditure curve shifts *upward* to AE_2, which intersects the 45° line at point *C*. Equilibrium expenditure increases to $1,900 billion.

We've just seen that when the price level changes, other things remaining the same, the aggregate expenditure curve *shifts* and the equilibrium expenditure changes. But when the price level changes and other things remain the same, there is a *movement along* the aggregate demand curve.

Figure 11.8(b) shows the movements along the aggregate demand curve. At a price level of 110, the aggregate quantity of goods and services demanded is $1,800 billion—point B on the AD curve. If the price level rises from 110 to 130, the aggregate quantity of goods and services demanded decreases to $1,700 billion and there is a movement up along the aggregate demand curve from point B to point A. If the price level falls from 110 to 90, the aggregate quantity of goods and services demanded increases to $1,900 billion and there is a movement down along the aggregate demand curve to point C.

Each point on the aggregate demand curve corresponds to a point of equilibrium expenditure. The equilibrium expenditure points A, B, and C in Fig. 11.8(a) correspond to the points A, B, and C on the aggregate demand curve in Fig. 11.8(b).

Changes in Aggregate Expenditure and Aggregate Demand

When any influence on aggregate planned expenditure other than the price level changes, both the aggregate expenditure curve and the aggregate demand curve shift. For example, an increase in investment or exports increases both aggregate planned expenditure and aggregate demand and shifts both the AE curve and the AD curve. Figure 11.9 illustrates the effect of such an increase.

Initially, the aggregate expenditure curve is AE_0 in part (a) and the aggregate demand curve is AD_0 in part (b). The price level is 110 and real GDP is $1,800 billion. The economy is at point A in both parts of Fig. 11.9. Now suppose that investment increases by $100 billion. At a constant price level of 110, the aggregate expenditure curve shifts upward to AE_1. This curve intersects the 45° line at an equilibrium expenditure of $2,000 billion (point B). This equilibrium expenditure of $2,000 billion is the aggregate quantity of goods and services demanded at a price level of 110, as shown by point B in part (b). Point B lies on a new aggregate demand curve. The aggregate demand curve has shifted rightward to AD_1 to pass through point B.

But how do we know by how much the AD curve shifts? The multiplier determines the answer. The

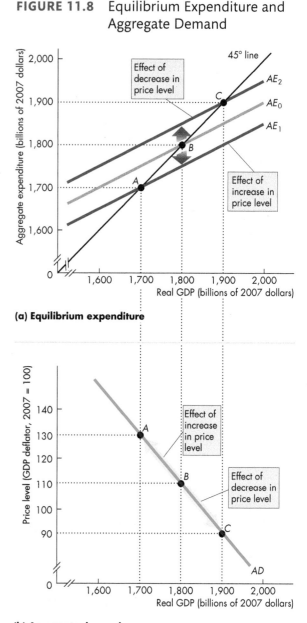

FIGURE 11.8 Equilibrium Expenditure and Aggregate Demand

(a) Equilibrium expenditure

(b) Aggregate demand

A change in the price level *shifts* the *AE* curve and results in a *movement along* the *AD* curve. When the price level is 110, the *AE* curve is AE_0. Equilibrium expenditure is $1,800 billion at point *B*. A rise in the price level from 110 to 130 shifts the *AE* curve downward to AE_1. Equilibrium expenditure decreases to $1,700 billion at point *A*. A fall in the price level from 110 to 90 shifts the *AE* curve upward to AE_2. Equilibrium expenditure increases to $1,900 billion at point *C*. Points *A*, *B*, and *C* on the *AD* curve in part (b) correspond to the equilibrium expenditure points *A*, *B*, and *C* in part (a).

 MyLab Economics Animation and Draw Graph

FIGURE 11.9   A Change in Aggregate Demand

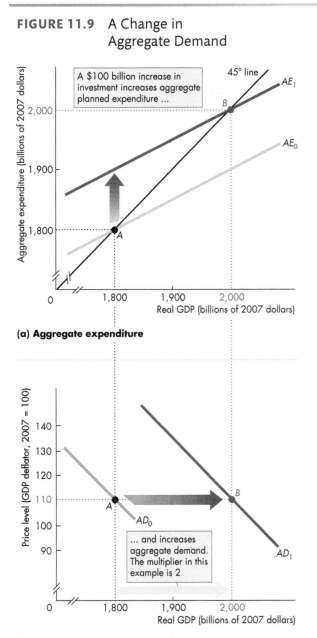

(a) Aggregate expenditure

(b) Aggregate demand

An increase in autonomous expenditure increases aggregate demand. The price level is 110. When the aggregate expenditure curve is AE_0 in part (a), the aggregate demand curve is AD_0 in part (b). The economy is at point A in both parts of the figure. An increase in autonomous expenditure shifts the AE curve upward to AE_1. In the new equilibrium, real GDP is $2,000 billion at point B in part (a). Because the quantity of real GDP demanded at a price level of 110 increases from $1,800 billion to $2,000 billion, the AD curve shifts rightward to AD_1.

larger the multiplier, the larger is the shift in the aggregate demand curve that results from a given change in autonomous expenditure. In this example, the multiplier is 2. A $100 billion increase in investment produces a $200 billion increase in the aggregate quantity of goods and services demanded at each price level. That is, a $100 billion increase in autonomous expenditure shifts the aggregate demand curve rightward by $200 billion.

A decrease in autonomous expenditure shifts the aggregate expenditure curve downward and shifts the aggregate demand curve leftward. You can see these effects by reversing the change that we've just described. If the economy is initially at point B on the aggregate expenditure curve AE_1 and on the aggregate demand curve AD_1, a decrease in autonomous expenditure shifts the aggregate expenditure curve downward to AE_0. The aggregate quantity of goods and services demanded decreases from $2,000 billion to $1,800 billion, and the aggregate demand curve shifts leftward to AD_0.

Let's summarize what we have just discovered:

> If some factor other than a change in the price level increases autonomous expenditure, then the AE curve shifts upward and the AD curve shifts rightward. The size of the AD curve shift equals the change in autonomous expenditure multiplied by the multiplier.

Equilibrium Real GDP and the Price Level

In Chapter 10, we learned that aggregate demand and short-run aggregate supply determine equilibrium real GDP and the price level. We've now put aggregate demand under a more powerful microscope and have discovered that a change in investment (or in any component of autonomous expenditure) changes aggregate demand and shifts the aggregate demand curve. The magnitude of the shift depends on the multiplier. But whether a change in autonomous expenditure results ultimately in a change in real GDP, a change in the price level, or a combination of the two depends on aggregate supply. There are two time frames to consider: the short run and the long run. First we'll see what happens in the short run.

An Increase in Aggregate Demand in the Short Run

Figure 11.10 describes the economy. Initially, in part (a), the aggregate expenditure curve is AE_0 and equilibrium expenditure is $1,800 billion—point A. In part (b), aggregate demand is AD_0 and the short-run aggregate supply curve is SAS. (Chapter 10, pp. 245–246, explains the SAS curve.) Equilibrium is at point A in part (b), where the aggregate demand and short-run aggregate supply curves intersect. The price level is 110, and real GDP is $1,800 billion.

Now suppose that investment increases by $100 billion. With the price level fixed at 110, the aggregate expenditure curve shifts upward to AE_1. Equilibrium expenditure increases to $2,000 billion—point B in part (a). In part (b), the aggregate demand curve shifts rightward by $200 billion, from AD_0 to AD_1. How far the aggregate demand curve shifts is determined by the multiplier when the price level is fixed.

But with this new aggregate demand curve, the price level does *not* remain fixed. The price level rises, and as it does, the aggregate expenditure curve shifts downward. The short-run equilibrium occurs when the aggregate expenditure curve has shifted downward to AE_2 and the new aggregate demand curve, AD_1, intersects the short-run aggregate supply curve at point C in both part (a) and part (b). Real GDP is $1,930 billion, and the price level is 123.

When price level effects are taken into account, the increase in investment still has a multiplier effect on real GDP, but the multiplier is smaller than it would be if the price level were fixed. The steeper the slope of the short-run aggregate supply curve, the larger is the increase in the price level and the smaller is the multiplier effect on real GDP.

An Increase in Aggregate Demand in the Long Run

Figure 11.11 illustrates the long-run effect of an increase in aggregate demand. In the long run, real GDP equals potential GDP and there is full employment. Potential GDP is $1,800 billion, and the long-run aggregate supply curve is LAS. Initially, the economy is at point A in parts (a) and (b).

Investment increases by $100 billion. In Fig. 11.11, the aggregate expenditure curve shifts to AE_1 and the aggregate demand curve shifts to AD_1. With no change in the price level, the economy would move to point B and real GDP would increase to $2,000 billion. But in the short run, the price level rises to 123 and real GDP increases to only $1,930 billion. With the higher price level, the AE curve shifts downward from AE_1 to AE_2. The economy is now in a short-run equilibrium at point C in both part (a) and part (b).

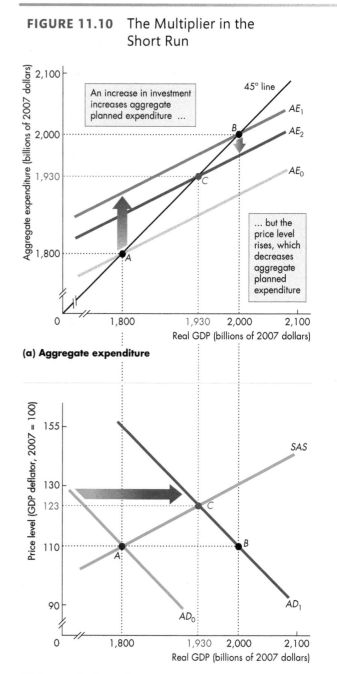

FIGURE 11.10   The Multiplier in the Short Run

An increase in investment increases aggregate planned expenditure ...

... but the price level rises, which decreases aggregate planned expenditure

(a) Aggregate expenditure

(b) Aggregate demand

An increase in investment shifts the AE curve from AE_0 to AE_1 and the AD curve from AD_0 to AD_1. The price level rises, and the higher price level shifts the AE curve downward from AE_1 to AE_2. The economy moves to point C in both parts of the figure. In the short run, when prices are flexible, the multiplier effect is smaller than when the price level is fixed.

MyLab Economics Animation

FIGURE 11.11   The Multiplier in the Long Run

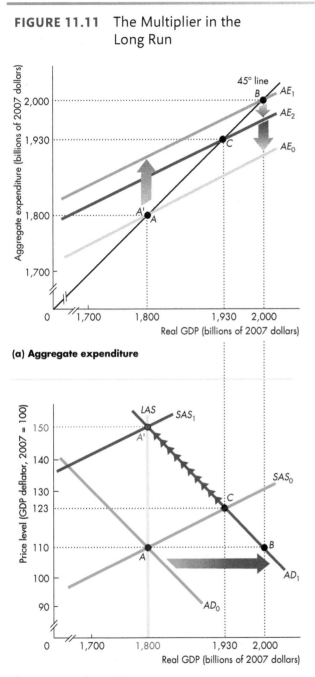

(a) Aggregate expenditure

(b) Aggregate demand

Starting from point A, an increase in investment shifts the AE curve upward to AE_1 and the AD curve rightward to AD_1. In the short run, the economy is at point C and at an above full-employment equilibrium. In the long run, the money wage rate rises and the SAS curve shifts leftward toward SAS_1. As the price level rises, the AE curve shifts downward. In the long run, the economy moves to point A' and the multiplier is zero.

MyLab Economics Animation

Real GDP now exceeds potential GDP. The labour force is more than fully employed, and in the long run shortages of labour increase the money wage rate. The higher money wage rate increases firms' costs, which decreases short-run aggregate supply and the SAS curve shifts leftward toward SAS_1. The price level rises above 123 and real GDP decreases. There is a movement up along AD_1, and the AE curve shifts downward from AE_2 toward AE_0. When the money wage rate and the price level have increased by the same percentage, real GDP is again equal to potential GDP and the economy is at point A'. In the long run, the multiplier is zero.

REVIEW QUIZ

1 How does a change in the price level influence the AE curve and the AD curve?

2 If autonomous expenditure increases with no change in the price level, what happens to the AE curve and the AD curve? Which curve shifts by an amount that is determined by the multiplier and why?

3 How does an increase in autonomous expenditure change real GDP in the short run? Does real GDP change by the same amount as the change in aggregate demand? Explain why or why not.

4 How does real GDP change in the long run when autonomous expenditure increases? Does real GDP change by the same amount as the change in aggregate demand? Why or why not?

Work these questions in Study Plan 11.4 and get instant feedback.   MyLab Economics

◆ You are now ready to build on what you've learned about aggregate expenditure fluctuations. We'll study the business cycle and the roles of fiscal policy and monetary policy in smoothing the business cycle while achieving price stability and sustained economic growth.

In Chapter 12, we study the Canadian business cycle and inflation; and in Chapters 13 and 14, we study fiscal policy and monetary policy, respectively. But before you leave the current topic, look at *Economics in the News* on pp. 286–287 and see the aggregate expenditure model in action in the Canadian economy during 2017.

Expenditure Changes in the 2017 Expansion

Gross Domestic Product, Income and Expenditure, Second Quarter 2017

The Daily
August 31, 2017

Real gross domestic product (GDP) rose 1.1 percent in the second quarter, following a 0.9 percent gain in the first quarter. . . .

Household final consumption expenditure and exports of goods were important contributors to second quarter growth. . . .

Household spending on goods advanced 1.9 percent, with outlays on durables, semi-durables and non-durables all increasing. Outlays on services rose 0.5 percent. Overall, household final consumption expenditure advanced 1.1 percent in the second quarter, after increasing 1.2 percent the previous quarter.

Growth in export volumes accelerated to 2.3 percent following a 0.4 percent gain in the first quarter. Exports of goods rose 2.8 percent, with energy products (+9.2 percent) contributing the most to the increase. Exports of services edged down 0.1 percent as commercial services fell 0.6 percent.

Imports rose 1.8 percent, about half the pace of the previous quarter. Imports of goods increased 2.5 percent while those of services declined 1.0 percent.

Business gross fixed capital formation slowed to 0.5 percent growth, following a 3.1 percent increase in the first quarter. The deceleration was mostly attributable to lower investment in housing (–1.2 percent). Business investment in non-residential structures rose 2.4 percent after increasing 1.0 percent in the first quarter.

Businesses accumulated another $11.5 billion in inventories in the second quarter, after adding $10.5 billion to their stocks in the first. Despite the strong inventory accumulation, the stock-to-sales ratio declined 0.8 percent.

Expressed at an annualized rate, real GDP rose 4.5 percent in the second quarter. In comparison, real GDP in the United States grew 3.0 percent. . . .

ESSENCE OF THE STORY

- Real GDP grew at an annual rate of 4.5 percent during the second quarter of 2017.

- The increase was due mainly to increases in consumer expenditure and exports.

- Business investment growth slowed.

- Business inventories increased.

ECONOMIC ANALYSIS

- Statistics Canada reports that real GDP increased in the second quarter of 2017 and identifies consumer expenditure and exports as being mainly responsible. Business inventories also increased.

- Table 1 shows the real GDP and aggregate expenditure numbers for the first two quarters of 2017 along with the change in the second quarter.

- You can see that exports increased, which means that much of the increase was autonomous expenditure rather than induced expenditure.

- The increase in consumption expenditure—mainly induced expenditure—was also large.

- The role played by inventories depends on whether their change was planned or unplanned.

- Figure 1 shows the changes in inventories and real GDP. The two variables fluctuate together at some times and move in opposition at other times.

- Most likely, inventories increased by less than planned, and you can see why in Fig. 2, which interprets the data for 2017 using the aggregate expenditure model.

- In 2017 Q1, the AE curve was AE_0 and real GDP was $1,829 billion, which we assume to be equilibrium expenditure at point A.

- The slope of the AE curve is 0.5 (an assumption).

- In Fig. 2(a), an increase in autonomous expenditure shifted the AE curve upward to AE_1 and aggregate planned expenditure temporarily exceeded real GDP at point B.

- In Fig 2(b), an unplanned decrease in inventories occurred as real GDP increased toward its second quarter equilibrium.

- When real GDP reached its second quarter equilibrium at point C, unplanned inventory changes had returned to zero.

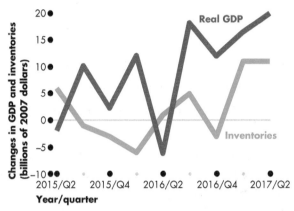

Figure 1 Inventories and Real GDP

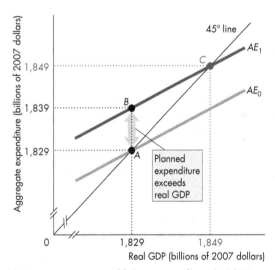

(a) Convergence to equilibrium expenditure in 2017

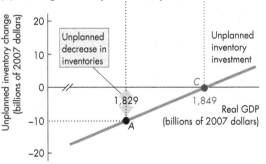

(b) Unplanned inventory change in 2017

Figure 2 Equilibrium Expenditure in 2017

Table 1 The Components of Aggregate Expenditure

Item	2017 Q1	2017 Q2	Change
	(billions of 2007 dollars)		
Consumption expenditure	1,074.1	1,086.1	11.9
Investment	322.6	324.4	1.8
Government expenditure	416.8	419.1	2.3
Exports	584.7	598.3	13.6
Imports	583.4	593.9	10.5
Real GDP*	**1,829.3**	**1,849.3**	**20.0**

*Chained-dollar real variables are calculated for each expenditure component independently of chained-dollar real GDP and the components don't exactly sum to real GDP.

MATHEMATICAL NOTE

The Algebra of the Keynesian Model

This mathematical note derives formulas for equilibrium expenditure and the multipliers when the price level is fixed. The variables are:

- Aggregate planned expenditure, AE
- Real GDP, Y
- Consumption expenditure, C
- Disposable income, YD
- Investment, I
- Government expenditure, G
- Exports, X
- Imports, M
- Net taxes, T
- Autonomous consumption expenditure, a
- Autonomous taxes, T_a
- Marginal propensity to consume, b
- Marginal propensity to import, m
- Marginal tax rate, t
- Autonomous expenditure, A

Aggregate Expenditure

Aggregate planned expenditure (AE) is the sum of the planned amounts of consumption expenditure (C), investment (I), government expenditure (G), and exports (X) minus the planned amount of imports (M). That is,

$$AE = C + I + G + X - M.$$

Consumption Function Consumption expenditure (C) depends on disposable income (YD), and we write the consumption function as

$$C = a + bYD.$$

Disposable income (YD) equals real GDP minus net taxes ($Y - T$). So if we replace YD with ($Y - T$), the consumption function becomes

$$C = a + b(Y - T).$$

Net taxes, T, equal autonomous taxes (that are independent of income), T_a, plus induced taxes (that vary with income), tY.

So we can write net taxes as

$$T = T_a + tY.$$

Use this last equation to replace T in the consumption function. The consumption function becomes

$$C = a - bT_a + b(1 - t)Y.$$

This equation describes consumption expenditure as a function of real GDP.

Import Function Imports depend on real GDP, and the import function is

$$M = mY.$$

Aggregate Expenditure Curve Use the consumption function and the import function to replace C and M in the AE equation. That is,

$$AE = a - bT_a + b(1 - t)Y + I + G + X - mY.$$

Collect the terms that involve Y on the right side of the equation to obtain

$$AE = (a - bT_a + I + G + X) + [b(1 - t) - m]Y.$$

Autonomous expenditure (A) is ($a - bT_a + I + G + X$), and the slope of the AE curve is $[b(1 - t) - m]$. So the equation for the AE curve, which is shown in Fig. 1, is

$$AE = A + [b(1 - t) - m]Y.$$

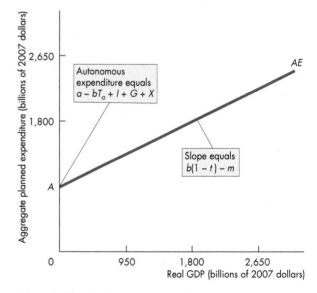

Figure 1 The AE Curve

Equilibrium Expenditure

Equilibrium expenditure occurs when aggregate planned expenditure (AE) equals real GDP (Y). That is,

$$AE = Y.$$

In Fig. 2, the scales of the x-axis (real GDP) and the y-axis (aggregate planned expenditure) are identical, so the 45° line shows the points at which aggregate planned expenditure equals real GDP.

Figure 2 shows the point of equilibrium expenditure at the intersection of the AE curve and the 45° line.

To calculate equilibrium expenditure, solve the equations for the AE curve and the 45° line for the two unknown quantities AE and Y. So starting with

$$AE = A + [\,b(1 - t) - m\,]Y$$

$$AE = Y,$$

replace AE with Y in the AE equation to obtain

$$Y = A + [\,b(1 - t) - m\,]Y.$$

The solution for Y is

$$Y = \frac{1}{1 - [\,b(1 - t) - m\,]}A.$$

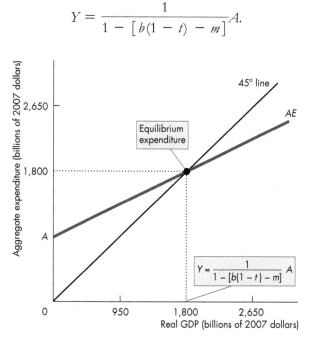

Figure 2 Equilibrium Expenditure

The Multiplier

The *multiplier* equals the change in equilibrium expenditure and real GDP (Y) that results from a change in autonomous expenditure (A) divided by the change in autonomous expenditure.

A change in autonomous expenditure (ΔA) changes equilibrium expenditure and real GDP by

$$\Delta Y = \frac{1}{1 - [\,b(1 - t) - m\,]}\Delta A.$$

$$\text{Multiplier} = \frac{1}{1 - [\,b(1 - t) - m\,]}.$$

The size of the multiplier depends on the slope of the AE curve, $b(1 - t) - m$. The larger the slope, the larger is the multiplier. So the multiplier is larger,

- The greater the marginal propensity to consume (b)
- The smaller the marginal tax rate (t)
- The smaller the marginal propensity to import (m)

An economy with no imports and no income taxes has $m = 0$ and $t = 0$. In this special case, the multiplier equals $1/(1 - b)$. If b is 0.75, then the multiplier is 4, as shown in Fig. 3.

In an economy with imports and income taxes, if $b = 0.75$, $t = 0.2$, and $m = 0.1$, the multiplier equals 1 divided by $(1 - [0.75(1 - 0.2) - 0.1])$, which equals 2. Make up some alternative examples to show the effects of b, t, and m on the multiplier.

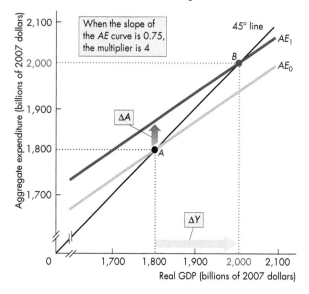

Figure 3 The Multiplier

Government Expenditure Multiplier

The **government expenditure multiplier** equals the change in equilibrium expenditure and real GDP (Y) that results from a change in government expenditure (G) divided by the change in government expenditure. Because autonomous expenditure is equal to

$$A = a - bT_a + I + G + X,$$

the change in autonomous expenditure equals the change in government expenditure. That is,

$$\Delta A = \Delta G.$$

You can see from the solution for equilibrium expenditure Y that

$$\Delta Y = \frac{1}{1 - [b(1 - t) - m]} \Delta G.$$

The government expenditure multiplier equals

$$\frac{1}{1 - [b(1 - t) - m]}.$$

In an economy in which $t = 0$ and $m = 0$, the government expenditure multiplier is $1/(1 - b)$. With $b = 0.75$, the government expenditure multiplier is 4, as Fig. 4 shows. Make up some examples and use the above formula to show how b, m, and t influence the government expenditure multiplier.

Autonomous Tax Multiplier

The **autonomous tax multiplier** equals the change in equilibrium expenditure and real GDP (Y) that results from a change in autonomous taxes (T_a) divided by the change in autonomous taxes. Because autonomous expenditure is equal to

$$A = a - bT_a + I + G + X,$$

the change in autonomous expenditure equals *minus* b multiplied by the change in autonomous taxes. That is,

$$\Delta A = -b\Delta T_a.$$

You can see from the solution for equilibrium expenditure Y that

$$\Delta Y = \frac{-b}{1 - [b(1 - t) - m]} \Delta T_a.$$

The autonomous tax multiplier equals

$$\frac{-b}{1 - [b(1 - t) - m]}.$$

In an economy in which $t = 0$ and $m = 0$, the autonomous tax multiplier is $-b/(1 - b)$. In this special case, with $b = 0.75$, the autonomous tax multiplier equals -3, as Fig. 5 shows. Make up some examples and use the above formula to show how b, m, and t influence the autonomous tax multiplier.

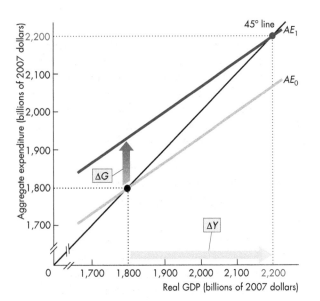

Figure 4 Government Expenditure Multiplier

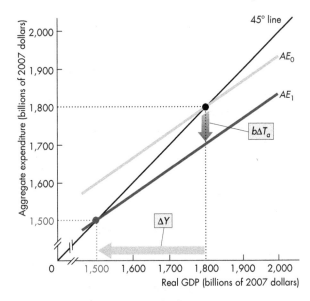

Figure 5 Autonomous Tax Multiplier

Balanced Budget Multiplier

The **balanced budget multiplier** equals the change in equilibrium expenditure and real GDP (Y) that results from equal changes in government expenditure and autonomous taxes divided by the change in government expenditure. Because government expenditure and autonomous taxes change by the same amount, the budget balance does not change.

The change in equilibrium expenditure that results from the change in government expenditure is

$$\Delta Y = \frac{1}{1 - [b(1 - t) - m]} \Delta G.$$

And the change in equilibrium expenditure that results from the change in autonomous taxes is

$$\Delta Y = \frac{-b}{1 - [b(1 - t) - m]} \Delta T_a.$$

So the change in equilibrium expenditure resulting from the changes in government expenditure and autonomous taxes is

$$\Delta Y = \frac{1}{1 - [b(1 - t) - m]} \Delta G +$$

$$\frac{-b}{1 - [b(1 - t) - m]} \Delta T_a.$$

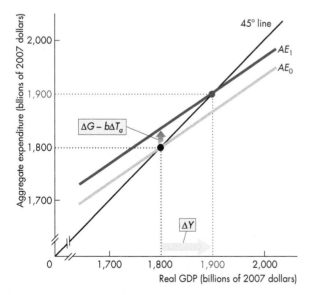

Figure 6 Balanced Budget Multiplier

Notice that

$$\frac{1}{1 - [b(1 - t) - m]}$$

is common to both terms on the right side. So we can rewrite the equation as

$$\Delta Y = \frac{1}{1 - [b(1 - t) - m]} (\Delta G - b\Delta T_a).$$

The AE curve shifts upward by $\Delta G - b\Delta T_a$ as shown in Fig. 6.

But the change in government expenditure equals the change in autonomous taxes. That is,

$$\Delta G = \Delta T_a.$$

So we can write the equation as

$$\Delta Y = \frac{1 - b}{1 - [b(1 - t) - m]} \Delta G.$$

The balanced budget multiplier equals

$$\frac{1 - b}{1 - [b(1 - t) - m]}.$$

In an economy in which $t = 0$ and $m = 0$, the balanced budget multiplier is $(1 - b)/(1 - b)$, which equals 1, as Fig. 6 shows. Make up some examples and use the above formula to show how b, m, and t influence the balanced budget multiplier.

Exercise

In an economy, autonomous consumption expenditure is $50 billion, investment is $200 billion, and government expenditure is $250 billion. The marginal propensity to consume is 0.7 and net taxes are $250 billion. Exports are $500 billion and imports are $450 billion. Assume that net taxes and imports are autonomous and the price level is fixed.

  a. What is the consumption function?

  b. What is the equation of the AE curve?

  c. Calculate equilibrium expenditure.

  d. Calculate the multiplier.

  e. If investment decreases to $150 billion, what is the change in equilibrium expenditure?

  f. Describe the process in part (e) that moves the economy to its new equilibrium expenditure.

WORKED PROBLEM

MyLab Economics Work this problem in Chapter 11 Study Plan.

You are given the following data about an economy that has a fixed price level, no imports, and no taxes:

Disposable income	Consumption expenditure
(billions of dollars per year)	
0	5
100	80
200	155
300	230
400	305

Questions

1. Calculate the marginal propensity to consume.
2. Calculate autonomous consumption expenditure.
3. Calculate saving at each level of disposable income and the marginal propensity to save.
4. Calculate the multiplier.
5. Calculate the increase in real GDP when autonomous spending increases by $5 billion. Why does real GDP increase by more than $5 billion?

Solutions

1. The marginal propensity to consume equals the fraction of an increase in disposable income that is spent on consumption.

   When disposable income increases from $100 billion to $200 billion, consumption expenditure increases from $80 billion to $155 billion. The increase in disposable income of $100 billion increases consumption expenditure by $75 billion. The marginal propensity to consume equals $75 billion ÷ $100 billion, which equals 0.75.

Key Point: The marginal propensity to consume is the fraction of an increase in disposable income that is spent on consumption.

2. Autonomous consumption expenditure is the amount of consumption expenditure when disposabale income is zero. From the table, autonomous consumption expenditure is $5 billion.

Key Point: Autonomous consumption expenditure is the amount of consumption expenditure that depends on things other than disposable income.

3. Disposable income is spent on consumption or saved.

   Saving = Disposable income − Consumption expenditure.

For example, when disposable income is $100 billion, consumption expenditure is $80 billion, so saving is $20 billion.

The table below sets out saving at each level of disposable income.

Disposable income	Saving
(billions of dollars per year)	
0	−5
100	20
200	45
300	70
400	95

The marginal propensity to save is the fraction of an increase in disposable income that is saved. When disposable income increases by $100 billion, saving increases by $25 billion, so the marginal propensity to save equals 0.25.

Key Point: The marginal propensity to consume plus the marginal propensity to save equals 1.

4. When the price level is fixed, the multiplier equals $1/(1 −$ Slope of the AE curve). With no income taxes, the slope of the AE curve equals the marginal propensity to consume (MPC), which is 0.75.

   The multiplier $= 1/(1 − 0.75) = 1/0.25 = 4$.

   Because $(1 − MPC) = MPS$, the multiplier also equals $1/MPS$.

Key Point: With a fixed price level, the multiplier equals $1/(1 − MPC)$ or $1/MPS$.

5. The increase in real GDP when the price level is fixed equals the change in autonomous spending multiplied by the multiplier. That is,

   Change in real GDP = Change in autonomous spending × Multiplier

   Change in real GDP = $5 billion × 4
   $= $20 billion.

An increase in autonomous spending increases income, which increases induced consumption, which in turn increases income. The quantity of real GDP demanded increases.

Key Point: With a fixed price level, real GDP increases by more than the increase in autonomous spending because induced consumption expenditure increases.

![SUMMARY banner]

Key Points

Fixed Prices and Expenditure Plans (pp. 268–271)

- When the price level is fixed, expenditure plans determine real GDP.
- Consumption expenditure is determined by disposable income, and the marginal propensity to consume (*MPC*) determines the change in consumption expenditure brought about by a change in disposable income. Real GDP determines disposable income.
- Imports are determined by real GDP, and the marginal propensity to import determines the change in imports brought about by a change in real GDP.

Working Problem 1 will give you a better understanding of fixed prices and expenditure plans.

Real GDP with a Fixed Price Level (pp. 272–275)

- Aggregate *planned* expenditure depends on real GDP.
- Equilibrium expenditure occurs when aggregate planned expenditure equals actual expenditure and real GDP.

Working Problems 2 to 5 will give you a better understanding of real GDP with a fixed price level.

The Multiplier (pp. 276–280)

- The multiplier is the magnified effect of a change in autonomous expenditure on equilibrium expenditure and real GDP.

- The multiplier is determined by the slope of the *AE* curve.
- The slope of the *AE* curve is influenced by the marginal propensity to consume, the marginal propensity to import, and the income tax rate.

Working Problems 6 to 8 will give you a better understanding of the multiplier.

The Multiplier and the Price Level (pp. 281–285)

- The *AD* curve is the relationship between the quantity of real GDP demanded and the price level, other things remaining the same.
- The *AE* curve is the relationship between aggregate planned expenditure and real GDP, other things remaining the same.
- At a given price level, there is a given *AE* curve. A change in the price level changes aggregate planned expenditure and shifts the *AE* curve. A change in the price level also creates a movement along the *AD* curve.
- A change in autonomous expenditure that is not caused by a change in the price level shifts the *AE* curve and shifts the *AD* curve. The magnitude of the shift of the *AD* curve depends on the multiplier and on the change in autonomous expenditure.
- The multiplier decreases as the price level changes, and the long-run multiplier is zero.

Working Problems 9 to 14 will give you a better understanding of the multiplier and the price level.

Key Terms

Aggregate planned expenditure, 268

Autonomous expenditure, 272

Autonomous tax multiplier, 290

Balanced budget multiplier, 291

Consumption function, 268

Disposable income, 268

Equilibrium expenditure, 274

Government expenditure multiplier, 290

Induced expenditure, 272

Marginal propensity to consume, 270

Marginal propensity to import, 271

Marginal propensity to save, 270

Multiplier, 276

Saving function, 268

STUDY PLAN PROBLEMS AND APPLICATIONS

MyLab Economics Work Problems 1 to 15 in Chapter 11 Study Plan and get instant feedback.

Fixed Prices and Expenditure Plans (Study Plan 11.1)

1. In an economy, when income increases from $400 billion to $500 billion, consumption expenditure increases from $420 billion to $500 billion. Calculate the marginal propensity to consume, the change in saving, and the marginal propensity to save.

Real GDP with a Fixed Price Level (Study Plan 11.2)

Use the following figure to work Problems 2 and 3. The figure illustrates the components of aggregate planned expenditure on Turtle Island. Turtle Island has no imports or exports, no incomes taxes, and the price level is fixed.

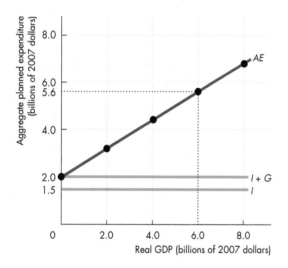

2. Calculate autonomous expenditure and the marginal propensity to consume.

3. a. What is aggregate planned expenditure when real GDP is $6 billion?

   b. If real GDP is $4 billion, what is happening to inventories?

   c. If real GDP is $6 billion, what is happening to inventories?

4. Explain why induced consumption expenditure differs from autonomous consumption expenditure. Why isn't all consumption expenditure induced expenditure?

5. Explain how an increase in business investment at a constant price level changes equilibrium expenditure.

The Multiplier (Study Plan 11.3)

Use the following data to work Problems 6 and 7.
An economy has a fixed price level, no imports, and no income taxes. *MPC* is 0.80, and real GDP is $150 billion. Businesses increase investment by $5 billion.

6. Calculate the multiplier and the change in real GDP.

7. Calculate the new real GDP and explain why real GDP increases by more than $5 billion.

8. An economy has a fixed price level, no imports, and no income taxes. An increase in autonomous expenditure of $200 billion increases equilibrium expenditure by $800 billion. Calculate the multiplier and explain what happens to the multiplier if an income tax is introduced.

The Multiplier and the Price Level (Study Plan 11.4)

9. Explain the link between equilibrium expenditure and the quantity of real GDP demanded.

Use the following data to work Problems 10 to 14.

Suppose that the economy is at full employment, the price level is 100, and the multiplier is 2. Investment increases by $100 billion.

10. What is the change in equilibrium expenditure if the price level remains at 100?

11. a. What is the immediate change in the quantity of real GDP demanded?

    b. In the short run, does real GDP increase by more than, less than, or the same amount as the immediate change in the quantity of real GDP demanded?

12. In the short run, does the price level remain at 100? Explain why or why not.

13. a. Compare the change in real GDP in the long run with the increase in investment.

    b. Explain how the price level changes in the long run.

14. Are the values of the multipliers in the short run and the long run larger or smaller than 2?

Mathematical Note (Study Plan 11.MN)

15. Use the data in the Worked Problem on p. 292 to calculate the change in equilibrium expenditure when investment decreases by $50 billion.

ADDITIONAL PROBLEMS AND APPLICATIONS

MyLab Economics You can work these problems in Homework or Test if assigned by your instructor.

Fixed Prices and Expenditure Plans

Use the following data to work Problems 16 and 17.
You are given the following information for the economy of Australia:

Disposable income	Saving
(billions of dollars per year)	
0	0
100	25
200	50
300	75
400	100

16. Calculate the marginal propensity to save.
17. Calculate consumption at each level of disposable income. Calculate the marginal propensity to consume.

Use the following information to work Problems 18 to 20.

Canadians' Wealth Rises

Canadian net saving in the first quarter of 2017 was $22 billion. Holdings of financial assets increased by $162 billion and the value of shares in corporations increased by $113 billion.

Source of data: Statistics Canada,
CANSIM Table 378-0119

18. Explain why higher share prices are equivalent to saving.
19. Explain how a rise in household financial assets would be expected to influence consumption expenditure and saving and how the consumption function and the saving function would change.
20. Draw a graph to illustrate how a rise in household financial assets would change the consumption function and the saving function.

Real GDP with a Fixed Price Level

Use the spreadsheet in the next column to work Problems 21 and 22.

The spreadsheet lists real GDP (Y) and the components of aggregate planned expenditure in billions of dollars.

21. Calculate autonomous expenditure. Calculate the marginal propensity to consume.

	A	B	C	D	E	F	G
1		Y	C	I	G	X	M
2	A	100	110	50	60	60	15
3	B	200	170	50	60	60	30
4	C	300	230	50	60	60	45
5	D	400	290	50	60	60	60
6	E	500	350	50	60	60	75
7	F	600	410	50	60	60	90

22. a. What is aggregate planned expenditure when real GDP is $200 billion?
    b. If real GDP is $200 billion, explain the process that moves the economy toward equilibrium expenditure.
    c. If real GDP is $500 billion, explain the process that moves the economy toward equilibrium expenditure.

23. **U.S. Wholesale Inventories Post Biggest Gain in Six Months**

The U.S. Commerce Department reported that wholesale inventories rose 0.7 percent in May and by 0.6 percent in June. Inventory investment had a neutral effect on second quarter GDP growth.

Source: *U.S. News and World Report*,
August 9, 2017

Explain why an increase in inventories might bolster economic growth, while a fall in inventories might be a sign of recession. In your explanation, distinguish between planned and unplanned changes in business inventories.

The Multiplier

24. **South Korea Plans $10 Billion Stimulus Package to Boost Jobs**

The government of South Korea announced a $10 billion (11.2 trillion won) fiscal stimulus package. It will increase social welfare subsidies for maternity leave and for the healthcare needs of older people. It will also create new public sector jobs.

Source: CNBC, June 4, 2017

If the slope of the *AE* curve is 0.7, calculate the immediate change in aggregate planned expenditure and the change in real GDP in the short run if the price level remains unchanged.

25. **Japan Cabinet Approves $132 Billion in Fiscal Stimulus**

Japan's government will spend $132 billion (13.5 trillion yen) on cash handouts to low-income earners and on infrastructure projects.

Source: CNBC, August 2, 2016

If Japan spends $66 billion (half the total) on cash handouts and $66 billion on infrastructure projects, which of these expenditures would have the larger effect on equilibrium expenditure, other things remaining the same?

The Multiplier and the Price Level

Use the following news item to work Problems 26 to 28.

Statistics Canada reported that in the second quarter of 2017 Canadian exports increased by $14 billion.

26. Explain and draw a graph to illustrate the effect of an increase in exports on equilibrium expenditure in the short run.

27. Explain and draw a graph to illustrate the effect of an increase in exports on equilibrium real GDP in the short run.

28. Explain and draw a graph to illustrate the effect of an increase in exports on equilibrium real GDP in the long run.

29. Compare the multiplier in the short run and the long run and explain why they are not identical.

Use the following news clip to work Problems 30 to 32.

Consumer Sentiment Rose to a Three-Month High

Consumer sentiment was up in August, helped by merchant discounts, especially from auto dealerships who received incentives from automakers Honda, General Motors, and Toyota to lower prices.

But consumers are worried about the future. They are worried about tax changes and government budget cuts that are on the horizon. Capital spending fell somewhat.

Source: Bloomberg, September 1, 2012

30. For each of the expenditures listed in the news clip, say which is part of induced expenditure and which is part of autonomous expenditure.

31. Which of the events reported in the news clip would change aggregate demand and which would change the quantity of real GDP demanded? Provide a graphical illustration of the distinction.

32. Explain and draw a graph to illustrate how increasing consumer confidence influences aggregate expenditure and aggregate demand.

33. **Japan Slides into Recession**

In Japan, consumer prices slid at a faster pace in July and industrial production unexpectedly slumped.

Source: Bloomberg, September 1, 2012

Contrast what the news clip says is happening in Japan with what is happening in Canada in Problem 30 and provide a graphical analysis of the differences.

Economics in the News

34. After you have studied *Economics in the News* on pp. 286–287, answer the following questions.
    a. If the second quarter 2017 change in inventories was a planned change, what role did it play in shifting the *AE* curve and changing equilibrium expenditure? Use a two-part figure (similar to Fig. 2 on p. 287) to answer this question.
    b. The Statistics Canada report says that an increase in consumption expenditure was the main reason why real GDP increased. How do we know that most of the increase in consumption expenditure was induced?
    c. Using the assumptions made in Fig. 2 on p. 287, what is the slope of the *AE* curve and what is the value of the autonomous expenditure multiplier?

Mathematical Note

35. In an economy with a fixed price level, autonomous spending is $20 billion and the slope of the *AE* curve is 0.6.
    a. What is the equation of the *AE* curve?
    b. Calculate equilibrium expenditure.
    c. Calculate the multiplier.
    d. Calculate the shift of the aggregate demand curve if investment increases by $1 billion.

12

THE BUSINESS CYCLE, INFLATION, AND DEFLATION

After studying this chapter, you will be able to:

◆ Explain how aggregate demand shocks and aggregate supply shocks create the business cycle

◆ Explain how demand-pull and cost-push forces bring cycles in inflation and output

◆ Explain the causes and consequences of deflation

◆ Explain the short-run and long-run tradeoffs between inflation and unemployment

We fear deflation because it brings stagnant incomes and high unemployment. And we worry about inflation because it raises our cost of living. We want low inflation, low unemployment, and rapid income growth. But can we have all these things at the same time? Or do we face a tradeoff among them? As this chapter explains, we face a tradeoff in the short run but not in the long run.

At the end of the chapter, in *Economics in the News*, we examine a stagnating European economy and the lessons it holds for Canada and other countries.

◆ The Business Cycle

The business cycle is easy to describe but hard to explain and the next peak or trough is impossible to predict. We'll look at two approaches to understanding the business cycle:

- Mainstream business cycle theory
- Real business cycle theory

Mainstream Business Cycle Theory

The mainstream business cycle theory is that potential GDP grows at a steady rate while aggregate demand grows at a fluctuating rate. Because the money wage rate is sticky, if aggregate demand grows faster than potential GDP, real GDP moves above potential GDP and an inflationary gap emerges. And if aggregate demand grows slower than potential GDP, real GDP moves below potential GDP and a recessionary gap emerges. If aggregate demand decreases, real GDP also decreases in a recession.

Figure 12.1 illustrates this business cycle theory. Initially, potential GDP is $1.2 trillion. The long-run aggregate supply curve is LAS_0, the aggregate demand curve is AD_0, and the price level is 100. The economy is at full employment at point A.

An expansion occurs when potential GDP increases and the LAS curve shifts rightward. During an expansion, aggregate demand also increases, and usually by more than potential GDP, so the price level rises. Assume that in the current expansion, the LAS curve shifts rightward to LAS_1, the price level is expected to rise to 110, and the money wage rate has been set based on that expectation. The short-run aggregate supply curve is SAS_1.

If aggregate demand increases to AD_1, real GDP increases from $1.2 trillion to $1.8 trillion, the new level of potential GDP, and the price level rises, as expected, to 110. The economy remains at full employment but now at point B.

If aggregate demand increases more slowly to AD_2, real GDP grows by less than potential GDP and the economy moves to point C, with real GDP at $1.7 trillion and the price level at 107. Real GDP growth is slower and inflation is lower than expected.

If aggregate demand increases more quickly to AD_3, real GDP grows by more than potential GDP and the economy moves to point D. Real GDP is $1.9 trillion and the price level is 113. Real GDP growth is faster and inflation is higher than expected.

Growth, inflation, and the business cycle arise from the relentless increases in potential GDP, faster (on average) increases in aggregate demand, and fluctuations in the pace of aggregate demand growth.

FIGURE 12.1   The Mainstream Business Cycle Theory

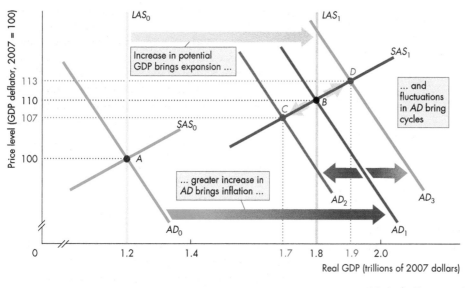

In a business cycle expansion, potential GDP increases and the *LAS* curve shifts rightward from LAS_0 to LAS_1. An increase in aggregate demand that is greater than expected brings inflation.

If the aggregate demand curve shifts to AD_1, the economy remains at full employment. If the aggregate demand curve shifts to AD_2, a recessionary gap arises. If the aggregate demand curve shifts to AD_3, an inflationary gap arises.

MyLab Economics Animation and Draw Graph

This mainstream theory comes in a number of special forms that differ regarding the source of fluctuations in aggregate demand growth and the source of money wage stickiness.

Keynesian Cycle Theory In **Keynesian cycle theory**, fluctuations in investment driven by fluctuations in business confidence—summarized by the phrase "animal spirits"—are the main source of fluctuations in aggregate demand.

Monetarist Cycle Theory In **monetarist cycle theory**, fluctuations in both investment and consumption expenditure, driven by fluctuations in the growth rate of the quantity of money, are the main source of fluctuations in aggregate demand.

Both the Keynesian and monetarist cycle theories simply assume that the money wage rate is rigid and don't explain that rigidity.

Two newer theories seek to explain money wage rate rigidity and to be more careful about working out its consequences.

New Classical Cycle Theory In **new classical cycle theory**, the rational expectation of the price level, which is determined by potential GDP and *expected* aggregate demand, determines the money wage rate and the position of the *SAS* curve. In this theory, only *unexpected* fluctuations in aggregate demand bring fluctuations in real GDP around potential GDP.

New Keynesian Cycle Theory The **new Keynesian cycle theory** emphasizes the fact that today's money wage rates were negotiated at many past dates, which means that *past* rational expectations of the current price level influence the money wage rate and the position of the *SAS* curve. In this theory, both unexpected and currently expected fluctuations in aggregate demand bring fluctuations in real GDP around potential GDP.

The mainstream cycle theories don't rule out the possibility that aggregate supply shocks might occur. An oil price rise, a widespread drought, a major hurricane, or another natural disaster, could, for example, bring a recession. But supply shocks are not the normal source of fluctuations in the mainstream theories. In contrast, real business cycle theory puts supply shocks at centre stage.

Real Business Cycle Theory

The newest theory of the business cycle, known as **real business cycle theory** (or RBC theory), regards random fluctuations in productivity as the main source of economic fluctuations. These productivity fluctuations are assumed to result mainly from fluctuations in the pace of technological change, but they might also have other sources, such as international disturbances, climate fluctuations, or natural disasters. The origins of RBC theory can be traced to the rational expectations revolution set off by Robert E. Lucas, Jr., but the first demonstrations of the power of this theory were given by Edward Prescott and Finn Kydland and by John Long and Charles Plosser. Today, RBC theory is part of a broad research agenda called dynamic general equilibrium analysis, and hundreds of young macroeconomists do research on this topic.

We'll explore RBC theory by looking first at its impulse and then at the mechanism that converts that impulse into a cycle in real GDP.

The RBC Impulse The impulse in RBC theory is the growth rate of productivity that results from technological change. RBC theorists believe this impulse to be generated mainly by the process of research and development that leads to the creation and use of new technologies (see *Economics in Action*, p. 300).

The pace of technological change and productivity growth is not constant. Sometimes productivity growth speeds up, sometimes it slows, and occasionally it even *falls*—labour and capital become less productive, on average. A period of rapid productivity growth brings a business cycle expansion, and a slowdown or fall in productivity triggers a recession.

It is easy to understand why technological change brings productivity growth, but how does it *decrease* productivity? All technological change eventually increases productivity. But if, initially, technological change makes a sufficient amount of existing capital—especially human capital—obsolete, productivity can temporarily fall. At such a time, more jobs are destroyed than created and more businesses fail than start up.

The RBC Mechanism Two effects follow from a change in productivity that sparks an expansion or a contraction: Investment demand changes and the demand for labour changes. We'll study these effects and their consequences during a recession. In an

ECONOMICS IN ACTION

The Real Business Cycle Impulse

To isolate the RBC impulse, economists measure the change in the combined productivity of capital and labour—called *total factor productivity*. The figure shows the RBC impulse for Canada from 1971 through 2015.

You can see that the productivity growth rate fluctuations are not directly correlated with real GDP fluctuations. Their influence on real GDP growth is spread out over time.

You can also see that the fluctuations in real GDP growth have wider swings than those of productivity growth.

Real business cycle theory explains these facts.

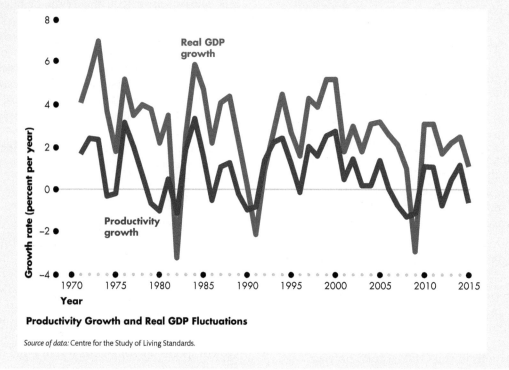

Productivity Growth and Real GDP Fluctuations

Source of data: Centre for the Study of Living Standards.

expansion, they work in the direction opposite to what is described here.

Technological change makes some existing capital obsolete and temporarily decreases productivity. Firms expect future profits to fall and see their labour productivity falling. With lower profit expectations, they cut back their purchases of new capital, and with lower labour productivity, they plan to lay off some workers. So the initial effect of a temporary fall in productivity is a decrease in investment demand and a decrease in the demand for labour.

Figure 12.2 illustrates these two initial effects of a decrease in productivity. Part (a) shows the effects of a decrease in investment demand in the loanable funds market. The demand for loanable funds curve is DLF and the supply of loanable funds curve is SLF (both of which are explained in Chapter 7, pp. 170–172). Initially, the demand for loanable funds

curve is DLF_0 and the equilibrium quantity of funds is $200 billion at a real interest rate of 6 percent a year. A decrease in productivity decreases investment demand, and the demand for loanable funds curve shifts leftward from DLF_0 to DLF_1. The real interest rate falls to 4 percent a year, and the equilibrium quantity of loanable funds decreases to $170 billion.

Figure 12.2(b) shows the demand for labour and supply of labour (which are explained in Chapter 6, pp. 142–143). Initially, the demand for labour curve is LD_0, the supply of labour curve is LS_0, and equilibrium employment is 20 billion hours a year at a real wage rate of $35 an hour. The decrease in productivity decreases the demand for labour, and the demand for labour curve shifts leftward from LD_0 to LD_1.

Before we can determine the new level of employment and the real wage rate, we need to look at a ripple effect—the key effect in RBC theory.

FIGURE 12.2 Loanable Funds and Labour Markets in a Real Business Cycle

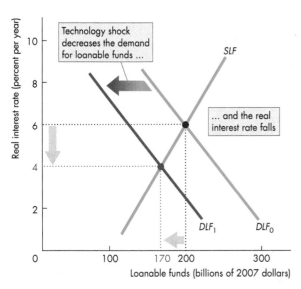

(a) Loanable funds and interest rate

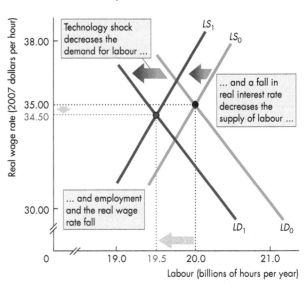

(b) Labour and wage rate

In part (a), the supply of loanable funds *SLF* and the initial demand for loanable funds DLF_0 determine the real interest rate at 6 percent a year. In part (b), the initial demand for labour LD_0 and the supply of labour LS_0 determine the real wage rate at $35 an hour and employment at 20 billion hours. A technological change temporarily decreases productivity, and both the demand for loanable funds and the

demand for labour decrease. The two demand curves shift leftward to DLF_1 and LD_1. In part (a), the real interest rate falls to 4 percent a year. In part (b), the fall in the real interest rate decreases the supply of labour (the when-to-work decision) and the supply of labour curve shifts leftward to LS_1. Employment decreases to 19.5 billion hours, and the real wage rate falls to $34.50 an hour. A recession is under way.

MyLab Economics Animation

The Key Decision: When to Work? According to RBC theory, people decide *when* to work by doing a cost-benefit calculation. They compare the return from working in the current period with the *expected* return from working in a later period. You make such a comparison every day in university. Suppose your goal in this course is to get an A. To achieve this goal, you work hard most of the time. But during the few days before the midterm and final exams, you work especially hard. Why? Because you believe that the return from studying close to the exam is greater than the return from studying when the exam is a long time away. So during the term, you take time off for the movies and other leisure pursuits, but at exam time you study every evening and weekend.

RBC theory says that workers behave like you. They work fewer hours, sometimes zero hours, when the real wage rate is temporarily low, and they work more hours when the real wage rate is temporarily high. But to properly compare the current wage rate

with the expected future wage rate, workers must use the real interest rate.

If the real interest rate is 6 percent a year, a real wage of $1 an hour earned this week will become $1.06 a year from now. If the real wage rate is expected to be $1.05 an hour next year, today's real wage of $1 looks good. By working longer hours now and shorter hours a year from now, a person can get a 1 percent higher real wage. But suppose the real interest rate is 4 percent a year. In this case, $1 earned now is worth $1.04 next year. Working fewer hours now and more next year is the way to get a 1 percent higher real wage.

So the when-to-work decision depends on the real interest rate. The lower the real interest rate, other things remaining the same, the smaller is the supply of labour today. Many economists believe this *intertemporal substitution* effect to be of negligible size. RBC theorists believe that the effect is large, and it is the key feature of the RBC mechanism.

You saw in Fig. 12.2(a) that the decrease in the demand for loanable funds lowers the real interest rate. This fall in the real interest rate lowers the return to current work and decreases the supply of labour today.

In Fig. 12.2(b), the labour supply curve shifts leftward to LS_1. The effect of the decrease in productivity on the demand for labour is larger than the effect of the fall in the real interest rate on the supply of labour. That is, the demand curve shifts farther leftward than does the supply curve. As a result, the real wage rate falls to $34.50 an hour and employment decreases to 19.5 billion hours. A recession has begun and is intensifying.

What Happened to Money? The name *real* business cycle theory is no accident. It reflects the central prediction of the theory. Real things, not nominal or monetary things, cause the business cycle. If the quantity of money changes, aggregate demand changes. But with no real change—with no change in the use of resources or in potential GDP—the change in the quantity of money changes only the price level. In RBC theory, this outcome occurs because the aggregate supply curve is the *LAS* curve, which pins real GDP down at potential GDP. So a change in aggregate demand changes only the price level.

Cycles and Growth The shock that drives the business cycle of RBC theory is the same as the force that generates economic growth: technological change. On average, as technology advances, productivity grows; but as you saw in *Economics in Action* on p. 300 it grows at an uneven pace. Economic growth arises from the upward trend in productivity growth and, according to RBC theory, the mostly positive but occasionally negative higher frequency shocks to productivity bring the business cycle.

Criticisms and Defences of RBC Theory There are three main criticisms of RBC theory:

1. The money wage rate *is* sticky, and to assume otherwise is at odds with a clear fact.

2. Intertemporal substitution is too weak a force to account for large fluctuations in labour supply and employment with small real wage rate changes.

3. Productivity shocks are as likely to be caused by *changes in aggregate demand* as by technological change.

If aggregate demand fluctuations cause the fluctuations in productivity, then the traditional aggregate demand theories are needed to explain them. Fluctuations in productivity do not cause the business cycle but are caused by it!

Building on this theme, the critics point out that the so-called productivity fluctuations that growth accounting measures are correlated with changes in the growth rate of money and other indicators of changes in aggregate demand.

The defenders of RBC theory claim that the theory explains the macroeconomic facts about the business cycle and is consistent with the facts about economic growth. In effect, a single theory explains *both growth and the business cycle*. The growth accounting exercise that explains slowly changing trends also explains the more frequent business cycle swings. Its defenders also claim that RBC theory is consistent with a wide range of *micro*economic evidence about labour supply decisions, labour demand and investment demand decisions, and information on the distribution of income between labour and capital.

REVIEW QUIZ

1 Explain the mainstream theory of the business cycle.

2 What are the four special forms of the mainstream theory of the business cycle and how do they differ?

3 According to RBC theory, what is the source of the business cycle? What is the role of fluctuations in the rate of technological change?

4 According to RBC theory, how does a fall in productivity growth influence investment demand, the market for loanable funds, the real interest rate, the demand for labour, the supply of labour, employment, and the real wage rate?

5 What are the main criticisms of RBC theory and how do its supporters defend it?

Work these questions in Study Plan 12.1 and get instant feedback.   MyLab Economics

In this first section, we've focused on the cycles in real GDP and the loanable funds and labour markets. Next, we're going to look at the causes and effects of cycles in the inflation rate.

◆ Inflation Cycles

In the long run, inflation is a monetary phenomenon. It occurs if the quantity of money grows faster than potential GDP. But in the short run, many factors can start an inflation, and real GDP and the price level interact. To study these interactions, we distinguish between two sources of inflation:

- Demand-pull inflation
- Cost-push inflation

Demand-Pull Inflation

An inflation that starts because aggregate demand increases is called **demand-pull inflation**. Demand-pull inflation can be kicked off by *any* of the factors that change aggregate demand. Examples are a cut in the interest rate, an increase in the quantity of money, an increase in government expenditure, a tax cut, an increase in exports, or an increase in investment stimulated by an increase in expected future profits.

Initial Effect of an Increase in Aggregate Demand

Suppose that last year the price level was 110 and real GDP was $1.8 trillion. Potential GDP was also $1.8 trillion. Figure 12.3(a) illustrates this situation. The aggregate demand curve is AD_0, the short-run aggregate supply curve is SAS_0, and the long-run aggregate supply curve is LAS.

Now suppose that the Bank of Canada cuts the interest rate. The quantity of money increases and the aggregate demand curve shifts from AD_0 to AD_1. With no change in potential GDP and no change in the money wage rate, the long-run aggregate supply curve and the short-run aggregate supply curve remain at LAS and SAS_0, respectively.

The price level and real GDP are determined at the point where the aggregate demand curve AD_1 intersects the short-run aggregate supply curve. The price level rises to 113, and real GDP increases above potential GDP to $1.9 trillion. Unemployment falls below its natural rate. The economy is at an above full-employment equilibrium and there is an inflationary gap. The next step in the unfolding story is a rise in the money wage rate.

FIGURE 12.3   A Demand-Pull Rise in the Price Level

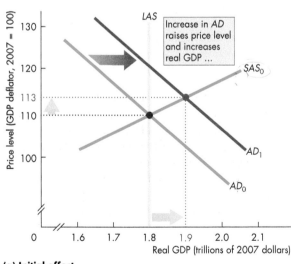

(a) Initial effect

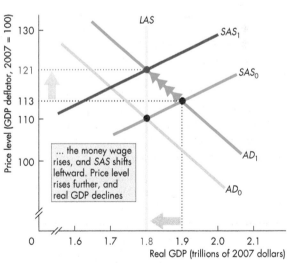

(b) The money wage adjusts

In part (a), the aggregate demand curve is AD_0, the short-run aggregate supply curve is SAS_0, and the long-run aggregate supply curve is LAS. The price level is 110, and real GDP is $1.8 trillion, which equals potential GDP. Aggregate demand increases to AD_1. The price level rises to 113, and real GDP increases to $1.9 trillion.

In part (b), starting from the above full-employment equilibrium, the money wage rate begins to rise and the short-run aggregate supply curve shifts leftward toward SAS_1. The price level rises further, and real GDP returns to potential GDP.

Money Wage Rate Response Real GDP cannot remain above potential GDP forever. With unemployment below its natural rate, there is a shortage of labour. In this situation, the money wage rate begins to rise. As it does so, short-run aggregate supply decreases and the *SAS* curve starts to shift leftward. The price level rises further, and real GDP begins to decrease.

With no further change in aggregate demand—that is, the aggregate demand curve remains at AD_1—this process ends when the short-run aggregate supply curve has shifted to SAS_1 in Fig. 12.3(b). At this time, the price level has increased to 121 and real GDP has returned to potential GDP of $1.8 trillion, the level at which it started.

A Demand-Pull Inflation Process The events that we've just described bring a *one-time rise in the price level*, not an inflation. For inflation to proceed, aggregate demand must *persistently* increase.

The only way in which aggregate demand can persistently increase is if the quantity of money persistently increases. Suppose the government has a budget deficit that it finances by selling bonds. Also suppose that the Bank of Canada buys some of these bonds. When the Bank of Canada buys bonds, it creates more money. In this situation, aggregate demand increases year after year. The aggregate demand curve keeps shifting rightward. This persistent increase in aggregate demand puts continual upward pressure on the price level. The economy now experiences demand-pull inflation.

Figure 12.4 illustrates the process of demand-pull inflation. The starting point is the same as that shown in Fig. 12.3. The aggregate demand curve is AD_0, the short-run aggregate supply curve is SAS_0, and the long-run aggregate supply curve is *LAS*. Real GDP is $1.8 trillion, and the price level is 110. Aggregate demand increases, shifting the aggregate demand curve to AD_1. Real GDP increases to $1.9 trillion, and the price level rises to 113. The economy is at an above full-employment equilibrium. There is a shortage of labour, and the money wage rate rises. The short-run aggregate supply curve shifts to SAS_1. The price level rises to 121, and real GDP returns to potential GDP.

But the Bank of Canada increases the quantity of money again, and aggregate demand continues to increase. The aggregate demand curve shifts rightward to AD_2. The price level rises further to 125, and real GDP again exceeds potential GDP

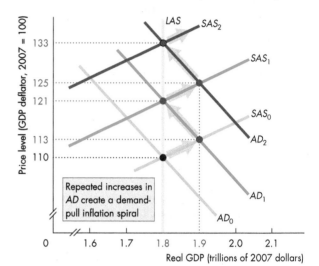

FIGURE 12.4 A Demand-Pull Inflation Spiral

Each time the quantity of money increases, aggregate demand increases and the aggregate demand curve shifts rightward from AD_0 to AD_1 to AD_2, and so on. Each time real GDP increases above potential GDP, the money wage rate rises and the short-run aggregate supply curve shifts leftward from SAS_0 to SAS_1 to SAS_2, and so on. The price level rises from 110 to 113, 121, 125, 133, and so on. There is a demand-pull inflation spiral. Real GDP fluctuates between $1.8 trillion and $1.9 trillion.

—— MyLab Economics Animation and Draw Graph ——

at $1.9 trillion. Yet again, the money wage rate rises and decreases short-run aggregate supply. The *SAS* curve shifts to SAS_2, and the price level rises further, to 133. As the quantity of money continues to grow, aggregate demand increases and the price level rises in an ongoing demand-pull inflation process.

The process you have just studied generates inflation—a persistently rising price level.

Demand-Pull Inflation in Chatham You may better understand the inflation process that we've just described by considering what is going on in an individual part of the economy, such as a Chatham cola-bottling plant. Initially, when aggregate demand increases, the demand for cola increases and the price of cola rises. Faced with a higher price, the bottling plant works overtime and increases production. Conditions are good for workers in Chatham and the cola-bottling factory finds it hard to hang on to its best people. To do so, it offers a higher money wage rate. As the wage rate rises, so do the bottling factory's costs.

What happens next depends on aggregate demand. If aggregate demand remains constant, the firm's costs increase but the price of cola does not increase as quickly as its costs. In this case, the firm cuts production. Eventually, the money wage rate and costs increase by the same percentage as the rise in the price of cola. In real terms, the bottling factory is in the same situation as it was initially. It produces the same amount of cola and employs the same amount of labour as before the increase in demand.

But if aggregate demand continues to increase, so does the demand for cola and the price of cola rises at the same rate as the money wage rate. The bottling factory continues to operate at an above full employment equilibrium and there is a persistent shortage of labour. Prices and the money wage rate chase each other upward in a demand-pull inflation spiral.

Demand-Pull Inflation in Canada A demand-pull inflation like the one you've just studied occurred in Canada during the late 1960s. In 1960, inflation was a moderate 2 percent a year, but its rate increased slowly during the mid-1960s. Then, between 1966 and 1969, the inflation rate surged upward. Inflation then decreased slightly during 1970 and 1971, but it took off again in 1972. By 1973, the inflation rate was almost 10 percent a year.

These increases in inflation resulted from increases in aggregate demand that had two main sources. The first was a large increase in U.S. government expenditure and the quantity of money in the United States, which increased aggregate demand in the entire world economy. The second source was an increase in Canadian government expenditure and the quantity of money.

With unemployment below its natural rate, the money wage rate started to rise more quickly and the *SAS* curve shifted leftward. The Bank of Canada responded with a further increase in the money growth rate, and a demand-pull inflation spiral unfolded. By 1974, the inflation rate had reached double digits.

Next, let's see how shocks to aggregate supply can create cost-push inflation.

Cost-Push Inflation

An inflation that is kicked off by an increase in costs is called **cost-push inflation**. There are two main sources of cost increases:

1. An increase in the money wage rate
2. An increase in the money prices of raw materials

At a given price level, the higher the cost of production, the smaller is the amount that firms are willing to produce. So if the money wage rate rises or if the prices of raw materials (for example, oil) rise, firms decrease their supply of goods and services. Aggregate supply decreases, and the short-run aggregate supply curve shifts leftward.[1] Let's trace the effects of such a decrease in short-run aggregate supply on the price level and real GDP.

Initial Effect of a Decrease in Aggregate Supply

Suppose that last year the price level was 110 and real GDP was $1.8 trillion. Potential real GDP was also $1.8 trillion. Figure 12.5(a) illustrates this situation. The aggregate demand curve was AD_0, the short-run aggregate supply curve was SAS_0, and the long-run aggregate supply curve was LAS. In the current year, the world's oil producers form a price-fixing organization that strengthens their market power and increases the relative price of oil. They raise the price of oil, and this action decreases short-run aggregate supply. The short-run aggregate supply curve shifts leftward to SAS_1. The price level rises to 117, and real GDP decreases to $1.7 trillion. The economy is at a below full-employment equilibrium and there is a recessionary gap.

This event is a *one-time rise in the price level*. It is not inflation. In fact, a supply shock on its own cannot cause inflation. Something more must happen to enable a one-time supply shock, which causes a one-time rise in the price level, to be converted into a process of ongoing inflation. The quantity of money must persistently increase. Sometimes it does increase, as you will now see.

---

[1]Some cost-push forces, such as an increase in the price of oil accompanied by a decrease in the availability of oil, can also decrease long-run aggregate supply. We ignore such effects here and examine cost-push factors that change only short-run aggregate supply. Real business cycle theory that you studied earlier in this chapter emphasizes the effects of shocks to long-run aggregate supply.

FIGURE 12.5 A Cost-Push Rise in the Price Level

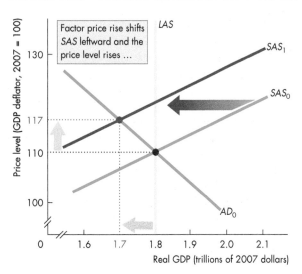

(a) Initial cost push

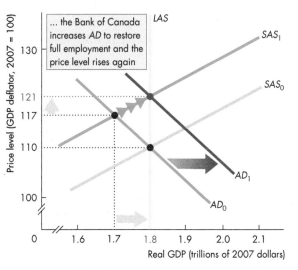

(b) The Bank of Canada responds

Initially, the aggregate demand curve is AD_0, the short-run aggregate supply curve is SAS_0, and the long-run aggregate supply curve is LAS. A decrease in aggregate supply (for example, resulting from a rise in the world price of oil) shifts the short-run aggregate supply curve to SAS_1. The economy moves to the point where the short-run aggregate supply

curve SAS_1 intersects the aggregate demand curve AD_0. The price level rises to 117, and real GDP decreases to $1.7 trillion.

In part (b), if the Bank of Canada responds by increasing aggregate demand to restore full employment, the aggregate demand curve shifts rightward to AD_1. The economy returns to full employment, but the price level rises further to 121.

MyLab Economics Animation

Aggregate Demand Response When real GDP decreases, unemployment rises above its natural rate. In such a situation, there is an outcry of concern and a call for action to restore full employment. Suppose that the Bank of Canada cuts the interest rate and increases the quantity of money. Aggregate demand increases. In Fig. 12.5(b), the aggregate demand curve shifts rightward to AD_1 and full employment is restored. But the price level rises further to 121.

A Cost-Push Inflation Process The oil producers now see the prices of everything they buy increasing, so oil producers increase the price of oil again to restore its new high relative price. Figure 12.6 continues the story. The short-run aggregate supply curve now shifts to SAS_2. The price level rises and real GDP decreases.

The price level rises further, to 129, and real GDP decreases to $1.7 trillion. Unemployment increases

above its natural rate. If the Bank of Canada responds yet again with an increase in the quantity of money, aggregate demand increases and the aggregate demand curve shifts to AD_2. The price level rises even higher—to 133—and full employment is again restored. A cost-push inflation spiral results. The combination of a rising price level and decreasing real GDP is called **stagflation**.

You can see that the Bank of Canada has a dilemma. If it does not respond when producers raise the oil price, the economy remains below full employment. If the Bank of Canada increases the quantity of money to restore full employment, it invites another oil price hike that will call forth yet a further increase in the quantity of money.

If the Bank of Canada responds to each oil price hike by increasing the quantity of money, inflation will rage along at a rate decided by oil producers. But if the Bank of Canada keeps the lid on money growth, the economy remains below full employment.

FIGURE 12.6   A Cost-Push Inflation Spiral

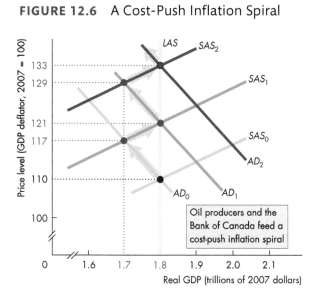

Each time a cost increase occurs, the short-run aggregate supply curve shifts leftward from SAS_0 to SAS_1 to SAS_2, and so on. Each time real GDP decreases to below potential GDP, the Bank of Canada increases the quantity of money and the aggregate demand curve shifts rightward from AD_0 to AD_1 to AD_2, and so on. The price level rises from 110 to 117, 121, 129, 133, and so on. There is a cost-push inflation spiral. Real GDP fluctuates between $1.8 trillion and $1.7 trillion.

———— MyLab Economics Animation and Draw Graph ————

Cost-Push Inflation in Chatham What is going on in the Chatham cola-bottling plant when the economy is experiencing cost-push inflation?

When the oil price increases, so do the costs of bottling cola. These higher costs decrease the supply of cola, increasing its price and decreasing the quantity produced. The bottling plant lays off some workers.

This situation persists until either the Bank of Canada increases aggregate demand or the price of oil falls. If the Bank of Canada increases aggregate demand, the demand for cola increases and so does its price. The higher price of cola brings higher profits, and the bottling plant increases its production. The bottling factory rehires the laid-off workers.

Cost-Push Inflation in Canada A cost-push inflation like the one you've just studied occurred in Canada during the 1970s. It began in 1974 when the

Organization of the Petroleum Exporting Countries (OPEC) raised the price of oil fourfold. The higher oil price decreased Canadian aggregate supply, which caused the price level to rise more quickly and real GDP to shrink. The Bank of Canada then faced a dilemma: Would it increase the quantity of money and accommodate the cost-push forces, or would it keep aggregate demand growth in check by limiting money growth? In 1975, 1976, and 1977, the Bank of Canada repeatedly allowed the quantity of money to grow quickly and inflation proceeded at a rapid rate.

In 1979 and 1980, OPEC was again able to push the price of oil higher. On that occasion, the Bank of Canada decided not to respond to the oil price hike with an increase in the quantity of money. The Canadian economy went into a recession but also, eventually, the inflation rate fell.

Expected Inflation

If inflation is expected, the fluctuations in real GDP that accompany demand-pull and cost-push inflation that you've just studied don't occur. Instead, inflation proceeds as it does in the long run, with real GDP equal to potential GDP and unemployment at its natural rate. Figure 12.7 explains why.

Suppose that last year the aggregate demand curve was AD_0, the aggregate supply curve was SAS_0, and the long-run aggregate supply curve was LAS. The price level was 110, and real GDP was $1.8 trillion, which is also potential GDP.

To keep things as simple as possible, suppose that potential GDP does not change, so the LAS curve doesn't shift. Also suppose that aggregate demand is *expected to increase* to AD_1.

In anticipation of this increase in aggregate demand, the money wage rate rises and the short-run aggregate supply curve shifts leftward. If the money wage rate rises by the same percentage as the price level is expected to rise, the short-run aggregate supply curve for next year is SAS_1.

If aggregate demand turns out to be the same as expected, the aggregate demand curve is AD_1. The short-run aggregate supply curve, SAS_1, and AD_1 determine the actual price level at 121. Between last year and this year, the price level increased from 110 to 121 and the economy experienced an inflation rate equal to that expected.

If this inflation is ongoing, aggregate demand increases (as expected) in the following year and the aggregate demand curve shifts to AD_2. The money

FIGURE 12.7 Expected Inflation

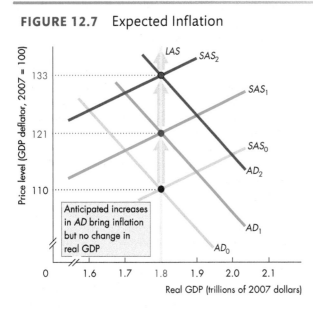

Potential real GDP is $1.8 trillion. Last year, aggregate demand was AD_0 and the short-run aggregate supply curve was SAS_0. The actual price level was the same as the expected price level: 110. This year, aggregate demand is expected to increase to AD_1 and the price level is expected to rise from 110 to 121. As a result, the money wage rate rises and the short-run aggregate supply curve shifts to SAS_1. If aggregate demand actually increases as expected, the actual aggregate demand curve AD_1 is the same as the expected aggregate demand curve. Real GDP is $1.8 trillion and the actual price level rises to 121. The inflation is expected. Next year, the process continues with aggregate demand increasing as expected to AD_2 and the money wage rate rising to shift the short-run aggregate supply curve to SAS_2. Again, real GDP remains at $1.8 trillion and the price level rises, as expected, to 133.

—— MyLab Economics Animation and Draw Graph ——

wage rate rises to reflect the expected inflation, and the short-run aggregate supply curve shifts to SAS_2. The price level rises, as expected, to 133.

What caused this inflation? The immediate answer is that because people expected inflation, the money wage rate increased and the price level increased. But the expectation was correct. Aggregate demand was expected to increase, and it did increase. It is the actual and expected increase in aggregate demand that caused the inflation.

An expected inflation at full employment is exactly the process that the quantity theory of money predicts. See Chapter 8, pp. 202–203 to review the quantity theory of money.

This broader account of the inflation process and its short-run effects shows why the quantity theory of money doesn't explain the *fluctuations* in inflation. The economy follows the course described in Fig. 12.7 but, as predicted by the quantity theory, only if aggregate demand growth is forecasted correctly.

Forecasting Inflation

To anticipate inflation, people must forecast it. Some economists who work for macroeconomic forecasting agencies, banks, insurance companies, labour unions, and large corporations specialize in inflation forecasting. The best forecast available is one that is based on all the relevant information and is called a **rational expectation**. A rational expectation is not necessarily a correct forecast. It is simply the best forecast that can be made with the information available. The forecast will often turn out to be wrong, but no other forecast that could have been made with the information available could do better.

Inflation and the Business Cycle

When the inflation forecast is correct, the economy operates at full employment. If aggregate demand grows faster than expected, real GDP increases to above potential GDP, the inflation rate exceeds its expected rate, and the economy behaves like it does in a demand-pull inflation. If aggregate demand grows more slowly than expected, real GDP decreases to below potential GDP and the inflation rate slows.

REVIEW QUIZ

1 How does demand-pull inflation begin?
2 What must happen to create a demand-pull inflation spiral?
3 How does cost-push inflation begin?
4 What must happen to create a cost-push inflation spiral?
5 What is stagflation and why does cost-push inflation cause stagflation?
6 How does expected inflation occur?
7 How do real GDP and the price level change if the forecast of inflation is incorrect?

Work these questions in Study Plan 12.2 and get instant feedback.　　MyLab Economics

Deflation

An economy experiences *deflation* when it has a persistently *falling* price level. Equivalently, during a period of deflation, the inflation rate is negative.

In most economies and for most of the time, the inflation rate is positive—the price level is rising—and deflation is rare. But deflation does happen, and most recently it was present in Japan (see *Economics in Action* on p. 310).

We're going to answer three questions about deflation:

- What causes deflation?
- What are the consequences of deflation?
- How can deflation be ended?

What Causes Deflation?

The starting point for understanding the cause of deflation is to distinguish between a one-time fall in the price level and a persistently falling price level. A one-time *fall* in the price level is not deflation. Deflation is a persistent and ongoing *falling* price level.

A One-Time Fall in the Price Level The price level can fall either because aggregate demand decreases or because short-run aggregate supply increases. So any of the influences on aggregate demand and short-run aggregate supply that you studied in Chapter 10 can bring a one-time fall in the price level.

Some examples on the demand side are a fall in global demand for a country's exports, or a fall in profit expectations that lowers business investment. Some examples on the supply side are an increase in capital or an advance in technology that increases potential GDP, or (unlikely but possible) a fall in the money wage rate.

But none of these sources of a decrease in aggregate demand or increase in aggregate supply can bring a persistently falling price level.

A Persistently Falling Price Level The price level falls persistently if aggregate demand increases at a persistently slower rate than aggregate supply. The trend rate of increase in aggregate supply is determined by the forces that make potential GDP grow. These forces are the growth rates of the labour force and capital stock and the growth rate of productivity that results from technological change. Notice that all these variables are real, not monetary, and they have trends that change slowly.

In contrast, the forces that drive aggregate demand include the quantity of money. And this quantity can grow as quickly or as slowly as the central bank chooses.

In most situations, the central bank doesn't have a target for the money stock or its growth rate and instead sets the interest rate. But the money stock is under central bank control, and its growth rate has a powerful effect on the growth rate of aggregate demand. To see the effect of growth in the money stock in the long term, we need to return to the quantity theory of money.

The Quantity Theory and Deflation The quantity theory of money explains the trends in inflation by focusing on the trend influences on aggregate supply and aggregate demand.

The foundation of the quantity theory is the *equation of exchange* (see Chapter 8, p. 202), which in its growth rate version and solved for the inflation rate states:

$$\text{Inflation rate} = \text{Money growth rate} + \text{Rate of velocity change} - \text{Real GDP growth rate}$$

This equation, true by definition, derives from the fact that the amount of money spent on real GDP, MV, equals the money value of GDP, PY. (M is the money stock, V is its velocity of circulation, P is the price level, and Y is real GDP.)

The quantity theory adds two propositons to the equation of exchange. First, the trend rate of change in the velocity of circulation does not depend on the money growth rate and is determined by decisions about the quantity of money to hold and to spend. Second, the trend growth rate of real GDP equals the growth rate of potential GDP and, again, is independent of the money growth rate.

With these two assumptions, the equation of exchange becomes the quantity theory of money and predicts that a change in the money growth rate brings an equal change in the inflation rate.

For example, suppose velocity increases by 2 percent per year and potential GDP grows by 3 percent per year. Then the quantity theory predicts that the trend inflation rate equals the money growth rate minus 1 percent. If the central bank makes the quantity of money grow by 1 percent, the inflation rate will be zero. If money grows at a rate faster than 1 percent, the economy will experience inflation. And if money grows at a slower rate than 1 percent, the economy will experience deflation.

ECONOMICS IN ACTION

Fifteen Years of Deflation in Japan

Japan experienced deflation for the 15 years from 1998 to 2013.

Japan's Deflation Rate

Figure 1 shows the inflation rate in Japan from 1991 to 2016. During the deflation years, the inflation rate fluctuated between −1 percent and −2 percent per year and accumulated to a 17 percent fall in the price level.

Cause of Japan's Deflation

Deflation, like its opposite, inflation, is primarily a monetary phenomenon. Japan's money stock grew too slowly during the deflation years.

Figure 2 shows the facts about inflation and money growth in Japan from 1996 to 2016. The relevant money growth rate that brings inflation or deflation is that of money itself *plus* the trend rate of change in the velocity of circulaton *minus* the growth rate of potential GDP. That is the money growth rate shown in Fig. 2. The inflation rate from 1998 to 2013 was negative, which means that Japan's money stock did not grow fast enough to accommodate the growth of potential GDP and a trend rise in velocity.

Consequences of Japan's Deflation

At first, Japan's deflation was unexpected and loan and wage contracts had been entered into that anticipated an ongoing low but positive inflation rate. So when the price level started to fall, the real value of debt increased and the real wage rate increased.

With higher real debt and wages, businesses cut back on both investment and hiring labour and cut production. Real GDP fell and the recessionary gap increased.

Because investment decreased, the capital stock increased more slowly and the growth rate of potential GDP slowed. From being one of the world's most dynamic rich economies, Japan became the world's most sluggish.

Figure 3 tells the story. The 1960s saw Japan doubling its real GDP in seven years. The growth rate slowed in the 1970s and 1980s but remained one of the world's fastest. Then, during the deflation years, the growth rate dropped to 1.5 percent in the 1990s, 0.8 percent in the 2000s, and 0.6 percent in the 2010s.

Japan's money growth rate increased in 2013 and the inflation rate turned positive in 2014. With sustained higher money growth, Japan can end its deflation.

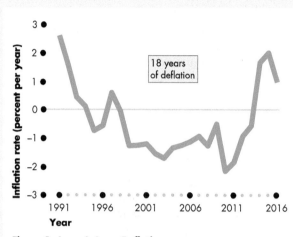

Figure 1 Japan's Long Deflation

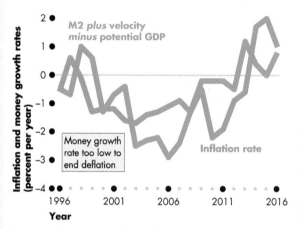

Figure 2 Money Growth Rate Too Low

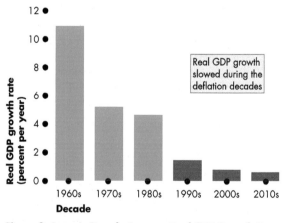

Figure 3 Japan's Decade Average Real GDP Growth Rates

Sources of data: Financial Statistics and *World Economic Outlook,* International Monetary Fund, Washington, DC.

Japan Example In the example of Japan during the 1990s and 2000s (see *Economics in Action*), the money (M2) growth rate during the 15 years 1998–2013 was 2.5 percent per year. The velocity growth rate was negative, and it *decreased* at a rate of 3 percent per year. Potential GDP grew at an average rate of 0.8 percent per year. Combining these numbers, the quantity theory predicts an inflation rate equal to −1.3 percent per year:

$$+2.5 + (-3) - 0.8 = -1.3.$$

In fact, the average inflation rate was −1.2 percent per year. So the quantity theory prediction is not exactly correct, but it is close. Its prediction of the deflation rate of 1.3 percent per year is off by only 0.1.

You now know what causes deflation. Let's turn to its consequences.

What Are the Consequences of Deflation?

Chapter 5 (p. 122) discusses why deflation and inflation are problems. But with what you now know about aggregate supply and aggregate demand and the determinants of potential GDP and its growth rate, you can gain deeper insight into the costs of deflation (and the related costs of inflation).

The effects of deflation (like those of inflation) depend on whether it is anticipated or unanticipated. But because inflation is normal and deflation is rare, when deflation occurs it is usually unanticipated.

Unanticipated deflation redistributes income and wealth, lowers real GDP and employment, and diverts resources from production.

Workers with long-term wage contracts find their real wages rising. But on the other side of the labour market, employers respond to a higher and rising real wage by hiring fewer workers. So employment decreases and output falls.

With lower output and profits, firms re-evaluate their investment plans and cut back on projects that they now see as unprofitable. This fall in investment slows the pace of capital accumulation and slows the growth rate of potential GDP.

Another consequence of deflation is a low nominal interest rate, which, in turn, brings an increase in the quantity of money that people plan to hold and a decrease in the velocity of circulation. A lower velocity adds to the deflationary forces and, if unattended to, lowers the inflation rate yet further.

So, what is the cure for deflation?

How Can Deflation Be Ended?

Deflation can be ended by removing its cause: The quantity of money is growing too slowly. If the central bank ensures that the quantity of money grows at the target inflation rate *plus* the growth rate of potential GDP *minus* the growth rate of the velocity of circulation, then, on average, the inflation rate will turn out to be close to target.

In the example of Japan, if the Bank of Japan, the central bank, wanted to get a 2 percent inflation rate, and other things remained the same, it would have needed to make the quantity of money grow at an annual average rate of 5.8 percent. (Money growth of 5.8 *plus* velocity growth of −3 *minus* potential GDP growth of 0.8 equals target inflation of 2 percent.) If raising the inflation rate brought faster potential GDP growth, a yet higher money growth rate would be needed to sustain the higher inflation rate.

Money Growth, Not Quantity Notice that it is an increase in the *growth rate* of the money stock, not a one-time increase in the quantity of money, that is required to end deflation. Central banks sometimes increase the quantity of money and fail to increase its growth rate. An increase in level with no change in the growth rate brings a temporary inflation as the price level adjusts, but not ongoing inflation, so it does not end deflation.

REVIEW QUIZ

1 What is deflation?
2 What is the distinction between deflation and a one-time fall in the price level?
3 What causes deflation?
4 How does the quantity theory of money help us to understand the process of deflation?
5 What are the consequences of deflation?
6 How can deflation be ended?

Work these questions in Study Plan 12.3 and get instant feedback.   MyLab Economics

In the final section of this chapter, we're going to look at an alternative model of short-run fluctuations—a model that focuses on the tradeoff between inflation and unemployment.

◆ The Phillips Curve

The *Phillips curve* is a relationship between inflation and unemployment. It is so named because it was first suggested by New Zealand economist A.W. (Bill) Phillips. We distinguish between two time frames for the Phillips curve (similar to the two aggregate supply time frames). We study:

- The short-run Phillips curve
- The long-run Phillips curve

The Short-Run Phillips Curve

The **short-run Phillips curve** is the relationship between inflation and unemployment when:

1. The expected inflation rate is held constant
2. The natural unemployment rate is constant

Expected inflation is the best available forecast of future inflation (see p. 308) and natural unemployment is frictional and structural unemployment in Chapter 5 (pp. 119–120).

Figure 12.8 shows a short-run Phillips curve, *SRPC*. Suppose that the expected inflation rate is 10 percent a year and the natural unemployment rate is 6 percent, point *A* in the figure. A short-run Phillips curve passes through this point. If inflation rises above its expected rate, unemployment falls below its natural rate in a movement up along the short-run Phillips curve from point *A* to point *B*. Similarly, if inflation falls below its expected rate, unemployment rises above its natural rate in a movement down along the short-run Phillips curve from point *A* to point *C*.

The Long-Run Phillips Curve

The **long-run Phillips curve** is the relationship between inflation and unemployment when the actual inflation rate equals the expected inflation rate. The long-run Phillips curve is vertical at the natural unemployment rate because, in the long run, any expected inflation rate is possible. In Fig. 12.9(a), the long-run Phillips curve is the vertical line *LRPC*.

Change in Expected Inflation A change in the expected inflation rate shifts the short-run Phillips curve, but it does not shift the long-run Phillips curve. In Fig. 12.9(a), if the expected inflation rate is 10 percent a year, the short-run Phillips curve is *SRPC*$_0$. If the expected inflation rate falls to 6 percent a year, the short-run Phillips curve shifts downward

FIGURE 12.8 A Short-Run Phillips Curve

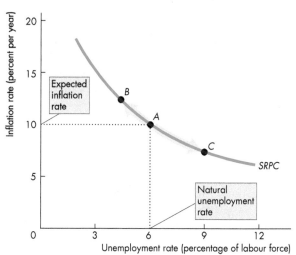

The short-run Phillips curve, *SRPC*, is the relationship between inflation and unemployment at a given expected inflation rate and a given natural unemployment rate. Here, the expected inflation rate is 10 percent a year and the natural unemployment rate is 6 percent at point *A*.

A change in the actual inflation rate brings a movement along the short-run Phillips curve from *A* to *B* or from *A* to *C*.

to *SRPC*$_1$. The vertical distance by which the short-run Phillips curve shifts from point *A* to point *D* is equal to the change in the expected inflation rate. If the actual inflation rate also falls from 10 percent to 6 percent, there is a movement down the long-run Phillips curve from *A* to *D*. An increase in the expected inflation rate has the opposite effect to that shown in Fig. 12.9(a).

The other source of a shift in the Phillips curve is a change in the natural unemployment rate.

Change in Natural Unemployment Rate A change in the natural unemployment rate shifts both the short-run and long-run Phillips curves. Figure 12.9(b) illustrates such shifts.

If the natural unemployment rate increases from 6 percent to 9 percent, the long-run Phillips curve shifts from *LRPC*$_0$ to *LRPC*$_1$, and if expected inflation is constant at 10 percent a year, the short-run Phillips curve shifts from *SRPC*$_0$ to *SRPC*$_1$. Because the expected inflation rate is constant, *SRPC*$_1$ intersects the long-run curve *LRPC*$_1$ (point *E*) at the same inflation rate at which *SRPC*$_0$ intersects the long-run curve *LRPC*$_0$ (point *A*).

FIGURE 12.9 Short-Run and Long-Run Phillips Curves

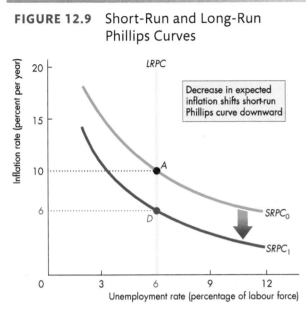

(a) A change in expected inflation

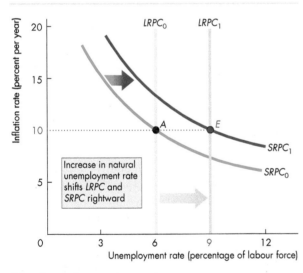

(b) A change in natural unemployment

In part (a), the long-run Phillips curve is *LRPC*. A fall in expected inflation shifts the short-run Phillips curve downward from $SRPC_0$ to $SRPC_1$. The long-run Phillips curve does not shift. In part (b), a change in the natural unemployment rate shifts both the short-run and long-run Phillips curves.

MyLab Economics Animation

Economics in Action on this page looks at the Canadian Phillips curve from 2001 to 2016, a period through which the expected inflation rate and the natural unemployment rate didn't change much. Over longer periods, big changes in the expected inflation rate have shifted the Canadian Phillips curve.

ECONOMICS IN ACTION

The Canadian Phillips Curve

The figure is a scatter diagram of the Canadian inflation rate (measured by the GDP deflator) and the unemployment rate from 2001 to 2016. *LRPC* is at a natural unemployment rate of 7 percent and *SRPC* is at an expected inflation rate of 1.7 percent a year. The dots for each year (some of which are identified) show that the *SRPC* jumps around as inflation expectations change.

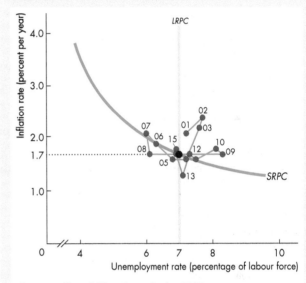

The Canadian Phillips Curve in the 2000s

REVIEW QUIZ

1 How would you use the Phillips curve to illustrate an unexpected change in inflation?
2 If the expected inflation rate increases by 10 percentage points, how do the short-run Phillips curve and the long-run Phillips curve change?
3 If the natural unemployment rate increases, what happens to the short-run Phillips curve and the long-run Phillips curve?
4 Does Canada have a stable short-run Phillips curve? Explain why or why not.

Work these questions in Study Plan 12.4 and get instant feedback. MyLab Economics

◆ *Economics in the News* on pp. 314–315 looks at the stagnating economy of Europe and the plans of the European Central Bank to revive it.

The Stagnating Eurozone

Eurozone Unemployment Falls to Lowest Level in 8 Years

The Financial Times
July 31, 2017

Eurozone unemployment fell to its lowest level in eight years in June, while a key inflation figure picked up to its fastest pace since 2013 in July, underscoring the gathering momentum of the bloc's economic expansion.

Annual unemployment in the Eurozone fell to 9.1 percent in June, down from 9.2 percent in May, according to data from Eurostat.

The bloc's unemployment rate has declined from over 10 percent in June 2016 as growth in the continent has been spurred by low interest rates and a strengthening world economy. ...

Policymakers at the European Central Bank are keeping a close eye on the bloc's labour market for signs of upward wage pressures. Higher wages would underpin higher inflation but as of yet, wage growth has been notable by its absence in the eurozone. ...

"At the current pace of decline, unemployment would be down to pre-crisis levels in the first half of 2019," said Christian Schulz, senior European economist at Citi.

Eurozone inflation data for July presented a more ambiguous picture.

Core inflation in the Eurozone, which strips out volatile food and energy prices, accelerated unexpectedly, picking up to a four-year high of 1.3 percent from 1.2 percent in June.

However, the headline inflation figure held steady at 1.3 percent in July. That is comfortably below the central bank's target rate of 2 percent, and a joint low for 2017 after price growth surged to a four-year high of 2 percent in February. ...

Mehreen Khan, Published July 31, 2017, *Financial Times*

ESSENCE OF THE STORY

- The Eurozone unemployment rate fell to 9.1 percent in June 2017, down from 10 percent a year earlier, and its lowest level in eight years.

- The Eurozone inflation rate was 1.3 percent per year in July and June.

- The Eurozone core inflation rate (which excludes food and energy prices) was 1.3 percent in July and 1.2 percent in June.

- Wage growth has been steady.

- The Eurozone target inflation rate is 2 percent per year.

ECONOMIC ANALYSIS

- The Eurozone is the group of 18 European countries that use the euro as their money and for which the European Central Bank (ECB) makes monetary policy decisions.

- The Eurozone economy is stagnating and has a high unemployment rate.

- Figure 1 shows the Eurozone unemployment rate compared with that of Canada.

- The Eurozone unemployment rate has been persistently higher than that of Canada and the average difference is structural, not cyclical.

- A high structural unemployment rate in the Eurozone results from high minimum wages, generous unemployment benefits and welfare payments, and extensive regulation of the labour market.

- ECB monetary policy can do nothing to lower the structural unemployment rate. But it can act to lower the cyclical unemployment rate.

- The Eurozone also has a low inflation rate that is below the ECB target rate of 2 percent per year.

- Figure 2 shows the Eurozone inflation rate compared with that of Canada. Both economies had inflation rates below 2 percent per year in 2016, but in the Eurozone inflation had been below 2 percent for 8 years.

- The high unemployment and stagnating real GDP result from real structural problems that make the Eurozone natural unemployment rate high and from high cyclical unemployment and below-target inflation that result from insufficient aggregate demand.

- The aggregate demand problem arises from the fact that the ECB has not expanded the money stock quickly enough.

- Figure 3 shows the growth rate of money plus the growth rate of velocity minus the growth rate of potential GDP.

- The growth rate of money plus the growth rate of velocity minus the growth rate of potential GDP equals the inflation rate that can be sustained at full employment.

- To lower cyclical unemployment, the growth rate of money plus the growth rate of velocity minus the growth rate of potential GDP must *exceed* the target and expected inflation rate.

- If, as in 2009 and 2010, the growth rate of money plus the growth rate of velocity minus the growth rate of potential GDP decreases, cyclical unemployment will increase and inflation will decrease.

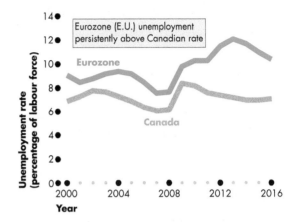

Figure 1 The Stagnating Eurozone Economy

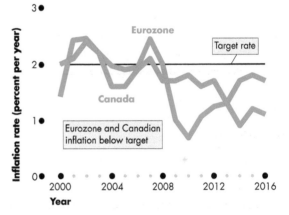

Figure 2 Inflation Rates Miss Targets

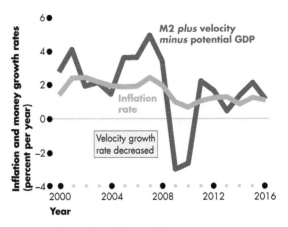

Figure 3 Money Growth Rate Too Low

- To end stagnation, the ECB must buy assets and increase the growth rate of money. A big one-off asset purchase will not do the job required.

WORKED PROBLEM

MyLab Economics Work this problem in Chapter 12 Study Plan.

The table shows the aggregate demand and short-run aggregate supply schedules of Shell Island, in which potential GDP is $600 billion. The economy is at full employment.

Price level	Real GDP demanded	Real GDP supplied in the short run
	(billions of 2007 dollars)	
100	650	550
110	625	575
120	600	600
130	575	625
140	550	650

Questions

1. An unexpected increase in exports increases aggregate demand by $50 billion. What happens to the price level and real GDP? Has Shell Island experienced inflation or deflation, and what type of output gap does it now have?

2. Starting at full employment, the price of oil falls unexpectedly and aggregate supply increases by $50 billion. What type of output gap appears? If the central bank responds to close the output gap, does Shell Island experience inflation or deflation?

3. Starting from full employment, the government of Shell Island announces an increase in spending of $50 billion a year and the central bank will increase the quantity of money to pay for the spending. Does the economy go into a boom? Will there be inflation?

Solutions

1. When aggregate demand increases by $50 billion, the price level rises from 120 to 130 and real GDP increases from $600 billion to $625 billion and the economy is at an above full-employment equilibrium.

   Shell Island experiences a one-time change in the price level and not inflation. The output gap is an inflationary gap, but demand-pull inflation does not take off until businesses respond to the labour shortage by raising the money wage rate.

Key Point: For an increase in aggregate demand to create demand-pull inflation, the shortage of labour must put pressure on the money wage rate to rise to close the inflationary gap.

2. When the price of oil falls unexpectedly, aggregate supply increases. The price level falls from 120 to 110 and real GDP increases from $600 billion to $625 billion. The economy is at an above full-employment equilibrium. An inflationary gap arises. Shell Island experiences a one-time change in the price level and not inflation.

   If the central bank responds to close the output gap, it cuts the quantity of money. Aggregate demand shifts leftward and a cost-push deflation is created. See the figure.

Key Point: A cost-push deflation is created if the central bank responds to a fall in costs by decreasing the quantity of money.

3. When the government announces an increase in spending of $50 billion a year, aggregate demand increases and the increase in aggregate demand is anticipated. Because the central bank increases the quantity of money, businesses anticipate the rise in the price level, so the money wage rate rises. Aggregate supply decreases.

   Real GDP remains at $600 billion and no output gap is created, but an anticipated inflation occurs.

Key Point: An anticipated increase in aggregate demand, accompanied by an increase in the quantity of money, created an anticipated inflation spiral with the economy at full employment.

Key Figure

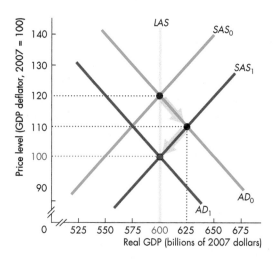

MyLab Economics Interactive Animation

SUMMARY

Key Points

The Business Cycle (pp. 298–302)

- The mainstream business cycle theory explains the business cycle as fluctuations of real GDP around potential GDP and as arising from a steady expansion of potential GDP combined with an expansion of aggregate demand at a fluctuating rate.

- Real business cycle theory explains the business cycle as fluctuations of potential GDP, which arise from fluctuations in the influence of technological change on productivity growth.

Working Problem 1 will give you a better understanding of the business cycle.

Inflation Cycles (pp. 303–308)

- Demand-pull inflation is triggered by an increase in aggregate demand and fuelled by ongoing money growth. Real GDP cycles above full employment.

- Cost-push inflation is triggered by an increase in the money wage rate or raw material prices and is fuelled by ongoing money growth. Real GDP cycles below full employment in a stagflation.

- When the forecast of inflation is correct, real GDP remains at potential GDP.

Working Problems 2 to 5 will give you a better understanding of inflation cycles.

Deflation (pp. 309–311)

- Deflation is a falling price level or negative inflation rate.

- Deflation is caused by a money growth rate that is too low to accommodate the growth of potential GDP and changes in the velocity of circulation.

- Unanticipated deflation brings stagnation.

- Deflation can be ended by increasing the money growth rate to a rate that accommodates the growth of potential GDP and changes in the velocity of circulation.

Working Problem 6 will give you a better understanding of deflation.

The Phillips Curve (pp. 312–313)

- The short-run Phillips curve shows the tradeoff between inflation and unemployment when the expected inflation rate and the natural unemployment rate are constant.

- The long-run Phillips curve, which is vertical, shows that when the actual inflation rate equals the expected inflation rate, the unemployment rate equals the natural unemployment rate.

Working Problems 7 and 8 will give you a better understanding of the Phillips curve.

Key Terms

MyLab Economics Key Terms Quiz

Cost-push inflation, 305
Demand-pull inflation, 303
Keynesian cycle theory, 299
Long-run Phillips curve, 312

Monetarist cycle theory, 299
New classical cycle theory, 299
New Keynesian cycle theory, 299
Rational expectation, 308

Real business cycle theory, 299
Short-run Phillips curve, 312
Stagflation, 306

STUDY PLAN PROBLEMS AND APPLICATIONS

MyLab Economics Work Problems 1 to 8 in MyEconLab Chapter 12 Study Plan and get instant feedback.

The Business Cycle (Study Plan 12.1)

1. **Debate on Causes of Unemployment**

   Two economists are debating the cause of a high unemployment rate. One economist argues that there is not enough government spending. The other says high unemployment is a structural problem—people who can't move to take new jobs because they are tied down to burdensome mortgages or firms that can't find workers with the skills they need to fill job openings.

   a. Which business cycle theory would say that the first economist is correct and why?

   b. Which business cycle theory would say that the second economist is correct and why?

Inflation Cycles (Study Plan 12.2)

2. **U.S. Inflation Rises at Faster Pace**

   With the consumer price index rising at a faster pace, President-elect Donald Trump wants to slash taxes and boost infrastructure spending, which could cause inflation to rise further.

   Source: *Washington Post*, January 19, 2017

   Explain what type of inflation the news clip is describing and provide a graphical analysis of it.

Use the following figure to work Problems 3 to 5.

The economy starts out on the curves AD_0 and SAS_0.

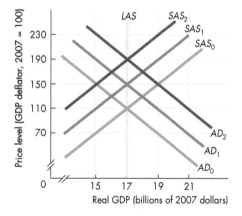

3. Some events occur and the economy experiences a demand-pull inflation. What might those events have been? Describe their initial effects and explain how a demand-pull inflation spiral results.

4. Some events occur and the economy experiences a cost-push inflation. What might those events have been? Describe their initial effects and explain how a cost-push inflation spiral develops.

5. Some events occur and the economy is expected to experience inflation. What might those events have been? Describe their initial effects and what happens as an expected inflation proceeds.

Deflation (Study Plan 12.3)

6. Suppose that the velocity of circulation of money is constant and real GDP is growing at 3 percent a year.

   a. To achieve an inflation target of 2 percent a year, at what rate would the central bank grow the quantity of money?

   b. At what growth rate of the quantity of money would deflation be created?

The Phillips Curve (Study Plan 12.4)

7. **Central Bankers Are Baffled**

   Another month with a low unemployment number and with no rise in the inflation rate has the Federal Reserve baffled. The Phillips curve has disappeared.

   Source: *The Financial Times*, July 27, 2017

   a. What does the Phillips curve model say about the relationship between the unemployment rate and the inflation rate?

   b. Explain the event in the news clip in terms of what is happening to the short-run and long-run Phillips curves.

8. **From the Fed's Minutes**

   FOMC participants saw the data on aggregate expenditure and unemployment as little changed since June but expected the unemployment rate to fall. Participants expected that inflation would remain below 2 percent per year in the near term but stabilize around the 2 percent objective over the medium term.

   Source: FOMC Minutes, July 25–26, 2017

   Are FOMC participants predicting that the U.S. economy will move along a short-run Phillips curve or that the short-run Phillips curve will shift through 2017 and 2018? Explain.

ADDITIONAL PROBLEMS AND APPLICATIONS

MyLab Economics You can work these problems in Homework or Test if assigned by your instructor.

The Business Cycle

Use the following information to work Problems 9 to 11.

Suppose that the Canadian business cycle is best described by RBC theory and that a new technology increases productivity.

9. Draw a graph to show the effect of the new technology in the market for loanable funds.

10. Draw a graph to show the effect of the new technology in the labour market.

11. Explain the when-to-work decision when technology advances.

12. **Workers: You've Never Had It So Bad**

    Working men and women had not had it so bad since the middle of the 19th century. During the 1860s, like the 2000s and 2010s, real wages grew slowly. Those mid-Victorian years were a lost decade for workers, disrupted by new technology such as steam engines and the telegraph. Today's lost decades are disrupted by information technologies.

    Source: *The Globe and Mail*, December 9, 2016

    Explain the relationship between wages and technology in this news clip in terms of real business cycle theory.

Inflation Cycles

Use the following information to work Problems 13 and 14.

Inflation Should Be Feared

Economist John H. Cochrane thinks the Fed must be careful not to over-stimulate the economy. He thinks inflation remains a danger because U.S. debt is skyrocketing, with no visible plan to pay it back. For the moment, foreigners are buying that debt. But they are buying out of fear that their governments are worse. They are short-term investors, waiting out the storm, not long-term investors confident that the United States will pay back its debts. If their fear passes, or they decide some other haven is safer, the Fed must watch out. For in that situation, inflation will come with a vengeance. It's not happening yet: Interest rates are low now. But if inflation takes off, it will happen with little warning, the Fed will be powerless to stop it, and it will bring stagnation rather than prosperity.

13. What type of inflation process does John Cochrane warn could happen? Explain the role that inflation expectations would play if the outbreak of inflation were to "happen with little warning."

14. Explain why the inflation that John Cochrane fears would "bring stagnation ..."

Deflation

15. **Europe's Deflation Fears**

    Consumer prices in the Eurozone fell in January for a second consecutive month reinforcing fears of sustained deflation, higher unemployment, and stagnant incomes.

    Source: *The New York Times*, January 31, 2015

    a. Explain the process by which deflation occurs.

    b. How might aggregate demand in Europe be increased? Might the increase in aggregate demand create demand-pull inflation?

The Phillips Curve

Use the following data to work Problems 16 and 17.

An economy has an unemployment rate of 4 percent and an inflation rate of 5 percent a year at point *A* in the figure. Then some events occur that move the economy from *A* to *B* to *D* to *C* and back to *A*.

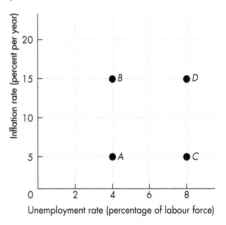

16. Describe the events that could create this sequence. Has the economy experienced demand-pull inflation, cost-push inflation, expected inflation, or none of these?

17. In the graph, draw the sequence of the economy's short-run and long-run Phillips curves.

Use the following information to work Problems 18 and 19.

The Reserve Bank of New Zealand signed an agreement with the New Zealand government in which the Bank agreed to maintain inflation inside a low target range. Failure to achieve the target would result in the governor of the Bank losing his job.

18. Explain how this arrangement might have influenced New Zealand's short-run Phillips curve.

19. Explain how this arrangement might have influenced New Zealand's long-run Phillips curve.

20. **Where Is the Phillips Curve?**

    One of the central propositions of macroeconomic theory is the Phillips curve, a pressure cooker model of the inflationary process. If the economy runs too hot, inflation will follow. If the economy cools and the pressure drops, wage and price inflation will ease. Yet in the United States, United Kingdom, and Japan, unemployment is low but inflation is nowhere in sight. The Phillips curve has gone flat.

    Source: *The Financial Times*, July 27, 2017

    a. Evaluate the claim that the Phillips curve has gone flat.

    b. How does the Phillips curve model account for the facts reported in the news clip?

21. **Stephen Poloz Press Briefing**

    The economy is absorbing excess capacity more rapidly than we projected in April, and it now appears that the output gap will close around the end of this year. ... Meanwhile, inflation has continued to fluctuate in the bottom half of our target range. ... All things considered, Governing Council judges that in the absence of temporary factors, inflation would be running at around 1.8 percent. ... [and] as the [output] gap closes in the months ahead, we expect inflation to head toward 2 percent.

    Source: Monetary Polcy Report Press Conference Opening Statement, July 12, 2017

    a. Is Stephen Poloz predicting that the Canadian economy is moving along a short-run Phillips curve or that the short-run Phillips curve is shifting? Or both? In which direction is the economy moving?

    b. Sketch an example of the Phillips curve and show on the graph how the Canadian economy is changing.

Economics in the News

22. After you have studied *Economics in the News* on pp. 314–315, answer the following questions.

    a. What are the macroeconomic problems in the Eurozone economy that the ECB is seeking to address?

    b. Is the European unemployment problem structural, cyclical, or both, and how can we determine its type?

    c. Explain which type of unemployment the ECB can help with.

    d. Use the *AS-AD* model to show the changes in aggregate demand and/or aggregate supply that created the Eurozone's macroeconomic problems.

    e. Use the *AS-AD* model to show the changes in aggregate demand and/or aggregate supply that the ECB must bring about to achieve its goal.

23. **British Economy Suffers Slowdown**

    The UK economy grew by 0.3 percent in the second quarter of 2017 after 0.2 percent growth in the first quarter. These slow growth rates are seen as confirming the predicted effects of the country exiting the European Union. Some worry that Britain might be heading toward recession. Household saving and business investment have fallen, credit card borrowing is at record high, wages are stagnating, and consumer confidence is crashing.

    Source: CNN, July 26, 2017

    a. How does a fall in business investment influence Britain's aggregate demand, aggregate supply, unemployment, and inflation?

    b. Use the *AS-AD* model to illustrate your answer to part (a).

    c. Use the Phillips curve model to illustrate your answer to part (a).

    d. What does the news clip mean by "Britain might be heading toward recession"?

    e. Use the *AS-AD* model to illustrate your answer to part (d).

    f. Use the Phillips curve model to illustrate your answer to part (d).

Boom and Bust

UNDERSTANDING MACROECONOMIC FLUCTUATIONS

To cure a disease, doctors must first understand how the disease responds to different treatments. It helps to understand the mechanisms that operate to cause the disease, but sometimes a workable cure can be found even before the full story of the causes has been told.

Curing economic ills is similar to curing our medical ills. We need to understand how the economy responds to the treatments we might prescribe for it. And sometimes, we want to try a cure even though we don't fully understand the reasons for the problem we're trying to control.

You've seen how the pace of capital accumulation and technological change determine the long-term growth trend. You've learned how fluctuations around the long-term trend can be generated by changes in aggregate demand and aggregate supply. And you've learned about the key sources of fluctuations in aggregate demand and aggregate supply.

The *AS-AD* model explains the forces that determine real GDP and the price level in the short run. The model also enables us to see the big picture or grand vision of the different schools of macroeconomic thought concerning the sources of aggregate fluctuations. The Keynesian aggregate expenditure model provides an account of the factors that determine aggregate demand and make it fluctuate.

An alternative real business cycle theory puts all the emphasis on fluctuations in long-run aggregate supply. According to this theory, money changes aggregate demand and the price level but leaves the real economy untouched. The events of 2008 and 2009 provide a powerful test of this theory.

John Maynard Keynes, *born in England in 1883, was one of the outstanding minds of the twentieth century. He represented Britain at the Versailles peace conference at the end of World War I, was a master speculator on international financial markets (an activity he conducted from bed every morning and which made and lost him several fortunes), and played a prominent role in creating the International Monetary Fund.*

He was a member of the Bloomsbury Group, a circle of outstanding artists and writers that included E. M. Forster, Bertrand Russell, and Virginia Woolf.

Keynes was a controversial and quick-witted figure. A critic once complained that Keynes had changed his opinion on some matter, to which Keynes retorted: "When I discover I am wrong, I change my mind. What do you do?"

Keynes' book, The General Theory of Employment, Interest and Money, *written during the Great Depression and published in 1936, created macroeconomics and revolutionized the way economists study aggregate fluctuations.*

"The ideas of economists and political philosophers, both when they are right and when they are wrong, are more powerful than is commonly understood. Indeed the world is ruled by little else."

JOHN MAYNARD KEYNES
The General Theory of Employment, Interest and Money

PETER HOWITT is Lyn Crost Professor of Social Sciences in the Department of Economics at Brown University. Born in 1946 in Toronto, he was an undergraduate at McGill University and a graduate student at Northwestern University.

Professor Howitt began his research and teaching career at the University of Western Ontario in 1972, where he spent many productive years before moving to the United States in 1996.

Professor Howitt is a past president of the Canadian Economics Association and is one of the world's leading macroeconomists. He has done research on all aspect of macroeconomics, with a focus in recent years on economic growth.

Michael Parkin and Robin Bade talked with Peter Howitt about his work and the major macroeconomic problems facing Canada today.

Peter, what attracted you to economics?

When I was in high school I had a part-time job as office boy with a small company that imported wool from around the world and sold it to textile mills in Ontario and Quebec. I was fascinated by the way wool prices went up and down all the time, and this curiosity led me to enroll in an honours economics course. My interests soon switched to macroeconomics, but I was always driven by curiosity to find out more about the workings of the human anthill.

You have made outstanding contributions to our understanding of all the major problems of macroeconomics, notably unemployment, economic growth, and inflation. Which of these issues do you believe is the most serious one for Canada today? Can they be separated?

> My biggest concern ... is that we may be headed for a credit crisis that would result in high unemployment and low economic growth.

Canada has suffered much less from the global financial crisis than the United States and most other countries. There are a number of reasons for this: Canadian banks have been more prudent in their lending and investment strategies; we did not have the explosion of household debt, especially mortgage debt, or the bubble in housing prices that occurred in the United States; and both the Bank of Canada's inflation-targeting policy and our relatively small government deficits gave our policymakers more room to stimulate the economy without stoking fears of inflation.

My biggest concern is that Canada seems to be losing many of these advantages, and we may be headed for our own crisis. In particular, household debt is still rising at a rapid rate in Canada, to the point where it is now a larger proportion of household income than in the United States. The longer this credit boom continues, the more exposed our financial system becomes in the event of a downturn in housing prices or a rise in unemployment.

Either of these events would lead to a rise in loan defaults, as it has already in the United States where people are walking away from mortgages on houses whose prices have fallen below the amount owed (i.e., mortgages that are "underwater") and where many unemployed people find themselves no longer able to pay back their debts.

*Read the full interview with Peter Howitt in MyLab Economics.

13

FISCAL POLICY

After studying this chapter, you will be able to:

◆ Describe the federal budget process and the recent history of outlays, revenues, deficits, and debt

◆ Explain the supply-side effects of fiscal policy

◆ Explain how fiscal stimulus is used to fight a recession

The Government of Canada has had a budget deficit for eight of the last nine years and its debt has grown. Does it matter if the government doesn't balance its books? How does a government deficit influence the economy? Does it create jobs, or does it destroy them? Does it speed or slow economic growth?

This chapter studies the effects of the government's budget on the economy. It looks at the effects of taxes, government expenditure, and budget deficits. In *Economics in the News* at the end of the chapter, we look at the effects of lowering the taxes on corporate profits, a move that Canada made a few years ago and that the U.S. government says it wants to follow.

◆ The Federal Budget

The annual statement of the outlays and revenues of the Government of Canada, together with the laws and regulations that approve and support those outlays and revenues, make up the **federal budget**. Similarly, a *provincial budget* is an annual statement of the revenues and outlays of a provincial government, together with the laws and regulations that approve or support those revenues and outlays.

Before World War II, the federal budget had no purpose other than to finance the business of government. But since the late 1940s, the federal budget has assumed a second purpose, which is to pursue the government's fiscal policy. **Fiscal policy** is the use of the federal budget to achieve macroeconomic objectives such as full employment, sustained long-term economic growth, and price level stability. Our focus is this second purpose.

Budget Making

The federal government and Parliament make fiscal policy. The process begins with long, drawn-out consultations between the Minister of Finance and Department of Finance officials and their counterparts in the provincial governments. These discussions deal with programs that are funded and operated jointly by the two levels of government. The minister also consults with business and consumer groups on a wide range of issues.

After all these consultations, and using economic projections made by Department of Finance economists, the minister develops a set of proposals, which are discussed in Cabinet and which become government policy. The minister finally presents a budget plan to Parliament, which debates the plan and enacts the laws necessary to implement it.

The Federal Budget in 2016

Table 13.1 shows the main items in the federal budget. The numbers are the amounts for the calendar year 2016 in the *National Income and Expenditure Accounts.* The three main items shown are:

- Revenues
- Outlays
- Budget balance

TABLE 13.1 Federal Budget in 2016

Item	Calendar year 2016 (billions of dollars)	
Revenues	**278**	
Personal income taxes		138
Corporate income tax		40
Indirect and other taxes		54
Investment income		46
Outlays	**296**	
Transfer payments		204
Expenditure on goods and services		70
Debt interest		22
Deficit	**18**	

Source of data: Statistics Canada, CANSIM Table 380-0080.

Revenues Revenues are the federal government's receipts, which were $278 billion. These revenues come from four sources:

1. Personal income taxes
2. Corporate income taxes
3. Indirect and other taxes
4. Investment income

The largest revenue source is personal income taxes. In 2016, personal income taxes were $138 billion. These are the taxes paid by individuals on their incomes. The second largest source of revenue is indirect taxes, which in 2016 were $54 billion. These taxes include the Goods and Services Tax (GST) and taxes on the sale of gasoline, alcoholic drinks, and a few other items.

The smallest revenue sources are corporate income taxes, which are the taxes paid by companies on their profits, and investment income, which is the income from government enterprises and investments. In 2016, corporate income taxes were $40 billion and investment income was $46 billion.

Outlays Total federal government outlays in 2016 were $296 billion. Outlays are classified in three categories:

1. Transfer payments
2. Expenditure on goods and services *Circular flow (G)*
3. Debt interest

The largest outlay, and by a big margin, is *transfer payments*. Transfer payments are payments to individuals, businesses, other levels of government, and the rest of the world. In 2016, this item was $204 billion. It includes unemployment cheques and welfare payments to individuals, farm subsidies, grants to provincial and local governments, aid to developing countries, and dues to international organizations such as the United Nations.

Expenditure on goods and services is the government's expenditure on final goods and services, and in 2016 this item totalled $70 billion. This expenditure includes the expenditure on national defence, computers for the Canada Revenue Agency, government cars, and highways.

This component of the federal budget is the government expenditure on goods and services that appears in the circular flow of expenditure and income and in the national income and product accounts (see Chapter 4, pp. 89–90).

Debt interest is the interest on the government debt. In 2016, this item was $22 billion. At its peak

percentage in 1990, debt interest exceeded government expenditure on goods and services. This interest payment was large because the government has a large debt—$709 billion. The large debt arose because, from the mid-1970s to 1997, the federal government had a large and persistent budget deficit.

Budget Balance The government's budget balance is equal to its revenues minus its outlays. That is,

$$\text{Budget balance} = \text{Revenues} - \text{Outlays}.$$

If revenues exceed outlays, the government has a **budget surplus**. If outlays exceed revenues, the government has a **budget deficit**. If revenues equal outlays, the government has a **balanced budget**.

In 2016, with outlays of $296 billion and revenues of $278 billion, the government had a budget deficit of $18 billion.

How typical is the federal budget of 2016? Let's look at its recent history.

The Budget in Historical Perspective

Figure 13.1 shows the government's revenues, outlays, and budget balance from 1961 to 2016. To get a better sense of the magnitudes of these items, they are shown as percentages of GDP. Expressing them in this way lets us see how large the government is relative to the size of the economy, and also helps us to

---

FIGURE 13.1   The Budget Surplus and Deficit

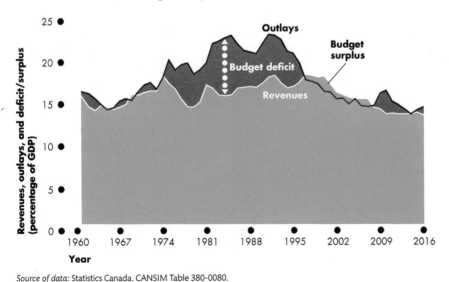

The figure records the federal government's revenues, outlays, and budget balance as percentages of GDP from 1961 to 2016. During the 1960s, outlays and revenues increased. During the late 1970s and through the 1980s, outlays continued to rise but revenues fell and then remained steady, so a large budget deficit arose. During the 1990s, expenditure cuts eliminated the budget deficit, and after 1997, the federal government had a budget surplus. A deficit re-emerged during the 2008–2009 recession.

Source of data: Statistics Canada, CANSIM Table 380-0080.

study changes in the scale of government over time. You can think of the percentages of GDP as telling you how many cents of each dollar that Canadians earn get paid to and are spent by the government.

During the 1960s, government expanded but tax revenues and outlays kept pace with each other. But from the mid-1970s through 1996, the federal budget was in deficit, and the average deficit over these years was 4.5 percent of GDP. The deficit climbed to a peak of 7.1 percent of GDP in 1985. It then decreased through the rest of the 1980s. During the recession of 1990–1991, the deficit increased again. The deficit remained close to 5 percent of GDP for most of the 1980s and early 1990s.

In 1997, the federal government finally eradicated its deficit. And it did so by cutting outlays, especially transfer payments to provincial governments. But another deficit emerged after the 2008–2009 recession.

Why did the government deficit grow during the early 1980s and remain high through the early 1990s? The immediate answer is that outlays increased while revenues remained relatively constant. But which components of outlays increased? And did all the sources of revenues remain constant?

To answer these questions, we need to examine each of the sources of revenues and outlays in detail. We'll begin by looking at the sources of revenues.

Revenues Figure 13.2 shows the components of government revenues since 1961. Total revenues have no strong trends. They increased through the 1960s and again through the 1980s, but they decreased during the 1970s and the 2000s.

The main source of the fluctuations in revenues was personal income taxes. Indirect taxes also fluctuated, but corporate income taxes and investment income were more stable than the other two revenue components.

The increase in personal income taxes during the 1980s resulted from increases in tax rates in successive budgets.

Indirect taxes decreased during the 1990s mainly because an old federal sales tax was replaced by the Goods and Services Tax, GST, or the Harmonized Sales Tax, HST. Initially, this switch maintained revenues at a constant level, but gradually, the revenue from indirect taxes (as a percentage of GDP) fell.

Outlays Figure 13.3 shows the components of government outlays since 1961. Total outlays increased steadily from 1971 through 1985, were relatively high through 1993, and then decreased sharply after 1993. The main source of the changing trends in outlays is transfer payments to provincial governments. These payments swelled during the 1980s and were cut drastically during the mid-1990s.

FIGURE 13.2 Federal Government Revenues

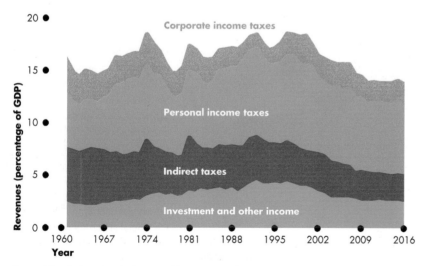

The figure shows four main components of government revenues (as percentages of GDP): personal income taxes, corporate income taxes, indirect taxes, and investment income. Revenues from personal income taxes fluctuate the most. They increased during the 1960s and early 1970s, decreased during the late 1970s, increased again during the 1980s and 1990s, and then decreased again during the 2000s. Indirect taxes have fallen during the 2000s. The other two components of revenues remained steady.

Source of data: Statistics Canada, CANSIM Tables 380-0080 and 380-0064.

MyLab Economics Animation

FIGURE 13.3 Federal Government Outlays

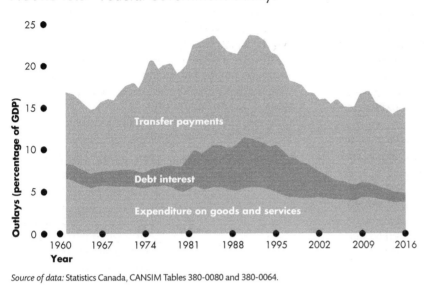

The figure shows three components of government outlays (as percentages of GDP): expenditure on goods and services, debt interest, and transfer payments. Expenditure on goods and services have had a downward trend. Transfer payments increased from 1965 to 1990 but decreased sharply during the 1990s and continued to fall until the 2008–2009 recession when they increased. Debt interest increased steadily during the 1980s as the budget deficit fed on itself, but decreased during the late 1990s as surpluses began to reduce the government's debt.

Source of data: Statistics Canada, CANSIM Tables 380-0080 and 380-0064.

MyLab Economics Animation

To understand the changes in debt interest, we need to see the connection between the budget deficit and government debt.

Deficit and Debt The government borrows to finance its deficit. And **government debt** is the total amount of government borrowing, which equals the sum of past deficits minus the sum of past surpluses.

When the government budget is in deficit, government debt increases; and when the government budget is in surplus, government debt decreases.

A persistent budget deficit emerged during the mid-1970s, and in such a situation, the deficit begins to feed on itself. A budget deficit increases borrowing; increased borrowing leads to larger debt; a larger debt leads to larger interest payments; and larger interest payments lead to a larger deficit and yet larger debt. That is the story of the increasing budget deficit and rising debt of the 1980s and early 1990s.

Similarly, a persistent budget surplus creates a virtuous cycle of falling interest payments, larger surpluses, and declining debt.

Figure 13.4 shows the history of the Government of Canada debt since 1971. In 1971, debt (as a percentage of GDP) was at a low of 4.4 percent. This almost zero debt resulted from 25 years of surpluses to pay off a huge debt built up during World War II that exceeded 100 percent of GDP.

FIGURE 13.4 The Federal Government Debt

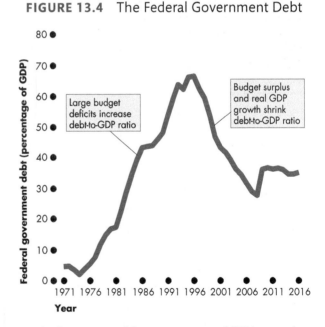

Federal government debt as a percentage of GDP increased from 1974 through 1996 and then began to decrease. It increased slightly during the 2008–2009 recession and has remained constant at 35 percent of GDP.

Source of data: Statistics Canada, CANSIM Tables 380-0080 and 191-0002.

MyLab Economics Animation

ECONOMICS IN ACTION

Provincial and Local Governments

The total government sector of Canada includes provincial and local governments as well as the federal government. In 2016, when federal government outlays were $296 billion, provincial and local government outlays were $520 billion and total government outlays were $816 billion.

Most provincial and local government outlays are on public hospitals and public schools, colleges, and universities.

Figure 1 shows the revenues, outlays, and deficits of the federal government and of total government from 1961 to 2016.

You can see that federal government outlays and revenues and total government outlays and revenues fluctuate in similar ways, but the total government is much larger than the federal government. In other words, the provincial and local governments are a large component of total government. You can also see that total government outlays fluctuate more than federal government outlays.

Both the federal and total government budgets moved into and out of deficit at similar times, and both were in surplus from the late 1990s to 2008.

Provincial government outlays and revenue sources vary a great deal across the provinces. Figure 2 shows the range of variation.

Part (a) shows outlays as a percentage of provincial GDP. You can see that outlays are greatest in the Atlantic provinces and smallest in Alberta, Ontario, and Saskatchewen.

Part (b) shows the sources of provincial revenues as a percentage of total outlays. Again, the Atlantic provinces receive the largest transfers from the federal government, while Alberta, Saskatchewan, Ontario, and British Columbia receive the least.

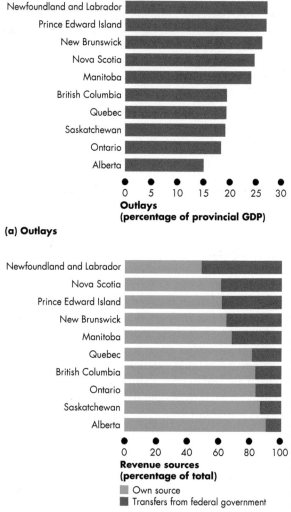

(a) Outlays

(b) Revenues

Figure 2 Provincial Government Budgets

Source of data: Part (a) Royal Bank of Canada, Canadian Federal and Provincial Fiscal Tables based on the public accounts of provincial governments, September 8, 2017. www.rbc.com/economics/economic-reports/pdf/provincial-forecasts/prov_fiscal.pdf.
Part (b) Statistics Canada, Tables by province or territory.

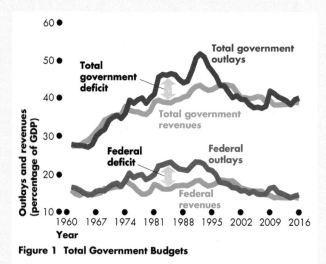

Figure 1 Total Government Budgets

Source of data: Statistics Canada, CANSIM Tables 380-0080 and 380-0064.

ECONOMICS IN ACTION

The Canadian Government Budget in Global Perspective

How does the Canadian government budget deficit compare with those of other major economies?

Comparing Like with Like

To compare the budget deficits of governments across economies, we must take into account the fact that some countries, and Canada is one of them, have large provincial and local governments, while others, and the United Kingdom is one, have a large central government and small local governments. These differences make the international comparison more valid at the level of total government.

Deficits Almost Everywhere

The figure shows the budget balances of all levels of government in Canada and other economies in 2017. Fiscal stimulus to fight the global recession of 2008 resulted in deficits almost everywhere. Of the countries shown here, only Germany had a budget surplus in 2017. Japan had the largest deficit and the United States had the second largest. Canada's budget deficit is in the middle of the pack.

Italy and other advanced economies as a group, which includes the newly industrialized economies of Asia (Hong Kong, South Korea, Singapore, and Taiwan), had the smallest deficits.

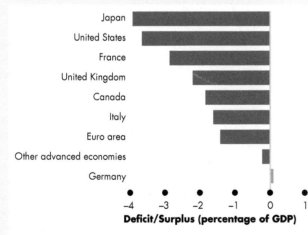

Government Budgets Around the World

Source of data: International Monetary Fund, *World Economic Outlook*, September 2017.

Small budget deficits increased the debt-to-GDP ratio slightly through the 1970s, and large budget deficits increased it dramatically between 1981 and 1986. During the late 1980s, the ratio continued to increase but at a more moderate rate. The debt-to-GDP ratio grew quickly again during the 1990–1991 recession and its growth rate slowed after 1995 and debt interest as a percentage of GDP decreased.

The 2008–2009 recession lowered revenues and increased outlays, so the debt-to-GDP ratio increased again and has remained fairly steady.

Debt and Capital When individuals and businesses incur debts, they usually do so to buy capital—assets that yield a return. In fact, the main point of debt is to enable people to buy assets that will earn a return that exceeds the interest paid on the debt. The government is similar to individuals and businesses in this regard. Some government expenditure is investment—the purchase of public capital that yields a return. Highways, major irrigation schemes, public schools and universities, public libraries, and the stock of national defence capital all yield a social rate of return that probably far exceeds the interest rate the government pays on its debt.

But Canadian government debt, which is $709 billion, is much larger than the value of the public capital stock. This fact means that some government debt has been incurred to finance public consumption expenditure.

REVIEW QUIZ

1 What are the main items of government revenues and outlays?

2 Under what circumstances does the government have a budget surplus?

3 Explain the connection between a government budget deficit and a government debt.

Work these questions in Study Plan 13.1 and get instant feedback.   MyLab Economics

It is now time to study the *effects* of fiscal policy. We'll begin by learning about the effects of taxes on employment, aggregate supply, and potential GDP. Then we'll look at fiscal stimulus and see how it might be used to speed recovery from recession and stabilize the business cycle.

◆ Supply-Side Effects of Fiscal Policy

How do taxes on personal and corporate income affect real GDP and employment? The answer to these questions is controversial. Some economists, known as *supply-siders*, believe these effects to be large, and an accumulating body of evidence suggests that they are correct. To see why these effects might be large, we'll begin with a refresher on how full employment and potential GDP are determined in the absence of taxes. Then we'll introduce an income tax and see how it changes the economic outcome.

Full Employment and Potential GDP

You learned in Chapter 6 (pp. 142–144) how the full-employment quantity of labour and potential GDP are determined. At full employment, the real wage rate adjusts to make the quantity of labour demanded equal the quantity of labour supplied. Potential GDP is the real GDP that the full-employment quantity of labour produces.

Figure 13.5 illustrates a full-employment situation. In part (a), the demand for labour curve is *LD*, and the supply of labour curve is *LS*. At a real wage rate of $30 an hour and 25 billion hours of labour a year employed, the economy is at full employment.

In Fig. 13.5(b), the production function is *PF*. When 25 billion hours of labour are employed, real GDP and potential GDP are $1.9 trillion.

Let's now see how an income tax changes potential GDP.

The Effects of the Income Tax

The tax on labour income influences potential GDP and aggregate supply by changing the full-employment quantity of labour. The income tax weakens the incentive to work and drives a wedge between the take-home wage of workers and the cost of labour to firms. The result is a smaller quantity of labour and a lower potential GDP.

Figure 13.5 shows this outcome. In the labour market, the income tax has no effect on the demand for labour, which remains at *LD*. The reason is that the quantity of labour that firms plan to hire depends only on how productive labour is and what it costs—its real wage rate.

FIGURE 13.5 The Effects of the Income Tax on Aggregate Supply

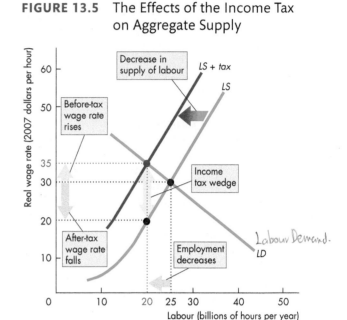

(a) Income tax and the labour market

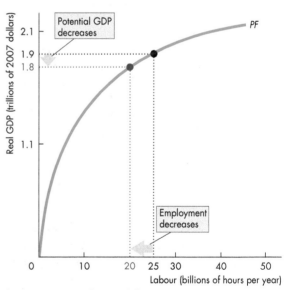

(b) Income tax and potential GDP

In part (a), with no income tax, the real wage rate is $30 an hour and employment is 25 billion hours. In part (b), potential GDP is $1.9 trillion. An income tax shifts the supply of labour curve leftward to *LS + tax*. The before-tax wage rate rises to $35 an hour, the after-tax wage rate falls to $20 an hour, and the quantity of labour employed decreases to 20 billion hours. With less labour, potential GDP decreases.

 MyLab Economics Animation and Draw Graph

But the supply of labour *does* change. With no income tax, the real wage rate is $30 an hour and 25 billion hours of labour a year are employed. An income tax weakens the incentive to work and decreases the supply of labour. The reason is that for each dollar of before-tax earnings, workers must pay the government an amount determined by the income tax code. So workers look at the after-tax wage rate when they decide how much labour to supply. An income tax shifts the supply curve leftward to *LS + tax*. The vertical distance between the *LS* curve and the *LS + tax* curve measures the amount of income tax. With the smaller supply of labour, the *before-tax* wage rate rises to $35 an hour but the *after-tax* wage rate falls to $20 an hour. The gap created between the before-tax and after-tax wage rates is called the **tax wedge**.

The new equilibrium quantity of labour employed is 20 billion hours a year—less than in the no-tax case. Because the full-employment quantity of labour decreases, so does potential GDP. And a decrease in potential GDP decreases aggregate supply.

In this example, the tax rate is high—$15 tax on a $35 wage rate is a tax rate of about 43 percent. A lower tax rate would have a smaller effect on employment and potential GDP.

An increase in the tax rate to above 43 percent would decrease the supply of labour by more than the decrease shown in Fig. 13.5. Equilibrium employment and potential GDP would also decrease still further. A tax cut would increase the supply of labour, increase equilibrium employment, and increase potential GDP.

Taxes on Expenditure and the Tax Wedge

The tax wedge that we've just considered is only a part of the wedge that affects labour-supply decisions. Taxes on consumption expenditure add to the wedge. The reason is that a tax on consumption raises the prices paid for consumption goods and services and is equivalent to a cut in the real wage rate.

The incentive to supply labour depends on the goods and services that an hour of labour can buy. The higher the taxes on goods and services and the lower the after-tax wage rate, the less is the incentive to supply labour. If the income tax rate is 25 percent and the tax rate on consumption expenditure is 10 percent, a dollar earned buys only 65 cents worth of goods and services. The tax wedge is 35 percent.

ECONOMICS IN ACTION
Some Real-World Tax Wedges

Edward C. Prescott of Arizona State University, who shared the 2004 Nobel Prize for Economic Science, has estimated the tax wedges for three countries: the United States, the United Kingdom, and France. We have estimated the tax wedge for Canada.

The wedges are a combination of taxes on labour income and taxes on consumption. They include all taxes on labour, including social insurance taxes. And the wedges are based on marginal tax rates—the tax rates paid on the marginal dollar earned.

The figure shows the tax wedges in these four countries. In the United States, the consumption tax wedge is 13 percent and the income tax wedge is 32 percent. Canada is very similar. In France, the consumption tax wedge is 33 percent and the income tax wedge is 49 percent. The tax wedges in United Kingdom fall between those of France and Canada.

Does the Tax Wedge Matter?

Differences in potential GDP per person arise partly from productivity differences and partly from choices influenced by the tax wedge. Potential GDP (per person) in France is 30 percent below that of the United States and the entire difference is attributed to the difference in the tax wedge in the two countries. Potential GDP in Canada is 12 percent below that of the United States, but this difference is due to different productivities. Potential GDP in the United Kingdom is 28 percent below that of the United States, and about a third of the difference arises from the different tax wedges and two-thirds from productivity difference.

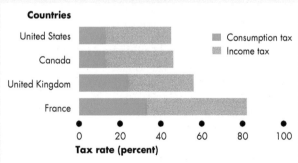

Four Tax Wedges

Sources of data: Edward C. Prescott, "Prosperity and Depression," *The American Economic Review*, Vol. 92, No. 2, Papers and Proceedings (May 2002), pp. 1–15, and authors' calculations.

Taxes and the Incentive to Save and Invest

A tax on interest income weakens the incentive to save and drives a wedge between the after-tax interest rate earned by savers and the interest rate paid by firms. These effects are analogous to those of a tax on labour income, but they are more serious for two reasons.

First, a tax on labour income lowers the quantity of labour employed and lowers potential GDP, while a tax on capital income lowers the quantity of saving and investment and slows the growth rate of real GDP.

Second, the true tax rate on interest income is much higher than that on labour income because of the way in which inflation and taxes on interest income interact. Let's examine this interaction.

Effect of Tax Rate on Real Interest Rate The interest rate that influences investment and saving plans is the real after-tax interest rate. The real after-tax interest rate subtracts the income tax rate on interest income from the real interest rate. But the taxes depend on the nominal interest rate, not the real interest rate. So the higher the inflation rate, the higher is the true tax rate on interest income. Here is an example. Suppose the real interest rate is 4 percent a year and the tax rate is 40 percent.

If there is no inflation, the nominal interest rate equals the real interest rate. The tax on 4 percent interest is 1.6 percent (40 percent of 4 percent), so the real after-tax interest rate is 4 percent minus 1.6 percent, which equals 2.4 percent.

If the inflation rate is 6 percent a year, the nominal interest rate is 10 percent. The tax on 10 percent interest is 4 percent (40 percent of 10 percent), so the real after-tax interest rate is 4 percent minus 4 percent, which equals zero. The true tax rate in this case is not 40 percent but 100 percent!

Effect of Income Tax on Saving and Investment In Fig. 13.6, initially there are no taxes. Also, the government has a balanced budget. The demand for loanable funds curve, which is also the investment demand curve, is *DLF*. The supply of loanable funds curve, which is also the saving supply curve, is *SLF*. The equilibrium interest rate is 3 percent a year, and the quantity of funds borrowed and lent is $200 billion a year.

A tax on interest income has no effect on the demand for loanable funds. The quantity of investment and borrowing that firms plan to undertake depends only on how productive capital is and what

---

FIGURE 13.6 The Effects of a Tax on Capital Income

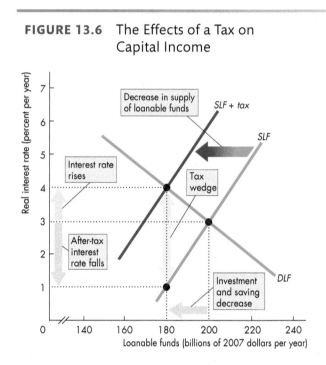

The demand for loanable funds and investment demand curve is *DLF*, and the supply of loanable funds and saving supply curve is *SLF*. With no income tax, the real interest rate is 3 percent a year and investment is $200 billion. An income tax shifts the supply curve leftward to *SLF + tax*. The interest rate rises to 4 percent a year, the after-tax interest rate falls to 1 percent a year, and investment decreases to $180 billion. With less investment, the real GDP growth rate decreases.

—— MyLab Economics Animation and Draw Graph ——

it costs—its real interest rate. But a tax on interest income weakens the incentive to save and lend and decreases the supply of loanable funds. For each dollar of before-tax interest, savers must pay the government an amount determined by the tax code. So savers look at the after-tax real interest rate when they decide how much to save.

When a tax is imposed, saving decreases and the supply of loanable funds curve shifts leftward to *SLF + tax*. The amount of tax payable is measured by the vertical distance between the *SLF* curve and the *SLF + tax* curve. With this smaller supply of loanable funds, the interest rate rises to 4 percent a year but the after-tax interest rate falls to 1 percent a year. A tax wedge is driven between the interest rate and the after-tax interest rate, and the equilibrium quantity of loanable funds decreases. Saving and investment also decrease.

Tax Revenues and the Laffer Curve

An interesting consequence of the effect of taxes on employment and saving is that a higher tax *rate* does not always bring greater tax *revenue*. A higher tax rate brings in more revenue per dollar earned. But because a higher tax rate decreases the number of dollars earned, two forces operate in opposite directions on the tax revenue collected.

The relationship between the tax rate and the amount of tax revenue collected is called the **Laffer curve**. The curve is so named because Arthur B. Laffer, a member of President Reagan's Economic Policy Advisory Board, drew such a curve on a table napkin and launched the idea that tax cuts could increase tax revenue.

Figure 13.7 shows a Laffer curve. The tax rate is on the *x*-axis, and total tax revenue is on the *y*-axis. For tax rates below T^*, an increase in the tax rate increases tax revenue; at T^*, tax revenue is maximized; and a tax rate increase above T^* decreases tax revenue.

Most people think that Canada is on the upward-sloping part of the Laffer curve; so is the United Kingdom. But France might be close to the maximum point or perhaps even beyond it.

The Supply-Side Debate

Before 1980, few economists paid attention to the supply-side effects of taxes on employment and potential GDP. Then, when Ronald Reagan took office as president, a group of supply-siders began to argue the virtues of cutting taxes. Arthur Laffer was one of them. Laffer and his supporters were not held in high esteem among mainstream economists, but they were influential for a period. They correctly argued that tax cuts would increase employment and increase output. But they incorrectly argued that tax cuts would increase tax revenues and decrease the budget deficit. For this prediction to be correct, the United States would have had to be on the "wrong" side of the Laffer curve. Given that U.S. tax rates are among the lowest in the industrial world, it is unlikely that this condition was met. And when the Reagan administration did cut taxes, the budget deficit increased, a fact that reinforces this view.

Supply-side economics became tarnished because of its association with Laffer and came to be called "voodoo economics." But mainstream economists, including Martin Feldstein, a Harvard professor who was Reagan's chief economic advisor, recognized the

FIGURE 13.7   A Laffer Curve

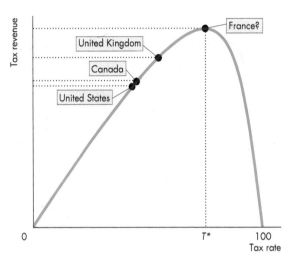

A Laffer curve shows the relationship between the tax rate and tax revenues. For tax rates below T^*, an increase in the tax rate increases tax revenue. At the tax rate T^*, tax revenue is maximized. For tax rates above T^*, an increase in the tax rate decreases tax revenue.

MyLab Economics Animation

power of tax cuts as incentives but took the standard view that tax cuts without spending cuts would swell the budget deficit and bring serious further problems. This view is now widely accepted by economists of all political persuasions.

REVIEW QUIZ

1 How does a tax on labour income influence the equilibrium quantity of employment?
2 How does the tax wedge influence potential GDP?
3 Why are consumption taxes relevant for measuring the tax wedge?
4 Why are income taxes on capital income more powerful than those on labour income?
5 What is the Laffer curve and why is it unlikely that Canada is on the "wrong" side of it?

Work these questions in Study Plan 13.2 and get instant feedback.   *MyLab Economics*

You now know how taxes influence potential GDP and saving and investment. Next, we look at the demand-side effects of fiscal policy.

◆ Fiscal Stimulus

The most recent recession (2008–2009) brought Keynesian macroeconomic ideas (see p. 258) back into fashion and put a spotlight on **fiscal stimulus**— the use of fiscal policy to increase production and employment. But whether fiscal policy is truly stimulating, and if so, how stimulating, are questions that generate much discussion and disagreement. You're now going to explore these questions.

Fiscal stimulus can be either *automatic* or *discretionary*. A fiscal policy action that is triggered by the state of the economy with no action by government is called **automatic fiscal policy**. The increase in total unemployment benefits triggered by the higher unemployment rate through 2009 is an example of automatic fiscal policy.

A fiscal policy action initiated by an act of Parliament is called **discretionary fiscal policy**. It requires a change in a spending program or in a tax law. A fiscal stimulus act passed by the U.S. government in 2008 (see *Economics in Action* on p. 337) is an example of discretionary fiscal policy.

Whether automatic or discretionary, an increase in government outlays or a decrease in government revenues can stimulate production and jobs. An increase in expenditure on goods and services directly increases aggregate expenditure. And an increase in transfer payments (such as unemployment benefits) or a decrease in tax revenues increases disposable income, which enables people to increase consumption expenditure. Lower taxes also strengthen the incentives to work and invest.

We'll begin by looking at automatic fiscal policy and the interaction between the business cycle and the budget balance.

Automatic Fiscal Policy and Cyclical and Structural Budget Balances

Two items in the government budget change automatically in response to the state of the economy. They are *tax revenues* and *transfer payments*.

Automatic Changes in Tax Revenues The tax laws that Parliament enacts don't legislate the number of tax *dollars* the government will raise. Rather they define the tax rates that people must pay. Tax dollars paid depend on tax rates and incomes. But incomes vary with real GDP, so tax revenues depend on real GDP. When real GDP increases in a business cycle expansion, wages and profits rise, so tax revenues from these incomes rise. When real GDP decreases in a recession, wages and profits fall, so tax revenues fall.

Automatic Changes in Outlays The government creates programs that pay benefits to qualified people and businesses. The spending on these programs results in transfer payments that depend on the economic state of individual citizens and businesses. When the economy expands, unemployment falls and the number of people receiving unemployment benefits decreases, so transfer payments decrease. When the economy is in a recession, unemployment is high and the number of people receiving unemployment benefits increases, so transfer payments increase.

Automatic Stimulus Because government revenues fall and outlays increase in a recession, the budget provides automatic stimulus that helps to shrink the recessionary gap. Similarly, because revenues rise and outlays decrease in a boom, the budget provides automatic restraint to shrink an inflationary gap.

Cyclical and Structural Budget Balances To identify the government budget deficit that arises from the business cycle, we distinguish between the **structural surplus or deficit**, which is the budget balance that would occur if the economy were at full employment, and the **cyclical surplus or deficit**, which is the actual surplus or deficit *minus* the structural surplus or deficit.

Figure 13.8 illustrates these concepts. Outlays *decrease* as real GDP *increases*, so the outlays curve slopes downward; and revenues *increase* as real GDP *increases*, so the revenues curve slopes upward.

In Fig. 13.8(a), potential GDP is $1.8 trillion. If real GDP equals potential GDP, the government has a balanced budget. There is no structural surplus or deficit. But there might be a cyclical surplus or deficit. If real GDP is less than potential GDP at $1.7 trillion, outlays exceed revenues and there is a cyclical deficit. If real GDP is greater than potential GDP at $1.9 trillion, outlays are less than revenues and there is a cyclical surplus.

In Fig. 13.8(b), if potential GDP equals $1.8 trillion (line *B*), the *structural balance is zero*. But if potential GDP is $1.7 trillion (line *A*), the government budget has a *structural deficit*. And if potential GDP is $1.9 trillion (line *C*), the government budget has a structural surplus.

FIGURE 13.8 Cyclical and Structural
Surpluses and Deficits

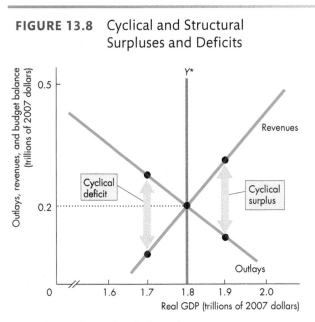

(a) Cyclical deficit and cyclical surplus

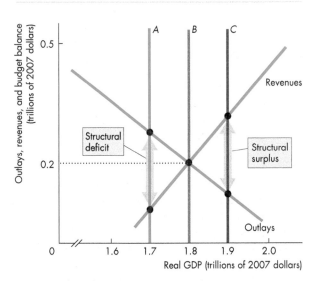

(b) Structural deficit and structural surplus

In part (a), potential GDP is $1.8 trillion. If real GDP is $1.7 trillion, the budget balance is a *cyclical deficit*. If real GDP is
$1.9 trillion, the budget balance is a *cyclical surplus*. If real
GDP is $1.8 trillion, the government has a *balanced budget*.

   In part (b), if potential GDP is $1.7 trillion, the budget
balance is a *structural deficit*. If potential GDP is $1.9 trillion,
the budget balance is a *structural surplus*. If potential GDP is
$1.8 trillion, the *structural balance* is zero.

MyLab Economics Animation

Canadian Structural Budget Balance in 2016 The
Canadian federal budget in 2016 was in deficit at
$18 billion and the recessionary gap (the gap between
real GDP and potential GDP) was estimated by the
Bank of Canada to be less than 1 percent of potential
GDP, or about $13 billion. This recessionary gap is
small. With a small recessionary gap and a substantial
budget deficit, most of the deficit was structural.

   We don't now exactly how much of the deficit was
structural and how much was cyclical, but *Economics
in Action* on the next page provides an illustration and
possible breakdown of the deficit into its two parts.

Discretionary Fiscal Stimulus

Most discussion of *discretionary* fiscal stimulus focuses
on its effects on aggregate demand. But you've seen
(on pp. 330–333) that taxes influence aggregate supply and that the balance of taxes and spending—the
government budget deficit—can crowd out investment and slow the pace of economic growth. So
discretionary fiscal stimulus has both supply-side and
demand-side effects that end up determining its overall effectiveness.

   We're going to begin our examination of discretionary fiscal stimulus by looking at its effects on
aggregate demand.

Fiscal Stimulus and Aggregate Demand Changes in
government expenditure and changes in taxes change
aggregate demand by their influence on spending
plans, and they also have multiplier effects.

   Let's look at the two main fiscal policy multipliers:
the government expenditure and tax multipliers.

   The **government expenditure multiplier** is the quantitative effect of a change in government expenditure
on real GDP. Because government expenditure is a
component of aggregate expenditure, an increase in
government spending increases aggregate expenditure
and real GDP. But does a $1 billion increase in gov-
ernment expenditure increase real GDP by $1 billion,
more than $1 billion, or less than $1 billion?

   When an increase in government expenditure
increases real GDP, incomes rise and the higher
incomes bring an increase in consumption expenditure. If this were the only consequence of increased
government expenditure, the government expenditure multiplier would be greater than 1.

   But an increase in government expenditure
increases government borrowing (or decreases government lending if there is a budget surplus) and raises

ECONOMICS IN ACTION

Canada's 2016 Budget Deficit

Canada's Conservative government places a high priority on maintaining a federal budget surplus for two reasons. First, it believes that the debt created by the long run of deficits during the 1980s and 1990s remains too large, so it wants to see that debt lowered every year. Second, it believes that aiming for a surplus places a discipline on a Parliament that can always find reasons to spend ever larger amounts on public projects and social programs.

From 2001 to 2004, Canada had a negative output gap, but the budget balance was a structural surplus. In the recession of 2008–2009, the budget moved into

a structural deficit, and as the economy expanded in 2010–2016, the budget deficit decreased but remains (see Fig. 1).

In the recession of 2008–2009, the government faced a dilemma. Should it stick to its surplus priority or join the call for fiscal stimulus to lessen the recession's impact? The government's decision was to stimulate and move to a structural deficit.

Figure 2 illustrates the situation in Canada in 2016. Potential GDP was (our estimate) $1,809 billion, and if actual real GDP had been at that quantity, the budget balance would have been a structural deficit.

Actual real GDP in 2016 was $1,796 billion, with a recessionary gap of $13 billion. At that real GDP, the budget was both a structural and a cyclical deficit.

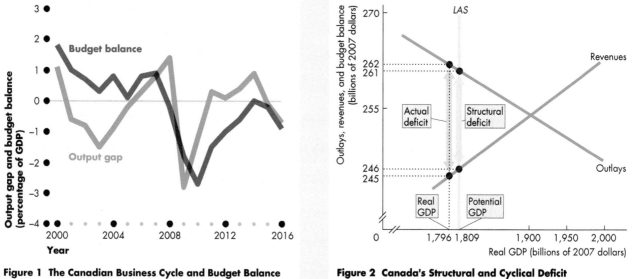

Figure 1 The Canadian Business Cycle and Budget Balance

Figure 2 Canada's Structural and Cyclical Deficit

Sources of data: Statistics Canada, CANSIM Tables 380-0080 and 380-0064, and the Bank of Canada's estimate of the output gap.

the real interest rate. With a higher cost of borrowing, investment decreases, which partly offsets the increase in government spending. If this were the only consequence of increased government expenditure, the multiplier would be less than 1.

The actual multiplier depends on which of the above effects is stronger, and the consensus is that the crowding-out effect is strong enough to make the government expenditure multiplier less than 1.

The **tax multiplier** is the quantitative effect of a change in taxes on real GDP. The demand-side effects of a tax cut are likely to be smaller than an equivalent

increase in government expenditure. The reason is that a tax cut influences aggregate demand by increasing disposable income, only part of which gets spent. So the initial injection of expenditure from a $1 billion tax cut is less than $1 billion.

A tax cut has similar crowding-out consequences to a spending increase. It increases government borrowing (or decreases government lending), raises the real interest rate, and cuts investment.

The tax multiplier effect on aggregate demand depends on these two opposing effects and is probably quite small.

Graphical Illustration of Fiscal Stimulus Figure 13.9 shows how fiscal stimulus is supposed to work if it is perfectly executed and has its desired effects.

Potential GDP is $1.8 trillion and real GDP is below potential at $1.7 trillion, so the economy has a recessionary gap of $0.1 trillion.

To restore full employment, the government passes a fiscal stimulus package. An increase in government expenditure and a tax cut increase aggregate expenditure by ΔE. If this were the only change in spending plans, the AD curve would shift rightward to become the curve labelled $AD_0 + \Delta E$ in Fig. 13.9. But if fiscal stimulus sets off a multiplier process that increases consumption expenditure and does not crowd out much investment, aggregate demand increases further and the AD curve shifts rightward to AD_1.

With no change in the price level, the economy would move from point A to point B on AD_1. But

FIGURE 13.9   Expansionary Fiscal Policy

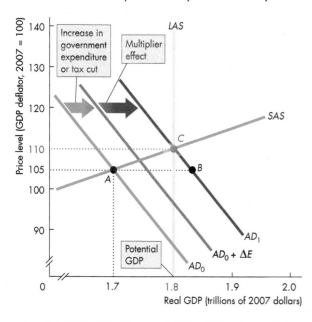

Potential GDP is $1.8 trillion, real GDP is $1.7 trillion, and there is a $0.1 trillion recessionary gap. An increase in government expenditure and a tax cut increase aggregate expenditure by ΔE. The multiplier increases consumption expenditure and the AD curve shifts rightward to AD_1. The price level rises to 110, real GDP increases to $1.8 trillion, and the recessionary gap is eliminated.

MyLab Economics Animation

ECONOMICS IN ACTION

Fiscal Stimulus in the United States

As recession fears grew, the Economic Stimulus Act of 2008, a discretionary fiscal policy, aimed to increase aggregate demand.

Tax rebates were the key component of the package, and their effect on aggregate demand depends on the extent to which they are spent and saved.

The last time the U.S. federal government boosted aggregate demand with a tax rebate was in 2001, and a statistical investigation of the effects estimated that 70 percent of the rebates were spent within six months of being received.

The rebates in the 2008 fiscal package were targeted predominantly at low-income individuals and families, so the experience of 2001 would be likely to apply: Most of the rebates would be spent.

The cost of the package in 2008 was about $160 billion, so aggregate demand would be expected to increase by close to this amount and then by a multiplier as the initial spending became someone else's income and so boosted their spending.

The figure illustrates the effects of the package. Before the rebates, aggregate demand was AD_0 and real GDP was $14.8 trillion. The rebates increased aggregate demand to $AD_0 + \Delta E$, and a multiplier increased it to AD_1. Real GDP and the price level increased and the recessionary gap narrowed.

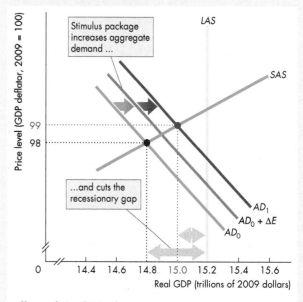

Effects of Fiscal Stimulus

the increase in aggregate demand brings a rise in the price level along the upward-sloping *SAS* curve and the economy moves to point *C*.

At point *C*, the economy returns to full employment and the recessionary gap is eliminated.

When Fiscal Stimulus Is Removed When fiscal stimulus brings a structural budget deficit, government debt grows. Concern about the effect of a deficit on debt often makes the government want to get back to a balanced budget. To do that, government expenditure must be cut and/or taxes must be increased. When these restraining discretionary fiscal policy actions are taken, aggregate demand decreases and a process the reverse of that described and illustrated in Fig. 13.9 kicks in. Care must be taken to try to time this restraint to coincide with an increase in investment and increasing aggregate demand.

Fiscal Stimulus and Aggregate Supply You've seen earlier in this chapter that taxes influence aggregate supply. A tax on labour income (on wages) drives a wedge between the cost of labour and the take-home pay of workers and lowers employment and output (p. 330). A tax on capital income (on interest) drives a wedge between the cost of borrowing and the return to lending and lowers saving and investment (p. 332). With less saving and investment, the real GDP growth rate slows.

These negative effects of taxes on real GDP and its growth rate and on employment mean that a tax *cut* increases real GDP and its growth rate and increases employment.

These supply-side effects of a tax cut occur along with the demand-side effects and are probably much larger than the demand-side effects and make the overall tax multiplier much larger than the government expenditure multiplier—see *Economics in Action*.

An increase in government expenditure financed by borrowing increases the demand for loanable funds and raises the real interest rate, which in turn lowers investment and private saving. This cut in investment is the main reason why the government expenditure multiplier is so small and why a deficit-financed increase in government spending ends up making only a small contribution to job creation. And because government expenditure crowds out investment, it lowers future real GDP.

So a fiscal stimulus package that is heavy on tax cuts and light on government spending works. But an increase in government expenditure alone is not an effective way to stimulate production and create jobs.

The description of the effects of discretionary fiscal stimulus and its graphical illustration in Fig. 13.9 make it look easy: Calculate the recessionary gap and the multipliers, change government expenditure and taxes, and eliminate the gap. In reality, things are not that easy.

Getting the magnitude and the timing right is difficult, and we'll now examine this challenge.

Magnitude of Stimulus Economists have diverging views about the size of the government spending and tax multipliers because there is insufficient empirical evidence on which to pin their size with accuracy. This fact makes it impossible for Parliament to

ECONOMICS IN ACTION
How Big Are the Fiscal Stimulus Multipliers?

When a U.S. 2009 fiscal stimulus package cut taxes by $300 billion and increased government spending by almost $500 billion, by how much did aggregate expenditure and real GDP change? How big were the fiscal policy multipliers? Was the government expenditure multiplier larger than the tax multiplier? These questions are about the multiplier effects on *equilibrium real GDP*, not just on aggregate demand.

President Obama's chief economic advisor in 2009, Christina Romer, a University of California, Berkeley, professor, expected the government expenditure multiplier to be about 1.5. So she was expecting the spending increase of $500 billion to go a long way towards closing the $1 trillion output gap by some time in 2010.

Robert Barro, a professor at Harvard University, says this multiplier number is not in line with previous experience. Based on his calculations, an additional $500 billion of government spending would increase aggregate expenditure by only $250 billion because it would lower private spending in a crowding-out effect by $250 billion—the multiplier is 0.5.

Harald Uhlig, a professor at the University of Chicago, says that the government expenditure multiplier on real GDP is even smaller and lies between 0.3 and 0.4, so that a $500 billion increase in government spending increases aggregate expenditure by between $150 billion and $200 billion.

determine the amount of stimulus needed to close a given output gap. Further, the actual output gap is not known and can only be estimated with error. For these two reasons, discretionary fiscal policy is risky.

Time Lags Discretionary fiscal stimulus actions are also seriously hampered by three time lags:

- Recognition lag
- Law-making lag
- Impact lag

Recognition Lag The *recognition lag* is the time it takes to figure out that fiscal policy actions are needed. This process involves assessing the current state of the economy and forecasting its future state.

Law-Making Lag The *law-making lag* is the time it takes Parliament to pass the laws needed to change taxes or spending. This process takes time because each member of Parliament has a different idea about what is the best tax or spending program to change, so long debates and committee meetings are needed to reconcile conflicting views. The economy might benefit from fiscal stimulation today, but by the time Parliament acts, a different fiscal medicine might be needed.

Impact Lag The *impact lag* is the time it takes from passing a tax or spending change to its effects on real GDP being felt. This lag depends partly on the speed with which government agencies can act and partly on the timing of changes in spending plans by households and businesses. These changes are spread out over a number of quarters and possibly years.

Economic forecasting is steadily improving, but it remains inexact and subject to error. The range of uncertainty about the magnitudes of the spending and tax multipliers make discretionary fiscal stimulus an imprecise tool for boosting production and jobs and the consequences of crowding out raise serious questions about the effects of fiscal stimulus on long-term economic growth.

There is greater agreement about tax multipliers. Because tax cuts strengthen the incentive to work and to invest, they increase aggregate supply as well as aggregate demand.

These multipliers get bigger as more time elapses. Harald Uhlig says that after one year, the tax multiplier is 0.5 so that the $300 billion tax cut would increase real GDP by about $150 billion after 1 year. But with two years of time to respond, real GDP would be $600 billion higher—a multiplier of 2. And after three years, the tax multiplier builds up to more than 6.

The implications of the work of Barro and Uhlig are that tax cuts are a powerful way to stimulate real GDP and employment, but spending increases are not effective.

Christina Romer agrees that the economy didn't perform in line with a multiplier of 1.5 but says other factors deteriorated and without the fiscal stimulus the outcome would have been even worse.

Christina Romer: 1.5

Robert Barro: 0.5

Harald Uhlig: 0.4

REVIEW QUIZ

1 What is the distinction between automatic and discretionary fiscal policy?
2 How do taxes and transfer payments programs work as automatic fiscal policy to dampen the business cycle?
3 How do we tell whether a budget deficit needs discretionary action to remove it?
4 How can the federal government use discretionary fiscal policy to stimulate the economy?
5 Why might fiscal stimulus crowd out investment?

Work these questions in Study Plan 13.3 and get instant feedback.   MyLab Economics

◆ To complete your review of fiscal policy, look at *Economics in the News* on pp. 340–341 and examine the effects of lowering the tax rate on the profits of corporations.

Cutting the Corporate Tax Rate

Trump Plans to Slash Corporation Tax Rate to 15 Percent

The Financial Times
April 24, 2017

The Trump administration is seeking a dramatic reduction in the rate of corporation tax to 15 per cent, a White House official said, as the president seeks to accelerate growth by easing burdens on U.S. business. …

The proposed reduction comes as the administration places a higher priority on easing taxes than on curbing the U.S. budget deficit. As such, it will encounter a rocky reception among fiscal conservatives in Congress, who worry about America's escalating public debt and will be the arbiters of what tax legislation is proposed and passed.

Steven Mnuchin, the Treasury secretary, has suggested that tax reductions would pay for themselves by galvanising higher growth and generating fresh revenue for the government.

Mr Mnuchin told the *Financial Times* last week that so-called dynamic models for scoring tax changes could show an extra $2tn of revenue under differing growth assumptions, saying the impact of growth of about 3 percent was "staggering."

The administration's tax-cutting plans may show an increased budget deficit under static models that do not account for the impact of higher growth on tax receipts, Mr Mnuchin had added. …

While the Treasury may be relying on "dynamic" economic models to suggest that deep tax cuts do not add to the deficit, Congress will have to use more conservative assumptions used by the Joint Committee on Taxation.

If these show the tax reductions adding to the deficit, it could create procedural headaches within Congress. To get through the Senate without Democratic party support, the tax package cannot add to the deficit over a 10-year timeframe.

Barney Jopson, Published September 27, 2017, *Financial Times*.

ESSENCE OF THE STORY

- The Trump administration wants to lower the rate of corporation income tax to 15 percent.

- Treasury Secretary Steven Mnuchin says the tax cut would increase real GDP growth to 3 percent per year and increase tax revenue.

- Congress will assume a more modest real GDP growth rate and support the tax cuts only as part of a package that does not add to the deficit over a 10-year timeframe.

MyLab Economics Economics in the News

ECONOMIC ANALYSIS

- Figure 1 shows the corporation income tax rates for 10 countries. U.S. corporations are among the most highly taxed in the world. Canadian corporations face a lower tax rate than the average of the 10 countries shown here.

- The U.S. rate of 40 percent is the sum of the federal rate of 35 percent and an average of state tax rates on the profits of corporations.

- The country with the lowest corporation tax rate, Ireland, lowered the rate in stages during the 1990s from 50 percent to the current 12.5 percent.

- The argument for cutting the tax rate is that a smaller tax wedge will increase private saving and investment and boost the growth rate of real GDP.

- Figure 2 illustrates the effects of the corporate income tax wedge in the market for loanable funds.

- The demand for loanable funds is *DLF* and with no corporate income tax, the supply of loanable funds is *SLF*. The equilibrium real interest rate is 3.4 percent a year and private saving and investment are $2.5 trillion. (The numbers are assumed but realistic.)

- With the tax wedge from the U.S. 40 percent corporate tax rate, the supply of loanable funds curve is *SLF + U.S. tax*. The real interest rate is 4 percent a year and investment and saving are only $2 trillion.

- Suppose that the U.S. tax rate is lowered to that of Canada, a rate of 26 percent.

- With the smaller tax wedge from Canada's 26 percent corporate tax rate, the supply of loanable funds curve is *SLF + Canada tax*. The real interest rate is lower at 3.8 percent a year and investment and saving are greater at $2.2 trillion.

- A higher amount of saving and investment means a larger capital stock, larger potential GDP, and a faster growth rate of potential GDP.

- A larger capital stock also means that labour is more productive, the demand for labour is greater, and the quantity of labour employed is larger.

- With higher real GDP and a faster growth rate, tax revenues increase, as argued by Steven Mnuchin.

- What is the evidence that these predicted effects occur?

- One test is to compare growth and real GDP (per person or per hour of work) in the United States and Canada.

- This comparison does not support the predictions. Canada has lower labour productivity than the United States and a similar growth rate.

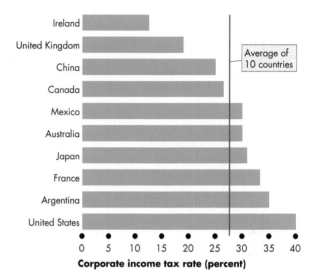

Figure 1 International Comparison of Corporate Income Tax Rates

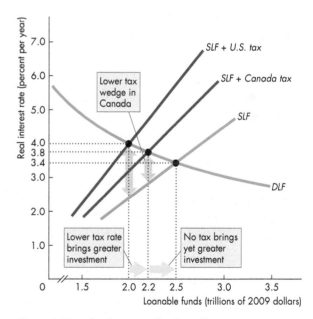

Figure 2 How the Corporate Tax Rate Changes Saving and Investment

- Another test is to compare Ireland's real GDP growth rate at a 50 percent tax rate with that at a 12.5 percent rate. There is no significant difference and other things have influenced Ireland's growth rate.

- Bottom line: There is no strong evidence to support claims for beneficial effects from corporate tax cuts.

341

WORKED PROBLEM

MyLab Economics Work this problem in Chapter 13 Study Plan.

The economy is at full employment, the inflation rate is 2 percent a year, and the government has a budget deficit. The government wants to make real GDP grow faster and is debating whether to spend more on infrastructure or to cut income taxes.

Questions

1. What would be the short-run effects of new infrastructure expenditure?
2. What would be the long-run effects of new infrastructure expenditure?
3. How would lower income taxes change the macroeconomic variables?
4. Which policy would increase the economic growth rate?

Solutions

1. With no change in government receipts, infrastructure expenditure will increase government outlays and the budget deficit. To fund the infrastructure work, the government goes to the loanable funds market. The demand for loanable funds increases and, with no change in the supply of loanable funds, the real interest rate rises. A higher real interest rate increases private saving and decreases private investment. The increased government expenditure crowds out some private investment.

   Aggregate demand increases by an amount equal to the infrastructure expenditure minus the crowded-out private investment plus the induced increase in consumption expenditure. With no change in aggregate supply, real GDP increases to above full employment and creates an inflationary gap.

Key Point: In the short run, a change in government expenditure changes the budget balance, the real interest rate, the quantities of private saving and private investment, aggregate demand, real GDP, and the output gap.

2. Two further things change in the long run. (1) An inflationary gap makes the money wage rate rise, and (2) the increase in infrastructure capital increases potential GDP.

   The higher money wage rate decreases short-run aggregate supply and the increase in potential GDP lessens that decrease. The price level rises,

and real GDP decreases to its new, higher full-employment level.

Key Point: An output gap brings changes in the labour market and the goods market, and increased capital increases potential GDP. In the long run, real GDP is at a higher full-employment equilibrium.

3. A cut in the tax rate on wage income increases the supply of labour, increases the quantity of labour employed, and increases potential GDP. A cut in the tax rate on interest income increases saving and investment, increases the quantity of capital, and increases potential GDP.

   Lower tax receipts increase the budget deficit, which sends the government to the loanable funds market. The demand for loanable funds increases, which lessens the effect of the cut in the tax on interest income.

   In the short run, the tax cut increases aggregate demand and brings an inflationary gap, which increases the money wage rate and decreases short-run aggregate supply.

   In the long run, the economy returns to full-employment equilibrium, but one in which more people are employed and real GDP is larger.

Key Point: A change in the income tax rate changes the labour market equilibrium and the loanable funds market equilibrium. Employment, private investment, and potential GDP change.

4. A change in the real GDP growth rate is a long-run effect.

   In the long run, an increase in infrastructure capital increases potential GDP and crowds out private investment, which decreases potential GDP. If the crowding out is incomplete, a larger capital stock increases potential GDP. To make real GDP grow faster, capital must keep increasing at a faster pace. A one-shot expenditure on new infrastructure does not have this effect.

   A lower tax rate on interest income increases private investment, the rate of capital accumulation, and the growth rate of real GDP.

Key Point: A one-shot investment in infrastructure increases real GDP but not economic growth. A cut in the tax rate on interest income increases investment, which increases the rate of capital accumulation and the real GDP growth rate.

SUMMARY

Key Points

The Federal Budget (pp. 324–329)

- The federal budget is used to achieve macroeconomic objectives.
- Revenues can exceed, equal, or fall short of outlays—the budget can be in surplus, balanced, or in deficit.
- Budget deficits create government debt.

Working Problem 1 will give you a better understanding of the federal budget.

Supply-Side Effects of Fiscal Policy (pp. 330–333)

- Fiscal policy has supply-side effects because taxes weaken the incentive to work and decrease employment and potential GDP.
- The Canadian labour market tax wedge is similar to that in the United States, but smaller than that in France or the United Kingdom.
- Fiscal policy has supply-side effects because taxes weaken the incentive to save and invest, which lowers the growth rate of real GDP.

- The Laffer curve shows the relationship between the tax rate and the amount of tax revenue collected.

Working Problems 2 to 4 will give you a better understanding of the supply-side effects of fiscal policy.

Fiscal Stimulus (pp. 334–339)

- Fiscal policy can be automatic or discretionary.
- Automatic fiscal policy might moderate the business cycle by stimulating demand in a recession and restraining demand in a boom.
- Discretionary fiscal stimulus influences aggregate demand *and* aggregate supply.
- Discretionary changes in government expenditure or taxes have multiplier effects of uncertain magnitude, but the tax multiplier is likely the larger one.
- Fiscal stimulus policies are hampered by uncertainty about the multipliers and by time lags (law-making lags and the difficulty of correctly diagnosing and forecasting the state of the economy).

Working Problems 5 to 11 will give you a better understanding of fiscal stimulus.

Key Terms

MyLab Economics Key Terms Quiz

Automatic fiscal policy, 334
Balanced budget, 325
Budget deficit, 325
Budget surplus, 325
Cyclical surplus or deficit, 334
Discretionary fiscal policy, 334

Federal budget, 324
Fiscal policy, 324
Fiscal stimulus, 334
Government debt, 327
Government expenditure
    multiplier, 335

Laffer curve, 333
Structural surplus or deficit, 334
Tax multiplier, 336
Tax wedge, 331

STUDY PLAN PROBLEMS AND APPLICATIONS

MyLab Economics Work Problems 1 to 11 in Chapter 13 Study Plan and get instant feedback.

The Federal Budget (Study Plan 13.1)

1. At the end of 2015, China's government debt was ¥25.8 trillion (¥ is yuan, the currency of China). In 2016, the government spent ¥18.7 trillion and ended the year with a debt of ¥28 trillion. What was the government tax revenue in 2016? How can you tell?

Supply-Side Effects of Fiscal Policy (Study Plan 13.2)

2. The government is considering raising the tax rate on labour income and asks you to report on the supply-side effects of such an action. Use appropriate graphs and report *directions* of change, not exact magnitudes. What will happen to:
   a. The supply of labour and why?
   b. The demand for labour and why?
   c. Equilibrium employment and why?
   d. The equilibrium before-tax wage rate and why?
   e. The equilibrium after-tax wage rate and why?
   f. Potential GDP?

3. What fiscal policy action might increase investment and speed economic growth? Explain how the policy action would work.

4. Suppose that instead of taxing *nominal* capital income, the government taxed *real* capital income. Use graphs to explain and illustrate the effect that this change would have on:
   a. The tax rate on capital income.
   b. The supply of and demand for loanable funds.
   c. Investment and the real interest rate.

Fiscal Stimulus (Study Plan 13.3)

5. The economy is in a recession, and the recessionary gap is large.
   a. Describe the discretionary and automatic fiscal policy actions that might occur.
   b. Describe a discretionary fiscal stimulus package that could be used that would not bring an increase in the budget deficit.
   c. Explain the risks of discretionary fiscal policy in this situation.

6. The economy is in a recession, the recessionary gap is large, and there is a budget deficit.
   a. Do we know whether the budget deficit is structural or cyclical? Explain your answer and use a graph to illustrate it.
   b. Do we know whether automatic fiscal policy is increasing or decreasing the output gap? Explain your answer.
   c. If a discretionary increase in government expenditure occurs, what happens to the structural deficit or surplus? Explain.

Use the following news clip to work Problems 7 and 8.

Ottawa Posts Small Surplus for First Quarter

The federal government ran a surplus of $16 million for the first quarter of the 2017–18 fiscal year but projected a $28.5-billion deficit for the full year. (A fiscal year begins on April 1 and ends on March 31.)

Source: *The Globe and Mail*, August 25, 2017

7. What would be the effect of the first quarter budget surplus on real GDP and jobs?

8. What would be the effect of the budget deficit for the full fiscal year 2017–18 on real GDP and jobs? Which effect would be larger, the first quarter surplus or the full year deficit, and why?

Use the following news clip to work Problems 9 to 11.

Recession Threat Demands Immediate Action

When the economy was slowly recovering from recession, in 2011, the NDP called for government spending on infrastructure and green energy and said that corporate tax cuts did not give sufficient stimulus.

Source: CBC News, September 29, 2011

9. Was the NDP's proposed infrastructure spending a fiscal stimulus? Would such spending be a discretionary or an automatic fiscal policy?

10. Explain whether, and if so how, spending on infrastructure and green energy would create jobs. Use graphs to illustrate your answer.

11. What would have a larger effect on aggregate demand: corporate tax cuts or an equivalent scale increase in government expenditure on infrastructure and green energy projects?

ADDITIONAL PROBLEMS AND APPLICATIONS

The Federal Budget

12. **Canada's Economy Surges 4.5 Percent**

    Canadian real GDP unexpectedly accelerated to a 4.5 percent pace in the second quarter of 2017. This faster-than-expected growth was the fastest among Group of Seven countries. It was led by the biggest rise in household spending since before the 2008–2009 global recession.

    Source: *Bloomberg*, August 31, 2017

    a. How would an unexpected increase in the economic growth rate influence federal government outlays?

    b. How would an unexpected increase in the economic growth rate influence federal government revenues?

Supply-Side Effects of Fiscal Policy

Use the following information to work Problems 13 and 14.

Suppose that investment is $160 billion, saving is $140 billion, government expenditure on goods and services is $150 billion, exports are $200 billion, and imports are $250 billion.

13. What is the amount of tax revenue? What is the government budget balance?

14. a. Is the government's budget exerting a positive or negative impact on investment?

    b. What fiscal policy action might increase investment and speed economic growth? Explain how the policy action would work.

15. Suppose that capital income taxes are based (as they are in Canada and most countries) on nominal interest rates. If the inflation rate increases by 5 percent a year, explain and use appropriate graphs to illustrate the effect of the rise in inflation on:

    a. The tax increase on capital income.

    b. The supply of loanable funds.

    c. The demand for loanable funds.

    d. Equilibrium investment.

    e. The equilibrium real interest rate.

16. **Fiscal Policy Sheltered Canada's Economy from the Worst Effects of the Global Recession**

    The Conference Board of Canada says that Canada weathered the global financial crisis and recession better than many other countries because of better policies already in place. Canada was in a much stronger position going into the recession thanks to its low and declining government debt and budget surpluses. The design of government policy and the speed of the policy response can make a huge difference in preventing or mitigating the worst of a recession.

    Source: Conference Board of Canada

    a. Explain the potential demand-side effects of "low and declining government debt and budget surpluses."

    b. Explain the potential supply-side effects of "low and declining government debt and budget surpluses."

    c. Draw a graph to illustrate the combined demand-side and supply-side effects of "low and declining government debt and budget surpluses."

Use the following information to work Problems 17 and 18.

Job Destruction and Job Creation

William Watson, an economics professor at McGill University, Montreal, says job creation is the flip side of job destruction. Jobs get destroyed when a new technology replaces workers with machines. Job creation occurs when someone who is now free from the drudgery of a now mechanized task wants to sell a product or service and contracts with someone else to help them do it. It's not rocket science, he says. To create jobs, the most obvious imperative is "Do no harm." Don't complicate, regulate, or overtax it.

17. Does William Watson think that job creation is primarily a problem that needs an increase in aggregate demand or aggregate supply?

18. Explain how lowering taxes on employment will create jobs. Use a graph to illustrate your answer.

Fiscal Stimulus

19. The economy is in a boom and the inflationary gap is large.
    a. Describe the discretionary and automatic fiscal policy actions that might occur.
    b. Describe a discretionary fiscal restraint package that could be used that would not produce serious negative supply-side effects.
    c. Explain the risks of discretionary fiscal policy in this situation.

20. The economy is growing slowly, the inflationary gap is large, and there is a budget deficit.
    a. Do we know whether the budget deficit is structural or cyclical? Explain your choice and sketch a graph to illustrate your answer.
    b. Do we know whether automatic fiscal policy is increasing or decreasing aggregate demand? Explain your answer.
    c. If a discretionary decrease in government expenditure occurs, what happens to the structural budget balance? Explain your answer.

Use the following news clip to work Problems 21 to 23.

China's Reliance on Infrastructure Stimulus at Record High

China's reliance on infrastructure spending to drive overall investment hit a new high in 2017. Chinese economic planners have turned more heavily to infrastructure as stimulus since 2015, preferring this approach over further investment in manufacturing, where earlier stimulus brought excess capacity in steel and coal. Stimulus spending is bringing increased government debt.

Source: *The Financial Times*, August 24, 2017

21. Explain the possible reasons why fiscal stimulus is needed in China.
22. Is the stimulus described in the news clip discretionary or automatic? Explain your answer.
23. What challenges that make fiscal stimulus difficult to implement does the news clip illustrate? What are the potential consequences of a stimulus being too much and being pursued for too long?

Economics in the News

24. After you have studied *Economics in the News* on pp. 340–341, answer the following questions.
    a. On which factor incomes does the corporation income tax fall?
    b. How does the corporation income tax influence investment and saving and the real interest rate? Draw a graph to illustrate your answer.
    c. How does the corporation income tax rate influence potential GDP and the real GDP growth rate?
    d. Explain why a cut in the rate of corporation income tax might speed economic growth. What does the evidence from Canada and Ireland imply about the strength of the effect?

25. **More Fiscal Stimulus Needed?**

    In *The New York Times* articles and in blogs, economists Paul Krugman and Joseph Stiglitz say that, with slow recovery from recession, there is a need for more fiscal stimulus in both the United States and Europe despite the large federal budget deficit and large deficits in some European countries.
    a. Do you agree with Krugman and Stiglitz? Why?
    b. What are the dangers of not engaging in further fiscal stimulus?
    c. What are the dangers of embarking on further fiscal stimulus when the budget is in deficit?

26. **The Fears About Japan's Debt Are Overblown**

    One quadrillion yen. ¥1,000,000,000,000,000. That's the scale of Japan's government debt. There are only five things a country with a large public debt can do: grow faster to shrink its burden, repay it, default, inflate, or live with it. In the case of Japan, the first four look unlikely. And the fifth option is surprisingly do-able with low interest rates and by keeping the deficit under control.

    Source: *The Financial Times*, September 5, 2017

    a. How does keeping the deficit under control enable Japan to live with a large debt-to-GDP ratio?
    b. What are the challenges Japan would face if it experienced a severe recession?

14 MONETARY POLICY

After studying this chapter, you will be able to:

◆ Describe Canada's monetary policy objective and the framework for setting and achieving it

◆ Explain how the Bank of Canada makes its interest rate decision and achieves its interest rate target

◆ Explain the transmission channels through which the Bank of Canada influences real GDP, jobs, and inflation

◆ Explain how monetary policy and macroprudential regulation seek to prevent financial crisis

How does the Bank of Canada make its interest rate decision? How does a change in the interest rate influence the economy? Can the Bank speed up economic growth and lower unemployment by lowering the interest rate, and can the Bank keep inflation in check by raising the interest rate?

This chapter answers these questions. It applies and extends what you learned in Chapters 8–12 to explain the Bank's monetary policy strategy and its effects on the economy. In *Economics in the News* at the end of the chapter, you will see how the Bank of Canada tries to maintain full employment and hit its inflation target.

◆ Monetary Policy Objectives and Framework

Canada's monetary policy objective and the framework for setting and achieving that objective stem from the relationship between the Bank of Canada and the Government of Canada.

We'll first discuss the objective of monetary policy and then describe the framework and assignment of responsibility for achieving the objective.

Monetary Policy Objective

The objective of monetary policy is ultimately political, and it stems from the mandate of the Bank, which is set out in the Bank of Canada Act.

Bank of Canada Act The objective of monetary policy as set out in the preamble to the Bank of Canada Act of 1935 is as follows:

> To regulate credit and currency in the best interests of the economic life of the nation … and to mitigate by its influence fluctuations in the general level of production, trade, prices, and employment, so far as may be possible within the scope of monetary action …

reduce

In simple language, these words have come to mean that the Bank's job is to control the quantity of money and interest rates in order to avoid inflation and, when possible, prevent excessive swings in real GDP growth and unemployment.

This emphasis on inflation has been made concrete by an agreement between the Bank and the government.

Joint Statement of the Government of Canada and the Bank of Canada

In a joint statement (the most recent of which was made in 2016), the Government of Canada and the Bank of Canada agree that:

- The target will continue to be defined in terms of the 12-month rate of change in the total CPI.
- The inflation target will continue to be the 2 percent midpoint of the 1 to 3 percent inflation-control range.
- The agreement will run for another five-year period, ending December 31, 2021.

A monetary policy strategy in which the central bank commits to an explicit inflation target and to explaining how its actions will achieve that target is called **inflation rate targeting**.

Interpretation of the Agreement The inflation-control target uses the Consumer Price Index (or CPI) as the measure of inflation. So the Bank has agreed to keep trend CPI inflation at a target of 2 percent a year.

But the Bank pays the closest attention to three measures of *core inflation* (see Chapter 5, pp. 124–125), which the Bank calls its operational guide. The Bank believes that the core inflation measures provide a better view of the underlying inflation trend and better predict future CPI inflation.

Although the Bank watches three core inflation measures closely, it must watch for the possibility that the volatile elements that they exclude have a trend inflation rate that differs from the core items. As it turns out, over the past 20 years, the core trends and CPI trend were very similar.

Actual Inflation The performance of Canada's inflation since the 1990s, when the current target was initially set, has been close to target. Figure 14.1 shows just how close. Part (a) shows the average of the three core inflation measures—the average of CPI-common, CPI-median, and CPI-trim. And part (b) shows the price level, measured by the CPI.

In part (a), you can see the target range of 1 to 3 percent a year. And you can see that the core inflation rate has never gone outside the target range. You can also see that the core inflation rate has been both above and below 2 percent, but with a bias or tendency for inflation to be below 2 percent for more of the time.

In part (b), you can see the trend of inflation at the 2 percent target midpoint. The CPI was on trend from 1997 through 2011. But since 2011, when core inflation was below 2 percent in part (a), the CPI drifted further and further below the 2 percent trend line.

The general message of Fig. 14.1 is that the Bank of Canada has done a remarkable job of holding inflation close to its 2 percent target with only small deviations from that goal.

Rationale for an Inflation-Control Target Two main benefits flow from adopting an inflation-control target. The first benefit is that the purpose of the Bank of Canada's policy actions is more clearly understood

FIGURE 14.1   Inflation-Control Target and Outcome

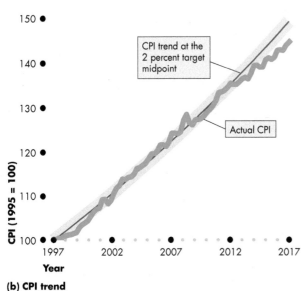

(a) Inflation target and outcome

(b) CPI trend

The Bank of Canada has kept the inflation rate close to the inflation-control target. In part (a), the average of the three core inflation measures has never left the target range. In part (b), the CPI remained close to the 2 percent trend line until 2011, after which inflation was below 2 percent.

Sources of data: Statistics Canada, CANSIM Tables 326-0020 and 326-0022, and Bank of Canada, Joint Statement of the Government of Canada and the Bank of Canada on the Renewal of the Inflation-Control Target, November 24, 2016.

―――――――――――――― MyLab Economics Animation ―――――――

by financial market traders, which leads to fewer miscalculations by savers and investors.

The second benefit is that the target provides an anchor for expectations about future inflation. Firmly held expectations of low inflation make the short-run output-inflation (or unemployment-inflation) tradeoff as favourable as possible. (See Chapter 12, pp. 312–313.) Firmly held (and correct) inflation expectations also help to make better economic decisions, which in turn help to achieve a more efficient allocation of resources and more stable economic growth.

Controversy About the Inflation-Control Target Not everyone agrees that the adoption of an inflation-control target brings benefits. Critics argue that by focusing on inflation, the Bank of Canada sometimes permits the unemployment rate to rise or the real GDP growth rate to suffer.

The fear of these critics is that if the inflation rate begins to edge upward towards and perhaps beyond the upper limit of the target range, the Bank of Canada might rein in aggregate demand and push the economy into recession. Related, the Bank might end up permitting the value of the dollar on the foreign exchange market to rise, which will make exports suffer.

One response of supporters of inflation targeting is that by keeping inflation low and stable, monetary policy makes its maximum possible contribution towards achieving full employment and sustained economic growth.

Another response is, "Look at the record." The last time the Bank of Canada created a recession was at the beginning of the 1990s when it was faced with the threat of ongoing double-digit inflation. Since that time, monetary policy has been sensitive to the state of employment while maintaining its focus on achieving its inflation target.

Responsibility for Monetary Policy

The Government of Canada and the Bank of Canada jointly agree on the monetary policy target, but the Bank of Canada Act places responsibility for the conduct of monetary policy on the Bank's Governing Council.

Governing Council of the Bank of Canada The members of the Bank's Governing Council are the Governor, Senior Deputy Governor, and four Deputy

Governors. All the members of the Governing Council are experts in monetary economics and monetary policymaking and, normally, they are people who have been promoted from within the ranks of economists working in the Bank's research and policy departments.

The current Governor (appointed in 2013) is Stephen Poloz, an economist who has had wide experience at the Bank of Canada, in the private sector, at the IMF, and at Export Development Canada.

Bank of Canada Economists The Bank of Canada employs research economists who write papers on monetary policy and the state of the Canadian and international economies. These economists provide the Governing Council with extensive briefings that guide monetary policy.

Consultations with the Government The Bank of Canada Act requires regular consultations on monetary policy between the Governor and the Minister of Finance. The Act also lays out what must happen if the Governor and the Minister disagree in a profound way.

In such an event, the Minister would direct the Bank in writing to follow a specified course and the Bank would be obliged to accept the directive. The Governor would most likely resign in such a situation. While in the past there have been disagreements between the government and the Bank, no formal directive has ever been issued.

You now know the objective of monetary policy and can describe the framework and assignment of responsibility for achieving that objective. Your next task is to see how the Bank of Canada conducts its monetary policy.

◆ REVIEW QUIZ

1 What is the Bank of Canada's monetary policy objective?
2 What are the two parts of the inflation-control target?
3 How does the core inflation rate differ from the overall CPI inflation rate?
4 What is the Bank of Canada's record in achieving its inflation-control target?

Work these questions in Study Plan 14.1 and get instant feedback.
MyLab Economics

◆ The Conduct of Monetary Policy

We're now going to describe how the Bank of Canada conducts its monetary policy. To do so, we're going to answer three questions:

■ What is the Bank's monetary policy instrument?
■ How does the Bank make its policy decision?
■ How does the Bank implement its policy?

The Monetary Policy Instrument

As the sole issuer of Canadian money, the Bank of Canada can decide to control the quantity of money (the monetary base), the price of Canadian money on the foreign exchange market (the exchange rate), or the opportunity cost of holding money (the short-term interest rate). If you need a refresher, check back to Chapter 8, pp. 202–203 to see how the quantity of money affects the interest rate and to Chapter 9, pp. 218–219 and pp. 225–227 to see how the interest rate or direct intervention in the foreign exchange market affects the exchange rate.

The Bank of Canada can set any one of these three variables, but it cannot set all three. The values of two of them are the consequence of the value at which the third one is set. If the Bank decreased the quantity of money, both the interest rate and the exchange rate would rise. If the Bank raised the interest rate, the quantity of money would decrease and the exchange rate would rise. And if the Bank lowered the exchange rate, the quantity of money would increase and the interest rate would fall.

So the Bank must decide which of these three instruments to use. It might decide to select one and stick with it, or it might switch among them.

The Overnight Loans Rate The Bank of Canada's choice of policy instrument (which is the same choice as that made by most other central banks) is a short-term interest rate. Given this choice, the Bank permits the exchange rate and the quantity of money to find their own equilibrium values and has no preset views about what those values should be.

The specific interest rate that the Bank of Canada targets is the **overnight loans rate**, which is the interest rate on overnight loans that the big banks make to each other.

Figure 14.2 shows the overnight loans rate for the 20 years from 1997 to 2017. The overnight loans rate was 3 percent a year in 1997, a bit more than its 20-year average of 2.44 percent. The rate was twice

FIGURE 14.2 The Overnight Loans Rate

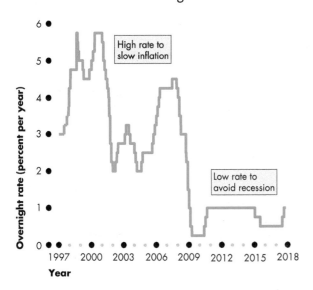

The Bank of Canada sets a target for the overnight loans rate and then takes actions to keep the rate close to its target. When the Bank wants to slow inflation, it raises the overnight loans rate. When inflation is low and the Bank wants to avoid recession, it lowers the overnight loans rate.

Source of data: Statistics Canada, CANSIM Table 176-0048.

—————————— MyLab Economics Animation ——————————

increased to 5.75 percent and once to 4.5 percent. These periods with a high overnight loans rate are ones in which inflation was a concern.

In recent years, the overnight loans rate has been at historically low levels. With inflation well anchored inside its target range, the Bank wanted to lean in the direction of avoiding recession.

Since 2000, the Bank has established eight fixed dates on which it announces its overnight loans rate target for the coming six-week period. Before 2000, the Bank announced changes in the overnight loans rate whenever it thought a change was required. And even now, the Bank sometimes acts in an emergency between normal announcement dates.

Although the Bank can change the overnight loans rate by any (reasonable) amount that it chooses, it normally changes the rate by only a quarter of a percentage point.[1]

How does the Bank decide the appropriate level for the overnight loans rate?

——————————
[1]A quarter of a percentage point is also called 25 *basis points*. A basis point is one hundredth of one percentage point.

The Bank's Interest Rate Decision

To make its interest rate decision, the Bank of Canada gathers a large amount of data about the economy, the way it responds to shocks, and the way it responds to policy. It then processes all this data and comes to a judgment about the best level for the overnight loans rate.

The Bank's staff economists use a model of the Canadian economy—a sophisticated version of the aggregate supply–aggregate demand model—to provide the Governor and Governing Council with a baseline forecast. All the available regional, national, and international data on macroeconomic performance, financial markets, and inflation expectations are reviewed, discussed, and weighed in a careful deliberative process that ends with the Governing Council finding a consensus on the interest rate level to set.

After announcing an interest rate decision, the Bank engages in a public communication to explain the reasons for its decision. Twice a year, the Bank publishes a highly detailed *Inflation Report* that describes the forces operating on the economy, the outlook for inflation and real GDP growth, and the reasons for the Bank's interest rate decision.

Having made a decision, how does the Bank ensure that the overnight loans rate is on target?

Hitting the Overnight Loans Rate Target

Once an interest rate decision is made, the Bank of Canada achieves its target by using two tools: the operating band and open market operations.

The **operating band** is the target overnight loans rate plus or minus 0.25 percentage points. The Bank creates the operating band by setting two other interest rates: *bank rate* and a rate called the *settlement balances rate*.

Bank rate is the interest rate that the Bank of Canada charges big banks on loans. If a bank is short of reserves, it can always obtain reserves from the Bank of Canada, but the bank must pay bank rate on the amount of borrowed reserves.

The Bank of Canada sets bank rate at the target overnight loans rate plus 0.25 percentage points. Because the Bank of Canada is willing to lend funds to banks at this interest rate, bank rate acts as a cap on the overnight loans rate. If a bank can borrow from the Bank of Canada at bank rate, it will not borrow from another bank unless the interest rate is lower than or equal to bank rate.

The Bank of Canada pays banks interest on their reserves at the Bank of Canada—called the **settlement balances rate**—set at the target overnight loans rate minus 0.25 percentage points. Banks won't make overnight loans to other banks unless they earn a higher interest rate than what the Bank is paying.

The alternative to lending in the overnight market is to hold reserves. And the alternative to borrowing in the overnight market is to hold smaller reserves. The demand for reserves is the flip side of lending and borrowing in the overnight market.

Figure 14.3 shows the demand curve for reserves as the curve labelled *RD*. If the entire banking system is borrowing from the Bank of Canada, reserves (on the *x*-axis) are negative. If the overnight loans rate (on the *y*-axis) equals bank rate, banks are indifferent between borrowing reserves and lending reserves. The demand curve is horizontal at bank rate. If the overnight loans rate equals the settlement balances rate, banks are indifferent between holding reserves and lending reserves. The demand curve is horizontal at the settlement balances rate.

You can see that the overnight loans rate always lies inside the operating band.

The overnight loans rate cannot exceed bank rate because if it did, a bank could earn a profit by borrowing from the Bank of Canada and lending to another bank. But all banks can borrow from the Bank of Canada at bank rate, so no bank is willing to pay more than bank rate to borrow reserves.

The overnight loans rate cannot fall below the settlement balances rate because if it did, a bank could earn a profit by borrowing from another bank and increasing its reserves at the Bank of Canada. But all banks can earn the settlement balances rate at the Bank of Canada, so no bank is willing to lend reserves at a rate below the settlement balances rate.

The Bank of Canada's open market operations determine the actual quantity of reserves in the banking system, and equilibrium in the market for reserves determines the actual overnight loans rate. (We describe how an operation works to change the monetary base in Chapter 8, p. 192–194.)

If the overnight loans rate is above target, the Bank buys securities to increase reserves, which increases the supply of overnight funds and lowers the overnight loans rate. If the overnight loans rate is below target, the Bank sells securities to decrease reserves, which decreases the supply of overnight funds and raises the overnight loans rate. If the overnight loans rate is at the target level, the Bank neither buys nor

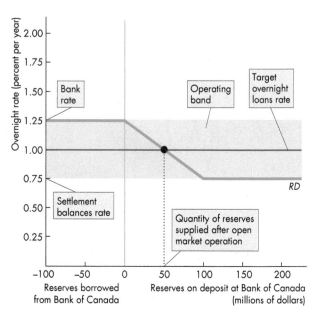

FIGURE 14.3 The Market for Reserves

The demand curve for reserves is *RD*. If the overnight loans rate equals bank rate, banks are indifferent between borrowing reserves and lending reserves. The demand curve is horizontal at bank rate. If the overnight loans rate equals the settlement balances rate, banks are indifferent between holding reserves and lending reserves. The demand curve is horizontal at the settlement balances rate. Equilibrium, where the quantity of reserves demanded equals the quantity supplied, determines the overnight loans rate.

———— MyLab Economics Animation ————

sells. By using open market operations, the Bank of Canada keeps the overnight loans rate on target.

◆ REVIEW QUIZ

1 What is the Bank of Canada's monetary policy instrument?
2 Summarize the Bank of Canada's monetary policy decision-making process.
3 What is the operating band?
4 What happens when the Bank of Canada buys securities in the open market?
5 How is the overnight loans rate determined in the market for bank reserves?

Work these questions in Study Plan 14.2 and get instant feedback.   MyLab Economics

◆ Monetary Policy Transmission

You've seen that the Bank of Canada's goal is to keep the inflation rate as close as possible to 2 percent a year. And you've seen how the Bank can use its policy tools to keep the overnight loans rate at its desired level.

We're now going to trace the events that follow a change in the overnight loans rate and see how those events lead to the ultimate policy goal—keeping inflation on target.

We'll begin with a quick overview of the transmission process and then look at each step a bit more closely.

Quick Overview

When the Bank of Canada wants to lower the overnight loans rate to a new target, it buys securities in the open market. Other short-term interest rates and the exchange rate also fall. The quantity of money and the supply of loanable funds increase. The long-term real interest rate falls. The lower real interest rate increases consumption expenditure and investment. And the lower exchange rate makes Canadian exports cheaper and imports more costly, so net exports increase. Easier bank loans reinforce the effect of lower interest rates on aggregate expenditure. Aggregate demand increases, which increases real GDP and the price level relative to what they would have been. Real GDP growth and inflation speed up.

When the Bank raises the overnight loans rate, it sells securities in the open market and as the sequence of events that we've just reviewed plays out, the effects are in the opposite directions.

Figure 14.4 provides a schematic summary of these ripple effects for both a cut and a rise in the overnight loans rate.

These ripple effects stretch out over a period of between one and two years. The interest rate and exchange rate effects are immediate. The effects on money and bank loans follow in a few weeks and run for a few months. Real long-term interest rates change quickly and often in anticipation of the short-term interest rate changes. Spending plans change and real GDP growth changes after about one year. The inflation rate changes between one year and two years after the change in the overnight loans rate. But these time lags are not entirely predictable and can be longer or shorter.

We're going to look at each stage in the transmission process, starting with the interest rate effects.

Think of the demand.

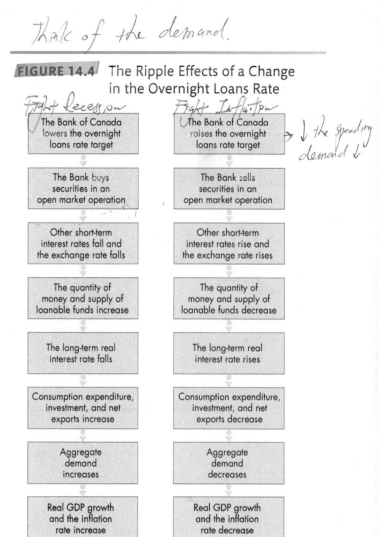

FIGURE 14.4 The Ripple Effects of a Change in the Overnight Loans Rate

Fight Recession

Fight Inflation

→ ↓ the spending demand ↓

The Bank of Canada lowers the overnight loans rate target	The Bank of Canada raises the overnight loans rate target
The Bank buys securities in an open market operation	The Bank sells securities in an open market operation
Other short-term interest rates fall and the exchange rate falls	Other short-term interest rates rise and the exchange rate rises
The quantity of money and supply of loanable funds increase	The quantity of money and supply of loanable funds decrease
The long-term real interest rate falls	The long-term real interest rate rises
Consumption expenditure, investment, and net exports increase	Consumption expenditure, investment, and net exports decrease
Aggregate demand increases	Aggregate demand decreases
Real GDP growth and the inflation rate increase	Real GDP growth and the inflation rate decrease

— MyLab Economics Animation —

Interest Rate Changes

The first effect of a monetary policy decision by the Bank of Canada is a change in the overnight loans rate. Other interest rates then change. These interest rate effects occur quickly and relatively predictably.

Figure 14.5 shows the fluctuations in three interest rates: the overnight loans rate, the short-term bill rate, and the long-term bond rate.

Overnight Loans Rate As soon as the Bank of Canada announces a new setting for the overnight loans rate, it undertakes the necessary open market operations to hit the target. There is no doubt about where the interest rate changes shown in Fig. 14.5 are generated. They are driven by the Bank of Canada's monetary policy.

FIGURE 14.5 Three Interest Rates

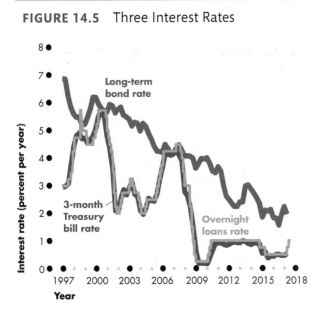

The short-term interest rates—the overnight loans rate and the 3-month Treasury bill rate—move closely together. The long-term bond rate is higher than the short-term rates, and it fluctuates less than the short-term rates.

Source of data: Statistics Canada, CANSIM Tables 176-0043 and 176-0048.

——————— MyLab Economics Animation ———————

3-Month Treasury Bill Rate The 3-month Treasury bill rate is the interest rate paid by the Government of Canada on 3-month debt. It is similar to the interest rate paid by Canadian businesses on short-term loans. Notice how closely the 3-month Treasury bill rate follows the overnight loans rate. The two rates are almost identical.

A *powerful substitution effect* keeps these two interest rates close. Chartered banks have a choice about how to hold their short-term liquid assets, and an overnight loan to another bank is a close substitute for short-term securities such as Treasury bills. If the interest rate on Treasury bills is higher than the overnight loans rate, the quantity of overnight loans supplied decreases and the demand for Treasury bills increases. The price of Treasury bills rises and the interest rate falls.

Similarly, if the interest rate on Treasury bills is lower than the overnight loans rate, the quantity of overnight loans supplied increases and the demand for Treasury bills decreases. The price of Treasury bills falls and the interest rate rises.

When the interest rate on Treasury bills is close to the overnight loans rate, there is no incentive for a bank to switch between making an overnight loan and buying Treasury bills. Both the Treasury bill market and the overnight loans market are in equilibrium.

The Long-Term Bond Rate The long-term bond rate is the interest rate paid on bonds issued by large corporations. It is this interest rate that businesses pay on the loans that finance their purchase of new capital and that influences their investment decisions. Two features of the long-term bond rate stand out: It is higher than the short-term rates, and it fluctuates less than the short-term rates.

The long-term interest rate is higher than the two short-term rates because long-term loans are riskier than short-term loans. To provide the incentive that brings forth a supply of long-term loans, lenders must be compensated for the additional risk. Without compensation for the additional risk, only short-term loans would be supplied.

The long-term interest rate fluctuates less than the short-term rates because it is influenced by expectations about future short-term interest rates as well as current short-term interest rates. The alternative to borrowing or lending long term is to borrow or lend using a sequence of short-term securities. If the long-term interest rate exceeds the expected average of future short-term interest rates, people will lend long term and borrow short term. The long-term interest rate will fall. And if the long-term interest rate is below the expected average of future short-term interest rates, people will borrow long term and lend short term. The long-term interest rate will rise.

These market forces keep the long-term interest rate close to the expected average of future short-term interest rates (plus a premium for the extra risk associated with long-term loans). The expected average future short-term interest rate fluctuates less than the current short-term interest rate.

Exchange Rate Fluctuations

The exchange rate responds to changes in the interest rate in Canada relative to the interest rates in other countries—*the Canadian interest rate differential.* We explain this influence in Chapter 9 (see pp. 220–221).

When the Bank of Canada raises the overnight loans rate, the Canadian interest rate differential rises and, other things remaining the same, the Canadian dollar appreciates. And when the Bank lowers the overnight loans rate, the Canadian interest rate differential falls and, other things remaining the same, the Canadian dollar depreciates.

Many factors other than the Canadian interest rate differential influence the exchange rate, so when the Bank changes the overnight loans rate, the exchange rate does not usually change in exactly the way it would with other things remaining the same. So while monetary policy influences the exchange rate, many other factors also make the exchange rate change.

Money and Bank Loans

The quantity of money and bank loans change when the Bank changes the overnight loans rate target. A rise in the overnight loans rate decreases the quantity of money and bank loans, and a fall in the overnight loans rate increases the quantity of money and bank loans. These changes occur for two reasons: The quantity of deposits and loans created by the banking system changes and the quantity of money demanded changes.

You've seen that to change the overnight loans rate, the quantity of bank reserves must change. A change in the quantity of bank reserves changes the monetary base, which in turn changes the quantity of deposits and loans that the banking system can create. A rise in the overnight loans rate decreases reserves and decreases the quantity of deposits and bank loans created; and a fall in the overnight loans rate increases reserves and increases the quantity of deposits and bank loans created.

The quantity of money created by the banking system must be held by households and firms. The change in the interest rate changes the quantity of money demanded. A fall in the interest rate increases the quantity of money demanded; and a rise in the interest rate decreases the quantity of money demanded.

A change in the quantity of money and the supply of bank loans directly affects consumption and investment plans. With more money and easier access to loans, consumers and firms spend more; with less money and loans harder to get, consumers and firms spend less.

The Long-Term Real Interest Rate

Demand and supply in the loanable funds market determine the long-term *real interest rate*, which equals the long-term *nominal* interest rate minus the expected inflation rate. The long-term real interest rate influences expenditure decisions.

In the long run, demand and supply in the loanable funds market depend only on real forces—on saving and investment decisions. But in the short run, when the price level is not fully flexible, the supply of loanable funds is influenced by the supply of bank loans. Changes in the overnight loans rate change the supply of bank loans, which changes the supply of loanable funds and changes the interest rate in the loanable funds market.

A fall in the overnight loans rate that increases the supply of bank loans increases the supply of loanable funds and lowers the equilibrium real interest rate. A rise in the overnight loans rate that decreases the supply of bank loans decreases the supply of loanable funds and raises the equilibrium real interest rate.

These changes in the real interest rate, along with the other factors we've just described, change expenditure plans.

Expenditure Plans

The ripple effects that follow a change in the overnight loans rate change three components of aggregate expenditure:

- Consumption expenditure
- Investment
- Net exports

Consumption Expenditure Other things remaining the same, the lower the real interest rate, the greater is the amount of consumption expenditure and the smaller is the amount of saving.

Investment Other things remaining the same, the lower the real interest rate, the greater is the amount of investment.

Net Exports Other things remaining the same, the lower the interest rate, the lower is the exchange rate and the greater are exports and the smaller are imports.

So eventually, a cut in the overnight loans rate increases aggregate expenditure and a rise in the overnight loans rate curtails aggregate expenditure. These changes in aggregate expenditure plans change aggregate demand, real GDP, and the price level.

Change in Aggregate Demand, Real GDP, and the Price Level

The final link in the transmission chain is a change in aggregate demand and a resulting change in real GDP and the price level. By changing real GDP and the price level relative to what they would have been without a change in the overnight loans rate, the Bank of Canada influences its ultimate goals: the inflation rate and the output gap.

The Bank of Canada Fights Recession

If inflation is low and real GDP is below potential GDP, the Bank acts to restore full employment. Figure 14.6 shows the effects of the Bank's actions, starting in the market for bank reserves and ending in the market for real GDP.

Market for Bank Reserves In Fig. 14.6(a), which shows the market for bank reserves, the Bank lowers the target overnight loans rate from 2 percent to 1 percent a year. To achieve the new target, the Bank

buys securities and increases the supply of reserves of the banking system from RS_0 to RS_1.

Money Market With an increase in reserves, banks create deposits by making loans, which increases the supply of money. The short-term interest rate falls and the quantity of money demanded increases.

In Fig. 14.6(b), the supply of money increases from MS_0 to MS_1, the interest rate falls from 2 percent to 1 percent a year, and the quantity of money increases from \$800 billion to \$900 billion. The interest rate in the money market and the overnight loans rate are kept close to each other by the powerful substitution effect described on p. 354.

Loanable Funds Market Banks create money by making loans. In the long run, an increase in the supply of bank loans is matched by a rise in the price level and the quantity of *real* loans is unchanged. But in the short run, with a sticky price level, an increase in the supply of bank loans increases the supply of (real) loanable funds.

FIGURE 14.6 The Bank of Canada Fights Recession

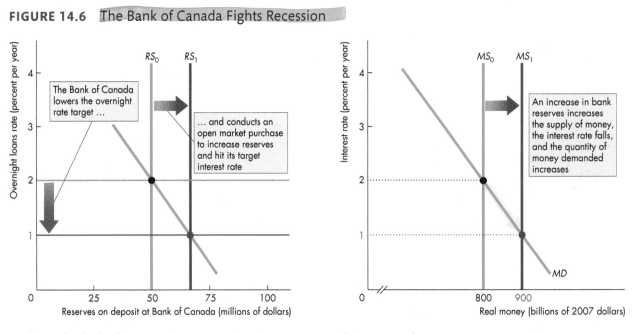

(a) The market for bank reserves

(b) Money market

In part (a), the Bank of Canada lowers the overnight loans rate target from 2 percent to 1 percent. The Bank buys securities in an open market operation and increases the supply of reserves from RS_0 to RS_1 to hit the new overnight loans rate target.

In part (b), the supply of money increases from MS_0 to MS_1, the short-term interest rate falls, and the quantity of money demanded increases. The short-term interest rate and the overnight loans rate change by similar amounts.

In Fig. 14.6(c), the supply of loanable funds curve shifts rightward from SLF_0 to SLF_1. With the demand for loanable funds at DLF, the real interest rate falls from 3 percent to 2.5 percent a year. (We're assuming a zero inflation rate so that the real interest rate equals the nominal interest rate.) The long-term interest rate changes by a smaller amount than the change in the short-term interest rate for the reason explained on p. 354.

The Market for Real GDP Figure 14.6(d) shows aggregate demand and aggregate supply—the demand for and supply of real GDP. Potential GDP is $1.8 trillion, where LAS is located. The short-run aggregate supply curve is SAS, and initially, the aggregate demand curve is AD_0. Real GDP is $1.6 trillion, which is less than potential GDP, so there is a recessionary gap. The Bank of Canada is reacting to this recessionary gap.

The increase in the supply of loans and the decrease in the real interest rate increase aggregate planned expenditure. (Not shown in the figure, a fall

in the interest rate lowers the exchange rate, which increases net exports and aggregate planned expenditure.) The increase in aggregate expenditure, ΔE, increases aggregate demand and shifts the aggregate demand curve rightward to $AD_0 + \Delta E$. A multiplier process begins. The increase in expenditure increases income, which induces an increase in consumption expenditure. Aggregate demand increases further, and the aggregate demand curve eventually shifts rightward to AD_1.

The new equilibrium is at full employment. Real GDP is equal to potential GDP. The price level rises to 110 and then becomes stable at that level. So after a one-time adjustment, there is price stability.

In this example, the Bank of Canada makes a perfect hit, achieving full employment and a stable price level. It is unlikely that the Bank would be able to achieve the precision of this example. If the Bank stimulated demand by too little and too late, the economy would experience a recession. And if the Bank hit the gas pedal too hard, it would push the economy from recession to inflation.

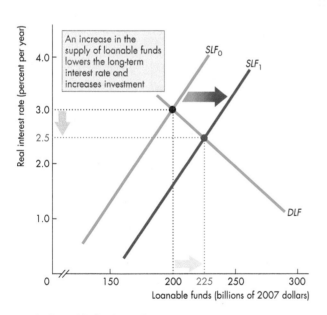

(c) The loanable funds market

In part (c), an increase in the supply of bank loans increases the supply of loanable funds and shifts the supply curve from SLF_0 to SLF_1. The real interest rate falls and investment increases.

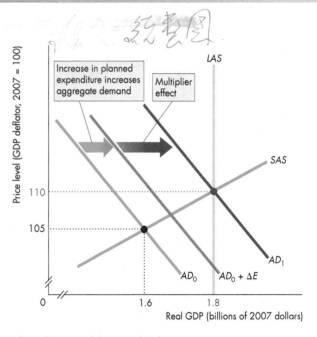

(d) Real GDP and the price level

In part (d), the increase in investment increases aggregate planned expenditure, and the aggregate demand curve shifts from AD_0 to $AD_0 + \Delta E$. Eventually, it shifts rightward to AD_1. Real GDP increases to potential GDP, and the price level rises.

The Bank of Canada Fights Inflation

If the inflation rate is too high and real GDP is above potential GDP, the Bank takes actions that are designed to lower the inflation rate and restore price stability. Figure 14.7 shows the effects of the Bank's actions starting in the market for reserves and ending in the market for real GDP.

Market for Bank Reserves In Fig. 14.7(a), which shows the market for bank reserves, the Bank raises the target overnight loans rate from 2 percent to 3 percent a year. To achieve the new target, the Bank sells securities and decreases the supply of reserves of the banking system from RS_0 to RS_1.

Money Market With decreased reserves, the banks shrink deposits by decreasing loans The supply of money decreases. The short-term interest rate rises and the quantity of money demanded decreases. In Fig. 14.7(b), the supply of money decreases from MS_0 to MS_1, the interest rate rises from 2 percent to

3 percent a year, and the quantity of money decreases from $800 billion to $700 billion.

Loanable Funds Market With a decrease in reserves, banks must decrease the supply of loans. The supply of (real) loanable funds decreases, and the supply of loanable funds curve shifts leftward in Fig. 14.7(c) from SLF_0 to SLF_1. With the demand for loanable funds at DLF, the real interest rate rises from 3 percent to 3.5 percent a year. (Again, we're assuming a zero inflation rate so that the real interest rate equals the nominal interest rate.)

The Market for Real GDP Figure 14.7(d) shows aggregate demand and aggregate supply—the market for real GDP. Potential GDP is $1.8 trillion where LAS is located. The short-run aggregate supply curve is SAS and initially the aggregate demand curve is AD_0. Now, real GDP is $1.9 trillion, which is greater than potential GDP, so there is an inflationary gap. The Bank is reacting to this inflationary gap.

FIGURE 14.7 The Bank of Canada Fights Inflation

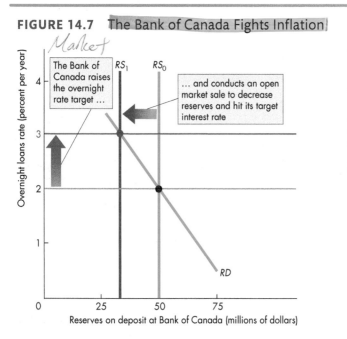

(a) The market for bank reserves

In part (a), the Bank of Canada raises the overnight loans rate from 2 percent to 3 percent. The Bank sells securities in an open market operation to decrease the supply of reserves from RS_0 to RS_1 and hit the new overnight loans rate target.

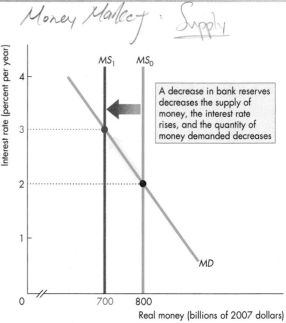

(b) Money market

In part (b), the supply of money decreases from MS_0 to MS_1, the short-term interest rate rises, and the quantity of money demanded decreases. The short-term interest rate and the overnight loans rate change by similar amounts.

The increase in the short-term interest rate, the decrease in the supply of bank loans, and the increase in the real interest rate decrease aggregate planned expenditure. (Not shown in the figure, a rise in the interest rate raises the exchange rate, which decreases net exports and aggregate planned expenditure.)

The decrease in aggregate expenditure, ΔE, decreases aggregate demand and shifts the aggregate demand curve to $AD_0 - \Delta E$. A multiplier process begins. The decrease in expenditure decreases income, which induces a decrease in consumption expenditure. Aggregate demand decreases further, and the aggregate demand curve eventually shifts leftward to AD_1.

The economy returns to full employment. Real GDP is equal to potential GDP. The price level falls to 110 and then becomes stable at that level. So after a one-time adjustment, there is price stability.

Again, in this example, we have given the Bank a perfect hit at achieving full employment and keeping the price level stable. If the Bank decreased

aggregate demand by too little and too late, the economy would have remained with an inflationary gap and the inflation rate would have moved above the rate that is consistent with price stability. And if the Bank hit the brakes too hard, it would push the economy from inflation to recession.

Loose Links and Long and Variable Lags

The ripple effects of monetary policy that we've just analyzed with the precision of an economic model are, in reality, very hard to predict and anticipate.

To achieve price stability and full employment, the Bank needs a combination of good judgment and good luck. Too large an interest rate cut in an underemployed economy can bring inflation, as it did during the 1970s. And too large an interest rate rise in an inflationary economy can create unemployment, as it did in 1981 and 1991. Loose links between the overnight loans rate and the ultimate policy goals make unwanted outcomes inevitable, and long and variable time lags add to the Bank's challenges.

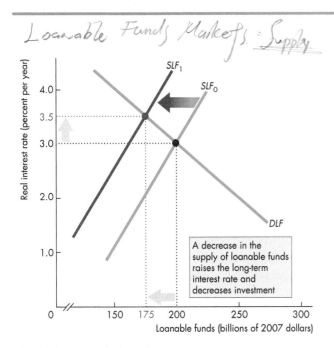

(c) The loanable funds market

In part (c), a decrease in the supply of bank loans decreases the supply of loanable funds and the supply curve shifts from SLF_0 to SLF_1. The real interest rate rises and investment decreases.

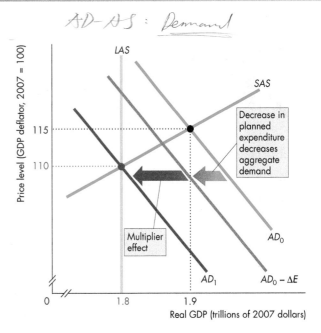

(d) Real GDP and the price level

In part (d), the decrease in investment decreases aggregate planned expenditure and the aggregate demand curve shifts from AD_0 to $AD_0 - \Delta E$. Eventually, it shifts leftward to AD_1. Real GDP decreases to potential GDP and the price level falls.

ECONOMICS IN ACTION

A View of the Long and Variable Lag

You've studied the theory of monetary policy. Does it really work in the way we've described? It does, and the figure opposite provides some evidence to support this claim.

The blue line in the figure is the overnight loans rate that the Bank of Canada targets *minus* the long-term bond rate. (When the long-term bond rate exceeds the overnight loans rate, the blue line is negative.)

We can view the difference between the overnight loans rate and the long-term bond rate as a measure of how hard the Bank of Canada is trying to steer a change in the economy's course.

When the Bank is more concerned about recession than inflation and is trying to stimulate real GDP growth, the Bank cuts the overnight loans rate target and the overnight loans rate *minus* the long-term bond rate falls.

When the Bank is more concerned about inflation than recession and is trying to restrain real GDP growth, the Bank raises the overnight loans rate target and the overnight loans rate *minus* the long-term bond rate rises.

The red line in the figure is the real GDP growth rate *one year later*. You can see that when the Bank of Canada raises the overnight loans rate, the real GDP growth rate slows one year later. And when the Bank

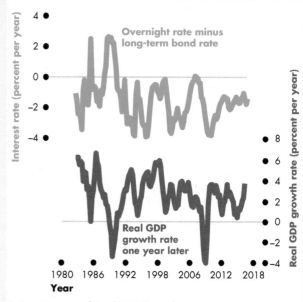

Interest Rate and Real GDP Growth

Source of data: Statistics Canada, CANSIM Tables 176-0043 and 380-0064.

lowers the overnight loans rate, the real GDP growth rate speeds up one year later.

Not shown in the figure, the inflation rate increases and decreases corresponding to the fluctuations in the real GDP growth rate. But the effects on the inflation rate take even longer and are not as strong as the effects on the real GDP growth rate.

Loose Link from Overnight Loans Rate to Spending
The real long-term interest rate that influences spending plans is only loosely linked to the overnight loans rate. Also, the response of the *real* long-term interest rate to a change in the nominal interest rate depends on how inflation expectations change. And the response of expenditure plans to changes in the real interest rate depend on many factors that make the response hard to predict.

Time Lags in the Adjustment Process The Bank of Canada is especially handicapped by the fact that the monetary policy transmission process is long and drawn out. Also, the economy does not always respond in exactly the same way to a policy change. Further, many factors other than policy are constantly changing and bringing new situations to which policy must respond.

REVIEW QUIZ

1 Describe the channels by which monetary policy ripples through the economy and explain how each channel operates.
2 Do interest rates fluctuate in response to the Bank of Canada's actions?
3 How do the Bank of Canada's actions change the exchange rate?
4 How do the Bank's actions influence real GDP and how long does it take for real GDP to respond to the Bank's policy changes?
5 How do the Bank's actions influence the inflation rate and how long does it take for inflation to respond to the Bank's policy changes?

Work these questions in Study Plan 14.3 and get instant feedback.   MyLab Economics

Financial Crisis: Cure and Prevention

During the financial crisis and recession of 2008–2009, the Bank of Canada, the U.S. Federal Reserve, the European Central Bank, the Bank of England, and other central banks lowered their overnight loans rate targets to the floor. The overnight loans rate can't go below zero, so what can a central bank do to stimulate the economy when it can't lower the interest rate?

Central banks answered this question with some extraordinary policy actions, and none more extraordinary than those of the U.S. Federal Reserve (the U.S. Fed). To understand those actions, we need to dig a bit into the anatomy of the financial crisis to which central banks responded. That's what we'll now do. We'll look at the key elements in the financial crisis and then look at the U.S. Fed's response and the responses of some other central banks. To understand these actions, we first need to describe the anatomy of the crisis.

The Anatomy of the Financial Crisis

A financial crisis is a situation in which a bank or other financial firm is unable to make payments that it has contracted to make. If one financial firm fails to pay its debts, other firms receive less than they need to pay theirs. A financial crisis arises when many financial firms fail to pay their debts.

We can describe the anatomy of a financial crisis by identifying the events that change the values of the assets and liabilities of a bank, representing all financial firms. Three main events can put a bank under stress:

- Widespread fall in asset prices
- Large currency drain
- Run on the bank

Widespread Fall in Asset Prices A widespread fall in asset prices means that the bank suffers a capital loss. The bank must write down the value of its assets (its loans and securities), and the value of its own capital (its equity) decreases by the same amount as the fall in the value of its securities. If the fall in asset prices is large, the bank's equity might fall to zero, in which case the bank is insolvent. It fails.

Large Currency Drain A large currency drain means that depositors withdraw funds and the bank loses reserves. This event puts the bank in a liquidity crisis. It is short of cash reserves.

Run on a Bank A run on a bank occurs when depositors lose confidence in the bank and massive withdrawals of deposits occur. The bank loses reserves and must call in loans and sell off securities at unfavourable prices. Its equity shrinks.

All these events and problems were present in the 2007–2008 financial crisis. The bursting of a house-price bubble triggered a widespread fall in the prices of mortgage-backed securities and derivatives whose values are based on these securities. People with money market mutual fund deposits withdrew them, which created a fear of a large withdrawal of these funds. With low reserves and even lower equity, banks turned their attention to securing their balance sheets and called in loans.

The U.S. Fed's Policy Actions

The U.S. Fed's policy actions in response to the financial crisis dribbled out over a period of more than a year. With substantial interest rate cuts, open market operations were used on a massive scale to keep the banks well supplied with reserves. This action lowered bank holdings of securities and swelled their reserves.

The Fed even purchased mortgage-backed securities from the banks and provided interest-earning reserves in exchange.

The U.S. Congress also acted to contain the crisis.

Congress Crisis Policy Action

Congress took two main actions to help limit the scope of the financial crisis:

- Extended deposit insurance
- Authorized the Treasury to buy "troubled" assets

Extended Deposit Insurance By extending the scope of deposit insurance to cover the deposits of a wider range of institutions, depositors had greater security and less incentive to withdraw their bank and other deposits.

Authorized the Treasury to Buy "Troubled" Assets A "troubled" asset is a security that has crashed in value and that no one wants to own. The *Troubled Asset Relief Program* (TARP) enabled the U.S. Treasury to use $700 billion of national debt. The original intent was to swap troubled assets held by banks and others for U.S. government securities. But instead of buying troubled assets, the Treasury decided to buy equity stakes in troubled institutions. This action directly increased the institutions' reserves and equity.

Taken as a whole, a huge amount of relief was thrown at the financial crisis, but the economy continued to perform poorly and didn't return to full employment until 2017.

Low interest rates, a massive injection of reserves, and a government stake in troubled institutions are aimed at coping with and hopefully curing a current crisis, but they don't lower the risk of the next crisis. That is a task for regulation.

Macroprudential Regulation

Macroprudential regulation is financial regulation to lower the risk that the financial system will crash. The global financial crisis of 2007–2008 brought this type of regulation to centre stage.

Macro Versus Micro Traditional financial regulation is microprudential: It seeks to lower the risk of failure of individual financial institutions. Macroprudential regulation focuses on the interconnections among individual financial institutions and markets and their shared exposure to common shocks.

The Tools The main macroprudential regulation tools are rules about the balance sheets of banks and other financial institutions. They are microprudential tools, with a macro twist. They are rules about ratios of loans to net worth or loans to cash and other liquid asset reserves that vary with respect to the macroeconomic environment. For example, a microprudential regulation requires banks to better a minimum ratio of net worth to loans, while a macroprudential regulation might make that minimum ratio increase during a recession and decrease in an expansion.

Canadian Macroprudential Policy

The Minister of Finance is responsible for maintaining Canada's financial stability, but the front line of Canada's macroprudential policy is performed by three agencies:

- The Bank of Canada
- The Office of the Superintendent of Financial Institutions
- The Canada Deposit Insurance Corporation

The Bank of Canada's policy goal is to achieve its inflation-control target, and achieving that goal makes an enormous contribution to financial stability for the reasons we explained earlier in this chapter. But three of the Bank's specific duties add further support to financial stability.

First, as lender of last resort, the Bank provides financial institutions with liquidity that ensures they can pay their debts.

Second, the Bank oversees and manages the payment system that enables banks to transfer funds between themselves and their customers.

Third, the Bank conducts financial system stress tests—assessments of risks to the stability of the financial system.

The Office of the Superintendent of Financial Institutions regulates and supervises financial institutions.

The Canada Deposit Insurance Corporation (see Chapter 8, p. 188) insures the deposits of banks and other depository institutions.

The Minister of Finance plays a direct role in macroprudential policy by defining the risk-management standards for mortgages insured by government-backed institutions. This feature of Canadian housing finance make the problems encountered in the U.S. mortgage market very unlikely here.

The macroprudential work that we've just described is coordinated and overseen by the Senior Advisory Committee (SAC).

This committee is chaired by the Deputy Minister of Finance and includes representatives from the Bank of Canada and the other two federal agencies. The main task of the SAC is to facilitate collaboration and information sharing, and to encourage the separate agencies to reinforce one another in countering financial stability risks.

We'll conclude this review of monetary policy and its contribution to financial stability by looking further at the role of inflation targeting and at a suggested policy rule that some economists say brings even greater clarity and stability.

Policy Strategies and Clarity

Unlike the Bank of Canada, with its clear *inflation rate targeting* strategy, the U.S. Fed pursues what is called a *dual mandate*, which is to keep *both* the inflation rate and the unemployment rate low. The pursuit of this dual mandate is a source of confusion and uncertainty about monetary policy. The central problem with the U.S. dual mandate is that it seeks to acheive the impossible. You've seen in Chapter 12 (pp. 312–313) that stabilization policy faces a *tradeoff* between inflation and unemployment in the short run. If policy seeks to lower the inflation rate, the unemployment rate rises in the short run. If policy seeks to lower the unemployment rate, the inflation rate rises in the short run.

In the *long run*, monetary policy influences the inflation rate but has no effect on the unemployment rate, which is determined by the natural unemployment rate.

It is because monetary policy influences only the inflation rate in the long run that inflation rate targeting is an attractive monetary policy strategy. This approach is now used not only by Canada but also by Australia, New Zealand, Sweden, the United Kingdom, and the European Union.

Inflation targeting focuses the public debate on what monetary policy can achieve and the best contribution it can make to attaining full employment and sustained growth. The central fact is that monetary policy is about managing inflation expectations. An explicit inflation target that is taken seriously and towards which policy actions are aimed and explained is a sensible way to manage those expectations.

It is when the going gets tough that inflation targeting has the greatest benefit. It is difficult to imagine a serious inflation-targeting central bank permitting inflation to take off in the way that it did during the 1970s. And it is difficult to imagine deflation and ongoing recession such as Japan has endured for the past 10 years if monetary policy is guided by an explicit inflation target.

One way to pursue an inflation target is to set the policy interest rate (for the Bank of Canada, the overnight loans rate) by using a rule or formula. The most famous and most studied interest rate rule is the *Taylor rule* described in *Economics in Action*.

Supporters of the Taylor rule argue that in computer simulations, the rule works well and limits fluctuations in inflation and output. By using such a rule, monetary policy contributes towards lessening uncertainty—the opposite of current U.S. monetary policy. In financial markets, labour markets, and markets for goods and services, people make long-term commitments. So markets work best when plans are based on correctly anticipated inflation. A well-understood monetary policy helps to create an environment in which inflation is easier to forecast and manage.

The debates on inflation targeting and the Taylor rule will continue!

ECONOMICS IN ACTION

The Taylor Rule

The idea of setting the overnight loans rate based on a rule was suggested by Stanford University economist John B. Taylor, and the rule bears his name.

The Taylor rule is a formula for setting the overnight loans rate. Calling the overnight loans rate R, the inflation rate INF, and the output gap GAP (all percentages), the Taylor rule formula is:

$$R = 2 + INF + 0.5(INF - 2) + 0.5GAP.$$

In words, the Taylor rule sets the overnight loans rate at 2 percent plus the inflation rate plus one-half of the deviation of inflation from 2 percent plus one-half of the output gap.

If the Bank of Canada had followed the Taylor rule, the overnight loans rate would have been higher on some occasions and lower on others. During 2008, when the overnight loans rate was 1.5 percent, the Taylor Rule would have kept it close to 4 percent.

The Bank of Canada believes that because it uses more information than just the current inflation rate and the output gap, it is able to set the overnight loans rate more intelligently than the Taylor rule would set it.

◆ REVIEW QUIZ

1 What are the three ingredients of a financial and banking crisis?
2 What are the policy actions taken by central banks in response to the financial crisis?
3 What are the institutions that conduct Canada's macroprudential policies?
4 How might inflation targeting improve U.S. monetary policy?
5 How might using the Taylor rule improve the Fed's monetary policy?

Work these questions in Study Plan 14.4 and get instant feedback.   MyLab Economics

◆ To complete your study of monetary policy, take a look at *Economics in the News* on pp. 364–365, which examines effects of the Bank of Canada's interest rate increases in 2017.

The Bank of Canada Applies a Gentle Brake

Bank of Canada Raises Benchmark Rate to 1%, Adding to July Increase

The Financial Times
September 6, 2017

The Bank of Canada (BoC) raised its benchmark interest rate by a quarter of a percentage point on Wednesday, adding to a rate increase in July amid robust growth in the North American country's economy.

Policymakers lifted the main interest rate to 1 percent. Economists were essentially 50–50 on whether or not the central bank would raise rates on Wednesday. The BoC lifted the rate in July for the first time since 2010, joining the U.S. Federal Reserve in tightening monetary policy.

"Recent economic data have been stronger than expected, supporting the Bank's view that growth in Canada is becoming more broadly-based and self-sustaining. Consumer spending remains robust, underpinned by continued solid employment and income growth. There has also been more widespread strength in business investment and in exports," the BoC said in a statement.

Canada's gross domestic product increased in the first six months of this year at the best rate in 15 years, according to official data. The G10 economy has benefited from a rebound in oil prices, that has helped the energy industry and the sectors that supply it. Overall, growth has been "widespread" both in the services and goods-producing sectors, according to Statistics Canada.

Still, though, the rate of price growth has cooled since the end of last year and remains "weak," according to Dana Peterson, an economist at Citigroup. She adds that "downside risks stemming mainly from the U.S." could be another factor for BoC policymakers.

The Canadian dollar jumped sharply on the decision, with the U.S. dollar dropping by over 1.5 percent on the day to a low of C$1.2134.

Adam Samson, Published September 6, 2017, *Financial Times.*

ESSENCE OF THE STORY

- Canadian real GDP growth in the first half of 2017 was the fastest in 15 years.
- The Bank of Canada saw the growth as broadly based and self-sustaining.
- Inflation remained low.
- The Bank raised the overnight interest rate by a quarter of a percentage point to 1 percent on September 6.
- The Canadian dollar jumped sharply on the decision.

ECONOMIC ANALYSIS

- In September 2017, the Bank of Canada announced a surprise 0.25 percentage point rise in the overnight loans rate to 1 percent.

- In explaining the increase, the Bank said that it saw growth that was broadly based and self sustaining, and at a faster rate than previously expected.

- Historically, an overnight loans rate of 1 percent would have meant that the Bank is boosting aggregate demand with monetary stimulus. But in 2017, the rise to 1 percent was seen as withdrawing monetary stimulus and decreasing aggregate demand.

- In 2017, the economy was at full employment, CPI inflation was inside its target range, and real GDP growth and employment growth were strong.

- Figure 1 illustrates the economy in mid-2017 with the Bank of Canada's estimate of no output gap and Statistics Canada's GDP data.

- Figure 2 shows an interpretation of what the Bank expected for 2018 in the absence of an interest rate rise.

- In Fig. 2, potential GDP grows by 2 percent per year but aggregate demand grows faster so that, without monetary restraint, an inflationary gap would open and the inflation rate would rise above 2 percent per year.

- Figure 3 shows the outcome in 2018 that the Bank wants to achieve and that it might achieve by raising the overnight loans rate to 1 percent, and thereby reducing monetary stimulus.

- The higher interest rate should dampen business and housing investment, and the stronger dollar should dampen exports and increase imports, so this policy action should decrease aggregate demand.

- If the Bank gets it right, aggregate demand in 2018 is AD^*, and the price level rises to 117. Inflation at just under 2 percent per year takes the price level from 115 in 2017 to 117 in 2018, and real GDP increases from $1,849 billion to equal potential GDP.

- If the Bank gets it wrong by over-restricting aggregate demand, in 2018 the price level will have risen to less than 117—the inflation rate will be further below 2 percent per year—and a deflationary gap will appear.

- If the Bank gets it wrong by restricting aggregate demand too little, by 2018 the price level will have risen to more than 117—the inflation rate will exceed 2 percent per year—and an inflationary gap will open up.

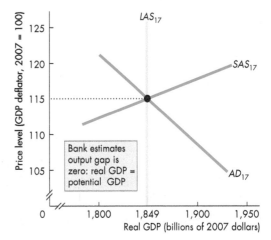

Figure 1 The Economy in 2017

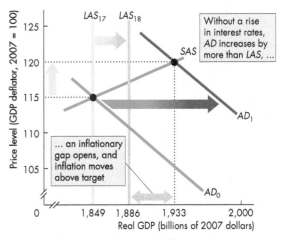

Figure 2 The Economy in 2018 Without Monetary Tightening

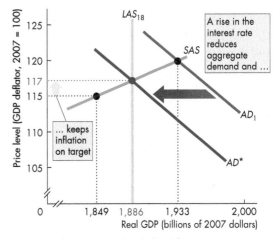

Figure 3 The Economy in 2018 With Monetary Tightening

◆ **WORKED PROBLEM**

MyLab Economics Work this problem in Chapter 14 Study Plan.

The economy is at full employment, the inflation rate is 2 percent a year, and the overnight loans rate is at 4 percent a year. But real GDP is growing more slowly than average, so the Bank of Canada decides to lower interest rates.

Questions

1. Which macroeconomic variables change immediately and in which direction?
2. Which macroeconomic variables change over the next few weeks or months and in which direction?
3. Which macroeconomic variables change over the next year or two and in which direction?
4. Does the economic growth rate increase?

Solutions

1. The Bank of Canada lowers its overnight loans rate target and buys securities on the open market. An increase in the monetary base creates excess reserves, and the interest rate at which banks lend and borrow reserves—the overnight loans rate—falls.

    The banks buy short-term bills, the price of which rises and the interest rate on which falls. The lower interest rate makes the Canadian dollar depreciate on the foreign exchange market.

Key Point: A change in the overnight loans rate flows immediately into the market for overnight loans, the short-term securities market, and the foreign exchange market, changing the short-term interest rate and the Canadian dollar exchange rate.

2. Over the next weeks and months, the banks increase loans. The quantity of money increases and the supply of loans increases. In the loanable funds market, an increase in supply lowers the real interest rate, so saving starts to decrease and investment starts to increase.

    The lower dollar on the foreign exchange market increases exports and decreases imports.

Key Point: A few weeks and months after the Bank changes the interest rate, ripples reach the loanable funds market and a change in the real interest rate starts to change investment.

Net exports begin to respond to the changed exchange rate.

3. Over the next year, the lower real interest rate increases consumption expenditure and business investment, and the lower dollar continues to increase net exports. With these components of aggregate expenditure increasing, aggregate demand increases and real GDP increases.

    The increase in real GDP is also an increase in income, which induces a further increase in consumption expenditure—an expenditure multiplier process.

    If aggregate demand increases before investment in new capital and new technology changes aggregate supply, the economy moves above full employment and an inflationary gap appears. Businesses face a shortage of labour. As time goes on, wage rates and prices start to rise, and after about two years the inflation rate rises.

Key Point: A change in the real interest rate influences the goods market. Aggregate demand changes and, with no change in aggregate supply, real GDP increases. But the inflation rate changes about two years after the Bank of Canada lowers the interest rate target.

4. The increase in aggregate demand increases real GDP, but will the economic growth rate be higher? With no change in aggregate supply, real GDP will eventually return to its initial level and a short burst of growth will have occurred. But in the long run, the economy will be back to its initial full-employment situation with no faster growth rate and a higher inflation rate.

    For the growth rate to increase, investment in new capital and new technologies must increase the rate of productivity growth to speed the growth rate of aggregate supply. Changing the interest rate will work its way through the economy to increase real GDP in the short term but not create economic growth.

Key Point: When the Bank of Canada changes the interest rate, changes ripple through all markets. The money market, the loanable funds market, the labour market, and the goods market all respond to the interest rate change one after the other, but unless the pace of productivity growth increases, the economic growth will not increase. Monetary policy cannot be used to increase the economic growth rate.

SUMMARY

Key Points

Monetary Policy Objectives and Framework
(pp. 348–350)

- The Bank of Canada Act requires the Bank to use monetary policy to avoid inflation and moderate cycles in real GDP and employment.
- The Government of Canada and the Bank of Canada have jointly agreed that the Bank will seek to keep CPI inflation between 1 percent and 3 percent a year and will aim for the 2 percent midpoint.
- The Bank has successfully achieved its inflation-control target.
- The Bank's Governing Council has the responsibility for the conduct of monetary policy, but the Bank and the government must consult regularly.

Working Problems 1 to 3 will give you a better understanding of monetary policy objectives and framework.

The Conduct of Monetary Policy (pp. 350–352)

- The Bank of Canada's monetary policy instrument is the overnight loans rate.
- The Bank sets the overnight loans rate target and announces changes on eight dates each year.
- To decide on the appropriate level of the overnight loans rate target, the Bank monitors the inflation rate and all the factors that influence inflation.
- The Bank sets the overnight loans rate at the level expected to keep inflation inside its target range and, on average, at the middle of the target range.

- The Bank achieves its overnight loans rate target by using open market operations.

Working Problems 4 to 8 will give you a better understanding of the conduct of monetary policy.

Monetary Policy Transmission (pp. 353–360)

- A change in the overnight loans rate changes other interest rates, the exchange rate, the quantity of money and loans, aggregate demand, and eventually real GDP and the price level.
- Changes in the overnight loans rate change real GDP about one year later and change the inflation rate with an even longer time lag.

Working Problems 9 to 12 will give you a better understanding of monetary policy transmission.

Financial Crisis: Cure and Prevention (pp. 361–363)

- A financial crisis has three ingredients: a widespread fall in asset prices, a currency drain, and a run on banks.
- Central banks responded to financial crisis with classic open market operations and by several other unconventional measures.
- Inflation targeting and the Taylor rule are monetary policy strategies designed to enable the central bank to manage inflation expectations and reduce uncertainty.

Working Problem 13 will give you a better understanding of the cure and prevention of a financial crisis.

Key Terms

MyLab Economics Key Terms Quiz

Bank rate, 351

Inflation rate targeting, 348

Macroprudential regulation, 362

Operating band, 351

Overnight loans rate, 350

Settlement balances rate, 352

STUDY PLAN PROBLEMS AND APPLICATIONS

MyLab Economics Work Problems 1 to 14 in Chapter 14 Study Plan and get instant feedback.

Monetary Policy Objectives and Framework
(Study Plan 14.1)

1. "Unemployment is a more serious economic problem than inflation and it should be the focus of the Bank of Canada's monetary policy." Evaluate this statement and explain why the Bank's policy goal is a target inflation rate.

2. "Monetary policy is too important to be left to the Bank of Canada. The government should be responsible for it." How is responsibility for monetary policy allocated between the Bank of Canada and the government?

3. **Inflation Control Target Renewal**
   The 2016 inflation control target agreement between the Government of Canada and the Bank of Canada runs to the end of 2021.

   Source: Bank of Canada, November 2016

   a. What does the inflation control agreement say about the Bank's control of the quantity of money?

   b. Why is it important that the agreement be renewed again in 2021 and what might be some obstacles to its renewal?

The Conduct of Monetary Policy (Study Plan 14.2)

4. What are the possible monetary policy instruments and which one does the Bank of Canada use? How has its value behaved since 1997?

5. How does the Bank of Canada hit its overnight loans rate target?

6. What does the Bank of Canada do to determine whether the overnight loans rate should be raised, lowered, or left unchanged?

Use the following news clip to work Problems 7 and 8.

'No Predetermined Path' for Interest Rates: Bank of Canada Chief

Bank of Canada governor, Stephen Poloz, said there is no prearranged route for further interest-rate hikes and signalled the bank would be taking a more cautious approach to any future increases.

Source: CTV News, September 27, 2017

7. Explain the situation faced by the Bank of Canada in 2017.

8. a. Why might the Bank of Canada take "a more cautious approach to any future increases" in interest rates?

   b. Why might the Bank of Canada decide to lower the interest rate in the future?

Monetary Policy Transmission (Study Plan 14.3)

Use the following data to work Problems 9 to 11.

How Will the Rise in Interest Rate Affect Us?

The Bank of Canada has hiked the interest rate for the first time in seven years. The increase will provide greater incentive for Canadians to save more, lead to a rise in mortgage rates, and increase the cost of borrowing to invest.

Source: *The Huffington Post*, July 18, 2017

9. Explain the effects of the Bank of Canada's interest rate rise on household saving and consumption and business investment. Draw a graph to illustrate your explanation.

10. Explain the effects of the changes in household saving and consumption and business investment on aggregate demand. Would you expect a multiplier effect? Why or why not?

11. How would the predicted rise in mortgage rates change aggregate demand?

12. **IMF Sees Global Economic Speedup**
    Global economic activity is picking up with a cyclical recovery in investment, manufacturing, and trade. World real GDP growth is expected to rise from 3.1 percent in 2016 to 3.6 percent in 2018.

    Source: International Monetary Fund, April, 2017

    a. If the IMF forecasts turn out to be correct, what would most likely happen to the output gap and unemployment in 2018?

    b. What actions taken by the Bank of Canada in 2015 and 2016 would you expect to have influenced real GDP growth in 2018? Explain how those policy actions would transmit to real GDP.

Financial Crisis: Cure and Prevention (Study Plan 14.4)

13. What is the role of the Bank of Canada in macroprudential policy and how does inflation targeting contribute to financial stability?

ADDITIONAL PROBLEMS AND APPLICATIONS

MyLab Economics You can work these problems in Homework or Test if assigned by your instructor.

Monetary Policy Objectives and Framework

Use the following information to work Problems 14 to 18.

The Bank of Canada and the Government of Canada have agreed that the Bank will achieve an inflation rate target.

14. Explain how inflation targeting promotes full employment in the long run.
15. Explain the conflict between inflation targeting and unemployment targeting in the short run.
16. Based on the performance of Canadian inflation and unemployment, has the Bank's inflation targeting been successful?
17. Suppose Parliament legislated interest rate changes. How would you expect the policy choices to change?
18. Which arrangement, inflation targeting or unemployment targeting, would most likely provide price stability?

Use the following news clip to work Problems 19 to 21.

Higher Interest Rates Will Increase Ottawa's Budget Deficits, Report Warns

A University of Ottawa Institute of Fiscal Studies and Democracy report says that rising interest rates will produce larger federal government deficits.

Source: *The Globe and Mail*, June 30, 2017

19. How does a government get funds to cover a budget deficit? How does financing a budget deficit affect the central bank's monetary policy?
20. How has Canada's budget deficit been influenced by the Bank of Canada's low interest rates?
21. a. How would the budget deficit change in 2018 and 2019 if the Bank of Canada moved interest rates up to 2 percent or higher?
    b. How would the budget deficit change in 2018 and 2019 if the Bank of Canada's monetary policy led to a rapid appreciation of the dollar?
22. The U.S. Federal Reserve Act of 2000 instructs the Federal Reserve to pursue its goals by "maintain[ing] long-run growth of the monetary and credit aggregates commensurate with the economy's long-run potential to increase production."

a. How would following this instruction make the U.S. monetary policy instrument different from Canada's monetary policy instrument?
b. Why might a central bank increase the quantity of money by more than the increase in potential GDP?

The Conduct of Monetary Policy

23. Looking at the overnight loans rate since 2000, identify periods during which, with the benefit of hindsight, the rate might have been kept too low. Identify periods during which it might have been too high.

Use the following information to work Problems 24 to 28.

In September 2015, the unemployment rate was 7.0 percent, the inflation rate was 0.1 percent, and the overnight loans rate target was 0.5 percent. In September 2017, the unemployment rate was 6.2 percent, the inflation rate was 1.4 percent, and the overnight loans rate target was 1.0 percent.

24. How might the Bank of Canada's decisions that raised the overnight loans rate from 0.5 percent to 1.0 percent have been influenced by the unemployment rate and the inflation rate?
25. Explain the dilemma that low inflation and low unemployment poses for the Bank of Canada.
26. Why might the Bank of Canada decide to keep the overnight loans rate at 1 percent in 2018?
27. Why might the Bank of Canada decide to raise the overnight loans rate in 2018?
28. Why might the Bank of Canada decide to lower the overnight loans rate in 2018?

Monetary Policy Transmission

Use the following data to work Problems 29 to 31.

From 2010 to 2017, the long-term *real* interest rate paid by the safest corporations decreased from 3 percent to less than 1 percent. During that same period, the overnight loans rate was between 1.0 percent and 0.25 percent a year.

29. What role does the long-term real interest rate play in the monetary policy transmission process?
30. How does the overnight loans rate influence the long-term real interest rate?

31. What do you think happened to inflation expectations between 2010 and 2017 and why?

32. **U.S. Dollar Falls as Fed Holds Rates, Raises Concern over Low Inflation**

    As expected, the Federal Reserve announced it would hold its key interest rate steady in the range of 1.00–1.25 percent. But the Fed's remark that inflation is expected to stay "somewhat below" 2 percent in the near-term spooked the foreign exchange market and the dollar fell.

    Source: *DailyFX*, July 26, 2017

    a. How does the U.S. interest rate influence the U.S. dollar exchange rate, other things remaining the same?

    b. How does an expected future change in the U.S. interest rate influence the U.S. dollar exchange rate, other things remaining the same?

    c. Explain why the Federal Reserve's remark about expected future inflation changed expectations about the federal funds rate and how that change influenced the U.S. dollar exchange rate.

33. Suppose that the Reserve Bank of New Zealand is following the Taylor rule and in 2018, it sets the official cash rate (its equivalent of Canada's overnight loans rate) at 4 percent a year. If the inflation rate in New Zealand is 2 percent a year, what is its output gap?

Use the following news clip to work Problems 34 and 35.

Bernanke on Inflation Targeting

Inflation targeting promotes well-anchored inflation expectations, which facilitate more effective stabilization of output and employment. Thus inflation targeting can deliver good results with respect to output and employment as well as inflation.

   Source: Federal Reserve Board, remarks by Ben Bernanke to the National Association of Business Economists

34. What is inflation targeting and how do "well-anchored inflation expectations" help to achieve more stable output as well as low inflation?

35. Explain how inflation targeting as described by Ben Bernanke is consistent with the central bank being also concerned about unemployment.

36. If the Bank of Canada had set the overnight loans rate according to the Taylor rule, how would the course of the overnight loans rate have been different from the course that it did take? How would inflation and the output gap have been different?

Financial Crisis: Cure and Prevention

Use the following news clip to work Problems 37 and 38.

Top Economist Says America Could Plunge into Recession

In December 2007, before the U.S. and global recession, Robert Shiller, Professor of Economics at Yale University, predicted that there was a very real possibility that the United States would be plunged into a slump.

   Source: timesonline.co.uk, December 31, 2007

37. If the U.S. Federal Reserve had agreed with Robert Shiller in December 2007, what actions might it have taken differently from those it did take? How could monetary policy prevent house prices from falling?

38. Describe the time lags in the response of output and inflation to the policy actions you have prescribed.

Economics in the News

39. After you have studied *Economics in the News* on pp. 364–365, answer the following questions.

    a. What was the state of the Canadian economy in 2017?

    b. What was the Bank of Canada's expectation about future real GDP growth and inflation in September 2017?

    c. How would maintaining the overnight loans rate at 1 percent influence the market for bank reserves, the loanable funds market, and aggregate demand and aggregate supply?

    d. How would you expect the Canadian dollar exchange rate to feature in the transmission of monetary policy to real GDP and the price level?

15 INTERNATIONAL TRADE POLICY

After studying this chapter, you will be able to:

◆ Explain how markets work with international trade

◆ Identify the gains from international trade and its winners and losers

◆ Explain the effects of international trade barriers

◆ Explain and evaluate arguments used to justify restricting international trade

iPhones, Wii games, and Nike shoes are just three of the items that you might buy that are not produced in Canada. Why don't we produce phones, games, and shoes in Canada? Isn't the globalization of production killing good Canadian jobs?

You will find the answers in this chapter. You will see that global trade is a win-win deal and also why governments restrict trade.

In *Economics in the News* at the end of the chapter, you'll see why Donald Trump's ideas about NAFTA and tariffs would end up costing Americans as well as Canadians and Mexicans. But first, we study the gains from international trade.

◆ How Global Markets Work

Because we trade with people in other countries, the goods and services that we can buy and consume are not limited by what we can produce. The goods and services that we buy from other countries are our **imports**, and the goods and services that we sell to people in other countries are our **exports**.

International Trade Today

Global trade today is enormous. In 2016, global exports and imports were $21 trillion, which is one-third of the value of global production. The United States is the world's largest international trader and accounts for 10 percent of world exports and 12 percent of world imports. Germany and China, which rank 2 and 3 behind the United States, lag by a large margin.

In 2016, total Canadian exports were $629 billion, which is 31 percent of the value of Canadian production. Total Canadian imports were $677 billion, which is about 33 percent of total expenditure in Canada.

We trade both goods and services. In 2016, exports of services were about 17 percent of total exports and imports of services were about 19 percent of total imports.

What Drives International Trade?

Comparative advantage is the fundamental force that drives international trade. Comparative advantage (see Chapter 2, p. 40) is a situation in which a person can perform an activity or produce a good or service at a lower opportunity cost than anyone else. This same idea applies to nations. We can define *national comparative advantage* as a situation in which a nation can perform an activity or produce a good or service at a lower opportunity cost than any other nation.

The opportunity cost of producing a T-shirt is lower in China than in Canada, so China has a comparative advantage in producing T-shirts. The opportunity cost of producing a regional jet is lower in Canada than in China, so Canada has a comparative advantage in producing regional jets.

You saw in Chapter 2 how Liz and Joe reap gains from trade by specializing in the production of the good at which they have a comparative advantage and then trading with each other. Both are better off.

This same principle applies to trade among nations. Because China has a comparative

ECONOMICS IN ACTION

We Trade Metals for Consumer Goods

The figure shows Canada's four largest exports and imports by value. Motor vehicles and parts are our biggest exports and second biggest imports. Consumer goods are our biggest imports. We export ores, oil, and lumber and import machinery and equipment.

Canadian Exports and Imports in 2016

Source of data: Statistics Canada, CANSIM Table 228-8059.

advantage at producing T-shirts and Canada has a comparative advantage at producing regional jets, the people of both countries can gain from specialization and trade. China can buy regional jets from Canada at a lower opportunity cost than that at which Chinese firms can produce them. And Canadians can buy T-shirts from China for a lower opportunity cost than that at which Canadian firms can produce them. Also, through international trade, Chinese producers can get higher prices for their T-shirts and Canadian firms can sell regional jets for a higher price. Both countries gain from international trade.

Let's now illustrate the gains from trade that we've just described by studying demand and supply in the global markets for T-shirts and regional jets.

Why Canada Imports T-Shirts

Canada imports T-shirts because the rest of the world has a comparative advantage in producing T-shirts. Figure 15.1 illustrates how this comparative advantage generates international trade and how trade affects the price of a T-shirt and the quantities produced and bought.

The demand curve D_C and the supply curve S_C show the demand and supply in the Canadian domestic market only. The demand curve tells us the quantity of T-shirts that Canadians are willing to buy at various prices. The supply curve tells us the quantity of T-shirts that Canadian garment makers are willing to sell at various prices—that is, the quantity supplied at each price when all T-shirts sold in Canada are produced in Canada.

Figure 15.1(a) shows what the Canadian T-shirt market would be like with no international trade.

The price of a shirt would be $8 and 4 million shirts a year would be produced by Canadian garment makers and bought by Canadian consumers.

Figure 15.1(b) shows the market for T-shirts with international trade. Now the price of a T-shirt is determined in the world market, not the Canadian domestic market. The world price of a T-shirt is less than $8, which means that the rest of the world has a comparative advantage in producing T-shirts. The world price line shows the world price at $5 a shirt.

The Canadian demand curve, D_C, tells us that at $5 a shirt, Canadians buy 6 million shirts a year. The Canadian supply curve, S_C, tells us that at $5 a shirt, Canadian garment makers produce 2 million T-shirts a year. To buy 6 million T-shirts when only 2 million are produced in Canada, we must import T-shirts from the rest of the world. The quantity of T-shirts imported is 4 million a year.

FIGURE 15.1   A Market with Imports

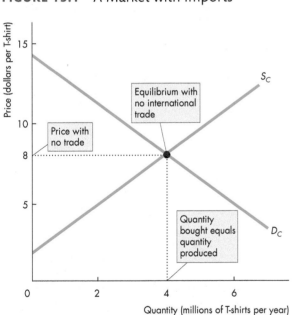

(a) Equilibrium with no international trade

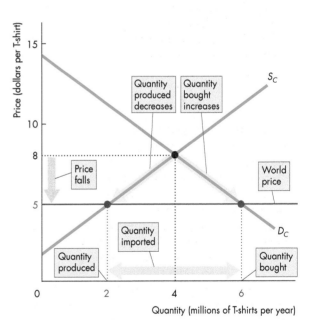

(b) Equilibrium in a market with imports

Part (a) shows the Canadian market for T-shirts with no international trade. The Canadian domestic demand curve D_C and Canadian domestic supply curve S_C determine the price of a T-shirt at $8 and the quantity of T-shirts produced and bought in Canada at 4 million a year.

Part (b) shows the Canadian market for T-shirts with international trade. World demand for and world supply of

T-shirts determine the world price of a T-shirt, which is $5. The price in the Canadian market falls to $5 a shirt. Canadian purchases of T-shirts increase to 6 million a year, and Canadian production of T-shirts decreases to 2 million a year. Canada imports 4 million T-shirts a year.

Why Canada Exports Regional Jets

Figure 15.2 illustrates international trade in regional jets. The demand curve D_C and the supply curve S_C show the demand and supply in the Canadian domestic market only. The demand curve tells us the quantity of regional jets that Canadian airlines are willing to buy at various prices. The supply curve tells us the quantity of regional jets that Canadian aircraft makers are willing to sell at various prices.

Figure 15.2(a) shows what the Canadian regional jet market would be like with no international trade. The price of a regional jet would be $100 million and 40 regional jets a year would be produced by Bombardier and bought by Canadian airlines.

Figure 15.2(b) shows the Canadian airplane market with international trade. Now the price of a regional jet is determined in the world market and the world price of a regional jet is higher than $100 million, which means that Canada has a comparative advantage

in producing regional jets. The world price line shows the world price at $150 million.

The Canadian demand curve, D_C, tells us that at $150 million each, Canadian airlines buy 20 regional jets a year. The Canadian supply curve, S_C, tells us that at $150 million each, Bombardier produces 70 regional jets a year. The quantity produced in Canada (70 a year) minus the quantity purchased by Canadian airlines (20 a year) is the quantity exported, which is 50 regional jets a year.

REVIEW QUIZ

1 Describe the situation in the market for a good or service that Canada imports.
2 Describe the situation in the market for a good or service that Canada exports.

Work these questions in Study Plan 15.1 and get instant feedback.   MyLab Economics

---

FIGURE 15.2   A Market with Exports

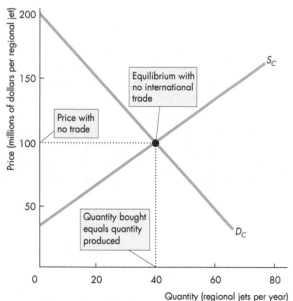

(a) Equilibrium without international trade

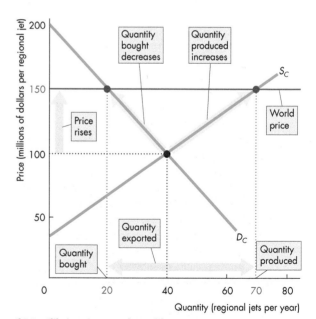

(b) Equilibrium in a market with exports

In part (a), the Canadian market with no international trade, the domestic demand curve D_C and the domestic supply curve S_C determine the price of a regional jet in Canada at $100 million and 40 regional jets are produced and bought each year.

In part (b), the Canadian market with international trade, world demand and world supply determine the world price of a regional jet at $150 million. The price in Canada rises. Canadian production increases to 70 a year, Canadian purchases decrease to 20 a year, and Canada exports 50 regional jets a year.

Winners, Losers, and the Net Gain from Trade

In Chapter 1 (see p. 6), we asked whether globalization is in the self-interest of the low-wage worker in Malaysia who sews your new running shoes and the displaced shoemaker in Toronto. Is globalization in the social interest? We're now going to answer these questions. You will learn why producers complain about cheap foreign imports, but consumers of imports never complain.

Gains and Losses from Imports

We measure the gains and losses from imports by examining their effect on the price paid and the quantity bought by domestic consumers and their effect on the price received and the quantity sold by domestic producers.

Consumers Gain from Imports When a country freely imports an item from the rest of the world, it is because the rest of the world has a comparative advantage at producing that item. Compared to a situation with no international trade, the price paid by the consumer falls and the quantity bought increases. It is clear the consumer gains. The greater the fall in the price and increase in the quantity consumed, the greater is the gain to the consumer.

Domestic Producers Lose from Imports Compared to a situation with no international trade, the price received by a domestic producer of an item that is imported falls. Also, the quantity sold by the domestic producer of a good or service that is also imported decreases. Because the domestic producer of an item that is imported sells a smaller quantity and for a lower price, this producer loses from international trade. Import-competing industries shrink in the face of competition from cheaper foreign-produced goods.

The profits of firms that produce import-competing goods and services fall, these firms cut their workforce, unemployment in these industries increases, and wages fall. When these industries have a geographical concentration an entire region can suffer economic decline.

Gains and Losses from Exports

We measure the gains and losses from exports just like we measured those from imports, by their effect on the price paid and the quantity consumed by domestic consumers and their effects on the price received and the quantity sold by domestic producers.

Consumers Lose from Exports When a country exports something to the rest of the world, it is because the country has a comparative advantage at producing that item. Compared to a situation with no international trade, the price paid by the consumer rises and the quantity consumed in the domestic economy decreases. The domestic consumer loses. The greater the rise in price and decrease in quantity consumed, the greater is the loss to the consumer.

Domestic Producers Gain from Exports Compared to a situation with no international trade, the price received by a domestic producer of an item that is exported rises. Also, the quantity sold by the domestic producer of a good or service that is also exported increases. Because the domestic producer of an item that is exported sells a larger quantity and for a higher price, this producer gains from international trade. Export industries expand in the face of global demand for their product.

The profits of firms that produce exports rise, these firms expand their workforce, unemployment in these industries decreases, and wages rise. When these industries have a geographical concentration, an entire region can boom.

Gains for All

You've seen that both imports and exports bring gains. Export producers and import consumers gain, export consumers and import producers lose, but the gains are greater than the losses. In the case of imports, the consumer gains what the producer loses and then gains even more on the cheaper imports. In the case of exports, the producer gains what the consumer loses and then gains even more on the items it exports. So international trade provides a net gain for a country.

REVIEW QUIZ

1 How is the gain from imports distributed between consumers and domestic producers?
2 How is the gain from exports distributed between consumers and domestic producers?
3 Why is the net gain from international trade positive?

Work these questions in Study Plan 15.2 and get instant feedback.   MyLab Economics

◆ International Trade Restrictions

Governments use four sets of tools to influence international trade and protect domestic industries from foreign competition. They are:

- Tariffs
- Import quotas
- Other import barriers
- Export subsidies

Tariffs

A **tariff** is a tax on a good that is imposed by the importing country when an imported good crosses its international boundary. For example, the government of India imposes a 100 percent tariff on wine imported from Ontario. So when an Indian imports a $10 bottle of Ontario wine, he pays the Indian government a $10 import duty.

Tariffs raise revenue for governments and serve the self-interest of people who earn their incomes in import-competing industries. But as you will see, restrictions on free international trade decrease the gains from trade and are not in the social interest.

The Effects of a Tariff To see the effects of a tariff, let's return to the example in which Canada imports T-shirts. With free trade, the T-shirts are imported and sold at the world price. Then, under pressure from Canadian garment makers, the government imposes a tariff on imported T-shirts. Buyers of T-shirts must now pay the world price plus the tariff. Several consequences follow and Fig. 15.3 illustrates them.

Figure 15.3(a) shows the situation with free international trade. Canada produces 2 million T-shirts a year and imports 4 million a year at the world price of $5 a shirt. Figure 15.3(b) shows what happens when the Canadian government imposes a tariff of $2 per T-shirt.

FIGURE 15.3 The Effects of a Tariff

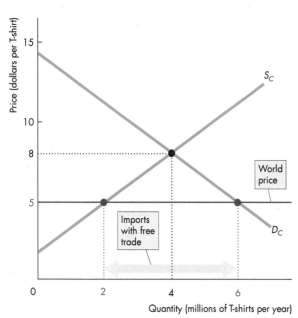

(a) Free trade

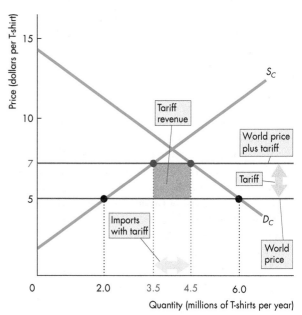

(b) Market with tariff

The world price of a T-shirt is $5. With free trade in part (a), Canadians buy 6 million T-shirts a year. Canadian garment makers produce 2 million T-shirts a year and Canada imports 4 million a year.

　　With a tariff of $2 per T-shirt in part (b), the price in the Canada rises to $7 a T-shirt. Canadian production increases,

Canadian purchases decrease, and the quantity imported decreases. The Canadian government collects a tariff revenue of $2 on each T-shirt imported, which is shown by the purple rectangle.

The following changes occur in the market for T-shirts in Canada:

- The price of a T-shirt rises by $2.
- The quantity of T-shirts bought decreases.
- The quantity of T-shirts produced in Canada increases.
- The quantity of T-shirts imported into Canada decreases.
- The Canadian government collects a tariff revenue.

Rise in Price of a T-Shirt To buy a T-shirt, Canadians must pay the world price plus the tariff, so the price of a T-shirt rises by the $2 tariff to $7. Figure 15.3(b) shows the new domestic price line, which lies $2 above the world price line. The price rises by the full amount of the tariff. The buyer pays the tariff.

Decrease in Purchases The higher price of a T-shirt brings a decrease in the quantity demanded along the demand curve. Figure 15.3(b) shows the decrease from 6 million T-shirts a year at $5 a shirt to 4.5 million a year at $7 a shirt.

Increase in Domestic Production The higher price of a T-shirt stimulates domestic production, and Canadain garment makers increase the quantity supplied along the supply curve. Figure 15.3(b) shows the increase from 2 million T-shirts at $5 a shirt to 3.5 million a year at $7 a shirt.

Decrease in Imports T-shirt imports decrease by 3 million, from 4 million to 1 million a year. Both the decrease in Canadian purchases and the increase in Canadian production contribute to this decrease in Canadian imports.

Tariff Revenue The government's tariff revenue is $2 million—$2 per shirt on 1 million imported shirts—shown by the purple rectangle.

Winners, Losers, and the Social Loss from a Tariff A tariff on an imported good creates winners and losers and a social loss. When the Canadian government imposes a tariff on an imported good:

- Canadian consumers of the good lose.
- Canadian producers of the good gain.
- Canadian consumers lose more than Canadian producers gain. Society loses.

Canadian Consumers of the Good Lose Because the price of a T-shirt in Canada rises, the quantity of T-shirts demanded decreases. The combination of a higher price and smaller quantity bought makes Canadian consumers worse off when a tariff is imposed.

ECONOMICS IN ACTION

Tariffs Almost Gone

Canadian tariffs were in place before Confederation. They increased sharply in the 1870s and remained high until the 1930s. In 1947, the **General Agreement on Tariffs and Trade (GATT)** was established to reduce international tariffs. Since then, tariffs have fallen in a series of negotiating rounds, the most significant of which are identified in the figure. Tariffs are now as low as they have ever been, but import quotas and other trade barriers persist.

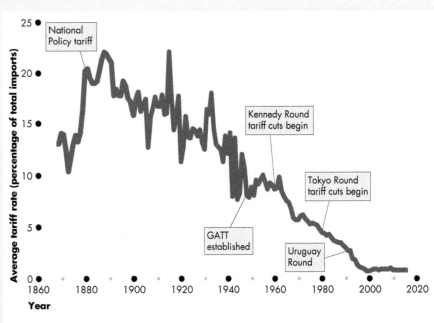

Canadian Tariffs: 1867–2016

Sources of data: Statistics Canada, *Historical Statistics of Canada*, Catalogue 11-516, July 1999 and CANSIM Tables 380-0002 and 380-0034.

Canadian Producers of the Good Gain Because the price of an imported T-shirt rises by the amount of the tariff, Canadian T-shirt producers are now able to sell their T-shirts for the world price plus the tariff, so the quantity of T-shirts supplied by Canadian producers increases. The combination of a higher price and larger quantity produced increases producers' profits. Canadian producers gain from the tariff.

Canadian Consumers Lose More Than Canadian Producers Gain Consumers lose from the tariff for three reasons:

1. They pay a higher price to domestic producers.
2. They buy a smaller quantity of the good.
3. They pay tariff revenue to the government.

The tariff revenue is a loss to consumers, but it is not a social loss. The government can use the tariff revenue to buy public services that consumers value. But the other two sources of consumer loss include some social loss.

There is a social loss because part of the higher price paid to domestic producers pays the higher cost of domestic production. The increased domestic production could have been obtained at lower cost as an import. There is also a social loss from the decreased quantity of the good bought at the higher price.

Import Quotas

We now look at the second tool for restricting trade: import quotas. An **import quota** is a restriction that limits the quantity of a good that may be imported in a given period.

Most countries impose import quotas on a wide range of items. Canada imposes them on food products such as meat, eggs, and dairy and manufactured goods such as textiles and steel.

Import quotas enable the government to satisfy the self-interest of the people who earn their incomes in the import-competing industries. But you will discover that, like a tariff, an import quota decreases the gains from trade and is not in the social interest.

ECONOMICS IN ACTION

Self-Interest Beats the Social Interest

The **World Trade Organization (WTO)** is an international body established by the world's major trading nations for the purpose of supervising international trade and lowering the barriers to trade.

In 2001, at a meeting of trade ministers from all the WTO member-countries held in Doha, Qatar, an agreement was made to begin negotiations to lower tariff barriers and quotas that restrict international trade in farm products and services. These negotiations are called the **Doha Development Agenda** or the **Doha Round**.

In the period since 2001, thousands of hours of conferences from Cancún in 2003 to Bali in 2013 and ongoing meetings at WTO headquarters in Geneva, costing millions of taxpayers' dollars, have made disappointing progress.

Rich nations, led by the United States, the European Union, and Japan, want greater access to the markets of developing nations in exchange for allowing those nations greater access to the markets of the rich world, especially those for farm products.

Developing nations, led by Brazil, China, India, and South Africa, want access to the markets of farm products of the rich world, but they also want to protect their infant industries.

With two incompatible positions, these negotiations are stalled and show no signs of a breakthrough. The self-interests of producers in both rich nations and developing nations are preventing the achievement of the social interest.

The Effects of an Import Quota The effects of an import quota are similar to those of a tariff. The price rises, the quantity bought decreases, and the quantity produced in Canada increases. Figure 15.4 illustrates the effects.

Figure 15.4(a) shows the situation with free international trade. Figure 15.4(b) shows what happens with an import quota of 1 million T-shirts a year. The Canadian supply curve of T-shirts becomes the domestic supply curve, S_C, plus the quantity that the import quota permits. So the supply curve becomes $S_C + quota$. The price of a T-shirt rises to \$7, the quantity of T-shirts bought in Canada decreases to 4.5 million a year, the quantity of T-shirts produced in Canada increases to 3.5 million a year, and the quantity of T-shirts imported into Canada decreases to the quota quantity of 1 million a year. All the effects of this import quota are identical to the effects of a \$2 per shirt tariff, as you can check in Fig. 15.3(b).

Winners, Losers, and the Social Loss from an Import Quota An import quota creates winners and losers that are similar to those of a tariff but with an interesting difference.

When the government imposes an import quota:

- Canadian consumers of the good lose.
- Canadian producers of the good gain.
- Importers of the good gain.
- Society loses.

Canadian Consumers of the Good Lose Because the price of a T-shirt in Canada rises, the quantity of T-shirts demanded decreases. The combination of a higher price and smaller quantity bought makes the Canadian consumers worse off. So Canadian consumers lose when an import quota is imposed.

Canadian Producers of the Good Gain Because the price of an imported T-shirt rises, Canadian T-shirt producers increase production at the higher domestic

---

FIGURE 15.4 The Effects of an Import Quota

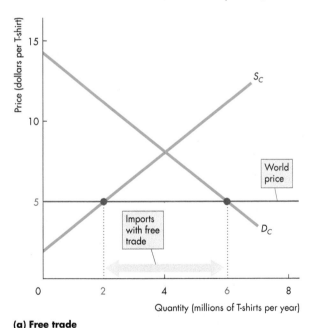

(a) Free trade

(b) Market with import quota

With free international trade, in part (a), Canadians buy 6 million T-shirts at the world price. Canada produces 2 million T-shirts and imports 4 million a year. With an import quota of 1 million T-shirts a year, in part (b), the supply of

T-shirts in Canada is shown by the curve $S_C + quota$. The price in Canada rises to \$7 a T-shirt. Canadian production increases, Canadian purchases decrease, and the quantity of T-shirts imported decreases.

ECONOMICS IN THE NEWS

The U.S.–Canada Lumber Dispute

20% Tariff on Canadian Softwood-Lumber Imports
The Trump administration wants to put a 20% tariff on Canadian softwood lumber that is used to build single-family homes. The U.S. International Trade Commission will need to find that U.S. loggers have been injured by low Canadian prices.

Source: *The Wall Street Journal,* April 24, 2017

SOME FACTS

Canada is one of the world's largest lumber producers and it has been exporting lumber to the United States since the 1800s. Most U.S. forests are privately owned and leased to lumber producers at market prices. Canadian forests are state owned and leased to lumber producers at low prices set by law. U.S. producers say Canadian producers receive a subsidy and are "dumping"—selling lumber on the U.S. market at a price lower than the cost of production or the selling price in Canada.

THE PROBLEM

Explain how U.S. lumber mills would gain from a tariff on imported lumber. Would everyone in the United States be better off? Illustrate your explanation and answer with a graph.

THE SOLUTION

- A tariff imposed on U.S. imports of lumber increases the price of lumber in the United States.

- The higher price decreases the quantity of lumber demanded in the United States, increases the quantity supplied by U.S. producers, and decreases U.S. imports of lumber.

- U.S. producers of lumber receive a greater profit but, faced with a higher price, the consumers of lumber are worse off. And the gain to producers is less than the loss to consumers—society's loss.

- The figure illustrates the U.S. market for lumber. The demand curve is D_{US} and the supply curve is S_{US}.

- With a Canadian and world price PW of $120 per cubic metre, Canada has a comparative advantage in producing lumber.

- At the world price PW, the United States produces 100 billion cubic metres a year, uses 150 billion, and imports 50 billion. The figure shows this quantity of U.S. imports.

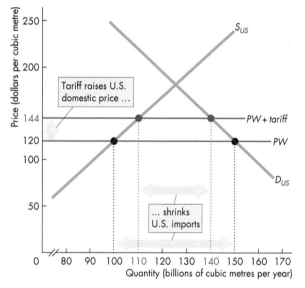

U.S. Market for Softwood Lumber

- If the United States imposes a 20 percent tariff, the price in the United States rises to $144 on the line *PW + tariff*.

- U.S. production increases to 110 billion cubic metres, the quantity bought decreases to 140 billion, and imports decrease to 30 billion.

- At the higher price and increased production, U.S. producers make bigger profit. But U.S. consumers buy less lumber and pay a higher price. Consumers lose more than producers gain, so U.S. society loses.

- The fact that the tariff is a response to Canada's alleged subsidy and dumping does not make the tariff efficient. Free trade in lumber, even if subsidized, brings a gain for U.S. consumers that exceeds the loss to U.S. producers.

price. The combination of a higher price and larger quantity produced increases producers' profit, so Canadian producers gain from the import quota.

Importers of the Good Gain The importer is able to buy the good on the world market at the world market price, and sell the good in the domestic market at the domestic price. Because the domestic price exceeds the world price, the importer gains.

Society Losses Society loses because the loss to consumers exceeds the gains of domestic producers and importers. Just like the social losses from a tariff, there is a social loss from the quota because part of the higher price paid to domestic producers pays the higher cost of domestic production. There is a social loss from the decreased quantity of the good bought at the higher price.

Tariff and Import Quota Compared You've looked at the effects of a tariff and an import quota and can now see the essential differences between them. A tariff brings in revenue for the government while an import quota brings a profit for the importers. All the other effects of an import quota are the same as the effects of a tariff, provided the quota is set at the same quantity of imports that results from the tariff.

Tariffs and import quotas are equivalent ways of restricting imports, benefiting domestic producers, and harming domestic consumers.

Let's now look at some other import barriers.

Other Import Barriers

Two sets of policies that influence imports are:

- Health, safety, and regulation barriers
- Voluntary export restraints

Health, Safety, and Regulation Barriers Thousands of detailed health, safety, and other regulations restrict international trade. For example, Canadian food imports are examined by the Canadian Food Inspection Agency, which is "mandated to safeguard Canada's food supply and the plants and animals upon which safe and high-quality food depends." The discovery of BSE (mad cow disease) in just one cow in 2003 was enough to close down international trade in Canadian beef. The European Union bans imports of most genetically modified foods, such as Canadian-produced soybeans. Although these types of regulations are not designed to limit international trade, they have that effect.

Voluntary Export Restraints A *voluntary export restraint* is like a quota allocated to a foreign exporter of a good. This type of trade barrier isn't common. It was initially used during the 1980s when Japan voluntarily limited its exports of car parts to the United States.

Export Subsidies

A *subsidy* is a payment by the government to a producer. When the government pays a subsidy to producers of a good, the cost of production falls by the amount of the subsidy, so the supply of the good increases. An *export subsidy* is a payment by the government to the producer of an exported good. Export subsidies are illegal under a number of international agreements, including the North American Free Trade Agreement (NAFTA), and the rules of the World Trade Organization (WTO).

Although export subsidies are illegal, the subsidies that the U.S. and European Union governments pay to farmers end up increasing domestic production, some of which gets exported. These exports of subsidized farm products make it harder for producers in other countries, notably in Africa and Central and South America, to compete in global markets.

Export subsidies bring gains to domestic producers, but they result in inefficient overproduction of some food products in the rich industrial countries, underproduction in the rest of the world, and create a social loss for the world as a whole.

REVIEW QUIZ

1 What are the tools that a country can use to restrict international trade?
2 Explain the effects of a tariff on domestic production, the quantity bought, and the price.
3 Explain who gains and who loses from a tariff and why the losses exceed the gains.
4 Explain the effects of an import quota on domestic production, consumption, and price.
5 Explain who gains and who loses from an import quota and why the losses exceed the gains.

Work these questions in Study Plan 15.3 and get instant feedback.   MyLab Economics

◆ The Case Against Protection

You've just seen that free trade promotes prosperity and protection is inefficient. Yet trade is restricted with tariffs, quotas, and other barriers. Why? Seven arguments for trade restrictions are that protecting domestic industries from foreign competition:

- Helps an infant industry grow.
- Counteracts dumping.
- Saves domestic jobs.
- Allows us to compete with cheap foreign labour.
- Penalizes lax environmental standards.
- Prevents rich countries from exploiting developing countries.
- Reduces offshore outsourcing that sends good Canadian jobs to other countries.

Helps an Infant Industry Grow

Comparative advantages change with on-the-job experience—*learning-by-doing*. When a new industry or a new product is born—an *infant industry*—it is not as productive as it will become with experience. It is argued that such an industry should be protected from international competition until it can stand alone and compete.

It is true that learning-by-doing can change comparative advantage, but this fact doesn't justify protecting an infant industry. Firms anticipate and benefit from learning-by-doing without protection from foreign competition. For example, when Research In Motion started to build its smartphone, BlackBerry, productivity was at first low. But after a period of learning-by-doing, huge productivity gains followed. Research In Motion didn't need a tariff to achieve these productivity gains.

Counteracts Dumping

Dumping occurs when a foreign firm sells its exports at a lower price than its cost of production. Dumping might be used by a firm that wants to gain a global monopoly. In this case, the foreign firm sells its output at a price below its cost to drive domestic firms out of business. When the domestic firms have gone, the foreign firm takes advantage of its monopoly position and charges a higher price for its product.

Dumping is illegal under the rules of the World Trade Organization and is usually regarded as a justification for temporary tariffs, which are called *countervailing duties*.

But it is virtually impossible to detect dumping because it is hard to determine a firm's costs. As a result, the test for dumping is whether a firm's export price is below its domestic price. But this test is weak because it is rational for a firm to charge a low price in a market in which the quantity demanded is highly sensitive to price and a higher price in a market in which demand is less price sensitive.

Saves Domestic Jobs

First, free trade does destroy some jobs, but it also creates other jobs. It brings about a global rationalization of labour and allocates labour resources to their highest-valued activities. International trade in textiles has cost tens of thousands of jobs in Canada as textile mills and other factories closed. But tens of thousands of jobs have been created in other countries as textile mills opened. And tens of thousands of Canadian workers have better-paying jobs than as textile workers because Canadian export industries have expanded and created new jobs. More jobs have been created than destroyed.

Although protection can save particular jobs, it does so at a high cost. For example, until 2005, U.S. textile jobs were protected by an international agreement called the Multifibre Arrangement. The U.S. International Trade Commission (ITC) estimated that because of import quotas, 72,000 jobs existed in the textile industry that would otherwise have disappeared and that the annual clothing expenditure in the United States was $15.9 billion ($160 per family) higher than it would have been with free trade. Equivalently, the ITC estimated that each textile job saved cost $221,000 a year.

Imports don't only destroy jobs. They create jobs for retailers that sell imported goods and for firms that service those goods. Imports also create jobs by creating income in the rest of the world, some of which is spent on Canadian-made goods and services.

Allows Us to Compete with Cheap Foreign Labour

With the removal of tariffs on trade between Canada, the United States, and Mexico, people said we would hear a "giant sucking sound" as jobs rushed to Mexico. That didn't happen. Why?

It didn't happen because low-wage labour is low-productivity labour. If a Canadian autoworker earns $40 an hour and produces 20 units of output an hour, the average labour cost of a unit of output is $2. If a Mexican autoworker earns $4 an hour and produces 1 unit of output an hour, the average labour cost of a unit of output is $4. Other things remaining the same, the higher a worker's productivity, the higher is the worker's wage rate. High-wage workers have high productivity; low-wage workers have low productivity.

It is *comparative advantage*, not wage differences, that drives international trade and that enables us to compete with Mexico and Mexico to compete with us.

Penalizes Lax Environmental Standards

Another argument for protection is that it provides an incentive to poor countries to raise their environmental standards—free trade with the richer and "greener" countries is a reward for improved environmental standards.

This argument for protection is weak. First, a poor country cannot afford to be as concerned about its environmental standards as a rich country can. Today, some of the worst pollution of air and water is found in China, Mexico, and Eastern Europe. But only a few decades ago, London and Los Angeles topped the pollution league chart. The best hope for cleaner air in Beijing and Mexico City is rapid income growth, which free trade promotes. As incomes grow, emerging countries have the *means* to match their desires to improve their environment. Second, a poor country may have a comparative advantage at doing "dirty" work, which helps it to raise its income and at the same time enables the global economy to achieve higher environmental standards than would otherwise be possible.

Prevents Rich Countries from Exploiting Developing Countries

Another argument for protection is that international trade must be restricted to prevent the people of the rich industrial world from exploiting the poorer people of the developing countries and forcing them to work for slave wages.

Child labour and near-slave labour are serious problems. But by trading with poor countries, we increase the demand for the goods that these countries produce and increase the demand for their labour. When the demand for labour in developing countries increases, the wage rate rises. So, rather than exploiting people in developing countries, trade can improve their opportunities and increase their incomes.

Reduces Offshore Outsourcing That Sends Good Canadian Jobs to Other Countries

Offshore outsourcing—buying goods, components, or services from firms in other countries—brings gains from trade identical to those of any other type of trade. We could easily change the names of the items traded from T-shirts and regional jets (the examples in the previous sections of this chapter) to banking services and call-centre services (or any other pair of services). A Canadian bank might export banking services to Indian firms, and Indians might provide call-centre services to Canadian firms. This type of trade would benefit both Canadians and Indians, provided Canada has a comparative advantage in banking services and India has a comparative advantage in call-centre services.

Despite the gain from specialization and trade that offshore outsourcing brings, many people believe that it also brings costs that eat up the gains. Why?

A major reason is that it seems to send good Canadian jobs to other countries. It is true that some manufacturing and service jobs are going overseas. But others are expanding at home. Canada imports call-centre services, but it exports education, healthcare, legal, financial, and a host of other types of services. The number of jobs in these sectors is expanding and will continue to expand.

The exact number of jobs that have moved to lower-cost offshore locations is not known, and estimates vary. But even the highest estimate is small compared to the normal rate of job creation and labour turnover.

Gains from trade do not bring gains for every single person. Canadians, on average, gain from offshore outsourcing, but some people lose. The losers are those who have invested in the human capital to do a specific job that has now gone offshore.

Unemployment benefits provide short-term temporary relief for these displaced workers. But the long-term solution requires retraining and the acquisition of new skills.

Beyond bringing short-term relief through unemployment benefits, government has a larger role to play. By providing education and training, it can enable the labour force of the twenty-first century to engage in the ongoing learning and sometimes rapid retooling that jobs we can't foresee today will demand.

Schools, colleges, and universities will expand and become better at doing their job of producing a more highly educated and flexible labour force.

AT **ISSUE**

Is Offshore Outsourcing Bad or Good for Canada?

The Royal Bank of Canada, Bell Canada, and the Hudson Bay Company engage in offshore outsourcing. They buy services from firms in other countries. Buying goods and components has been going on for centuries, but buying *services* such as customer support call-centre services is new and is made possible by the development of low-cost telephone and Internet service.

Should this type of offshore outsourcing be discouraged and penalized with taxes and regulations?

Bad

- Whenever a major company announces job cuts and a decision to send some jobs abroad, there is an outcry from not only the affected workers but also the broader community. It seems clear: Offshore outsourcing is bad for Canadians.

- Surveys of opinion find that around 70 percent of people in advanced economies such as Canada think outsourcing hurts jobs and incomes at home and only a small minority think it helps.

Have these Indian call-centre workers destroyed Canadian jobs? Or does their work benefit Canadian workers?

Good

- Economist N. Gregory Mankiw speaking about the U.S. situation, but relevant to all countries, says, "I think outsourcing ... is probably a plus for the economy in the long run."

- Mankiw goes on to say that it doesn't matter whether "items produced abroad come on planes, ships, or over fibre-optic cables ... the economics is basically the same."

- What Greg Mankiw is saying is that the economic analysis of the gains from international trade—exactly the same as what you have studied on p. 375—applies to international trade in all types of goods and services.

- Offshore outsourcing, like all other forms of international trade, is a source of gains for all.

Avoiding Trade Wars

We have reviewed the arguments commonly heard in favour of protection and the counterarguments. But one counterargument to protection that is general and quite overwhelming is that protection invites retaliation and can trigger a trade war.

A trade war is a contest in which when one country raises its import tariffs, other countries retaliate with increases of their own, which trigger yet further increases from the first country.

A trade war occurred during the Great Depression of the 1930s when the United States introduced the Smoot-Hawley tariff. Country after country retaliated with its own tariff, and in a short period, world trade had almost disappeared. The costs to all countries were large and led to a renewed international resolve to avoid such self-defeating moves in the future. The costs are also the impetus behind current attempts to liberate trade.

Why Is International Trade Restricted?

Why, despite all the arguments against protection, is trade restricted? There are two key reasons:

- Tariff revenue
- Rent seeking

Tariff Revenue Government revenue is costly to collect. In developed countries such as Canada, a well-organized tax collection system is in place that can generate billions of dollars of income tax and sales tax revenues.

But governments in developing countries have a difficult time collecting taxes from their citizens. Much economic activity takes place in an informal economy with few financial records. The one area in which economic transactions are well recorded is international trade. So tariffs on international trade are a convenient source of revenue in these countries.

Rent Seeking Rent seeking is the major reason international trade is restricted. **Rent seeking** is lobbying for special treatment by the government to create economic profit or to divert benefits away from others. Free trade increases consumption possibilities *on average*, but not everyone shares in the gain and some people even lose. Free trade brings benefits to some and imposes costs on others, with total benefits exceeding total costs. The uneven distribution of costs and benefits is the principal obstacle to achieving more liberal international trade.

Returning to the example of trade in T-shirts and regional jets, the benefits from free trade accrue to all the producers of regional jets and to those of T-shirts that do not bear the costs of adjusting to a smaller garment industry. These costs are transition costs, not permanent costs. The costs of moving to free trade are borne by the garment producers and their employees who must become producers of other goods and services in which Canada has a comparative advantage.

The number of winners from free trade is large, but because the gains are spread thinly over a large number of people, the gain per person is small. The winners could organize and become a political force lobbying for free trade. But political activity is costly. It uses time and other scarce resources and the gains per person are too small to make the cost of political activity worth bearing.

In contrast, the number of losers from free trade is small, but the loss per person is large. Because the loss per person is large, the people who lose *are* willing to incur considerable expense to lobby against free trade.

Both the winners and losers weigh benefits and costs. Those who gain from free trade weigh the benefits it brings against the cost of achieving it. Those who lose from free trade and gain from protection weigh the benefit of protection against the cost of maintaining it. The protectionists undertake a larger quantity of political lobbying than the free traders.

Compensating Losers

If, in total, the gains from free international trade exceed the losses, why don't those who gain compensate those who lose so that everyone is in favour of free trade?

Some compensation does take place. When Canada entered the North American Free Trade Agreement (NAFTA) with the United States and

Mexico, the United States set up a $56 million fund to support and retrain workers who lost their jobs as a result of the new trade agreement. During NAFTA's first six months, only 5,000 workers applied for benefits under this scheme.

The losers from international trade are also compensated indirectly through the normal unemployment compensation arrangements. But only limited attempts are made to compensate those who lose.

The main reason full compensation is not attempted is that the costs of identifying all the losers and estimating the value of their losses would be enormous. Also, it would never be clear whether a person who has fallen on hard times is suffering because of free trade or for other reasons that might be largely under her or his control. Furthermore, some people who look like losers at one point in time might, in fact, end up gaining. The young autoworker who loses his job in Windsor and gets a job on Alberta's oil patch might resent the loss of work and the need to move. But a year later, looking back on events, he counts himself fortunate.

Because we do not, in general, compensate the losers from free international trade, protectionism is a popular and permanent feature of our national economic and political life.

REVIEW QUIZ

1 What are the infant industry and dumping arguments for protection? Are they correct?
2 Can protection save jobs and the environment and prevent workers in developing countries from being exploited?
3 What is offshore outsourcing? Who benefits from it and who loses?
4 What are the main reasons for imposing a tariff?
5 Do the winners from free trade win the political argument? Why or why not?

Work these questions in Study Plan 15.4 and get instant feedback.   MyLab Economics

◆ We end this chapter on international trade policy with *Economics in the News* on pp. 386–387, where we apply what you've learned by looking at why Donald Trump's ideas about trade protection are wrong.

The Cost of a Tariff

A 20% Mexico Tariff Would Pay for the Wall. But It Would Hurt Americans

Shortly after President Donald Trump took office, his now former press secretary Sean Spicer gave a news conference aboard Air Force One in which he talked about the U.S. imposing an import tariff as a way of making Mexico pay for Trump's proposed border wall.

"When you look at the plan that's taking shape right now, using comprehensive tax reforms as a means to tax imports from countries that we have a trade deficit from like Mexico—if you tax that $50 billion at 20% of imports, which is, by the way, a practice that 160 other countries do right now (our country's policy is to tax exports and to let imports flow freely in, which is ridiculous), but by doing it that way, we could do $10 billion a year and easily pay for the wall just through that mechanism alone."

A tariff on Mexican imports would raise the prices faced by U.S. consumers. *The Washington Post* did some calculations, providing pre- and post-tariff pricing for some common Mexican imports:

Item	Price	Price + Tax
An avocado	$3.00	$3.60
Papermate pen refills	$5.54	$6.65
Six pack of Tecate beer	$6.00	$7.20
LG refrigerator	$1,600	$1,920
Ford Fiesta	$21,435	$25,722

In response to the idea shared by Spicer, Senator Lindsey Graham (R-South Carolina) employed one of the president's favourite communication methods by tweeting: "Simply put, any policy proposal which drives up costs of Corona, tequila, or margaritas is a big-time bad idea. Mucho Sad."

Sources: Based on Gillespie, Patrick, "A 20% Mexico Tariff Would Pay for the Wall. But It Would Hurt Americans." CNNMoney, January 26, 2017; Bump, Philip, "Americans Might Need to Buy 25 Billion Avocados so Mexico Could Pay for the Wall." *The Washington Post*, January 26, 2017; Sean Spicer on C-SPAN video; Lindsey Graham on Twitter.

ESSENCE OF THE STORY

- The Trump administration floated the idea of paying for a border wall with the revenue from a 20% tariff on imports from Mexico.

- A 20% tariff would raise enough revenue to pay for a border wall.

- American consumers, not Mexico, would be paying for the wall.

- Americans would bear the cost of the tariff by paying higher prices for cars, refrigerators, avocados, beer, and many other products imported from Mexico.

ECONOMIC ANALYSIS

- You might think a border wall is a bad idea, or you might think it is a good idea. This news article is not taking sides on that question, and nor is this analysis.

- The questions addressed are would a 20 percent tariff on imports from Mexico bring in enough revenue to pay for a wall, and who would end up paying?

- The article says the tariff would generate enough revenue, and Americans, not Mexicans, would pay.

- The article is correct about who would pay, but it makes a mistake in its revenue calculation.

- To see why, we'll look at the U.S. market for just one of the items that the United States imports from Mexico—avocados.

- In Fig. 1, the demand curve D_{US} shows the demand for avocados in the United States, and the supply curve S_{US} shows the supply of avocados produced in the United States.

- The world price of avocados is $1,750 a ton, shown by the line PW. The United States can import avocados at this price, so this is the price in the United States.

- With free trade, the United States produces 200,000 tons of avocados a year, imports 600,000 tons, and consumes 800,000 tons.

- Figure 2 shows what happens when a 20 percent tariff is imposed on avocados. The U.S. demand curve and the U.S. supply curve don't change. But the United States is no longer able to buy avocados from Mexico for $1,750 a ton.

- The U.S. price now rises by 20 percent to $2,100 per ton. At that price, the quantity of avocados demanded decreases to 555,000 tons, the quantity supplied by U.S. growers increases to 240,000 tons, and imports decrease to 315,000 tons a year. (These quantities are based on realistic assumptions about the elasticities of demand and supply of avocados.)

- U.S. avocado producers receive a higher price and sell more avocados, but U.S. consumers take a hit. They pay a higher price and buy fewer avocados.

- The U.S. government receives a tariff revenue (the purple rectangle).

- The tariff revenue is not 20 percent of the value of imports with free trade. It is 20 percent of a lower value of imports that results from the 20 percent higher price.

- So, a U.S. tariff to pay for a wall would mean American consumers pay for the wall; and a 20 percent tariff might not generate enough revenue to pay for a wall.

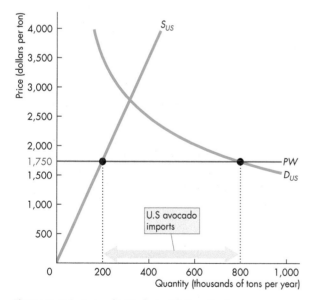

Figure 1 U.S. Avocado Market with Free Trade

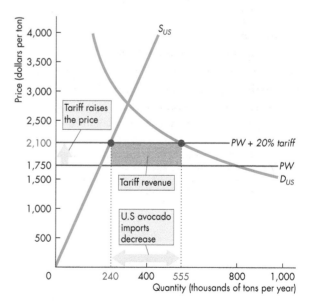

Figure 2 U.S. Avocado Market with 20% Tariff

WORKED PROBLEM

MyLab Economics Work this problem in Chapter 15 Study Plan.

The table shows the Canadian demand schedule for honey and the supply schedule of honey by Canadian producers. The world price of honey is $8 a jar.

Price (dollars per jar)	Quantity demanded	Quantity supplied
	(millions of jars per year)	
5	10	0
6	8	3
7	6	6
8	4	9
9	2	12
10	0	15

Questions

1. With no international trade, what is the price of honey and the quantity bought and sold in Canada? Does Canada have a comparative advantage in producing honey? With free international trade, does Canada export or import honey?

2. With free international trade, what is the Canadian price of honey, the quantity bought by Canadians, the quantity produced in Canada, and the quantity of honey exported or imported?

3. Does Canada gain from international trade in honey? Do all Canadians gain? If not, who loses and do the gains exceed the losses?

Solutions

1. With no international trade, the price of honey is that at which the quantity demanded equals the quantity supplied. The table shows that this price is $7 a jar at which the equilibrium quantity is 6 million jars a year.

   The price of honey in Canada is less than the world price, which means that the opportunity cost of producing a jar of honey in Canada is *less* than the opportunity cost of producing it in the rest of the world. So Canadian producers have a comparative advantage in producing honey, and with free international trade, Canada exports honey.

Key Point: Comparative advantage is determined by comparing the opportunity cost of producing the good in Canada and the world price.

2. With free international trade, the price of honey in Canada rises to the world price of $8 a jar. Canadians cut their consumption of honey to 4 million jars a year while Canadian honey producers expand production to 9 million jars a year. Canada exports 5 million jars of honey a year. The figure shows the quantities bought and produced in Canada and the quantity exported.

Key Point: As the domestic price rises to the world price, the quantity demanded decreases and the quantity supplied increases, and the difference is exported.

3. With free international trade in honey, Canada gains from exporting honey.

   The higher price and the larger quantity of honey produced increase the honey producers' profit.

   Consumers lose because the price of honey rises and they buy less honey.

   Canada gains because the gain of honey producers exceeds the loss of honey consumers.

   There is a social gain from free trade.

Key Point: Free trade brings gains to domestic exporters and losses to domestic consumers of the exported good, but the exporting country has a net social gain.

Key Figure

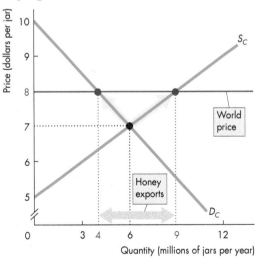

MyLab Economics Interactive Graph

SUMMARY

Key Points

How Global Markets Work (pp. 372–374)

- Comparative advantage drives international trade.
- If the world price of a good is lower than the domestic price, the rest of the world has a comparative advantage in producing that good and the domestic country gains by producing less, consuming more, and importing the good.
- If the world price of a good is higher than the domestic price, the domestic country has a comparative advantage in producing that good and gains by producing more, consuming less, and exporting the good.

Working Problems 1 to 3 will give you a better understanding of how global markets work.

Winners, Losers, and the Net Gain from Trade (p. 375)

- Compared to a no-trade situation, in a market with imports, consumers gain and producers lose but the gains are greater than the losses.
- Compared to a no-trade situation, in a market with exports, producers gain and consumers lose but the gains are greater than the losses.

Working Problem 4 will give you a better understanding of winners, losers, and the net gains from trade.

International Trade Restrictions (pp. 376–381)

- Countries restrict international trade by imposing tariffs, import quotas, and other import barriers.
- Trade restrictions raise the domestic price of imported goods, lower the quantity imported, make consumers worse off, make producers better off, and damage the social interest.

Working Problems 5 to 10 will give you a better understanding of international trade restrictions.

The Case Against Protection (pp. 382–385)

- Arguments that protection helps an infant industry to grow and counteracts dumping are weak.
- Arguments that protection saves jobs, allows us to compete with cheap foreign labour, is needed to penalize lax environmental standards, and prevents exploitation of developing countries are flawed.
- Offshore outsourcing is just a new way of reaping gains from trade and does not justify protection.
- Trade restrictions are popular because protection brings a small loss per person to a large number of people and a large gain per person to a small number of people. Those who gain have a stronger political voice than those who lose and it is too costly to identify and compensate losers.

Working Problem 11 will give you a better understanding of the case against protection.

Key Terms

MyLab Economics Key Terms Quiz

Dumping, 382
Exports, 372
Import quota, 378
Imports, 372
Offshore outsourcing, 383
Rent seeking, 385
Tariff, 376

STUDY PLAN PROBLEMS AND APPLICATIONS

MyLab Economics Work Problems 1 to 11 in Chapter 15 Study Plan and get instant feedback.

How Global Markets Work (Study Plan 15.1)

Use the following data to work Problems 1 to 3.

Wholesalers buy and sell roses in containers that hold 120 stems. The table provides information about the wholesale market for roses in North America. The demand schedule is the wholesalers' demand and the supply schedule is the North American rose growers' supply.

Price (dollars per container)	Quantity demanded	Quantity supplied
	(millions of containers per year)	
100	15	0
125	12	2
150	9	4
175	6	6
200	3	8
225	0	10

Wholesalers can buy roses at auction in Aalsmeer, Holland, for $125 per container.

1. a. With no international trade, what would be the price of a container of roses and how many containers of roses a year would be bought and sold in North America?

   b. At the price in your answer to part (a), does North America or the rest of the world have a comparative advantage in producing roses?

2. If North American wholesalers buy roses at the lowest possible price, how many do they buy from North American growers and how many do they import?

3. Draw a graph to illustrate the North American wholesale market for roses. Show the equilibrium in that market with no international trade and the equilibrium with free trade. Mark the quantity of roses grown in North America, the quantity imported, and the total quantity bought.

Winners, Losers, and the Net Gain from Trade
(Study Plan 15.2)

4. Use the data on the market for roses in Problem 1 to work this problem.

   a. Explain who gains and who loses from free international trade in roses compared to a

situation in which North Americans buy only roses grown locally.

   b. Calculate the value of the roses imported into North America.

International Trade Restrictions (Study Plan 15.3)

Use the information on the North American wholesale market for roses in Problem 1 to work Problems 5 to 10.

5. If a tariff of $25 per container is imposed on imports of roses, explain how the price of roses, the quantity of roses bought, the quantity produced in North America, and the quantity imported change.

6. Who gains and who loses from this tariff?

7. Draw a graph of the North American market for roses to illustrate the gains and losses from the tariff. On the graph, identify the government's tariff revenue from imported roses.

8. If an import quota of 5 million containers is imposed on roses, what happens to the price of roses, the quantity of roses bought, the quantity produced in North America, and the quantity imported?

9. Who gains and who loses from this import quota?

10. Draw a graph to illustrate the effects of the import quota, and on the graph, identify the importers' profit.

The Case Against Protection (Study Plan 15.4)

11. **Cheese Makers Brace for European Imports**

   The Canada–European Union Comprehensive Economic and Trade Agreement (CETA) becomes effective July 2017. It will increase Canada's European cheese import quota by 17,700 tonnes. The change could cost Canadian producers $230 million a year with up to 400 jobs lost.

   Source: *The Globe and Mail*, April 15, 2017

   a. What does the news clip imply about the comparative advantage of producing cheese in the European Union and Canada?

   b. Are any of the arguments for protection valid reasons for a cheese import quota?

ADDITIONAL PROBLEMS AND APPLICATIONS

MyLab Economics You can work these problems in Homework or Test if assigned by your instructor.

How Global Markets Work

12. Suppose that the world price of eggs is $1 a dozen, Canada does not trade internationally, and the equilibrium price of eggs in Canada is $3 a dozen. Canada then begins to trade internationally.
    a. How does the price of eggs in Canada change?
    b. Do Canadians buy more or fewer eggs?
    c. Do Canadian egg farmers produce more or fewer eggs?
    d. Does Canada export or import eggs and why?
    e. Would employment in the Canadian egg industry change? If so, how?

13. Suppose that the world price of steel is $100 a tonne, India does not trade internationally, and the equilibrium price of steel in India is $60 a tonne. India then begins to trade internationally.
    a. How does the price of steel in India change?
    b. How does the quantity of steel produced in India change?
    c. How does the quantity of steel bought by India change?
    d. Does India export or import steel and why?

14. A semiconductor is a key component in your laptop, smartphone, and iPad. The table provides information about the market for semiconductors in Canada.

Price (dollars per unit)	Quantity demanded	Quantity supplied
	(billions of units per year)	
10	25	0
12	20	20
14	15	40
16	10	60
18	5	80
20	0	100

Producers of semiconductors can get $18 a unit on the world market.
    a. With no international trade, what would be the price of a semiconductor and how many semiconductors a year would be bought and sold in Canada?
    b. Does Canada have a comparative advantage in producing semiconductors?

15. Food Versus Fuel

Biofuels (mainly ethanol) make up 10 percent of auto fuel in the United States and 5 percent in Canada, and the mandated shares have risen. Farmers are smiling because taxpayers subsidize the fuel. Using ethanol makes food prices higher than they should be.

Source: *The Globe and Mail*, October 28, 2016

    a. What is the effect on the world price of corn of the increased use of corn to produce ethanol in Canada and the United States?
    b. How does the change in the world price of corn affect the quantity of corn produced and consumed in a corn-exporting country?
    c. How does the change in the world price of corn affect the quantity of corn produced and consumed in a corn-importing country?

Winners, Losers, and the Net Gain from Trade

16. Draw a graph of the market for corn in the corn-exporting country in Problem 15(b) to show the changes in the price of corn, the quantity produced, and the quantity consumed by people in that country.

Use the following news clip to work Problems 17 and 18.

Beef Exporters Re-Focus on South Korea

South Korea recently lifted its temporary mad cow disease ban on Canadian beef and veal imports. Canadian beef exporters predict that with the free trade, beef exports to South Korea might exceed $50 million a year.

Source: *The Vancouver Sun*, January 11, 2016

17. Explain how South Korea's temporary import ban on Canadian beef affected beef producers and consumers in South Korea. Draw a graph of the South Korean market for beef to show how this ban changed the price of beef, the quantity produced, the quantity consumed, and the quantity imported.

18. Assuming that South Korea is the only importer of Canadian beef, explain how South Korea's ban on beef imports affected beef producers and consumers in Canada. Draw a graph of the market for beef in Canada to show how this ban changes the Canadian beef market.

International Trade Restrictions

Use the following information to work Problems 19 to 21.

Before 1995, trade between Canada and Mexico was subject to tariffs. In 1995, Mexico joined NAFTA and all Canadian and Mexican tariffs have gradually been removed.

19. Explain how the price that Canadian consumers pay for goods from Mexico and the quantity of Canadian imports from Mexico have changed. Who are the winners and who are the losers from this free trade?

20. Explain how the quantity of Canadian exports to Mexico and the Canadian government's tariff revenue from trade with Mexico have changed.

21. Suppose that this year, tomato growers in Ontario lobby the Canadian government to impose an import quota on Mexican tomatoes. Explain who in Canada would gain and who would lose from such a quota.

Use the following information to work Problems 22 and 23.

Suppose that in response to huge job losses in the Canadian textile industry, the Government of Canada imposes a 100 percent tariff on imports of textiles from China.

22. Explain how the tariff on textiles will change the price that Canadians pay for textiles, the quantity of textiles imported, and the quantity of textiles produced in Canada.

23. Explain how the Canadian and Chinese gains from trade will change. Who in Canada will lose and who will gain?

Use the following information to work Problems 24 and 25.

With free trade between Australia and Canada, Australia would export beef to Canada. But Canada imposes an import quota on Australian beef.

24. Explain how this import quota influences the price that Canadians pay for beef, the quantity of beef produced in Canada, and the Canadian and the Australian gains from trade.

25. Explain who in Canada gains from the quota on beef imports and who loses.

The Case Against Protection

26. **The Cost of Bringing Home American Jobs**
    Donald Trump says he'll bring home jobs lost to China and Mexico. It is possible but costly.

American consumers would face higher prices and those on low incomes would suffer most because they spend a high share of their income on clothes, shoes, and toys—things that are made at low cost and imported.

Source: CNNMoney, April 14, 2016

a. What are the arguments for bringing jobs back to America? Explain why these arguments are faulty.

b. Is there any merit in bringing jobs back?

Economics in the News

27. After you have studied *Economics in the News* on pp. 386–387, answer the following questions.

a. What was the value of U.S. imports from Mexico in 2015 and why would the value of imports fall if a 20 percent tariff were imposed on them?

b. How do the elasticities of demand and supply influence the revenue that a tariff generates?

c. Who in the United States would benefit and who would lose from a 20 percent tariff on imports from Mexico?

d. Illustrate your answer to part (c) with an appropriate graphical analysis.

28. **NAFTA: What Canada Could Gain from Renegotiation**
    NAFTA is light on trade in services. But it is services that have dominated Canada's export growth in the past decade. If U.S. President Donald Trump makes good on his election pledge to renegotiate NAFTA, reducing barriers to trading digitally delivered goods and services should be Canada's priority.

Source: *The Globe and Mail*, January 28, 2017

a. What is NAFTA? What is its aim?

b. Explain how barriers to free trade in e-commerce—delivering services digitally—influence the quantity of these services produced, consumed, and traded. Illustrate your answer with an appropriate graphical analysis.

c. Explain why U.S. producers of e-commerce services would be expected to oppose free trade in these services with Canada.

Tradeoffs and Free Lunches

A policy tradeoff arises if, in taking an action to achieve one goal, some other goal must be forgone. The Bank of Canada wants to avoid a rise in the inflation rate and a rise in the unemployment rate. But if the Bank of Canada raises the interest rate to curb inflation, it might lower expenditure and increase unemployment. The Bank of Canada faces a short-run tradeoff between inflation and unemployment.

A policy free lunch arises if, in taking actions to pursue one goal, some other (intended or unintended) goal is also achieved. The Bank of Canada wants to keep inflation in check and, at the same time, to boost the economic growth rate. If lower inflation brings greater certainty about the future and stimulates saving and investment, the Bank of Canada gets both lower inflation and faster real GDP growth. It enjoys a free lunch.

The first two chapters in this part describe the institutional framework in which fiscal policy (Chapter 13) and monetary policy (Chapter 14) are made, describe the instruments of policy, and analyze the effects of policy. This exploration of economic policy draws on almost everything that you learned in previous chapters. The final chapter (Chapter 15) explains a free lunch that arises from international trade and the gains that are achieved from *free* trade.

These policy chapters serve as a capstone on your knowledge of macroeconomics and draw together all the strands in your study of the previous chapters.

Milton Friedman, whom you meet below, has profoundly influenced our understanding of macroeconomic policy, especially monetary policy.

Milton Friedman *was born into a poor immigrant family in New York City in 1912. He was an undergraduate at Rutgers and a graduate student at Columbia University during the Great Depression. From 1977 until his death in 2006, Professor Friedman was a Senior Fellow at the Hoover Institution at Stanford University. But his reputation was built between 1946 and 1983, when he was a leading member of the "Chicago School," an approach to economics developed at the University of Chicago and based on the views that free markets allocate resources efficiently and that stable and low money supply growth delivers macroeconomic stability.*

Friedman has advanced our understanding of the forces that determine macroeconomic performance and clarified the effects of the quantity of money. For this work, he was awarded the 1977 Nobel Prize for Economic Science.

By reasoning from basic economic principles, Friedman (along with Edmund S. Phelps, the 2006 Economics Nobel Laureate) predicted that persistent demand stimulation would not increase output but would cause inflation.

Inflation is always and everywhere a monetary phenomenon.

MILTON FRIEDMAN
The Counter-Revolution in Monetary Theory

When output growth slowed and inflation broke out in the 1970s, Friedman seemed like a prophet, and for a time, his policy prescription, known as monetarism, was embraced around the world.

PIERRE SIKLOS is Professor of Economics and Director of the Viessmann European Research Centre at Wilfrid Laurier University in Waterloo, Ontario. He was an undergraduate at McGill University in Montreal, where he was born, and a graduate student at the University of Western Ontario and Carleton University, where he received his PhD in 1981.

Professor Siklos is a macroeconomist who studies inflation, central banks, and financial markets. His work is data driven and he uses statistical methods to uncover the mechanisms at work. His research is published in a variety of international journals.

He has been a visiting scholar at universities around Europe and North America, Australia, and New Zealand. Pierre is a member of the C.D. Howe Institute's Monetary Policy Council.

Michael Parkin and Robin Bade talked with Pierre Siklos about his work and about the problems facing Canada today.

Pierre, why did you become an economist and what attracted you to macroeconomics?

As an undergraduate at McGill University in Montreal I was majoring in mathematics. I was especially interested in statistics and I enrolled in an econometrics course. The econometrics lecturer emphasized how statistical tools could be used to help us understand economic phenomena. I became fascinated by the sheer breadth and scope of the economic phenomena that could be studied with econometric tools. I was particulary impressed by the range of macroeconomic questions that could be studied. After taking that econometrics course, I was hooked and I resolved to take economics in graduate school.

You've specialized in the study of monetary policy: How would you describe the most important principles that you and other economists have discovered for the conduct of monetary policy?

After much research I have come to the conclusion that monetary policy can help smooth business cycle fluctuations in the short to medium term (say around 2–3 years) but not beyond.

Consistently good monetary policy can lead to desirable economic outcomes with low and predictable inflation. Canada's monetary policy during the period of inflation targeting is an example of the achievement of good outcomes with good policy.

Similarly, consistently bad monetary policy can lead to disastrous economic outcomes with hyperinflation, perhaps the single best example of monetary policy that has utterly failed.

The clear and convincing communication of monetary policy decisions plays an important role in the achievement of good policy outcomes, although its vital importance is difficult to demonstrate.

> The clear and convincing communication of monetary policy decisions [is] vital.

*Read the full interview with Pierre Siklos in MyLab Economics.

394

Above full-employment equilibrium A macroeconomic equilibrium in which real GDP exceeds potential GDP. (p. 254)

Absolute advantage A person has an absolute advantage if that person is more productive than another person. (p. 40)

Aggregate demand The relationship between the quantity of real GDP demanded and the price level. (p. 248)

Aggregate planned expenditure The sum of planned consumption expenditure, planned investment, planned government expenditure on goods and services, and planned exports minus planned imports. (p. 268)

Aggregate production function The relationship between real GDP and the quantity of labour when all other influences on production remain the same. (p. 142)

Allocative efficiency A situation in which goods and services are produced at the lowest possible cost and in the quantities that provide the greatest possible benefit. We cannot produce more of any good without giving up some of another good that we *value more highly*. (p. 37)

Arbitrage The practice of seeking to profit by buying in one market and selling for a higher price in another related market. (p. 222)

Automatic fiscal policy A fiscal policy action that is triggered by the state of the economy with no action by the government. (p. 334)

Autonomous expenditure The sum of those components of aggregate planned expenditure that are not influenced by real GDP. Autonomous expenditure equals the sum of investment, government expenditure, exports, and the autonomous parts of consumption expenditure and imports. (p. 272)

Autonomous tax multiplier The change in equilibrium expenditure and real GDP that results from a change in autonomous taxes divided by the change in autonomous taxes. (p. 290)

Balanced budget A government budget in which receipts and outlays are equal. (p. 325)

Balanced budget multiplier The change in equilibrium expenditure and real GDP that results from equal changes in government expenditure and lump-sum taxes divided by the change in government expenditure. (p. 291)

Balance of payments accounts A country's record of international trading, borrowing, and lending. (p. 228)

Bank rate The interest rate that the Bank of Canada charges big banks on loans. (pp. 194, 351)

Below full-employment equilibrium A macroeconomic equilibrium in which potential GDP exceeds real GDP. (p. 255)

Benefit The benefit of something is the gain or pleasure that it brings and is determined by preferences. (p. 9)

Bond A promise to make specified payments on specified dates. (p. 165)

Bond market The market in which bonds issued by firms and governments are traded. (p. 165)

Budget deficit A government's budget balance that is negative—outlays exceed receipts. (p. 325)

Budget surplus A government's budget balance that is positive—receipts exceed outlays. (p. 325)

Business cycle The periodic but irregular up-and-down movement of total production and other measures of economic activity. (p. 95)

Canadian interest rate differential The Canadian interest rate minus the foreign interest rate. (p. 219)

Canadian official reserves The Canadian government's holdings of foreign currency. (p. 228)

Capital The tools, equipment, buildings, and other constructions that businesses use to produce goods and services. (p. 4)

Capital accumulation The growth of capital resources, including *human capital*. (p. 45)

Capital and financial account A record of foreign investment in a country minus its investment abroad. (p. 228)

Central bank A bank's bank and a public authority that regulates the nation's depository institutions and conducts *monetary policy*, which means it adjusts the quantity of money in circulation and influences interest rates. (p. 191)

Ceteris paribus Other things being equal—all other relevant things remaining the same. (p. 26)

Change in demand A change in buyers' plans that occurs when some influence on those plans other than the price of the good changes. It is illustrated by a shift of the demand curve. (p. 60)

Change in supply A change in sellers' plans that occurs when some influence on those plans other than the price of the good changes. It is illustrated by a shift of the supply curve. (p. 65)

Change in the quantity demanded A change in buyers' plans that occurs when the price of a good changes but all other influences on buyers' plans remain unchanged. It is illustrated by a movement along the demand curve. (p. 63)

Change in the quantity supplied A change in sellers' plans that occurs when the price of a good changes but all other influences on sellers' plans remain unchanged. It is illustrated by a movement along the supply curve. (p. 66)

Chartered bank A private firm, chartered under the Bank Act of 1991 to receive deposits and make loans. (p. 187)

Classical A macroeconomist who believes that the economy is self-regulating and always at full employment. (p. 258)

Classical growth theory A theory of economic growth based on the view that the growth of real GDP per person is temporary and that when it rises above subsistence level, a population explosion eventually brings it back to subsistence level. (p. 151)

Comparative advantage A person or country has a comparative advantage in an activity if that person or country can perform the activity at a lower opportunity cost than anyone else or any other country. (p. 40)

Competitive market A market that has many buyers and many sellers, so no single buyer or seller can influence the price. (p. 58)

Complement A good that is used in conjunction with another good. (p. 61)

Consumer Price Index (CPI) An index that measures the average of the prices paid by urban consumers for a fixed basket of consumer goods and services. (p. 121)

Consumption expenditure The total payment for consumer goods and services. (p. 89)

Consumption function The relationship between consumption expenditure and disposable income, other things remaining the same. (p. 268)

Core inflation rate A measure of the inflation rate that excludes volatile prices in an attempt to reveal the underlying inflation trend. (p. 124)

Cost-push inflation An inflation that results from an initial increase in costs. (p. 305)

Crawling peg An exchange rate that follows a path determined by a decision of the government or the central bank and is achieved in a similar way to a fixed exchange rate. (p. 226)

Creditor nation A country that during its entire history has invested more in the rest of the world than other countries have invested in it. (p. 231)

Crowding-out effect The tendency for a government budget deficit to raise the real interest rate and decrease investment. (p. 175)

Currency The notes and coins held by individuals and businesses. (p. 185)

Currency drain ratio The ratio of currency to deposits. (p. 195)

Current account A record of receipts from exports of goods and services, payments for imports of goods and services, net interest income paid abroad, and net transfers received from abroad. (p. 228)

Cycle The tendency for a variable to alternate between upward and downward movements. (p. 103)

Cyclical surplus or deficit The actual surplus or deficit minus the structural surplus or deficit. (p. 334)

Cyclical unemployment The higher-than-normal unemployment at a business cycle trough and the lower-than-normal unemployment at a business cycle peak. (p. 117)

Debtor nation A country that during its entire history has borrowed more from the rest of the world than other countries have lent it. (p. 231)

Default risk The risk that a borrower, also known as a creditor, might not repay a loan. (p. 171)

Deflation A persistently falling price level. (p. 120)

Demand The entire relationship between the price of the good and the quantity demanded of it when all other influences on buyers' plans remain the same. It is illustrated by a demand curve and described by a demand schedule. (p. 59)

Demand curve A curve that shows the relationship between the quantity demanded of a good and its price when all other influences on consumers' planned purchases remain the same. (p. 60)

Demand for loanable funds The relationship between the quantity of loanable funds demanded and the real interest rate when all other influences on borrowing plans remain the same. (p. 170)

Demand for money The relationship between the quantity of real money demanded and the nominal interest rate when all other influences on the amount of money that people wish to hold remain the same. (p. 199)

Demand-pull inflation An inflation that starts because aggregate demand increases. (p. 303)

Depository institution A financial firm that takes deposits from households and firms. (p. 187)

Depreciation The decrease in the value of a firm's capital that results

from wear and tear and obsolescence. (p. 90)

Desired reserve ratio The ratio of reserves to deposits that banks *plan* to hold. (p. 195)

Direct relationship A relationship between two variables that move in the same direction. (p. 20)

Discouraged searcher A person who currently is neither working nor looking for work but has indicated that he or she wants a job, is available for work, and has looked for work sometime in the recent past but has stopped looking because of repeated failure. (p. 115)

Discretionary fiscal policy A fiscal action that is initiated by an act of Parliament. (p. 334)

Disposable income Aggregate income minus taxes plus transfer payments. (pp. 250, 268)

Dumping The sale by a foreign firm of exports at a lower price than the cost of production. (p. 382)

Economic growth The expansion of production possibilities. (pp. 45, 136)

Economic model A description of some aspect of the economic world that includes only those features of the world that are needed for the purpose at hand. (p. 11)

Economics The social science that studies the *choices* that individuals, businesses, governments, and entire societies make as they cope with *scarcity* and the *incentives* that influence and reconcile those choices. (p. 2)

Efficient Resource use is efficient if it is *not* possible to make someone better off without making someone else worse off. (p. 5)

Employment rate The percentage of people of working age who have jobs. (p. 115)

Entrepreneurship The human resource that organizes the other three factors of production: labour, land, and capital. (p. 4)

Equilibrium expenditure The level of aggregate expenditure that occurs when aggregate *planned* expenditure equals real GDP. (p. 274)

Equilibrium price The price at which the quantity demanded equals the quantity supplied. (p. 68)

Equilibrium quantity The quantity bought and sold at the equilibrium price. (p. 68)

Excess reserves A bank's actual reserves minus its desired reserves. (p. 195)

Exchange rate The price at which one currency exchanges for another in the foreign exchange market. (p. 214)

Expansion A business cycle phase between a trough and a peak—a period in which real GDP increases. (p. 95)

Exports The goods and services that we sell to people in other countries. (pp. 90, 372)

Factors of production The productive resources used to produce goods and services. (p. 3)

Federal budget The annual statement of the outlays and receipts of the Government of Canada, together with the laws and regulations that approve and support those outlays and taxes. (p. 324)

Final good An item that is bought by its final user during the specified time period. (p. 88)

Financial capital The funds that firms use to buy physical capital and that households use to buy a home or to invest in human capital. (p. 164)

Financial institution A firm that operates on both sides of the market for financial capital. It borrows in one market and lends in another. (p. 166)

Firm An economic unit that hires factors of production and organizes those factors to produce and sell goods and services. (p. 48)

Fiscal policy The use of the federal budget, by setting and changing tax rates, making transfer payments, and purchasing goods and services, to achieve macroeconomic objectives such as full employment, sustained economic growth, and price level stability. (pp. 250, 324)

Fiscal stimulus The use of fiscal policy to increase production and employment. (p. 334)

Fixed exchange rate An exchange rate the value of which is determined by a decision of the government or the central bank and is achieved by central bank intervention in the foreign exchange market to block the unregulated forces of demand and supply. (p. 225)

Flexible exchange rate An exchange rate that is determined by demand and supply in the foreign exchange market with no direct intervention by the central bank. (p. 225)

Foreign currency The money of other countries regardless of whether that money is in the form of notes, coins, or bank deposits. (p. 214)

Foreign exchange market The market in which the currency of one country is exchanged for the currency of another. (p. 214)

Frictional unemployment The unemployment that arises from normal labour turnover—from people entering and leaving the labour force and from the ongoing creation and destruction of jobs. (p. 117)

Full employment A situation in which the unemployment rate equals the natural unemployment rate. At full employment, there is no cyclical unemployment—all unemployment is frictional and structural. (p. 117)

Full-employment equilibrium A macroeconomic equilibrium in which real GDP equals potential GDP. (p. 255)

Goods and services The objects that people value and produce to satisfy human wants. (p. 3)

Government debt The total amount that the government has borrowed. It equals the sum of past budget deficits minus the sum of past budget surpluses. (p. 327)

Government expenditure Goods and services bought by government. (p. 90)

Government expenditure multiplier The quantitative effect of a change in government expenditure on real GDP. It is calculated as the change in real GDP that results from a change in government expenditure divided by the change in government expenditure. (pp. 290, 335)

Government sector balance An amount equal to net taxes minus government expenditure on goods and services. (p. 232)

Gross domestic product (GDP) The market value of all final goods and services produced within a country during a given time period. (p. 88)

Gross investment The total amount spent on purchases of new capital and on replacing depreciated capital. (pp. 90, 164)

Growth rate The annual percentage change of a variable—the change in the level expressed as a percentage of the initial level. (p. 136)

Human capital The knowledge and skill that people obtain from education, on-the-job training, and work experience. (p. 3)

Hyperinflation An inflation rate of 50 percent a month or higher that grinds the economy to a halt and causes a society to collapse. (p. 120)

Import quota A restriction that limits the quantity of a good that may be imported in a given period. (p. 378)

Imports The goods and services that we buy from people in other countries. (pp. 90, 372)

Incentive A reward that encourages an action or a penalty that discourages one. (p. 2)

Induced expenditure The sum of the components of aggregate planned expenditure that vary with real GDP. Induced expenditure equals consumption expenditure minus imports. (p. 272)

Inferior good A good for which demand decreases as income increases. (p. 62)

Inflation A persistently rising price level. (p. 120)

Inflationary gap An output gap in which real GDP exceeds potential GDP. (p. 254)

Inflation rate targeting A monetary policy strategy in which the central bank makes a public commitment to achieve an explicit inflation rate and to explain how its policy actions will achieve that target. (p. 348)

Interest The income that capital earns. (p. 4)

Interest rate parity A situation in which the rates of return on assets in different currencies are equal. (p. 222)

Intermediate good An item that is produced by one firm, bought by another firm, and used as a component of a final good or service. (p. 88)

Inverse relationship A relationship between variables that move in opposite directions. (p. 21)

Investment The purchase of new plant, equipment, and buildings, and additions to inventories. (p. 90)

Keynesian A macroeconomist who believes that, left alone, the economy would rarely operate at full employment and that to achieve full employment, active help from fiscal policy and monetary policy is required. (p. 258)

Keynesian cycle theory A theory that fluctuations in investment driven by fluctuations in business confidence—summarized by the phrase "animal spirits"—are the main source of fluctuations in aggregate demand. (p. 299)

Labour The work time and work effort that people devote to producing goods and services. (p. 3)

Labour force The sum of the people who are employed and who are unemployed. (p. 113)

Labour force participation rate The percentage of the working-age population who are members of the labour force. (p. 114)

Labour productivity The quantity of real GDP produced by an hour of labour. (p. 146)

Laffer curve The relationship between the tax rate and the amount of tax revenue collected. (p. 333)

Land The "gifts of nature" that we use to produce goods and services. (p. 3)

Law of demand Other things remaining the same, the higher the price of a good, the smaller is the quantity demanded of it; the lower the price of a good, the larger is the quantity demanded of it. (p. 59)

Law of supply Other things remaining the same, the higher the price of a good, the greater is the quantity supplied of it; the lower the price of a good, the smaller is the quantity supplied. (p. 64)

Lender of last resort The Bank of Canada is the lender of last resort—depository institutions that are short of reserves can borrow from the Bank of Canada. (p. 191)

Linear relationship A relationship between two variables that is illustrated by a straight line. (p. 20)

Loanable funds market The aggregate of all the individual markets in which households, firms, governments, banks, and other financial institutions borrow and lend. (p. 170)

Long-run aggregate supply The relationship between the quantity of real GDP supplied and the price level when the money wage rate changes in step with the price level to maintain full employment. (p. 244)

Long-run macroeconomic equilibrium A situation that occurs when real GDP equals potential GDP—the economy is on its long-run aggregate supply curve. (p. 252)

Long-run Phillips curve A curve that shows the relationship between inflation and unemployment when the actual inflation rate equals the expected inflation rate. (p. 312)

M1 A measure of money that consists of currency held by individuals and businesses plus chequable deposits owned by individuals and businesses. (p. 185)

M2 A measure of money that consists of M1 plus all other deposits—non-chequable deposits and fixed term deposits. (p. 185)

Macroeconomics The study of the performance of the national economy and the global economy. (p. 2)

Macroprudential regulation Financial regulation to lower the risk that the financial system will crash. (p. 362)

Margin When a choice is made by comparing a little more of something with its cost, the choice is made at the margin. (p. 10)

Marginal benefit The benefit that a person receives from consuming one more unit of a good or service. It is measured as the maximum amount that a person is willing to pay for one more unit of the good or service. (pp. 10, 38)

Marginal benefit curve A curve that shows the relationship between the marginal benefit of a good and the quantity of that good consumed. (p. 38)

Marginal cost The *opportunity cost* of producing *one* more unit of a good or service. It is the best alternative forgone. It is calculated as the increase in total cost divided by the increase in output. (pp. 10, 37)

Marginal propensity to consume The fraction of a *change* in disposable income that is spent on consumption. It is calculated as the *change* in consumption expenditure divided by the *change* in disposable income. (p. 270)

Marginal propensity to import The fraction of an increase in real GDP that is spent on imports. It is calculated as the *change* in imports divided by the *change* in real GDP, other things remaining the same. (p. 271)

Marginal propensity to save The fraction of a *change* in disposable income that is saved. It is calculated as the *change* in saving divided by the *change* in disposable income. (p. 270)

Market Any arrangement that enables buyers and sellers to get information and to do business with each other. (p. 48)

Means of payment A method of settling a debt. (p. 184)

Microeconomics The study of the choices that individuals and businesses make, the way these choices interact in markets, and the influence of governments. (p. 2)

Monetarist A macroeconomist who believes that the economy is self-regulating and that it will normally operate at full employment, provided that monetary policy is not erratic and that the pace of money growth is kept steady. (p. 259)

Monetarist cycle theory A theory that fluctuations in both investment and consumption expenditure, driven by fluctuations in the growth rate of the quantity of money, are the main source of fluctuations in aggregate demand. (p. 299)

Monetary base The sum of Bank of Canada notes, coins, and depository institution deposits at the Bank of Canada. (p. 192)

Monetary policy The Bank of Canada conducts the nation's monetary policy by changing interest rates and adjusting the quantity of money. (p. 250)

Money Any commodity or token that is generally acceptable as a means of payment. (pp. 48, 184)

Money multiplier The ratio of the change in the quantity of money to the change in the monetary base. (p. 196)

Money price The number of dollars that must be given up in exchange for a good or service. (p. 58)

Mortgage A legal contract that gives ownership of a home to the lender in the event that the borrower fails to meet the agreed loan payments (repayments and interest). (p. 165)

Mortgage-backed security A type of bond that entitles its holder to the income from a package of mortgages. (p. 166)

Multiplier The amount by which a change in autonomous expenditure is magnified or multiplied to determine the change in equilibrium expenditure and real GDP. (p. 276)

National saving The sum of private saving (saving by households and businesses) and government saving. (p. 169)

Natural unemployment rate The unemployment rate when the economy is at full employment—natural

unemployment as a percentage of the labour force. (p. 117)

Negative relationship A relationship between variables that move in opposite directions. (p. 21)

Neoclassical growth theory A theory of economic growth that proposes that real GDP per person grows because technological change induces an amount of saving and investment that makes capital per hour of labour grow. (p. 151)

Net borrower A country that is borrowing more from the rest of the world than it is lending to it. (p. 230)

Net exports The value of exports of goods and services minus the value of imports of goods and services. (pp. 90, 232)

Net investment The amount by which the value of capital increases—gross investment minus depreciation. (pp. 90, 164)

Net lender A country that is lending more to the rest of the world than it is borrowing from it. (p. 230)

Net taxes Taxes paid to governments minus cash transfers received from governments. (p. 168)

Net worth The market value of what a financial institution has lent minus the market value of what it has borrowed. (p. 167)

New classical A macroeconomist who holds the view that business cycle fluctuations are the efficient responses of a well-functioning market economy bombarded by shocks that arise from the uneven pace of technological change. (p. 258)

New classical cycle theory A rational expectations theory of the business cycle in which the rational expectation of the price level, which is determined by potential GDP and *expected* aggregate demand, determines the money wage rate and the position of the SAS curve. (p. 299)

New growth theory A theory of economic growth based on the idea that real GDP per person grows because of the choices that people make in the pursuit of profit and that growth will persist indefinitely. (p. 152)

New Keynesian A macroeconomist who holds the view that not only is the money wage rate sticky, but also that the prices of goods and services are sticky. (p. 259)

New Keynesian cycle theory A rational expectations theory of the business cycle that emphasizes the fact that today's money wage rates were negotiated at many past dates, which means that *past* rational expectations of the current price level influence the money wage rate and the position of the SAS curve. (p. 299)

Nominal GDP The value of the final goods and services produced in a given year valued at the prices that prevailed in that same year. It is a more precise name for GDP. (p. 93)

Nominal interest rate The number of dollars that a borrower pays and a lender receives in interest in a year expressed as a percentage of the number of dollars borrowed and lent. (p. 169)

Normal good A good for which demand increases as income increases. (p. 62)

Official settlements account A record of the change in official reserves, which are the government's holdings of foreign currency. (p. 228)

Offshore outsourcing A Canadian firm buys finished goods, components, or services from firms in other countries. (p. 383)

Open market operation The purchase or sale of government securities by the Bank of Canada in the loanable funds market. (p. 192)

Operating band The target overnight loans rate plus or minus 0.25 percentage points: bank rate and the settlement balances rate. (p. 351)

Opportunity cost The highest-valued alternative that we must give up to get something. (pp. 9, 35)

Output gap The gap between real GDP and potential GDP. (pp. 118, 254)

Overnight loans rate The interest rate on overnight loans that the big banks make to each other. (p. 350)

Positive relationship A relationship between two variables that move in the same direction. (p. 20)

Potential GDP The value of production when all the economy's labour, capital, land, and entrepreneurial ability are fully employed; the quantity of real GDP at full employment. (p. 94)

Preferences A description of a person's likes and dislikes and the intensity of those feelings. (pp. 9, 38)

Price level The average level of prices. (p. 120)

Private sector balance An amount equal to saving minus investment. (p. 232)

Production efficiency A situation in which goods and services are produced at the lowest possible cost. (p. 35)

Production possibilities frontier The boundary between those combinations of goods and services that can be produced and those combinations that cannot. (p. 34)

Profit The income earned by entrepreneurship. (p. 4)

Property rights The social arrangements that govern the ownership, use, and disposal of anything that people value. Property rights are enforceable in the courts. (p. 48)

Purchasing power parity A situation in which the prices in two countries are equal when converted at the exchange rate. (p. 222)

Quantity demanded The amount of a good or service that consumers plan to buy during a given time period at a particular price. (p. 59)

Quantity supplied The amount of a good or service that producers plan to sell during a given time period at a particular price. (p. 64)

Quantity theory of money The proposition that, in the long run, an increase in the quantity of money brings an equal percentage increase in the price level. (p. 202)

Rational choice A choice that compares costs and benefits and achieves the greatest benefit over cost for the person making the choice. (p. 9)

Rational expectation The best forecast possible; a forecast that uses all the available information. (p. 308)

Real business cycle theory A theory of the business cycle that regards random fluctuations in productivity as the main source of economic fluctuations. (p. 299)

Real exchange rate The relative price of Canadian-produced goods and services to foreign-produced goods and services. (p. 224)

Real GDP The value of final goods and services produced in a given year when valued at the prices of a reference base year. (p. 93)

Real GDP per person Real GDP divided by the population. (pp. 94, 136)

Real interest rate The nominal interest rate adjusted to remove the effects of inflation on the buying power of money. It is approximately equal to the nominal interest rate minus the inflation rate. (p. 169)

Real wage rate The money (or nominal) wage rate divided by the price level. The real wage rate is the quantity of goods and services that an hour of labour earns. (p. 143)

Recession A business cycle phase in which real GDP decreases for at least two successive quarters. (p. 95)

Recessionary gap An output gap in which potential GDP exceeds real GDP. (p. 255)

Relative price The ratio of the price of one good or service to the price of another good or service. A relative price is an opportunity cost. (p. 58)

Rent The income that land earns. (p. 4)

Rent seeking The lobbying for special treatment by the government to create economic profit or to divert consumer surplus or producer surplus away from others. The pursuit of wealth by capturing economic rent. (p. 385)

Reserves A bank's reserves consist of notes and coins in its vaults plus its deposit at the Bank of Canada. (p. 187)

Rule of 70 A rule that states that the number of years it takes for the level of any variable to double is approximately 70 divided by the annual percentage growth rate of the variable. (p. 137)

Saving The amount of income that is not paid in taxes or spent on consumption goods and services. (p. 164)

Saving function The relationship between saving and disposable income, other things remaining the same. (p. 268)

Scarcity Our inability to satisfy all our wants. (p. 2)

Scatter diagram A graph that plots the value of one variable against the value of another variable for a number of different values of each variable. (p. 18)

Self-interest The choices that you think are the best ones available for you are choices made in your self-interest. (p. 5)

Settlement balances rate The interest rate that the Bank of Canada pays on bank reserves held at the Bank of Canada. (p. 352)

Short-run aggregate supply The relationship between the quantity of real GDP supplied and the price level when the money wage rate, the prices of other resources, and potential GDP remain constant. (p. 245)

Short-run macroeconomic equilibrium A situation that occurs when the quantity of real GDP demanded equals the quantity of real GDP supplied—at the point of intersection of the AD curve and the SAS curve. (p. 252)

Short-run Phillips curve A curve that shows the tradeoff between inflation and unemployment, when the expected inflation rate and the natural unemployment rate are held constant. (p. 312)

Slope The change in the value of the variable measured on the y-axis divided by the change in the value of the variable measured on the x-axis. (p. 24)

Social interest Choices that are the best ones for society as a whole. (p. 5)

Stagflation The combination of inflation and recession. (pp. 257, 306)

Stock A certificate of ownership and claim to the firm's profits. (p. 166)

Stock market A financial market in which shares of stocks of corporations are traded. (p. 166)

Structural surplus or deficit The budget balance that would occur if the economy were at full employment and real GDP were equal to potential GDP. (p. 334)

Structural unemployment The unemployment that arises when changes in technology or international competition change the skills needed to perform jobs or change the locations of jobs. (p. 117)

Substitute A good that can be used in place of another good. (p. 61)

Supply The entire relationship between the price of a good and the quantity supplied of it when all other influences on producers' planned sales remain the same. It is described by a supply schedule and illustrated by a supply curve. (p. 64)

Supply curve A curve that shows the relationship between the quantity supplied of a good and its price when all other influences on producers' planned sales remain the same. (p. 64)

Supply of loanable funds The relationship between the quantity of loanable funds supplied and the real interest rate when all other influences on lending plans remain the same. (p. 171)

Tariff A tax that is imposed by the importing country when an imported good crosses its international boundary. (p. 376)

Tax multiplier The quantitative effect of a change in taxes on real GDP. It is calculated as the change in real GDP that results from a change in taxes divided by the change in taxes. (p. 336)

Tax wedge The gap between the before-tax and after-tax wage rates. (p. 331)

Technological change The development of new goods and of better ways of producing goods and services. (p. 45)

Time-series graph A graph that measures time (for example, years, quarters, or months) on the x-axis and the variable or variables in which we are interested on the y-axis. (p. 102)

Tradeoff A constraint that involves giving up one thing to get something else. (p. 9)

Trend The tendency for a variable to move in one general direction. (p. 103)

Unemployment rate The percentage of the people in the labour force who are unemployed. (p. 114)

Velocity of circulation The average number of times a dollar of money is used annually to buy the goods and services that make up GDP. (p. 202)

Wages The income that labour earns. (p. 4)

Wealth The value of all the things that people own—the market value of their assets—at a point in time. (p. 164)

Working-age population The total number of people aged 15 years and over who are not in jail, hospital, or some other form of institutional care. (p. 113)

Note: Key terms and the pages on which they are defined are **bolded.** References to "*f*" denote a figure and "*t*" denote a table.

NOTES

NOTES

NOTES

NOTES

NOTES

NOTES

Economics in the News

Economics in the News boxes show students how to use the economic toolkit to understand the events and issues they are confronted with in the media. An extended *Economics in the News* at the end of each chapter helps students think like economists by connecting chapter tools and concepts to the world around them.

Economics in Action

Economics in Action boxes apply economic theory to current events to illustrate the importance of economic forces in the world around us.